Air War Over Spain

To
my brother Ignacio

all those who fought nobly and without
bitterness in defence of their ideals

all aviators who love their profession

Air War Over Spain

Jesus Salas Larrazabal

Translated from the Spanish by Margaret A. Kelley

English Translation Edited by David Mondey

LONDON

IAN ALLAN LTD

First published 1969

English edition first published 1974

ISBN 0 7110 0521 4

Published by Ian Allan Ltd, Shepperton, Surrey,
Photoset and printed
in Great Britain by
Redwood Burn Limited
Trowbridge & Esher

Contents

List of Maps

Introduction

Although the reader is unlikely to be very interested in the origin of this book, I feel obliged to give some explanation to throw light on the inequality with which subjects of similar interest have been treated.

Ten years ago I began collecting information to write a history of Spanish aviation, in collaboration with the well-known aeronautical engineer, José Warleta Carrillo. For the preparatory work we decided to divide the subject so that Warleta should collect and compile information for the period prior to July 18th, 1936, leaving me to deal with the period subsequent to that date.

In order to pinpoint the role of aviation in the Civil War, I had to read every possible book on this latter subject. Unfortunately, the majority of them either ignored aviation completely, or treated it casually in passing and with a remarkable lack of factual information. This forced me to go back to primary sources: communiqués of operations, books dealing with the activities of different units, news bulletins, records of when aircraft entered or left repair workshops, flight logs of the most important pilots, as well as interviews with pilots, crew members, mechanics etc, who could clarify the details and bring some life to the data collected.

I began my researches in Madrid, where I located some vital sources of information, the most important of which was the Military History Archives. Another source was in Seville, where I live at present. On account of the distance to Madrid, and my short holiday periods, I found great difficulty in following up the vital investigations there, and since 1963 these have been continued diligently by my brother Ramón. He has been concerned principally with the strength of the land armies, and more recently he has continued his researches in other centres and towns, among them the Fondo Documental in Salameinca.

In Seville I located interesting documents and data in the archives of Región Aérea, Tablada aerodrome, Maestranza Aérea, Hispano Aviación etc, and have been able to interview many pilots of both sides, together with technicians and workmen from Construcciones Aeronáuticas and Hispano Aviación, companies who undertook the repair and manufacture of the most commonly used aircraft (Fiat, Chato and Rata).

Since this information complemented that obtained by my brother, we decided to write jointly a History of the Civil War, and we applied for a historical research grant from the Juan March Foundation, to allow us time for more detailed study, as well as the opportunity to learn more from certain foreign centres, particularly the Congress Library in Washington. The grant was not approved, we had to give up the idea of writing the history for the time being.

Under these circumstances, the *Revista del Servicio Histórico Militar* suggested that, instead, I should write something about aviation history in the Civil War, and we agreed on the subject of Spanish National aircraft. When the work was half finished, and despite the extremely concise manner in which it was written, the number of pages far exceeded that which the *Revista* felt reasonable. We decided to limit the length of this history by ending it at the time of the formation of the Morato Group.

However, I wanted to continue independently with the work I had begun. Several people encouraged me to write this, adding something about the other aircraft involved: those of the Spanish Government, as well as the Russian, Italian, German, French and International contributions.

Recently, my brother Ramón has thought it desirable to increase the coverage of the activities of the land armies, and to add comments on the situation, both on land and in the air, at representative periods of the war. I decided also to add some details of the part played by the Navy, to avoid a complete gap on this subject.

Given the great disparity between what I set out to write and what has been written, this may help to explain the inequalities between the different chapters and their subjects.

I have not attempted to correct this inbalance, since I hope to rectify this in the projected History of the Civil War. Neither did I want to add more information regarding aviation (air lifts across the Straits and to Santuario de la Cabeza; training schools, manufacture and servicing). This is not simply because it would unbalance still further the relationship between the coverage of aviation activities by comparison with those of the land and sea forces, but because it belongs to the book to be written on this subject in collaboration with José Warleta.

I think that the present book, now that I have pointed out these inequalities, gives sufficient new information to justify its publication, and I hope that the reader will judge this to be so.

It gives a general picture of aviation activities during this bitter period in Spanish history, although preference is given to Spanish aircraft. The activities of the Fiat, Rata, Messerchmitt and Heinkel machines, quoted in relation to their numbers, have been clarified basically. Further investigation is necessary to fill in some of the gaps regarding the record of the Chatos—the aircraft used most extensively (380, plus 200 in an advanced state of construction found abandoned at Sabadell-Reus in January 1939)—and to throw some light on the activities of aircraft used in small numbers such as Dewoitine, Letov, Spad, Hawker Fury, Bristol Bulldog, etc, and the Nieuport 52s used before the war in the Government Zone.

As far as aviation in general is concerned the entire number of airborne units of the Nationalist Zone, with the dates of their formation, their commands and deployment, together with an acceptable approximation of the same data for the Government Zone, is given for the first time. I have also made efforts to find

Government Sector. In this field there is still scope for a lot of additional checking and investigation.

As far as the land forces are concerned, I think that I have managed to finalise the details of people, commands and material on both sides. Until now details of the army corps, the divisions taking part at each stage, and their deployment over the whole of Spain, have not been presented. With reference to the first phases of the War, when divisions had not been organised successfully, data is given as to the number of men or, where possible, the number of battalions, together with the number of aircraft, tanks and guns available.

I also considered it necessary to throw some light on the way in which the brigades and divisions of the *Cuerpo de Ejército de Madrid* (Madrid Army Corps), the initial nucleus of the Popular Army, were formed. Details of the units which came from Africa by sea and air, with an indication of the date when they were formed; and information on the decisive sea battles of Vizcaya and Aragón, in which the Government Units present and their activities, are given in a concise, but clear form.

As far as the Navy is concerned, I have only studied in detail men and materials at the beginning of the Uprising, and their difficulties during the first three months. For the rest I have made use of reports already published.

Throughout this book I have tried to be as impartial as possible, considering my obvious link with one of the sides. This spirit of equanimity was imposed on me by family tradition. For example, as soon as the war was over my father came into contact with a man who had previously been sent to arrest him in the tragic summer of 1936: he conducted his business without even reminding him of the incident. My eldest brother, Ángel, fought in the air and saluted a defeated enemy on the same day that our second brother, Ignacio, was killed in an air raid. Brother Ramón, during his year and a half of voluntary military service (which covered the whole period of the Northern Campaign), managed to avoid being detailed as a member of any firing squad. When the war was ended he became a court clerk and considered it fortunate that during the six months he spent in this office only two or three death sentences were awarded, none of which was carried out.

But these attitudes did not interfere with their determination to defend their ideals. This is proven by the fact that all my brothers, plus five sisters and the writer, who was then just eleven years old, crossed over from the Government Zone to the Nationalist Zone; one by plane, seven across the frontier, and one, accompanied by our mother, across France. Our father, who was saved by the anarchist leader Melchor, for whom he had not the slightest friendship, refused not only to serve in the Government Army, but also to collect the pension due to him as a retired soldier, and he had to be confined for almost three years in the Guatemalan Embassy. (Protected by Chile from the time when Franco was recognised by that nation).

I did not wish this book to be published until a period of thirty years had elapsed from the end of the war for, although little detailed information of any individual person is given, I would not like to feel that this book could in any way aggravate previous antagonisms but that, on the other hand, it might serve to illustrate our mistakes and avoid their repetition.

If there are any statements in this book that are not strictly accurate, this is due to a wrong interpretation of facts by the author, who will be pleased to receive details of any errors.

I have to express my thanks in the first place to José Warleta and Ramón Salas who unselfishly allowed me to use information gained in collaboration with them, as well as for other data provided by them. Warleta supplied most of the details regarding the Ratas and Katiuskas, and Ramón Salas gave me many new facts concerning the Popular Army, particulary about the defence of Madrid and the operations of the Northern Army. Also of great help were Tarazona and Larios who gave me permission to quote from their books.

Secondly, I must express my thanks for the facilities provided by the Military History Archives, to the various photographic and document archives belonging to what were then the *Región Aérea del Estrecho* in Hispano Aviación and, more recently, in the Air Ministry, and to the library of works dealing with the Spanish war kept by the Ministry of Information and Tourism. I must mention in particular Colonel Salcedo and Lieutenant Colonels Escartín and Martínez Bande, who were in charge of the Military History Archives when I began my investigations; Lieutenant General Cuesta Monereo, who opened the doors of this Centre for me, and to Generals Eduardo Gonzalez Gallarda and Julio Salvador, Colonel José Antonio del Val, Lieutenant Colonel del Valle, Commanders Salvador and Martínez de Velasco, and Captain Ruiz Cabello, who provided many facilities in Seville, and Commanders Fernández Suárez and Egea in Madrid.

I have also been helped by Ricardo de la Cierua and Domingo Balaguer, thanks to whose kindness I have been able to read books which were difficult to locate, and by José Gutiérrez Ravé who presented me with an almost complete collection of *Official War Communiqués, Nationalist and Red*, which were published between July 1936 to March 1937. Similarly, Tomás Martín Barbadillo gave me pamphlets issued by the *Servicio Antiaeronáutica*, and Santiago Gala has allowed me to have the *Historia de la Cruzada* (History of the Crusade) for constant reference.

Finally, I must say thank you for the kindness shown to me by Lieutenant Generals Asensio, Cuesta Monereo, Eduardo Sáenz de Buruaga, Eduardo González Gallarza, Apolinar Sáenz de Buruaga, Llop, Eduardo Prado, Luis Pardo, Ángel Salas and Luis Bengoechea, who made my task easier by answering so many oral and written questions; likewise the ex-minister José Antonio Girón (who was the only surviving member of the *Junta de Defensa Nacional*), the Italian Lieutenant General Aldo Remondino and the Aviation General Alfonso de Orleáns y Borbón. Generals Salvador, Guerrero, Cuadra, Jiménez, Ugarte and Alonso Pimentel, added to my information in an important way by placing their flight records at my disposal, as did the widows of the famous pilots Carlos Haya, José Muñoz and José Ugarte, and Manuel Vázquez Sagastizábal's family. General Murcia was also willing to let me have his flight records, but for various reasons it has not yet been possible for me to make use of his offer, although he has written me two letters containing much important detail. A large number of generals, chiefs and officials have helped me in various ways. The most important information has come from Generals

Alvarez Rementería, Alvarez Pardo, Ramiro Pascual and Noreña, Colonels Soler, Senra, Queipo de Llano, Amores, Larrauri, Julián del Val, Torres, Prol, Madrano, Lacour and Eduardo Camino, from Lieutenant Colonels Lacalle, Gómez del Barco, Isidro Comas, Cabenza and Juan Prieto, Commanders Sánchez Gallicher and Santa Cruz, Captain Pablo Atienza, and mechanics Guereta, Merenciano, Aristegui, Cumplido etc.

From the Government side, Gaspar Company, Francisco Tarazona and Luis Burgos answered my questionnaires, as did a large number of workmen from Hispano Aviación, among them Marcelino Viejo, Luis Peñalver, Félix Jardo, etc and I have managed to obtain indirect information from a large number of people; the most important details coming from Mariano Perea, Martínez Lledó and Parrondo.

Helmut Bolz, the ex-*Luftwaffe* pilot and member of the third Fighter Squadron of the Cóndor Legión gave me a lot of information about this unit before his death, and the Italian ex-Colonels Bonzano and Pittoni gave me other information about the Legionary Fighters.

To all these I express my gratitude, as well as to my sister Pilar, to my nephew José Ignacio Salas Collantes, and to Señorita Loli Giroult who somehow managed to type my disorderly manuscript.

Seville, November 1968

CHAPTER ONE

The Background

Historical

To be able to understand the terrible Civil War which ravaged Spain for three years, one must know a little of the state of the country prior to that time.

It is not reasonable to suggest that national characteristics such as intransigence, our warlike spirit or the cruelty of our race were responsible for the war. Spaniards, like all peoples of the world, have been intransigent, moderate, warlike, pacifist, cruel or generous, according to time and circumstance. And one should not forget that Spain is one of the few nations that succeeded in avoiding participation in the last two world wars, and not under the most favourable of circumstances.

Our country was shaken violently by the loss of our last overseas provinces; a result of the war of 1898, into which we were dragged unfairly by the United States and which brought us into a situation that was more ridiculous than dishonourable.

Everyone knew that we could not fight a war against the United States; everyone except the Spanish. Even to the most humble of our sailors it was clear that our naval vessels were incapable of confronting the North American squadron; but the Government continued to believe that battles could be won by history and heroism alone. This disaster made them alive to cruel reality: Spain, after its slow and continuous decadence for centuries, had become a second-class nation.

But Spain was not dead. Our great disasters initiated an important intellectual movement: the 98 Generation, whose most representative figurehead was Unamuno, seemed the incarnation of all the worries, doubts and grandeur of the country. Spain also tried to surge forward in other activities: the greatest musicians in our history (Falla, Albéniz, Turina) made their appearance; scientists of the stature of Ramón and Cajal emerged, and world famous technicians such as Torres Quevedo and La Cierva became known as the process of industrialisation was intensified in the north and in Catalonia.

These were symptoms of vitality, a reaction to the tremendous set-backs, both cultural and economic, social and political, which Spain had received in relation to the rest of Europe. They served to illustrate that there were small groups of the population who would not resign themselves to the situation. Unfortunately, these nuclei were not united in a common aim. Large sectors of Spain were discontented, many were looking for solutions: because of the widely differing backgrounds of these most of the answers were contradictory.

So far as aviation was concerned Spain was not far behind the pioneer nations—the United States and France—and was almost on a par with England, Germany, Italy and Russia. In 1909 Antonio Fernández met his death in an attempt to fly from France to Spain in a biplane of his own design. In 1910, Benito Loygorri and Alfonso de Orleáns received their pilot's licences from the French school at Mourmelon, and in that same year the first aircraft flew in Spain. In the following year the first international air route was inaugurated between Paris and Madrid.

The year of 1911 also saw the establishment of the Aerodynamics Laboratory; construction of the first military aerodrome; organisation of the first flying training school for pilots in Cuatro Vientos; and the acquisition by the Army of its first aircraft, supplied by Benito Loygorri. Before the end of the year the first five pilots to enter the flying school (Kindelán, Barrón, Ortiz Echagüe, Herrea and Arrillaga) had been given their licences.

It is interesting to record a few brief notes regarding Spain's first seven pilots: Loygorri still likes to travel by air, albeit as a passenger on commercial aircraft; Orléans is the oldest pilot in the world still in active service and Ortiz Echagüe is the president of Construcciones Aeronáuticas; Kindelán and Herrera died only a few years ago, the former having become the leader of national aviation, the latter is remembered for being in control of the Government in exile; Arrillaga lived for more than 55 years in a wheelchair and Barrón, who was the first of the seven to die, had become general of the Aeronautical Engineers and was responsible for the design of several aircraft. I must mention also Quesada, who was the first mechanic at Cuatro Vientos: he became commander of the Corps of Aeronautical Engineers and remained in the service for many years after reaching retirement age.

It does not seem possible that the success of these pioneer pilots was a matter of chance, at a time when even a simple routine flight was an heroic thing, attempted only by those who felt they were in excellent mental and physical condition. Possibly the fact that they were selected by the expert eye of Colonel Pedro Vives, the man who guided the first halting steps of Spanish aviation, had something to do with their achievements.

Also in the year 1911 Julio Adaro and Heraclio Alfaro received their civil pilot's licences. Both became distinguished engineers, especially the latter, who returned to Spain a few years before his death after achieving many brilliant successes in North America.

In 1913 the civil school of Getafe began to function and Vives and Kindelán went across to Africa with the first expeditionary squadron (Orleáns and Barrón were members of this unit), which was equipped with bombing and photographic equipment. Before the year was out Spain counted its first pilots injured in action, and they received the Laurel Cross for saving their aircraft. By 1914 there were two squadrons in Africa; one in Tetuan and the other in Melilla.

At this time the prototypes of at least five Spanish aircraft had been constructed: Condé's seaplane and machines designed by Montero, La Cierva-Barcala, Adaro and Acedo. Hispano Suiza had also built the prototype of what proved to be the most successful aero-engine of the European War. No less than 49,893 examples of this engine were built in France and allied countries (a number never since equalled) and Fonck attributed the wartime achievements of air power to this engine.

In 1915 the first seaplanes used by the Spanish Army began to operate from the new aerodrome at Los Alcázares. This, like the aerodrome at Tablada, had been selected by Vives just before he was replaced by Colonel Rodríguez Mourelo as commander of the Air Force.

At the beginning of the century, by tradition, Spain held little respect for manual workers or merchants, an attitude that impeded the country's progress within Europe and as a nation of the world as a whole. Society frowned on people who devoted their lives to productive work, and this was probably the most important reason for loss of prestige by the Spanish nobility.

As far as the economic aspect was concerned the loss of the colonies had a marked influence, since enterprising people were returning to the homeland bringing capital they had been using overseas. This caused the process of industrialisation to speed up and introduced a new political factor in Spain. In Barcelona in 1902 an organisation called *Solidad Obrera* (Workers Solidarity) was formed. In 1907 this extended across the whole of Catalonia and in October 1910, after the dreadful events of the *Semana Trágica* (Tragic Week) of 1909, it gave rise to the formation of the *Confederación Nacional del Trabajo* (CNT; National Work Confederation). The Socialist Union, the *Unión General de Trabajadores* (UGT; General Workers Union), was much older, but until the loss of the colonies its members numbered less than 10,000, and they did not exceed 200,000 until 1918. At that time the anarchosyndicatists had about 700,000 members.

The CNT succeeded in gaining a foothold in the old anarchist districts (the rural zones of Andalucia, Catalonia etc) while the UGT stretched across the mining areas (Asturias, Almáden, Peñarroya, Río Tinto etc) and the industrial zones of Navarre.

In 1912 the third important workers' union, the *Federación Nacional de Sindicatos Católicos Libres* (National Federation of Free Catholics Syndicate) was formed. This predominated in the Basque and Navarre regions and in the northern half of the Meseta, particularly in Burgos and Palencia, and in any area where Catholics formed the overwhelming majority of the population.

Spanish neutrality in the first world war provided unexpected prosperity. This, together with the existence of two strong, but moderate workers' unions, seemed to suggest that the transformation of Spanish industrialisation had begun.

But, in 1917, the UGT started its first swing towards the left, probably influenced by events in Russia and by the fact that Largo Caballero was taking a much more influential part in the affairs of the UGT, due to the ill health of Pablo Inglesias. The Lliga, the right wing Catalan party, adopted a similar attitude, deceived probably by the effervescence that could be noted in the Army and which culminated in the creation of the Defence Juntas. When a general strike was called, at the instigation of Largo Caballero, the Army stood out against it, despite Pablo Iglesias' opposition.

In order to pacify the country a predominantly Nationalist government had to be formed. This was presided over by Maura, a politician who was kept in power during 1918 and 1919, with brief interventions by García Prieto and the Count of Romanones. In 1919 street warfare began in Barcelona, and this lasted for four years.

The ending of the European war had an unfavourable effect on the Spanish aviation industry which, despite its lack of technical experience and finance, had been making steady progress because of the enthusiasm shown by all sections of the industry.

On September 5th, 1918, Colonel Rodríguez Mourelo initiated a national design competition for military aircraft. In this competition, held in 1919, Hispano Suiza scored a resounding success, thanks to the prototypes designed by Barrón, who was then in charge of the new factory at Guadalajara. These aircraft took the first prize in the section for fighters and second prize for reconnaissance machines: the first prize in this latter section was not awarded and the second prize in the fighter section went to Amalio Díaz. Alfaro and Loring-Hedilla's contenders, both built in Barcelona by Hereter S.A., and La Cierva's three-engined aircraft—the only bomber entered in the competition, and which was destroyed during trials—failed to win prizes.

Hispano Suiza's misfortunes began from this time. They were the company who had achieved the most technical success in Spain, but they were always troubled with economic problems. At the end of the war in Europe the Allies swamped our country with war surplus materials, in particular with aircraft which had been tested under the severe conditions of active service. As a result our own promising national designs were not built. Barrón left Hispano and went back to the workshops at Cuatro Vientos since he did not wish to abandon his military career. Hereter closed down; Hispano managed to survive, thanks to their manufacture of cars, but they were not able to nationalise their outstanding aero-engines since the essential factory was not built in Spain.

In 1921 another ridiculous national event took place at Annual, this time at the hands of the guerrilla Abd-el-Krim. At that time there was no politician in Spain with sufficient prestige and authority to take control. When Sagasta had died, Cánovas del Castillo, Canalejas and Dato had all been assassinated, and Maura had retired soon after, leaving no one capable of directing the country's affairs. This complete lack of authority led to the dictatorship of General Primo de Rivera.

The disaster at Annual had also one serious effect on military aviation, causing the squadron based at Melilla to be attacked one night. The crew members were billeted in the town, and those left behind on guard feared they would be overpowered. In order to deprive the attackers of success they destroyed all the squadron's aircraft.

The chief of aeronautics, Colonel Echagüe, had fortunately created an establishment for 132 pilots in 1920. Of the 95 applicants for training 63 were granted licences in due course. There were, in addition, pilots coming from the flying training school at Cuatro Vientos (from the first course held in 1919 ten licences were granted). This allowed a rapid growth of aviation forces in Africa and, at the same time, provided a means of transit for urgently-needed goods from abroad, since national industries were not always able to meet requirements. In order to improve the postal service with Africa the first Spanish air route, from Seville to Larache, was inaugurated in 1921. This was the work of Loring and Barrón, who pushed further forward in this field, soon providing a link with Italy.

The seven years of the dictatorship saw an impressive attempt at national resurgence. The prosperity which had begun during the European war reached a peak in 1929. The economic structure of the nation changed in such a way that the agrarian population began to increase. In 1927 this class of worker was outnumbered by the total of those employed in industry and the services.

This explains the paradoxical collaboration of socialism with the Dictatorship. Socialism benefited from the great rise in the standard of living and the majority of the new workers joined the UGT which, by the end of 1931, could count over a million members. By then, this organisation could equal in strength the old anarchist syndicates (CNT). The UGT predominated in Castilla la Nueva and Extremadura, but the CNT was stronger in the East (Levante).

The beginning of the Dictatorship coincided with a new growth of activity in Spanish aviation, encouraged by Soriano and Kindelán. At the end of 1923 the C-4 autogiro, piloted by Alejandro Gómez Spencer, flew for the first time at Cuatro Vientos. This was an important event and one which was documented in detail by Emilio Herrera, chief of the Aerodynamics Laboratory. At about the same time, Pescara, who had worked in collaboration with Alfaro, was having great success in France with his helicopter. In the same year Construcciones Aeronauticas moved from Getafe and Loring founded the new factory in Carabanchel (now Aeronautica Industrial, SA). Barrón transferred there, with an insatiable desire to build aircraft of his own design. At that time, however, Alfaro was in America and La Cierva was preparing to go to England, so Barrón was left without the necessary support to develop his ideas, which had begun with the C-1 in 1920.

A decree of February 13th, 1926, brought the first attempt to make the Spanish air arm an independent force, and the names of the first 50 officers, who had to be either pilots or observers, were promulgated. This was followed by three similar announcements in succeeding years.

Also in 1926, while the Moroccan campaign continued, the age of epic flights began. First, between January 22nd and February 10th, came a crossing of the South Atlantic in a Dornier Wal flying-boat named *Plus Ultra* (with Ramón Franco, Julio Ruiz de Alda, Durán and Pablo Rada) and a flight to the Philippines made by Eduardo González Gallarza and Lórigo. These were followed in 1929 by the direct crossing from Seville to Bahia, Brazil, by Captains Francisco Ingelesias and Ignacio Jiménez in *Jesús del Gran Poder*. In 1928, the C-8.11 autogiro was flown across the English Channel and, in the following year—piloted by Luis Rambaud—it successfully completed a journey from Madrid to Lisbon.

The prosperity created during the Dictatorship aggravated another of the nation's political problems. Economic advancement began, as one would

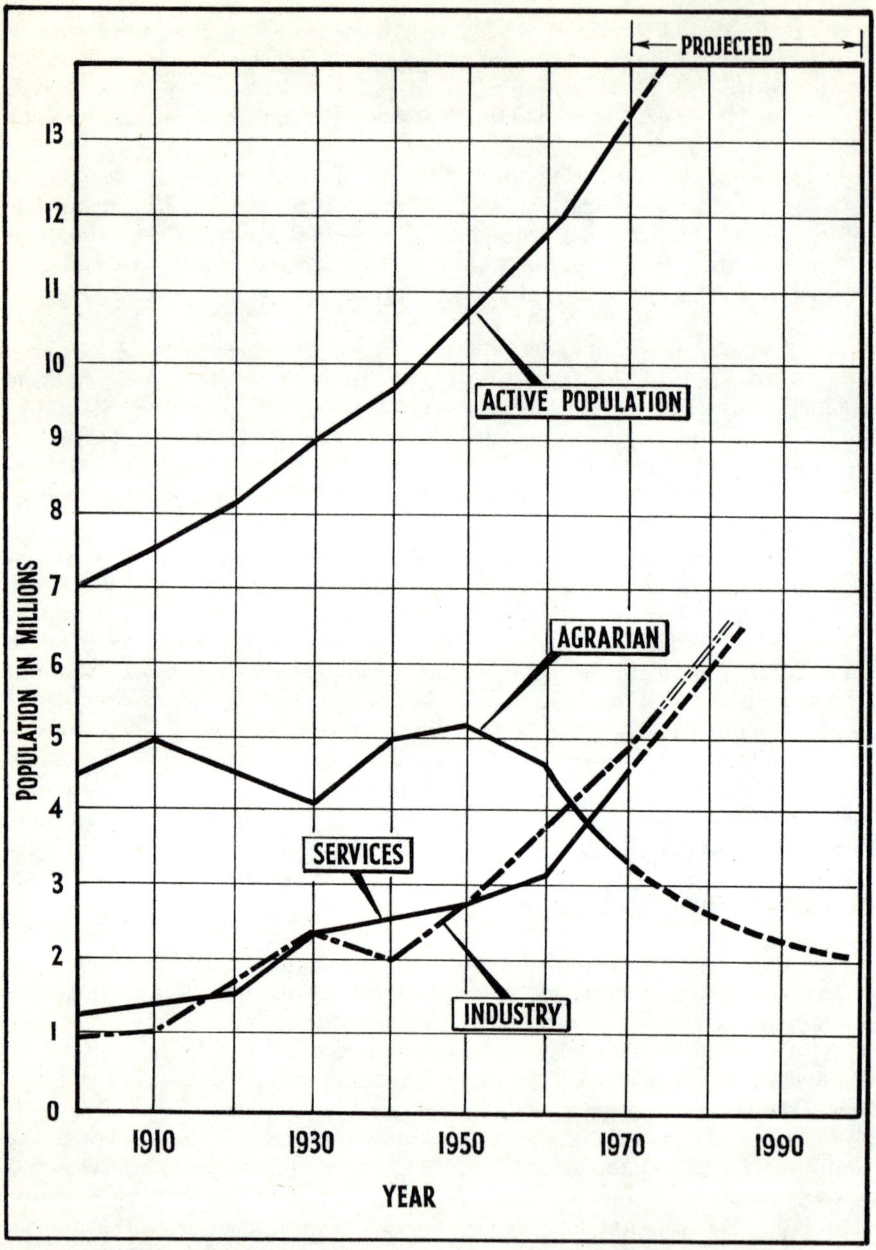

Graph showing population and employment trends throughout the 20th century.

expect, in those areas blessed with the most financial and cultural resources, and led to a pronounced difference in regional standards of living. This aggravated Catalan and Basque regionalism and separatism and led to revolution in Asturias. In the case of Catalonia, the lack of tact shown by the Dictatorship helped the growth of the extremist parties, who joined together in Colonel Maciá's 'Esquerra', to the cost of Cambó's 'Lliga'.

The lack of authority from the governments of the period 1930–31, nicknamed the *Dictablanda*, encouraged regionalism, which was also fostered by the republicans who recognised the need for assistance if they were to bring about the downfall of the Monarchy. The Republican-Socialist-Regionalist alliance was not opposed by the Anarchists, because of their old federal doctrine. This alliance was to divide Spaniards into two large blocks, those who thought that all the evils came from the disorder, and those who could not see any possibility of progress without a radical change in the political structure.

1930 proved to be an unfortunate year for aviation. As a result of the unsuccessful Republican uprising in Cuatro Vientos, the embryo air arm ceased to be judged an independent force and lost its bright green uniform. The pilots produced by the four training courses held since 1926 were returned to their original units, but remained available for aviation duties if needed.

Until now this military Republican movement, which began a year before the end of the Dictatorship and three years before the end of the African war, has not been studied in sufficient detail. In 1923, the army were unquestionably behind General Primo de Rivera, although they found his early decisions at the beginning of the Moroccan war (as, for example, retreating from Xauen to Tetuan) rather disconcerting. With the successful landing at Alhucemas (September 1925), he reinforced the confidence of the Army and of the nation in general.

The year 1926 saw also a strange incident concerning the artillery, which concluded with this force being disbanded temporarily. It arose because, by tradition, officers of the artillery received promotion according to their success in battle. This had been considered one means of maintaining the pre-eminent position of this force, gained by a combination of training and tradition.

Prior to 1926 officers of the artillery had gained a promise from the Military Academy that this system of promotion would be waived because it was unjust, since by the fortunes of war a new officer on his first day of active service could be promoted over an experienced man with many years of service in an officer capacity. Primo de Rivera sought to force the artillerymen to revert to the old system of promotion, but he had little success. The stubbornness of both sides led to a state of deadlock, which was harmful to all. As a result the artillery were disbanded for several months, but the incidents continued and finally led to an unsuccessful uprising of the Valencian artillery regiments in January 1929 under the leadership of the ex-war minister, Sánchez Guerra. Joaquín Pérez Salas, who was to become well known at a later date, was also implicated in this.

These incidents divided the Army and contributed to the fall of the Dictatorship, which had also made enemies of the University and the intellectuals.

The air services had maintained a neutral position to this time, although many pilots came from the artillery. The first airmen to turn against the Dictatorship, Martínez de Aragón, Cascón, Legorburu and Ramón Franco, for example, were not artillerymen. Arturo Menéndez, Alvarez, Buylla, Ángel Pastor and Warleta, who were to play important parts during the Republic, were members of the artillery. The uprising at Cuatro Vientos was led by Ramón Franco, who had been in opposition since 1926. This originated from a confrontation with Primo de Rivera resulting from the unfortunate situations of protocol on his return from his magnificent journey in *Plus Ultra*. He was supported by González Gil, Martínez de Aragón, Rexach, Rada, Ángel Pastor, Carlos Roa, Julián Rubio and José Mazas, and over twenty more officials, as well as Commander Hidalgo de Cisneros, Lieutenant Mellado and Second Lieutenant Valle who had been sent from Melilla by Camacho. Luis Riaño and Díaz Sandino did the liaison work with Alcalá Zamora, Maura and the remaining members of the revolutionary Junta.

In the uprising, which had to be simultaneous with those at Jaca and Burgos, two important generals of the Land Army (Queipo de Llano and Núnez̃ de Prado) were implicated. Queipo's mission was to assume command of the artillery regiments of Campamento and Nunez de Prado was to go to Burgos. Ramón Franco, who was hoping for support by a general strike, decided to continue with his rash attempt. Queipo accepted the task of going to Cuatro Vientos, from where he hoped to occupy Campamento and then Madrid. Meanwhile Mola, at that time director general of security, had managed to detain Alcala Zamora and Maura, and to sever all connections. Franco, Hidalgo de Cisneros, Álbarez Buylla and Martinez de Aragón, amongst others, flew over Madrid and dropped leaflets calling for support, but in view of the overall situation they decided not to bombard the city.

Because of the obvious failure of their attempts Queipo, Franco, Pastor, Hidalgo de Cisneros and Martinéz de Aragón took refuge in Portugal. Their exile did not last for long and in April 1931 Ramón Franco returned as director of Aeronautica (soon replaced by Álvarez Buylla and later by Warleta), Pastor became the principal of Fuerzas Aéreas and Martínez de Aragón civil governor of Vizcaya.

Carlos Roa, González Gil, José de la Roquette and Collar also escaped and at the end of February they were declared deserters, since their whereabouts had been unknown for two months.

A little later Cuatro Vientos was occupied by Orgaz's column, which included Commander Jurado, one of the artillerymen who had been promoted under the old system, and Lieutenant Faraudo; Romerales was named examining magistrate. The majority of officials at Cuatro Vientos had supported the uprising in a half-hearted manner. Only a few had stood up resolutely against it, among them Berberán, Alberto Álvarez Rementería, Ramón Escario, Fernando Valenciano and others, and they were arrested.

At that time, as one can see from the people named, the factions were far from well defined; we find Queipo, Ramón Franco and Julián Rubio amongst the revolutionaries and Romerales, Jurado and Faraudo in opposition.

A point which illustrates the sporting attitude of airmen at that time, and in the difficult times to come, was that although Collar and Barberán served in opposing factions this did not stop them, three years later, joining forces for a daring transatlantic flight which led to fame and death.

As a result of the uprising at Cuatro Vientos, the air arm gained the favour of the Republic. They did not, however, convert it back into an independent force, but they did give them their own uniform, this time navy blue. During the period of the Republic military, naval and civil aviation were all grouped together under the Dirección General de Aeronáutica, which depended, according to the date, either on the Presidency or on the Ministers of Communications or War.

In 1931 the Second Republic was proclaimed. A large part of the nation greeted this with satisfaction thinking that here, at last, was an inauguration of the resurgence. Another large group greeted it with fear, remembering the terrible failure of the previous attempt in 1873.

In Madrid, on April 14th, 1931, the atmosphere was one of joy, as the author can well remember despite the fact that he was then quite young. In spite of the incessant, alarming shouting of slogans such as, "today or tomorrow Albiñana's head", the impression was not one of anxiety.

During the first two years the atmosphere continued to be peaceful, despite the first scars of violence left by the burning of the convents on May 10–12th, 1931, and Azaña's comment: "all the churches in Spain are not worth the life of one republican". This would not have been considered important if it had come from the opposition, but was regarded as serious coming from the lips of the strongest man in the government.

General Sanjurgo's monarchial uprising (August 8th, 1932) failed through lack of enthusiasm. The military were not active, despite a recent law reducing their numbers, discontent produced by suppression of the General Military Academy (controlled by Francisco Franco), sentences passed by the Honour Courts, revision of some of the recompense for overseas service in Africa and a system of promotions by election. The reduction in strength, now that Morocco was peaceful, was logical and had been recommended publicly by Mola: however, one could not expect such a move to be popular amongst the forces. Together with the other steps which have been quoted, and an unfortunate selection of commanders, it seemed as if there was a deliberate plan to destroy the Army.

At that time the Catholics had not yet taken up an attitude of systematic opposition. The author can well remember how the President of the Republic was applauded as he arrived and left twelve o'clock Mass at the Milagrosa Basilica. Because of his opposition to article 26 of the Constitution he resigned from the presidency of the provisional government in October 1931, but this did not prevent him from accepting the presidency of the Republic in December of the same year.

The outbreaks of violence (Seville in July 1931; Castilblanco on the last day of that year; Arnedo and Llobregat in January 1932; Villa de Don Fadrique in July 1932, and Casas Viejas in January 1933) were the responsibility of Anarchists or Communists, since the Socialist Party—as during the Dictatorship—were in collaboration with those in power.

The repression of Casas Viejas made way for Azaña's downfall, but he managed to stay in power until June. Under a third government, he was conceded additional time (until September) for the completion of some fundamental laws. However, the Socialist Party did not wish to take over power (they were not interested in the bourgeois revolution which was trying to influence the Republic: their designs were for a proletarian revolution) so there was no solution other than to dissolve the *Cortes* (Parliament). When Lerroux failed to obtain sufficient parliamentary support his second, Martínez Barrio, managed to form a cabinet in order to prepare for new elections, which were fixed for November.

Azaña's period of government, which had lasted for almost two years, was then one of the longest in the 20th century and one of the most productive for legislative reforms. But, as his own admirers would be first to admit, he placed far too much importance on political problems and his anti-religious phobia than on economic and social matters, which were those needing the most urgent attention. Agrarian reform was not put into operation and industrialisation was completely forgotten. Azaña tried to give a new impetus to education but, through lack of time, he achieved very little (his anti-Catholic prejudices also hindered him in this).

On the whole, right-wing reaction to his politics was democratic and well ordered. In March 1933 the moderate CEDA (Conservative) party was formed. This led the right-wing block and triumphed in the elections held in November 1933, although it did not manage to achieve a majority. At the same time the monarchial party, the *Renovación Española* (Spanish Restoration) had been formed and this, like the Traditionalist party, obtained very few seats. The Falange, established a few days before the elections, was represented in the *Cortes* by José Antonio Primo de Rivera, who was included in the right-wing list of candidates.

The Agrarian Party, which numbered 26 deputies in the previous Parliament, raised this figure to 36 and became a second right-wing party, behind the CEDA, and the fourth in the *Cortes*.

On the left-wing the Socialist Party, due to over confidence in their own strength, made the mistake of standing alone, and the number of their deputies was reduced from 117 to 60. The Radical Party exceeded this number and obtained 102 seats as opposed to 93 in the previous Parliament. Azaña's party was barred.

The CEDA, with its 115 seats, could not govern on its own, but was able to do so in alliance with the Radicals and Agrarians, since this gave them a total of 253 votes as opposed to 100 on the right and some 125 on the left. The Agrarian minority accepted the 'regime legally established', and prepared to collaborate and even to govern, although this produced a split which reduced it to 26 deputies. The CEDA realised that this was not an opportune moment for a right wing government and decided that a solution was to rule from the centre.

Lerroux formed his government on December 16th, supported by the CEDA and the Agrarians. The left wing of the Socialist Party did not accept its electoral downfall lightly; it abandoned the impartial attitudes it had held until then and the first skirmishes broke out with members of the Falange, a movement that was beginning to be noticed. Here was the origin of the later drama. Assassination of some of the first Falangists occurred, and soon after a merging of the Falange and the JONS the reprisals started. Juan Antonio Ansaldo undertook the organisation of these in March 1934.

Matías Montero of the Spanish University Syndicate (SEU), had been buried on February 10th, and was the third of the Falangists to be assassinated. Prieto, a moderate Socialist said in a public speech, "if it is necessary to shed blood, then it must be shed", thus following in the footsteps of the intransigent Largo Caballero. In the *Cortes* he exclaimed, "we are being pushed beyond the legal limits". The right wing Socialists (Besteiro, Saborit and Trifón Gómez) resigned their posts to show their disapproval of the tactics being adopted.

The CNT maintained its previous attitude and, after the events at Aragón, organised general strikes in Saragossa and Valencia.

The Centralist middle of the road) Government, was harassed by the Socialists, Anarchists and Communists. They also made enemies of the Basques and Catalans on account of the Basque Statute and the law for farming contracts, approved by the Catalan Parliament on April 11th, 1934, both of which they were unprepared to recognise. Lerroux managed to bring forward the amnesty law and that of the passive rights of the clergy, but he had to leave the government on April 28th. Gil Robles claimed power at the *Congreso de la Juventud de Acción Popular* (Congress of Popular Action Youth Group) but the President, supported by Socialist opinion, whisked him out of sight. The Radical, Samper, formed an insignificant government which lasted until the end of September.

In May the position became more radical. On the first day of the month *el Socialista* asked for "a Spanish October". Two days later the Carlist Pretender named Fal Conde as secretary general and forbade all union with the Alphosine monarchists, despite the fact that a joint commission, only a short while before, had succeeded in obtaining a promise of help from Mussolini. Varela began to give military instruction to the Monarchist volunteers. Calvo Sotelo returned to Spain and adopted a much less transigent role in the *Cortes* than that of Gil Robles. On May 16th Martinez Barrio stood up in opposition at the Radicalist Party Congress and the Centralist majority was reduced even further.

On June 5th there was a Socialist strike, on the 6th two deposits of arms were found in Madrid, and the Falangists held a demonstration near Cuatro Vientos to show their strength. The government wasted the whole of the summer in its dispute with the Basques and Catalans, whose deputies had walked out of the *Cortes*, without finding time to do anything about the 700,000 out of work.

Asturias was also beginning to make itself heard. On September 8th Gil Robles announced to his followers in Covadonga, "we will not tolerate this state of affairs one moment longer. . . ." Two days later eighty cases of armaments were disembarked from the ss *Turquesa* in San Esteban de Pravia, showing that the Socialists were determined to do something about the situation.

When the *Cortes* resumed in October, Gil Robles attacked the government, which resigned. Lerroux formed his fourth cabinet (on the 9th) with three

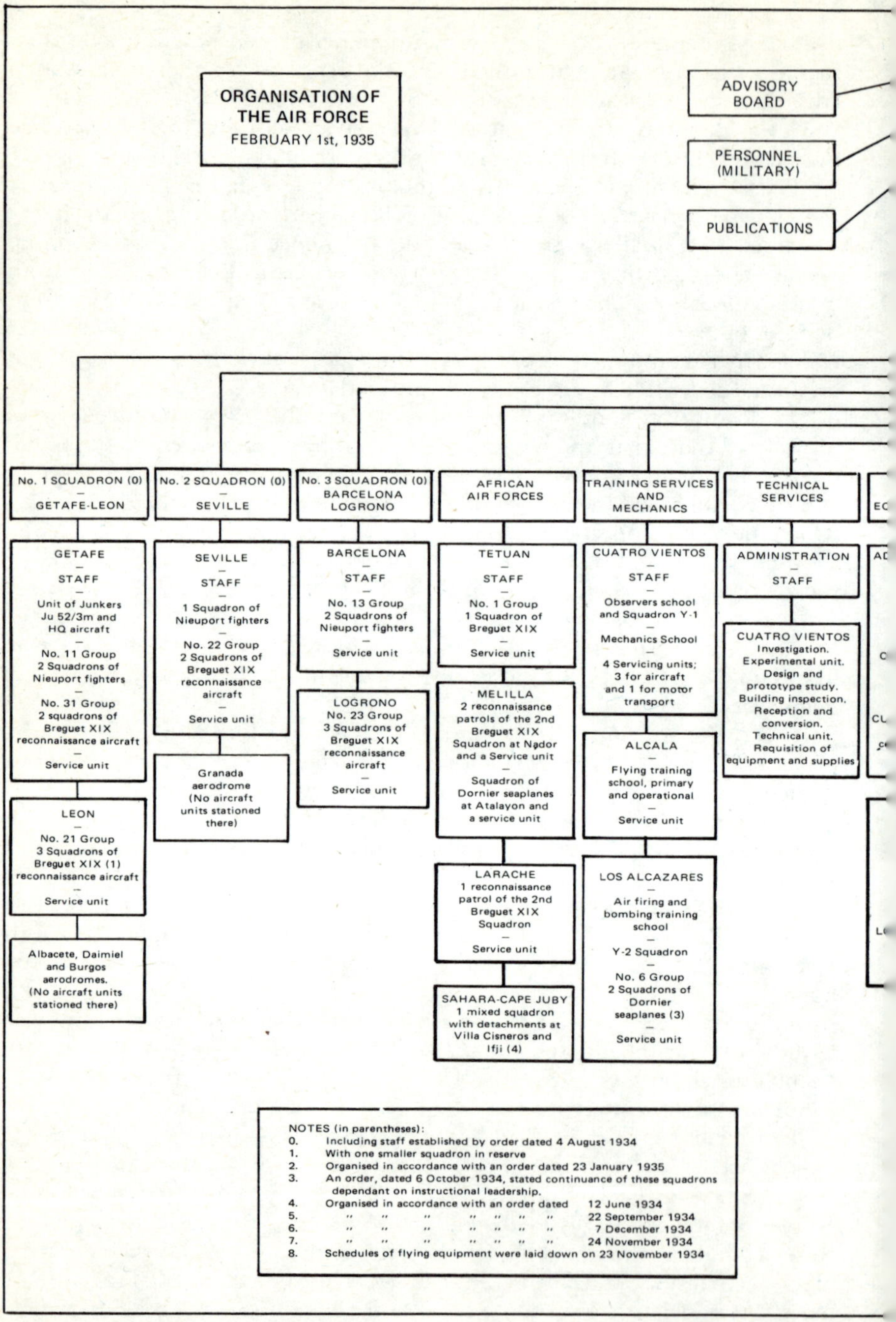

A chart showing the organisation of the Spanish Air Force which became effective on February 1st, 1935.

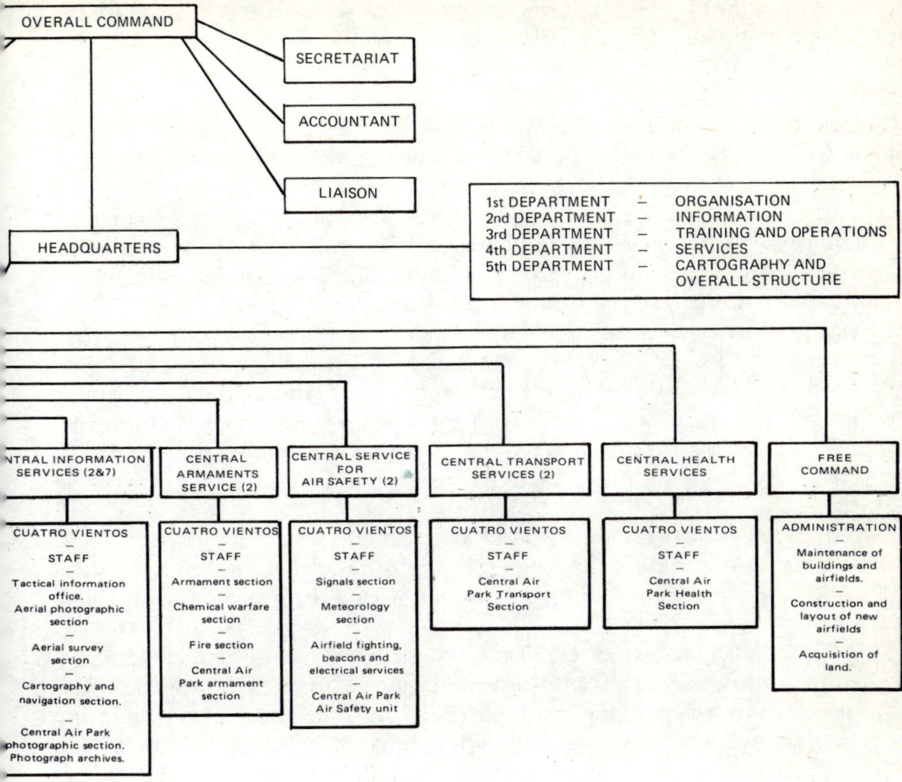

EFFECTIVE AIR FORCE UNITS	Squadron Staff	Group Staff	Groups of Three Squadrons	Groups of Two Squadrons	Squadrons	Service Squadrons
Fighters	–	2	–	2	1	–
Strategic Reconnaissance	1	1	–	1	–	–
Reconnaissance	2	4	2(1)	2	–	–
Seaplanes	–	1	–	1	1	–
Colonial (Fokker, Bregnet XIX and light aircraft)	–	–	–	–	1(4)	–
Training Services	–	–	–	–	2	–
Cuatro Vientos Aerodrome (various)	–	–	–	–	–	3
TOTALS	3	8	2	6	5	3

ministers from the CEDA, six Radicals, two Agrarians, a Democratic-Liberal and an Independent. The Socialist Party seized this pretext to launch the revolution which they had been preparing, almost in the open, for many months.

On the 5th of the month a general strike was declared in Madrid and Barcelona and there was a rebellion in Asturias. The following day this insurrection spread to Catalonia and the Basque regions. The strike affected the majority of Spain and the cabinet declared a state of war. On the 7th peace returned to Catalonia but in Asturias, where forces and aircraft from Africa had been used, the battle lasted until the 19th. The balance sheet at the end of this period showed more than a thousand dead and two thousand wounded.

On that occasion the Army acted as a co-ordinated force, despite the existence of opposing groups (the UME and the UMRA) which, in fact, were never very strong and had little prestige. General Batet, a Catalan and a confirmed republican, promptly quelled the uprising in Barcelona; the Republican, López Ochoa successfully completed his assignment of linking up with those besieged in Oviedo. Moriones, the military commander of Gijón, also contributed to this.

Aviation, now under the direction of Warleta and Sáenz de Buruaga, took an active part, to the extent that the 1st Squadron was awarded collectively a military medal. One pilot had objected to attacking the miners, but received no backing.

Hidalgo de Cisneros escorted Prieto out of Spain, as an act of personal friendship, and not as an act of insubordination. This does not mean to say that the Army was reactionary, but progress is one thing and armed revolution another. The Army acted in a disciplined manner, obeying the Government's orders, which it accepted without qualms. It was different at a later date when the Army had to act against the Government. Then, many of its members restricted themselves to obedience, some acted according to their personal conscience, while others accepted the situation to suit their own convenience—or were carried away by fear.

Gil Robles did not take advantage of the quelling of the revolution to take control of the Government, leaving responsibility for repression with the Radicals. This meant that he faced much the same problems as Azaña had after the incidents at Casas Viejas. The CEDA lost little support, given the enormous ideological difference which separated its followers from those who had revolted.

The judgement of responsibility consumed all the Government's energies until March 29th, the day when three ministers resigned as a protest against the pardon granted to González Peña who had led the uprising in Asturias. Earlier, in November, some twenty people had been pardoned, among them Lieutenant Colonel Ricart, Commander Pérez Farrás and Captain Escofet, together with some others in December. Two men were executed in November and Sergeant Vázquez and Jesús Argüelles 'Pichilatu' at the beginning of January. The journalist Luis de Sirval, responsible for distorted reports regarding the repression, was killed during a dispute with an official of the troops who fled the country. Later, four other miners were condemned to death.

Calvo Sotelo, whose authority was increasing and who was now at the head of the *Bloque Nacional*, pronounced in the House: "the Government's attitude has been hesitant, unconstitutional and, finally, unjust". The Government according to José Antonio, also committed the folly of refusing to judge Azaña, on the grounds that it had insufficient evidence.

To solve the crisis the President did not call on Gil Robles. Despite the successive failure of Lerroux and Martínez de Velasco (agrarian), he suspended the *Cortes* for a month to allow Lerroux to form a government, this time with Radicals alone. When the House met again on May 3rd there was a new crisis, also solved by Lerroux. This time he brought in five ministers from the CEDA, among them their leader who occupied the portfolio for war and who nominated Franco chief of staff.

A year and a half after the elections Gil Robles consented to take his place in the Government, although not as president. This did not happen until September 20th, although there were two months of prorogation by Chapaprieta's two governments. During this year and a half things had changed a great deal and it was not easy to undertake any constructive work. José Antonio prophesied that, "in the next elections the left wing parties will win and Azaña will return to power" and on July 13th, one year before the final act of the play, this same politician was able to proclaim that, "the political initiative has passed into our hands".

Gil Robles concentrated his political activity on obtaining constitutional reform. A committee was nominated to examine the proposed law, which was to be discussed in the last quarter of the year. The Agrarian ministers resigned, despite the fact that the government had brought forward a new law for agrarian reform, one which was described by José Antonio as, "the most reactionary that has ever been brought before us". Chapaprieta was given the task of forming a new government, which included Gil Robles and Lerroux, until the latter resigned one month later.

The left wing opposition, recognising the President's resistance when he handed over power to Gil Robles, persisted until they obtained Lerroux's political destruction. Chapaprieta was still forming his second government when the CEDA issued a warning to form a government or dissolve the *Cortes*. In December the Constitution had been in force for four years, after which period it could be revised. Alcalá Zamora, despite an earnest desire to bring about a revision, decided to dissolve the *Cortes* for the second time.

Politically, the nine governments of the years 1934–1935 did little more than destroy much of what had been achieved in the first two years of Republican rule. This only increased a desire for revenge, so far as those who had been defeated in 1934 were concerned, and sowed seeds of doubt amongst the members of the right wing block. There was nothing more positive on the balance sheet than a law for the intensification of farming, one relating to retirement pensions for the clergy, a law for amnesty, Giménez Fernández's law for country rents, one dealing with mixed juries, Salmón's law and Chapaprieta's good economic programme.

The Spanish Falange appealed to the rest of the nation, arguing that there was no hope of salvation with either the right or left wing elements and that it was vital to adopt a completely new approach. The Traditionalists also broke away from the right wing block. In opposition, at the instigation of Russia, Popular Fronts had just been formed throughout Europe, as a result of directions of the VIIth Congress of the 'Komintern' (July–September 1935).

With this background elections were held in February 1936. They were organised by Portela Valladares' government (one of the president's friends) and brought the Popular Front into power. The total number of votes cast did not vary appreciably in 1931, 1933 or 1936: the percentage wavered between 45 and 55 per cent. Victory or failure depended on the electoral tactics of the small group of floating voters. The CEDA continued to be the largest minority party, with 120 deputies (more than in 1933), although many certificates of election were later annulled.

With the Popular Front in power normality quickly turned to abnormality, and the most incomprehensible things became a part of everyday life. It is difficult for those who did not live in Spain to realise that the menfolk of many Madrid families slept away from their homes for months on end. This was not to protect their own lives, but to prevent groups of revolutionaries from destroying all churches within the district. These men were also exposed to the constant danger of being arrested if they failed to hide their guns quickly enough during one of the frequent visits by the police. It is a fact that many 'provocation' arrests were made, of those who dared to shout in public, "long live Spain", at a time when paramilitary organisations roamed the streets of Madrid shouting, "long live Russia", and when many were exalting Euzcadi or free Catalonia.

During the month of April, after Alcalá Zamora's dismissal on April 7th, the author was able to follow the progressive worsening of the situation from his house in Garcia de Paredes. On April 14th, the fifth anniversary of the proclamation of the Republic, Second Lieutenant Reyes of the Civil Guard was assassinated in la Castellana. A crowd of more than 100,000 people accompanied his body as it was carried along la Castellana. At the corner of García de Paredes they were met by bursts of fire from machine-guns mounted on a building that was under construction adjoining the Costellana Hilton Hotel. The only intervention on the part of the authorities was to prevent the funeral procession from passing along Colon de Cibeles, thence to Manuel Becerra Square. Forces of the Assault Corps, led by Lieutenant Castillo, enforced this order with weapons fired at point-blank range. The following day a general strike was declared in Madrid.

Generals Orgaz and Varela, hoping to take advantage of the reaction provoked by these events, planned to take the War Ministry by surprise on the 20th, but they were arrested before they could put this plan into action.

One afternoon, some days later, members of the Socialist Party attempted to burn down the Milagrosa Basilica. Police on duty outside General Orgaz's door (who was under house arrest) acted with indifference. However, the attempt was foiled by the spontaneous intervention of people living in nearby houses, among them General Queipo de Llano. A little later these same policemen informed the director general of security of the event, using the author's telephone.

On May 1st, the workers' holiday, Madrid looked like a Bolshevik city. On the 3rd day elections were held in Cuenca, but the results, like those in Granada, were invalidated. Under a pretext many churches were burned down. Despite this, José Antonio, who was still in detention, received the largest number of votes, although he was ultimately stripped of his office. Two days later the right wing parties withdrew from the elections in Granada. As a reprisal, on May 8th, Captain Faraudo, instructor of the armed Militia, was assassinated.

On the 10th, Azaña was eliminated from politics by the elegant procedure of electing him president of the Republic. Two days later the CNT Congress ended and on the 16th a large Communist meeting was held in Valencia. This party had gained importance in Spain because of the merging of its youth groups with the Socialists. On the 19th, in his presentation of the Government to the *Cortes*, Casares Quiroga declared himself, "ready for war against Fascism". For some time the CEDA had kept in touch with Prieto, considering the possibility of forming a government presided over by this moderate Socialist. He, however, could not count on the authorisation of his party; it would have been necessary to hold a Socialist Party Congress, but this had been deferred until the autumn when the other parties (the left wing Republican, Republican Union and 'Unió de Rabassaires') were to have Congressional meetings. Meanwhile the 'hot' war continued, centred in Madrid, principally by the sale of the newspapers *FE* and *Mundo Obrero*. But with the same regularity that newspapers were printed Spaniards were being killed.

Mola began his first campaign of action on May 25th. On June 3rd the director general of security went to Pamplona in the hope of surprising Mola. He failed in this attempt, but had his first interview with the Carlists on that day. José Antonio sent a circular to all provincial chiefs before being transferred to Alicante prison, where he arrived on June 6th. The following day Mola had his first interview with Cabanellas, an official of the Saragossan Division who, until then, had been a fervent Republican.

On June 16th, at a pathetic meeting of the Permanent Commission of the *Cortes*, Calvo Sotelo made an impressive speech about the outrages committed in recent times and had a long argument with the president of the cabinet, during which he exclaimed, "I consider myself well aware of the threat . . . it is better to die honourably than to live with scorn". Obviously this situation could not continue. Power had passed to the street but the street, like the ballot boxes, was divided.

None of the various factions made any attempt to conceal the fact that they were prepared to obtain power by violence. The political ineptitude of the Spaniards meant there was no other way. The Socialists were certainly not going to accept defeat now that they had control within their grasp. The Falange and Carlists were not prepared to lose, presuming they were given the opportunity to win.

On June 23rd Franco, in his capacity as war minister, wrote a courteous but positive letter to Casares Quiroga. The end of the drama was drawing near. On July 12th Lieutenant Castillo was assassinated. On the 13th, Calvo Sotelo, chief of the national block, was dragged from his house by police and, despite his parliamentary immunity, was assassinated and his body abandoned in the Eastern Cemetery.

Nobody doubted that this was the last straw. All that remained to be decided was the moment of the uprising.

Preparation of the Uprising

An operation as important as a *coup d'état* (nobody had considered the prospect of a long term war) could not be attempted, not even in Spain, without a leader.

It was a difficult task to find one. The right wing block, which brought together half the nation in 1933, lost a great deal of prestige because of its indecision and lack of plans in the key years of 1934 and 1935. The most energetic groups, the Falange and the Carlists, had their own leaders and had broken away from the other associated parties.

In order to avoid political rivalry they needed to find a suitable military leader. Sanjurjo seemed the best choice, despite his earlier failure, because of the freedom of action he enjoyed through not living in the country, and also because he was the most senior general prepared to take part in an uprising.

In Madrid, en route to Pamplona for Africa, Mola was encouraged by Franco and Goded to accept the post of director for the preparation of the Uprising in the Peninsula, acting as Sanjurjo's representative. In April he sent out the first general instruction, ordering the formation within twenty days of provincial, civil and military juntas in each *División Orgánica* (Organic Division, the old *Capitanias Generales*).

On May 25th he organised his first campaign of action, in which the 5th (Saragossa), 6th (Burgos) and 7th (Valladolid) Divisions were assigned the task of taking Madrid, whose garrison, together with all the 1st (Madrid), 2nd (Seville) and 4th (Barcelona) Divisions, were to remain neutral. The 3rd (Valencia) Division had to support the march on Madrid with an attack to divert attention, so the main body could advance towards Barcelona. In this plan the only job assigned to the Navy was to prevent the government bringing in reinforcements from Africa.

This campaign had been carefully thought out. The divisions which had to attack the capital were those to which vast popular support was assured. They counted on this to increase the military forces by up to 75 per cent. Since it was realised that their task was difficult it was considered necessary for each of the chosen divisions to utilise at least two-thirds of their troops, because the strength of the opposing forces centred around Madrid was much greater than in other towns. The 8th (Galicia) Division and the Asturias Command were ordered to be on the defensive, because the socialist potential in the latter area was still strong. Valencia, where the atmosphere was also favourable, was to try and prevent Barcelona from turning against Aragón, so supporting the attack on Madrid. There was to be no attempt to do anything in the south since the political climate was uncertain and it was a long way from the capital.

On June 5th, Mola dispatched new instructions, in which he indicated that once they had attained their objective a directorate of five military officers would assume power. Throughout the month of June he distributed special instructions to the 5th, 6th and 7th Divisions and to the Navy, giving plans for defence from air attacks, together with means of overcoming opposition from the riot police, whose 29 recently-acquired armoured cars were likely to prove a tough obstacle. Goded also sent instructions to the Valencian garrison.

On June 23rd Franco sent his now-famous letter of protest to the Prime Minister and the War Minister, Casares Quiroga. On the following day Mola drew up instructions for the African Army, which involved an important alteration from the original plan in the sense that he was now trying to achieve control in all areas. The African Army was instructed to revolt as soon as Franco arrived to assume command. The Generals Queipo de Llano, González Carrasco and Villegas each accepted their difficult assignments of taking control of Seville, Barcelona and Madrid, although only the first was to accomplish his mission successfully. Saliquet replaced Queipo in Valladolid.

The fiestas at San Fermin presented Mola with a perfect occasion for meeting emissaries from throughout Spain. On the 7th, however, following the letters exchanged between Fal Conde and the 'director', it seemed that all roads that might lead to an understanding with the Carlists were closed. However, Sanjurjo's intervention from Lisbon (on the 9th) opened the doors to new discussions. José Antonio Primo de Rivera distributed instructions to his followers, recommending them to collaborate with the military, but only at provincial level.

Calvo Sotelo's death removed all the difficulties. The Carlist pretender, Alfonso Carlos, authorised the mobilisation of his followers, with an order that this should be done to the cry of, 'God and our Fatherland'. The de Havilland Dragon Rapide which was needed to take General Franco to Tetuán had been standing by at Cabo Juby, and it was flown immediately to Las Palmas.

At this date it was decided to switch the assignments of Generals Goded and González Carrasco and this caused great confusion in both Barcelona and Valencia, especially the latter.

Meanwhile, the leaders of the Popular Front had not remained inactive. Belarmino Tomás had announced in Sama during October 1934: "Our present surrender is only a halt along the way . . . ready for our next battle which will end in final victory." At that time the weapons which the Revolutionaries had at their disposal consisted of a collection of arms held in Catalonia and guarded by the *Generalidad* (Catalan Autonomous Government of 1931–36). In Asturias there was a hoard of 17,456 weapons, comprising everything from pistols to artillery weapons, and there were also quantities hidden in various places. Hugh Thomas put this last number as high as 90,000 guns, 33,000 pistols, 30,000 shells, 330,000 cartridges and 10,000 sticks of dynamite, a number which was clearly exaggerated to impress the 30,000 'political' prisoners.*

Until December 1935, with Gil Robles as minister of war, Fanjul as under secretary and Franco chief of staff, the possibilities of a revolution or for an increase in their stock of arms was greatly reduced.

The political 'atmosphere' began to show itself during October 1935, with the formation of the Popular Front and the clever way in which Lerroux was

* Hugh Thomas, *The Spanish Civil War*.

made to lose prestige over the 'straperlo' affair. A little later, coinciding with Portela Valladares' formation of a transitional government and General Molero's entry into the Ministry of War, the Army began to 'operate' through the UMRA (Military Republican Antifascist Union). This was led by General Núñez del Prado, who had the support, amongst others of Lieutenant Colonels Asensio Torrado, Luis Romero Bassar, del Rosal, Díaz Sandino, Victor Lacalle, Commanders Pérez Farrás, Pérez Salas, Burguete, díaz Sandino and Guarner, and Officers La Roquette, Burguete, Faraudo, Castillo, Condes, Moreno, Adonis Rodriguez.*

On January 31st, 1936, before the general elections, Largo Caballero, having taken over the presidency of the executive commission of the Socialist Party was bold enough to say: "When we launch into. . . ."

With the arrival of the Government of the Popular Front the Antifascist Workers and Peasants Militias (MAOC) came out into the open and Captain Francisco Galan, in his capacity as commissar of the Militia of the Central Revolutionary Committee—or the 'Soviet National' over which Largo Cabellero presided—opposed them.

Largo Caballero, together with the commissars for the Militia and the Interior (Hernández Zancajo) formed a supreme *troika* to offer armed insurrection, and were determined to carry out the proposed revolutionary plan of action. For their liaison with the exterior and the provinces they also created the 'Liaison Organisation' and nominated officials to take charge in these regions.

When Azaña, who was then president of the Council of Ministers, heard of these revolutionary proposals, he called together the National Congress of the Popular Front and obtained a promise that this plan would only be put into action if there were "fascist provocation".

From May 1st–12th the Congress of the CNT (National Workers' Confederation, with anarchist tendency) was held in Saragossa. They maintained their traditional revolutionary and anti-political attitudes. On the 16th there was a meeting in the Casa del Pueblo in Valencia, presided over by a delegate of the III International (Ventura, better known as 'Codovila' or 'Luis Medina') and attended by representatives of the Central Revolutionary Committee and of the Russian Party. They approved a ten-point programme, of which the following were paramount:

(2) To unleash, on the same day as the movement breaks out, a campaign of agitation throughout the world, to be called 'antifascist', and which should express itself so clearly that the whole proletariat is behind this movement.

(3) To provoke strikes systematically . . . so that they serve as a preparation . . . and to test the solidarity of the organisation.

(6) To bring discredit on the central figures of the Socialist Party (Prieto, Besteiro, etc).

(9) To entrust to 'Radio' No 25 Madrid (composed of active members of the police force) the task of eliminating prominent military and political characters.

* Comin Colomer, *Secret History of the Second Republic.*

Preparations for the revolution were expected to be finished by June 29th, when it was hoped that Léon Blum, the Socialist, would have attained power in France.*

After all the right wing parties had left the *Cortes*, following the dramatic session of June 16th, the danger of revolution was imminent.

The moderate Republicans and Socialists realised that things had gone too far and that some appeasement was necessary if normal life was to continue. On July 9th, taking advantage of Largo Caballero's absence (he was in London to attend the VIII Congress of the International Syndical Federation which began on July 6th), the leaders of the minorities of the Popular Front met together under the presidency of Marcelino Domingo.

On the following day the Socialist executive met, called together by the vice president Jimenéz Asúa. At this meeting, Prieto triumphed by one vote to gain presidency of the Council.

Meanwhile, Largo Caballero was declaring in London: "There are no longer any neutral states. On one side there is Russia and the Popular Front of the democratic countries, and on the other side there are the dictatorships of the right wing. Spain is a member of the League of Nations and will remain loyal to the pact; but if the League of Nations fails we will not be neutral. No. We will be the allies of the enemies of fascism".†

As soon as news of events in Madrid reached London, Largo Caballero hastened his return, without stopping in Paris as he had planned. But his presence was no longer required: assassination of the leader of the opposition (Calvo Sotelo) by members of the police had shattered any attempt at peacemaking.

Even the moderates realised that the die was cast. Prieto advised Condes (organiser of Sotelo's assassination) to remain in hiding. The following day he was a member of a group of people who gave 'evidence' that Sotelo's death was an act of revenge for the earlier assassination of Señor Castillo, a member of the riot police.

The authorities could see that conflict was imminent, as the following comment by Colonel Luis Romero Basart shows: "Days before the Uprising, General Nunez de Prado (who was then director general of aviation) ordered Captain La Roquette to organise a battalion composed of civil aviation workers. The aerodrome at Cuatro Vientos and, if possible, the artillery park were to be used as bases for men and weapons. This plan was confirmed later at a meeting which the three republican generals held in the office of the director general of the Civil Guard, and which was also attended by the director general of the Merchant Navy, the aviators González Gil, Mellado, Núñez Maza and Captain La Roquette. Within a few hours, however, La Roquette was advised personally by General Núñez de Prado that the War Ministry disapproved of the meeting and of the agreements reached. This did not stop the aviation workers from continuing preparations."‡

* This information was obtained from four documents found in Communist centres in the provinces of Seville, Cádiz and Badajoz, and in the Cuartel General at Bayo in Mallorca.

† *News Chronicle*: July 9th, 1936.

‡ Jacinto Toryho: *The Independence of Spain*.

The order to begin the Uprising could not be given immediately, since the African Army was then carrying out manoeuvres in Llano Amarillo. On July 16th Mola dispatched orders to the leaders in Africa that they should be ready to leave on the 17th at 17.00hrs, since according to the latest plan, Africa and the vital centres in the Peninsula should have started to revolt on the 18th; the rest on the 19th.

In fact, the leaders at Melilla were forced to bring events forward to the afternoon of the 17th. During the night the whole of Morocco joined their companions at Melilla. In the early morning, with the surrender of the aerodrome at Sania Ramel, resistance in the Protectorate ended.

Franco, informed of the happenings in Morocco on the morning of the 18th, declared a state of war in his military command in the Canaries, and flew to Tetuán. Also on July 18th, at 14.00hrs, the Uprising began in the Peninsula when Queipo de Llano took over command of the 2nd Division in Seville; the garrisons at Córdoba, Cádiz and Algeciras immediately gave their support.

In the north, at Valladolid, Saliquet seized the building of the 7th Division at 23.00hrs on the night of the 18th. At 06.00hrs on the 19th, as had been agreed, Mola assumed command of the 6th Division (Burgos) from Pamplona, Miguel Cabanellas declared a state of war to his 5th Division (Saragossa) and the garrison at Barcelona tried to seize the city. At the same time, Franco arrived in Tetuán to take over the African Army.

The 1st (Madrid), 3rd (Valencia), and the 8th (Galicia) Divisions, together with the Asturian Military Command, waited in readiness until the 20th.

Failure of the Coup d'Etat

The Uprising began in Melilla before orders were received from the leaders in Spain. As soon as the Government became aware of the events at Melilla, including the arrest of General Romerales, they initiated a search for the head of the African Army, General Gómez Morato, who had departed by air for Larache on a tour of inspection. Without being aware of events General Morato returned to Melilla and had the misfortune to land at Tauima aerodrome, which was occupied by the forces in revolt, and he was taken prisoner.

When Yagüe in Ceuta learned that Melilla had risen, he ordered the African Army to occupy key points in the territory during the night of July 17th, and this was accomplished without difficulty. Under the respective leadership of Arturo Alvarez Buylla, an artillery captain and fighter pilot, and Commander Ricardo de la Puente Bahamonde, the *Alta Comisaría* (High Commissariat) and the Sania Ramiel aerodrome resisted until the following morning. The seaplane base at Atalayón (Melilla) had been reduced by force the previous afternoon and the aerodromes of Tauima (Melilla) and Auamara (Larache) had been occupied without any resistence. At these air bases there were about twenty Breguet 19s, half of which had been sabotaged, and about ten unserviceable Dornier-Wal seaplanes at Atalayón. (These seaplanes were not available for service because of a succession of engine failures which led, eventually, to their being exchanged for a new type; in the Government Zone this problem was solved in a different way).

Before resistance in Tetuan died down the director general of aeronautics, General Núñez del Prado, made preparations to fly there to take over command. As he was about to take off from Barajas a breakdown of radio communication with Tetuán decided him to abandon his plan. Immediately an order was given to bombard Africa from Tablada.

Franco learned of the Uprising in Africa on the morning of July 18th and immediately declared a state of war in the Canaries, and travelled to Agadir and Casablanca in the de Havilland Dragon which had been hired by Bolin in London. Whilst Franco's Dragon was being refuelled at Agadir, two Fokker F-VIIs of the Cabo Juby squadron put down at the same aerodrome. They were en route to Tablada on Government orders to take part in the bombardment of Africa, begun early in the morning by the Fokkers, a Douglas DC-2 of the Compañía Aérea L.A.P.E. and a Breguet machine. In fact, the DC-2 failed to take off from that aerodrome because of the action of Captain Carlos Martínez Vara de Rey, who damaged it by small-arms fire.

During the morning of July 18th, General Queipo de Llano went to Seville, after evading police vigilance in Huelva, and daringly visited Government offices to ask whether the news from Africa was correct. He also used his visit to give details of his future movements. Naturally, these were false.

Meanwhile, the Navy was carrying out government orders to move the battleship *Jaime I* the cruisers *Libertad* and *Miguel de Cervantes*, together with four destroyers, into the waters of the Straits. The Government's intention was to prevent forces crossing from Africa, and to threaten and shell Ceuta and Melilla if this became necessary.

At 14.00hrs on July 18th Queipo, who had been hiding in the 2nd Division's building for half an hour, decided to confront its chief, General Vallaabrille. Both the general and the chief of staff refused to join the Uprising, but allowed themselves to be removed from office without putting up any strong resistance. From that moment, aided only by Commander Cuesta Monereo who took over as chief of staff, a few official followers and a small number of volunteers managed, by means of several daring moves, to take control of the centre of Seville, contrary to all predictions. That night they made their first broadcast from Radio Seville.

Late in the afternoon the two three-engined military Fokkers arrived at Tablada. Before nightfall they made reconnaissance flights over Seville, at it was intended that this town was to be subjected to bombing attacks on the morning of July 19th. The chief of Tablada aerodrome, Commander Martínez Esteve, handed over control to his second-in-command before the hour fixed for the bombing attack and made himself scarce. Realising that the situation was precarious the civil aircraft from Madrid managed to escape, but not the Fokkers from Cabo Juby or the damaged DC-2, and this gave a great boost to the Uprising. Ureña, the pilot of the third Fokker in West Africa, disobeyed Government orders and flew his aircraft to Larache (The fourth three-engined Fokker in the Colonial Squadron had been taken to Madrid before the Uprising by Captain Félix Sampil).

While these events were taking place in Seville, the aero-naval base at San Javier adopted a favourable attitude towards the Uprising, without actually taking any action, other than to sever communications with Captain Fernando Navarro sent from Madrid. The naval base at Cartagena was sympathetic to this attitude, but it was not seconded by Admirals Márquez and Molíns.

The four destroyers had already sailed from Cartagena and reached the African coast in mid-afternoon. The *Churruca* went to Ceuta, where her crew came out strongly in favour of the Uprising. The *Lepanto*'s crew took the opposite view and waited in readiness outside the port of Melilla. The *Sánchez Barcáiztegui* and the *Almirante Valdés* went into port and their crews held conversations with the rioters, but they decided not to join them. Once out of port the sailors imprisoned the officers of the Cuerpo General and sailed the vessels to Cartagena and Malaga, where the mere presence of the *Sánchez Barcáiztegui* forced the surrender of the irresolute General Patxot.

The cruisers *Libertad* and *Miguel de Cervantes* had sailed from Ferrol and the battleship *Jaime I* and the destroyer *Almirante Antequera* had left Santander, where they had been waiting for the President of the Republic.

During the late hours of July 18th, Casares Quiroga dismissed the Government and the dissident Radical leader, Martínez Barrio, was given the task of forming a moderate cabinet. At 02.00hrs on July 19th, the new president of the cabinet and General Miaja (minister of war and an old friend and superior of Mola) telephoned Pamplona and, so it seems, offered Mola the portfolio for war if he would quell the Uprising. Mola, knowing that Yagüe, Franco, Queipo and Saliquent had rebelled, that the regiments of Barcelona had withdrawn to barracks, and without any possibility of warning the other people involved, decided he could not accept.

That night, July 18–19th, the garrison in Barcelona revolted, but this came as no surprise.

On the morning of July 19th, the 5th Division (Miguel Cabanellas), 6th (of which Mola assumed command once Batet had been arrested) and 7th (under the orders of Saliquet, who had arrested Molero at 23.00hrs on July 18th) and the Military Command of the Balearics, joined the Uprising. This moment, chosen by Mola, should really have been exactly right, since it was a Sunday in the midst of the summer holidays: Saturday afternoon had been kept for the Uprising in Africa. Since progress in Africa was well advanced, it would perhaps have been more logical to rush the Rising in the Peninsula, just as Yagüe had done in Morocco.

The 1st (Madrid), 5th (Valencia) and the 8th (Galicia) Divisions, together with the *Comandancia Exenta* from Asturias, stood by in readiness.

Once a state of war had been declared in the Balearics, Goded embarked on one of Mahón's seaplanes (which had landed at Palma de Mallorca en-route from Cartagena) and took off for Barcelona at midday on July 19th, when the situation in the city was desperate. In this action Goded showed great courage but, strangely, he would not show himself in Barcelona until his garrison had revolted, and this contributed to failure of the *coup*. For their part, those who had risen not only failed to arrest the leader of the division, but allowed him to report to his superiors by telephone.

At 09.00hrs on the morning of July 19th the African Army had begun the crossing of the Straits as ordered by Franco. With the arrival of two units of regulars at the ports of Cádiz and Algeciras, who were expected to advance to Seville and Córdoba, the northern half of the Central Meseta was controlled by Mola, and Barcelona, Gerona, Lénido and Seo de Urgel had risen. It seemed as if the Uprising would be an overwhelming success.

During the course of the morning the situation changed completely when the crew of the *Churruca* (which had joined the *Lepanto* to patrol off Morocco) rebelled, followed by the crews of the cruisers *Libertad* and *Miguel de Cervantes* and the battleship *Jaime I* which was *en route* to the Straits. It was also confirmed that the Uprising was not meeting with success in Barcelona. This change of attitude of the ship's crew was due partially to the action of a radio telegraphist, Benjamín Balboa, who had worked hard to incite them to riot during the afternoon of July 18th and the morning of the 19th. He had taken over control of the broadcasting station after imprisoning the officer in charge, and lost no time in converting the ships' crews to support the Uprising.

At midday on Sunday 19th, Giral's government was formed in Madrid. This was after a big proletarian protest at the excessively compliant attitude of Martínez Barrio's government. When Castelló arrived in Badajoz to assume command of the 1st Division he found himself named as an official of the War Ministry. Giral kept the portfolio for the Navy. The new minister of the interior, General Pozas, was assigned the task of finding out the current situation in each province, encouraging his followers and threatening and sowing doubt amongst his opponents.

Pozas was compelled to use the telephone for his fact-finding task, and this could only be counteracted by Queipo's broadcasts and the message broadcast from Tetuán by General Franco to the various headquarters of the Guardia Civil. This was done because Pamplona, Seville and Tetuan, were so far apart that there was no possibility of any telephone link between them or between distant provinces. The isolation of the north and south zones was such that the government historian, Ramos Oliveria, quoted as vital the assistance given by Portugal, which had allowed telephone communication between the two zones, via a room in the Hotel Avis in Lisbon.

The order to arm the militia, given by the new president of the Council, caused the quartering of the Covadonga Regiment (No 4) in Madrid, and a close watch was kept on the bolts of 45,000 rifles deposited in the artillery park. Up to this time Madrid had remained peaceful: that very morning the troops had paraded for Mass. At midday, with the arrival of General Fanjul at the Montaña barracks, the rebellion of the No 4 Regiment became official. In the afternoon, at Carabanchel, the Zapadores Battalion and the Regiment of Mounted Artillery joined the Uprising under the orders of General García de Herrán.

Casares Quiroga, Martínez Barrio and leaders of the Madrid Division including Virgilio Cabanellas, Miaja, Cardenal, Castelló and García Antúnez did not want an order to arm the militia to be given. They were all aware that such action would signal the beginning of a Marxist revolution. Furthermore, such a course seemed absolutely unnecessary since, in Madrid, the number of troops likely to be loyal to the government far exceeded the doubtful element. In addition, in the capital there were many leaders and officials who were absolutely loyal to the Government and capable of taking command of the troops wherever they were needed. The best proof of this is that a massive distribution of arms could only take place when the 45,000 bolts deposited in the Montaña Barracks were available. That is to say when the Rising had been conquered in Madrid.

At the same time as the militia was being armed in Madrid, Mola sent Commander Juan Antonio Ansaldo to Lisbon to bring back Sanjurjo, and then to Cordoba for Captain Salas, one of the three pilots who went from Getafe to Pamplona. Salas was required to liaise with General Franco.

The Boundaries are Defined

By July 20th the possibility of an occupation of Madrid from outside the city was slight: that of an internal coup was nil, having regard to the inactivity of the rioters throughout the previous afternoon. Barcelona was lost for the Nationalists, despite the fact that Colonel Lacasa with his Santiago Chasseur Regiment was continuing to resist. In the remaining garrisons in Catalonia despondency was spreading to the extent that a few hours later they surrendered without resistance. All that remained uncertain was the situation within the 3rd and 8th Divisions and the Asturian Command.

Mola, convinced that only vigorous and speedy action could bring him victory, put into operation his plan for a concentric advance on Madrid. On the night of July 19–20th he ordered two columns of his 6th Division to attack the city. These comprised the Burgos column (Colonel Gistau) which was en route to Aranda de Duero and, most important, that of Pamplona (Colonel García Escámez), which was routed via Logrono, where it was to pick up the artillery. The column of the 7th Division (Colonel Serrador) had to remain at Valladolid until the night of July 20th, when the news from Galicia and Asturias seemed to be more encouraging. The 5th Division, overwhelmed by the premature loss of Catalonia and Valencia which left its flank exposed, failed to organise its column.

The instructions which Mola had given to the 5th, 6th and 7th Divisions were very detailed and specified how each column should be organised. One battery of guns was to accompany each battalion, with a gun mounted on a motorised truck to lead each column. They were told how to obtain supplies, how to defend themselves from air attack, and the stages that should have been reached at 24, 48 and 72 hours from the beginning of the Uprising. The Pamplona column was free to go to Somosierra—via Riaza—or to Guadalajara, according to the expeditionary leader's decision in Soria.

Once support of the fleet had been lost, Franco knew that he could not attempt to advance towards the capital until Mola could gain sufficient time to allow him to bring the Army across by air transport. On the afternoon of July 19th the first forces began to arrive in Seville and Algeciras, carried by the Fokkers of the Cabo Juby Squadron and the Navy's Dornier-Wal seaplanes, which had been made serviceable at the CASA factory in Cadiz.

At 14.00hrs on July 20th resistance ended in the Montaña barracks, following air and artillery bombardment (the latter from three guns taken from the artillery park under Colonel Rodrigo Gil's orders). This destroyed the morale of the troops, especially when they saw General Fanjul and Colonel Serra injured by a bomb. In the surrounding district resistance lasted until dawn on July 21st. An attack by aircraft from Getafe killed General García de la Herrán and Lieutenant Colonel Alberto Álvarez Rementería as they were briefing their troops for an advance towards the centre of the capital; as a result the march was abandoned.

The failure of the Uprising in Madrid was compensated, in part, by success in Galicia and Quiedo. This was achieved due to the action of Colonel Aranda, who refused to arm the two columns of miners which the Government had ordered him to send to Madrid via Valladolid and Zamora. In Galicia, Colonel Cánovas of the Engineers succeeded General Salcedo, overthrown by the Corunna garrison.

Throughout July 21st the military forces of Madrid, reinforced by conscripts, spilled out in all directions, occupying Alcalá and a large part of Toledo (including the arms factory), and the towns of Guadarrama and Robregordo, at the foot of Alto del León and the entrance to Somosierra respectively. Taking advantage of this great troop movement the El Pardo Signals Regiment, under the pretext of joining the fight in the Sierra, went instead to La Granja, where they helped capture and defend the Alto del León.

By 18.00hrs the Valladolid, Burgos and Saragossa columns should have reached Alto del León, Aranda and Guadalajara respectively in accordance with Mola's plans. In fact, the first two spent the night in Villacastín and Aranda, and the Pamplona column, which was intended to replace the Saragossan unit on the following day, spent the night on the outskirts of Soria.

Madrid newspapers gave optimistic reports on July 21st. The government triumph in the three principal capitals of the nation (Madrid, Barcelona and Valencia) and in the industrial area of Catalonia and the Cantabrican Coast; their control of communications and central organisation and the possession of the gold reserves seemed to assure them victory.

Latterly, much emphasis has been given to the crisis of the State, without considering the fact that in the Nationalist Zone the crisis was really a lack of State. In a country governed as centrally as Spain, with transport and communications radiating out from this hub, loss of the capital would have an immediate and overwhelming effect. This was why Mola, and then Franco, made it their first task to occupy it as quickly as possible.

July 21st was a difficult day for General Mola. In the morning he learned of the death of General Sanjurjo—in an aircraft accident at Lisbon—and of his brother, Ramón, in Barcelona. Since he was acting as 'director' in Sanjurjo's name, it was vital to stabilise the situation as quickly as possible, since several generals of higher rank were taking part in the Uprising. The oldest of them all was Cabanellas, so Mola flew to Saragossa to confer with him. At midday, on his return to Recajo (Logrono aerodrome), he met Captain Salas, who had left Pamplona on July 19th on his liaison mission. The news he brought was not promising, although Franco and Queipo had done their utmost to improve the situation. In Tetuán, on July 20th, Franco had shown his displeasure at the Navy's action, but remained resolute in his decision to fly the Army across from Africa. He corroborated this, stating: "I have sent a commission to Rome to acquire the necessary Capronis". In Seville, on the morning of July 21st, Queipo appeared full of confidence despite the critical situation in the city.

Mola realised that at that moment the entire responsibility lay on his shoulders. He could not hide his disappointment at the situation, but lost no time lamenting. He ordered García Escámez, who had lost a whole day in La Rioja, to set out for Soria without delay, and then to continue his journey to Burgos to complete the formation of the National Defence Junta.

Mola had some compensation on July 21st when Granada joined the Uprising, but disappointment at Almeria where the arrival of Lepanto foiled Nationalist aims.

July 22nd saw the first battle in the open country, when the Valladolid column arrived at Alto de León 20 hours later than had been planned. Troops of the 1st Railway Regiment from Leganés which, under the command of Colonel Castillo and Lieutenant Colonel Moriones, had occupied Alto in the early morning, were unable to resist a resolute attack by Colonel Serrador's 7th Division.

A little earlier on the same day the section of volunteers who were attacking Somosierra were forced to withdraw from the port following the death of their commander, lack of reinforcement from the Burgos column and in the face of superior defence mounted by Civil Guard and Aviation forces commanded by Lieutenants Francisco Galán and José Ma. Valle respectively.

Before that García Escámez's Pamplona column, intending to reinforce the Aragón column, began an impressive march of 86 miles (139km) which brought them to Miralrio at nightfall, 210 miles (338km) from Pamplona and 18½ miles (30km) from Guadalajara, where they learnt that the city was occupied by the Government troops of Lieutenant Colonel Puigdendolas and Commanders Jurado and Ristori.

Four hours later than had been planned the Burgos column also arrived at Cerezo de Abajo, where they found a Battalion from Bailen. Both groups were waiting in vain for the arrival of the Navarrese troops which, as we have just seen, had made a detour.

That night three Nationalist columns were camping 36½, 61 and 59 miles (59, 98 and 95km) from Madrid, but there were Government troops of similar numbers barring their way to the capital.

García Escámez received orders to proceed to Somosierra, where the situation had worsened following Colonel Gistau's unsuccessful attempt to recapture the position. The Navarrese column reached Aranda at nightfall on the 23rd, after an exhausting withdrawal of 119 miles (192km) which, together with the 210 miles (338km) of the previous days gave a total distance of 329 miles (530km) travelled in four days. The gap left by this column was filled by the Saragossan battalion (which camped in Medinaceli 48 hours after the deadline set by Mola), and by volunteers from the local area, who defended the Sigüenza-Atienza zone. Government troops occupied all the lowland area of the province of Guadalajara and even extended so far as to establish contact with the Nationalist troops.

In the western part of the Madrid Sierra the battles were more violent. Government forces under Lieutenant Colonel Gaspar Morales, and later

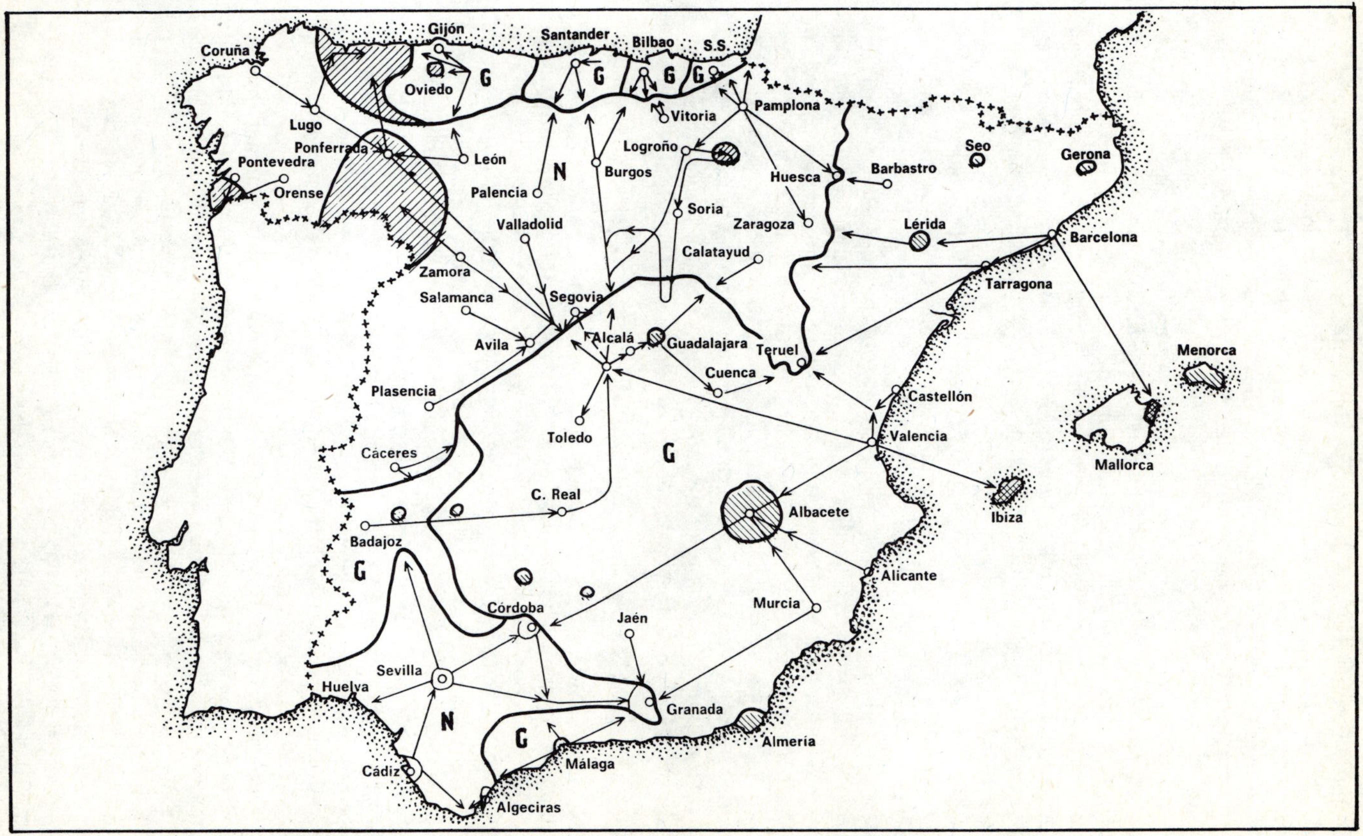

1. First troop movements. The letters N and G indicate areas occupied by Nationalist and Government forces respectively.

Lieutenant Colonel Puig, made repeated attempts to recover Alto del León, which had been lost the day before. Despite intensive aerial assistance they failed in their attempts, due to heroic resistance by Serrador's troops and his efficient use of available artillery. On his left flank Lieutenant Colonel Mangada managed to occupy El Tiemblo, Navalperal, and the routes through the Avila Sierra, and to his right Commander Burillo and Captains Gil and Perea occupied Puerto de Navacerrada.

On that same day, a column led by Commander Salavera, and comprising infantry of the 13th and 14th regiments, left Barcelona for Aragón.

Queipo de Llano was successful in occupying the whole of Seville, and Mola announced over Radio Burgos the formation of a National Defence Junta, comprised exclusively of soldiers from the North Zone. Beorlegui's Navarrese troops arrived at Oyarzun, but they did not succeed in meeting up with the rioters in Loyola barracks.

On July 24th the battle began in Aragón, when Caspe was attacked by Pérez Farrás-Durruti's column. He then established his headquarters in Bujaradoz, 43½ miles (70km) from Saragossa, 45 miles (73km) from Lerida and 146 miles (235km) from Barcelona. The troops of the Montana de Barbastro Battalion (Colonel Villalba) reached Tardienta, 17 miles (28km) from Huesca, and then Lanaja, 37 miles (60km) from Saragossa, before beginning their march to Boltaña (Acaso column). A new Catalan column left Barcelona and Tarragona on its way to Alcañiz, Híjar, Muniesa and Montalbán. This was led by Colonel Martinez Peñalver, Commander of the 15th Regiment. General Riquelme assumed command of the troops who were still attacking Alto del Leon, leaving Morales in charge of the artillery, but the situation did not change.

The last important act of Nationalist initiative in the North Zone was taken on St James the Apostle's day. When Colonel Garcia Escamez had reorganised the columns of the 6th Division, which were under his command, he seized Puerto de Somosierra from General Bernal's forces. In the South Zone, however, the Nationalists were just beginning to regain the initiative. Utrera and Morón were occupied, and there were sufficient forces available to send assistance to Cordoba, which was being defended by Colonel Eduardo Saenz de Buruaga, who had recently arrived from Tetuan.

In Aragón, the centre and the east, the initiative was held by the Government, whose troops had occupied Caspe and Sigüenza, and were subduing the little island of Albacete, which they used to restore communications from the east with Madrid and Andalucia.

In the Sierra, Alto del León was still holding out, despite the fact that the War Ministry had announced its fall, but the situation became critical for the Nationalists on July 26th. The Government side had brought together their best leaders and concentrated their forces to launch a decisive attack. There, amongst others, were Generals Castelló, Cruz Boullosa and Riquelme, who had at their disposal two battalions of the Ferrocarriles Regiment No 1, one battalion of the Wad Ras Regiment, one battalion of the Castilian Regiment (which had arrived from Badajoz), one expeditionary battalion from Valencia (composed of soldiers from the Otumba Regiment and civil guards), the 2nd group of Riot Police, various groups of civil guards, the 'October' battalion and approximately two thousand other soldiers.

Behind the defences of Alto were the 1st battalion of the San Quintin Regiment, the 2nd battalion from Victoria, several hundred Falangists from Valladolid, a squadron from the Farnesio Regiment, two companies from the Signals Regiment and one company from the Plasencia machine-gunners battalion, together with two batteries of the 13th Ligero Regiment, two from the 14th Ligero and one from the 4th Pesado.

The Government forces had far greater strength in artillery, being able to deploy a mounted artillery group, a group of machine-guns and cannons, the 155mm batteries commanded by Captains Alau and Zamarro, the 105mm battery under Captain Pérez Alvarez, the 75mm batteries of Captains Lirón and Grande, as well as some tanks belonging to the 1st Tank Regiment.

The battle followed a similar pattern to that of the previous days, with continuous attacks supported from the air, since there were several aerodromes within close range. A new element was introduced by advancing the 105mm and 155mm batteries to within one kilometre of the town of Guadarrama. Nationalist aircraft from the distant bases at León and Burgos were also able to join the battle, since landing facilities had been provided at Arevalo and Grajera. Government despatches reported the destruction of two Nationalist bomber aircraft that were operating without fighter protection.

The situation became so serious that General Mola ordered his staff to make an immediate study of the possibility of using the Duero as a defence line. When he heard that Colonel Serrador had been wounded, he decided to go in person to Alto del León, but this was vetoed by Colonel Moreno Calderon, his chief of staff. Finally General Ponte was sent, but he too was wounded within hours of his arrival. At night a Government armed truck succeeded in forcing its way to the perimeter of Alto, but it was driven back by the opportune arrival of the 2nd Battery, 13th Ligero.

During the day the Nationalist forces had suffered 215 casualties, amongst them three battalion commanders, one of which, Commander Toribio de Dios of the Victoria Battalion, was killed. In the preceeding days a number of leaders had been lost, including Commanders Moyano and J. Martín Montalvo, both killed in attacks from the air.

Forces in Navarre had moved in all directions: one battalion, a regiment of Carlist soldiers and two hundred Falangists had gone to Somosierra; 1,200 Carlist soldiers to Saragossa, a similar number to Logroño and 275 to Jaca. Abárzuza's regiment of Carlist soldiers were despatched to the front on the 27th, and together with the 1st Toledo and the 1st Victoria battalions, two squadrons from Calatrava and two companies of the Arapiles Battalion, they helped to stabilise the situation.

On the same day García Escámez brought his lines forward to the hills above Buitrago, beyond Robregordo. When he proposed to occupy Navafría and Sigüenza, Mola replied: "No more shots. There are only 26,000 rounds of ammunition available for the whole of the Northern Army." This genuine lack of ammunition provided an excellent excuse for Mola to terminate his advance on Madrid, without giving a direct order.

On the Aragón front a semicircle had been formed around Saragossa, to the north of the river Ebro, extending from the mountains at Alcubierre to Pina and Gelsa. To the south of the river, the battle was being fought in Azaila and La Zaida, but had not extended beyond Belchite. In Huesca, Colonel Villalba had made the capital yield and Teruel was beginning to be threatened by Colonel Carabineros Bujanda's column, stationed in Mora de Rubielos, and soon to be reinforced by Castellón and Catalan columns led by Commander Sirera and Deputy Casas Salas respectively.

In the north-west when the initial fighting ended in Tuy, Noya and the mining zone of Ponferrada-Puebla de Sanabria, the first Galician expeditionary columns were organised. Led by Lieutenant Colonels Ceano and Nevado they were despatched to Oviedo and Alto de León respectively. León. Palencia, Burgos and Álava continued to be relatively undefended.

In the south, towards the end of July, the Nationalists achieved some important victories, occupying all the low lying areas in the provinces of Seville, Cadiz and Huelva (the capital of this last province, occupied on the 28th, was the first to change hands during the struggle). Cordoba, however, was in a dangerous situation, and one that was deteriorating following the surrender of Albacete which allowed government troops to move from the east. On July 26th a machine-gun battalion, commanded by Lieutenant Colonel Peire arrived from Castellon, followed on the 28th by General Miaja who took over command. Granda continued to be isolated, and although resistance in the Albaicín district was stifled, it was considered desirable to strengthen the situation and the 6th Standard Legion was flown in.

The situation in Valencia remained uncertain for, despite orders from General Martinez Monge, some units refused to take up arms. This was resolved on August 1st with the arrival of the war minister, followed by the surrender, after a short struggle, of the 10th Guadalajara Regiment, the Lusitania (Cavalry) and the 3rd Zapadores (Sappers) Battalion.

This was to be General Castelló's last service to the government. A few days later, on learning of his brother's assassination in Extremadura, he took refuge in an embassy. He was succeeded by his under secretary, Lieutenant Colonel Hernández Saravia.

By this time the boundaries had been almost completely defined, although inside the Government Zone (approximately 60 per cent of the nation) there were small Nationalist islands at Oviedo, Gijón barracks, Toledo fortess and the Santuario de Nuestra Señora de la Cabeza. Except in Extremadura and Granada, the month of August saw stabilisation of the front: the Galician columns were halted in Luarca, and those of the Navarrese in Guipúzcoa after they had occupied Tolosa. The Catalan troops failed at Saragossa, Huesca, Teruel and Mallorca, and those of Biscay at Villareal. After breaking down the resistance of the Gijón barracks, the Asturian column was halted at Oviedo; that from Madrid at the Toledo fortess. The lines in the Sierra also remained stable.

Initial Balance of Forces

During the 1930s there were two groups of Nieuport 52 fighters in Spain, aircraft built under licence by Hispano Suiza at Guadalarjara, plus one independent squadron. No 11 Group, comprising two squadrons, was stationed at Getafe (Madrid), and No 13 Group, also with two squadrons was at Prat (Barcelona). The independent squadron was stationed in Seville.

In 1935 No 12 Fighter Group was formed in Granada. This comprised the independent squadron from Seville plus one of the squadrons from Barcelona, but this group was broken up some days before the Nationalist Uprising. Captain Méndez Iriarte's squadron then went to reinforce No 11 Group at Getafe, while Pérez y Martínez de la Victoria's squadron was disbanded. The aircraft of this latter unit were sent to the Southern Regional Park (now the Maestranza Aérea in Tablada) for overhaul, with the exception of one patrol which remained at Los Alcázares under the command of Lieutenant Villimar.

Thus, when the Uprising began four fighter squadrons were available to support Government forces, (three in Getafe and one in Barcelona), plus the single patrol at Los Alcázares.

There were also three Hawker Fury fighters at Guadalajara, but these, too, were unarmed since they had just arrived from England. Licence rights had been obtained from Hawker Aircraft for production of a series of these aircraft for the Government, and at that particular moment a Spanish-built prototype was under construction. Air power in the Navy consisted of a few ageing Martinsydes, all unserviceable.

There were no organised units in the Nationalist Zone. All the aircraft available to them comprised some unarmed Nieuport 52s in the Southern Regional Park (between 7 and 10), and one unserviceable Nieuport 52 in Granada.

So far as fighter pilots were concerned the situation in the Nationalist camp was more promising. Captain Pérez y Martínez de la Victoria and Lieutenants Miguel Guerrero, Narciso Bermúdez de Castro and Antonio Peñafiel had remained in Granada; Lieutenants Julio Salvador, Jesús Fernandez Tudela, and Staff-Sergeant Ramón Senra were still in Seville, remnants of the disbanded No 12 Fighter Group, together with Captain Gancedo. They were joined on July 20th by Lieutenant Pablo Benavides who came from Cuatro Vientos flying a Breguet machine which he had been detailed to deliver to the aerodrome at Getafe. On July 26th Lieutenant Timoteo Valiente came from La Línea de la Concepción and on August 1st Captain Joaquín García Morato arrived from England, via France.

In Africa there were other good fighter pilots: Captains Luis Rambaud and Manrique Montero, as well as Lieutenant Alfredo Arija who arrived at Larache from Cabo Juby as co-pilot of Urena's Fokker-VII. Captain Ángel Salas (who had fled from Getafe to Pamplona on July 18th, leading a patrol of three Breguet 19s, just before the rising in the Peninsula began) was at Burgos, together with Lieutenants Miguel García Pardo and Ramiro Pascual. Lieutenant César Martin Campos also joined these other pilots at Burgos.

At the beginning of the Uprising there were eighteen Nationalist fighter pilots, comprising six captains, eleven lieutenants and a staff-sergeant. This represented a remarkable total for the small number of aircraft available to them. It was, however, far less than the number of staff in the Government units at Getafe, Barcelona and Los Alcazares. Nevertheless, the inferiority in numbers was far outweighed by their superiority as pilots. With the exceptions of those who were killed, Ramiro Pascual who spent many years in hospital following a flying accident, and Timoteo Valiente, also injured in a crash, they all continued in aviation and ten of them are still flying. Four were killed during the war (Arija, Bermúdez de Castro, Martín Campos and Montero). Morato, Salas, Garcia Pardo, Salvador, Guerrero and Senra were the founder members of three fighter groups which were formed later. Other professional pilots, including José Muñoz, Javier Murcia and Mariano Cuadra, had been involved from the start of the Uprising, using their expert knowledge to train new pilots. At a later date they were to join the fighter squadrons.

It was not long before there was a large number of young pilots who, gathered around the nucleus of veterans, formed excellent units. From amongst these Queipo, Vázquez Sagastizábal, Arístices García López, Allende and Carlos Serra eventually became squadron commanders.

The Government Air Force did not have such a select nucleus of pilots around which to form its units. The veteran leader of the Getafe Group, Captain Manuel Cascón soon retired from the force, and the squadron commanders, Captains Avertano González and Méndez Iriarte, died in the Sierra at the beginning of August, 1936.* Lieutenant De Haro was killed in action at Gaudix, Lieutenant Prieto landed in error at Granada and was arrested and Lieutenant Martín Campos joined the Nationalist forces at Burgos. There were some first-class auxiliaries, including Second Lieutenant Giménez, Sergeants García Herguido, Aguirre, García la Calle, Cabré, Urtubi, and Jiménez Bruguet, and Corporals Peña and Alonso Santamaría, together with others from the naval air force. Capable and keen pilots, they lacked the experience to cope with the responsibility placed on their shoulders. Cabré, Urtubi and García Herguido were soon killed and Peña had to have a leg amputated. Aguirre, García La Calle, Alonso Santamaría and Jiménez Bruguet commanded the first Spanish squadrons to operate Russian fighters, but their inexperience made them poor leaders. The real leaders of the Government fighter force, pilots of the first months of the war, suffered the same lack of combat experience.

What has been said about the enemy forces applied generally to the entire Air Force. Of the five hundred military pilots in service before the war, approximately two hundred remained loyal to the Government, about one hundred did not serve on either side, and the remainder went over to the Nationalists, although many of them joined only in the later stages of the conflict.

In the Republican Gazette No.50, dated February 19th, 1937, details were given of Air Force personnel (air crew and others) who had been dismissed from the service for disloyalty. This gave a total of 333 names, some included in error. From this one can deduce that initially the proportion of air crew was in the ratio of two to three in favour of the government, and this proportion is increased if one takes naval pilots into consideration.

This disproportion was even greater in the higher and lower ranks, for there were hardly any senior Air Force officers in the Nationalist Zone, but in the key

* Alejandro Manso de Zúñiga, Paulino Leon Triguero and Lieutenant Serrano Arenas did not serve with the Government forces. Lieutenant Ruiz Mas was executed.

ranks of captain and lieutenant they had the edge. Due to this distribution of personnel, the Government Air Force was more technical and better organised, but less effective in combat.

It should not be thought, however, that the Air Force was peculiar in this respect. The last paragraph could equally well apply to the infantry. If things had not been as they were it would have been absolutely impossible to have a civil war lasting for three years.

In order to provide some comparison, it is necessary to give brief details of the organisation of the Army in July 1936. There were eight basic divisions—the old General Captaincies—each comprising two infantry brigades (a total of four battalions), one artillery brigade (with four groups of three batteries), one battalion of Sappers and a squadron of Breguet 19s. These eight divisions and the cavalry were grouped together in three Inspecciones Generales, all based in Madrid. The nine squadrons of aircraft were also assembled in three groups, stationed at Leon, Seville and Logrono (Nos 21, 22 and 23 Groups respectively).

Apart from the thirty-two infantry batallions mentioned above, there were another eight, one at each main naval base (Ferrol, Cadiz and Cartagena), two in the Balearics (Mallorca and Menorca), two in the Canaries (Las Palmas and Tenerife) and one in Gijon. There were also two mountain brigades, with a total of eight battalions, the Presidential Battalion, a Ministry Group and the African Forces.

These latter forces had two Legionary Regiments (*Legiones del Tercio,*)* each with three Colour groups, five groups of Regulars (each with three units of Moroccan Troops), and six battalions of Cazadores. Thus, in all, there were eighty infantry battalions, eight mountain, six Cazadores, six Legionary Colours and fifteen groups of Moroccan regulars, making one hundred and fifteen battalion-type units. One must add to this at least four hundred Civil Guard, Revenue Guard, Riot Police or Security Corps Companies, which were the equivalent of another hundred battalions. The total number of police was 67,610, comprising 34,320 Civil Guards, 17,500 Security and Riot Police, and 15,790 Revenue Guards; the call-up in 1935 brought this to a total of 140,000 men.†

Of these forces the following remained in the Nationalist Zone: 45 battalions in the Peninsula, six in the Islands, 27 in Africa, and troops equivalent to another 33 battalions. This made a total of 111 battalions, representing 52 per cent of the total.

The distribution of the other Army units was roughly the same as that of the infantry. The most favourable proportion for the Nationalists was in the cavalry, with seven regiments in their zone and a further three in Barcelona and Valencia. The most unfavourable was in respect of the engineer units, whose five regiments and six of the eight battalions of Sappers remained in the Government Zone.

As regards the artillery, fifteen of the twenty-seven regiments stayed in the Nationalist Zone, together with one of the three special groups (anti-aircraft

* During the war this name was changed to *Tercios de la Legion*—Regiments of the Legion.

† For more details see Appendices 32, 34 and 37.

defence, automatic machine-guns and cannons), the joint groups of African Artillery (Ceuta and Melilla) and two of the three Mixed Island Groups (Palma, Tenerife and Las Palmas). Of the four machine-gun battalions one remained in the Nationalist Zone; the two tank regiments divided, one on each side, and the Cycle Battalion remained in Alcala de Henares.

The majority of the Navy remained loyal to the Government. Of the 11 destroyers based at Cartagena (nine of the *Lepanto* class and two of the *Alsedo* class), only the *Churruca* went over to the Nationalist side for a few hours. Crews of the *Almirante Valdés* and *Sánchez Barcáiztegui* were undecided. The majority of the larger ships were at El Ferrol, with the exception of the battleship *Jaime I*, and the cruisers *Libertad* and *Méndez Núñez* raised anchor, under Government orders, and sailed towards the Straits. During the voyage, the ship's crews imprisoned the officers of the Cuerpo General, leaving the majority of the remaining officers at their posts. The only opposition arose in the *Jaime I*, led by its third commander (Corvette Captain Carlos Aguilar Tablada), the watch officer (Ship's Lieutenant Jose Ma. Otero Goyanes) and the Ship's Second Lieutenant (Carlos Falquina).

The battleship *España*, the cruiser *Almirante Cervera* and the destroyer *Velasco*, were not in a fit condition to set sail and remained in the Naval dockyard at El Ferrol.

Of the smaller vessels, torpedo boats Nos 2, 7 and 19 remained in the Nationalist Zone, and Nos 3, 9, 14, 16, 17, 20, 21 and 22 in the Government Zone, together with twelve submarines (six class B and six class C). The coastguard vessels were divided equally between each zone, and the Nationalists had a four to one advantage with regard to gunboats.

As well as the vessels already mentioned, the cruisers *Canarias* and *Baleares* were in an advanced state of construction at El Ferrol, as well as five destroyers of the *Lepanto* class, and four series D submarines in Cartagena.

So far as the Air Force was concerned, three army co-operation Groups remained in the Nationalist Zone (León, Logroño and Seville), although one of the squadrons from Logroño and another from Seville, had been transferred to Madrid just before the Uprising began.

In Africa there was another group of Breguet 19s: No 1 Group, with its aircraft based in Tetuan (Sania Ramel), Melilla (Tauima) and Larache (Auamara). The Independent Air Force, comprising No 31 Group of Breguets from Getafe, the fighter groups, the Bomber Squadron, the Colonial Squadron together with squadrons from Cuatro Vientos, Alcalá, Barcelona and Los Alcázares, and the Seaplane Group from Los Alcázares, remained in the Government Zone. This latter Group operated Dornier-Wals, plus others of the same type built under licence by CASA in Cadiz. Some of the Dornier-Wal seaplanes remained in Atalayon (Melilla) and Pollensa (Mallorca). Two of the four Fokker-VIIs from Cabo Juby passed into Nationalist hands at Tablada, and a third landed at Larache. (All had been built at Loring, in Carabanchel; the fourth, built in Holland, remained in the Government Zone).

The Naval Air Force had one squadron of bombers, equipped with CASA-built Dornier-Wal seaplanes; three squadrons of Vickers Vildebeest torpedo-bombers built by CASA in Getafe; a squadron of Hispano Suiza E-40 trainers, designed and built by Hispano in Guadalajara; plus a squadron of Martinsyde fighters in San Javier; the reconnaissance fleet of Savoia-62 seaplanes, with squadrons at San Javier, Mahon and Marin; and the Pilots School and Workshops in Barcelona, which was equipped with Macchi M. 18s plus a few Martinsyde fighters.

All these machines remained in the Government Zone, apart from five S-62 in Marin and six Do-Wals undergoing repairs in Cadiz. The air-sea base at San Javier joined the Uprising for a few hours, but this action was soon put down by troops from the Los Alcázares aerodrome.

All the aircraft belonging to the LAPE Aviation Company (a total of 18 machines), except for the DC-2 damaged by Vara del Rey in Tablada, remained in Government hands, together with the majority of all other civil and military aircraft.

In all, about 100 aircraft remained in the Nationalist Zone, comprising some 60 Breguet Br 19 reconnaissance planes, ten Nieuport Ni 52 fighters, three Fokker F-VIIs, one de Havilland Dragon Rapide, a dozen light aircraft (nearly all from the Aero Club in Andalucia) and 15 seaplanes (five Savoia S-62 reconnaissance aircraft and ten Dornier Do-Wal bombers).

Government forces could boast a total of nearly 200 aircraft amongst them 60 Breguet 19s, (209 had been acquired between 1927 and 1935, and 30 were rebuilt in 1935), 50 Nieuport 52s (altogether about 100 were built between 1929 and 1936 and very few had been lost) five Fokker-VIIs (only those still airworthy have been counted), four de Havilland Dragon Rapides, four Douglas DC-2s, three Hawker Furies, 27 Vickers Vildebeest, 20 Dornier Do-Wals (the Army had acquired 34, the Navy 12 and LAPE another two), 20 Savoia S-62s (at one stage there was a total of 40 but many fell by the wayside). In addition to the foregoing 'military' aircraft, there were some fifty light landplanes and seaplanes and over one hundred civil light aircraft.

A Critical Judgement of the Development of the War

The fact that, from the beginning, the forces were fairly well matched, explains why the *coup d'état* failed and developed, instead, into a long war. During the first few months one could see clearly the calibre of the African Army (the only trained troops), who were far better equipped than the Peninsula Army.

The Air Force took part only when ground forces were disorganised or lacking in morale, or where the leaders were uncertain of themselves. Where there were bold leaders and enthusiastic troops the Uprising triumphed, despite their initial disadvantage in the air.

Throughout the war it was clear that aircraft were most effective in the field of morale, especially in the early stages when their aggressive capability was only slight and their numbers few. In western Andalucia, a key point at the beginning, the Nationalists managed during the first 10 days of August to achieve local superiority in the air, due to the availability of a few Nieuport fighters in Seville, eight Savoia S-M.81s which joined in the battle and nine Junker Ju 52s. The incomprehensible failure of the Madrid Air Force in the south was also a contributory factor.

The Land Army was even worse than the Air Force in its lack of foresight, with the inconceivable order to transfer forces from Badajoz to the Madrid Sierra.

During September and October, with the entire African Army in the Peninsula, and with air supremacy now that the Fiats had arrived, the Nationalists could have won the war. They did not succeed because of diversification of their efforts, attacking Madrid, San Sebastian, Oviedo, Ronda and Penarroya simultaneously. They soon realised their mistake and nominated one officer to ensure that, in future, great opportunities should not be missed by overcommitting their forces. By then, however, it was too late.

In November the Nationalist troops lost much of their early superiority, both on the ground and in the air, primarily as a result of their predominantly defensive attitude and the stabilisation of the fronts. Government troops, greater in number and with better air support, provided stubborn defence but were unable to launch a successful attack. The mixed brigades, organised by Largo Caballero's Military team (there were six Spanish and two International Brigades active in November) lacked combat experience.

The Nationalist command, which had not expected the Government to display such organisational ability, had forgotten to plan the formation of new units, and this was the reason for their momentary weakness during November. The foregoing explains the Madrid 'case', together with its derivatives, Jarama and Guadalajara.

The Air Force showed a greater degree of inequality than the Infantry. The Government fighter force had not only increased in numbers by this stage, but had better equipment: the Ratas were quite clearly better than the Fiats, and the Chatos superior to the Heinkel He 51s. Nor was there any possible comparison between the very fast twin-engined Russian Katiuska bombers and the slow Junkers Ju 52s or medium-slow Savoia S-M.81s.

At the height of the crisis only the high calibre of the personnel brought the Nationalists a ray of hope. García Morato, Julio Salvador, and Narciso Bermúdez de Castro in El Jarama, and Salas, Allende, Muntadas, Joaquín Ansaldo, Mazarredo and Palmero in Teruel, showed that with courage and determination one could overcome the disadvantages of inferior equipment. The German pilots, with great skill and admirable tenacity, maintained the struggle which the Italians (under a hesitant leader) were beginning to abandon. But it remained for the Spaniards to show the possibility of victory. This needed not only courage, but also flying competence and experience. García Morato had been Spain's undisputed aerobatic champion long before the war; Salas and Salvador had led his air shows; and all three had served in the war for many months.

From the beginning of April 1937 Nationalist troops had achieved local superiority in all their offensives (Vizcaya, Santander, Asturias), in much the same way as they had gained success in Málaga. These victories were due to a careful geographical selection of their objectives, for they were still inferior in manpower and equipment. For example, the north of the country was very isolated, providing fewer possibilities of moving troops and supplies than in the rest of the country, and the mountainous terrain made it difficult to site aerodromes. The Nationalists exploited such situations to the maximum.

Government leaders, on the other hand, lacked such tactical expertise. This was primarily for political reasons, as when the proposed offensive in Extremandura was postponed indefinitely and the crucial months of April and May were marked by inactivity. There were also purely military causes, such as a lack of troops for the offensive at La Granja or the wrong choice of Huesca as a key point for attack. If these offensives had been made simultaneously they would have put the Nationalists in a tight spot. Instead, they made the same mistake the Nationalists had made at the battles of Jarama and Guadalajara. Attacks at Brunete were by now serious, but too late; the northern campaign was decided and the Nationalist leaders were able to make use of various divisions of reserves.

Nobody can understand why the Navy made no determined attempt to defend Bilbao and break through the Cantabrian blockade. Quite clearly this operation was risky, but they were risking much more with the loss of Bilbao.

The Government Air Force deployed significant numbers of Ratas in the north only after Brunete had fallen. Chatos were sent to Vizcaya and they, too, were insufficient in number. In defence of the Air Force one must accept the logic of a decision not to deploy large numbers of aircraft in territory from which they would find it difficult to operate.

Once the battles of Santander and Belchite were over, the prolonged defence of Asturias gave the Valencian Government just sufficient time to mobilise reserves and organise new units to substitute for those lost in the north (30 per cent of the total). But these new units lacked the experience of men that had been fighting continuously for over a year, and from which only a few high ranking leaders and fighter pilots had survived.

As regards Naval activity, only three submarines were detailed for operations in the north. The *Ciscar* and the submarine C-6 were sunk at Gijón; the others finally took refuge in France, where they remained inactive for a long time.*

Once the northern campaign had ended the Nationalist Army had both quantitative and qualitative superiority. In the air, the arrival of the Heinkel He llls and the Savoia 79s (with support from Do 17s and BR 20s), wiped out the advantage held by the Katiuskas and certainly outnumbered them. The new Grumman and Vultee aircraft operated by the Government Air Force could not, on account of their limited payload, offset Nationalist superiority and restore the balance.

The Government forces still maintained superiority as far as fighter aircraft were concerned, for there were only two squadrons of Nationalist Me 109Bs to oppose the six squadrons of Ratas. The Nationalists held an advantage in the ability and perseverance of their flying crews.

It is difficult to make any comparison between the Russian, German and Italian pilots, whom we must therefore consider of equal merit, since their effectiveness varied from time to time owing to frequent changes in personnel. In general one could see a drop in efficiency each time there was a periodic change

* The destroyer *José Luis Díez* and submarines C-2 and C-4. Prior to this the B-6 and C-5 had been sunk in the North, and B-5 and C-3 were lost off the coast of Málaga.

in crews, since even the most expert pilots lose out through lack of combat experience. As far as the Spanish pilots were concerned, government leaders chose also to change the veterans and they sent Cascón to the North in 1936 (and then to Russia as leader of the 1st promotion of pilots), García La Calle was also sent to Russia, with the 2nd promotion (in the spring of 1937), Alonso Santamaría, Jiménez and Jover, and later Riverola, were brought back from the front to Santander at the same time as the Russians left. Comas, Zarauza and Sambudio remained in the thick of the battle throughout 1937 and, from the beginning of July, so did the leading pilots from the 1st Russian promotion. Of the veterans the only one to continue in combat was Aguirre.

By contrast, in the Nationalist Zone, the first Morato Group (2-G-3) was composed only of veterans from the first days of the war, the majority of which had been professional pilots when the Uprising began. This different selection of personnel certainly gave the Nationalists a qualitative advantage. When, later on, the new 3-G-3 Group was formed, the decisive importance of Morato's rigorous selection for 2-G-3 was proven. It was only after several months in battle, and when Morato himself took over command, that 3-G-3 began to achieve the successes of its predecessor.

It would seem that with their superiority on the ground and with good air support the Nationalists should have been able to end the war during the early months of 1938. But a sudden attack upon Teruel made its leaders hesitate, since they thought that the Popular Army had acquired new efficiency. Kindelán's report showed that, in fact, the Army had never been stronger than at the time of Brunete, but they had just retreated from the offensive in Guadalajara and many of the troops intended for this battle had been re-directed to Teruel.

While the battle was reduced to a small area the Popular Army, by concentrating its few select units there, was able to resist all Nationalist efforts. When in March the battle ranged over a much wider area the collapse of the army, hoped for since the autumn, was finally brought about. The brilliant geographical victory at Aragón was not decisive, because it was not followed up by a bold offensive on Barcelona; the material gains were very important, but the number of prisoners was small.

In the face of this serious defeat, Negrín managed to provoke a typical reaction of 'Spanish fury'. By strict mobilisation he managed, quantatively, to increase his forces to equal those of the opposition. What was even more remarkable, he even managed to outnumber them in the essential area. At this time there was a grave shortage of material for the air forces of both sides, especially for the fighter units. Because of the international situation (the annexation of Austria by Germany) all outside help had been suspended. These facts explain the successful defence of Valencia.

One more, in the summer, the mistake of fighting in a small area was made, and this put off until December the big, decisive battle in Catalonia.

In the days of the Ebro, the Government fighter force went through a period of great vigour, as a result of the arrival of a large number of Super-Ratas and Super-Chatos piloted, in the main, by veterans of the 1st Russian promotion, who now had a year's combat experience behind them. The substitution of

Spaniards for the Russian pilots increased the aggressiveness of the Government fighter force during the months of September to November, and this was at a time when the second Spanish group of Fiat fighters had reached the height of its effectiveness and the Me 109s had been increased to three squadrons. But in these battles they lost their equipment and their hope of victory.

For the Government forces Catalonia was a defensive battle with no other purpose than to prolong the war, in anticipation of the imminent outbreak of a world war.

The last serious attempt at victory was the offensive at Pozoblanco-Peñarroya where, with hardly any support from the air, without international assistance and famous names, the Popular Army achieved their biggest success of the whole war. If they had begun this offensive a few weeks earlier and it had been combined with the proposed landing at Motril they could, perhaps, have put back the Catalan disaster until the Spring.

But the disproporation of forces available in 1939 was such that the process of the war was now irreversible. During the last three months, once the Catalonian campaign had been decided, 40 new Messerschmitt Me 109s (the Model E, which was far superior to the earlier machines), 15 Heinkel He 112s and a further 15 Fiat G. 50s arrived, which made a body of seventy fighters technically superior, or at least equal to, the Super-Ratas, which could not be reinforced easily.

CHAPTER TWO

The War Begins

The First Fighter Patrols in the South

The first fighter operations in the south began at Tablada, on July 20th, with aircraft supplied by the Parque Regional (now Maestranza Aérea). On the same day Sergeant-Major Senra was instructed to take Nieuport aircraft No 66 to Tetuan, and while he was there Captain Manrique Montero suggested that they should join forces to try and form a fighter squadron. Senra would not fall in with this suggestion as he had orders to return to his base at Tablada.

On the morning of July 21st, Lieutenant Salvador intercepted a Breguet 19 with a Getafe serial number. This aircraft from Pamplona, which had landed at Burgos, had been sent by General Mola to liaise with General Franco. The pilot, Captain Salas, had to extend his journey to Tetuan, which brought him the unexpected satisfaction of meeting Franco sooner than he had hoped.

One must appreciate that it was not easy to verify the situation at Tablada, since the aerodrome had been bombed at 23.00hrs on the night of July 19th by Fokker-VIIs, and at 06.00hrs on the morning of July 20th by DC-2s. During the night of July 19th–20th the Nationalists made use of the 1st fighter force, which was being maintained at constant readiness, but the DC-2 attack was so sudden that the defenders did not have time to take off. Three hours later, the first Nationalist Fokker-VII arrived bringing legionaries, and this received a cool reception, despite the fact that it had come from Africa.

Meanwhile, in Granada, which was and would continue to be isolated for a long time, reinforcements arrived on July 21st in the form of a patrol of three Nieuport 52s from the Getafe group. Unfortunately, these were sent there without knowledge of the fact that the aerodrome had changed hands only a few hours before. The three pilots, Lieutenant Juan Prieto, Sergeant Gerardo Marín and Corporal Laurentino Lozano were all taken prisoner. With one of these aircraft Lieutenant Bermudez de Castro shot down a Nieuport 52 at Piñar on July 23rd, and Miguel Guerrero, the pilot who recorded the greatest number of victories during the opening stages of the war, celebrated his first combat success on July 25th. While returning from a liaison mission in Africa he shot down a Málaga-based Dornier-Wal over the Straits of Gibraltar. A few days later, on July 29th, Guerrero destroyed a Vickers Vildebeest at Iznájar, another machine of the same type at Iznalloz on July 31st, and added a Breguet 19 to his score on August 1st.

After Salvador and Senra had gone to Burgos on July 27th, Captain

Gancedo, Lieutenants Arija, Fernandez Tudela and Valiente and an aero club pilot, Manolo Camino, (who was killed in a flying accident on August 1st), flew their Nieuport aircraft into Seville. In Africa, Rambaud and Manrique Montero took on the task of protecting the aircraft used in the air lift and they waited until the sea convoy had crossed (August 5th), before transferring to the Peninsula.

The Seville fighters sometimes operated from Cordoba, in an attempt to avoid frequent attacks by the Government Air Force. On July 31st Lieutenant Fernandez Tudela was shot down at Cordoba by a Douglas aircraft belonging to the enemy. On August 2nd, Lieutenant Timoteo Valiente joined the forces at Cordoba, but he was replaced on the following day by Captain García Morato, who had recently arrived in the Nationalist Zone from England.

Until August 7th, Morato operated on his own in Cordoba and then, for the following two days, he joined with Captain Gancedo who was in command of the Nieuports at Seville. On August 12th Morato shot down his first aircraft, a Vickers Vildebeest which was opposing General Varela's advance on Antequera. Two days later he returned the Nieuport to Lieutenant Valiente and joined the Heinkel He 51 squadron which was being formed in Seville. Valiente was able to make little use of this machine, for on August 15th he was involved in an accident which prevented him from flying in fighter aircraft again.

Meanwhile, Benavides had gone to Granada to replace Bermúdez de Castro. This latter pilot had been shot down by ground fire at Transmulas, made a forced landing and escaped with an injured arm. On August 5th Miguel Guerrero moved first to Seville, proceeding to Burgos on the following day. On August 7th a Nieuport from Granada shot down in error a Breguet 19 from Seville, flown by Lieutenant Jesús Lassala Liñán. Another Breguet from Seville, flown by Arístides García López, narrowly missed the same fate. Attacks upon Granada by machines of this type were frequent and this, together with poor visibility at the time, explains the mistakes. Apart from the Breguets in Seville some of those from Africa were also being used in the south. These aircraft went into action for the first time over Algeciras on July 23rd, led by A. Llorente.

On the same day the first aircraft from Seville was shot down near to Puente Genil, and its crew, Francisco Medina and Jacinto Bada, were taken prisoner and executed.

A squadron of light aircraft from the Aero Club were also operating from Seville. A few days later they lost their first two members, Sebastián Recasens and Tomás Murube, whose aircraft were shot down at La Roda.

As soon as Antequera had been occupied an aerodrome was built there to support Varela's advance on Granada. Fighter aircraft sometimes operated from this base, but when contact was established with the defenders of Granada, on August 18th, Antequera's aerodrome soon fell into disuse.

At this time Captain Montero and Lieutenant Fernández Tudela, and occasionally Captains Gancedo and López Cantero (the latter in command of the Seville Breguet squadron, then based at Cordoba) were operating from Cordoba in Nieuports.

It is remarkable how little importance the Government Air Force attached to these operations in the south. After their failure to establish a fighter patrol at Granada on July 21st, during the rest of the month they succeeded only in establishing Villimar's patrol, from Los Alcázares, in Malaga.

The Getafe Fighter Group, like the rest of Madrid, was too occupied with the battles in the Sierra to pay any attention to what was going on in the south. This had already caused them to lose one patrol through lack of information.

In fact, these three fighter squadrons were wasted in the Sierra, since the opposing side had few aircraft. Half of this force could easily have been sent to the province of Málaga, to stop the airlift between Morocco and Seville, using bases which they could have established between Estepona and Algeciras.

The truth was that nobody in Madrid thought this airlift could work. On July 28th the Information Office of the Ministry of the Interior was still saying: "The Republican battleships have complete control over the Straits, so that any attempt to bring troops and aircraft across to the Peninsula to save the opposing forces is quite impossible". Only the chief of Naval operations, Pedro Prados, realised that Algeciras was more important than Cordoba and Granada, but his field of vision was limited to ships.

On the other hand, Franco and Mola were well aware that the war was being decided in the south. By July 21st Franco had sent Captain Salas to reassure Mola that the Army would fly across from Morocco, and had already sent a mission to Rome to obtain the necessary transport. Instead of the Capronis which they wanted they obtained military Savoia S-M.81s, but this did not stop people talking about the Capronis as if they had arrived; it was only at the end of the war that they obtained some light bombers, and these were quickly christened 'Capronchinos'.

From July 23rd Mola gave up the idea of an immediate conquest of Madrid, restricting operations to the occupation and defence of the gateways to the Sierra, until such time as the promised crossing from Morocco became a reality. He did not have to wait long for on August 3rd, with the nine Savoia S-M.81s still unserviceable and when only a few of the 29 Ju 52s which had been promised had arrived, Asensio and Castejón began the advance on Merida with troops of which nearly all had been airlifted across. This had required a tremendous effort on the part of the Spanish crews of the three Fokker-VIIs from Cabo Juby (Ureña, R. Guerrero and Arija), the DC-2 captured at Seville (Haya) and two Dornier-Wal seaplanes (Ruiz de la Puente and José María Moreno) belonging to the Navy. These latter aircraft had been modified at Cadiz since they had to serve te dual role of transport and bombing aircraft. During the first month of the war, Captain Ureña logged 180 flying hours and Haya 108; second place went to Salas, in the North, with a total of 117 hours.

The sea convoy of August 5th was used to send reinforcements and heavy armour, but when these reached Seville, Asensio was already in Almendralejo.

The air force at Malaga did not attempt to stop the Tetuan–Seville air traffic, but they did try to prevent it reaching Granada, since their aim was to force this city to surrender. In order to achieve this, on August 3rd, Lieutenant Villimar requested Malaga to supply two more fighters and some mechanics.

A new squadron, which was soon put under Villimar's command, was based at Andújar to support the advance of General Miaja's columns on Cordoba. From this aerodrome Sergeant Major Benito López Trinidad and Sergeant Manuel Aguirre López, who was later to be the first Spanish leader of No 21 Group Ratas, operated with Nieuports. Captain Abelardo Moreno Miró was left in charge of Malaga, with a squadron of Breguet 19s and three Nieuport fighters. During the night of July 29th–30th the aerodrome at Andújar was bombed by Haya with the DC-2.

A third squadron was installed at Guadix. On August 6th the order was given from Tetuan for attacks upon the two Guadix aerodromes, where there were said to be twenty 'planes. The next day word spread that two out of five Potez 54s had been shot down over the Nationalist lines in the Guadix sector.

This was almost certainly the first time that the Government Air Force had used aircraft of foreign origin for their attacks in the south, although Malraux says that at the beginning of August the Seville-Cordoba railway was bombed by them. The Savoia S-M.81s had been put into operation by the Nationalists for the first time two days earlier, to support the sea convoy from Ceuta to Algeciras: they entered active service over the Peninsula one day later.

In the north Potez 54s had been used before, both at Aragón and in the Madrid Sierra (the *Paris-Soir* attributed the bombing of Saragossa to Potez 54s led by Gayoso). In the north, on the Nationalist side, from July 25th they were using a Dragon Rapide, which had been bought from an airline, as we shall see later.

In the middle of August some Dewoitine fighters were sent to Guadix and, together with three Breguets and three Nieuports they formed Captain Juan Carmona Rey's squadron. Lieutenant Antonio de Haro commanded the Dewoitine 371 patrol, and he crash-landed on his own airfield in one of these aircraft. The Dewoitines had arrived in Barcelona around August 16th, flown by French pilots, and one machine broke up as it landed; a further two suffered damage at Santa Cruz de Mudela, and another before it made the journey to Guadix.

The Nationalist Fighters Operate in the North

In the Nationalist Northern Zone there was a complete lack of fighter aircraft. This, together with the proximity of several aerodromes around Madrid, gave the Government forces, which were much more active, overwhelming supremacy in the air.

On July 20th, the same day as the attack on the Montaña Barracks, Captain Manuel Cascon, leader of the Getafe Nieuport group, claimed the first aerial victory of the war, although I have been unable to find any confirmation of this. At this time the Government Air Force managed to delay the advance of the Burgos column by attacking it at Aranda and Cerezo de Abajo. This was one of the reasons why Colonel Gistau's column was late in arriving at Puerto de Somosierra. In this sector an aircraft with overall black paint scheme became very prominent. Known as 'El Negus' it was apparently flown by Rexach, yet it had nothing to do with the Negus aircraft which arrived in Spain much later.

On July 25th, the day of Garcia Escámez's counter-attack on Somosierra, Mola gathered together all the aircraft he could find from various aerodromes. Eduardo Prado returned from Saragossa to join Logroño, and Jiménez Ugarte arrived in a Breguet from Leon. Since they were unescorted, Government fighter aircraft forced the Breguets piloted by Gregorio Gomez Martin (Number 31-21) and Augusto Puga (with Lieutenant José Antonio de Val as observer) to land before reaching their base. Lieutenant Gómez Martín, who was fired at by the Nieuport No 11-41, managed to land on an emergency aerodrome at Grajera.

The previous day the base at Logroño had lost its first aircraft when one of the bombs it was carrying exploded as the machine landed, causing the death of the two crew members, Captains Miguel Rubio and Luis Calderón. A few days later there was another explosion at Getafe, causing the death of several people.

At about the same time, a Nationalist Breguet, piloted by Ramiro Pascual, forced down one of the opposing Nieuports, thanks to a lucky shot by the observer, Julían del Val (José Antonio's brother). This shot wounded the fighter pilot (Corrochano) in his thigh and forced him to make an emergency landing. Apart from this isolated event, the Nationalist Air Force was able to make only sporadic appearances over the Sierra sector, where hard battles were being fought at this time, particularly at Alto del León where Government aircraft provided almost continuous support. Alto del León was, in fact, the furthest point from the three Nationalist aerodromes at Logroño, Burgos and León, thus making it extremely difficult to give air cover. Aerodromes at Olmedo and Escalona were established in the middle of August and one at Avila in September; there was also an auxiliary airfield at Arévalo and one at Grajera, near Somosierra. Later, another airfield came into use at La Ventosilla in Aranda de Duero.

General Mola was continually asking for fighters, but the Southern Zone was unable to supply him with them immediately. In view of this deficiency, Captain Salas decided to mount a machine-gun on the Dragon Rapide transport aircraft, which Juan de la Cierva had acquired from the Airways company in England. Salas relied on the help of an old friend, Captain Del Monte of the artillery arsenal in Burgos, for installation of the gun. It was mounted within the fuselage, so that the pilot could have direct access to it, and an aperture cut in the fuselage covering the muzzle of the machine-gun. In this way a civil aircraft, which had first been turned into a bomber, became the first fighter-bomber to see service in the war.

Initially, there were two Dragon Rapides operating from Burgos, a military version which, piloted by Navarro, took Núñez de Prado to Saragossa, and a civil machine. This was similar to one which took Koltsov from Barcelona to Madrid (when Koltsov referred to it as being very poorly equipped); and the aircraft which brought Franco from the Canaries to Tetuan. Later, other Dragon Rapides arrived and, on August 17th, the first Fokker F-XII. Its pilot, a Pole with very little experience, was not exactly enthusiastic about the machine. He abandoned it at Vitoria, saying that he never wanted to see it again: he even refused to fly as co-pilot to the Spaniard detailed to collect the Fokker and fly it to its destination. Another Fokker force landed at Burgos and two more were lost en route, due to the inexperience of their pilots. During the first few days of the Uprising there was also a Beechcraft lightplane at Burgos. Piloted by an Englishman, it disappeared without trace after being sent on a war mission.

The first aerial combat in the North involved Salas. Over Somosierra, on July 27th, he had to fight off a Nieuport attacking the Breguets he was escorting. His Dragon Rapide received two direct hits, but Salas continued to fly this machine until the middle of August, when a mixed Dragon-Fokker group was formed. This comprised two F-VIIs from the Cabo Juby squadron (which were flown up from the south on August 6th), a single-engined Fokker and three or four Dragon Rapides. The last aerial combat took place on August 10th, against a Hawker Fury in the Buitrago sector, the engagement lasting for 15 minutes. The Furys were armed at Cuatro Vientos, at the same time as the Dewoitines, Spads and Loires which had come from France, although it seems that they had entered service in July before being armed. The Dewoitines and Loires were armed with two Vickers 7·7mm machine-guns, firing outside the propeller disc. The Spads had a single Vickers machine-gun. Installation of this gun took six to eight days, but as the firing controls were very long its operation was erratic: at critical moments it frequently stopped firing. Warleta bomb-sights were also fitted, and these were better than those of Russian design which arrived later.

On July 27th the two Nieuport 52s had still not reached Burgos from Seville (Nos 43 and 66 piloted by Lieutenant Julio Salvador y Díaz-Benjumea, and Sergeant Major Ramón Senra), although these fighters had been requested a long time before. On July 21st Franco had requested: "Please send two fighters and a Breguet to Mola, following the route Seville—Cáceras—Zamora—Grajera". Queipo's reply on the 22nd was: "I will send the only two available". Days later Franco advised Mola: "I am sending three fighters to Arevalo, prepare fuel". Mola replied: "They did not arrive on the 26th; 1,000 litres of fuel available".

The journey made by these two Nieuports is worth telling in some detail, since it was full of incident. They left Seville on July 27th, accompanied by a Breguet 19 with Captain Carlos Pombo Somoza and Corporal Pedro Álvarez García as crew. These aircraft should have been decorated with the insignia ordered by Mola, consisting of circles with black stripes painted on the fuselage and wings, but due to an error, either in the transmission or the interpretation of the order, black stripes had been omitted. The order for the tail unit to be painted white and this to carry the insignia of a St Andrews cross was given by Franco on August 8th, at the same time as he ordered all the bicoloured and tricolour flags to be painted out. The first stage of the journey, as had been agreed, was from Seville to Caceres, passing directly over Mérida.

When the aircraft landed at Cáceres their crews were asked what the situation was like at Mérida. Unfortunately, they did not know how to reply, even though they had flown low over the town.

Their uncertainty was regarded as suspicious and it was decided to detain them, and they were told that the military governor wanted to interrogate them. They were then taken to a hotel, where they were kept under close confinement until, a few days later, some 'experts' arrived and assured their captors that none of the four crew members was either Pombo or Benjumea from Seville. Apparently they had confused Captain Pombo Somoza with the civil pilot Juan Ignacio Pombo, who had recently gained fame by a flight across the South Atlantic in a light aircraft. The situation was beginning to look serious when, fortunately, news was received from Tablada, announcing the departure of three military aircraft for Burgos, via Cáceres. On the 28th Benjumea, Senra and Somoza were able to continue their journey to Burgos, although Senra was forced to return to Caceres with engine trouble. On the 30th he had to make another forced landing at Valladolid. His travelling companions, after the experiences of the previous day, asked Colonel Apolinar Sáez de Buruaga, the chief of aviation in the north, to send new instructions without delay. On the 31st Senra made two flights in his aircraft, to Buitrago and Navacerrada, and the same machine made a third sortie in conjunction with a fighter piloted by Salas.

On August 4th, two Dragon Rapides (at that time there were three in use) gained some success at Atienza, making a surprise attack on Jiménez Orge's column which they threw into confusion. Nationalist forces in this sector amounted to a mere 100 volunteers. Opposing them was Jiménez Orge who had at his disposal two companies of Riot Police, two of Civil Guards, and a squadron of Security Corps., with eleven 75mm guns, eleven armoured trucks, nine lorries, three light trucks and eleven buses. Thus, the Nationalists had to rely on the Dragon Rapides, which at that time operated from Leon and were busy bombing the armament factory in Trubia and supporting Ceano's Galician column which was being challenged at Luarca. On the 5th these aircraft flew for almost eight hours to give assistance to both fronts.

On August 6th Lieutenant Guerrero, the man who had overthrown Granada, flew with his aircraft to join the forces in Burgos. On the 9th, García Pardo achieved his first victory in the air, and on the 10th Lieutenant César Martín Campos joined the Nationalists in a Nieuport, accompanied by Camacho and Sebastián Rubio's Breguet. To illustrate the general feeling in the Nationalist Zone at this time, it is interesting to see the way in which Martín Campos was received. He was reviled for having taken so long to join the Nationalist cause, and was told that he had only made his mind up now that the war was won. Campos defended himself by saying that not only was the war not won, but that as yet nobody knew who would win it.

Martín Campos brought interesting news from the enemy zone. He gave more information about the shooting down of Captain Mendez Iriarte on the 6th, which had been confirmed by land armies in Alto del Leon, despite the fact that the three members of the Nationalist patrol that flew over the sector on that particular day made no claims for combat success. In fact, Méndez Iriarte, who had taken off from Alcalá, was shot down by another Government patrol. This had taken off from Villalba aerodrome alerted by the presence of the three Nationalist Nieuport 52s, and Iriarte had the misfortune of being mistaken for the enemy.

A small fighter squadron was formed in Burgos and for a brief period it was under the command of Captain Chamorro, although he soon went on to pilot Dragon Rapides and an Airspeed Envoy, in which he was killed whilst escorting General Mola. Pilots who flew with this squadron included Salvador, Guerrero, Martín Campos and Senra, Lieutenants García Pardo and Ramiro Pasual, and occasionally Captain Salas.

I have not been able to ascertain the origin of the Airspeed Envoy which Chamorro flew, although I think it was probably bought by La Cierva. The Government had several machines of this type which, according to Oloff de Wett, were bought from Jersey Airways at the beginning of the war.

Apart from this fighter squadron, Juan Antonio Ansaldo's Dragon/Fokker Group and a Breguet 19 squadron, led by Luis Pardo until the middle of August, (later by Francisco Inglesias), also operated from Burgos. This latter squadron consisted mainly of aircraft which had escaped from Getafe and Barcelona, and included the one which was captured in Soria (usually flown by Lieutenant Colonel Ángel Pastor), one which had come from Seville and one from León.

Jiménez Ugarte's Breguet squadron had its base at León and was active at first in Alto del León and later in Asturias.

The Getafe Breguet Group was nominally under the command of Maza and Carlos Tourné at the beginning of the war. However, the former was in Portugal, from whence he went to the Nationalist Zone, and the latter was in a sanatorium in the mountains. Thus, Besonia was effectively in control, with Urzaiz in charge of the observers. Álvarez Monteagudo and Valle were in charge of squadrons, Rafael Jiménez Benamú was also made a squadron leader, but during his first mission he went across to Gamonal.

Along the Cantabrian coast there were no aviation units until July 19th, when Felipe del Rio arrived at San Sebastian. Later, a few odd fighters appeared at Lasarte, Lamiaco and Carreño, together with some Breguet 19s and Fokkers, Hernandez Franch's Dragon Rapide, Eloy Fernández Navamuel's Monospar, and from time to time some Potez 54s. These aircraft plagued Oviedo and the Nationalist warships, which were attacking the forts at San Sebastian, and also assisted those defending the Simancas and Zapadores barracks in Gijón. During a flight made on August 11th, the Breguet crewed by Esteban Farreras and Esteban Bruno was forced to land at Palencia, where both were taken prisoner and shot.

In the middle of August, the Dragon/Fokker Group was based at a new aerodrome at Olmendo and the Burgos Breguet squadron ('Cinderella') went first to Grajera, then to La Ventosilla and finally Escalona del Prado. At the aerodrome of La Ventosilla, which was situated close to a farm of the same name, such vast quantities of milk were consumed that a mechanic named Cerderiña refused to drink any more, commenting:

"The cows are already giving me strange looks".

During mid-August in this sector, the single-engined Fokker, which had previously been used in the airlift across the Straits was briefly put into action. Towards the end of August, the three engined Fokkers were also in operation

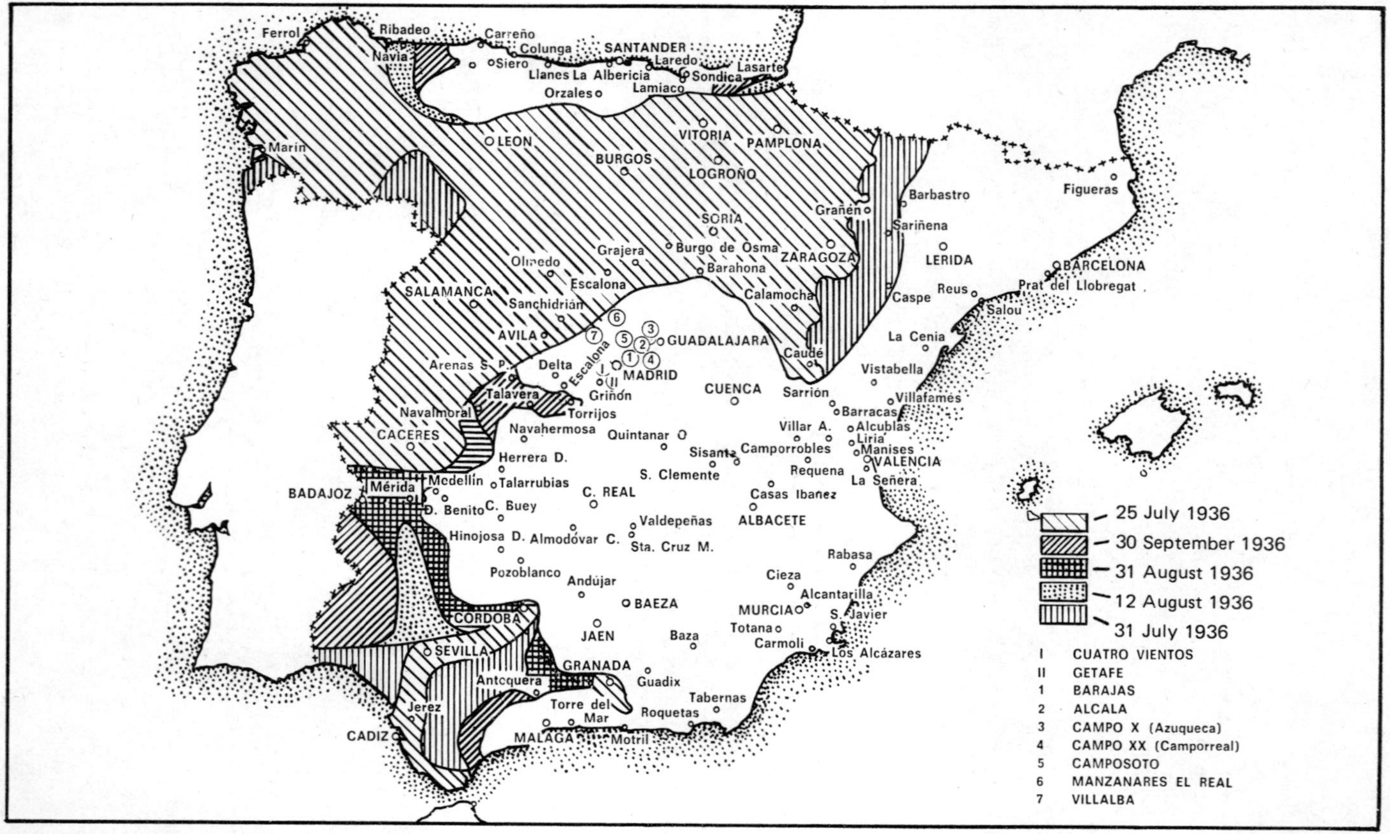

II. Zones occupied by both armies in the summer of 1936 and aerodromes used in the early stages.

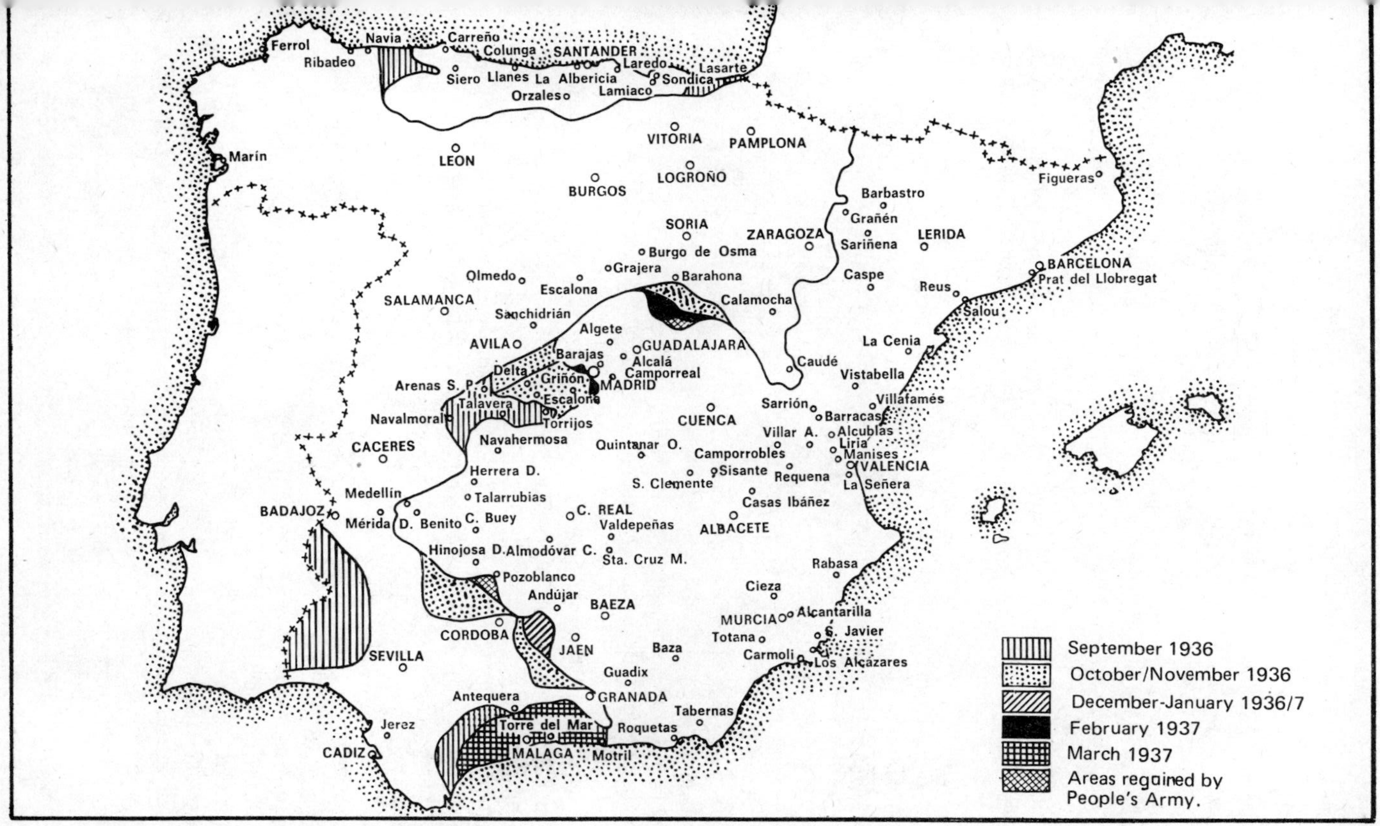

III. Zones occupied in the autumn of 1936 and winter of 1936–37. The main aerodromes in use at the time are shown, with the exception of those in the vicinity of Madrid which can be found on map IX.

to support the Guipuzcoan front. Luis Pardo, Tasso, Carlos Pombo, Llop, José Calderón, José Ugarte, and others, flew in these aircraft.

The Malraux Squadron

Direct French help for the Government of the Republic, requested by Giral on the 19th and authorised by León Blum, following consultation with his Minister of External Affairs and with Delbos Daladier of the National Defence, failed initially. This was due to the action of Cárdenas, the Spanish Ambassador, backed up by Castrillo, the Embassy Secretary, and by Barroso and Carmelo de las Morenas the military and air attachés respectively. Cárdenas and Castrillo resigned their posts rather than sign the agreement for the transference of arms, thus delaying matters for a few days. Meanwhile, Barroso gave details of the proposed agreement to the *Echo de Paris*, which started a violent press campaign that aroused public opinion.

León Blum, who had been delayed in London by discussions with Anthony Eden, the British Foreign Secretary, was told of the changed situation by his Minister. At half past nine in the evening he called to his house the new acting Ambassador, Fernando de los Ríos, who had been sent urgently from Madrid. The four ministers involved in the matter were also present at the meeting.

In the morning Charles Maurras wrote: "Today two trains are leaving for Marseilles with aircraft bombs, four Potez 54 and seventeen Potez 25 aircraft, belonging to the French Army, which are to be put aboard the *Ciudad de Cadiz*. These have been given by the Government to two Spanish officials who arrived at Le Bourget today".

The news was not completely accurate. In fact, France had offered the Potez 25s, but these had been turned down by the Spanish because, although new, they had been in storage for three years. So far as the bombs were concerned the news was correct, for the *Ciudad de Tarragona* and the torpedo boat No 17 of the Spanish Navy berthed at Marseilles on the night of July 24th/25th to load equipment.

In payment for the supplies, according to F. Belforte, a deposit of six million francs was made to the Banque de Paris et des Pays Bas on July 24th.

Even before these facts were made public, León Blum promised immediate transfer of the aircraft, but the Minister of External Affairs would only agree to allow the French pilots to fly the aircraft to Perpignan. Fernando de los Ríos, however, was anxious to retain the French pilots to operate their aircraft. As a result of these difficulties, André Malraux put forward the idea of forming an international squadron, a proposal which received full support of the Air Minister, Pierre Cot.

León Blum, at the instigation of the Presidents of the Republic (Lebrun), of the House (Herriot) and of the Senate (Jeanneney), called an extraordinary meeting of the Government at 4 o'clock in the afternoon of Saturday July 25th. Together with the Council, he had an hour's meeting with Fernando de los Ríos. By half past nine at night the Spanish Ambassador had adopted the resolution "not to hand anything over from one Government to the other, but to give private industry special authorisation to supply and distribute the armaments we acquire". This statement formed the text of a letter, sent by

Fernando de los Ríos during the night of July 25th/26th to the President of the Madrid Government, in which he also stated that the aircraft would be brought out before the 27th. The *French Diplomatic Documents 1932-39* which were published recently, confirm that the French Government ordered the Customs to allow the aircraft to pass through, and this was ratified later, following a meeting of the Council of Ministers on August 1st.

Getting the aircraft out of the country was not as easy as Fernando de los Ríos had expected since, as one of the pilots testified, by that time opinions had begun to change. The Breguet Company decided it wanted no part in the operation and the Potez Company had lost a great deal of its early enthusiasm. The Dewoitine Company was first to take action and began delivering aircraft in Spain, but the Government had to fly 3,306lb (1,500kg) of gold to Paris on July 30th and a further 15,432lb (7,000kg) the following week (Belforte, Volume II). So far as arms were concerned, the Hotchkiss Company were the most co-operative.

Malraux solved the problem of recruiting men to fly these aircraft by offering pilots a renewable, monthly contract, based on a monthly salary of 50,000 pesetas and a life insurance of 500,000 pesetas.

To appreciate the significance of these figures it is necessary to understand that the monthly pay of a second lieutenant was 333 pesetas and that a workman's average daily wage was only 5 pesetas. Militamen in the Government Zone took home 10 pesetas a day (ministerial order of August 15th, 1936) and in the Nationalist Zone 3 pesetas (National Defence Junta Order of August 24th, 1936: 2·50 for board and lodging and 0·50 to take home) and a supplement of 1·10 pesetas a day when they were involved in combat (Order of September 17th, 1936). The exchange rate was 0·50 pesetas for the franc and 8 pesetas to the dollar. Both the franc and the Government peseta lost a great deal of their value during the second half of 1936; at the beginning of 1937 the Government peseta was worth only half the National peseta (for more details see Appendix 38).

In 1937 these incredible rates of pay were slashed; Tinker says that he earned 18,000 pesetas a month, while a lieutenant pilot took home 1,500 and a sergeant pilot 800.

Malraux arrived in Madrid on the last day of July and found the French Air Attaché very helpful. News had already been received that a Savoia, which was armed and being flown by an Italian crew, had landed near the frontier between Algeria and French Morocco. The crew of this aircraft, which was bound for Melilla, had been interrogated by General Denain.

For a short time, León Blum reverted to his idea of direct Government assistance, but this was rejected finally when Lord Chatfield, First Lord at the Admiralty, would not accept Admiral Darlan's suggestion of recalling the British Parliament to discuss assistance for the Spanish Government. During the meeting of the French Cabinet, on August 8th, it was announced that the last 13 Dewoitines had left France (of a total of between 40 and 50 available at the time). The Cabinet decided immediately to put into action their plan of Non-Intervention.

From the beginning of August the 'Spain' squadron (this was its official title) began to be effective over the Madrid Sierra, using Barajas airport as its base. Spanish crews, led by J. de la Roquette and Urzaiz, were also operating from this aerodrome. Malraux, who was not a pilot, flew in the Potez 54s or single Marcel Bloch belonging to this squadron. It would seem that there were never more than five of the former aircraft available at any one time. At a later date the squadron received other aircraft, including the one which had belonged to Negus. According to Malraux's accounts in *L'Espoir*, it would appear that there were 11 bomber aircraft, but there must have been more than this since six were rebuilt in Barcelona and four more were lost (two in the Sierra, one at Getafe and one at Valdelinares).

The squadron had its own fighter cover, led by Abel Guídes, and used Barajas or Getafe as bases. At the end of the year Guídes took over from Malraux as leader of the 'Spain' squadron. Other fighter pilots who operated with the squadron included Labit, Veniel, Darry Valbert, Bernay, Gouinet, Thomas, Bourgeois, Poulain, Isard, Hant, Heilmann, Castaneda di Campo, Renant, Henri Gensons and various Belgians, British, Italians and the Czech Kozek.

The aircraft they used were solely Dewoitines, for although Segnaire, the squadron's political commissary, said that Malraux planned to buy Czech machines, he does not seem to have taken any positive steps to do so. He limited himself to obtaining the Dewoitines and to recruiting the pilots to fly them.

There is very little information available regarding the activities of the fighter aircraft attached to the 'Spain' squadron, although the Russian correspondent Koltsov attributed the destruction of ten enemy aircraft (four bombers and six fighters) to Abel Guídes. Jean Gisclon, Jean Darry and Michel Bernay each claimed three victories and various other pilots shot down one or more.

The Short-Lived Rambaud Squadron

Early on the morning of August 6th, the ship *Usaramo* arrived at Cadiz with six Heinkel He 51 fighters. These were unloaded on the 7th, whilst a Government squadron was bombing the port.

These aircraft were then taken to Tablada where they were used on operations from August 15th, piloted by Captains Rambaud and García Morato, together with Lieutenants García Pardo, Salvador and Ramiro Pascual.

Under the supervision of Captain Francisco Arranz Monasterio, these aircraft had been loaded on board the *Usaramo* at Hamburg during the night of July 31st, as a result of permission granted in Berlin on the 27th. Arranz, who had been serving in the Air Force in Morocco, was commissioned by General Franco to go to Germany and negotiate for the supply of 20 Junkers Ju 52 transport aircraft, similar to those used by Lufthansa for their flights across the South Atlantic. It was, in fact, in one of Lufthansa's aircraft, piloted by Alfred Henke, that Arranz flew to Berlin, accompanied by a representative of the Nationalist-Socialist Party in Tetuan and Herr Bernhart, a German businessman, who was later to become director of the Hispano-Moroccan Transport Company (HISMA).

This aircraft left Tetuan during the afternoon of July 22nd, following the route Seville—Albacete—Valencia—Marseilles—Stuttgart—Berlin, with a stop at Marseilles to refuel. During the flight to Marseilles, as the Lufthansa machine was over Albacete, a Government fighter came alongside, but when the pilot saw that it was a German commercial aircraft he banked away to continue his patrol. This is not surprising for, at that time, Germany was completely neutral, and had also offered some Junkers Ju 52 transport aircraft to the Republican Government. It was natural, also, that the pilot of the patrolling fighter should be suspicious, since Ureña had managed to reach Albacete in his Fokker, where he intended to assist in its defence.

Whilst the Lufthansa aircraft was at Marseilles, the French Government were meeting in Paris, where they decided to supply aircraft to the Republican Government. Simultaneously, and even more close at hand, aircraft bombs intended for use by the Spanish Government were being loaded on to shipping in the Port of Marseilles.

The aircraft carrying Arranz and his companions reached Berlin very late on Friday 24th, and they managed to talk with Hitler on the following day when he returned from the Wagner Festival at Bayreuth. On Sunday afternoon, July 26th, the first official talks were held in Berlin, General Blomberg (war minister and leader of the Wehrmacht) representing the German Government.

While these discussions were taking place, the situation was complicated by the arrival of a second Nationalist mission. This had been sent by General Mola, unaware of the initiative taken by Franco, and it seemed barely credible to the Germans that not only was this second mission unaware of that sent by Franco, but that Mola's team did not know Arranz. This duplication of missions made the task of negotiation far more difficult, and also pinpointed the lack of communication between the Nationalist Northern and Southern Zones.

The problems were overcome eventually, and permission was given for the Junkers firm to supply twenty Ju 52s, and these were flown direct from Dessau to Seville, across the Alps and the Mediterranean. Ground staff to maintain the aircraft were recruited at Döveritz aerodrome, near Berlin, and they, together with six Heinkel He 51 fighters, were embarked at Hamburg on board the *Usaramo*, which sailed from that port at 01.30hrs on August 1st.

In order to regularise the transit of so many people, eighty-six in all, a travel society was formed, and supplies were transferred from the German firm of Rowak, to the Spanish Company La Hisma.

Arranz returned to Spain on July 28th in the same aircraft in which he had travelled to Germany, the machine taking off from Stuttgart at 04.00hrs and landing at Tetuan at 15.00hrs. In order to make this eleven-hour non-stop flight, the machine had been provided with auxiliary fuel tanks.

Although the Heinkel He 51 was but little better than the Nieuport and was, apparently, inferior to the Hawker Fury, it had some initial success. Morato, for example, was able to celebrate General Varela's link-up with the defenders of Granada by shooting down a fighter at Loja and a twin-engined Potez 54 at Antequera on August 18th. On the same day, Salvador shot down a Nieuport and a Breguet 19 at Merida, and it is thought probable that he shot down one other Breguet. The remaining pilots in the squadron were not so fortunate, two aircraft becoming damaged, one with a broken propeller for which there was no replacement. This lack of success by the majority of the Nationalist pilots prompted the German pilots, who had accompanied the aircraft to Spain, (Eberhard, Trautloft, Knüppel, Von Houwald, Klein and Hefter) to seek permission to fly on operations against Government aircraft. This permission was granted by General Kindelán, chief of the Air Services, who became later air chief (*Jefe del Aire*). (Decrees Nos 16 and 52 of the Nationalist Defence Junta Bulletins Nos 3 and 8, dated July 30th and August 18th, 1936).*

Commander von Scheele was in command of all the German forces, and he was surprised to find that the Spanish mechanics at Tablada had made an entirely satisfactory repair to the broken propellor of the He 51, without access to any specialised equipment. At a later date von Scheele proposed the establishment of a workshop for the repair of propellors at Tablada, but this proved impossible as the small number of technical staff there were already too heavily involved in other work.

The squadron of He 51s, complete with their German pilots, were transferred on August 22nd to the aerodrome at Escalona del Prado, between Cuéllar and Segovia, from where Captain Francisco Inglesias Brage's squadron of Br 19s was already operating. The five Spanish pilots at Escalona del Prado were ferried in a Ju 52 to San Fernando aerodrome (Salamanca), where the first of three Fiats were due to arrive.

On August 23rd the three squadrons of Ju 52s (led by Carrillo, Ricardo Guerrero and Gil Mendizabál) were detailed to bomb the aerodrome at Getafe. The Fiats did not join in this operation because, as we shall see later, they got lost en route and did not reach Salamanca.

Since it was necessary to penetrate a long way into enemy territory, it was considered prudent to provide fighter escort and that Spanish pilots should fly the He 51s that were serviceable. The attack was fixed for early morning, but due to a shortage of bombs it had to be put back to midday. García Pardo, who flew as co-pilot in a Junker since there was no fighter aircraft available for him, recorded the comments of one of the crew members. "The sun, almost at its zenith, will make the task of the anti-aircraft guns more difficult; there seems little doubt that we will catch them napping . . ." The eight Junkers and the three escorting He 51s, which joined them at Escalona, passed over Getafe where they could see many aircraft. Despite heavy anti-aircraft fire they pressed home their attack. By the time they were over Avila on their return journey, the crews could congratulate themselves on the success of their mission. Rambaud's machine received a hit which made the landing gear inoperative, and he damaged the aircraft on landing: Ramiro Pascual's aircraft was also damaged by landing short of the runway.

The Germans seized this opportunity to ask Kindelán to allow them to be the only ones to fly the He 51s, a request that was granted, although Morato made three more sorties on the 24th. Koltsov, the Pravda correspondent, re-

* Warlimont is quoted frequently as being leader of the initial German forces (eighty-six in all), that arrived in Spain on August 6th. In fact, Warlimont did not arrive in Spain until September and remained there until the Cóndor Legion arrived.

ferred to the bombing of Getafe, but he attributed the attack to eight Savoias, although he did admit that the bombs were of German origin.

Juan Antonio Ansaldo's mixed Dragon-Fokker Group, which had been in operation since August 19th from the new aerodrome at Olmendo, soon regretted Kindelán's decision. When their escorting Nieuports were reinforced by the He 51s on August 27th, the pilot of one of the Heinkels accidentally shot down the Dragon Rapide flown by Captains José Pouso Cabanas and Joaquín Vela de Almazán.

According to German sources the Eberhard patrol, formed by Lieutenants Eberhard, Trautloft and Knüppel, destroyed six Government aircraft, and this seems to be confirmed by Nationalist reports of August 25th–27th. Lieutenant Matias Iglesias Romo was shot down on the 25th (Republican Gazette, No 37 of the 6-2-37), and on the 27th, the Englishman Cartwright, (Oloff de Wett, page 14).

When the Spanish squadron was disbanded at the end of August, Rambaud and Morato applied for transfer to the Regulars, Salvador and Pascual to the Legion, but Kindelán did not acknowledge their applications. Morato and Salvador flew the He 51s again on September 2nd, during the battle of Talavera de la Reina, and Morato destroyed a Nieuport. Rambaud went to Cadiz to fly seaplanes; Ramiro Pascual entered hospital with a serious illness that prevented him from flying for the remainder of the war; García Pardo went back to the Nieuports at Aragon and in September he was flying with Guerrero and Senra.

Although the break-up of this short-lived squadron caused considerable disappointment to its members, the fact that Spaniards and Germans had been living and working together in harmony was important for the future. Moreover, Morato's success on operations with the He 51 indicated that provided the Spanish pilots had a good basic knowledge of combat techniques, and took the trouble to gain a detailed knowledge of the imported aircraft allocated to them, they could be assured of a fair measure of success against their enemy. This knowledge was valuable at a later date when new units were formed.

On August 27th Captain Salas took off from Aragon in a Nieuport aircraft, eventually arriving at Olmedo. He had written to Morato, from Saragossa hospital, asking if he could occupy the vacant place in the He 51 squadron. Morato had replied to the effect that the situation, so far as the He 51s were concerned, was not very hopeful, but that he had heard some Fiat fighters were due to arrive in Seville, and suggested that it might be better for him to try to get one of these machines allocated to him.

In fact, Salas went to Cáceres, where for some days he acted as a machine-gunner in Ricardo Guerrero's squadron of Ju 52s, and from there he went to Seville in company with Salvador.

On the days he was not detailed for fighter operations, Morato acted as Haya's co-pilot. They bombed the aerodrome at Cuatro Vientos on the nights of August 27th and 28th, as well as the station at Villalba on the latter date, where they hit an ammunition dump. On the same night, according to Koltsov, Morato and von Morau dropped a bomb on the patio of the War Ministry.

Von Morau, who had led the German crews en route to Spain, carried out his first operation of the war on August 13th when he bombed the *Jaime I* at Málaga. Later, on August 20th, he became the first pilot to bring in supplies to the Alcázar at Toledo.

When the German pilots took charge of the He 51s, six Ju 52s were withdrawn from Spanish service and two German squadrons formed with them. These were known as *Pedros y Pablos* (Peters and Pauls) and they were led by Von Morau.

The Centre of Operations in Aragon

The first Nationalist fighter did not appear at Saragossa until August 13th. This was Sergeant Major Senra's Nieuport, which had been sent from Burgos by the order of Colonel Apolinar Sáez de Buruaga, acting chief of the Nationalist Air Force in the Northern Zone. Before then the only aircraft available in this sector were the Breguet 19s of Prado's squadron, which had arrived from Logroño on July 20th. These aircraft suffered from the lack of escorts and on August 4th the leader of the squadron was shot down by García Herguido.

On the Government side the 'Red Wings' squadron, which included a Dragon Rapide, a Fokker VII and various other aircraft from Catalonia, was stationed at Sariñena aerodrome. At about this time the Multi-engine Flying School, which had J. de la Roquette and Gayoso as leaders, was established at Reus.

Alfonso Reyes came back from retirement, re-entering the service with the rank of commander, and acted as leader of air operations on the Aragón front. Under him he had Squadron Leader Isidoro Giménez, and the following officers: Manuel Valle, Salueña, López Garro, Adonis Rodríguez, Bercial and Castero.

Lieutenant Colonel Díaz Sandino was based in Barcelona as chief of the Air Force in Catalonia, and later he became adviser for the defence of Generalidad. At the beginning of August the Barcelona aerodromes of Prat, Muntadas, Canudas, and the Air France base, served as reception centres for the Potez 54s and the Dewoitine 371s coming from France. According to Francisco Belforte it was not until August 7th that the first thirteen Dewoitine fighters arrived from Toulouse. On August 8th the Russian correspondent Koltsov arrived in an aircraft flown by Abel Guides. At this time Lufthansa civil transports were still refuelling at Barcelona, and those of Air France at Mallorca.

At Tardienta, on the day after his arrival at Saragossa, Senra shot down a Nieuport 52 flown by Cabré. Senra was acting as escort to a Breguet patrol led by Eduardo Prado, maintaining station some 1,400ft (500m) above the Breguets. As they were returning from their mission another Nieuport, which had red stripes painted on the upper surface of the wings, burst into the middle of the formation without noticing Senra's machine overhead. Senra streaked in to attack, but both machine-guns failed to fire. Climbing steeply he wheeled into a second attack when, to his utter frustration, one of the machine-guns jammed. A collision between the two opposing Nieuports was avoided only by a hairsbreadth; after banking steeply and gaining height Senra made his third attack, this time successful. Cabré's Nieuport dived steeply, a trail of smoke in its wake as the pilot baled out over the side: within seconds it plunged into the ground exploding on impact. Cabré had managed to inflict some damage to two of the Breguets before being attacked by Senra, one being hit in the cockpit area and its pilot, Julio Andrés, was wounded. Koltsov, who was visiting the Aragón front at this time, writes of a Fascist attack on Tardienta, under the cover of aerial support.

The destruction of this aircraft in the Aragón area was regarded as a matter of some importance as, until that time, the Nationalists had achieved little success in this centre of operations. Officials at Saragossa received news of the destruction of Cabré's Nieuport even before Senra's 'plane had landed, for a motorist who saw the duel from Almudévar brought word of the event. During the afternoon Senra was taken to Military Headquarters, where he was interviewed by the Press. The following day he received a telegram of congratulation from the leader of the Northern Air Forces, another from the President of the Huesca Congress, who also sent an award of 1,000 pesetas, and the Nationalist Junta which administered Saragossa presented him with a further 10,000 pesetas.

Four days later Captain Salas (who had just ferried from Vitoria to Burgos the first Fokker-XII received in Spain) arrived at Saragossa with another Nieuport. During the succeeding days Salas operated at Teruel and Senra at Huesca. On August 23rd, over the Teruel front, Salas attacked and destroyed a light aircraft. The following day he was admitted to hospital suffering from exhaustion, after completing 50 operational sorties totalling 116 flying hours, which had been amassed within four weeks.

On August 28th Captain Larrauri, flying a Farman light aircraft, took to General Franco currency collected by the Saragossan banks to buy aeroplanes. With this money they bought three He 51s which were named *Huesca*, *Saragossa* and *Teruel*.

Salas was replaced on September 1st by García Pardo who, together with Guerrero and Senra, formed a fighter patrol which operated from El Palomar (Saragossa) aerodrome throughout the whole of September. On the same day Guerrero attacked a Potez and a Fokker, wounding the pilot of the latter machine. According to a bulletin issued by the Catalan legislative assembly, the observer in one of Guerrero's aircraft (Picañol) was wounded in the leg when they were attacked by four fighters.

At this time, Juan Antonio Ansaldo's bomber group was also operating from Saragossa, having been rushed there to defend Huesa. Despite the gravity of the situation there, this group was sent to Logroño on September 2nd to assist the Navarrese assault on the important position at San Marcial, the last Government stronghold before Irún. On the 3rd one of the Dragon Rapides in José Muñoz's squadron caught fire and Lieutenant Ignacio Ansaldo, brother of the group leader, was injured. During these missions the Fokker XIIs operated for the first time with bomb gear, which had been assembled in Logroño by the Larrauri brothers.

When San Sebastian was occupied, Colonel Beorlegui and some of his forces were sent to Huesca, where the situation improved so much that Ansaldo's group was able to return to Olmedo. On September 15th Captain Jose Munoz was wounded while in action over Cueva Valiente (Sierra de Guadarrama), and had to relinquish command of the squadron of Dragon Rapides to Captain Gregorio Gómez Martín. Three days earlier the pilot Francisco Cuesta had died as a result of wounds received when his 'plane No 12-10 (a Nieuport from the old No 12 group) had been shot down by anti-aircraft fire.

García Pardo and Guerrero did not return to Olmedo with Ansaldo's Group, but together with Senra they remained in Aragón throughout September. On the 15th, when García Pardo was escorting four Breguets to Almudevar, he fought off three enemy Nieuports, one of which was damaged severely. The 5th Division offered its congratulations for the air support at Huesca, particularly for supplies brought in by air.

The Aerial Battle at Extremadura

As we have seen earlier, on August 3rd Lieutenant Colonel Asensio's column, together with Commander Castejón's column, began their march towards Mérida. By the 7th Asensio was already at Almendralejo, 105 miles (170km) from his base at Seville and less than 18½ miles (30km) from Mérida. Ahead was General Mola's advance guard, comprising troops from the Argel Regiment at Cáceres barracks.

Asensio had to wait for Castejón's arrival, as he had inadequate forces with which to continue his advance and, at the same time, oppose enemy forces who had made a strongpoint at Almendralejo church.

It was at this point that Government officials in Madrid realised the great danger to which they were exposed by this daring advance in the North, and decided at once to send aircraft to Herrera del Duque and Medellín Don Benito.

Nationalist squadrons from Seville began operations on the Extremadura front, and on August 4th Haya attacked Badajoz in a DC-2, and then chased off a Government machine of the same type. That day also marked the arrival of the first of the three squadrons that were formed with nine of the twenty Junkers Ju 52s, which had been withdrawn from the airlift and armed at Tablada. On the following day, near Badajoz, the leader of the second squadron, Captain Díaz Trechuelo, was killed by small-arms fire from the ground. The Fokkers, which were no longer required in a transport rôle were all sent to the north, with the exception of one which crashed at Jérez with Asensio on board.

On August 10th it was planned to bomb both of the Madrid aerodromes (Getafe and Cuatro Vientos), since information had been received that a large number of bomber aircraft had arrived from France and were being assembled there. This attack was to be carried out by Savoia S-M.81s and Junkers Ju 52s, led by Haya's DC-2. This latter pilot had already bombed Barajas on the night of August 2nd/3rd.

Von Morau, leader of the German crews ferrying the Ju 52s, stated that his Government would not authorise these aircraft to penetrate as far as Madrid. On August 9th one of these aircraft, unarmed, had landed at a Government aerodrome while being ferried from Germany to Spain. Bonomi, whose aircraft were equipped for military operations, had volunteered to serve in the Foreign Legion, and was therefore required to obey orders. However, two of his aircraft were unserviceable, forcing him to postpone the operation. Later, he had to cancel it when Jesús Camacho and Sebastián Rubio arrived with the news that there were eleven modern fighter aircraft on the aerodromes to be attacked.

On August 11th Asensio and Castejón continued their advance and, supported from the air by three Savoia S-M.81s, occupied Mérida at midday. A third column, led by Tella, arrived to reinforce them and Lieutenant Colonel Yagüe took command of the force formed from these three columns. On August 11th he established his headquarters at Santos de Maimona, but on the following day transferred this to Mérida. At 20.00hrs on August 12th he gave orders for the attack upon and occupation of the walled city of Badajoz. Four battalions, taken from Asensio's and Castejón's columns, were to be used for the attack upon the city, and one of Tella's battalions was to be held in reserve. Tella was to remain at Mérida with one of his battalions and one from the Northern Army, ready to deal with an expected Government counter-attack.

On August 13th the Breguets from Seville began to fly over Badajoz, using an improvised aerodrome at Mérida as their base. Haya made two long reconnaissance flights over Badajoz, (totalling six hours in all) and the first squadron of Ju 52s made a reconnaissance of Guadalupe and Navalmoral. On the same day, General Mola flew to Seville for discussions with Franco and Queipo de Llano.

On August 14th Badajoz was taken by storm and the Government counter-attack was unleashed on Mérida. Three aircraft came from Madrid to give support and three more from Malraux's squadron. Malraux wrote that they encountered six Ju 52s which they were able to leave behind, since they were much slower than either the Potez 54s or DC-2s. This was the first time that imported bomber aircraft had met face to face.

Captain Soler's Breguet patrol was too late to be able to land at Seville, and had to land instead at Elvas, a frontier post near to Badajoz. The Portuguese authorities said they would be allowed to take off again, providing they did so before daybreak.

On August 16th an amusing incident was caused by Sgt Major Álvaro Fernández Matamoros, pilot of the first Nationalist fighter aircraft—a Nieuport 52—to operate in Extremadura. Matamoros had been sent to Mérida to support Tella's column, which was being strongly counter-attacked by land forces and by Don Benito and Herrera del Duque's air units. When Matamoros saw two Breguets in a field near the Guadiana he landed, thinking that it was Mérida aerodrome. When Moroccan troops from Commander Del Oro's unit surrounded him and asked his name, all he could reply was 'Matamoros!', the humour arising from the fact that Matamoros translates as 'Kill the Moors'. A little later Tella asked Captain Carlos Vara del Rey, leader of the two-machine Breguet patrol which had landed near the Guardiana, "Do you think that those two aeroplanes will still be by the river?", to which the latter replied: "No, my Lieutenant Colonel, there are now three".

On August 16th and 17th the Ju 52s bombed Don Benitos aerodrome, which was occupied on the 17th. Franco also paid a visit to Mola, travelling to Burgos in Haya's DC-2.

Successful aerial attacks upon Castejón's column at Santa Amalia forced the Nationalists to send another fighter to Extremadura. On the 18th Salvador arrived in a Heinkel He 51 and, as already recorded, he made a good start by shooting down a Nieuport and a Breguet and damaging a second Breguet. It was confirmed later that this latter machine was destroyed, giving Salvador three victories on the first day.

Three days later a Government Nieuport attempted to revenge Captain Soler, leader of the Breguets at Mérida, but this failed. Haya, who at this time was leader of operations for the Southern Air Force, observed the fruitless pursuit while travelling in his DC-2 near Guadalupe.

On August 15th Uribarri, leader of the column in the Badajoz sector, sent a teletype to the Army for Central Operations. Re-transmitted to Madrid this message stated that at Badajoz on the previous night the governor, mayor, a deputy, a commander and the governor's chauffeur had been taken to Portugal where they had been executed. The message was exaggerated, at least so far as the governor was concerned, since he fled to Portugal, together with Lieutenant Colonel Puigdendolas, commander of the garrison.

On August 13th at least 104 priests had been executed in the Government Zone, the largest number eliminated in a single day, and on the night of August 14th/15th more than 100 Naval officials in Cartagena were dismissed. These facts, although not directly related to events at Badajoz, were not isolated incidents. These, and others, were the result of the first important Nationalist victory, when their North and South Zones met. The Nationalists found themselves with the task of having to judge those who were responsible for these and other atrocities, and their judgement was not always impartial. There were more of these atrocities in the provinces than in the capital, where the Riot Police had promised that three hundred persons held prisoner would not be killed. For the first time the Government began to fear that they might lose the war, and they began a second wave of terror which was far worse than that of July.

The Fiats Enter the Battle

The first three Fiat C.R.32s arrived in Seville on the afternoon of August 18th. Until this point Italy had supplied only the nine Savoia S-M.81s which reached Melilla on July 30th. If one adds to these aircraft the twenty Junkers Ju 52s and six Heinkel He 51s sent by Germany, plus the Dragon Rapides, Fokker XIIs and the single-engined Fokkers bought from airlines, this makes a total of 40 aircraft received by the Nationalist side, slightly less than the total number of machines handed over to the Government side by France alone.

The Fiats had only just arrived at Seville, when General Miaja made a surprise attack on Córdoba, having crossed the Pedroches Valley. On August 20th Miaja's columns occupied Adamuz and Torres Cabrera and were then 3¾ miles (6km) north and 3 miles (5km) south of Córdoba, but lack of co-ordination between the two columns deprived the attack of its continued initiative. The most daring move came from the south, under the command of Pérez Salas, but his men were driven back when Morato dived to attack them with machine-gun fire and Haya caught one battery by surprise, straddling it with bombs. The Fiats and Savoia S-M.81s also joined in the action, attacking the forces advancing along the Madrid road.

Anticipating that the Government attack would be repeated on the following day, three of the six Fiats which had been prepared for operations were transferred urgently to Córdoba, under the command of Sub-Lt Ceccarelli (known in Spain as 'Vacaresse'). Their task was to support the three Nieuports which were being flown by Gancedo, Manrique Montero and Fernández Tudela.

According to a communiqué from Córdoba, in their first operation the Fiats shot down a Nieuport and, as they were landing, one of them collided with a Breguet. This was confirmed by Bonomi, who attributed both of these incidents to Ceccarelli.

During the battles at Espejo in the following days, the Savoia S-M.81s were flown by Spanish crews for the first time. Antonio Llorente, who had recovered from injuries received during an attack on Tauima on July 26th, was the leader of the Spanish crews.

On August 22nd the Monico patrol of three Fiats were sent to Salamanca, but failed to find the aerodrome and landed in a field, the landing gear of two machines being damaged. At that time, of the twelve Fiats which had arrived at Melilla, two were unserviceable at Salamanca, two at Córdoba and one at Seville. This left two serviceable Fiats in the Peninsular and five in Africa. On August 24th Dequal arrived at Tablada leading four of the Fiats from Africa, and Cenni arrived with the fifth on the following day. With the receipt of these reinforcements, the Nationalists were able to send two Fiats to Granada (Ceccarelli and Magistrini) and one to Cáceras, where it joined the two from Salamanca which had been repaired and were fit for operations. At this time the He 51s began to operate from Escalona del Prado, escorting the two Nieuport patrols from Olmedo to Saragossa and from Córdoba to Granada.

At Granada, on August 27th, Magistrini scored a second victory for the Fiats when he attacked the Dewoitine flown by Lieutenant de Haro, which crashed at Guadix.

The first notable success for the Fiats came at Mallorca on August 28th. 'Cerruti' attacked four seaplanes anchored in Cala Morlanda Bay, damaging two which had to be towed ashore. At 14.15hrs a second Fiat, flown by Carestiato, a well-known test pilot of the Italian Macchi Company, attacked Captain Freire's Savoia S-M.62 seaplane over Punta Amer bay. This seaplane had aboard Captain Bayo, leader of the on-shore Catalan Forces. Freire was fatally wounded in the attack and Bayo* had to take over the controls, and make an emergency landing at Cabo Pera. The *Mar Negro* later took the seaplane aboard and delivered it to Mahón.

During the first few days of the battle at Espezo three light aircraft of the Nationalist Air Force had been making reconnaissance sorties, but these were

* Bayo was a captain at this time, although later given the rank of commander, backdated to July 18th, and almost immediately afterwards was promoted to the rank of lieutenant colonel.

soon destroyed by Government aircraft during bombing attacks which met little resistance.

Earlier on August 19th, three Italian seaplanes had taken some part in the action, but these were damaged during an attack on Palma made on August 20th by seven aircraft operating from Barcelona and Mahón. On the same day an aerodrome was completed in the Mallorcan disembarkation zone, from which Government fighters were able to operate, and the Nationalist seaplanes were withdrawn.

On August 23rd the bombing of Palma was intensified, and as a result the inhabitants subscribed money with which to buy aircraft for their defence. On the 26th, the forces which had disembarked on the island made a frontal attack and occupied a line of hills. This allowed the Mahón seaplanes to anchor in Cala Morlanda Bay on the 28th, and it was at this moment that the Fiats appeared, with the success mentioned earlier.

With the support of the Air Force, the Mallorcan forces launched a successful counter-attack, and on September 4th the Bayo forces had to withdraw. The island's commander sent the following telegram to the Balearic Air Force: "In the spirit of justice and impelled by gratitude, I wish to make it known that the actions of your worthy command were the main reason for the victory". It is worth remembering that the earlier overwhelming aerial supremacy held by the Bayo forces had not brought success to them.

In the Peninsula the Fiats began to operate from Cáceres at the end of August, but they failed to maintain the success of their initial sorties. This was at the period when Yagüe began his advance along the Tajo Valley.

On August 31st two Fiats, flown by Monico and Castellani, were shot down in a battle with the Dewoitines, Hawker Furys and Nieuports from Talavera. These latter aircraft belonged to Captain Martín Luna's International squadron and to the Getafe No 11 Fighter Group (Manuel Cascón).

Amongst the fighter pilots then flying in the International squadron were the Russians Iván Kopets, Evgueni Erlikin and Kovalievski; the Englishmen Cartwright, Clifford and Collins; the Italian Locatelli; and others of various nationalities. The Russians Gueorgui Túpikov, Victor Jalzunov, Iván Proskúrov and the Italian Primo Gibelli were pilots of the bomber aircraft.

It would appear that the combat victories on August 31st were scored by Spanish pilots, for on September 3rd Andrés García La Calle was prompted to the rank of second lieutenant, and seven days later Rafael Peña Dugo and Roberto Alonso Santamaría received similar promotions.

Another squadron of Dewoitines flown by foreign pilots was led by Captain Abel Guides, also operating from the Madrid aerodromes. Their principal task was to escort Malraux's squadron of bombers, although some of the operations carried out in Extremadura by this latter squadron were made without fighter escort. The first squadron of No 21 Group was based at Andújar, and this was equipped with Breguet Br 19s and Nieuport 52s and Aguirre took command of the squadron on September 6th.

A first comparison of the imported fighters seemed to favour the Dewoitines, but during the months of September and October the Fiats proved their superiority against these machines, as well as against the Loires and Spads, which were also of French origin. This superiority was not gained without significant losses.

In view of the poor beginning made by the Fiat patrols (the second patrol, for example, got lost, landed in a field and was not available for operations for several days), Mola made an urgent request for experienced fighter pilots. And on September 1st Queipo complained that there were only two Nieuports (one unserviceable) in Granada. Franco replied to Queipo to the effect that he had four Nieuports and two Fiats in his Organic Division, and that nine more Fiats were being assembled in Seville.

Mola and Queipo took due note of requests for help from Cáceres, Garcia Morató and Salvador being despatched in two Heinkel He 51s to take part in the battles at Talavera. Lieutenant Fernández Tudela's Nieuport was shot down when he tried to defend Camacho and Solsona's Breguets, and a second Nieuport was shot down by Morato.

The Nationalist communiqué claimed the destruction of one fighter and two Breguets. The Government communiqué stated that two of their aircraft had been shot down in Extremadura, but that they had destroyed four Ju 52s which caught fire in an attack on Olmedo. Malraux has written a very detailed description of this attack on Olmedo, but Olmedo was not the Junker's base (they operated from Salamanca), but that of the Dragon/Fokker Group.

The Nieuport patrol had left its base on the morning of August 30th, but returned in the afternoon. Thus, on the 31st, Garcia Pardo was able to pursue a Potez as far as Peguerinos, but had to break off the engagement when he saw that a Dewoitine patrol was airborne.

Fernández Tudela's performance in his old Nieuport won him the Military Medal seven years later. This pilot had been shot down earlier at Córdoba, from where he had been operating until this time.

The nine Fiats which Franco had said were being assembled in Seville had reached Vigo at the end of August, and were sent from there by rail to Seville. The union with the Northern Zone was beginning to have an effect in the south. The troops had been led by Lieutenant Dante Oliviero, but he was killed in an accident at Tablada before the battle began. In view of this, and other losses suffered by the first squadron, it was decided to leave all the Fiats together in Seville and to form them into a single squadron under Dequal's command.

On September 5th Dequal arrived in Seville, and immediately ordered the inexperienced pilots to fly on the Seville-Salamanca route, so that they could familiarise themselves with the lie of the land and thus minimise the risk of any more of them losing their way.

On the following day Morato arrived in Seville, where he was warmly received by the squadron, since his experience and knowledge of the area could be very useful to them. (One must appreciate that at this time there were no military maps or aviation charts available for use in the Nationalist Zone).

At this period the aircraft based at Seville had a vital task, maintaining a keen look out for the merchant ship *Magallanes*, then one of the largest of the Spanish mercantile fleet, which was due to arrive from Mexico with an important cargo of arms.

The Military Situation During the Month of September

At the beginning of September the general situation was turning out very favourably for the Nationalist troops. In the Tajo Valley they occupied Talavera de la Reina on the 2nd. (capturing two aircraft on the aerodrome) and on the same day they broke through the Guipúzcoa front and occupied San Marcial and Behovia. On the following day, in Asturias, Salas advanced to within 18½ miles (30km) of Oviedo. During the night of September 3rd/4th the Bayo forces had to withdraw from Mallorca, abandoning several seaplanes. On the 4th Mola occupied Irún and Fuenterrabia, cutting off the Cantabrian zone from France, and on the 5th the situation in Córdoba became extremely favourable when Cerro Muriano was occupied. It was only in Huesca that the situation remained difficult.

Under these circumstances the Socialists decided to take over power in Madrid, and Largo Caballero succeeded Giral in the presidency of the Government, which included some Communists and Basque Nationalists. Largo Caballero decided to concentrate his forces near Talavera de la Reina, with the objective of retaking it from the Nationalists. On September 4th the overall commander in that sector, Burillo, had under his control Jurado, Uribarri and Fernández Navarro's columns, with a total of 11,247 men. By the 19th these columns had increased to 24,264 men, not counting those stationed in Toledo under the command of Rubert and later Barceló, the strength of which increased, from 2,305 to 3,960 over the same period.

On the Nationalist side, Yagüe's three columns that had fought at Badajoz (Asensio, Castejón and Tella) were joined by Delgado Serrano's new columns at the beginning of September and by Barron on September 15th, and they all increased the number of their battalions from two to three. Yagüe then had under his command a total of fifteen batallions, fourteen from the African Army (more than half the total number of troops involved at the time of the Uprising).

These troops from Africa had been ferried across to the mainland by sea and air during July, August and early September. Of these forces, four tabores* remained in the south, one in the Madrid Sierra and another in Asturias, and two banderas* went to Guipúzcoa (later to Aragón) and Asturias. The remainder, five banderas and nine tabores, together with a battalion from the Argel Regiment, came under Yagüe's command. Remembering that the tabores of regular soldiers were small battalions, with only 550 men (those from Mehala had only 350 men), Yagüe did not have more than 10,000 experienced soldiers which, together with the auxiliaries and other services, gave him a total of about 15,000 men. However, because of their training and experience he did not consider that Asensio Torrado's forces represented a strong enemy, even though they had a similar number of regular soldiers, civil guards and riot police.

September was also a favourable month for the Nationalists so far as the air force was concerned. We have already seen that towards the end of August the assistance given to the Government by France was much greater than the total help given to the Nationalists by the Germans and Italians. But at this time the

* Tabor and bandera are the names of Moroccan and African army units. They have no direct translation into English equivalents.

French aviation industry was in a very weak state, as proved soon after in World War II, and they were unable to maintain production of aircraft at the required speed. In October Russia replaced France as the main supplier of aviation requirements, but there was a lull in supplies during September which gave the Nationalists superiority in the air although, as we shall see, this was short lived.

In the middle of September the Nationalists received about twenty Heinkel He 46 reconnaissance fighters, nine more Heinkel He 51 fighters, and three or four Junkers Ju 52s from airlines. In October they received the first ten, of an order for 21, Romeo Ro 37 army co-operation machines and a third squadron of Fiat C.R.32 fighters; these aircraft began to operate after Russian supplies had arrived in Spain.

The He 46s, known as 'Turkeys' by the Air Force (this was also the name given to the Ju 52 by the Land Army) showed little improvement over the Breguet 19s. They were formed into three squadrons, led by Carlos Martínez Vara del Rey, Emilio Jiménez Ugarte and José Gancedo Saenz, and were sent initially to the Madrid front, to relieve Camacho's Breguet squadron. Their indifferent performance meant that they were soon moved to less important operational centres. These three squadrons were designated as 1-E-11, 2-E-11 and 3-E-11, the terminal numerals 11 being used to designate the type of aircraft (Heinkel He 46).

The Romeo Ro 37s were much more advanced aircraft. Two squadrons of them were formed and at the end of October they began operations at the Madrid front, led by José Muñoz Jiménez, known as 'el Corto' (the short one) and Colacicchi. They replaced the He 46 squadrons which were sent to Asturias and Aragón. The old Breguet biplanes were used to form five groups, each of two squadrons, which were numbered from 1-G-10 to 5-G-10. The first group was based at León (led by Eyaralar), the second at Lasarte-Vitoria (Llop), the third at Seville-Córdoba (Rueda), the fourth in Granada (initially led by Perez y Martínez de la Victoria, later by Navarro), and the fifth in Africa (initially Manual Ugarte and Julio Meléndez). Three more Ju 52s, which had been withdrawn from the airlift, formed a fourth squadron led by Luis Pardo.

So far as fighters were concerned, the Heinkel He 51s were outdated before they entered service. The Fiats, on the contrary, were the best fighters in Spain until the Ratas arrived. In some respects the Dewoitine 510s and Spad 510s were superior to the Fiats, but there was not enough of them. The Dewoitine 371s, of which there were more in service, were far inferior.

At this time the Nationalists acquired their first heavy anti-aircraft battery, commanded by Captain Aldinger, and a short time before they had received some anti-aircraft machine-guns and searchlights.

The Government fleet, which had been inactive in the Mediterranean since the re-embarkation of the Bayo forces from Mallorca, assembled at Málaga on September 20th, and were joined there by the cruiser *Méndez Núñez*, which had just come from Fernando Poo. Guinea was occupied by the Nationalists as soon as this warship had left there; the same thing happened in Ibiza when the fleet sailed to Málaga.

After occupying Guipúzcoa, Mola delivered an ultimatum to the defenders of Bilbao, to the effect that he would occupy the town on September 25th. Prieto, Government Minister for Sea and Air, and himself a native of Bilbao, decided to send the bulk of the fleet there to raise morale and to keep the small Nationalist Fleet in check. The submarine B-6, which was sent in advance of the fleet, was intercepted by the tug *Galicia* and later sunk by the destroyer *Velasco*.

On the afternoon of September 21st (not the 26th as reported in some chronicles), the battleship *Jaime I*, cruisers *Libertad* and *Miguel de Cervantes*, together with the destroyers *Almirante Valdés*, *José Luis Díez*, *Almirante Antequera*, *Almirante Miranda*, *Lepanto* and *Escaño*, set sail for Bilbao. On board the *Libertad* was Miguel Buiza, commander of the Fleet, the central committee and the Russian advisers Nikolai Juznetsov (now an Admiral) and N. Anin. *Jaime I* was commanded by Carlos Esteban, the *Miguel de Cervantes* by Luis Gonzalez Ubieta, and the escorting destroyers were under the overall command of Vicente Ramírez.

This fleet crossed the Straits of Gibraltar during the night of 21st/22nd, and remained undiscovered until they were off the northwest tip of Spain, at El Ferrol. Here they were spotted at 13.00hrs on September 23rd by Leopoldo Brage, commander of Naval Artillery, who was flying a Savoia S-M.62 seaplane.

During the voyage of this fleet, Prieto had learned that the new Nationalist cruiser *Canarias* had put to sea for tests, and he decided to attack it with the Potez 54s. On September 23rd this vessel was attacked by Mellado off El Ferrol and it was claimed that he hit it with heavy bombs, the subsequent Government communiqué reporting that it was seriously damaged.

The validity of this claim may be judged by the fact that on the same day Mola ordered the naval Capt Francisco Moreno to move to the South with the *Canarias* and *Almirante Cervera*, and to report to Franco, who had been proposed as Generalissimo two days before. This voyage took place during the night of September 27th/28th.

The Nationalist destroyer *Velasco* laid mines in the bay at Bilbao before the Fleet arrived, and then steamed as far north as Brest on the return journey to its base at Ferrol, so that the Fleet would not catch sight of it.

In the Straits, the Nationalist cruisers surprised the destroyers *Almirante Ferrándiz* and *Gravina* whilst they were on patrol at low speed. The *Almirante Ferrándiz* was sunk and the *Gravina* damaged so badly that it had to put in at Casablanca for repairs. The commander of the *Almirante Ferrándiz*, José Luis Barbastro, was picked up by a French vessel and landed at Casablanca, where he took command of the *Gravina* whose commander, De Caso y Montaner, had taken the opportunity of arriving in a neutral port to make good his escape from Government service.

The cruiser *Méndez Núñez*, then commanded by Pedro Prados, and three other destroyers sailed from Cartagena to seek out the Nationalist cruisers, but through lack of enthusiasm for their task failed to make contact.

Soon after, the *Almirante Cervera* put the finishing touches to Nationalist victory in these naval moves by sinking the coastguard cutters *Uad Muluya* and *Uad Lucas* off Málaga.

Top: Nieuport-Delage ND 52 fighter in service in 1936. Approximately 125 were built under licence by Hispano-Suiza at Guadalajara./*La Hispano Aviación*

Above: Hawker 'Spanish Fury' after repair at Tablada. Three production Fury Mk IIs were supplied to Spain by the British Hawker company./*Región Aérea del Estrecho*

Top left: Dewoitine D 510./*Air Classics*

Centre left: D 371, the first fighter aircraft imported by the Government./*Air Classics*

Bottom left: Heinkel He 51, the first fighter type obtained from Germany./*Balaguer*

Below and bottom: Italian-built Fiat C.R.32s, the most outstanding fighter in the early stages of the war./*Maestranza Aérea de Tablada*

Top: A Nieuport-Delage ND 52 shot down at the Madrid front./*Serrano*

Above and right: Aquí te espero, a famous Potez 540, which was shot down by Salas at the Madrid front. Its bomb load is still carried securely on the under-wing racks./*Serrano*

ESPERO

Top: Breguet 19s of 22 Group, from Tablada, provided cover for Yagüe as far as the outskirts of Madrid. The two shown are at Arenas de San Pedro aerodrome, in the Tiétar valley./*Serrano*

Above: Hispano E-30, a Spanish-designed and built advanced trainer, called in for more active service in the early days of the war./*La Hispano Aviación*

The Vickers Vildebeest, designed as a two-seat torpedo-bomber, was built under licence by CASA for the Naval Air Force. Powered by Hispano-Suiza engines, both land (*top*) and seaplane (*above*) versions were produced, and saw considerable service with Government forces during 1936./*CASA*

Top: A Fokker F.VII of a colonial squadron. That illustrated, No 1, was of Dutch origin and three more were built by Loring. Generally similar to those in use with LAPE, they were armed for war service./*Guereta*

Above: Fokker F.XII transport aircraft acquired from British Airways in August 1936./*Guereta*

Top: The de Havilland D.H. 89 Dragon Rapide, which was used by both sides in the Civil War. A number of D.H. 84 Dragons were also in use./*Región Aérea del Estrecho*

Above: A Douglas DC-2 transport aircraft which had been in service with LAPE in early 1936. The aircraft shown is that captured by Vara de Rey in Tablada, and carries his name as captain./*Región Aérea del Estrecho*

Top: Savoia-Marchetti S.M.81, the first Italian type to be sent to Franco's aid. *Above:* An S.M. 81 with a Junkers Ju 86 in the background./*Ėjercito de Aire*

The Junkers Ju 52m, which was responsible for airlifting the majority of the troops across the straits and which proved to be a slow but robust bomber aircraft. The upper photograph (*top right*) was taken during the airlift. A squadron of Ju 52s (*centre right*) fly in formation over Burgos Cathedral. The festoon of bunting on the aircraft (*bottom right*) celebrates a task well done./*Región del Estrecho, Guereta*

ARGANDA
1822
1E

Top: Polikarpov I-15 single-seat fighter ('Chato'), called Curtiss by the Nationalists, was the first Russian-built fighter to see service in Spain. The aircraft illustrated is one captured by the Nationalists and is shown in the illustration (*above*) behind a line-up of Fiats./*Meastranza Aérea de Tablada*

Top and above: Polikarpov I-16 ('Mosca' or 'Rata'), the most advanced Russian fighter which arrived on the Madrid front in November 1936. Illustrated is a captured aircraft at Tablada. The I-16 was the first low-wing single-seat fighter monoplane with retractable landing gear to achieve service status./ *Región Aérea del Estrecho*

Top: Another view of a captured I-16 'Rata'./*Región Aérea del Estrecho*

Above: I-16 'Rata' in squadron service.

Top: The prototype Messerschmitt Me 109V-4 was evaluated in Spain in December 1936, and Me 109B-2s were the first to be used operationally in Spain, as the fighter component of the Cóndor Legion.

Above: Koolhoven F.K. 51 imported from Holland. They were used operationally in the north, and for night flying training./*Servicio Fotografico y Cartografico*

Top: A Hucks starter in use, then still essential to achieve a quick start of many aero-engines./*Ministerio de Información y Turismo*

Above: A Hucks starter was the only means possible of starting engines in such conditions as those at El Toro, during the battle of Teruel.

The Dequal ('Limonesi') Squadron, Basis for the Future García Morato Group

At the beginning of September Morato requested Colonel Bonomi ('Federici') for permission to serve with the Fiats. He asked him: "Who is the squadron leader?", to which the colonel replied: "Dequal". Morato thought he had said "de cuál?" (of what) and replied "Of my squadron". The answer came back the same: "Dequal".

This captain was a superb pilot and in Spain they had christened him 'Limonesi'. Whilst the Fiat squadron was under his command morale was high and their co-ordination perfect. Unfortunately, he returned to Italy in the middle of November, soon after being surprised and shot down by the first Chatos (called Curtis in the Nationalist Zone) to arrive in Spain. When he left, Commander Fagnani ('Faroni') took over leadership of the squadron, and we shall see the consequence of this change at a later date.

García Morato joined the Tablada forces on September 6th. Three days later there was a sufficiently large number of Fiats flying for them to be able to transfer the squadron, consisting of three patrols, to Cáceres. These were led by Dequal, Morato and Mantelli. A fourth patrol, Ceccarelli's, remained in the south.

The day after the Fiats arrived in Cáceres, Delgado Serrano's column, which had been following the Tiétar valley, joined with Colonel Monasterio's cavalry, which had taken possession of Puerto del Pico four days before. At Ramacastañas they were joined by Tella's column from Talavera. On the 11th and 12th Castejon's column reached El Real de San Vicente, dominating the mountains of that name, a dividing line between the valleys of the rivers Tiétar and Alberche.

On September 11th the three patrols from Dequal's squadron entered into the battle, with remarkable success, destroying two Breguet 19s and five other fighters. Morato, who was leading the second patrol, shot down a Nieuport 52 over Talavera, scoring his first victory in a Fiat. Dequal and Franceschi each scored a victory, and Magistrini destroyed two enemy fighters. Mantelli had no success on this occasion.

Two days later, Morato, Patriarco and Baschirotto between them shot down two more fighters, but shortly afterwards Patriarco ('Boccolari'), an Italian-born naturalised American, was himself shot down.

On September 16th Morato and Mantelli's patrols were successful in destroying a Breguet, two other fighters and a Potez 54. The latter was shot down by Morato, near Navalcarnero. Lieutenant Giorgio Franceschi ('Saletti'), from Mantelli's patrol, was shot down and taken prisoner.

At this time Salas and Salvador arrived at Tablada, offering to serve with the Italians. Initially they were unwilling to accept them in the squadron, but after Captain Salas had given them a demonstration of his flying ability, including some manoeuvres which even the Italians had not attempted in the Fiats, they were finally convinced.

Salas led his first war sortié in a Fiat on September 15th, his mission to strafe Andújar aerodrome, which had been the base for the first bombing attack on Santuario de la Cabeza. According to the Nationalist communiqué three aircraft were damaged by fire, one was destroyed, and eight more holed by machine-gun fire. The Air Force bulletin announced only the destruction of two Breguet 19s by the Fiats. Salvador went into action for the first time on the following day, when he supported General Varela's column near Ronda.

In the middle of September Yagüe re-organised his forces, and was joined by Barrón's new column which, like the others, now consisted of three battalions.

At about this date the troops at Avila (Valdés Cabanillas) fought some hard local battles at Navalperal, Peguerinos and Cabeza Guijar, with some air support, and José Muñoz ('El Corto') leader of the Dragons group was wounded. He was replaced by Gregorio Gómez Martín.

Meanwhile, in the north, the Guipuzcoan campaign came to an end after San Sebastián and Eibar had been occupied.

On September 20th Salas and Salvador joined the forces in Cáceres, where they continued to operate with the Fiat squadron. They were able to intervene in Yagüe's decisive advance towards the Santa Olalla—Maqueda defensive line, known as the Masquelet line. Santa Olalla was occupied on the 20th and Maqueda on the 21st, when Yagüe handed over his command provisionally to Asensio. The next day they reached Torrijos and by September 23rd they were within sight of the River Guadarrama.

On September 24th, following his occupation of Ronda, Varela arrived to replace Yagüe and on the same day, in Cáceres, Franco issued the order for operations to begin for the conquest of Toledo, a task which was allocated a period of three days for completion. As had been planned, on the third day of the offensive they reached the Alcázar of Toledo, but a fourth day was needed to gain complete control of the city. Knowing Yagüe's character, it seems likely that the sudden illness which he suffered at this time was a pretext to cover up a difference of opinion he had held regarding the direction of the advance.

On the day that Salas and Salvador arrived in Cáceres, Morato shot down a Hawker Fury at Santa Olalla, his third success in a Fiat, and his seventh since the beginning of the war. On September 22nd Dequal and Buffali each recorded their second victory, a feat which had already been accomplished by Salvador, Magistrini, Patriarca, Chianese and Mentelli.

On the 24th the Fiat squadron transferred from Cáceres to Talavera (Gamonal aerodrome), where they would be better placed to follow the advance on Toledo. At the same time the He 51 squadron and the Dragon-Fokker group left the Madrid front and moved to León aerodrome.

That same day, Salas scored his second victory, shooting a Potez 54 named *Aqui le espero* ("I will wait for you here"). It was flown by Captain Mellado and Moreno (a lieutenant from the Riot Police who had been involved in the assassination of Calvo Sotelo) and had gained some distinction two days before when it bombed the *Canarias* in Galician waters. It had also been involved in incidents across the whole of Spain from Asturias to Málaga. Mellado had, from the very beginning, been the most active pilot on his side, performing outstanding services at Seville, Madrid and in the Sierra.

The next day Morato shot down a Breguet at Bargas, and a Government fighter shot down a Junkers Ju 52 from Carrillo's squadron, in full view of those defending the Alcazar. It was piloted by Eustaquio Ruiz de la Alda and he and the rest of his crew, except Sgt Joaquin Sanjuan Gongora who survived and was taken prisoner, died when the aircraft crashed.

It seems strange that during two months of continuous activity not a single Ju 52 (much slower and with inferior equipment to the Potez 54) had been shot down until this time. In fact, several Potez 54s had already been shot down by that date. However, no Fokkers had been destroyed either, and they were even slower than the Ju 52s, and the only Dragon Rapide destroyed in the air had been the victim of one of its own fighters. Captain Díaz Trechuelo had been killed in a Ju 52, hit by small-arms fire from the ground at Badajoz, but the aircraft was flown back to its base at Tablada by the co-pilot, Fernández Matamoros.

At this time the slowest aircraft used in the battle were Breguet 19s and Dornier-Wals, followed by the Savoia S-M.62s, Fokker F-VIIs and the Vickers Vildebeeste, all having a cruising speed of less than 124mph (200km/h). The Fokker F-XIIs were a little faster, with a cruising speed of 124mph (200km/h), as were the Heinkel He 46, Junkers Ju 52 and the Cant Z.501, with a cruising speed of 137mph (220km/h) and a maximum speed of 155mph (250km/h). The Nieuport 52 was capable of the same speed as these, but the de Havilland Dragon Rapide was slightly faster. The DC-2, the Potez 54, the Marcel Bloch M.B.210 (which had retractable landing gear) and the Savoia S-M.81 were much faster, with a cruising speed of 168-174mph (270–280km/h) and a maximum speed of more than 186mph (300km/h). The Heinkel He 51 and Dewoitine 371 fighters had a maximum speed of around 224mph (300km/h), but the Fiat C.R.32, Dewoitine 510, Loire Nieuport 46, and the Spad Bleriot 510, were the fastest machines at the time, capable of speeds up to 248mph (400km/h). All of these fighters had fixed landing gear.

During the battles on September 25th, 26th and 27th the Fiats shot down four fighters which gave Morato his eighth victory, and Montegnacco and Presel their second.

On September 27th the land armies reached the Alcázar, and Toledo was occupied on the 28th. On the same day there was considerable activity in the air, but this produced no results. At about this time, during a violent land battle at Olías del Rey, the famous Commander Ristori was fatally injured.

At the end of September, as mentioned before, the other nine Heinkel He 51 fighters arrived, under the leadership of Strümpell. The Germans then handed over to the Nationalists the three He 51s from the first batch that were still operationally serviceable. These three aircraft were flown for some days by Morato, Salas and Salvador, being alternated with Fiats.

The German He 51 squadron moved to León on September 24th, the eve of the attack on Toledo, because the columns advancing on Oviedo had no fighter support, and Mola demanded aerial assistance to speed up their progress. The Dragon/Fokker Group was also moved to León, and the Ureña-Larrauri pair of Ju 52s, aided by the *Pedros y Pablos*, attacked the Government naval squadron at Bilbao.

The following day, the Nationalist Air Force destroyed a Breguet and a Dragon Rapide on the ground, and seriously damaged a Fokker. In the Eibar-

Elgueta sector of Guipúzcoa another Breguet and a Vickers Vildebeeste were shot down. (Von Houwald's patrol had been operating in this sector for several days, before being moved to Aragón).

During the last month of this battle the famous Government fighter pilots Antonio de Haro, Urtubi and Rafael Peña were shot down, the first at Andalusia, and the other two at Toledo. Peña escaped with injuries to his legs, one of which became gangrenous and had to be amputated. In spite of this, he escaped from Toledo hospital shortly before Varela's troops arrived. He later became an inspector at a French flying school which trained pilots for the Spanish Government, and eventually returned to flying, occupying the position of chief of staff of the 7th Squadron. It was not the first time that Urtubi had come off worst in an encounter with the Nationalist Air Force. Earlier he had been shot down over enemy lines, but had managed to get through to his own forces.

These victories were not achieved without cost. At the end of September, according to Goma, there were seven Fiats available for operations and five more being repaired. If this information is correct, then nine of the Fiats had been lost: of these four had been shot down (Monico, Castellani, Patriarca and Franceschi), one wrecked in an accident (Oliviero) and the remainder destroyed in varying circumstances.

October: The Organization Begins To Increase

The month of October was notable because of the great efforts made by both sides to organize themselves.

In the Nationalist Zone the leadership was finally handed over to one person. This originated on September 21st, the day that Maqueda was occupied, when Franco was chosen as prime military leader at a Defence Junta meeting. On the 28th of the month, the day that Toledo was occupied, it was considered important to make public Franco's position, and at a second meeting he was elected Generalissimo of the Armies and Leader of the Government of the Spanish State. Both of these meetings were held near San Fernando aerodrome (Salamanca), at a farm worked by Pérez Tabernero.

Almost all the members of the National Defence Junta attended the meeting. Cabanellas, Saliquet, Ponte, Mola, Dávila, Montaner and Moreno Calderón were founder members (Decree No 1, dated July 24th, 1936); Franco joined under Decree No 25 (Official Bulletin No 4), Gil Yuste under Decree No 47 (O.B. No 8), Queipo under Decree No 114 (O.B. No 24) and Orgaz under Decree No 115 (O.B. No 24). I have not been able to ascertain the Decree under which Kindelán was named as a member of the Junta, but I think he must have been nominated in his capacity as chief of air. The naval Captain Francisco Moreno, leader of the Fleet, was named in Decree No 18 (O.B. No 3), but he was not able to attend the meeting since, on the night of September 28th/29th he was busily occupied in the Straits of Gibraltar, sinking the *Almirante Ferrándiz*, and chasing the *Gravina* into Casablanca.

Decree No 138, dated September 29th, 1936, and signed by Cabanellas, sanctioned Franco's nomination, and he assumed his new powers in Burgos on October 1st. On the same day the law for the structure of the New Spanish

State was passed, and this created a Technical Junta for the State, the General Government, a Foreign Office and the Chief of State's general office. Decree No 1 of this new Nationalist Government confirmed Mola as leader of the Northern Army and named Queipo de Llano as leader of the Southern Army. It issued also a general Army order in which Lieutenant Colonel Apolinar Saéz de Buniaga was promoted to colonel and made Chief of State for Air. Two days later Decree No 9 was published, creating a War Office with three sections, Land, Sea and Air. The Air section only had two departments, for staff and supplies.

Dávila was named President of the Technical Junta and Chief of the Generalissimo's State, Gil Yuste went to the War Office, Nicolás Franco the General Office, Serrat the Foreign Office and General Fermoso the General Government, where he was soon replaced by Valdés Cabanilles.

During the month of September, as mentioned earlier, all the battalions of the African Army, apart from six battalions of light infantry, had crossed to the Peninsula. During October four battalions of light infantry, ten units from Mehala and five newly formed units of regulars also crossed from Africa. This represented a draining of the main source of reserves. In the Peninsula, by the beginning of October, about fifty voluntary battalions had been formed (Navarre alone provided sixteen corps and Valladolid more than 8,500 volunteers) and several others from the Regular Army.

By March 1937 the number of battalions of volunteers exceeded a hundred, and it was logical that Nationalist leaders were anxious to strengthen their combat forces by increasing the number of battalions of regulars. From September 4th the Academies for Provisional Officers began to function (Nationalist Defence Junta Decree No 94), so that later in the autumn there were sufficient officers available to form the backbone of the new units.

The African Army alone, up to the end of 1936, recruited twenty battalions of light infantry, four legionary units and twenty five units of regulars. In the Peninsula, over the same period, many of the twenty regiments which remained in the Nationalist Zone recruited up to six new battalions; three times their initial forces.

If one includes the new battalions of volunteers, from October 1936 to January 1937 about two hundred new battalions were created, a total which was greater than Franco's entire Army at the beginning of October 1936 (about forty battalions initially in the Peninsula, twenty-five from Morocco and five newly formed, some with volunteers, some with regulars). At the beginning of 1937 the number of battalions of volunteers was approximately one-third of the total Nationalist forces.

In the Government Zone, the month of October was marked by a revival of activity in the organisation of the Popular Army.

On the 16th, Largo Caballero, as minister of war, assumed command of the Army, created his consultative staff and introduced the Commissariat. The first chief of staff (a position which had been vacant since General Sánchez Ocaña resigned at the beginning of the war) was Commander Estrada, who was soon replaced by General Martínez Cabrera. Álvarez del Vayo was named as general commissary and Antonio Mije, Crescenciano Bilbao, Ángel

Pestaña and Angel Gil Roldán as sub-commissaries. Largo Caballero had previously created three Instruction Centres (Infantry/Cavalry, Artillery and Engineers) for the training of officers, similar to those which had been functioning in the Nationalist Zone since September. Theoretically, Giral had started these Schools on August 12th, 1936, but they had not begun to function because of Largo Caballero's opposition when he was leader of the UGT.

On October 20th Largo Caballero dissolved the *Inspección General de Milicias* and created the *Comandancia de Milicias* (Military Command) whose battalions had to be identified only by number. On the 27th an order was published in the Madrid Gazette No 301, which required all soldiers operating in the central area, less than 30,000 of them, to be formed into battalions of 872 men, with four mortars, eight heavy and 24 light machine-guns per battalion. Three days later all men between the ages of twenty and forty were called up and a decree drawn up on October 20th was made public (Madrid Gazette No 304) increasing the Carabineers Corps by 12,000 men. Finally, the *Consejo Superior de Guerra* (Supreme Council of War) was established by decree on November 9th, which was published in the second edition of the Republican Gazette (which was identified as No 315, continuing the numerical sequence of its predecessor, the Madrid Gazette).

So far as the organisation of new units was concerned, five mixed Spanish brigades were created at Albacete in October. These were numbered from 2 to 6: No 1 was reserved for a brigade formed at Alcalá de Henares, which originated as a handful of men from the 5th Regiment. Two International brigades were formed at the same time, and these were initially designated as the 9th and 10th, but at an early date they were re-designated as the 11th and 12th Brigades.

Simultaneously with the creation of these new units, vast quantities of modern arms and equipment began to reach the Government Zone: together with the build up of infantry forces, they decided the fate of Madrid. The supplies came mainly from Russia, which had elected to intervene directly once the Zinoviev and Kamenev trials ended, and now that Spanish gold reserves were on their way to Moscow. The gold left Spain at the end of September, carried aboard the ships *Neva, Kine, Volgotes* and *Kuban.* Loaded at Cartagena on October 25th, it arrived at Odessa on November 6th, its safe transit from Spain assured by a naval escort comprising the squadron that had been withdrawn from Bilbao for this purpose.

Towards the end of the year twenty-five mixed brigades, each with four battalions, were formed in the Central-Southern Zone (twenty Spanish and five International). The old columns were organised into mixed brigades, starting with those at the Madrid front, which were given identifying numbers between 26 and 50. This re-organisation lasted until March, when the last Anarchist force in the Central-Southern Zone (Hierro's column) was re-designed as the 83rd brigade. The brigades from the Eastern and Northern Armies had higher numbers, because they were formed later (from 116 to 135 and 154 to 204 respectively). At the end of 1936 the Eastern Army had some fifty battalions and the North had more than one hundred.

So far as the Air Force was concerned, when Largo Caballero came to power a Ministry for Sea and Air was formed with Prieto at its head, aided by two under-secretaries. Lieutenant Colonel Angel Pastor (now Colonel), who had been acting as chief of Military Aviation, became the under-secretary for Air, although he was soon replaced by Antonio Camacho. Hidalgo de Cisneros became leader of the Air Forces and Angel Riãno remained as chief of staff. Despite all this re-organisation, Civil Aviation continued until December 1936 and Naval Aviation until May 1937.

The creation of an Under-Secretary for Air also brought about a re-organisation of the Air Force and the formation of a new framework. On August 20th a pilot's course was initiated at the Alcalá School. The leader of the course was Commander Alejandro Gómez Spencer, who had under his command the following instructors: J. Doménech, J. Rubio, L. Besonía and Staff Sergeant Emilio Roig Aira. Prior to this, pilots had been trained at Barajas. Later, specialised instruction for observers was arranged at Cuatro Vientos, and architects, engineers and science graduates were invited to apply for training.

In the middle of September the scope of specialised training was expanded considerably, beginning with an elementary pilot's course which was held at San Javier. On October 14th the first steps were taken to begin courses for fighter-bomber pilots at Los Alcazares. The Corps of Air Force Armourers (*Cuerpo de Armores de Aviación*) was formed, and shortly afterwards a course for ground crews began at the Air Force Mechanics' School in Valencia, under the command of Commander Mariano de la Iglesia.

Later, in December, a fighter school was formed, with Captain Félix Sampil, (formerly leader of the 'Marcel Bloch' group) in command. Additional training courses were arranged for wireless operators, armourers, mechanics and observers. In addition, regulations were drawn up for pilot's courses, recruiting of Air Force personnel, uniformity in Aviation, and militarisation of the Staff of LAPE etc.

At this time No 12 Group (mixed fighter and bomber), No 14 (the Nieuport 14-26s in Manises) and No 15 (Multi-engine School) were formed. The Potez group was led by Martin Luna and the Marcel-Bloch Group by J. de la Roquette, following the transfer of F. Sampil to the Fighter School. The Multi-engine School was under Gayoso's command and No 14 Group under Arceaga.

The March Towards Madrid

When Franco took over Supreme Command he decided to amalgamate the African expeditionary Army and the Northern Army, and Mola assumed responsibility for the advance on Madrid. Mola sent out his first directive on October 3rd and the advance began on the 6th. But circumstances had changed: now that Toledo was taken the front had become considerably wider, and Varela did not have sufficient troops to advance along the entire length of the line. This meant that for the first fortnight of October progress could be made only on the left flank. Although it would have been logical to continue as far as Aranjuez, along the Tajo, it was impossible unless the entire Nationalist line could advance.

The defeat of the Government destroyers in the Straits, and later of the gunboats *Uad Muluya* and *Uad Lucas*, meant that between October 5th and 14th the sea passage between Morocco and the Peninsula was open to the Nationalists and ten tabores from Mehala (the equivalent of five battalions), five of regulars and, a little later, four battalions of light infantry and Moroccan Falange, and a battalion from the Canaries, all crossed the Straits safely.

Sea passage of troops across the Straits had to stop in the middle of October, when the *Canarias* and *Almirante Cervera* were ordered out into the Atlantic to intercept the Government squadron due to return from Bilbao. All available aircraft from Cadiz, Seville and Africa were detailed to search for the enemy's naval force. Kuznetsov dates this event for October 12th, but in fact it was the 16th when both squadrons passed unseen within a comparatively short distance of each other, possibly with great relief on both sides. In view of their inferior numbers the Nationalist cruisers would have had a desperate fight if they had been surprised by the enemy.

The first Cant Z.501 to arrive in Spain took part in the aerial reconnaissance, but had to make a forced landing on the sea due to the fact that its Spanish crew had not familiarised themselves with the fuel system and starved the power plant of fuel.

On October 17th the Government Naval Squadron passed through the Straits en route to Cartagena. At about this time the submarine B-5 sank, but the reason for the loss of this vessel was unknown.

Of the forces which crossed from Africa in the first fortnight of October, only three tabores from Mehala were sent to the Madrid front, the remainder of these reinforcements were dispersed between Oviedo, where the siege was raised on October 17th, Aragón and the south.

On October 16th the right flank of Mola's forces (commanded in the field by Varela) began to advance towards Madrid, following the Toledo-Madrid road. However, the left flank, which was once again under Yagüe's command, was unable to advance in concert. Commander Pujalte's Column No 5, took part in this attack, because Tella's troops remained in their barracks on the Tajo line.

On October 20th, to speed up the advance, Franco ordered the formation of three new columns, using Asturian, Moroccan and Canarian forces, and these were ready for action on the 28th. On November 1st Varela still had only twenty battalions (six legionary battalions, four battalions of volunteers, one battalion from the peninsula and nine tabores) and the Monasterio cavalry to oppose the 42,786 men on the Government side.

On September 25th the Nationalists began a general attack, which resulted in considerable gains of land, but had no appreciable influence on the situation in Madrid. In Guadalajara, the town of Sigüenza was besieged on September 30th, but Anarchist soldiers remained within the Cathedral until the middle of October.

In the south, during October, Sáez de Buruaga, Gómez Cobián and Álvarez Rementerias's Nationalist columns occupied the mining valley of Peñarroya-Belmez-Espiel which, apart from its economic importance, was of great strategic interest in so far as the safety of Córdoba and Seville was concerned. This important campaign was totally obscured by the more spectacular action at Madrid and Oviedo. In Aragón, following the hard battles at Huesca in September, there was relative calm throughout October.

On October 2nd Lieutenant Salvador escorted General Mola to Toledo, where he inspected Varela's forces.

As mentioned earlier, Mola had issued his first directive for the advance on Madrid on October 3rd. His principal objective was to improve contact between Varela's troops and those in Avila, since the stretch of land as far as Toledo was exposed on the left flank. On October 6th the Government line was broken at Torrijos and pushed back to Santa Cruz de Retamar, and by the 8th the advance towards the North had reached San Martín de Valdeiglesias. These sudden moves by the Nationalists met little serious resistance from the air. Contact with the four Avila columns (commanded by Merlo, Rada, Santa Pau and Nevado) was made on October 12th. On the 7th Mola had issued his second directive, under which the forces which had advanced towards the north turned eastwards towards Madrid. By the 16th they reached the line Hoyo de Pinares, Robledo de Chavela, Chapinería, Aldea de Fresno, Méntrida, Valmojado, Arniel de Toledo. On the same day, forces on the right flank broke through the Government lines at Bargos, and advanced towards Olías del Rey. During these operations Morato shot down a Loire at Valmojado. Also on the 16th Salas led a Fiat patrol to León, their task being to protect the three Savoia S-M.81s which had been sent to reinforce the Oviedo columns. On October 18th, Morato shot down two Breguets at Illescas, the most forward point of the Nationalist advance towards Madrid.

Prior to this, in the period October 14th to 17th, the Fiats had destroyed six Dewoitines at the Madrid front, without incurring any losses. During the same month they shot down three more fighters and two Breguets near Córdoba. One occasion is recorded when five Government Dewoitines, led by Bonneval, took off for a sortie, but only two of these returned to base as a result of Nationalist air supremacy at that period.

Government air power was weak mainly because their French equipment, which consisted of Dewoitine, SPAD, Bleriot, Nieuport and Loire fighters; and Potez and Marcel Bloch bombers, as well as the pre-war Breguet 19, Nieuport ND 52, Hawker Fury, de Havilland Dragon Rapide and Fokker F-VII, were fast disappearing through losses and old age.

But Government pilots could take heart from the sure signs of massive reinforcement as Russian equipment began to arrive at the southern ports, especially Cartagena.

Between July 31st and August 1st, a total of 16 Dewoitine D 372s were received in Spain (another was damaged at Toulouse and arrived later), and on August 8th 13 more machines of the same type arrived. Documents for the transfer of these last 14 aircraft were received from the manufacturer (Lioré et Olivier) on August 4th, together with other documents relating to six Potez 540s and six Amiots (Document 77 from Volume III of the French Diplomatic Documents 1932–39). Before the end of September ten more fighters of various types and 20 bombers arrived in Spain, making a total of 70 new aircraft for the Government Air Force.

At the same time, aircraft were arriving from France, Holland and England flown by foreign pilots who received large sums of money for delivering the machines, and many of these men enrolled in the International squadrons. To slow down this traffic, Franco ordered the President of the Technical Junta to offer 40,000 francs to any pilot who delivered an aircraft to the Nationalist Zone.

In September, Air France crews led by De Marmier flew seven Potez 540s (Nos 4.220 to 4.226) and some Bloch MB 210s (at least four) to the Nationalist Zone. At this time the Dewoitine factory completed 32 model 510 fighters, of which six appear to have entered Spain. According to information brought by Captain Guillermo Casares, who came over to the Nationalist side at the beginning of the month (he died soon after on a flight to Oviedo), the del Negus machine, armed with six machine-guns, was in Barcelona, together with two armed Air France transport aircraft, ten bombers undergoing repairs, six fighters, one secret fighter and seven seaplanes.

The arrival of Russian supplies and personnel was of much greater significance because of their quantity and quality, which promised to change the situation completely. With the purpose of hindering the unloading and assembly of Russian aircraft, the port of Cartagena was bombed on the 18th by a patrol of S-M.81s, Cieza aerodrome on the 19th by Captain Carrillo's squadron of Ju 52s, Hellín and Cartagena once again on the morning of the 21st. A Fiat patrol, which included García Pardo, was moved to Granada to provide escort for the bombers during their return flight to base.

On October 20th, the German He 51 squadron, plus the Junkers aircraft of the *Pedros y Pablos* squadron were centred in Avila, where they were reinforced by some Heinkel He 46s.*

On October 21st the Mantelli patrol, which had been based in the south, and a new Fiat patrol led by Lieutenant Miguel García Pardo (who had been flying Nieuports in Saragossa until the end of September), were transferred to Talavera. Commander Fagnani ('Faroni') also joined the air units at Talavera, but the bulk of the new Maccagno ('Pecori') squadron was still being assembled and tested in Seville.

The four Spanish Junkers squadrons were centred in Navalmoral de la Mata and Escalona. The Dragon/Fokker group remained in León for operations at the Cantabrian front.

The Romeo 37 squadrons led by José Muñoz and Colacicchi also operated from Talavera from the 19th, and for a short space of time they were both led by Commander Gerardo Fernández Pérez. The first aircraft to equip these squadrons, each of which initially had five machines, had reached Talavera on October 14th. With the arrival of these Romeos at the Madrid front, the slow He 46 squadrons were sent to less vital areas: Vara de Rey to Asturias, and Jiménez Ugarte to Aragón.

Of the Savoia-Marchetti S-M.81s which had arrived in Melilla at the end of July, three were operating from Talavera, three more from Seville and the rest

* By the end of October Germany had provided the Nationalist Army with 15 Heinkel He 51 fighters, 20 Junkers Ju 52 bombers (which arrived in the form of transport planes and were armed in Spain) and 20 Heinkel He 46 army co-operation aircraft, all of which had indifferent performance.

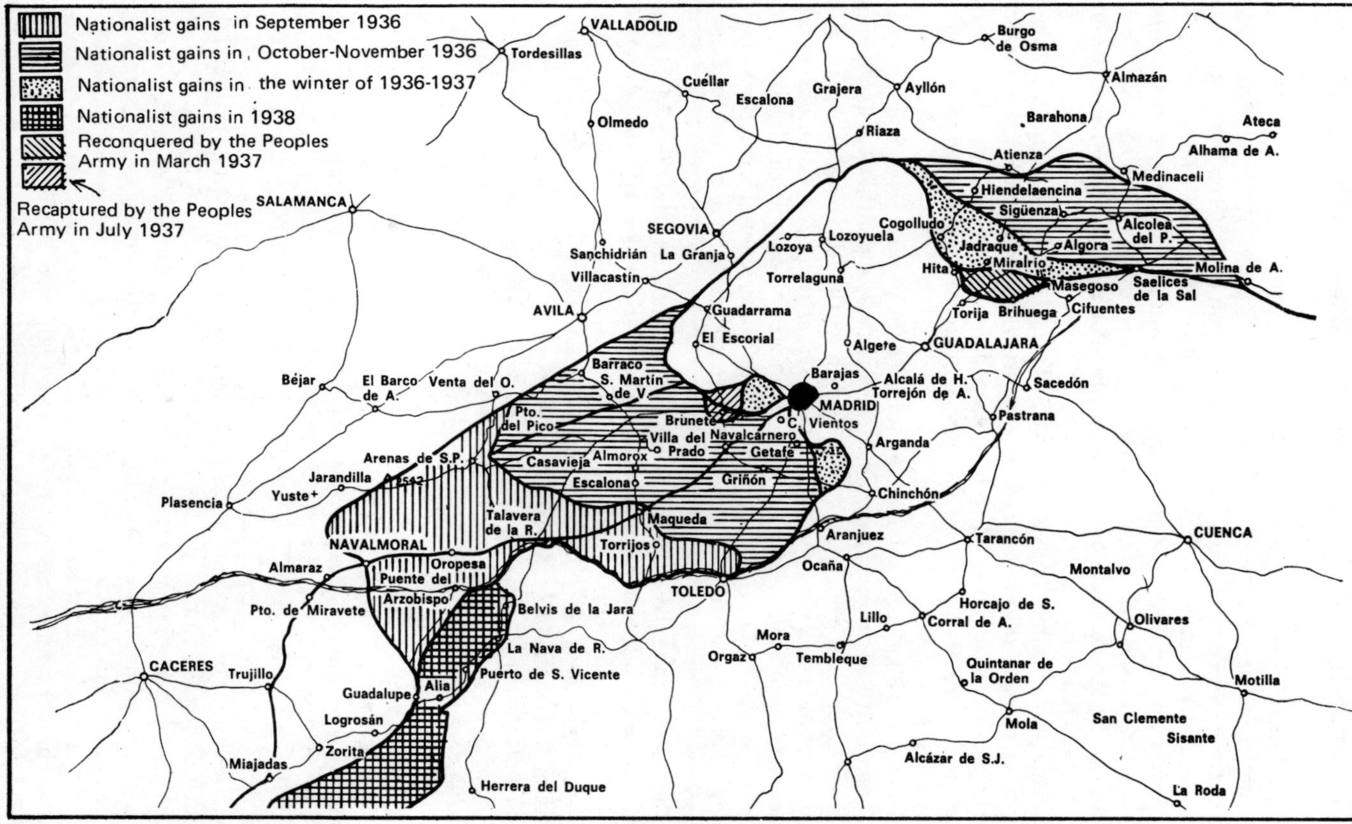

IV. The advance towards Madrid.

were out of action (one had collided with a Breguet at Melilla, another had exploded at Tablada on August 24th and a third ground-looped landing at Talavera).*

Some thirty Breguets were still flying (distributed among the Lasarte-Vitoria, León-Escalona, Seville-Córdoba, Granada and African groups), plus two or three Nieuports (flown by Senra in Aragón, and Pérez Martínez de la Victoria and Bermúdez de Castro in Granada). About ten Dornier Do Wal and S-62 seaplanes were still operating, mainly in the Straits, under the command of Cdr Luis Rambaud (one time leader of the short-lived Heinkel He 51 squadron). In the north, Leopoldo Brage and Torres Prol were operating from Ferrol and Ribadeo.

At this point in time the Nationalist Air Force had about 30 multi-engined machines, the same number of fighters, 70 Army co-operation aircraft (including the pre-war Breguets) and about ten seaplanes. Of these, 20 multi-engined machines, 10 fighters, 50 Army co-operation aircraft and the seaplanes were flown by Spanish crews.

On October 22nd Bonomi was summoned to headquarters at Salamanca to plan night attacks upon Cartagena, (where unloading of the Russian equipment was progressing without interference under the cover of darkness) and to study combined operations with the Fleet. The cruisers *Canarias* and *Almirante Cervera* had been able to operate with complete freedom at the beginning of October. But with the return of the bulk of the Government Fleet to Cartagena their task of intercepting traffic in the Mediterranean had become much more difficult.

The night bombing of Cartagena was carried out jointly by the S-M.81s and Ju 52s, which flew from Granada and crossed the Sierra Nevada on the night of the 27th/28th. On October 27th the *Canarias* made its first dash into the Mediterranean (the *Almirante Cervera* was in dock having its boilers re-tubed) and on October 30th shelled Rosas on the north-east coast.

After the fall of Navalcarnero on October 21st, the greatest activity was on the right flank towards Esquivias and Seseña, as a first step towards gaining Jarama, and at this stage the first small Italian tanks were used.

On October 23rd fighter patrols ranged over the outskirts of Madrid. That which comprised Morato, Salas and Cenni attacked two barrage balloons over Casa de Campo, Cenni destroying one which burst into flames: Salvador, flying in another patrol, destroyed the second balloon during his last sortie.

Also on October 23rd, Asensio Torrado handed over command of army operation in central Spain to General Pozas, following the receipt of an order to replace Colonel Rodrigo Gil as under-secretary at the War Ministry. Miajas took over from Pozas as leader of the Madrid Division, but not as leader of the Madrid Defence Junta.

On the following day Varela occupied Borox, Seseña and Esquivias, and on the 27th had gained a line formed by Griñón, Torrejón de Velasco, Torrejon de la Calzada and Cuesta de la Reina. On the left flank of the advance, Castejón had to resist violent counter-attacks from Chapinería.

Government bomber aircraft now began to be more active, but the fighters

* 9 Savoia-Marchetti S.M.81 bombers, 30 Fiat fighters, 21 Romeo Ro 37s, and a seaplane had reached the Peninsula from Italy. No more Italian aircraft arrived until the end of the year.

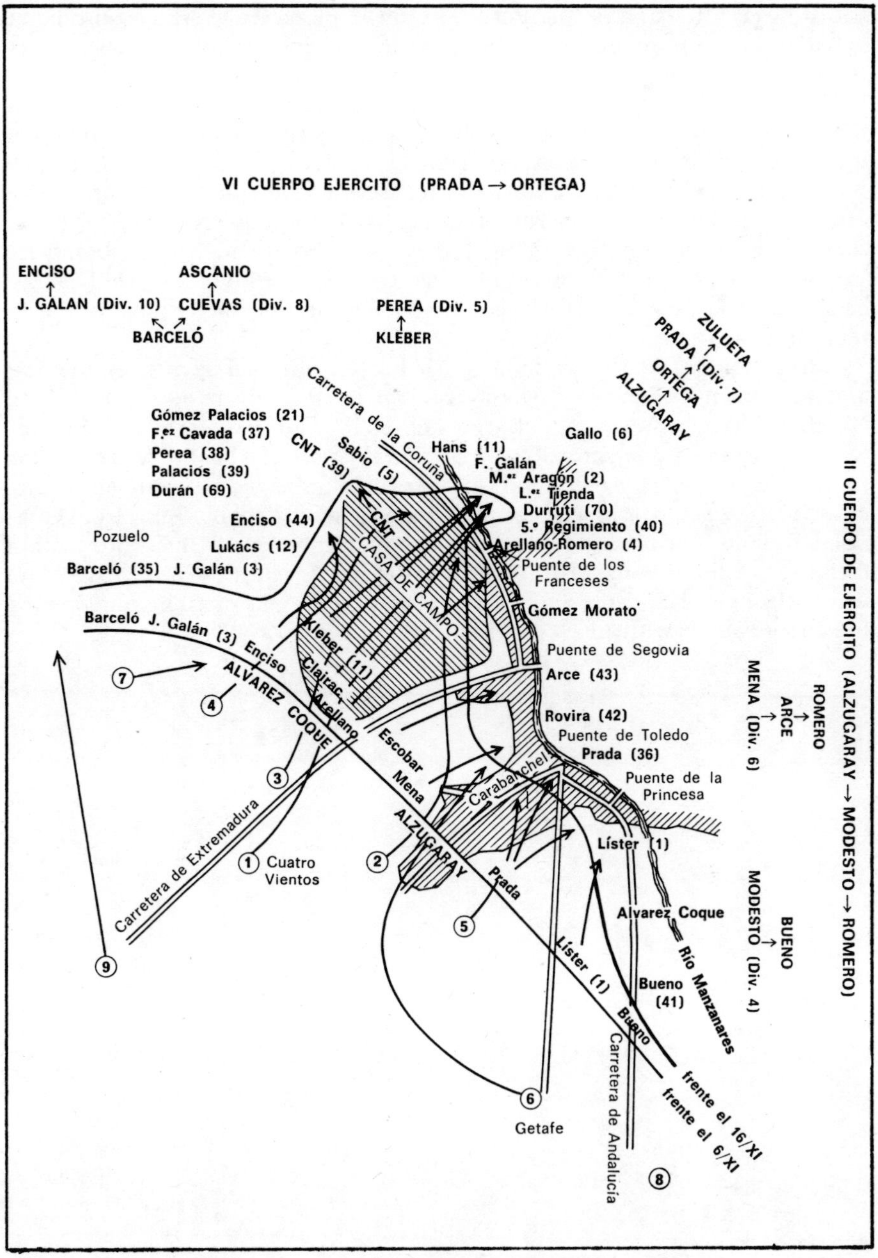

V. The attack on Madrid and the line-up of Brigades, Divisions and Army Corps on this front. The numbers in brackets indicate the Brigades which replaced the columns. Those in a circle are those of Gen Varela's columns. The two black lines indicate the front on November 6th and 16th.

still showed little sign of life. Potez aircraft bombed Talavera aerodrome at dawn and tried to repeat this action a little later in the day. They were prevented from doing so by a single Fiat, which showed sufficient aggression to drive them off. A Fiat formation surprised five Breguets and shot down two of them (a Nationalist communiqué claimed four destroyed), and one Fiat had to make a forced landing at Avila aerodrome.

On October 28th Cáceres, Granada and Seville (Tablada) aerodromes were attacked. At the latter, three Russian Katiuska bombers were seen for the first time, and the Nationalists thought they were American Martin bombers. When fragments of the bombs were collected they were found to be of Russian origin, code numbers on the fragments indicating that the bombs had been made in June 1936.

During this period the Nationalist Air Force continued its attacks on ports and aerodromes along the Mediterranean coast and on access routes to Madrid. The aerodromes at Albacete and Hellín, Los Alcazares and the railway link between Alcázar de San Juan and the port of Alicante, were regular targets. At Alicante the merchant ship *Kursk* had unloaded Russian fighter aircraft. These were to be assembled at Rabasa (where Hispano-Suiza from Guadalajara and Loring from Carabanchel had transferred their production facilities). Admiral Kuznetsov recorded that the Argentine cruiser *25 de Mayo* was in the port of Alicante at the time of these Nationalist attacks, and opened fire on the raiders with all available anti-aircraft guns.

CHAPTER THREE

The Formation of the Armies

Russian Supplies Enter the Battle

On October 28th, eve of the Government counter-attack, Largo Caballero, leader of the Government and minister in control of the Army, issued an address to the troops taking part. This opened with the words: "We now have in our hands a formidable selection of mechanised weapons, we have tanks and a powerful Air Force. . . ." In the *Madrid Gazette*, No 334 of October 29th, there was no reference to the tanks and aeroplanes. However, Communist writers confirm that this was the address published on the night of the 28th.

The counter-attack began on October 29th and the Russian T-26 tanks and fast twin-engined Katiuska bombers were used for the first time. Despite their speed, Salas, who was on patrol over Valdemoro, 16 miles (26km) south of Madrid, managed to climb above four Katiuskas, against which he made three attacks before running out of ammunition. He was successful in damaging one machine which lost formation and which, from the ground, could be seen falling in flames. Bonomi, in his memoirs, recalls that a Katiuska fell over enemy lines. Some days later Mantelli shot down another machine of this type, which landed in the Nationalist Zone.

These Katiuskas had been carried by cargo vessels to Cartagena. Each machine was packed in two crates, one of which contained the fuselage, wing centre-section and the engines and the other the wings, tail unit and accessories. Judging by the large number of cobwebs, these had been crated up for a long time. The first batch comprised a total of thirty-one Katiuskas, and these were used to form three squadrons, each with ten aircraft, and led by Ernst Schacht, Victor Jalzunov and Nesmeyánov, with Arkadi Zlatotsvietov in overall command of the group.

The 'Komsomol' squadron was the first to begin operations, and this was composed entirely of Russian personnel, with the exception of a few Spanish mechanics who had been given a 25-day course of instruction. This had been held in Los Alcázares from the middle of September, Russian instructors providing the tuition. This squadron was based initially at Albacete, and was moved first to Tomelloso and then to San Clemente. The other squadrons were based at Albacete, Argamasilla de Alba and Sisante.

During the battles on October 29th, Captain Paul Armáns' battalion of Russian tanks took part, together with the Madrid Renault Tank Regiment, providing an armoured unit of almost fourty vehicles. This was a powerful force which, if properly deployed, should have broken through the Nationalist lines. The Russian T-26 tank weighed 10·5 tons and was armed with a 45mm cannon and a machine-gun, both mounted in a turret which rotated to give a 360° field of fire. It was, at that time, the best light tank in military service. On the day of the attack the Nationalists had no anti-tank weapons and thus the only opposition consisted of some small Italian Ansaldo tanks. These weighed only 3·3 tons, their armament comprising two fixed forward-firing machine-guns. The 45mm armour-piercing shells of the T-26's cannon could easily penetrate the armour plate of the Ansaldo tanks, which was only 13mm thick. On the other hand, the machine-guns of the latter could make little impression on the armour plate of the T-26. The arrival of the German armoured scout cars, weighing almost six tons, had little effect on the situation since they, too, were armed only with machine-guns.

The Government military leaders made the mistake of deploying the tanks in small units. Those in the primary centre of action were under the control of Líster, Uribarri and Burillo in the area of Seseña-Esquivias-Illescas. Those in the secondary centre of action, controlled by Mena, Modesto and Bueno, were operating in the area of Humanes-Griñón, Parla-Torrejón de la Calzada and Pinto-Torrejón de Velasco.

The largest number was assigned to Líster, who had fifteen T-26 tanks at his disposal. These crossed the lines with ease, but failed to destroy the enemy's machine-gun nests. As a result the infantry, which should have been following closely behind the tanks, could not continue their advance. Nevertheless, making the most of the confusion resulting from their sudden attack, the tanks penetrated into Seseña and beyond. However, as soon as it was realised that the infantry was not following they had to withdraw. By the time they were moving through Seseña again, the Nationalist infantry had rallied and in a display of improvisation and courage they attacked the tanks with petrol bombs and put three out of action.

Things went slightly better in the secondary sector, where the infantry managed to follow within 1,300ft (400m) of the tanks. With support from artillery and armoured cars they managed to advance some $2\frac{1}{2}$–$3\frac{1}{2}$ miles (4–6km) and occupied Griñón and the Torrejones, losing only two armoured cars.

The failure of this counter-attack could not be attributed to incompetence of the leaders. Líster's advice was sought by P. Batov, who is now an army general, and by Paul Arman, who died in Russia while leading a tank corps. In the secondary sector were N. Voronov, who is now principal marshal in the artillery, and his second-in-command, V. Kolpakchi. The Spanish leaders, apart from Uribarri who soon faded from the limelight, were some of the most efficient of the war. Líster and Modesto, for example, could speak Russian and had completed a course at the Frunze Academy in Moscow. As a result of this they were well acquainted with Russian materials and tactics.

The principal mistake was the failure to concentrate all the tanks and armoured vehicles in one sector; which would have allowed them to form an echelon and gain a foothold. They lacked advanced tactical knowledge. This is quite obvious today, but at the time only a few experts appreciated the fact, amongst them Colonel Guderian who wrote the almost clairvoyant book *Achtung-Panzers*. Even a critic as famous as Helmut Klotz did not believe in the independent use of tanks, although he accepted the axiom of their collective use in a single action. And General Pavlov, who led the Tank Brigade at Guadalajara, paid dearly for his outdated tactics when, four years later, he had to face up to Guderian.

Maccagno's Fiat squadron did not take part in the battles on the 29th, for on that day they had to escort the second patrol of Savoia S-M.81s moving from Seville to Talavera. The Savoias arrived safely at Talavera, but Maccagno lost his way and had to return to Tablada aerodrome.

Government bomber aircraft attacked Seville, Granada, Cáceres, and Salamanca the next day, but the Russian fighters still failed to appear.

The attack in the area of Seseña was repeated on October 30th, with even worse results. In the air, the Mantelli patrol attacked a formation of three Potez machines, destroying one piloted by Gibelli and damaging those flown by Proskúrov and Goranov. Three Katiuskas attacked Talavera aerodrome, but as six Fiats took off at their approach they beat a hasty retreat without causing any damage. As there was no anti-aircraft defence at Tablada, a routine air patrol was started and permission was sought to move some of the machines to another aerodrome. Despite institution of this patrol, at 09.00hrs on November 1st three Katiuskas attacked the aerodrome and caused slight damage to six Fiats. These aircraft were repaired within a week, but that week proved to be vital, not only at the time, but so far as later events were concerned.

Although the counter-attack on October 29th had failed, it helped dissuade Mola from his first plan: to reach Jarama before attempting an assault on Madrid.

To decentralize Talavera, where six S-M.81s, two Romeo Ro 37 squadrons and the Fiats were all based, it was decided to send Dequal's squadron to a new airfield at Torrijos. Near to this aerodrome there was a wooded area where aircraft could be concealed. The scarcity of aerodromes in the Nationalist Zone contrasted sharply with the large number available in the Government Zone. This made it almost impossible to surprise Government aircraft on the ground. One exception was the achievement of the S-M.81s at Alcalá de Henares on November 2nd. On the same day a Katiuska attempted another surprise attack. Mantelli and Sozzi, who were on patrol, succeeded in shooting it down.

Ironically, an accident was responsible for more damage than had been caused by the Government attacks when a bomb fell from a Fiat that was being taxied. This exploded destroying the machine and killing the pilot, Vivarelli ('Guglielmotti'), and also injured the pilot Salvadori, a mechanic and an armourer.

On November 2nd the air chief (General Kindelan) sent the following communication to the leader of the air units operating from Toledo: "It is strictly forbidden for any aircraft to bomb the city of Madrid without your express order".

On November 3rd a second counter-attack was made with the tanks, this time carried out by the 2nd Battalion of the Tank Group, led by Lieutenant General S. Krivoshein. Paul Arman's tank group had been sent to defend

Madrid, opposite the Nationalist left wing (Yagüe) which at that time was occupying Móstoles and Villaviciosa de Odón.

This attack, with assistance from the columns of Burillo, Líster and Bueno, took them from Cerro de los Ángeles and Marañosa towards Pinto, which had been occupied by Varela the day before. As on October 29th, the tanks succeeded in surrounding Torrejón de Velasco, which was soon occupied by the infantry, and in this sector they captured five guns mounted on lorries. The 3rd Tank Company, which should have attacked Valdemoro, went to Pinto in error and had to withdraw, leaving behind two tanks.

Despite the fact that orders had been given to the effect that the infantry should make their advance some 550yds (500m) in the rear of the tanks, they soon fell behind. The Nationalist artillery concentrated its fire on the road and the tanks were forced to seek refuge in a nearby valley, but their position was soon discovered and two of them were put out of action. When experienced tank crews made an attempt to rescue them, a third tank was also damaged. In Seseña, where the heavy armoured vehicles were being used, two were damaged by artillery fire, but they were retrieved later.

Making a surprise attack by night, the Nationalists recovered Pinto, and the 1st Tank Company (Faorie) was forced to make a rapid withdrawal; the 3rd Section was cut off and lost all its tanks, with the exception of one which beat a hasty retreat to Aranjuez the following morning.

On November 4th, an attempt was made to launch a new counter-attack, spearheaded by the tanks, but this had to be cancelled at mid-day on receipt of the news that Yagüe had advanced to Alcorcón. To strengthen Government defences, all the armoured vehicles, together with Bueno's column and several of Burillo's battalions, were ordered to Madrid. To strengthen the air defences Kindelán had issued an order on the previous day suspending a planned bombing operation on Albacete and Santa Cruz de Mudela. The aim was to concentrate all available forces in Madrid.

On the same day, Russian fighter aircraft made an appearance at the Madrid front, damaging a Junkers Ju 52 (from Luis Pardo's squadron) which had to force-land at Esquivias; the observer, Captain Aguirre, was fatally wounded. They also attacked a Romeo Ro 37, injuring the observer, Lieutenant Alfaro de Pueyo, and shot down a Ju 52 from the *Pedros y Pablos* squadron, flown by Lieutenant Kolbitz.

Two machines from the Dequal squadron, flown by 'Limonesi' and Magistrini ('Mainetti'), were patrolling the area and attacked some Katiuskas without spotting the ten Chatos that were escorting them. They escaped unscathed from this initial clash, but in attempting to defend a Romeo they were both shot down. Magistrini was seriously injured and died in hospital; Dequal was wounded but escaped by parachute and dropped between the lines. To add to the Nationalist problems, two more Fiats were wrecked when landing at Torrijos. On the Government side the Russian pilots of two Chatos lost themselves and had to make forced landings in Segovia.

On November 5th came the first big aerial battle of the war. Nine Fiats from Torrijones, led by Maccagno (their pilots included Morato, Salas and Salvador) met about 15 Chatos and some Potez aircraft between Leganés and

Madrid. Without waiting for the support of five additional Fiats from Talavera, Maccagno led them in to attack, relying on superior performance to compensate for lack of numbers. Morato shot down a Chato, and then damaged the engine of a Potez, forcing it to land. Salas shot down a Chato, which crashed in flames, and 3 miles (5km) south east of Barajas he scored hits on two more Chatos. He, in turn, came under attack, but put his aircraft into a steep dive and made good his escape at tree-top level. Salvador chased a Chato as far as Barajas and attacked two Potez machines without success. The Nationalist bulletin claimed seven fighters and one Potez destroyed and admitted the loss of one Fiat, that of Captain Maccagno ('Pocori'), leader of the recently formed squadron. The Madrid bulletin claimed that one Fiat, number 384 (flown by Picoli), and four other aircraft had been destroyed. Maccagno was later exchanged for one of the Russian pilots.

Two air battles took place on the 6th, at 10.00hrs and 14.00hrs. In the latter, five Fiats led by Salas attacked seven Chatos. Salas was thought to have destroyed one machine from a patrol of three, this aircraft trailing smoke as it veered into a cloud and disappeared from sight. The Nationalist bulletin claimed two aircraft destroyed, while the Government bulletin, which referred only to the earlier engagement, claimed the destruction of two Heinkels. Bonomi confirmed that the Fiats had shot down two fighters, and this was also confirmed by the Air Force communiqué, which admitted the loss of a Fiat and a Junkers. This latter machine was probably flown by Captain Larrauri, who managed to reach Talavera with one engine out of action, the other developing only restricted power, and his aircraft riddled with bullet holes. Von Morau, leader of the *Pablos y Pedros*, also had to force-land near Madrid at this time.

Also on November 6th, the Madrid Government decided to move to Valencia, and power was handed over to the Madrid Defence Junta, which was presided over, from that day, by General Miaja. The Army for Operations in Central Spain (Pozas) established its headquarters in Alcalá de Henares.

At the same time as the Government left Madrid, Bonomi gave orders to the fighter forces to refrain from combat unless they had numerical superiority, and although this went much against the grain, Kindelán had no alternative but to accept. Ávila aerodrome, from where the He 51s, He 46s and Ju 52s were operating, was subjected to an attack on November 6th and the subsequent communiqué reported the destruction of two He 51s and some damage to equipment and supplies.

The Frontal Attack on Madrid

November 8th was the date fixed by the Nationalists for their attack on Madrid, but to their misfortune the order of operations fell into the hands of Madrid's leaders on the eve of the attack. Because of this, the Government were able to concentrate their forces at Casa de Campo, knowing that the attacks on Caranbanchel and Usera were of a secondary nature.

On the 7th, according to Miaja, Madrid had eight columns available for defence, those of Barceló, Clairac, Galán, Escobar, Mena, Prada, Líster and Bueno. Escobar was situated on the Extremadura road, the columns to his right being co-ordinated by Alvarez Coque and those to his left by Alzugaray.

Miaja had reinforced the defending troops by using the mixed brigades: the 1st (Líster), 3rd (J. Galán), 5th (Sabio) and the 11th International (Kleber), as well as the Enciso and Alicante columns, and Paul Arman's tank corp. Opposing them were about the same number of troops in the columns of Asensio, Barrón, Delgado, Serrano, Castejón, Bartomeu and Tella, although only the first five of these took part in the action. The 8th column (Rodrigo) and the 9th (being formed), remained on the flank; the 6th column was held in reserve until November 10th, and the 7th (Bartomeu) was later merged with the 4th.

On November 10th Varela had twenty-nine battalions to call upon, nine more than at the end of October. García Escámez and Rada had come from the Sierra with some of their troops, because the African reserve was exhausted. He had also two companies of light German tanks, plus some small Italian tanks. The first German anti-aircraft battery, the Aldinger battery, did not become operational until some days later.

On the eve of the attack the Nationalist Air Force dropped pamphlets over Madrid. Penned by Franco, it called upon the defenders to surrender. During the night a radio announcement said that the bombing of Madrid was about to begin, apart from one special area bounded by the Paseo de La Ronda in the north, Diego de León Street in the south, the Castellana in the east (including the new Ministries) and the Guindalera in the west.

On the first day of the attack the air force was concentrated in the centre of the action, at the Casa de Campo, where a squadron of Romeos was operating, escorted by nine Fiats, and six Junkers escorted by nine Heinkels. By then the Fiats damaged during the bombing of Talavera had been repaired, and there were eighteen aircraft of this type serviceable.

On November 9th the 1st and 3rd squadrons with Romeos and Fiats, and the 2nd with Ju 52s, made three sorties to the River Manzanares zone and the Northern Station. During the third sortie, at 12.25hrs, fourteen Fiats were in combat with the two squadrons of Chatos from Barajas and Alcalá, and were successful in destroying two of them. One crashed between Madrid and Vicálvaro, the other fell in flames between Madrid and Barajas. Morato shot down one of them, and this made his fourteenth victory.

The occupation of the Casa de Campo was completed the following day, when the military hospital and the bull ring in Carabanchel were also occupied; the Extremadura road was bombed as far as Segovia bridge, and up to Ferraz Street in Madrid, the agreed penetration zone. Ananías San Juan, the co-pilot of Ureña's Ju 52, made off with the aircraft while the engines were warming up. He went to Alcalá de Henares, leaving the mechanic helpless to do anything but report what had happened.

The Government bombers had one of their most notable successes of the war on November 11th, when they made a surprise attack on Avila aerodrome. The Ju 52s of the *Pedros y Pablos* squadron were there, together with Eberhard's fighter squadron and some Heinkel He 46 reconnaissance aircraft. According to the Valencian communiqué, eighteen 50kg bombs were dropped, landing on and among the parked aircraft.

This blow was partly compensated when the 3rd squadron of the Fiat Group arrived at Torrijos. Their arrival was marked by bad weather, and due to low cloud they lost their way. Morato had to take off to guide them back to their new base. Now that he had received reinforcements of aircraft, Bonomi issued an order that they were not to enter into combat unless their force numbered fifteen fighters.

On the 12th it was strange to note that the Nationalist communiqué did not claim any aircraft destroyed, while that of the Government reported the loss of two machines. These were Katiuskas piloted by Bazhénov and Fiódorov, which collided during a raid on Nationalist lines.

During the last two days the lines had hardly moved, and in Guadalajara there was even an attempt to recapture Almadrones, which had fallen into the hands of Moscardó's forces (Soria Division) only a few days before.

On November 13th, now that the Casa de Campo had been taken, Yagüe decided to press onwards towards the Manzanares. Miaja delivered a speech which began: "Fighters—today you are going to crush fifty thousand men . . ." At the same time Krivoshein's armoured column, the 12th International Brigade (Lukacs) and three other Spanish brigades, attacked Cerro de los Ángeles.

Above the Pasco de Rosales (Madrid), fourteen Fiats fought a fierce battle against Government Chatos. Morato shot down one, Salas damaged three and Salvador shot down another. On their return flight they encountered five Katiuskas, bombing Getafe and Cuatro Vientos from a height of 16,400ft (5,000m). Salas damaged one so severely that the crew had to take to their parachutes, and Morato damaged three others. On that day Morato recorded his fifteenth victory, both Salas and Salvador their fifth.

The Nationalist bulletin claimed the destruction of six fighters and a Russian bomber, and admitted one loss. The Government claimed five aircraft destroyed, admitted the loss of a Breguet and stated that two of their pilots had been wounded. A Russian pilot who landed in Madrid was attacked by the public because they thought he was a German; Koltsov identifies this pilot as Captain Antonio, leader of a Chato squadron, adding that he died of his injuries a few days later. It seems that he must have mistaken him for Serguei Tarjov, who died in Gómez Ulla hospital on the 22nd.

The Fiat that was lost was flown by Captain Mosca ('Massa'), whose pilot, badly injured, made a crash landing at Talavera. Mariotti force-landed outside the airfield at Getafe, but without damaging his aircraft. The He 51 squadron lost its leader, Eberhard, and Lieutenant Henrici.

In another battle, fought during the afternoon of the same day, the Nationalists claimed to have destroyed five of the enemy without loss. The opposing claim was for the destruction of four Nationalist aircraft for the loss of two of their own.

On November 14th, General Miaja issued the following order: "Any aviator who jumps from his aircraft using a parachute is out of the battle and, therefore, I order all forces defending Madrid not to shoot at parachutists under any circumstances. They may be our own men, but, if they prove to be enemies they can provide us with valuable information, which will be of great use for our operations".

On November 15th Krivoshein's tanks were ordered to Madrid to relieve those commanded by Paul Arman. The latter returned to the training centre at Archena, where fifty-six new tanks were expected, intended to form General D. Pávlov's Tank Brigade in December. A small factory was opened at Alcalá de Henares for the repair of these vehicles.

Between November 13th and 15th the Nationalist left wing, under command of Yagüe, made several unsuccessful attempts to cross the river Manzanares. Yagüe had excellent forces available to him, comprising the columns of Asensio, Barrón, Delgado Serrano and Bartomeu. The latter had taken command of the column commanded originally by Castejón, who had been wounded in the attacks on the Casa de Campo. The Manzanares could hardly be considered a serious obstacle by any reader who may have seen it at the point of San Isidro's shrine. But from the very beginning it was clear that Madrid could not be entered by that route. The river itself was no great obstacle, but its banks certainly were. The Casa de Campo, apart from the distant Garabitas, was no higher than the river. On the other hand, the houses in the Paseo de Rosales and, further north, Dehesa de la Villa, had a perfect view of the river valley and the positions from which the Nationalists began their attack on the Casa de Campo. Further inside Madrid, the telephone exchange provided a superb observation point for the artillery, from which they could survey all the Nationalist artillery sites.

Yagüe intended to begin his attack in the north of the Casa de Campo, towards El Pardo, and then to enter Madrid via Dehesa de la Villa and Estrecho, towards Cuatro Caminos, but his plan was not accepted. On the morning of the 15th he had to abandon command of the left wing, this time because of a genuine illness, and he was replaced a few hours later by Colonel García Escamez.

Meanwhile, Miaja had increased his reinforcements. Already there were in Madrid the Spanish Brigades Nos 1–6 (Líster, Martínez de Aragón, José María Galán, Arellano, Sabio and Gallo), the 11th and 12th Internationals (Kleber and Lukacs) and Krivoshein's Tank Group. Columns commanded by Lopez Tienda, Álvarez Coque, Gómez Morato, the 5th Regiment and Durrut's column, which had arrived from the distant Aragonese front, now joined the battle.

In the air, two Ratas (called Moscas in the Government Zone) entered the battle for the first time on November 15th. One of these, according to Bonomi, was shot down; the communiqué quoted one fighter but did not specify the type.

To offset the large shipments of Russian aircraft, the availability of which would complicate their entry into Madrid, the Generalissimo took steps to increase the Nationalist Air Force.

He came to an agreement with Germany who promised to keep one hundred aircraft permanently in Spain. This was the famous Condór Legion, which consisted of a fighter group of three or four squadrons, a reconnaissance squadron and a squadron of seaplanes. Acting in co-operation with the Condór Legion was a tank group, comprising two companies of light vehicles and a company of anti-aircraft artillery with three heavy and two light batteries and one with searchlights. By the middle of 1938 the number of tanks had been increased to four battalions.

The Condór Legion, which was led initially by Sperrle, with von Richthofen as chief of staff, began to operate on November 15th with a massive attack on the port of Cartagena, made by the three squadrons of Junkers Ju 52s under command of the group leader, Commander Fuchs. The Junkers took off from Melilla and attacked from the sea; on their return they went to Salamanca to prepare for operations at the Madrid front.

The Condór Legion fighter group (von Merhard) could not compensate for the arrival of the Ratas, since their Heinkel He 51s were manifestly inferior.

In fact, of the competing fighters the Ratas were the fastest and had the highest ceiling, the Chatos were the most manoeuvrable and had the best rate of climb, and the Fiats were the most robust and were very fast in a dive. The Heinkel He 51s were far inferior to all of these types.

With the three He 51s handed over by the Germans before the Condór Legion was formed, and three others bought with money subscribed in Aragón (those named *Sarragossa, Huesca* and *Teruel*), two Spanish patrols were formed and these were led by Captains Manrique Montero Mera and César Martin Campos.Other members of these patrols, which operated in the north and Aragón, were Arija, Senra, and the Portuguese Krug (who was of German origin).*

To add to their disadvantages as regards the performance of the He 51s, the number of Russian fighters reaching the Government Air Force was far greater than the fighter types received by the Nationalists. Within a short time the Government had formed six squadrons of Chatos and a similar number of Ratas (called Boeings in the Nationalist communiqués and Moscas by the Government Zone). The names Boeing, Curtis and Martin Bomber, which the Nationalists gave to the Russian aircraft, can be explained by the fact that they bore some similarity to aircraft of American design and manufacture. The US originals had been exhibited in Spain just before the Uprising, and licence rights for the manufacture of the Martin B-10B had been acquired. The Chato (Polikarpov I-15) was similar to the Boeing P-12 and the Rata (Polikarpov I-16) to the Boeing P-26.

On November 15th the Nationalist bulletin jubilantly announced the crossing of the Manzanares, which had been effected late in the afternoon. The Government bulletin ignored this, but reported attacks on Ávila, Torrijos, Navalmoral and Toledo aerodromes, and claimed the destruction of four aircraft in air combats and about sixteen more on the ground.

The 11th International Brigade, commanded by Kleber, which had been fighting on the Government right flank since November 8th, was moved to the Manzanares sector. When the Nationalists had fought their way across the Manzanares, continued opposition to the attackers in this sector was assigned to Alzugaray, who left the bridges sector in Mena's control. Alzugaray had under his direct command the forces led by López Tienda, Durruti, Heredia-Ortega and Kleber, while Mena had those of Rovira, Arce and Prada. Arel-

* The Condór Legion had initially about 100 aircraft: 36 Ju 52s, 36 He 51s, 12 He 70s, 9 He 59s and some He 45s and 46s. Russia sent 55 Chatos, 31 Ratas, 31 Katiuskas and 31 Rasantes in 1936. By the middle of March 1937, 92 more Chatos, 31 Ratas, 30 Rasantes and 31 Natachas arrived. A large quantity of Ratas and Natachas continued to arrive until July of the same year, at least 80 of the former and 75 of the latter.

lano and Gómez Morato held positions between these two groups. Outside Alzugaray's jurisdiction, but also in the University Campus sector, were the CNT columns and one led by Francisco Galán, with Sabio in reserve. The right flank was held by troops led by Barceló, J. Galán and Enciso and the left by Líster, Álvarez Coque and Bueno. The columns commanded by Álvarez Coque was later transferred to the Argüelles district as Alzugaray's reserve.

Asensio had received orders from Nationalist headquarters to cross the Manzanares at all costs, and he decided to do so without tank support. At the same time, defending forces led by Durruti were attempting to cross the river in the opposite direction. Asensio succeeded in his task and established camp near the University Campus, which meant that Government forces under the command of Arellano were to the south and Enciso to the north of his base.

The 11th International Brigade was moved to the northern sector, where a new group was formed under Kleber's command, comprising the 5th, 11th and 12th Brigades and the columns of the CNT and Enciso. Alzugaray continued to defend access to Moncloa and Arellano covered the route to the West Park, where Carlos Romero (later Arellano's successor) was defending the *Puente de los Franceses* (French Bridge) which had been damaged earlier. Much further south Nationalist aircraft had also damaged the bridge at Segovia.

On November 16th Asensio began his attack on the University Campus. In the sky overhead a Fiat squadron, with Morato as one of the pilots, fought a battle against four Ratas which were escorting nine Chatos. The Nationalist bulletin announced the destruction of two fighters; the Government bulletin claimed five victories and admitted the loss of one aircraft. The leader of one of the Chato squadrons (named as Capt Palancar by Koltsov) parachuted to the ground, landing uninjured in the Paseo de la Castellana, near the War Ministry.

On the 17th, Salas led seven Fiats into an attack against a group of Ratas that had intercepted a flight of their Ju 52s. Both sides suffered losses and, for the first time, the Government acknowledged the loss of a Rata.

November 18th was a critical day of the attack on Madrid. Ascencio's troops together with those of Barrón and Delgado Serrano attacked the University Campus and Kleber ordered Krivoshein to rush his tank corps to that sector.

Escorted by the Fiats, four Savoia S-M.81s (Llorente squadron), five Junkers Ju 52s (from Luis Pardo's and Carrillo's groups) the three Romeo Ro 37s (Munoz's squadron), bombed the Florida and del Rey bridges, and Marqúes, Urquijo and Rosales streets, leading from the University Campus to Montaña barracks. On the same day, in other air attacks, the buildings of the Ministry of the Interior, the Madrid-Paris building (now the SEPU) near to the telephone exchange and the San Carlos Hospital were all set on fire.

On November 18th, Italy and Germany officially recognised General Franco as leader of the Nationalist cause, waiving their earlier condition that he must first occupy the capital. During the night of the 18th/19th the cruisers *Canarias* and *Almirante* Cervera subjected the port of Barcelona to a heavy bombardment from their guns.

A determined attempt was still being made to occupy Madrid by a frontal attack, with the collaboration of the entire Nationalist Air Force and the

Condór Legion. Before these new attacks began, the neutral zone in Madrid was increased in area to include the sector between the Calle Zurbano in the west, the Pasco de La Ronda in the north, Calle Velázquez in the east and the Calles Goya and Velázquez in the south.

From a viewpoint on a tower in the town of Leganés, Mola and Bonomi watched the S-M.81s and Ju 52s, now numbering about fifty, as they made their attack on Madrid. They dropped a total of about 40 tons of bombs, a comparatively small quantity for a city with a million inhabitants, but it was the heaviest raid to that date.

The Government in Valencia protested violently about these attacks on Madrid, but the city had been allowed to become a military stronghold, containing the majority of the Popular Army. Earlier, Oviedo, Huesca, Teruel, Córdoba, Granada, Saragossa, Caceres, Salamanca, Seville, Cádiz, Huelva, Algeciras, Tarifa, Palma de Mallorca, Ceuta, Tetuan, Melilla, Larache etc, had all suffered air raids. From the beginning of the war until August 27th, the day of the first air raid upon Madrid, Government bulletins had quoted more than thirty-two air raids on Nationalist towns (see Appendix 43).

The air attacks on Madrid were really of little avail: their scale was such that they caused no significant number of military casualties, neither did they in any measure lower the morale of the military or civil population. Five three-engined bombers at Oviedo were worth more than fifty over Madrid.

During the first heavy air attack on November 19th, nine He 51s and sixteen Fiats fought against a large number of Ratas and Chatos. Salas fired off practically all his ammunition against one Rata, which was last seen in a dive behind its own lines. The Nationalist bulletin claimed four aircraft destroyed (three fighters and one bomber). The Ministry for Sea and Air admitted the loss of two fighters, but counter-claimed to have shot down three Junkers and three fighters. This was the last large air battle during 1936.

The attacks on Madrid lasted until the 22nd, and in these four days 133 deaths and the destruction of 110 houses were reported in the official Government communiques.

The Nationalist frontal attack on Madrid gradually lost impetus. It was clear to Mola that even though the three columns of Asensio, Barrón and Delgado had gained a foothold in the University Campus, in view of the enormous number of Government troops within the city, the possibility of a Nationalist occupation of Madrid was virtually nil.

The fighting in Madrid was the most violent that had taken place until that time. Three of the initial leaders of the five Nationalist columns, Castejón, Tella and Delgado Serrano, were all seriously wounded. In December Varela, too, had to relinquish his command for the same reason, and he spent a month in hospital. On the Government side Escobar, Clairac, Francisco Galán, José Galán, Arellano, Arce and Alzugaray were all injured.

The loss of these combat-hardened and popular leaders was a blow to the morale of the inexperienced rank and file, which meant that the weight of defending Madrid fell on the professional soldiers. Arellano-Romero and Enciso, leading Wad-Ras's Regiment and the Presidential Battalion respectively, and later Sabio, with battalions of carabineers, guarded the flanks without yielding the vital Franceses Bridge and San Fernando Bridge. This compelled Varela to retain his forces in a precarious situation within the University Campus, despite the fact that their tenuous supply route—a footbridge—had been destroyed by enemy fire.

At this same period the most efficient force in Carabanchel was the Elche Battalion, led initially by Rovira. So far as the Militia were concerned their most efficient battalion at that time was the 9th Syndicalist, with Cipriano Mera as their leader; Modesto also led a battalion, but he was soon wounded and replaced. Lister was in a fairly peaceful sector, and the only time his men fought in November was during a night attack on Cerro de los Ángeles.

Russian Aircraft Dominate

On November 20th the Nationalists were still putting pressure on certain districts of Madrid, and they confirmed that some houses and large buildings in Moncloa had been occupied. There was also evidence of activity in the Sigüenza sector. The Government countered with the claim that there was little activity in Madrid and announced that the Clinical Hospital had been recaptured and that the Casa de Velázquez had been set on fire.

During those days weather conditions had been bad and all air activity was greatly reduced. On November 20th six more Romeos arrived at Talavera, just before the airfield was closed by heavy storms. On the 15th, Gamonal aerodrome had been flooded and the Romeos there had been transferred to Prado del Arca which had once been a fighter airfield.

On November 22nd, in a move suggested by Yagüe, the Nationalist forces began to advance into the Pozuelo-Húmera section, supported by Italian tanks and German light armoured cars. Krivoshein's Russian tank corp was deployed immediately in support of the Galán Brigade and they succeeded in containing the advance, but losses on both sides were heavy.

The last Nationalist efforts, made on November 24th and 25th, were held by the heaviest mass of artillery fire mounted by the Government. According to N. Voronov's account, this involved the use of 22 batteries of field artillery.

On November 24th Government forces began a decoy manoeuvre on Talavera, mounted from the left bank of the Tagus, and their artillery shelled Prada del Arca aerodrome, a one-time fighter airfield then being used by the Italian and Spanish Savoia S-M.81s and the Romeo Ro 37s. To avoid destruction, these aircraft took off and flew to Talavera (Gamonal) airfield, having first requested assistance from the Fiats at Torrijos and the Spanish Junkers Ju 52s at Navalmoral. General Mola expressed his concern that an insignificant diversionary attack should deprive more important fronts of air support. But, in fact, this attack was the beginning of a strong offensive against the Nationalist Air Force.

On the 25th and 26th, the Katiuskas bombed Gamonal airfield, where the bomber and reconnaissance aircraft had flown for refuge, damaging two Romeos and a Savoia S-M.81. During the following days they attacked Prada del Arca aerodrome, which was now flooded, and it was not until the end of the month that Nationalist forces recaptured the hill from which the enemy artillery was dominating that aerodrome. In view of the situation it was decided to send six of the Romeos to Cáceres until a new aerodrome, which was being constructed at Veladas on the Arenas de San Pedro road, was ready for use.

On November 26th Nationalist bombers attacked the port of Cartagena, where the *Miguel de Cervantes* was lying at anchor. This cruiser had been seriously damaged when an Italian submarine had scored a direct hit with a torpedo. At the end of the month the Nationalist cruiser *Almirante Cervera* was also badly damaged when torpedoed twice by submarines. This cruiser had been damaged previously in August 1936; while operating off the Guipuzcoan coast she was hit by a torpedo from the submarine *Remigio Verdia*, but this failed to explode. At about this same time the submarine C-3 was sunk off Málaga.

On November 26th, Nationalist bombers made two attacks on Madrid, and these were the last made in daylight. The superiority of the Government fighters was such that they had to revert to making their attacks by night. Clearly the initiative was passing over to the Government Air Force. On December 2nd eighteen Rasantes attacked Talavera (Veladas) aerodrome, destroying a Savoia S-M.81 on the ground and damaging two others. In the course of this operation one of the Rasantes was shot down by anti-aircraft fire; its pilot, Lieutenant Tupikov, was taken prisoner and the observer killed. According to Bonomi, Cenni shot down three more Rasantes. Two days earlier Chianese's Fiat had been shot down south of the Tagus and on the 2nd a Romeo suffered the same fate.

On December 4th the Rasantes damaged three Ju 52s of Carrillo's group at Navalmoral, and also made an unsuccessful attack on the fighter airfield at Torrijos. The Ju 52s were sent by road to Tablada for repair and Carrillo took command of the He 46 group from León, comprising Vara de Rey and Larrauri's squadrons, the latter newly-formed.

The next day the Katiuskas attacked Tablada (Seville) aerodrome and the towns of Burgos, Salamanca, Seville, Granada and Cordoba. On December 7th the Rasantes attacked the fighter airfield at Torrijos, but the aircraft normally based there had already been moved to nearby Barcience. The Katiuskas also returned to attack Seville and lost one aircraft which, after being machine-gunned by Bermudez de Castro, crashed at Castilblanco. During the battles of the previous days two Fiat pilots (Larsimon and Ferrari) had been wounded, and both had been compelled to make forced-landings.

On December 10th (the Virgin de Loreto's day, patron of the Spanish Air Force) the Katiuskas made two attacks on Veladas, aerodrome, where Savoia S-M.81s were being temporarily patched-up so that they could be flown to Seville for a thorough overhaul. The four S-M.81s that were still serviceable were moved to a new aerodrome at Arenas de San Pedro. This aerodrome and that at Barcience were continually being attacked by the Rasantes. So frequently, in fact, that a patrol of fighters at Escalona became a little confused and mistook the Romeo flown by Jiménez Benamú and Compagni for one of the enemy machines and both men lost their lives in the incident.

Events were slowly undermining the morale of the Fiat squadrons, as might be expected. Of the first three squadron leaders the brilliant Dequal was wounded and had returned to Italy; Oliviero was killed in an accident; and

Maccagno had been taken prisoner. Of their three replacements only Nobili remained. Larsimon and Captain Mosca had both been wounded: the latter, following his discharge from Seville Hospital, was killed in an attack at Tablada. The officers who flew the squadron aircraft had also taken a great deal of punishment. In the first squadron Lt Monico had been shot down and was subsequently executed; Lt Cenni ('Stella') was taken prisoner and 2nd Lts Ceccarelli and Patriarca were killed and taken prisoner respectively. In the second squadron Franceschi was killed in combat, Chianese was taken prisoner and Mantelli ('Arrighi') was shot down over his own lines during the Málaga offensive.

By contrast, the three Spanish officers of these squadrons, Capts García Morato, Salas and Lt Salvador, all remained uninjured during the time they were attached to the Italian squadron; and the same could be said for Lt García Pardo who had joined the squadron at the Madrid front on October 21st. The Italian non-commissioned officers who flew with the squadrons were also more fortunate than their commissioned officers, although of the three most distinguished, Magistrini ('Mainetti'), Presel ('Sammartano') and Montegnacco ('Romualdino'), the first two were killed in combat.

The Spanish Capts Morato and Salas did not consider that the Italian commander was sufficiently aggressive, and as they sought continually to have their own way the situation daily became more tense. The Italian leader had ordered that on a particular occasion they were not to penetrate into enemy territory: Salas, who was leading the patrol, defied the order. Fagnani attempted to have him arrested when he returned to base, but Morato intervened violently and protested that in Spain nobody was arrested for displaying courage. The outcome of ensuing discussions between Morato and Salas was a decision to try and form their own independent squadrons.

On December 20th, Lt Col Bonomi (known in Spain as Col Federici) reiterated his order that the Fiats should not enter into combat unless there were at least 15 aircraft available, and that they should form three patrols of five machines, each operating at different heights. This formation gave good results on the same day: when four Ratas attacked the mid-altitude patrol, three of them were destroyed by the combined machine-guns of the patrol providing high-altitude cover.

On December 21st Bonomi went to Tablada to attend the funeral ceremony for Mosca and Ceccarelli, and then stayed in Seville to await the arrival of Col Velardi (known as General Velani in Spain) who was coming to take over his command.

On December 22nd the Fiats destroyed a Potez and a Rata, and Morato chose that day to fly to Seville in a light aircraft. On the following day he began to operate from Córdoba, giving support to the advance on Porcuna and Lopera. Salvador began to operate from Córdoba on the 24th and Bermúdez de Castro joined them almost immediately. The Blue Patrol had been formed.

Salas and Garcia Pardo remained in the Italian squadrons during the Rozas operations, but on January 9th they also moved to the south. During one of his last missions at Rozas, on January 3rd, and despite the most determined efforts, Salas was unable to prevent the Ratas from shooting down a Savoia

S-M.81 which had become separated from the main formation. This was piloted by Tasso, who had been one of his companions when he fled from Getafe. A few minutes later he gained a little revenge for the loss of a friend when he destroyed one of the attackers.

On the same day a Romeo of Lt Paternina's patrol, flown by 2nd Lt Mariano Garcia Alonso and staff sergeant Antonio Grimaldi was also shot down.

The Condór Legion Fighter Group had its 2nd squadron (Lehmann) based at León, one in Vitoria, leaving the remaining two at the Madrid front (Escalona and Ávila). The He 51 squadrons tried various tactics in their attempt to succeed in the fighter role, but it was soon clear that this was an impossibility. They could survive only by sending a patrol of three of their number to attack the enemy bombers, massing the remainder of the He 51s to take on the escorting fighters. It was a costly and completely ineffectual tactic, and they were soon forced to restrict their use to that of bomber escorts.

Towards the end of the year three prototypes of the Messerschmitt Bf 109* fighter aircraft (more usually designated Me 109), were received by the Condór Legion. This aircraft, a low-wing mono-plane with an enclosed cockpit, proved far superior to the He 51, despite the fact that it then had an engine of only 610hp, driving a two-blade wooden propeller.

The Heinkel factory had also sent to Spain a prototype of their new fighter, the He 112, which was evaluated by the *Luftwaffe* in competition with the Bf 109. These two new prototype aircraft had been designed and built to replace the obsolete He 51s and Arado Ar 68s, but the He 112 was rejected by the *Luftwaffe* despite favourable test reports.

Combat evaluation of the Bf 109 prototypes proved satisfactory, but the first squadron of Bf 109B-2s, which were powered by a Junkers Jumo engine driving a two-blade metal variable-pitch propeller, did not join the Condór Legion until March 1937. The only squadron of He 112s to operate in Spain did not enter service until January 1939.

The Nationalist Air Force, which had lost the initiative in the area of Madrid, was far more effective on other fronts which were less well supported by the opposing fighters, as we shall see.

Meanwhile, in Madrid, the Popular Army had achieved a high degree of organisation in the month of December. On November 26th, as proposed by Vicente Rojo, Miaja had divided the Madrid front into four sectors, under the commands of Kleber, Álvarez Coque, Mena and Líster. Initially the mixed brigades 1 to 5, 11, 12, 'X' (the former CNT column led by Palacios), 'Y' (5th Ortega Regiment), 'A' (Arce), 'B' (Rovira), 'C' (Prada), 'D' (Bueno), Barcelo's column (later designated Mixed Brigade No 35), and shortly afterwards the 6th Brigade, were all moved to the front. The Brigades C, X, Y, D, B, and A were later numbered 36, 39, 40, 41, 42 and 43 respectively; the numbers 37 and 38 were given to the brigades formed from the columns led by Fernandez Cavada and Perea, which also moved into Madrid at about this time, and 44 was the number allocated to the brigade formed from Enciso's column.

With these brigades, together with No 14 (Walter) and No 21 (Gomez Pala-

*The Initials Bf were those of the factory where they were built: Bayerische Flugzeugwerke.

cios) which arrived at the beginning of January, divisions numbered 4 to 8 were formed, commanded by Modesto, Perea, Mena, Prada and Cuevas respectively. These divisions formed part of the II Army Corps, initially under the overall command of Miaja and later Alzugaray. Divisions Nos 1 to 3 were formed of brigades from the Sierra (Nos 26 to 34) and they became part of the I Army Corps under the command of Moriones, which covered the sector from Brunete to Somosierra.

In January, the remaining forces in Madrid became Mixed Brigades which were allocated the Nos 48, 29 and 67 to 70. In addition there was the 1st Brigade and the 1st *Móvil de choque* (Mobile shock troops), and these later became Nos 9 and 10 Brigades. The 3rd Brigade returned from Andalucia, which became the base for the new 10th Division (J. Galan, later Enciso), and Nos 1 and 9 Mixed Brigades became the 11th Division (Lister). The 9th Division (Arce), covered the Aranjuez sector and did not belong to the Madrid Army Corps.

At this same time the Nationalist forces (nominally under Varela's orders, although he was still in hospital), comprised four brigades each of six battalions, commanded by Iruretagoyena, Sáenz de Buruaga, Barrón and Asensio, and Gavilan's Cavalry. Monasterio was second-in-command of the Militia, with his headquarters in Ávila, García Escámez, Bartomeu, Rada, Siro Alonso and Tella remained at the Madrid front, which had become stablised. Towards the Sierra were Cebrián and Nevado (in the Fuentes sector), who liaised with Palenzuela who was now out of the jurisdiction of the Reinforced Madrid Division. This Reinforced Division was, in fact, a reinforced Army Corps. The Avila Divisions (Serrador) and Soria (Moscardó) were dependent upon Mola via Saliquet.

The Villareal Offensive

The Basque country achieved self-government on October 7th, when Guipúzcoa and the majority of Álava were occupied by the Nationalists, and they immediately organised their own Army. The Basque front was divided into the three sectors of Guipúzcoa, Álava and Burgos, commanded by Vidal, Aizpuru and Irezábal respectively. Their overall commander was Arambarri, who had Montaud as his chief of staff, and all were subordinate to the president, José Antonio Aguirre.

The Central Government made General Llano de la Encomienda commander of the Northern Army. He had been the leader of the Barcelona División Orgánica at the time of the Uprising.

In Biscay the first massive Government offensive was mounted in November 1936. With forces equivalent to two divisions formed into nineteen battalions, six batteries of artillery, two companies of armoured vehicles in Cueto and Ibarrola's columns, and with Irezábal's column in reserve. Aizpuru remained in Amurrio with six more battalions and two batteries of artillery, ready to advance towards Orduna if their assistance was needed. The Biscay air force, organised by Luis Cerro, was subordinated to the Northern Region Air Force, then under the leadership of Commander Manuel Cascón (former leader of the Getafe Fighter Group).

The Villareal offensive began on November 30th, in conjunction with an attack by the Santander forces on the Lora Valley. Their objectives were somewhat ambitious, but because Nationalist leaders had based the majority of their troops in the Madrid sector, Llano de la Encomienda thought that it would be easy to occupy Vitoria and Miranda, and to demolish the whole Northern front.

However, by good fortune, aircraft of the Nationalist Air Force discovered preparations for the offensive before it was launched. A Dragon Rapide, a Fokker XII and three Breguet 19s had taken off from Burgos with orders to carry out reconnaissance of the Elgueta-Mondragón sector. The cloud base was very low that day and this Nationalist patrol, following a precarious course between ground and cloud, failed to locate the area designated for their reconnaissance. Following a somewhat erratic course on their return journey, they passed close to the south of Arlabán, where they spotted large numbers of men and some forty vehicles moving along a road in a narrow valley.

Julián del Val, pilot of the Fokker XII, decided to attack and the Breguets followed suit. The leader of the formation, Cdr Ansaldo flying the Dragon Rapide, was afraid that it might be one of their own columns, but there was really little doubt as some of the lorries carried the initials UHP in large letters.

The attack was shattering and completely blocked the road, but the attackers did not escape unscathed, both the Fokker and Breguets receiving many hits from small arms fire. One shot passed right through Lieutenant Loaysa's glasses, without injuring him.

As they left the valley to continue their return flight the patrol saw a town being strongly attacked, and this was identified later as Villareal. As soon as they landed at Burgos they informed General Álvarez,* who could not believe the news, since all previous information had suggested that the attack would take place at Mondragon. This had derived primarily from the fact that by night a large number of lorries with headlights burning had been seen travelling in that direction: this ruse was employed in the south by Queipo several months later, also with great success. However, news of this offensive was received some days later.

On November 13th General Davila, the Generalissimo's chief of staff, despatched a message to the effect that the ships *Bayo* and *Virrelise* would shortly anchor at Bilbao with some 30,000 artillery shells, 20,000 Mauser guns and 6 million rounds of ammunition, all of which suggested an imminent attack.

Two days later news was received that eleven infantry and one motorised battalion had been centred on Bilbao, and the following day came further news that there were thirty-five aircraft at Bilbao. The aircraft were at Sondica, (now Bilbao airport), which was then being extended and Lamiaco (a short distance from las Arenas). Sondica airfield was equipped with three hangars and had two bomb dumps, one on each side of the River Gobelas. However, the airfield was flooded, and the job of extending it had to be postponed.

The nearby heights of Mount Pagasarri and Santo Domingo were equipped

* A few days later López Pinto became commander of the 6th Division Organica, when Alvarez succeeded Benito in command on November 17th, 1936.

with anti-aircraft batteries, besides those already in existence at Archanda on Mount Artagán, los Baldes (Olaveaga) and Casa Menchaca (South of Las Arenas), and an attempt was also being made to convert for anti-aircraft use the 40mm cannon that had been destined for installation on the cruisers *Canarias* and *Baleares*.

According to information received in the Nationalist Zone, 97,000 rifles (40,000 good quality Belgian; 22,000 very poor quality Japanese; 20,000 Czech, 6,000 of which were Skodas; and 15,000 Russian), 550 machine-guns (350 of Russian origin)—although other sources quote them as Colts—and 200 Mexican; 60 field guns, 30 rapid-firing guns, 14 armoured cars, 30 Russian tanks and 13 more small tanks had reached Biscay. On the whole this information was fairly accurate. Tanks and armoured vehicles, totalling 120 in all, had arrived on the Russian ship *A. Andreu*, on November 1st, together with 15 aircraft, 46 field guns, 300 machine-guns and 30,000 rifles. Earlier, a total of 35,000 rifles had arrived. On the 9th, 18th and 21st respectively, the British ships *Hillfern*, *York Brook* and the Norwegian vessel *Saca* sailed into Bilbao, bringing, amongst other supplies, 54 field guns and 200 mortars.

Thus, as one can appreciate, there was ample information to suggest an attack was imminent, but the tactical surprise was complete. Despite this, Colonel Alonso Vega, commander of the Sector, and later of the Navarre Brigade, managed to force the enemy to raise the siege of Villareal and regained the position. The Air Force attacks on Ochandiano had helped a great deal towards achieving this result, as had been the case on July 22nd during the first advance on Villareal, when a single Breguet flown by Salas had succeeded in disrupting a counter-attack by Government troops.

The Nationalist Air Force continued to achieve success, despite serious enemy opposition. Julián del Val's Fokker XII was shot down only days later while being flown by Montesinos; another machine of the same type, flown by I. Ansaldo, was riddled with shrapnel. Pablo Bazán was wounded on the 16th, and Juan Antonio Ansaldo's Dragon Rapide force-landed at Lasarte aerodrome with an engine out of action, extensive damage and Perales, the observer, wounded.

Government aircraft were based at Lamiaco aerodrome, these comprising two squadrons of Chatos. One squadron was flown by Russian pilots, one of which, according to local inhabitants, was a woman. The other squadron had Spanish pilots and included the famous Felipe del Río. There were also seven Bristol Bulldogs, with one or two English pilots. Bomber aircraft were based at Sondica, these including the Potez machines, Douglas DC-2s and three-engined Farmans.

In the north at this time there were some thirty Slav pilots, probably all Russians, who were to fly the aircraft that were being assembled at Santander, and they eventually began to fly the Russian aircraft from La Albericia, because Nestares and Orzales were flooded. Four Savoia S-M.62 seaplanes from Santander were crewed by Spaniards, led by Beneito.

Nationalist news despatches announced the forthcoming arrival of several Dewoitines to reinforce the Government Air Force. In fact, four had arrived in 1936 and three more were received in the first half of 1937; apart from these they received 7 Potez 54s, one Marcel Bloch M.B.210, 8 Bristol Bulldogs, 4 Fokkers, 3 Lockheeds and eight other machines of various types.

The most important battles in the air took place over Vitoria. In one of them (on the 8th) the Chatos attacked a Heinkel He 51 and the pilot had to take to his parachute. In another (on the 11th), a twin-engined Government aircraft flown by Sergeant Sidney Holland was shot down.

Nationalist aircraft struck at the naval construction factory in Reinosa on December 19th, and with some success, as for days afterwards the factory could only function at a third of its normal capacity. Santander was attacked on December 27th and Bilbao on January 4th.

Battles in the Air Over Aragón During Autumn 1936

During the month of October the Heinkel He 46 Squadron of Captain José Gancedo (3-E-11) and Captain Emilio Jiménez Ugarte (4-E-11) arrived in Saragossa to replace the old Breguet squadron led by Eduardo Prado. The latter remained in command of the aerodrome until replaced by Commander Ignacio Jiménez, who had been Francisco Inglesias companion during the historic flight in *Jesús del Gran Poder*. Of the three Nieuports which had been operating in Aragón in September, only Senra's remained. In the middle of the month a German patrol of Heinkel He 51s arrived.

In the Government sector 6 Dewoitines arrived in October, piloted by Darry, Valbert, Bernay, Thomas, Heilmann (until his death) and Kozek. On October 12th four Gourdou-Leseurre aircraft arrived from Toulouse and the first 3 Chatos from los Alcázares, the latter with Russian pilots. Soon afterwards the French pilots returned home.

On October 17th von Houwald's patrol (which included also Strümpell and Henrici), was escorting Gancedo's squadron and fought off twelve enemy aircraft, amongst them five Nieuports and a Fokker. Henrici destroyed three aircraft and his two companions one each.

On the same day Jiménez Ugarte's squadron arrived, and he was shot down at Almudévar on October 22nd. Eight days later his aircraft was hit by small arms fire from the ground, and on this occasion his observer, Montel, was wounded. During November and the first fortnight of December, activity in the air over this front was greatly reduced.

At the end of December Government forces from Guadalajara, Cuenca and Teruel (led by Colonels Lacalle, del Rosal and Velasco) began to attack at Bustares and along the line from Gea de Albarracín as far as Santa Bárbara and Celadas. The names of these places, together with those of Mansueto, Corbalán, Muela de Villastar, Puerto Escandón and Campillo, were then hardly known nationally. They were soon to become renowned. At Bustares the attack was supported by a company of tanks, and at Teruel by twenty armoured vehicles which had arrived directly from Archena, together with ten batteries of artillery. Their combined guns loosed off a barrage of some 2,400 shells in half an hour, representing a total weight of about 30 tons.

The Nationalists had no reserves available to meet this attack, and decided to send to Caudé aerodrome (near Concud) the two Spanish patrols of Heinkel He 51s. These arrived on December 25th, and during a landing on the following day Senra's aircraft was wrecked, this reducing the number of fighters available to five.

On December 27th the Heinkels took off to intercept a patrol of Potez 54s, which were escorted by six Russian fighters. During the battle, the Potez flown by Lt Gregorio Garay Martin (promoted to the rank of Captain in the Republican Gazette No 49, of February 18th, 1937) and Captain Alfredo Arija's Heinkel were both shot down. The remaining four Heinkels while on the ground at Caudé aerodrome, which was close to the front and without any anti-aircraft defence, were badly shot up by six Chatos, and finally so severely damaged in a bombing attack that they had to be dismantled and sent by rail to Seville.

The Generalissimo sent the following telegram to the leader of the Northern Army: "Will you please inform the leader of the 5th Division that it is essential to take precautions to avoid cases such as the one at Teruel, where the enemy was able to fire at our fighter aircraft on the ground, rendering them useless, simply because sufficient precautions were not taken. It should be remembered that since we have no aeroplane factories in our territory, we must make every effort to defend the material we possess, as it will not be easy to replace".

The Government bombers did not escape from these attacks unscathed. Apart from Martin's aircraft which had been shot down on December 27th, a second Potez, from Malraux's squadron, had to make a forced-landing at Valdelinares, near to Mora de Rubielos, with one of its crew dead and six wounded. A third Potez, with Malraux on board, was wrecked on take off from La Señra aerodrome. Days later Malraux handed over command of the squadron to Abel Guídes.

The loss of the three Potez bombers was glossed over by the Aviation bulletin and by Julien Segnaire's report (political commissary for the Malraux squadron). The Aviation bulletin stated that in Teruel at the time there were, apart from the Potez bombers, a Breguet group in squadrons of six aircraft, a Nieuport group in pairs for reconnaissance, and six fast fighters. These had fought against four Fiats (in fact they were the He 51s as we have seen) and had destroyed two (in fact, only one). A little later the fighters had taken off again to escort the Potez and Breguet machines, during which sortie they had attacked with machine-guns the four fighters on the ground at Caudé aerodrome, and which were subsequently destroyed in an attack by bomber aircraft. This bulletin was, in the main, fairly accurate as we have seen.

Gea de Albarracin was recaptured by the Nationalists on December 30th and fighting continued until the middle of January, when the 22nd Brigade severed the road from Teruel to Puerto Escandón.

Action in the South

At the same time as the battles were being fought at Teruel, the Nationalist Army in the south improved its position on the Córdoba front, occupying Montoro, Villa del Río, Lopera and Porcuna. From this latter point they were able to establish heliographic contact with Santuario de la Cabeza. At the beginning this advance was easy, but from December 20th the struggle became fierce at Cañete de las Torres. Between December 20th and 24th the left wing was consolidated, and was able to advance as far as Montoro and Villa del Río. When an attempt was made to continue to advance in the centre of the front, bitter resistence was encountered at Lopera and Porcuna, areas which fell eventually on December 27th and January 1st respectively.

On December 20th, the overall commander of the Southern Army, Martínez Monje, had advised the central chief of staff that this was a major offensive and that his objective was to reach Jaén or to free Santuario. Initially, Cdr García Vallejo's eight hundred men undertook the task of defence; later, Cdr López Gómez defended Montoro and he was joined by the 3rd (José Galán) and 14th (Walter) International Brigades, and the 16th (Martínez Cartón) and 20th (Lopez Mejias) Mixed Brigades.

Nationalist support in the air was provided by the Breguet groups from Seville and Granada (Squadrons 3-G-10 and 4-G-10), led by Cdrs Rueda and Navarro. On December 23rd Morato arrived in Córdoba and immediately the Blue Patrol went into action. On January 3rd they were successful in destroying two Katiuskas which were approaching to attack the town of Andújar. Soon afterwards Capt García Pardo joined this patrol at Córdoba.

At Cañete de las Torres on December 20th one of the Breguet pilots, Antonio Romero Noriega, was wounded. On the following day another pilot, Francisco Pelayo, was wounded, as were Comas and Núñez on December 31st. On January 1st Arístide García López's Breguet was shot down at Porcuna, although the pilot escaped successfully through the enemy lines.

Salas, who also left the Italian Fiat group in the middle of January, arrived in the south with the intention of forming a fighter squadron from a number of P.W.S.10 single-seat fighters bought in Poland. These aircraft proved to be unsuitable for operations, and were used later in a trainer role.

At this time some of the Italian Fiats also moved to the south (there were then 4 squadrons: Nobili, Lodi, Viola and Francois) to participate in the Málaga offensive, the first operation in which Italian land troops had taken part.

This intensification of assistance for Spain had been agreed in Rome on December 6th, at a time when, in Britain, Edward VIII was preparing to abdicate and Baldwin was being replaced by Chamberlain.

This period was marked by great diplomatic activity after it had been agreed in Madrid that no quick military victory could be expected. Lord Plymouth presented a plan to prevent further volunteers from going to Spain once the Government side had achieved numerical superiority. Delbos proposed a 'gentlemen's agreement' with Eden, to stop arms traffic to Spain; and France and England proposed officially to Russia, Germany, Italy and Portugal a policy of joint mediation.

The Italian decision to increase their help was taken when their Government knew, via the Canaries, that Germany had rejected Von Faupel's alternative proposals: to pull out of Spain or to send an entire division.

Although on December 16th the Government in Valencia agreed in principal to accept the plan for mediation, and the Nationalists in Salamanca did not reject the idea, by the time that additional questions were asked on the 19th the general situation had become worse. This was as a result of the seizing of the German ship *Palos*, the sinking of the Russian ship *Komsomol* by the *Canarias* on December 15th, and the continuous arrival of Italian supplies and troops at Cadiz, Russian supplies at Cartagena and international volunteers at Albacete. To further complicate matters, the American policy of 'moral embargo' began on December 28th, although on January 8th the Act of Neutrality was enforced. On the same day the French began to concentrate troops on the frontier of the Spanish Protectorate in Morocco, alleging that Germany had military forces in Morocco. This referred to the squadron of He 59 seaplanes based at Melilla, a town which was not included in the area of the protectorate.

By this time, England and Italy had signed their 'gentlemen's agreement': Hitler had given assurances to France that Germany had no ambition to possess Spanish territory and that he would not accept the Italian suggestion to send more troops to Spain.

On January 20th, Hitler and Mussolini met in Rome and agreed that since there was now a similar number of volunteers (approximately 20,000) on each side, they could accept the French and English plan. They also agreed that, under no circumstances, should the Spanish Civil War be allowed to develop into a world war. In this decision Mussolini was probably sincere. Hitler, however, had discovered that under combat conditions his war machinery was not as invincible as he had imagined. He needed to gain time until the new weapons being prepared were ready to enter into service (Panzer II, III and IV tanks, more advanced Me 109 fighters, Heinkel He 111 and Junkers Ju 87 bombers etc).

On January 14th, the day when Estepona was occupied by the Bourbon Colonel's troops, Martínez Monje received an urgent order to leave his post as leader of the Southern Army and to go at once to Málaga to organise resistance there, despite the fact that his second-in-command, Colonel Salafranco, was in Valencia.

A squadron of six Katiuskas (probably the Air Detachment operating in conjunction with the Proskúrov Fleet) attacked the Nationalist Fleet which was supporting the advance between Estepona and San Pedro de Alcántara, and a Potez bomber and two fighters were sent to Almeria aerodrome to support Jover's Nieuport-Delage 52s which were operating from Tabernas.

According to the Government communiqué, one of the Katiuskas dropped two 100kg bombs on the *Almirante Cervera*, forcing the cruiser to retire to Ceuta. In fact, two Katiuskas dived to about 4,000ft (1,200m) above the *Canarias*, but because of the vicious anti-aircraft fire coming from the cruiser's 120mm and 44mm guns, they climbed to about 7,200ft (2,220m) before releasing their bombs. The first two fell some 1,300ft (400m) from the *Canarias*, the third was nearer and the last two about 650ft (200m) to port.

The Nationalist forces reached Marbella on January 17th, and this meant a pause in the advance along the coast. At this period the Spanish Nationalist Air Force operated from Los Barrios aerodrome, near to Algeciras. Marbella was bombed on January 19th by a Government squadron recently sent to the Málaga front, and they also attacked Ceuta the next day.

On January 22nd the Nationalists advance continued in Málaga, this time along the Alhama de Granda sector. On the same day the Katiuskas were sent to bomb the port of Cadiz, where the cruiser *Canarias* was at anchor. On the following day the Málaga fighters claimed to have scattered two squadrons of Nationalist Cavalry. The Russian pilot Nikolai Ostriakov, who died at Sebastopol years later when in command of air units belonging to the Black Sea Fleet, took part in these missions.

These operations were interrupted by very heavy rain storms which lasted from January 24th to 31st. Despite the weather, the Italian Fiats attempted to operate on the 29th, but met with ill-fortune. One of them crashed beside the Jandula reservoir (near to Santuario de la Cabeza), and its pilot was killed; another at Jaen, about 200 miles (324km) from Madrid; and two others in Extremadura, 9 miles (15km) from Castuera. The Italian pilots Cenni, Pelo and Resce were all taken prisoner.

A Government bulletin from Malaga, dated January 31st, said that: "Yesterday a seaplane forced the ship *Delfín* to run aground at Nerja" and went on to complain that despite the weather the Nationalist Air Force was continuing its operations, even though they had lost four aircraft on January 29th.

On February 1st there was a clash between two Italian bombers and two Russian Chatos, resulting in the destruction of a Chato, its Russian pilot, Cdr Casimiro, being killed. On February 2nd, in response to a request for the support of two bombers and six fighters, Martínez Cabrera told Villalba (who had replaced Martínez Monje as commander of the Southern Army) that he could only count on one fighter and five bombers from San Javier. He also promised to send the 25th Mixed Brigade to Jaen, so that the 16th Brigade could move to Málaga.

On the 4th a general assault on Malaga began, and by the 6th Loja's columns had reached Colmenar. Those advancing from the coast gained Fuengirola, and those from Alhama came within 7½ miles (12km) of Vélez-Málaga. On February 11th Puerto de León and Torremolinos were occupied, and in the early morning of the 8th Málaga also fell.

On the eve of the attack there was a great deal of activity in the air. Five Chatos had attacked three Nationalist bombers, and according to the Government bulletin they destroyed two and a third was compelled to make a forced-landing. In this engagment two Chatos were damaged. Bombers were also operating from Bobadilla, Marbella, Cádiz and Granada aerodrome, and for several days they attacked the Nationalist warships off Salobreña, Málaga, Torre del Mar and Fuengirola. On the 4th, five Chatos scattered three Nationalist seaplanes.

On February 5th, two damaged Fokkers landed at Tabernas aerodrome (Almería); one, flown by Lt Ezquerdo had its controls jammed; in the other the pilot, Capt Vila, was seriously injured.

On the night of February 6th/7th, six destroyers left Cartagena under orders to attack the Nationalist Naval Squadron that was blocking the entrance to Malaga, and to release the coastguard cutter *Xauen.* Having reached the Cape of Gata, these destroyers turned back without completing their mission, which resulted in a swift trial of two officers, two sub-officers and seven sailors from the *Almirante Valdés* which was leading the expedition. On the 7th, the Nationalist Squadron was dive-bombed by three aircraft which, taking advantage of the sun, dropped bombs which fell about 650ft (200m) ahead of them.

On the 11th two Potez bombers and five fighters left Almería, but they were intercepted by eight or ten Fiats over Motril. As a result of the attack one of the Potez machines fell into the sea off Cape Sacratif, (a fact confirmed by Malraux and Delpierre de Bayac) and the other made a crash landing at Llanos de Dalias. The leader of the fighter squadron claimed that one Fiat was set on fire and another was last seen in a steep dive. The Fiat shot down would be Mantelli's, which landed without further damage behind his own lines. Early in the morning of the same day Granada aerodrome was attacked.

Between February 10th and 12th the Blue Patrol was based at Málaga aerodrome, and they went to search for the second Fiat. This they found, eventually, upside down on the beach at Motril.

As we will see later, the Italian Fiats moved to Madrid in the middle of February and the Blue Patrol on the 16th. On the 19th the twelve Russian fighters stationed at Tabernas also moved from their base.

To counteract the bad effect caused by the action of the Government destroyers in the Málaga campaign, the Minister for Sea and Air went aboard the *Libertad* on March 2nd, and left with the rest of the Fleet for trials of a new Russian gun which, according to Colonel Salafranca, was not very successful. Two days later, six destroyers shelled Ceuta, taking advantage of the fact that the *Canarias* had sailed from the area, and the cruisers *Baleares* and *Almirante Cervera* were carrying out a raid in the Mediterranean.

The *Canarias* had been in Matagorda from February 13th (the day when it collided with a Greek vessel) until February 26th, when it sailed for Ferrol where it remained until March 4th. On that day the *Canarias* put to sea to await the *Mar Cantabrico* which was captured on March 8th. On February 26th the *Almirante Cervera* captured the vessel *Marqués de Comillas*. On the 1st it joined up with the *Baleares* off Barcelona, and from there they returned to the Straits.

The Struggle for Dominion of the Air—El Jarama

On February 6th, 1937, the Nationalist offensive on Jarama began. After the failure of the frontal attack on Madrid in November, the left wing had made two further attempts; firstly to the north-east of Casa de Campo, secondly towards the La Coruña road, but these moves had only succeeded in speeding up the Nationalist advances on Casa de Campo and the University Campus. The route proposed by Yagüe was also closed, and this encouraged Mola to try out his original idea of advancing towards the Valencia road.

Throughout the winter new troops had been arriving at such a speed that the thirty battalions of mid-November became fifty at the beginning of December and seventy-five at the beginning of February. The best of these were formed into five brigades, each of six battalions, commanded by Rada, Buruaga, Barrón, Asensio and García Escámez. All took part in the ensuing battle, as well as eleven battalions which arrived as reinforcements making a total of forty-one battalions, the largest number that had been used for any offensive. Cebollino's Cavalry also took part. García Escámez came down from

Pozuelo, leaving Iruretagoyena in his place, and took up a position at Ciempozuelos, on the right flank, opposite the Aranjuez Division. Rada, who had been in charge of the sector up until this point, remained on the left flank.

On the Government side there were even larger numbers involved, since the A, B and C Divisions (later given the Nos 13, 15 and 16), some of the 11th Division and one which was later designated No 14, were all operating together, making a total of more than fifty battalions, together with the Agrupación Modesto (formed basically from the 4th Division, plus reinforcements) and the 9th Division on the flanks. At the beginning of February the Government forces were also preparing another offensive, this to be in the Jarama sector, and for this they had called in Mena's and Chorda's groups. There were also the forces standing on the line, commanded by Col Espá.

Vicente Rojo, Miaja's chief of staff, tried to reverse the manoeuvre, by attacking Valdemorillo and supporting the offensive with a feigned attack in the Jarama sector, (a manoeuvre similar to the one carried out months later in the battle at Brunete). However, Pozas' idea of attacking Jarama and supporting the attack from the north prevailed although, in fact, neither of these operations were ever carried out. For the offensive fifteen brigades, twenty-four batteries and sixty armoured vehicles had been sent to the main sector and a force equivalent to half of this was in the secondary sector.

The Nationalists forged ahead and began the first phase of their advance on February 6th. This took place in four directions simultaneously: Pinto to Marañosa (Rada), Pinto to Gózquez de Abajo (Buruaga), Valdemoro to San Martín de la Vega (Asensio) and Valdemoro to Ciempozuelos (García Escámez). Initially the advances were very successful, despite strong resistance at Ciempozuelos. They crushed the front at Marañosa, and within two days had occupied the patch of high ground overlooking the right bank of the Jarama. One more day was needed to occupy the mountains at Vaciamadrid. On the 11th they forced their way to Puente Pindoque, where they surprised and routed a Franco–Belgian battalion of the 12th International Brigade, and this marked the beginning of the second phase of the battle.

On February 11th the leader of the Central Army went to Arganda in person to prepare the counter-attack. Andrés García La Calle's first Spanish squadron of Chatos, which had made its debut the day before, lost its leading pilot, José Calderón, whose Chato was hit by anti-aircraft fire. This squadron began by operating from Guadalajara aerodrome, but soon moved to 'Airfield X' (Azuqueca), which was bombed as soon as they arrived there on February 11th.

The next day the 11th International Brigade and the 17th Brigade fought hard to defend Cerro Pajares; the 12th International Brigade had an equally hard battle at Puente Arganda. Further to the south, Asensio crossed the river via San Martín de la Vega and occupied Pingarrón; Buruaya, who had crossed via Puente Pindoque behind Barrón, was situated between them both, although he did not manage to join up with Asensio.

On the flanks the 9th Division counter-attacked at Cuesta de la Reina and the 19th Brigade on the hills at Coberteras and Vaciamadrid, in accordance with orders issued by the central chief of staff at 24.00hrs on February 8th, to "recover this very night the hills in Coberteras, fortifying and defending them at all costs", and adding: "the leader involved should proceed with courage and energy . . . to set a good example so that others can imitate his actions".

In their bulletin for that day, the Central Army boasted that they had contained the enemy between Cerro Pajares and Pingarron, and claimed to have shot down five enemy aircraft as they attempted to bomb Titulcia and Seseña station. This number was later given as seven fighters. In fact, five of the twelve He 51s escorting the Ju 52s and Spanish Romeo Ro 37s, fought against seven Ratas. In this combat one Rata and two He 51s were destroyed.

The communiqué sent by the Albacete Air Forces to the central chief of staff said that during a mission carried out by twelve fighters, between 11.10hrs and 12.00hrs, they had fought against three three-engined machines and fifteen fighters, shooting down seven Heinkels without loss. It continued to mention various other missions, amongst them a reconnaissance flight by the Tabernas (Almería) fighters, and a list of objectives for the Katiuskas in that sector since, according to Commander Núñez Maza, the front was now stable. It also recorded an air raid on Albacete.

On February 13th there was a new battle in the air over Arganda, involving fourteen Fiats and twenty-four Ratas, during which the Caza Legionaria lost Capt Luigi Lodi ('Marcelli'), their third squadron leader to be killed and the fifth to be shot down.

On February 13th only Barrón managed to advance, towards Arganda, but he received orders to halt because Buruaga and Asensio's columns were lagging behind.

The next day all the available Fiats (fifteen), led by Capt Nobili ('Notabili') and Lt Degli Incerti ('Tocci') were in operation, and the latter pilot achieved his first victory. The Nationalist bulletins said nothing of these battles, but the Valencia bulletins reported two aircraft destroyed on the 12th, four on the 13th and two Heinkels on the 14th.

The breach opened on the 14th between the 11th and 15th Mixed Brigades was closed by a counter-attack of Pavlov's Tank Brigade, together with support from the 24th Brigade.

Commander Fagnani ('Faroni') insisted on the maintenance of earlier orders not to penetrate into enemy territory, and of only patrolling over their own lines.

On February 15th the Junkers were only able to carry out their bombing attacks by night, since there were no fighters to escort them. On the same day, Carrillo was named as the new leader of the 2nd Group; Groups 1 and 3 were still led by Pardo and Gil Mendizábal.

The central chief of staff, General Martinez Cabrera sent the following message to his commanders: "I am more optimistic, every day our morale is being boosted". Miaja, who took charge of the sector which had been attacked, disbanded Mena and Chorda's groups, and created the Jarama group under the command of Burillo. At this time the Government batteries were arranged in groups for the first time. Varela issued orders to continue the advance on the Arganda-Morato line, to achieve the objectives of the second phase, although any possibility of concluding the third and final phase now seemed slight.

During the night, the acting leader of the Carrillo group, Captain José Calderón Gaztelu, pronounced his famous words "Whoever falls, tomorrow my group will drop bombs"; words which ended with his death at the hands of the Russian fighters. In all, eleven Ju 52s went out on this mission, with Eduardo Prado, Larrauri and Alonso Pimentel from the 3rd Group at the head of the formation. Behind them were Rute, Aviles, Conejos and Ureña from the 1st Group, and at the rear José Calderón, Pablo Atienza, Presa and Pablo Benjumea. The leader of the 1st Group, Luis Pardo, went as co-pilot in one of the leaders' aircraft (this time Rute), as was his custom when his group was not leading the formation.

Calderón's co-pilot, Francisco Taillefer, and the machine-gunner, Corporal Felipe Gómez Rojas, died with him. The remainder of the crew took to their parachutes and were exchanged for Government prisoners some months later.

By a strange coincidence, the first pilot shot down from the Government squadron led by La Calle was also called José Calderón; they died within five days of one another.

Tinker makes reference to the fact that the Ju 52 which was set on fire was attacked by the squadron led by La Calle, and that the Russian Ratas also shot down two He 51s. He also quotes damage caused to another Ju 52, which force-landed in the centre of Jarama, but I have not been able to find any other reference to this.

On that day, February 16th, the honour of the Nationalist Air Force had been saved. But this was not enough, they needed to beat the enemy fighters if the advance on Madrid was to continue. Despite all setbacks this was still Mola's idea. After visiting Orgaz, Mola had succeeded in obtaining from Franco the last six reserve battalions.

On February 16th Morato's patrol was urgently called to the area. They abandoned their protection of the supply routes to Santuario de la Virgen de la Cabeza and flew directly to Veladas. All the Spanish squadron leaders met and decided to repeat the bombing attacks. Morato guaranteed that the fighters would not let them down, and on the 17th he flew to Salamanca in a Dragon Rapide to obtain express permission from Air Headquarters for this operation. Meanwhile, twenty Fiats escorted two Romeos on a mission, but they did not encounter any Government fighters.

Early in the morning of February 18th the operation was mounted. Two Spanish Romeo Ro 37s took off first, followed by three Ju 52s escorted by the Blue Patrol and the Italian Fiat Group, which now had twenty-four aircraft. When they arrived over the lines the Fiats turned so that they were patrolling parallel to the front, while the Chatos waited on the other side. The Romeos and Junkers crossed into enemy territory and were attacked immediately. Morato at once broke from the formation and, followed by Salvador and Bermúdez de Castro, launched himself into the battle. The Italians hesitated until the brave veteran, Captain Nobili, who was leading a squadron, also broke from formation and went to help his companions. Finally, all the group took part in the battle, and were so successful that they destroyed eight fighters for the loss of only one of their numbers. This battle was fought against La Calle's Chato squadron (the first to be formed with Spanish pilots, although one of the patrols was American) and Captain José's Russian squadron, which were joined during the battle by a Rata squadron. Tinker admits that Ben Leider, Jim Allison and Harold Dahl from La Calle's squadron, and two more aircraft from other squadrons, were all shot down. Ben Leider, who had been the first American pilot in the squadron to gain a victory in the air, was killed as he attempted to land.

In the afternoon, in a fresh battle, two Ratas were shot down. For his action on this day, Captain Garcia Morato was awarded the *Laureada*, (the Laureate Cross of San Fernando, Spain's highest military award).

On February 20th, nineteen Fiats fought against twenty-eight Government fighters. In this battle Bercial, deputy leader of the patrol, was killed when his aircraft was destroyed by Nobili. He was the fifth pilot from La Calle's squadron to be shot down. Garcia Pardo, whose turn it was to fly with the Blue Patrol on that day (the patrol had four pilots, but only three aeroplanes), was forced to break away from the mission and return to base, due to engine trouble.

At this time, Franco wrote to the Italian representative in Spain, pointing out that: ". . . so long as the enemy have fighter strength we cannot carry out our vital bombing missions . . . we lack aeroplanes, since the twenty promised to us (Fiat fighters) have not been handed over . . ." Similarly, Kindelán was asking for more fighters, but had set his sights somewhat higher, requesting forty, or if possible, eighty new aircraft.

Soon after these events, Fagnani returned to Italy. His successors, especially Zotti, Casero, Tessari and Remondino were, by their spirited leadership and example, able to eradicate the timorous image that the Italian Squadron had gained under Fagnani's command.

On February 18th fierce battles at Pingarrón began with a counter-attack by the 11th Division (Líster), whilst Modesto pressed on towards La Marañosa. Divisions 'A' (Walter), 'B' (Gal) and 'C' (Lister, later Güemes) were at battle readiness, and on the 20th they joined the 3rd Army Corps (Burillo) and the 2nd Army Corps (Miaja). On the 21st the general counter-attack by these divisions began, assisted by Modesto's Group and the 9th Division. The 46th and 63rd Brigades created a diversion to the south of the Tajo, in the 1st Army's zone (Pozas). By the 28th the battle was considered to be over, although Miaja had not succeeded in recapturing the banks of the Jarama.

At about this date the Cóndor Legion realised they could no longer avoid the obvious fact that the Heinkel He 51 was completely outclassed by the Government fighters. It was essential that they should be replaced by the Messerschmitt Me 109. Therefore, the Second Fighter Squadron was equipped with Me 109B-2s in March, and Lützow assumed command. The Fourth Squadron was disbanded, and with the equipment from these units and the Heinkel He 51s which had been rebuilt, three Spanish squadrons were formed, each with seven aircraft. They were led by Manrique Montero, Salas and Martín Campos, and began to operate during late February in Aragón, Asturias and Pozoblanco. The squadron numbers 1-E-2, 2-E-2 and 3-E-2, were allocated to them, the terminal numeral 2 indicating the type of aircraft (He 51).

All the forces involved, whether they fought in the air or on the land, remember the Battle of Jarama as one of the hardest of the war. It was the first time the Popular Army had managed to hold their ground on the battlefield and mount a counter-offensive. The casualties on each side were in the order of 10,000.

The majority of the fighter pilots taking part were of foreign nationality, although there was one Spanish unit on each side: García Morato's patrol and La Calle's squadron.

Bomber aircraft played no significant role in this battle, the Junkers Ju 52s and Romeo Ro 37s being used mainly as bait for the Nationalist fighters trap. On the Government side, the Katiuskas saw little employment, but this was because they had lost half the crews which had arrived in October. This situation became so bad that the 3rd squadron had to be disbanded, their aircraft being shared between the other two squadrons. Similarly, the pilots were apportioned: Proskúrov replaced Schacht in command of the 1st squadron, taking with him Nesmeyánov, Ostriákov, Skovoródnikov and Oproscheno. Bíbikov, Levenberg, Zótov and the Spaniards Pereira and Mendiola joined the 2nd squadron. When the battle began these squadrons were based on San Clemente and Sisante.

Lack of activity by bomber aircraft was compensated by the artillery which, although it had not reached the proportions of one battery per column as demanded by Mola, was skilfully deployed with up to twelve batteries concentrated on a single target area. There was also considerable assistance from the tanks.

The Fighter Forces in the Secondary Centres of Operations

While the battle was raging in Jarama, the Government's Northern Army began a fierce offensive on Oviedo, and were successful in cutting off the only access road to the city. However, they did not manage to take Oviedo, due to stubborn resistance by the gunners of artillery batteries at Escamplero who, because they had exhausted their supplies of shells, fought as infantrymen. The attack, which was carried out by four small Asturian divisions assisted by some Basque expeditionary battalions, began on February 21st, although the action at Escamplero began on the 16th.

There was no Nationalist fighter force in this sector, and the only aircraft consisted of the Heinkel He 46 squadrons led by Emilio Jiménez Ugarte and Vara del Rey (later Sebastián Rubio Sacristán), which were consolidated into one group under Carrillo's command. When the latter returned to the Ju 52s, Vara del Rey assumed command. The Breguets in León were still commanded by Eyaralar, with Francisco Iglesias and Manuel Bazán as squadron leaders.

On March 5th, the day before the beginning of the Nationalist offensive on Pozoblanco, the 2nd squadron of He 51s, led by Salas, was transferred to León since it was felt that they would be of more value there. In fact, when they reached León there was little need for them and at the end of the month they moved to Navia aerodrome, the home base of the He 46s, and remained there until April 10th.

The 1st Squadron of He 51s, led by Montero, arrived in Saragossa on February 16th. Two days later a Nationalist counter-attack began on the

Teruel front, in the same area as the December battles. On February 18th Sariñena aerodrome was attacked and, according to a Nationalist bulletin, four aircraft were destroyed.

The fighter squadron had a black day as the offensive began. Whilst escorting Capt Gancedo's He 46s on a mission, Francisco Bofill and Krug collided, the first pilot being killed and the second seriously injured. The third pilot of the patrol, Ernesto, had just arrived at this front and lost his way, but landed on the outskirts of Saragossa without damaging his aircraft.

During these days the Cóndór Legion's strategic reconnaissance squadron was busy attacking the trenches and hydro-electric power stations in the Catalan region.

On February 19th the Catalans asked the Centre for the fighter support which had been promised earlier. At that time it was impossible to spare any fighter aircraft from Jarama, and those in the north were involved in the struggle for Oviedo. Consequently, nine aircraft were transferred from Almería, but six of these were subsequently withdrawn to Guadalajara on March 6th.

Alonso Santamaría's squadron of Chatos was then based in Aragón, and Juan Comas Borras joined it at about this time. He eventually took over command of all Group 26 Chatos.

As a reprisal for the attack upon the hydro-electric power stations, two Potez machines attempted to bomb Saragossa on February 21st, but only one was able to press home its attack, as the other developed a mechanical fault and had to jettison its bombs into the sea.

In the south, General Queipo del Llano began the Nationalist offensive against Pozoblanco on March 6th, with the intention of occupying the Pedroches Valley and reaching Santuario de la Cabeza via Venta de Cardeña.

This attack came as no surprise to the Government, for on February 26th the central chief of staff had advised 'General Douglas' (whose real name was Smushkévich): "The enemy forces are being built up in Peñarroya, Belmez and Espiel. I repeat my order that the Air Force should despatch some aircraft to Andújar or Santa Cruz de Mudela aerodrome, whichever the leader of the Southern Army prefers . . . This mission is urgent and takes priority. Let me know as soon as it has been carried out". It is strange that Martínez Cabrera should have passed this order to Douglas and not to the chief of the Air Forces (Hidalgo de Cisneros) or his chief of operations (Luis Romero Bassart). This order was carried out, and on the same day as the offensive began Martinez Cabrera ordered seven of the thirteen fighters in the south to move to Guadalajara.

The attack was supported by the Spanish Ju 52 squadrons commanded by Capts Prado and Larrauri, the Seville Breguet group commanded by Rueda and by Díaz de Rivera's squadron from the Granada Breguet group. On March 11th a Breguet flown by Felipe de Francisco and Adolfo Miralles was lost.

A little later the Ju 52 squadron formed by Captain Haya (with surplus aircraft from the group led by José Calderón at Jarama) carried out a number of night attacks. The other group of Ju 52s, led by Luis Pardo, operated in Aragon and Biscay until being disbanded in May. Carrillo, Ricardo,

Guerrero, Ureña and Presa were sent to Germany to attend a pilot's course specialising in Instrument Flying.

Initially, Queipo's plan was remarkably successful, his forces managing to occupy Villanueva del Duque and Alcaracejas, to reach the outskirts of Pozoblanco and to advance as far as Villanueva de Córdoba. But then they were face to face with the most select brigades in the south, the 20th, 25th and 86th, as well as the 13th International Brigade. The leaders of the Pozoblanco sub-sector and the Córdoba sector, Francisco Blanco Pedraza and Joaquín Pérez Salas respectively, were among the most competent of the war.

On March 13th a general counter-attack was launched, in which the 63rd Brigade from the Ruiz Farrona sub-sector and the 46th and 62nd Brigade from the Tajo-Extremadura group took part. Queipo, who realised it would be impossible to mount an unyielding defence on the open plain, ordered a retreat by night to the port of Calatraveño. He managed to deceive his opponents by the strategy of sending lorries to the front with their headlamps blazing, but with their lights off as they carried equipment and supplies to the rear. The first Russian tanks to be seen in the south were used in this counter-offensive.

The 3rd squadron of He 51s was being formed in Seville at this time, under the leadership of Capt César Martín Campos. In view of General Queipo de Llano's complaints about the performance of Fagnani's Fiats and the 2nd He 51 squadron at Asturias, this squadron was sent to Córdoba, although it did not begin to operate until the 26th, during Pérez Salas' counter offensive.

Until that day the only fighters in the sector were those belonging to the Blue Patrol, which became the 1st Fiat Squadron at the end of the month, designated 1-E-3, the terminal number 3 indicating Fiat. This squadron of six aircraft was formed with the four pilots from the Blue Patrol (Garcia Morato, Salvador, Bermudez de Castro and García Pardo), who were joined by Miguel Guerrero from Squadron 3-E-2 and Manuel Vázquez Sagastizábal from Squadron 2-E-2.

From March 24th the few Fiats in the sector devoted their activities to individual sorties. Bermúdez de Castro surprised a formation of bombers at Peñarroya, with a fighter escort only 500ft (1,500m) above, but managed to sneak in and destroy one aircraft, a victory that was confirmed by forces on the ground.

On the 30th of the month an attack was mounted against Andújar aerodrome. This was carried out by three Junkers, four Fiats and five Heinkels, which took off at dawn in conditions of low cloud and with fog patches covering the ground. García Pardo, who was delayed on take off by a fault in the engine starting system, arrived over Andújar to find fires burning, and added his quota of machine-gun fire. Ten aircraft were claimed as destroyed on the ground by this attack.

The Battle of Guadalajara

As soon as the battle at Jarama was over, preparations for an attack on Guadalajara began. It is incomprehensible that these offensives were not simultaneous, as had been planned initially. In fact, the Italians arrived at Guadalajara much later than had been anticipated because the storms at the end of January had delayed the final assault on Málaga by two weeks. But considering the stubborn resistance encountered in Madrid during the last few months, it seemed a rash decision to attack Jarama alone, especially with inferior air support. In any event, it revealed a total lack of information about Government plans, who had strong forces in this sector preparing their own attack.

It was even more surprising that, after the failure at Jarama, they should continue with the idea of launching the offensive on Guadalajara; a fact which can be explained only by the unjustified optimism of the Italian leaders after the Málaga campaign. Málaga was, in fact, the only Government front where the troops were not then well organised, and their standard of discipline was low. Besides this, the Nationalist land forces had both strategic and numerical superiority at Málaga, and their air support was at least comparable to the enemy's.

General Mola took little part in the offensive at Guadalajara; this was because the Italians had asked to be independent of Mola's forces, although he did provide the 2nd Brigade from the Soria Division to protect the Italian right flank, in the zone between the rivers Badiel and Henares.

Once again, the Government were prepared for the attack. On March 16th the central chief of staff sent the following order to the chief of Air Forces in Albacete: "Send to Madrid urgently six of the nine fighters in Catalonia, plus seven from the south. Violent attack imminent".

The Italians attacked with eleven groups of banderas, in three small divisions, plus the *XXIII of March* Group and the *Littorio* Division, making a total of forty battalions. The *Plumas Negras* (Black Feathers, commanded by Coppi) and the *Llamas Negras* (Black Flames, commanded by Nuvoloni) led the attack, leaving the *Dio lo Vuole* (Rossi), *Littorio* (Bergonzoli), and the *XXIII of March* (Francisci) in reserve. Rodimtsev estimated that they would have at their disposal 1,300 lorries and cars and 150 motorcycles, but, in fact, they had four companies of light tanks and some 160 field guns.

The opening move was carried out by the *Llamas Negras* Division, which then veered towards Brihuega, leaving the way clear for the *Plumas Negras*, which was a motorised Division. During the first days of the offensive the 12th Division (Lacalle) was routed from this sector, and the Italians advanced rapidly on both sides of the Aragón road, in an area which lay between the rivers Badiel and Tajuna. The Spanish Marzo Brigade, which was not motorised, could not maintain the pace of the Italian advance and slowly slipped behind.

Government bombers were unable to operate until March 10th because of low cloud, but this did not keep the fighters on the ground. According to despatches from Los Llanos aerodrome (Albacete), dated March 10th and signed by 'General Douglas', sixteen fighters took off for patrol and were joined by eighteen others based in Valencia. On that day a number of Government bomber (and one fighter) airfields were unable to mount any supporting operations because of bad weather and floods. A Nationalist bulletin on March 10th announced the destruction of a single fighter on the previous day.

On March 10th the Italian 2nd Division occupied Brihuega, the Spaniards Jadraque, and this fulfilled the objectives of the second phase of the offensive.

On March 11th the Spaniards occupied Cogolludo and the 3rd Division Trijueque, but neither they, nor the 2nd could enter Torija, the final objective of the 3rd phase (the 4th phase being to reach Guadalajara).

In Madrid, at 21.15hrs, Lt Col Casado despatched a message to central headquarters advising the formation of the IV Army Corps, comprising the 11th Division (Lister), 14th Division (Mera), Lacalle's Division, the 72nd Brigade, one regiment and one squadron of cavalry and 4 battalions of reinforcements. This Army Corps was assigned the task of defending the line of the River Henares; Taracena, Lubiana, Romanones, Irueste, Budia, and Durón, which showed that there was some degree of pessimism in Madrid. With these forces, far superior in numbers to those of their attackers, they must have been contemplating a counter-attack, but they were still awaiting the promised arrival of the Carlos Marx Division (later designated No 27). When Jurado took command of this Army Corps, Lacalle objected and was replaced by Nino Nanetti, formerly commander of the 35th Brigade.

March 12th saw the first Government counter attacks at Ibarra Palace and Trijueque. Pavlov, commander of the Tank Brigade, arrived at this front with two of his battalions, which could deploy a total of more than 50 T-26 and T-5B tanks. This latter class of tank was referred to as the T-28 by Klotz. By this stage the Government had received between three and four hundred tanks, which were distributed amongst the six battalions of the Tank Brigade, the Combat Truck Regiment, the Armoured Vehicles Brigade (which had only recently been formed), and some independent companies. The Combat Truck Regiment was commanded at this time by Sánchez Paredes, who was later to lead the Armoured Vehicles Division. Navarro Abujas was the first commander of the Armoured Vehicles Brigade.

On March 12th and 13th Government fighter squadrons made repeated attacks on the Italian troops. A Nationalist bulletin announced the destruction of four aircraft at Guadalajara and two over Madrid. According to a bulletin from the Ministry of Sea and Air, 200,000 rounds of machine-gun ammunition and 492 bombs were discharged by their aircraft on March 12th. If one assumes that each fighter was armed with approximately 600 rounds of ammunition, this represents more than 300 sorties made by Government fighters during that day. Since Tinker's squadron carried out three sorties, and the Chato squadrons less than this (the bulletin quotes eight missions by biplane fighters), one can calculate that about 100 fighters took part. On the 13th, twenty-eight biplanes dropped 120 bombs and fired 50,000 rounds of ammunition at Brihuega, and the land forces recaptured Trijueque. The Marzo Brigade succeeded in stopping the advance at Copernal, which was approximately on the line that had been decided as the objective of the 3rd phase.

On March 15th the Rasantes and Natachas went into operation for the first time, protected by fighters, and they attacked several motorised columns at Ledanca with great success. On that same day Trijueque and Ibarra Palace were securely in Government hands.

General Roatta (nicknamed 'Mancini' in Spain) took the unfortunate step of moving the *Plumas Negras* and *Llamas Negras* Divisions to the rear, replacing them with the *Dio lo Vuole* and *Littorio*. Apart from the inherent difficulty of performing this operation in waterlogged and muddy terrain, with only a single access road, Government fighter aircraft ranged almost freely over the area, producing total confusion.

Air attacks on the 16th, supported by three squadrons of Chatos and various Ratas, were even more destructive, but they were unable to maintain this pressure on the 17th because of bad weather.

The decisive day was the 18th. At midday fifteen aircraft dropped 360 bombs over the Brihuega sector, and during a second attack the Tora squadron bombed for a whole hour, their forty-five escorting fighters strafing the enemy ground forces with some 25,000 rounds from their machine-guns. When there were only two hours of daylight remaining, the 14th Division began the final assault on Brihuega, which was evacuated before nightfall under General Rossi's orders, despite a spirited counter attack made by the *XXIII of March* Group. The *Littorio* Division, placed in a difficult situation by the loss of Brihuega, retreated along the Aragón road. A complete disaster was avoided largely by a skilled withdrawal under General Bergonzoli.

The counter-offensive continued until March 21st, but the Government forces did not press forward, being content to occupy the areas which had now been abandoned by the Italians. In their retreat the latter had not only lost a large number of vehicles, but also a long-held belief in their own superiority.

Strangely enough, the Nationalists did not seem to regard the battle of Guadalajara as a defeat. The Italians had some 5,000 casualties, the Spanish Nationalists nowhere near this number and so it was considered an Italian defeat, an attitude well expressed by the Italian Ambassador, Roberto Cantalupo, in his book *Embajada en España* (Ambassador in Spain).

The Nationalist outlook was celebrated in a popular song which began "Guadalajara is not Abyssinia . . ." and ended "the retreat was a dreadful thing; one Italian even arrived in Badajoz". The most surprising and admirable fact was that the Italians, despite this ungrateful display, did not withdraw their support (as advocated by Cantalupo) but decided to reinforce their Air Force in Spain, as we shall see later.

During this offensive in Guadalajara not a single Spanish Nationalist aircraft took part. The Legionnary air force employed all their available aircraft, comprising Raffaelli's Savoia S-M.81 group, Colacicchi-Sforza's Romeo Ro 37 group and Fagnani's group of Fiat C.R.32 fighters, which operated from aerodromes in the Province of Soria. A few aircraft from the Cóndor Légion also took part in a strategic role.

The Government Air Force employed at least three squadrons of Chatos (La Calle's and the Russian squadrons led by 'José' and Kosokov) as well as the Rata squadrons from Alcalá de Henares and the Rasante, Natacha and Katiuska groups. The Americans Harold Dahl, Tinker and 'Chang' Selles flew in La Calle's squadron, and Baumler flew in Kosokov's squadron.

On the afternoon of March 13th, La Calle's squadron lost its fourth member, Lieutenant Blanch. His aircraft had been attacked by one of the Savoia S-MM.81s from Raffaelli's group, which was strafing the old Hispano-Suiza airfield; he took to his parachute, but this failed to open.

Blanch had been a Navy pilot, and came to Malaga on December 15th, together with Carvalleira. He was promoted to Lieutenant and soon afterwards was sent to join a fighter squadron, a custom established at the beginning of December, and intended to strengthen the fibre of the squadrons that had been affected by Fagnani's example, by sending them pilots who had the courage to cross from the enemy zone.

The next day Tinker won his first victory in Spain, during a combat with the Fiats, fought in conditions of rain and low clouds. When he landed at Manises in the midst of a particularly violent storm, the wind was so strong that his landing run was only about 100ft (30m), and he had to maintain his engine at half-throttle to prevent the aircraft from being blown backwards. Fortunately his plight was realised and ground crews came running to his rescue.

Tinker returned to his base at Guadalajara on March 15th, landing just as his own squadron was returning from a sortie, and causing some consternation among the ground staff who could not at first understand how the squadron had gained a machine during their mission. During Tinker's brief absence Barbeitos and the Mexican Manuel Gómez García had joined the squadron.

The Nationalist Air Force was now beginning to be more active. During the night of the 15th bombers attacked Barajas, 'Campo X' and Alcalá aerodromes, and the next morning the Fiats shot down a Chato from the 'José' squadron. They, in turn, were attacked by Kosokov's squadron, which seemed to appear from nowhere, and lost two of their number, one destroyed by Baumler.

On the 17th and 19th the fighter squadrons were unable to operate because of bad weather, but on the intervening day, March 18th, Government bombers and fighters provided efficient support to their land forces as they recaptured Brihuega.

On March 20th La Calle's squadron took part in the last aerial combat during the battle of Guadalajara. They took off in four patrols, led by La Calle, Dahl, Tinker and Manuel Gómez, and were soon involved with three bombers and twenty Fiats. Gomez's patrol was jumped by the Fiats, which had been patrolling at a higher altitude, and in the first hail of bullets Gomez was shot down. Tinker gained his second victory, and from the two squadrons of fighters taking part five Fiats were destroyed. Degli Incerti ('Jocci') has said that one of the Fiat squadrons shot down a Chato piloted by an American.

Shortly after these events, La Calle was promoted, being replaced by Jiménez Bruguet and Dahl was admitted to hospital with a stomach ulcer. The squadron was re-formed in three patrols, led by Jiménez Bruguet, Tinker and Ortiz. Castañeda, Gerardo Gil, Riverola, Velasco, Lecha, Barbeitos, Francisco Alarcón, Justo García, Magriñá and Bastida were all members of this squadron at that time. 'Chang' Selles, who had been a member of the squadron, was accused of espionage and executed by a firing squad.

Activity in Spring 1937, a Critical Period

As we have seen earlier, re-organisation of the columns in the Central-Southern Zone was completed in March 1937. At that time there were already at least 93 organised mixed brigades, each of four battalions. In Aragón there were 6 more divisions, which had not been re-organised, and three more in Catalonia (later designated Nos 31, 32 and 33). All these forces together totalled about 475 battalions. In the Northern Zone, the number of organised battalions could not have been less than 150 at this time since, two months later, they totalled 192, comprising 74 Basque, 75 Asturian and 43 from Santander. Thus, in March 1937, the Government had available approximately 625 battalions.

In the Nationalist Zone the total number of organised battalions was a little below 500 at the same period, according to the following calculation:

		Battalions
25	Regiments or Groups of Regulars with 9 battalions each	225
9	Regiments of Mountain Chasseurs with 4 battalions each	36
14	Tabores from Mehala or Marksmen from Ifni	7
10	Banderas from the Legion	10
48	Groups of Requetés	48
66	Falange Banderas	66
20	Battalions of volunteers	20
11	Groups of Banderas and 1 Italian Division	40
2	Mixed Brigades of Flechas with 6 battalions	12
		464

This relative strength of troops largely explains the failures of the Nationalist offensives during the month of March (Guadalajara and Pozoblanco), especially if it is also appreciated that the Government had superiority in aircraft, tanks, and artillery. According to N. Voronov, in May 1937 the Popular Army had 451 batteries with a total of 1,681 guns of mixed calibre.

The overwhelming naval superiority held by the Nationalists during February was very important in deciding the Málaga campaign and this, in its turn, influenced later actions, when the Nationalist cruisers blockaded the Straits and confined the Government Fleet in the Mediterranean. However, in March the Cartagena Fleet recovered its full potential, its ships re-armed with Russian weapons, and their crews strengthened by the addition of about a hundred foreign officers, mainly American, Russian and French.

The balance of Naval power, as regards numbers of vessels, was also in the Government's favour as at that time there was a battleship and three cruisers on each side, but the Nationalists had only a single destroyer as opposed to fifteen, and two submarines (purchased from Italy) to compare with eight in the Government Fleet. It should be recorded, however, that the two Nationalist cruisers completed in September and December 1936 were far superior to those of the enemy.

Despite their numerical superiority in troops, in March the Government mobilised the 1932, 1933 and 1936 reserves, and warned those from the 1934 and 1935 registration that their mobilisation, which had been decreed in September 1936, was imminent. At the same time the Central Committee for the

Recruitment of Volunteers was made redundant. In the Northern Zone, isolated from the rest of the country, which had a population of just under two million people, no less than 150,000 men were recruited.

In this way, the Government forces continued to increase, and by June 1937 they had 153 mixed brigades properly organised, making a total of 612 battalions, as well as the 192 battalions in the North. From these battalions 17 Army Corps were established, the first six being formed basically from the Army for Central Operations. Numbers VII to IX covered the line from the Tajo to the Mediterranean coast and Numbers X to XII the Aragon front. The Basque Army Corps was later numbered VII and XIV. Subordinated to these Army Corps were 47 Divisions created in the Central Zone, 4 in Biscay, 4 in Santander and 7 in Asturias.

In the Nationalist Zone the number of battalions also increased rapidly, reaching a total of about 600, but the organisation of large units was lagging behind. The first five divisions were created in the Southern Army at the end of March, and the first Army Corps (at the Madrid front) was formed on April 3rd. In May the Army Corps numbered II, III and VIII were organised.

The composition of these Army Corps was fairly mixed. Those belonging to the Southern Army had initially two divisions each, with the 102nd Division serving as reserve for both of them. Army Corps VII was made up initially of five divisions, numbered from 71 to 75 (later re-designated Nos 11 to 14), four of which remained in the Madrid-Toledo Sector (these were numbered 11 to 14) and one (No 75) was sent to Ávila together with two brigades. The VIth Army Corps was organised in two divisions, No 61 Vitoria and No 62 Palencia. The Vth Army Corps had three Divisions, No 51 in Huesca-Saragossa, No 52 in Teruel and No 53 (later re-designated No 72) in Soria, together with the *Brigada de Posición y Etapas* and the Mobile Brigade. The VIIIth Army Corps also had three Divisions, No 81 in León and Nos 82 and 83 in Asturias, together with the Oviedo Brigade.

In June, after Mola's death, the Central Army was formed, under the overall command of Saliquet. This included the 1st Army Corps, commanded initially by Valdés Cavanilles and later by Yagüe, and the VIIth Army Corps commanded by Varela, with Nos 71 and 72 Divisions.

Of all these large units, the most effective were the four Madrid Divisions, led initially by Iruretagoyena, Asensio, Barrón and Yague; No 61 Division which was under the command of Solchaga and consisted of four Navarrese Brigades led by García Valiño, Cayuela, Latorre and Alonso Vega, and the Galician Divisions, led by Múgica, Ceano and Martín Alonso.

On April 3rd the Government formed its first Army Shock Corps, which was commanded by Modesto and designated No IV. It comprised initially 'A' Division (José Galán), 'B' Division (Walter) and these were soon joined by No 11 Division (Líster), and Nos 1, 2, 3, 9, 10, 11, 12, 14, 21, 68 and 69 Brigades. In May the 'A' and 'B' Divisions were re-designated as No 34 and 35 respectively. In the north they began organising three Shock Divisions in the month of July, Ibarrola's Basque Division and the Asturian (Bárzana) and Highland Expeditionary Forces (San Juan). Finally, shortly before the Battle of Brunete, the XVIIIth Army Shock Corps (Jurado) was organised in Madrid and this, together with the Vth, formed the *Ejército de Maniobra* (Army of Manoeuvre), which was to take part in the Battle of Brunete.

At the same time as military organisation was being finalised, political activity was also on the increase. In the Nationalist Zone the arrival of Serrano Súñer, the Generalissimo's brother-in-law, reinforced Franco's authority. Serrano Súñer was the originator of the Unification Decree (19th April), which caused several incidents in Valladolid and was responsible for the deportation of the leaders of the two strongest political parties, the Falangists and the Carlists. Franco forbade the formation of any new battalions of volunteers, although a year later he allowed recruits to choose in which of the surviving battalions they would like to serve, and also allowed some of the battalions which had been disbanded to reform. From January 21st, all the battalions of volunteers were under the command of General Monasterio (second-in-command of the Militia), who was then named as the direct leader of the Militia, with headquarters in Ávila.

The process of political re-organisation in the Nationalist Zone did not end until January 1938, when the first Burgos Government was formed.

In the Government Zone there were also political shake-ups, but these were more serious and had far-reaching results. Largo Caballero, against his wishes, had to confront the Anarchists in Barcelona, defeating them after a fierce struggle which lasted for three days. But this victory brought about his own downfall, instigated by the Communists, who succeeded in eliminating their two principal enemies at one stroke.

To discredit Largo Caballero, the Communist faction first directed their campaign against Asensio, the under-secretary for War, and Martínez Cabrera, the central chief of staff, accusing them of being responsible for the defeat of Málaga. It was conveniently forgotten that Ascensio and Cabrera had been primarily responsible for organisation of the five hundred battalions which had made possible the victories at Madrid, Jarama, Guadalajara and Pozoblanco. It was remarkable that nobody attacked Prieto, who was more directly responsible for the defeat at Málaga, since the Fleet failed completely and the Air Force was largely ineffective. Instead, he was elevated to the position of Minister of Defence after Largo Caballero had gone.

Finally, a direct attack was made on Largo Caballero because of the incidents in Barcelona during May. Incidents in which he had become involved by those who had criticised him. Taking advantage of the unsettled situation, the Government managed to get rid of the Trotskyite party, POUM, and their leader Andrés Nin.

In this way, with Negrín's sudden rise to power, the Communists acquired a political strength which they maintained until the last few days of the war, when Colonel Segismundo Casado attempted a coup d'état.

So far as diplomatic moves were concerned, Cardinal Valerio Valeri, papal nunciate in Paris, tried to achieve peace between Euzcadi and Franco, but this did not advance beyond preliminaries. Italy hesitated between the withdrawal of all her forces from Spain, as advised by their ambassador, or of increasing her aid. In the end she decided to increase air support and provide two submarines.

A secret agreement, signed on November 28th by Italy and Franco, had not been well received by Germany. As a result, at the end of January the Italian ambassador in Paris, Cerutti, informed Pierre Laval of his Government's wishes to begin negotiations with León Blum, with the object of opposing German politics in Central Europe.

Germany, who had provided the Cóndor Legion to intervene in Spanish internal affairs, considered they had been snubbed. Their immediate reaction had been to withdraw their assistance. In November, during a conference in Berlin, which was attended by Warlimont who had recently arrived from Spain, General Blomberg (German Minister of Defence), said that he was opposed to increasing aid to Spain. Later, their ambassador, Von Faupel, also advised a withdrawal, but by then Admiral Canaris and General Reichenau had been sent to Spain to study the situation. They favoured leaving the troops there, and their decision was accepted by the German High Command. In May the first reliefs for the Cóndor Legion arrived, as they continued to do every six months for the remainder of the war.

Not long after these events the Government Air Force created a serious international incident by bombing the Italian cruiser *Barletta* in Palma and the German battleship *Deutschland* at Ibiza. These two warships were components of the *Comisión de Control* (Control Commission), the incident ending by the *Leipzig* and *Admiral Scheer* shelling Almería, an action which terminated when the *Leipzig* was hit by a torpedo discharged by a submarine.

France continued her policy of indirect help to the Valencian Government; England sent a naval squadron to protect British shipping that wanted to use the port of Bilbao, which was being blockaded by the Nationalist Fleet; and the United States, despite the Neutrality Act, sent volunteer pilots, some aircraft and a reasonable number of aero-engines.

Russia continued to send large quantities of war supplies by sea, as proved by reports from the German military attaché in Turkey. It would appear that his ability as an accountant was somewhat sketchy, for the number of aircraft supplied in 1936 and 1937 considerably exceeded the numbers reported by him. In fact 148 aircraft arrived from Russia during 1936, comprising 55 Chatos (25 to the east and 30 to the north), 31 Ratas, 31 Rasantes and 31 Katiuskas, compared with a total of 49 recorded by the military attaché. During the first half of 1937 an additional 184 Russian aircraft were received in Spain (92 Chatos, 31 Ratas, 30 Rasantes and 31 Natachas), although only 66 were reported from Turkey. Similarly, in the latter half of 1937, the number of aircraft sent by Russia was approximately three times the number reported by the information services.

On May 1st a complete group of Katiuskas (31 aircraft) arrived at Santo Tomé, and these were sent to bomb the Fascist warships in Balearic waters. Prokófiev has recently made it clear that it was his successor, the chief observer of the group, who released the bombs which hit the *Deutschland*.

CHAPTER FOUR

The Northern Campaign, Key to the Nationalists Victory

The Campaign in Biscay

The campaign in Biscay was decisive for the final results of the battle. This was not only because of the economic importance of this province to the Nationalists (since they had no industrial areas within their zone), but more especially because the campaign came at an opportune moment.

During the month of March 1937, the Nationalist offensives at Guadalajara and Pozoblanco had ended in retreats. It was only at Oviedo that they were able to revert to the precarious situation that had existed before the Government's Northern Army made the offensive on their access route at the end of February.

In view of the Government's numerical superiority on land, in the air and at sea, it seemed as if the war could end in stalemate. The Valencian Government was well aware of this possibility, and President Azaña gave Besteiro the task of discovering Nationalist intentions. Whilst carrying out investigations in London, he attended the Coronation of George VI (May 1937), who had succeeded his brother Edward VIII after his abdication in December 1936.

Lieutenant Colonel Vigón (Mola's successor as commander of the Pamplona Brigade and later commander of all the forces on the Basque front), who was General Solchaga's chief of staff, had prepared a plan of campaign in Biscay. This seemed viable, as some of the Basque forces and almost all of their air units had moved to Asturias in the middle of February.

It was not until March 21st, when the attack in Guadalajara had failed that, supported by the air chief (Kindelán), this plan received Franco's approval. Prior to this, Mola had asked Ponte to study a plan of campaign in Aragón: Ponte's conclusions were that it would not be possible to mount an attack with only his División Orgánica (later the 5th Army Corps), and this made Mola decide in favour of the Biscay Campaign. Franco was still a little doubtful, since he did not want to risk a third, consecutive failure. However, Kindelán's approval, together with that of the Cóndor Legion, seemed to convince him.

Mola discussed plans for the attack in Salamanca on March 22nd. On the 28th, at Navalcarnero, he suggested to the *Flechas Negras* (Black Arrows) Brigade that they should take part in the campaign under his orders, and this proposal was accepted. On the 29th, the Navarrese Brigades' Headquarters issued their general order of operations.

The Northern Campaign had an enormous advantage, namely that the Nationalists could count on aerial superiority in that region and, when the Basque expeditionary troops returned from Oviedo, they even had numerical superiority for a short while. This made it possible to break through the outer line of defence and subsequently to occupy the hilltops along the dividing line. However, by moving the main centre of operations to the North it was clear that there was to be no swift ending to the war.

Local superiority in the air was easier to maintain because of geographical reasons. For one thing, the narrowness of the Cantabrian strip and the rugged terrain made it difficult, if not impossible, for the Government to establish new airfields. These were essential if the Government Air Force were to remain within striking range, for the distance from Bilbao to Madrid or Sariñena (Saragossa province) made it hazardous to fly fighter aircraft to the combat area. It was also risky to transport supplies by sea, since the Nationalists had naval superiority in the Cantabrian sea. This was demonstrated by the capture of the *Mar Cantábrico, Hordeana* and the *Forbea* by the *Canarias* and *Almirante Cervera*.

In the air, the Nationalists were fortunate that their bases in the province of Soria enabled the Savoias to operate at either the Northern or Central fronts. The light aircraft were restricted to operations within a short distance of their bases at Logrõno and Vitoria so that, in emergency, they could return quickly to the central front.

The Condór Legion moved from Ávila and Salamanca to Vitoria, where they established their headquarters on March 29th. The Spanish Air Force remained under the command of the leader of the Aerial Region in the north, Julián Rubio, who had Francisco Iglesias as his chief of staff.

The Biscay offensive began on March 31st, in the Villarreal sector, where the 4th Navarrese Brigade (Camilo Alonso Vega), the 1st (García Valiño) and part of the 3rd (Latorre) began the attack. The Navarrese Brigades each had five battalions, and these increased in size until they became authentic divisions. At the time when they started this offensive the three attacking brigades each had a total of twenty battalions and a slightly larger number of artillery batteries, to which were added seven or eight from Italian units. In general, throughout the Northern Campaign the artillery used was both small in number and obsolete.

Air Force fighters were in operation almost continuously, escorting bombers to reinforce the artillery. At 07.10hrs on March 31st, twenty Junkers Ju 52s, escorted by fighters, dropped heavy and medium bombs in the Ochandiano sector. At 09.00hrs the Heinkel He 111 squadron and a few Dornier Do 17s, which were being used on operations for the first time, added their quota of bombs. The infantry attacked at 09.40hrs, and used visual signalling methods to direct supporting aircraft to areas of strong enemy resistance. At 10.00hrs three fighter squadrons strafed enemy positions.

Within half an hour Maroto and Albertia were overrun, and Tarinto fell shortly afterwards. The air units made a fourth sortie, and this time the Savoias took part. By the end of the day the Nationalist Air Force had dropped more than 70 tons of bombs and fired 35,000 rounds of machine-gun ammunition. These figures are significant, for the 30 odd batteries taking part (20 of them supporting the 4th Brigade), had fired off only some 150 tons of shells.

On April 1st the attack slowed as enemy resistance became more resolute, and by the 2nd it had been brought to a halt. The next day, because of bad weather, only reconnaissance aircraft were in action.

On April 4th Ochandiano was occupied with moderate losses, due to support from some tank units on the ground and by more than fifty aircraft. The next day reinforcements from Bilbao began a counter-attack in the west, but they were deterred by the Nationalist Air Force and their allies: between them they dropped about 100 tons of bombs, the highest weight delivered in one day up to that moment. By April 7th the ports of Barâzar, Zumelzu and Urquiola were occupied, together with the hills of Gorbea Chiqui and Amboto, which lay behind the ports.

On April 4th, and for several days following, Nationalist aircraft attacked various aerodromes in the north, among them Lamiaco and Santander. At these airfields several fighters were destroyed or damaged. Two days later a new operation was planned, but this had to be cancelled due to bad weather. A little later fierce fighting began at Mount Sebigain, the Government forces using Russian tanks in their counter-attacks. The fortunes of war favoured first one side, then the other, but a third and bloody attack brought victory to the Nationalist forces.

A Government communiqué claimed that their fighters had destroyed a twin-engined German aircraft over Durango on the afternoon of the 13th, and had attacked other enemy machines over Bilbao. In fact, the aircraft shot down was a single-engined He 51 flown by Lt Vandel. At about this time the Spanish He 51s had gained ascendancy at the battle of Santa Quiteria in Huesca: thus, at a distance, they contributed to the success of the Biscay campaign.

Mola abandoned his plan to attack Urquiola-Durango and decided instead to make a further breach in the Vergara front, towards Lequeito, using a formidable combination of artillery and air power. García Valiño disagreed, since he considered it impractical to breach the front only 15 miles (25km) from the point at which they had broken through before. Valino favoured an attack on the three Inchortas mountains, the strongest and deepest fortifications of the whole front. A compromise was adopted, the 4th Brigade moving to Vergara to attempt a break through, whilst the 1st Brigade were to encircle Udala from the west, from their positions in Amboto, and to attack Elorrio, at the rear of the Inchortas.

On April 20th the second phase of the offensive began in the Mondragon sector, led by the 1st Navarre Brigade (García Valiño) reinforced by Tutor and Gual's brigades. The 4th Brigade, also reinforced, attacked from the Vergara sector.

On the first day of the attack Nationalist artillery discharged some 12,000 shells, equivalent to about 180 tons, and by the 24th the 1st Brigade had occupied Elorrio, after encircling mount Udala from the west, and the next day the Basques were forced to evacuate the three Inchortas. This left the Vergara –Elgueta–Elorrio road free, giving the Nationalists assurance of final victory in this area. The 1st Brigade continued their advance towards the north-west until reaching Durango, which they occupied on the 28th. Meanwhile, the 4th Brigade continued their successes towards the north and arrived at Marquina on the 27th. From here they turned west and reached Guernica on the 29th. The *Flechas Negras* Brigade, which had joined the line in the coastal sector at the beginning of April, began their advance towards Marquina on the 30th. Here they received orders from Mola not to proceed any further until the 4th Navarre Brigade arrived.

During the last ten days of April the Biscay campaign was decided. In these latter stages of the battle the Nationalist Air Force were unable to operate as freely as at the beginning. Captain José Antonio del Val, squadron leader of the Lasarte Breguet group, was shot down over the Inchortas and wounded. Shortly afterwards German Me 109Bs shot down two Government fighters. At this time Felipe del Río, hero of the Government Air Force in the north, was shot down and killed. His place in the squadron was taken by Miguel Zambudio.

On Monday April 26th the famous air attack on Guernica took place. On that day the entire eastern Basque front was in a state of collapse: the only feasible route by which their reinforcements could arrive was via the bridge at Guernica. The Cóndor Legion were given orders to destroy the bridge and, according to Galland, who arrived in Victoria only days afterwards, this unit must have excelled itself in this mission.

At the beginning of May the Basques made a great defensive effort, which succeeded in delaying the fall of Bilbao for a month. On May 5th Aguirre assumed command of the Basque Army Corps, with La Fuente as chief of staff. Seven new battalions (Nos 68 to 74) and two new brigades (Nos 17 and 18) were formed. Reinforcements arrived in the form of four Asturian and two Santander expeditionary brigades, each of three battalions, and this provided a defensive force of twenty-four brigades comprising ninety-two battalions. These troops were distributed between five divisions, with the 5th (Beldarrain) remaining on the coast, and the other four (Gómez, Vidal, Ibarrola and Irezábal), stretching from there to the borders of Santander.

On May 7th, the UGT and the CNT called up all available men between the ages of 18 and 50, to form new battalions of reinforcements. Euzkadi's Government mobilised a total of 14 drafts, but this extreme military effort had a disastrous effect on industry.

As a result of this increase in the defending forces, the Nationalists also had to bring in reinforcements. The recently-formed Navarre Brigade (Juan Bautista Sánchez González), arrived on May 3rd to relieve the 4th Brigade, which then took up the position it had occupied earlier, in the ports of Barázar and Urquiola. To strengthen the *Flechas Negras* Brigade, the Italian *XXIII of March* Brigade was brought in, its commander Francisci, arriving in Bermeo on May 3rd: the remainder of the group arrived by the 12th. Roatta, who had now handed over supreme command to Bastico, persuaded Mola to let him take over joint command of the *XXIII of March* and the *Black Arrows* brigades. When the 6th Navarre Brigade (Bartomeu) arrived in the sector on May 23rd, the *XXIII of March* Brigade was sent to the rear to be reorganised as a division, and it did not operate again in Biscay. As from April 30th the Navarrese Brigades became part of the 1st Division (later re-designated No 61) in the recently-formed VIth Army Corps (López Pinto). Solchaga continued to exercise overall command.

On May 5th Mola distributed a new general order, which modified the earlier plan of campaign, and by May 8th the 5th Brigade, with strong air support, had occupied mount Sollube. This was an excellent beginning for a new and untried unit.

During these battles at the beginning of May, the second squadron of the He 51 group (previously Martín Campos' 3-E-2 Squadron, now re-designated 2-E-2) and the first Ju 52 group (Luis Pardo's), both took part in the air operations. Only days later this Ju 52 group was disbanded, their pilots sent to Italy to collect new Savoia S-M.79s, and was replaced by Carrillo's night operations group (1-G-22). This was formed from Haya's old squadron and a new squadron led by Luis Bengoechea. Gil Mendizábal's old group became known as 2-G-22 and was led by Eduardo González Gallarza, who had recently arrived in the Nationalist Zone.

At about this time the first Heinkel He 45 army co-operation aircraft arrived. These were more modern then the He 46s, despite the lower type number, and were nicknamed *Pavo* (turkey). One of the first squadrons to be equipped with these aircraft was led by Manuel Bazán, and later by Manuel Lapuente.

On May 8th and 17th, attempts were made to transfer two squadrons of Chatos from Lérida to Bilbao, but these were forced to turn back to Toulouse and Pau.

From May 14th to 19th courageous attempts were made to occupy the mountains of Tollu and Jata. Colonel Piazzoni complained that the Cóndor Legion failed to provide adequate support for the attack on mount Jata on May 14th, but acknowledged that the operations of the Nationalist Air Force on the 19th were decisive. Further inland, the 1st Brigade had occupied mount Bizcargui on May 11th, having previously taken the famous 333 bench mark (survey datum level).

On May 22nd the 4th Navarre Brigade attacked the port of Barázar, and on the 29th they occupied Pena Lemona. This meant that the Nationalist Army had reached the line of the *Cinturón de Hierro* (Iron Ring) along its eastern flank. On the 26th the 3rd Brigade attempted to advance as far as Amurrio, to gain the San Pedro mines, and this caused many fierce and fruitless battles. Government resistance was particularly strong, not only because of the economic importance of the mines, but because this advance threatened to cut off the line of retreat from Bilbao.

On May 22nd Cdr Vara del Rey was wounded at Ochandiano, forcing him to relinquish leadership of the He 46 squadron, by then designated 5-G-11 (shortly afterwards re-designated 3-G-11). Also on May 22nd, the Me 109B squadron shot down a Chato, the Fiats destroying another aircraft of the same type on the following day. On the 24th Savoia S-M. 81s attacked the aerodrome at Santander where, according to the Nationalist bulletin, they destroyed two machines.

At the end of May, two squadrons of Aero-101s were formed with twenty-two aircraft siezed from an enemy ship. These squadrons were led by Cárdenas and Gómez Martín, and they became part of the old León and Lasarte Breguet groups (1-G-10 and 2-G-10). By June, sufficient He 45s had arrived to form a second squadron, and these were put under the leadership of Cardenas, the Leon group handing over all the Aero 101s to the Lasarte group. The León group was designated 6-G-15 (the terminal number 15 indicating He 45s nicknamed *Pavos*) and the Lasarte group 5-G-17, the terminal number 17 indicating the Aero 101s, which were given the nickname Ocas (*Geese*). Following these changes, the He 45 group was commanded by Eyaralar (later Cipriano Rodríguez) and the Aeros by Llop (later Antonio Llorente).

Genesis of the First Groups of Spanish Fighters

The April operations required three squadrons of the He 51s to be based in Saragossa. On April 7th, the date when the Huesca attack began, Squadron 1-E-2 had performed brilliantly at Carrascal, which is situated between Ayerbe and Huesca, but two more squadrons were needed to help defend positions to the south of the town. Squadron 2-E-2 arrived in Saragossa on the 10th, having flown from Navia, via Burgos, and Squadron 3-E-2 arrived from Seville.

At that time the pilots of these three squadrons included Capts Montero, Salas, Martín Campos, Murcia and Corsini, Lts Atienza and Carlos Serra (formerly Ju 52 pilots), and 2nd Lts Senra, Jesús Rubio, Arístides García Lopez, Ferrera, Palmero, Henricourt, Ernesto Nienhuisen, Mariano Ruiz de Alda, Jurado, Allende, Joaquín Ansaldo, Muntadas and Mazarredo.

Captain Corsini replaced Guerrero when he moved to the Fiats. Shortly afterwards Prieto, Careaga, Varona and Santamaría joined the squadron, followed in May by Rafael Simón and Comas.

Their aircraft were those no longer used by the Cóndor Legion, as well as the old *Huesca, Saragossa* and *Teruel*, which had been re-built. The first six Heinkel He 51s were given the serial numbers 2-1 to 2-6, and as they arrived in Spanish service succeeding aircraft of this type were numbered on from that beginning. The named aircraft (*Huesca, Saragossa* and *Teruel*) had the serial numbers 2-54, 2-55 and 2-56 respectively. This was a simple method of allocating serial numbers, and was probably adopted because the Germans used a similar system. By contrast, the first Fiats had been numbered from 3-51. The Italian system of numbering their aircraft was far more complicated, as within a squadron there was numerical duplication or triplication and colour identification (eg: No 1 red, No 1 blue, No 1 green, etc).

On April 12th the three He 51 squadrons took part in operations at Carrascal and Santa Quiteria. On the following day, supported by a squadron of He 46s, they ranged the sky above the battlefield and concentrated their fire power on the enemy troops below. They succeeded to the extent that the Nationalists were able to re-capture Santa Quiteria, the Government *Carlos Marx* Division suffering almost 400 fatal casualties as a direct result of the intensive air support. Orders to the Aragón Air Forces on the 12th, 13th and 15th, expressed congratulations from Cdr Galera, leader of the Tetuán Mehala, Cdr Amado, leader of the Almodóvar column, and from the Generalissimo. The general order from the 5th Army Corps, on the 15th, praised the activities of the Air Force on the 7th and the 13th, quoting especially Group 2.

Up to this time aircraft had made many machine-gun attacks against targets on the ground, but now the He 51 squadron employed a new tactic which later became known as the 'chain' formation. This consisted of attacking with the entire squadron in line astern. When the leader of the formation had made his first attack he manoeuvred into a position behind the last aircraft in line, each pilot following the same procedure in his turn, the cycle being maintained until their ammunition was exhausted. Three months later, following a suggestion from Morato, this tactic became accepted by the Nationalist Air Force as a standard method of attack against ground targets. As experience was gained it became possible to provide effective close support for infantry on the ground, who displayed a Nationalist flag to identify their position.

The potential of this close support operation had been demonstrated by Capt Salas. After completing a reconnaissance sortie, he reported one of their positions surrounded by a large number of the enemy, and immediately took off again leading Squadron 2-E-2 and eight He 46s to attack the enemy troops. They remained in the air above their hard-pressed infantry, providing machine-gun fire against enemy positions for 2hrs 8min, by which time their ammunition was exhausted. Salas then handed over to Squadrons 1-E-2 and 3-E-2 the task of maintaining the attack. By the time that another 1hr 45min had elapsed the enemy forces were in retreat. In due course Government bulletins acknowledged four hundred casualties, and complained that their own aircraft did not take a part in driving off the Nationalist squadrons.

In the middle of the month the main action on the ground, which had been centred around Huescal, moved to Teruel, where Cols Velasco and Lacalle led new attacks.

On April 16th, at Teruel, Salas and Montero's squadrons attempted to bring to combat a twin-engined low-wing monoplane, but were unable to get within range as it was flying at a much higher altitude. Later, when Salas was returning to Saragossa aerodrome in company with two other He 51s, they spotted seven Chatos overhead and climbed to attack them. One went into a dive and was followed down by Salas until it was near the ground, where it crashed and burst into flames. Tinker said that the pilot was Tuya, who had recently joined Kosákov's Russian squadron. On the same day 2nd Lt Arístides García López destroyed a Katiuska.

On April 17th the three squadrons were in operation with a total of seventeen aircraft. The 2nd squadron, with a total of five aircraft, saw an enemy bomber but were unable to close with it. Shortly after they were joined by another He 51, flown by 2nd Lt Palmero, and caught sight of ten Chatos patrolling well above their own altitude of 13,100ft (4,000m). They climbed to attack, determined to break off at the moment of interception, but Palmero was unable to evade one Chato that was coming down very fast in the dive, and the two machines collided. The ensuing air combat ranged all over the sky, and ten more Chatos and a third fighter squadron soon joined the battle against the five remaining aircraft of 2-E-2.

Tinker's account of this battle is both confused and contradictory. He obviously attached great importance to it, admitted that it was hard fought on both sides, and ended by claiming it as an overwhelming victory. Whilst it might have been difficult for him to be certain of the number of Nationalist aircraft involved, he should have been able to give reliable information about the number of Chatos taking part. Even these figures were confused; first he writes of three squadrons of six aircraft; then he acknowledges that his squadron, which was the third to join the battle, operated with six machines, and that the second squadron to join the battle (probably Kosákov's, which operated from the same aerodrome at Sarrion), had at its disposal three patrols of three aeroplanes. Government bulletins add further confusion by speaking of sorties in squadrons of six aeroplanes, apart from one in a group of twenty!

What is certain is that Squadron 2-E-2 alone was involved in this combat, the other two He 51 squadrons were unaware of the action and were patrolling peacefully over their own lines. Of the five pilots remaining after Palmero had collided with a Chato, Capt Salas had made attacks on four aircraft, and arrived at Calamocha with his petrol tanks almost dry and eighteen bullet holes ventilating the fuselage and wings. He had remained in the combat area until all the government fighters had disappeared. Muntadas, Mazarredo and Joaquín Ansaldo had already landed at Calamocha, and only Ansaldo's aircraft was free from damage. The fifth pilot, Allende, made a forced landing on his own side of the line, close to the front, having been shot down by Juan Comas Borrás. Palmero, who had joined them in the battle, died in the collision with Calvo's Chato during the first moments of the attack.

The remaining He 51 squadrons took no part and suffered no losses, so Tinker's claim that five aircraft fell behind their lines can, in reality, only be an admission of the loss of five Chatos. Nationalist observers on the ground saw seven aircraft fall, and if one discounts the two He 51s flown by Palmero and Allende, this confirms the destruction of five Chatos, but the Nationalist communiqué claimed a total of seven aircraft destroyed.

On the night of April 17th Salas received a warm telegram of congratulations from García Morato. The general order of the 5th Army Corps on the 19th highlighted the activities of Squadron 2-E-2 at Teruel on April 17th, and the leader of the Aragón Air Forces emphasised the distinguished efforts of Capt Salas and 2nd Lt Palmero.

On the 18th Salas and Muntadas went with another squadron to escort six He 46s to Celadas. They saw some enemy fighters but did not break away from their charges to attack. On the 19th, they made three sorties: by the following day Squadron 2-E-2 had only four aeroplanes flying, and on the 21st these were handed over to Squadron 1-E-2. The 2-E-2 pilots were flown to Seville on the 22nd in Haya's old DC-2, piloted by Navarro.

In Seville, on April 26th, aerobatic classes for fighter pilots began, Bücker Jungmeisters being used for training, and on the 30th more Fiat machines arrived, and were used to form the 2nd squadron of this type, which was given the designation 2-E-3.

Squadron 1-E-3 was formed of six aircraft numbered 3-51, 3-52 and 3-53 in the first patrol, and 3-61, 3-62 and 3-63 in the second. The pilots were the four veterans (Morato, Salvador, Bermúdez de Castro and García Pardo) and

Guerrero and Vázquez Sagastizábal, who had transferred their loyalties from Government to Nationalists. At this time Guerrero already had four confirmed victories, and Vázquez Sagastizábal had a magnificent record as a pilot in the Seville Aero-Club, and later as a member of Squadron 2-E-2.

This first Fiat squadron operated from Córdoba throughout the month of April, plaguing the recently-formed 19th and 20th Government Divisions, especially the 19th in the Pozoblanco sector. Their most noteworthy operations during the month included an attack on the 16th on Andújar aerodrome, the base used for supporting the final attacks on Santuario de la Cabeza, a fierce battle between three Fiats and eight Chatos over Cabeza Mesada on the 3rd, and a machine-gun attack on Puerto Calatraveño on the 21st.

During the month of May both squadrons joined together to form Morato's group, designated 2-G-3. Similarly, the two He 51 squadrons formed one group, designated 1-G-2, and this was commanded by Manrique Montero.

In Aragón, on May 26th, the He 51 squadrons distinguished themselves again during operations at Celadas and Santa Bàrbara. The He 46s (Gancedo), Ju 52s (Luis Pardo) and some Italian Fiats from the *As de Bastos* (Ace of Clubs) Group also took part. Attacks on the 22nd and 26th caused many losses amongst Government troops, and were decisive in preventing any break out by the enemy.

The Great Increase in the Legionary Fighter Force

When the battle of Guadalajara ended, the Italians debated whether to withdraw from Spain or whether to increase their assistance; in the end the latter decision prevailed.

During the first fortnight in April two convoys from Italy, escorted by the cruisers *Canarias* and *Baleares*, brought urgently needed supplies, especially aircraft. The Government Fleet was also busily involved in escorting ships carrying war materials between Cape Ténés and Cartagena. At the end of the month Government warships shelled Málaga, Melilla and Motril, until forced to retreat by Nationalist torpedo boats and the Ju 52s from Gil Mendizábal's group.

Admiral Moreno was called to Salamanca, where he remained from May 15th to 19th. On his return he directed the battle being fought off Cartagena between the *Canarias* and *Baleares* on the Nationalist side, and the *Lepanto* and *Sánchez Barcáiztegui* on the Government side, supported by the cruisers *Libertad* and *Méndez Núñez*, a flotilla of destroyers, and the coastal batteries at Cape Sines.

At the end of the month, when a third Italian convoy arrived, sufficient Fiat C.R.32 fighters were assembled in Seville to form a second Italian group and a second Spanish squadron. Cdrs Casero and Zotti were named as leaders of *La Cucaracha* (Cockroach) 16th Fighter Group and *As de Bastos* 23rd Fighter Group respectively. Brambilla, Viola and Francois were leaders of Nos 24, 25 and 26 squadrons which formed the *La Cucaracha* Group; the veterans Nobili ('Notabili'), Larsimont ('Laimo') and Degli Incerti ('Tocci') led Nos 18, 19 and 20. Squadrons which comprised the *As de Bastos* Group.

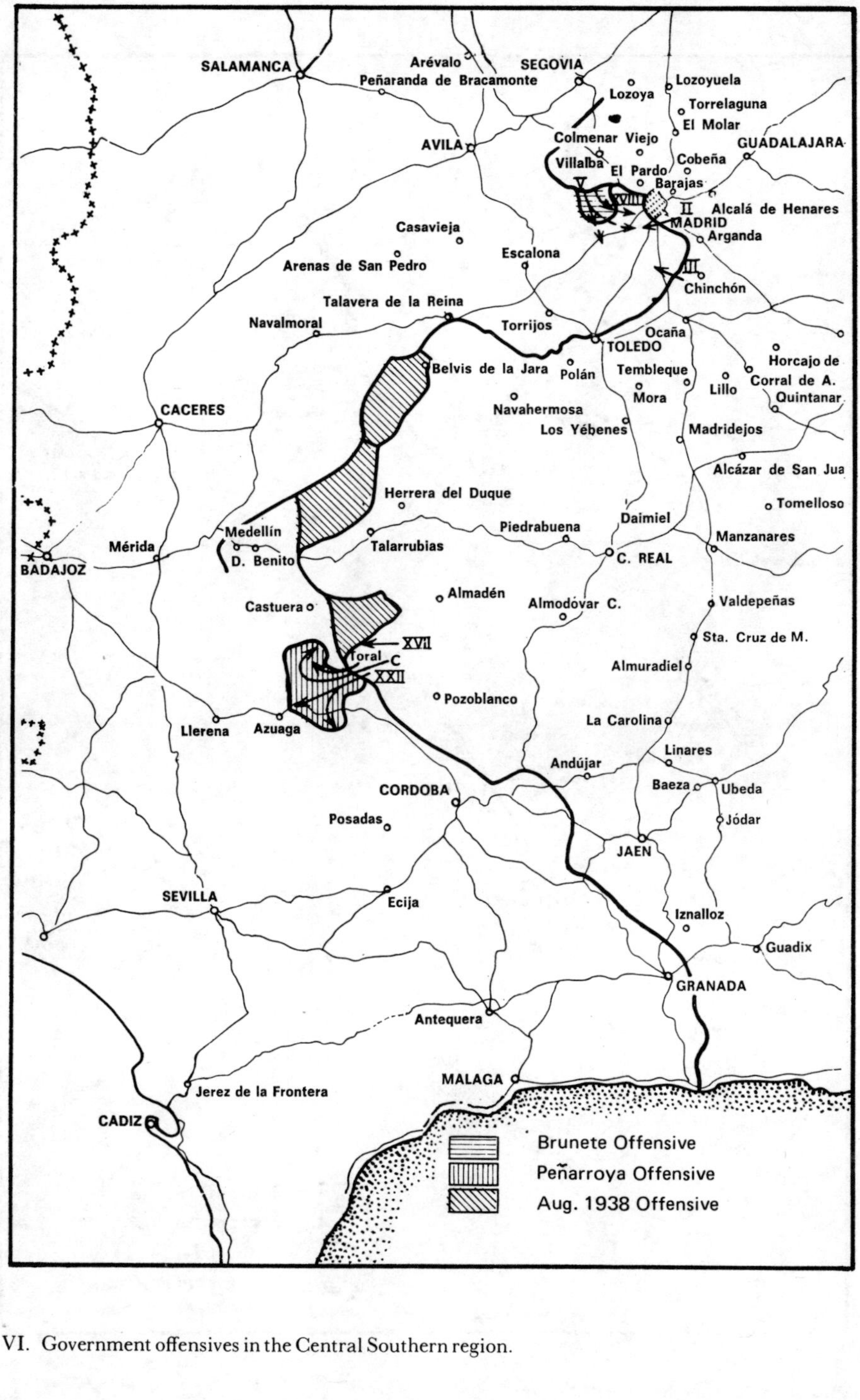

VI. Government offensives in the Central Southern region.

VII. Government offensives in Aragón—Catalonia.

The *La Cucaracha* Group began to operate in the north, and the *As de Bastos* Group remained in central Spain, save for one squadron sent to Alfamén at the end of April, during the period when the pilots of the 2nd squadron of He 51s went to Seville to collect their new Fiats.

During the month of May the *Baleares* sailed to Cádiz for completion of its armament, and the *Canarias* to the Ferrol Arsenal. The *Almirante Cervera* was forced to remain on patrol in the Cantabrian sea and thus, following the sinking of the *Espana*, the Nationalist Fleet had only the two submarines recently acquired from Italy to keep watch in the Mediterranean.

At this time two new Italian squadrons were formed, the 31st and 32nd, led by Borgogno and Botto. These became part of the 6th Fighter Group, commanded by Leotta ('Leonello'), and this group later adopted the name *Gamba de Ferro* in honour of Capt Botto. Simultaneously with the expansion of their fighter force, the Nationalist Air Force was also increasing the number of reconnaissance and bomber aircraft in service.

Colacicchi, veteran captain of the Romeos, returned to Italy, leaving Sforza and Romagnoli as squadron leaders. Both were in the 'Linci' 22nd Group, commanded by Lt Col Franciosa. Raffaelli's 24th Group of Savoia S-M.81s was joined by a new group of fast Savoia S-M.79 bombers, newly-arrived from Italy and commanded by Aramu. These two groups together formed a new bomber squadron. General Bernasconi ('Garda') arrived from Italy to assume supreme command of the Legionary Air Force. Velardi remained in command of the aircraft deployed in Mallorca.

For the time being the bombers remained at Soria aerodrome, although on May 21st Aramu's S-M.79s moved temporarily to the south to attack the *Jaime I*, which was anchored in the port of Almería, and on May 31st attacked also the *Miguel de Cervantes* at Cartagena. The Romeos were transferred to Vitoria and Logroño. With this considerable increase in the strength of the Legionary Air Force, both sides were once again on an almost equal footing.

The Government still maintained superiority in fighters. They had at their disposal six squadrons of Ratas and six of Chatos, each squadron consisting of twelve aircraft. This provided a force of almost one hundred and fifty modern fighters, and disregards the secondary Nieuports, Dewoitines, Bulldogs and Letovs.

The Nationalists had eight Fiat squadrons each with nine aeroplanes and two more with six, as well as a squadron of twelve Messerschmitt Me 109Bs, giving a total of nearly one hundred modern fighters. They also had a total of thirty-six Heinkel He 51s from the 1st and 3rd squadrons of the Cóndor Legion's J-8 fighter group and Manrique Montero's 1-G-2 group.*

For army co-operation the Government had some Aeros and Gourdou Lesseurres, and three groups of Natachas and Rasantes. The Nationalists had the Italian Romeo group, two squadrons of Romeo Ro 37s, four of Heinkel He 46s and one of Heinkel He 45s (which began operating in April), each with six aircraft. Breguet 19s continued in use on both sides. Although the Government

* By the middle of March 1937, 147 Chatos, 62 Ratas, 45 Dewoitines, 8 Bulldogs and about 10 fighters of various kinds had arrived in Spain for service with the Government Air Force: these were soon followed by 31 Ratas in the spring, and in the summer 80 were received. By this time 150 Fiats, 63 Heinkel He 51s and 12 Me 109Bs had been supplied to the Nationalists and their Allies.

had numerical superiority in Army co-operation types, the quality of the Romeo Ro 37s and He 45s was superior. During the month of May a second squadron of He 45s was formed.

With regard to bomber aircraft, the Nationalists were beginning to gain numerical superiority. Although they still had inferior numbers of fast bombers (the Government had received 31 Katiuskas in October 1936, and a similar number was received in May, as opposed to twelve Savoia S-M.79s and twelve Heinkel He 111Bs delivered to the Nationalists), they had greater strength in heavy bombers. Against the Governments 40 Potez 54s and 15 Marcel Bloch M.B.210s, they could deploy 56 Junkers Ju 52s and 21 Savoia S-M.81s.

This numerical disadvantage was almost compensated, so far as the Government were concerned, by their DC-2s, Fokkers and Dragon Rapides of which there were about 20, as opposed to 8 or 9 in the Nationalist side. But at about this time both sides stopped using these types in a bomber role.

An appreciable number of American Lockheed, Northrop and Vultee aircraft arrived in the Government Zone, although seven of these were captured when the cruiser *Canarias* intercepted the merchant ship *Mar Cantábrico* on March 8th. This vessel was sailing to Santander, under the assumed name *Adda Castle*. Because of this event, arrangements were made for future consignments of American aircraft, and pilots of the same nationality, to disembark at the French port of Le Havre, completing their journey overland.

At this time some Dutch aircraft also reached the Government Zone. These comprised a number of Koolhoven F.K.51s and one prototype each of the Fokker C.X and D.XXI models, and they were nearly all sent to training schools in the east (Los Alcázares, San Javier, Palmar, Carmolí, Totana, etc) where they joined other light aircraft which had arrived from England and France, and machines from the pre-war aero clubs. These schools also had some two-seat Ratas and several multi-engined aircraft.

The first Bücker trainers arrived in the Nationalist Zone at the end of 1936, and they were used to form elementary flying training schools at Copero and Cáceres. The latter school was later transferred to Las Bardocas, in Badajoz. The Breguet 19s and the Polish PWSs continued in use until the arrival of Gothas, first at Copero and later at Jerez, and the school at Tablada used Fokkers. The first pilots from these schools went to their units in January 1937, followed by other courses in April, May and July 1937. The first three courses for other crew members (which were more vital than pilots at this date, since about fifty men with civil pilots' licences had started military flight training before the formation of the Copero School in November), were posted to units in January, March and May 1937. Prior to this, in August 1936, some short courses had been held at Tablada for machine-gunners and bomb aimers, titles which were not recognised officially until much later.

Summary of Fighter Operations until the Formation of the Morato Group

Initially, the Nationalist fighter force was based on the three Nieuport 52s which had been captured in Granada and subsequently modified in the *Parque Regional del Sur* (Southern Region Air Park). With these machines they achieved at least ten victories, four by Miguel Guerrero, and one by each of the following, in chronological order, Bermúdez de Castro, García Pardo, García Morato, Senra, Salas and Pérez y Martínez de la Victoria. Of the pilots who flew these aircraft, Fernández Tudela was shot down twice, but both times parachuted to safety. Cuesta was killed when his aircraft was hit by anti-aircraft fire and Caimon died in an accident. Bermúdez de Castro was hit by small-arms fire from the ground and received slight injuries.

Sixteen victories were achieved by the Heinkel He 51s, 6 in August –September 1936 (3 Morato and 3 Salvador), 1 in December (Manrique Montero's squadron) and 9 in April 1937 (2 Salas, 1 Arístides García López, Allende, Mazarredo, Muntadas, Ansaldo, Palmero and Martín Campos' squadron). Arija and Palmero were killed in air combats, Bofill in an accident, and Krug was seriously injured in a collision.

The Fiats, before the Morato group was formed, destroyed 23 aircraft and 1 balloon (Morato 14, Salas 4, Salvador 3 and the balloon, and Bermúdez de Castro and García Pardo one each). No Fiats were lost.

García Morato's score of victories was unequalled by any ally or enemy pilot throughout the war. The most outstanding German pilot during these early stages was Sgt Maj Ihlefeld. Later Lt Harder and Sub Lt Bodden each achieved seven victories, almost all in the summer of 1937, and their record was only beaten by Oesau, Schellmann and Mölders in the summer of 1938. Mölders held the final record for the Cóndor Legion, with a total of fourteen confirmed victories.

Lt Degli Incerti ('Tocci'), who achieved his eighth and final victory in October 1937, had only destroyed two machines three months earlier. The most outstanding Italian pilots prior to this were Lieutenant Adriano Mantelli de Parma ('Arrighi')and Sgt Maj Guido Presel ('Sammartano'), who was killed in battle at Biscay on June 4th.

On the Government side, Felipe del Río (who also died during the Biscay battle), was promoted to the rank of captain from April 13th, 1937, for destroying six aircraft. According to Tinker, his first captain, Andrés García La Calle had shot down eleven machines by February 1937. Manuel Aguirre López, the first Spanish leader of the Ratas group, also gained ten victories. Among other outstanding pilots at this time were Roberto Alonso Santamaría, who was promoted to captain on February 1st 1937 for war services, and who later led a Chato squadron in Aragón; Alfonso Jiménez Bruguet, who replaced García de La Calle when he went to Russia; and the naval pilots Juan Alonso Vega, who also led a squadron, and Javier Jover.

The Russian writer Koltsov attributed the destruction of ten aircraft (six fighters and four bombers) to the Frenchman Abel Guídes, and five victories were also attributed to the Frenchman Rayneau. The French writer Jean Giselon also quotes Jean Darry and Michel Bernay with having achieved three victories each by November 1936.

According to the American historian, Raymond F. Tollver, the Americans Frank G. Tinker and Albert G. Baumler each destroyed eight aircraft, but these figures were not achieved until July 1937. In fact, Tinker shot down his fifth aircraft on June 16th and his eighth on July 18th. Harold Dahl is reputed to have destroyed five aircraft, but this may be doubtful as Tollver does not quote Dahl amongst his country's aces.

Very little information is known about the Russian pilots, although *Pravda* published a list of seventeen fighter pilots who were "Heroes of the USSR". Eight victories were attributed to the Turkish-Russian Ahmed Amba and six to Commander Tarrasov. Serov and Yakushin, known in Spain as Carlos Castejón and Rodrigo Mateo, were the first two pilots in Spain to achieve victories during night operations. According to Yakushin, Eriómenko, Stepánov and Finn also shot down aircraft at night. Dahms also quotes Bjev, Cosjainov Serov and Tscherkassov as outstanding Russian pilots. Koltsov has written that during the two months from November 3rd 1936 to January 3rd 1937, Russian pilots shot down 70 aircraft. The squadron leader 'Pablo Palancar', who landed by parachute over Castellana, was reputed to have shot down one machine for every six and a half hours of flight, his total including four Heinkels on January 3rd. It is obvious that this information is exaggerated, for while it is possible that 'Palancar' might have shot down five aircraft, a total of 32 hours flying time for two very active months seems very little. In addition, the total number of seventy aircraft destroyed is much higher than the numbers claimed by official bulletins at that time.

The First Morato Group

When the pilots of the 2nd squadron of He 51s changed their aircraft for Fiat C.R.32s, this provided two squadrons of each type, and these were formed into two groups. The He 51 group took the designation 1-G-2 and remained under Captain Manrique Montero's command, the two squadrons being led by Corsini and Martín Campos.

The Fiat group, with the designation 2-G-3, was formed in Cordoba on May 4th from the squadrons led by Morato and Salas. Morato assumed command of the group, and Salvador took over leadership of his old squadron. As García Pardo and Bermúdez de Castro were senior to Salvador, they moved to the 2nd squadron, changing places with Jesús Rubio and Mazarredo. Initially the squadrons were made up as follows:

1-E-3: Salvador, Guerrero, Mazarredo, Vázquez Sagastizábal, Jesús Rubio, Arístides García López and Senra.

2-E-3: Salas, Bermúdez de Castro, García Pardo, Murcia, Allende, Ansaldo and Muntadas.

Therefore, counting Morato, there were fifteen pilots, but with a total of only thirteen aircraft. At that time Morato had eighteen victories to his credit, Salas seven, Salvador five and one balloon, Guerrero four, Bermúdez de Castro three, García Pardo two and Arístides García López, Senra, Allende, Ansaldo, Mazarredo and Muntadas one each. Captain Murcia and second lieutenants Jesús Rubio and Vázquez Sagastizábal had only been flying fighters for a short time, but their exceptional merit was obvious and was confirmed within a short space of time.

The thirteen aircraft of 2-G-3 were allocated Spanish serial numbers 3-51 to 3-63, and their factory numbers were respectively 44, 111, 262, 331, 508, 587, 589, 594, 596, 597, 598, 601 and 603.

It is worthwhile recording that in May and June these two squadrons did not lose a single aircraft and succeeded in shooting down twenty-six enemy machines. Only one of their pilots, 2nd Lt Arístides, received a slight injury. Although this seems incredible, it was brought about by the exceptional skill of the pilots and their battle tactics. Of the twenty-six aircraft destroyed twenty-one fell during the Huesca-Saragossa operations and the other five at La Granja, showing that the activities of the 2-G-3 Group were fundamental in both these offensives.

The Morato group began their operations in Córdoba, where they stayed until May 11th. At that time their efforts were concentrated on machine-gun and dive bombing attacks, but they found time also to escort the Junkers Ju 52s (Gil Mendizábal's Group by day and Carrillo's at night) and Rueda's and Baquera's Breguet 19 groups during their attacks on the recently-formed lines of the VII and VIII Government Army Corps (which later became the Extremadura Army) and sporadically on those of the IV Army Corps.

On May 12th the Morato group were transferred to Torrijos, where they remained until the 15th, and then moved to Saragossa. Until the end of the month they spent their time primarily in escorting the *Pavas* (Gancedo and Pérez Cela's squadrons), although Morato carried out some reconnaissance flights and took part in a night attack with an He 51 from Corsini's squadron. The other squadron of the He 51 group, that led by Martín Campos, had left for Biscay on May 1st, and from there they went to León on the 10th. When this squadron was operating in Burgos on May 7th, the leading pair (Simón and Comas) took off from Gamonal to intercept an enemy bomber, but this proved to be the Generalissimo's DC-2, whose arrival had not been announced.

The Organisation of the Air Forces

In the Government Zone the Navy's Air Force continued in existence until May 1937, complete with their own training schools, although the majority of their crews flew in land units. The Military Air Force also displayed a degree of versatility by retaining several units of seaplanes. During May, and two days before establishment of the Ministry of Defence, these two branches of the Air Force were brought together by formation of the Air Army. The personnel of the military and naval air forces and of the civil aviation service then became members of three new aviation forces, known respectively as the General Corps, Auxiliary Corps and Maestranza Aviación.

The land-based units then came under the control of eight Air Regions—Madrid, Murcia, Barcelona, Valencia, Ciudad Real, Santander, Albacete and Baeza—each of which was divided into several Sectors. The three pre-war Air Squadrons were replaced by Nos 1, 2 and 3 Air Regions. In January 1937 the Valencia Air Zone had been created to provide air support for the Teruel front, and this now became the 4th Region. The 5th Air Region was allocated to the autonomous Extremadura Group, which had split away from the Madrid Region. The Air Forces in the north became the 6th Region and finally, when the 2nd Region was broken up, the 7th and 8th Air Regions were formed, the latter's task being to support the Southern Army. The 2nd and the 7th Air Regions were not allocated to any particular front: the 2nd continued the pre-war function of the Murcia air base as Instruction Command; the 7th, based at Albacete, was in effect a staff college and the source of a general reserve.

The number of aerodromes prepared in each of these regions was fantastic, with thirty as a minimum, and up to one hundred in the 1st and 2nd Regions, making a total of some 400 aerodromes in the Government Zone. In the Alcalá de Henares, Barajas and Guadalajara sectors alone there were 54 aerodromes. The aerodromes were classified as permanent and special, permanent, semi-permanent, occasional and emergency, and according to their category had an establishments of 100, 50, 30, 8 or nil men respectively.

In the Nationalist Zone the three air regions, established in August 1936, were increased to four by formation of the Levante Air Region, which was commanded by Julio García de Caceres from Saragossa. White had been transferred from Logrõno to Seville, to assume control of the Southern Air Region, leaving Julian Rubio as leader of the Northern Air Region. José Rodríguez y Díaz de Lecea continued to lead the Central Region.

The number of aerodromes in the Nationalist Zone at this time was below one hundred. This number increased considerably at a later date, because of those captured in the north and Aragón, but it always remained inferior to the number in the Government Zone. At the beginning of the final offensive, in March 1939, the number of Nationalist aerodromes totalled 264.

The Nationalists did not have a Naval Air Force, although initially five Navy Savoia S-M.62s operated from the naval base at el Ferrol, and the fleet's Dornier-Wal's were subordinated to the naval base at Cádiz. The Atalayon (Melilla) seaplanes, which later operated from Cádiz and Mallorca, and the Cant Z.501s and Z.506s acquired in Italy, all came under the direct control of Air Headquarters, as well as the Cóndor Legion's Heinkel He 59s. The Heinkel He 60s, intended for operation from the cruisers *Canarias* and *Baleares* were flown by Navy pilots, but were also a component of Air Headquarters.

An Anti-Aircraft Service was established on February 19th 1937, as the result of an order, dated February 11th, which gave Air Headquarters the task of creating this service. This was divided into an Active Defence group, comprising fighter aircraft, anti-aircraft batteries, searchlights and sound locators; and a Passive Defence group, responsible for information, an observation network, air raid shelters, camouflage, alarm signals, and fire-fighting and de-contamination services. The observation network was divided into zones, with a central observation HQ and local posts. At the headquarters of the air regions an officer was placed in command of anti-aircraft operations.

Shortly after the formation of the Anti-aircraft Service, a booklet was published in Seville under Tomás Martín Barbadillo's direction. This contained thirty-six pages of information and twenty-four plates, and was virtually an early aircraft recognition manual. It gave details of all aircraft in use by both sides and, on the whole, was a fairly useful booklet, although there were some errors. These were caused by including the Martin Model 139 (B-10) and the Boeing P-26A as Government equipment, referring to Chatos as

Boeings, including an inaccurate drawing of the Rata, and omitting both the Natacha and Rasante. Another important error came from inclusion of the Polish-built P.Z.L. P.24 fighter amongst Nationalist equipment. It included, also, an accurate description of the Heinkel He 112 fighter and Junkers Ju 87 dive bomber, (later the famous Stuka), although at the time they had only flown briefly as prototypes and were not used in operations until much later.

In fact, German behaviour in respect of the Ju 87 was rather strange. It seemed they were loath to display this machine and even at the end of the war, in 1939, they took back to Germany the five examples of this type that had been sent to Spain, although they had neither been flown nor seen by the Spaniards.

Each copy of the 'aircraft recognition' manual was numbered, and it was classified as restricted. But this did not prevent several copies from arriving in the Government zone within a few days, together with their original recipients, who had been based at an anti-aircraft observation post in the Sierra Morena. In this way the Government received fairly comprehensive information of the various types of aircraft being used in the Nationalist Zone. Perhaps even more importantly, they learned that the Nationalists were ignorant of the operational capabilities of most of their aircraft, especially those from Russia.

Coincident with the receipt of this information, Government anti-aircraft defence was re-organised and centralised, coming under the overall control of the under-secretary for Air (Antonio Camacho, who had replaced Ángel Pastor). On May 3rd the DECA (Special Anti-Aircraft Defence Group) was formed, this controlling the Anti-Aircraft No I Group; searchlight units; radio communications; the anti-aircraft batteries of the Artillery Regiments on the coast, No 3 (Cartagena) and 4 (Mahón); the local defences, searchlights and anti-aircraft batteries.

The Government's anti-aircraft guns were not particularly efficient until the battle at Brunete, and by the battle of Teruel the anti-aircraft defences of both sides were proving to be most effective. The Cóndor Legion used the magnificent 88mm anti-aircraft guns, which were used also as anti-tank weapons; there were eventually five batteries of these guns, which were usually sited in forward areas. Nationalist aerodromes, on the whole, were badly protected, although at the end of 1937 they acquired a number of 75 mm anti-aircraft weapons which helped to improve the situation.

The organisation of the Nationalist Air Units was also disturbed during the months of May and June. The five Breguet groups (each with six aircraft) were reduced to two, these retaining the designation 1-G-10 and 2-G-10. The first remained under Baquera's command, with one squadron in Granada (Micheo, later Antonio Bazán) and the other in Córdoba (A. Bazán, later Guitar). Group 2-G-10 remained in Africa, its two squadrons being led by Martínez Mejías (later Jofre), and Recuenco. The He 46 group became designated 3-G-11 and the Romeos 4-G-12. José Pérez Pardo took command of 3-G-11, with Gancedo and Pérez Cela leading its two squadrons, while Ansaldo remained in command of 4-G-12 for some time. The old Lasarte Breguet group became 5-G-17 (with Czech Aero-101 aircraft), and Antonio Llorente replaced Llop in command. The León Breguet group then became equipped with He 45 aircraft and Eyarlar handed over command to Cipriano Rodríguez. As we have already seen, the 1-G-2 and 2-G-3 fighter groups remained under the command of Montero and Morato.

Luis Pardo's first Junkers group was disbanded, some of the aircraft being sent to the Blind Flying School at Olmedo. The remainder were used to form a night bomber squadron, led by Bengoechea and which, together with Haya's squadron, formed group 1-G-22 commanded by Carrillo. Eduardo González Gallarza assumed command of group 2-G-22, with Eduardo Prado and Pedro Atauri as squadron leaders.

At this time the Germans withdrew three He 70s from the Cóndor Legion's reconnaissance squadron, these being replaced by the more modern Dornier Do 17Fs, nicknamed *Bacalaos* (Cod).

Manuel Martínez Merino replaced Julio Meléndez in command of the Cádiz seaplane group (Dornier-Wals), and Enrique de la Puente's squadron from this group was sent to operate in the Cantabrian sea area. The Mallorca seaplane group, with its Cant Z.501s, continued under the command of Federico Noreña, with squadrons led by Antonio Soriano and Carlos Pombo. Noreña later took over command in Pollensa after Miguel Ruiz de la Puente's death.

Antonio Llop was placed in command of the Crew Training School, which was then at Logrono. Gerardo Fernández Pérez continued at the head of the pilots' school and Juan Prieto was nominated commander of a new elementary school being formed in Cáceres, and which was transferred to Badajoz (Las Bardocas), soon afterwards.

At this time two specialist schools were established, one in Tetuan, led by Reixa; the other was at Málaga, founded by Colonel Sabatucci in collaboration with Francisco Iglesias Brage.

The Condor Legion at this stage comprised:

(1) Combat Group J-88, with two squadrons of He 51s and one of Me 109Bs (although Galland has mistakenly written that there were two). The group leader was then von Merhard, replaced by Handrick at the beginning of July. After Palm's death, the squadrons were led by Pitcarin, Lützow, and Harder. The official designation of these squadrons derived by placing a numeral prefix to the group numbers, thus 1/JG-88 etc. They were, however, more commonly known by the nicknames 'Marabau', 'Zylinder Hut' and 'Mickey Mouse'. The 2nd squadron (2/JG-88) was the one equipped with Me-109s, their nickname deriving from a joke that their faster speed was attributed to an extra cylinder (Zylinder).

The 4th squadron, the *Wilder Jäger*, had been disbanded at the beginning of the year.

(2) Bomber Group K-88, with two squadrons of Ju 52s and one of Heinkel He 111Bs, which was commanded initially by Fuchs and later by Wehnert. One of the Ju 52 squadrons continued to be led by von Morau until the end of July 1937.

(3) Reconnaissance Squadron A-88, with three patrols of He 70s and one of Do 17Fs, commanded by Kessel.
(4) A small squadron of dive bombers, VB-88, equipped with Henschel Hs 123s, a biplane powered by a BMW nine-cylinder radial engine, which was known in Spain as *Angelito* (Little Angel).
(5) A squadron of two-seat Heinkel He 59 seaplanes, A-88, which were nicknamed 'Zapatones' (Big Shoes), because of their large floats.
(6) Some Junkers Ju 52 transport aircraft.
(7) Seven anti-aircraft batteries, four heavy and three light. At a later stage there were nine batteries, two of them mixed German-Spanish.

The Cóndor Legion was led by Hugo von Sperrle (known in Spain as Sander) until the end of the Northern Campaign, with von Richthofen as chief of staff.

In the Government Air Force No 11 Fighter Squadron was formed, made up of Group 21 Ratas and Group 26 Chatos. It was led initially by the Russian Colonels Pablo and Julio, who were later joined by the Russian José, formerly the leader of a Chato Squadron. At that time all the Rata squadrons were led by Russians: Ujov, Lockiev, Goofy, Pligunov, Boris Smirnov, etc. Of the seven Chato squadrons, three were led by Spaniards, comprising those led originally by Roberto Alonso Santamaría, Andrés García La Calle, and the Basque Squadron. These were now led by Aguirre, Jimenez and Jover. The other Chato squadrons were led by the Russians I. Eriómenko (later Serov), I. Lakéiev, G. Pleschenko and possibly the American Dickinson. The group commander was Evggueni Ptujin.

There were three groups of Natachas, No 20 (Moreno Miró), Nos 25 and 30, one Russian group of Rasantes, another of Aeros, as well as the Koolhovens, Gourdou Lesseurre and Potez 25s from the north.

So far as bombers were concerned, there were 12 and 24 Groups with Katiuskas (Zlatotsvietov and Arcega), the Mixed Group No 22 (Núñez Maza), the Potez and Marcel Bloch groups. With these, No 5 squadron was formed, led initially by Alfredo Tourné. Later No 7 squadron was formed, from Nos 71, 72 and 73 groups, and the No 28 group of German aircraft.

Although the Government Air Forces were commanded theoretically by Hidalgo de Cisneros, in fact, the Russian General 'Douglas' (Smushkévich) was the man who made the important decisions.

Therefore, by way of summary, at this time there were 13 Government fighter squadrons (6 of Ratas, all Russian, and 7 of Chatos, of which three were Spanish), opposing 11 Nationalist fighter squadrons, 10 of Fiats (including those from the Morato group) and 1 of Me 109Bs. In this summary no account is taken of the out-of-date fighters, the He 51s on the Nationalist side and the Dewoitine, Letov, Bristol Bulldog and Nieuport Delage ND.52 aircraft used on the Government side.

So far as bombers were concerned, there was a predominance of outdated machines on both sides, Ju 52s and S-M.81s on the Nationalist side; Potez 54s and Marcel Bloch machines in Government service; as well as Fokkers and Dragon Rapides on both sides. The Popular Army had a group of 31 magnificent, light, twin-engined Katiuskas, with a large number in reserve at this time, opposing a squadron of 12 He 111Bs (twin-engined) and a similar number of S-M.79s (a fast three-engined aircraft). In all there were a total of about 100 bomber aircraft on each side.

In reconnaissance and army co-operation machines (ignoring the old Breguets which were nearly all obsolete), there were 6 groups in the Government Zone, equipped with Natachas, Rasantes and Aeros, all known as *Papagayos* (Parrots) in the Nationalist Zone, Koolhovens and Gourdour Lesseures, opposing 4 Nationalist Groups comprising He 46, He 45, Ro 37 and Aeros. For reconnaissance and light bombing operations Vultee V-1As and Heinkel He 70s, nicknamed *Rayos* (Lightning), were used by the Government and Nationalists respectively. These were modern aircraft, but were very scarce, with no more than a dozen on each side.

It is clear that at this period the Government still had superior numbers of fighters and light bombers, that the numbers of army co-operation and reconnaissance aircraft were about equal, and that Nationalist Air Forces had slightly more heavy bombers. So far as seaplanes were concerned, the Government side had a superior number of Dornier-Wals, but the Nationalists had a squadron of He 59s, six Cant Z.501s and four He 60s. Only the twin-engined He 59s had sufficient range for deep penetrations over land.

The Chatos are Moved to Santander

As we have seen, the Government held overall numerical superiority in fighters, but their inferior numbers in Biscay were very obvious, especially at the time when the fate of Bilbao was being decided as, in fact, was the fate of the whole war.

The logical action would have been to try and divert the main action to areas far away from Biscay (for which the offensive in Extremadura had been planned by Largo Caballero), and to reinforce the fighters in the north. The Extremadura offensive which was abandoned for political reasons was replaced, at a later date, by those at La Granja and Huesca.

As a result of street fighting in Barcelona, Alonso Jiménez Bruguet's squadron of Chatos was sent to Catalonia. It was divided into two flights, one of which remained in Reus under Gerardo Gil's command.

On Saturday May 8th, the day following an armistice in Barcelona, 15 Chatos and a Douglas DC-2, with Jiménez Bruguet in the lead, took off from Lérida and crossed the French frontier through the valley of the River Ariége, *en route* for Toulouse, where the sixteen aircraft landed at 09.30hrs, on the Francazal aerodrome. Here they were refuelled and prepared for the next stage of their flight. It is difficult to understand why the Valencian Government decided to have this stop at Toulouse, when the aircraft could quite easily have made the direct flight to Santander or Bilbao. At Toulouse they were, in fact, slightly more distant from their final goal than they had been at the moment of take off from Lérida. Also, at Toulouse, the French had instituted a Control Committee, which had been in operation since April 20th, and they insisted that the Spanish aircraft must return to their own country, crossing the frontier at the point of original entry. Strangely, they did not disarm them, although the French aircraft which escorted them over the border were themselves unarmed. On Sunday May 9th fifteen of the aircraft returned to Spain, leaving one behind at Toulouse in an unserviceable condition.

By this time the Navarrese Brigades had occupied Sollube and Bizcargui, which held a dominating position in the Iron Ring around Bilbao, but Euzcadi's forces were counter-attacking furiously.

The Spanish pilots from La Calle and Santamaría's old squadrons were based at Campo Soto, on the Duke of Albuquerque's farm, and these were under the overall command of Jover. The flight led by Gerardo Gil, which had remained in Reus, now returned to Madrid, although their leader had to force-land *en route* because of a mechanical failure.

On May 13th, a fresh attempt was made to send an expeditionary squadron to the Bilbao front. The aircraft selected for this squadron made an ostentatious departure along the route Campo Soto, Madrid, Alcalá, Guadalajara, suggesting that they were to attempt a direct flight north, as Mola's forces were getting closer to the Iron Ring. In fact, they then returned to Campo Soto and set out for Manises, where they were received by the Minister for Sea and Air and ordered to fly to Lérida. From there, on May 17th, Jover took off for France, with his reinforced squadron of Chatos, which was accompanied by two Douglas DC-2s, and several Natachas under Juan Alonso Vega's command.

This time they took a northern route from Lérida, and entered France via the Luchon Valley. Weather conditions in the mountain area were appalling, and the squadron battled through a snowstorm which made it extremely difficult to fly in formation. Fifteen Chatos, with the two DC-2s in the lead, gingerly threaded their way between the peaks of Tourmalet and Aspin. Eventually, some of the aircraft arrived safely at their destination, Port Long aerodrome at Pau. A Chato patrol from Zarauza and some of the Natachas turned back; others landed at Toulouse.

Due to the weather conditions, which were pretty grim even at Pau, it proved impossible to refuel the aircraft quickly so that they could continue to Bilbao. Once again, this gave the French Control Committee sufficient time to intervene and prevent the aircraft from taking off again.

On the first day that the expeditionary squadron was in Pau their leader was arrested, with the result that the world press learnt of the landing.

All the Italian and German newspapers detailed the happening. Within three days the French Communist press was in full spate, protesting that the aircraft were still being held in France. Eventually, the French Government decided to disarm the machines, with the exception of three which would have to serve as escorts in the event that they were attacked by Nationalist aircraft on their return flight into Spain. This flight was made on May 22nd.

At about this date, Gerardo Gil travelled by road to Algete aerodrome, where there were five Chatos which needed to be flown to La Albericia (Santander). He made arrangements and soon had four other pilots with whom he ferried the aircraft.

The arrival of fighter reinforcements in the North could not have been delayed any longer, as the 4th Navarre Brigade was beginning to advance along the direct road from Vitoria to Bilbao. Days later the 3rd Brigade was threatening Orduña and Amurrio, on the Burgos-Bilbao road.

Jover's squadron, based at Algete, and then led by Riverola, were ordered to the Cantabrian coast. On May 27th, eve of the beginning of a new offensive intended to divert troops from La Granja, Riverola led his squadron of Chatos to a new base at La Albericia: it could hardly be regarded as a successful operation. Of the twelve Chatos which left Algete, nine got lost *en route* and arrived over high country near San Sebastián. Here they met fierce fire from the ground and one of the fighters was hit and forced to crash-land, the pilot being taken prisoner; a second fighter was shot down shortly afterwards in a combat over Bilbao. One patrol of three aircraft maintained a correct route and arrived without incident at Santander.

Coincident with the arrival of these aircraft at their destination the entire north-eastern front, represented by the 'Iron Ring' stretching from Peña Lemona to the sea, erupted into battle.

But despite the battles fought on the ground, two fighter squadrons, with some of the most experienced Spanish pilots, remained inactive throughout almost the whole of May.

The arrival of 15 Chatos in Bilbao on May 8th should have balanced out local aerial potential on both sides, and one can imagine the consequences this could have had on the course of operations. But by the end of May the arrival of these Chatos had achieved nothing more than counteracting partially the effect of 18 new Fiats received by the Nationalists. They were unable to prevent a break-through into the 'Iron Ring' in front of Bilbao, an action in which Nationalist bombers played a very active part, and one which foretold the outcome of the war.

The Battle at La Granja

As a result of the battle being fought at La Granja, Group 2-G-3 was moved from Saragossa to Ávila on June 1st. *En route* they surprised a Government column at Navacerrada and, despite strong anti-aircraft fire, strafed the enemy with machine-gun fire at low level. On the same day the whole group, with the exception of two machines left in reserve, escorted Ansaldo's Romeo Ro 37s (also based at Ávila) in an attack near La Granja. This task completed, the Fiats made low-level sorties over the enemy lines, making machine-gun and dive-bombing attacks on armoured vehicles and, once again, they encountered fierce anti-aircraft fire.

On the Government side, Tinker made three sorties with his Rata squadron, accompanying fifteen Rasantes, but they did not encounter any enemy aircraft. According to Tinker, the Commander of the Russian Air Force, Smushkévich, arrived in Albacete that day, piloting a Chato.

Because of the scarcity of Nationalist fighters, Morato ordered the maintenance of a standing patrol from June 2nd, and this consisted of two aircraft at a time. When Guerrero and Vázquez Sagastizábal were on patrol, they destroyed two Rasantes and machine-gunned a Chato which beat a hasty retreat. During another of these patrols Jesús Rubio Paz shot down one Rata and one Rasante, and then continued his routine patrol for another thirty minutes until he was relieved. For this action his name was put forward for a Military Medal, and this was awarded some years later. On the same day two Fiat squadrons from the *As de Bastos* group, led by the veterans Nobili and Larsimont, arrived in the North to fight against Tinker's squadron.

According to Tinker, on the third sortie the Ratas shot down three Fiats, without suffering any losses, and on the fourth they fought against fifty Fiats and Heinkels, shooting down nine. Their own losses included one Rata from another squadron, the Russian leader of a Chato squadron and a Rasante piloted by the American Eugene Finnick. Tinker claimed the destruction of one Fiat.

The Government Air Force bulletin quoted three sorties on that day: in the first, seventeen aircraft from Group 20, four bombers from Group 15, seven Ratas and twelve Chatos, took off at 06.25hrs, but did not encounter the enemy. In a second sortie at 13.30hrs, six patrols from Group 20 went out and lost one aeroplane. In the final sortie of the day, at 17.30hrs, thirteen Ratas and twelve Chatos destroyed six or seven enemy aircraft that were escorting four bombers. The twin-engined aircraft from Group 12 were not in operation that day.

According to Degli Incerti 'Tocci', Leader of the 3rd Fiat Squadron, who remained at Olmedo to protect Salamanca and Valladolid, his companions fought against thirty fighters and five Rasantes on that day, of which four and three were destroyed respectively. The Nationalist Air Force bulletin claimed the destruction of ten Chatos, two Ratas and three Douglas aircraft.

On June 3rd Tinker's squadron of Ratas was not involved in operations, although the Government bulletin stated that seventeen Ratas and nine Chatos took off. Morato's Fiats went to the key sector at Cabeza Grande, where they dive-bombed the anti-aircraft batteries, and strafed two tanks and the enemy trenches. The first squadron of Aero 101s, led by Captain Cárdenas, attacked enemy concentrations in the valley situated behind the Cogorros.

Also on June 3rd, General Mola was killed in a flying accident. Despite bad weather, he refused to postpone his journey from the Biscay front to the Headquarters of the Northern Army in Valladolid, probably because he was worried about the situation at La Granja, where he knew that General Varela was involved in a fierce battle and that he had no reserves available.

Only days before he had sent his chief of operations to Segovia, to check with Varela on the minimum number of reinforcements needed to contain the attack. Taboada arrived just as Varela had organised his last reserve company, comprising office staff and wounded men, and was travelling to the front to direct the counter-attack personally. Varela, with typical idiosyncrasy, insisted to Taboada that: "I do not need any reinforcements, and what upsets me most is that Moriones should have attacked at this point, knowing that I am here".

Moriones was leader of the 1st Government Army Corps, which was defending the Madrid Sierra with Divisions I (Cueto), 2 (Cuevas) and 3 (Fernández Heredia). The attack took place in the 2nd Division's sector, with troops from Divisions 34 (J. Galán)and 35 (Walter), which had belonged to the disbanded

Vth Army Corps, all operating under Moriones command. Varela, who had to cover approximately the 1st Corps' Sector, had only the Ávila Division to hold the attack. This had recently been redesignated Division 75 and, days after, was again redesignated Division 71.

This offensive was the first organised by Prieto in his new office as Minister of Defence, and its objective was to prevent the attack on Bilbao and to occupy Segovia, unless the extent of their victory was such that they could attempt to attack in other directions.

The main action was entrusted to Brigades 14 (Dumont) and 31 (Cacho), the latter from the 2nd Division (Cuevas), and they were both under Walter's orders. The 14th International Brigade arrived at Balsaín, and Brigade 31 arrived within a mile of La Granja at midday on May 30th. Meanwhile, the 69th Brigade (Durán) was attempting to occupy Cabeza Grande, with air and tank support. During a second attack, Brigades 29 and 30 joined in.

On May 31st the 21 Brigade (De Pablo), which also came from the V Army Corps, reinforced the attack being made by the 14th and 69th Brigades, and they finally succeeded in occupying Cabeza Grande; throughout this day there were five attacks and counter-attacks, with the air forces of both sides providing support.

On June 1st Varela recovered Cabeza Grande, and the situation was consolidated by the arrival of some battalions from the 13 Division (Barrón). On that day Nationalist aircraft attacked the Headquarters of the Army Corps and on the next two days the Headquarters of the 34 Division. Galán failed at Cabeza Grande and Walter was unable to occupy La Granja, in spite of the intervention of the new 3rd Brigade.

Morato, as we have seen earlier, organised a standing patrol with his Fiats operating in pairs, and this led to several air combats.

On June 3rd the incessant activity of the Nationalist Air Force, which had now been increased by intervention of the Spanish Ju 52s from Olmedo, was hardly being counteracted by their opponents. On the night of the 4th Moriones ordered their withdrawal.

On the same day, whilst two Fiats flown by Salas and Garcia Pardo were on patrol, they were in combat against Ratas on three occasions. Morato shot down one when he arrived with Mazarredo to relieve Salas and Pardo. Also on that day, according to Tinker, his squadron leader Ujov shot down a solitary Fiat, while the Government bulletin claimed two Fiats as destroyed. On June 5th eight Fiats from the Morato group reconnoitred the whole sector Mujer Muerta—Navacerrada—El Paular without meeting opposition, and then returned to attack the anti-aircraft battery at Reventón.

Two days earlier General Varela had sent telegrams of congratulations to the leader of the Central Air Forces (Lecea) and to the Air Chief (General Kindelán). The first stated: "The behaviour of the Air Units and the activity of the fighter patrols merit special rewards, particularly for today. Suggest collective and individual rewards which I will send". Lecea sent enthusiastic congratulations to Group 2-G-3 for their activities at La Granja. For the part they played in this battle and later at Brunete and Belchite, the *As de Bastos* Group was jointly awarded the Military Medal.

When the battle at La Granja ended, the National Army was re-organised and a Central Army (Saliquet) was created as a separate unit from the Northern Army, where Dávila replaced the deceased Mola.

The information given by the three main Government leaders regarding this offensive shows that they had little faith in the ability of their own Air Force to provide cover or support, although one must remember that they had to blame their own failure on someone.

This is the text of what Moriones wrote:

"The action of the Air Force was not only deficient but bad and often prejudicial . . . their low efficiency and the length of their attacks, as opposed to the constant enemy activity, produced demoralising effects on our forces . . . Our Air Force carried out their bombing attacks hastily and from a great height . . . our fighters wisely stayed at a respectable height and seldom came down to fire at the enemy . . . In the air battles . . . they were far the weakest side.

"The enemy Air Force operated with extraordinary efficiency. Their bombers attacked our positions accurately at slow speed, at low level and with great determination, making it impossible, as at La Granja, for our forces to stand fast. The fighters, in daring attacks, came down low and machine-gunned our forces, including the Paris anti-aircraft battery . . . They did not stop their vigilance and reconnaissance flights continued throughout the whole day, their aircraft continually relieving one another."

Walter expressed himself in similar vein:

"We cannot say that our Air Force did not help us, but their help was certainly not noticeable over our lines. Their lack of punctuality and their very brief intervention greatly reduced their efficiency. My impression is that they could have done much more than they did to help the whole operation."

Other fragments commented:

"Our aircraft always arrived late . . . they were only active for a very short time . . . they just left it to the enemy air force which was master of the sky, bombing and machine-gunning our lines and even our Headquarters."

José María Galán wrote:

"The enemy aircraft were always masters of the air . . . they were continually over our lines . . . Whenever we asked for our Air Force they arrived so late that their help was of little use . . . their delays caused critical moments since infantry movements had to be carried out not under the cover of our own Air Force, but under the persistent fire of the enemy Air Force."

This constant presence of the Nationalist Air Force over the front, as shown unanimously by the Government leaders, was carried out by the 13 aircraft of the Morato group, and is related to in the following previously unpublished article by one of the members of the group, the ill-fated Captain García Pardo:

"Red Offensive Over Segovia"
"Urgent call to Ávila—journey Saragossa to Ávila—Morato 'looks out' at Puerto de Guadarrama to see what is going on—lorries!—How many? . . . Since the beginning of the war we had not seen greater numbers—the troops at the front were visible—Morato dives to machine-gun. S. follows him and then me—white clouds—anti-aircraft guns!—white barrier at 650ft (200m)—I cross it almost without thinking what it was. The second patrol cannot join in yet—we climb at full speed—bullets surround us and continue, we are not above them yet!

"Morato tells L. of a wonderful objective—they do not take any notice of him—on the ground they urge: we must recover Cabeza Gordo—Morato says 'We could have nipped the offensive in the bud without abandoning this objective.'

"Thanks to the operation Cabeza Gordo became ours again—the land forces are suffering a very harsh counter-attack—that same position was conquered twice by the enemy. The enemy air force, arriving in large groups, attacks the forces which can hardly contain the avalanche.

"We must free our forces from Air Force attacks! How? Morato takes charge of the direct defence of the forces. With twelve planes altogether he promises to mount a permanent patrol. The rest of the fighters (Olmedo group) will assist them. At Aeronautical Command there is little faith in Morato's resolution—how many planes will be constantly in the air on watch over the front?: Two.

"It seemed impossible for them to be effective against the masses of enemy fighters. Morato trusted in the tactics which had already been tried out over the Córdoba front. This resulted in circumstances favourable to us, when the Reds on their return flight from the front had to cross a 6,500 foot (2,000m) mountain range. To make the most of this advantage an order was given that the pair should never fly lower than the height of the mountain range.

"The permanent patrol began at dawn on that day. S. and I went out —greetings from the anti-aircraft guns—low, less than 5,000ft (1,500m) from the ground, and revolving around the same point we were a tempting target —first a few minutes of 'hopeful firing'—then shooting ceases. I think: 'their guns must have got hot'. We continue passing across the lines—more shooting. To divert them S. takes us low over the hill where the battery is situated—for a few moments they fire furiously—suddenly they stop and do not shoot again for the remaining hour and a quarter.

"The pairs are relieved—the anti-aircraft guns open fire a few more times during the morning—not once in the afternoon.

"Telephone call about the battle—a large number of Rasantes have arrived, escorted by Ratas and Curtis—the pair on patrol attack them.

"Another battle: this time the enemy's appearance coincides with the presence of two fighter squadrons on an offensive patrol at the front—the battle, begun by the pair on patrol, turns into a disaster for the enemy fighters.

"The bombings stop. On another day the pairs on patrol take advantage of

Top: First Morato Group (2-G-3) in June 1937. Muntadas, Allende, Salas, Morato, Arístides, Salvador, Murcía, Bermudez de Castro, Senra, Garcia Pardo, Joaquín Ansaldo, Jesús Rubio, Miguel Guerrero, Mazarredo y Vázquez Sagastizábal./*General Murcia*

Above: Manrique Montero's Fiat squadron (4-E-3) in January 1938: Santamaría, Velaz de Medrano, Figueroa, Barranco, Montero, Vela, Noguera, Núñez and Gil Escoain./*Región Aérea del Estrecho*

Top left: Pilots who joined 3-G-3 in February 1938: O'Connor, Lacour, Jurado, Vela, G. a Díaz and Bartolomé./ *Región Aérea del Estrecho*

Left: Morato with his three squadron commanders (Murcia, Barranco and Gautier), with other pilots of 3-G-3 in July 1938.

Above: Bravo, commander of 21 Group's 3rd Squadron, receives the barber's attention alongside his aircraft. The 'double-six' domino was the squadron's emblem./*Ministerio de Información y Turismo*

Right: Morato and Salas, leaders of the two Fiat fighter groups./*Teniente General Salas*

249

Top left: Tarazona, who succeeded Bravo as commander of the 3rd Squadron, is photographed in Rata CM-249./*Ministerio de Información y Turismo*

Left: A 'Super-Rata', a developed version of the original I-16, seen at Valls aerodrome.

Above and right: The Russian-built Tupolev SB-2 (ANT-40) 'Katiuska', most effective bomber in Government service. The two shown in flight are captured aircraft bearing Nationalist insignia./*Maestranza Aérea de Tablada, Región Aérea del Estrecho*

Top: Comas' I-15 'Chato at Liria aerodrome. The white square on the fin identifies the aircraft as that of the squadron leader.

Above: A group of Government fighter pilots at Santander (Comas, Zambudio, Panadero, Feo and Morquillas).

Top: The Savoia-Marchetti S.M.79-1, a fast Italian bomber, was used most widely./*Sánchez Gallicher*

Above: Another Italian bomber type was the Fiat B.R.20, which had a greater level speed than the Fiat C.R. 32 fighter. The aircraft was photographed after an unhappy entanglement with orange trees./*Maestranza Aérea de Tablada*

Top and above: Heinkel He 111B-2, which entered service with the Cóndor Legion at the beginning of 1937./*Región Aérea del Estrecho*

Top: In Nationalist insignia, a Vultee V-1A, an American-built transport aircraft, imported and adapted for use as a bomber./*Región Aérea del Estrecho*

Above: Polikarpov R-5 'Natasha', a lightweight bomber which was used in an army co-operation role by Government forces from October 1936./*Balaguer*

Top: The Czechoslovakian-built Aero A 101 medium bomber, which saw service in the Civil War from early 1937./ *Ministerio de Información y Turismo*

Above: Polish-built P.Z.L P. 23 bomber-reconnaissance aircraft in the spring of 1938./*Balaguer*

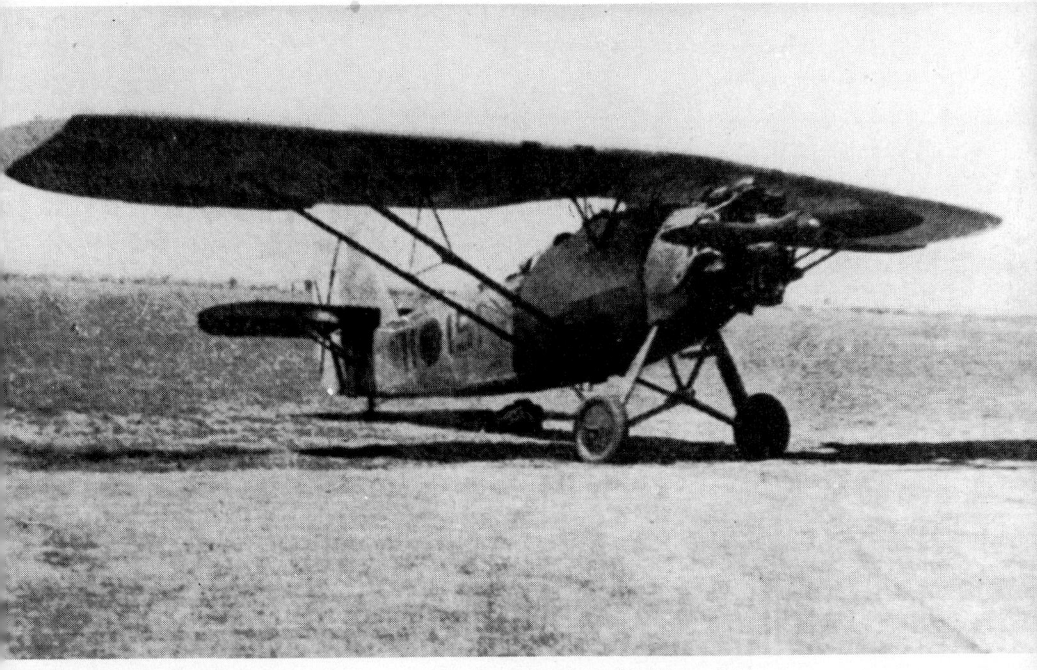

Top: Romeo Ro 37, built by the Meridionali company. A lightweight reconnaissance/army co-operation aircraft, it saw service from October 1936./*Región Aérea del Estrecho*

Above: Heinkel He 46 ('Pava'), short-range reconnaissance and army co-operation aircraft, which was service in Spain in September 1936./*Aviación*

Top: Heinkel He 45 ('Pavo') light bomber, serving in Spain in early 1937./*Región Aérea del Estrecho*

Above: Lockheed Electra civil transport aircraft imported from the USA./*Guereta*

Dornier Do 17F-1 (*top*) and Do 17P-1 (*above*) which served as light bomber/reconnaissance aircraft with the Cóndor Legion in Spain./*Sanchez Gallicher, Balaguer*

Top: A formation of Heinkel He 70Fs, used for reconnaissance and light bombing attacks./*Sanchez Gallicher*

Above: Built by the Canadian Car and Foundry Co, this two-seat biplane fighter was evolved from the Grumman FF-1. About 40 reached Spain, sold to that country by Turkey./*Balaguer*

Top: A Fiat of Morato's group damaged by enemy fire./*Maestranza Aérea de Tablada*

Above: Messerschmitt Me 109E, one of the more modern fighter aircraft which began to arrive in Spain in 1939./*La Hispano Aviación*

Top: Fiat G.50./*Servicio Cartografico y Fotografico del Aire*

Above: Heinkel He 112B-0./*Servicio Cartografico y Fotografico del Aire*

the low cloud closing in on the Sierra and spend their time harassing the forces on the ground, machine-gunning the trenches and lorries. The morale of our soldiers is increasing—the movement of vehicles along the tracks in the pine forests has almost stopped—we also realise that everything that is happening on the front seems to be revolving around the same place.

"Attack on the anti-aircraft batteries to attract attention, then he attacks with further supplies of 30kg bombs; the bombs fall amongst the guns—he has surprised them by flying through the valleys.

"The enemy, in large formations (eight or ten bombers and fifteen or twenty fighters) tries to retaliate, but on seeing our pair on patrol they decide not to cross the Sierra; slight skirmishes when another pair comes to relieve those already there; perhaps they thought we had more fighters following them.

"The offensive ended. Without a doubt the permanent pair on patrol influenced the Red failure. The Olmedo group understood the meaning of our operations perfectly, and when they were not out on an escorting mission they sent squadrons on an offensive patrol as frequently as possible."

The great difference, so far as the number of rival aeroplanes over the front is concerned, cannot be explained by an unequal distance from their respective aerodromes, since Ávila and Olmedo were no nearer to the front than Alcalá de Henares, Algete, Campo Soto and the remaining aerodromes in the Jarama Valley. Staying on patrol over the front until their fuel was almost exhausted was one of the tactics used throughout the war by the Spanish Nationalist fighters, and to a lesser degree by the Italians. This was never imitated by the German or Russian fighters, nor by the Spanish Government forces, thus reducing their time on patrol at the front.

The Battle of Huesca

In May 1937, after the struggle against the anarchists in Barcelona and the change of Government which this produced, the Eastern Army was formed, with the I, X and XII Army Corps being created in June. The Teruel front continued to be separate, with the XIII Army Corps being organised there on June 12th, 1937; later the XIX Army Corps was also established there, and both formed the basis of the Mediterranean Army.

In the Saragossa sector the Maciá Company, *Jovert, Durruti* and *Carlos Marx* Divisions were operating, and these became designated Nos 30, 25, 26, and 27 respectively, when they were incorporated in the XI and XII Army Corps. The X Army Corps remained in Huesca, with Divisions 28 and 29 (formerly 'Ascaso' and 'Lenin') and the Alpine Brigade, although Division 29 was disbanded on July 17th for failing to conform to the political evolution, but was later reformed in the Extremadura Army.

Before the creation of the X Army Corps, the Huesca sector organised two groups for operations in the June offensive under the command of Colonels Guillermo de la Peña and González Morales. One of the columns from the Northern Group remained under the command of General Lukacs, who had moved from Madrid to Aragon with his XII International Brigade. Nos 49, 72 and 108 mixed brigades had also arrived in Aragon. In this offensive Nos 25, 28 and 29 Divisions, one brigade from No 27 Division and two battalions of No. 31 Division, all from the Eastern Army, took part.

On June 10th, fighter Group 2-G-3 moved from Avila to Saragossa to reinforce Corsini's squadron of He 51s and the He 46 group (José Pérez Pardo), since the Nationalist leaders were aware that an attack on Huesca was imminent.

On June 11th the Ratas squadrons, led by Ujov and Lockiev, arrived at Barbastro. These were flown by Russian pilots, with the exception of the Americans Tinker and Baumler. These squadrons, which came from Alcalá, made the flight with two stops; one at Manises, the other at Liria. In fact, they would have been much more useful in Biscay, where on that same day the attack on the 'Iron Ring' was beginning.

On the same day that the Ratas arrived, in preparation for the offensive at Huesca, Government bombers made repeated attacks on Saragossa. During the various battles that followed, the Morato group destroyed five aircraft, Salvador and Vázquez Sagastizábal destroying two each; the fifth victory was claimed by Arístides García López. The aircraft destroyed were two Ratas (Vázquez and Arístides), one Potez (Vázquez) and two Rasantes (Salvador). On that day many of the pilots of the group were involved in five sorties, and Salvador made six.

On June 12th Tinker made five sorties, escorting Rasantes and Katiuskas (Groups 20 and 24), but he made no mention of combat with enemy aircraft. However, on that day, 2-G-3 had two confrontations with Ratas. During their second sortie over Huesca, made by two patrols of four machines, they encountered a formation of Ratas and destroyed four, the victories going to Salvador, García Pardo, Bermudez de Castro and Arístides. This is perhaps the combat to which Tinker refers as being between Fiats and another squadron of Ratas on the 13th.

Also on June 12th, during a patrol over the Huesca front, which was flown by Morato, Salas and Guerrero, four tanks were attacked with machine-gun fire and light bombs. In his book *Guerra en el Aire (War in the Air)* Morato says that he was surprised to see a gleaming black car, and could not understand why no attempt had been made to camouflage it. He dived at it with machine-guns blazing, and within seconds it left the road and stopped. Two motorists rushed to give assistance and, whilst Morato was gaining height, another car drew alongside and then dashed away at full speed. That night Radio Barcelona broadcast, "The Leader of the forces in the offensive on Huesca, General Lukacs, has died after being fired at by an enemy fighter."

Batov, who was travelling with Lukacs, related that while they were crossing a bridge built by the infantry there was a violent explosion which made him lose consciousness. Koltsov recorded in his 'Diary', that Lukacs was killed by an aircraft weapon and that his Chief of Staff, Regler, was also seriously wounded.

During the same sortie, Morato and Guerrero each destroyed a Rasante. Salas' guns had jammed, but despite this he continued the mission, which lasted for 2hrs 10mins; and during which time his aircraft was hit three times, one bullet shattering his windscreen.

On June 13th the Fiat group and the Heinkel He 51 squadron made two sorties to escort the Junkers and Pavas, which were detailed to bomb Huesca and Azuara, but they did not encounter any enemy aircraft.

The biggest air battle took place on June 14th. Tinker recorded that his squadron and two squadrons of Chatos were in combat with sixty Fiats and Heinkels, making a total of more than one hundred aircraft involved. In fact, eight Fiats and six Heinkel He 51s were detailed to escort five Heinkel He 46s and four Junkers Ju 52s, making a total of twenty-three aircraft. 2-G-3 claimed the destruction of six of the thirty fighters they met, victories being achieved by García Pardo, Muricia and each member of Morato's patrol.

Tinker acknowledged the loss of three Chatos, but claimed that they shot down fourteen aircraft. The bulletin issued by the 3rd Air Region (Barcelona) acknowledged the loss of four fighters, two of whose pilots escaped, and confirmed the destruction of seven of the 30 Fiats which fought against 24 Government fighters.

On the 15th Arístides succeeded in shooting down a Rasante, making his fourth victory in five days and the fifth in his overall total. On that day Barcelona mentioned only attacks on the Saragossa aerodromes, made by five patrols of bombers, but no mention was made of air combats.

On June 16th the last air battle was fought over Huesca. Vázquez Sagastizábal described it as hard fought and difficult. 2-G-3 was in combat with between 40 and 60 enemy aircraft and claimed three more victories: Vazquez a Rata, whose pilot landed by parachute behind his own lines; and Salvador and Guerrero one Aero each. Tinker recorded that they fought against fifty Fiats and Heinkels (in fact there were nine Fiats, four Heinkel He 51s and five Heinkel He 46s) and destroyed five aircraft, losing one Rasante. Tinker claimed one Fiat, making his fifth victory.

On June 18th, according to Tinker, the Government Air Force attacked Huesca with two squadrons of Katiuskas and three of Rasantes, escorted by two squadrons of Chatos and three of Ratas. In all a total of more than one hundred aircraft took part, and the town was damaged severely.

On June 19th Bilbao was occupied by the Navarrese Brigades. There was, therefore, no point in the Government Air Force continuing their offensive against Huesca and, on the 20th, Tinker's squadron of Ratas moved to Liria and los Alcázares. In retrospect, it is clear that if the offensive on Huesca was to have had any material effect in assisting the defence of Bilbao, it should have been made simultaneously with the attack at La Granja.

On June 21st, in company with two Italian Fiat squadrons that had flown in to relieve them, the Morato Group flew as escort to the day group of Ju 52s (then led by Commander Eduardo González Gallarza) in an attack upon Sariñena. The following day the Morato Group moved to Seville for their aircraft to be overhauled.

In the short period between June 11th and 16th, Morato's 2-G-3 had destroyed 21 enemy aircraft, of which Salvador had shot down five, Aristides four, Vázquez Sagastizábal three, Morato, García Pardo and Guerrero two each, Bermúdez de Castro, Murcia and Senra one each.

At the end of this stage of the war the list of aces in this group was led by

Morato, with a total of eighteen victories, followed by Salvador with ten, Salas with seven, Guerrero with six, and Vázquez Sagastizábal and Arístides García López with five each.

Assault on the 'Iron Ring'

The whole of May and part of June was spent in manoeuvring the Nationalist advance forces into position for their assault on the 'Iron Ring'. This had been achieved by putting up strong resistance to counter-attacks made by the Government forces at the key positions of Sollube, Jata, Bizcargui and Peña Lemona.

When Prieto took over the Ministry of Defence, he sent Gámir Ulibarri to take command of the Basque Army Corps, which had split from the Northern Army. Prieto gave Gamir Ulibarri instructions to offer maximum resistance on the Eastern front and around the ring of fortifications, especially on the outskirts of the town. He was assured that major operations would be carried out in concert on other fronts, thus easing the situation in Biscay, and authorised him to reorganise land, sea and air forces. Thus, on May 29th, General Gámir Ulibarri arrived to take command of Euzkadi's Army Corps.

On June 3rd, General Mola was killed in an air crash and this, together with poor weather conditions,, the counter-attack at Peña Lemona and the offensive at La Granja, delayed the assault on the 'Iron Ring' until June 11th.

The 'Iron Ring', a continuous line of fortifications, was considered impregnable by its builders, although it surrounded Bilbao very closely in order to reduce its perimeter. It has been written that 70,000 men would be needed to defend this line, and that Gámir had only half this number. In fact, according to military beliefs at that time, seventy battalions were needed to defend 43·5 miles (70km), in order to provide a forward line with a reserve line in the rear. Gámir had ninety-two battalions, although many of these men were battle weary. But of these the 3rd Division (Ibarrola) and 4th (Irezábal) were not available for defence of the 'Ring', as they were still involved at the Orduna front. During these difficult times the Liaison Division, (Hernández de Castillo) was formed in the Valmaseda sector, composed of Basque and Montaña troops, and two brigades of the 4th Division were sent to reinforce the defences of Bilbao, so that there were never less than 50 battalions available for its defence.

There were some defects in the 'Iron Ring': in the main it consisted of only a single defensive line, although in some sectors there was a reserve line; there were no trenches on the slopes forward of the main defences, which would have allowed more strategic scope; and there was a weak point to the north of Larrabezúa. Although there were two lines of defence in this sector, it was dominated by the Bizcargui, of which the flanks were undefended. Furthermore, the Nationalists knew the layout of these defences well since Captain Goicoechea, Commander of the Euzkadi fortifications, switched his allegiance from Government to Nationalists, bringing with him the plans of the defences.

On June 11th, the 'Ring' was attacked by the 1st, 2nd, 5th and 6th Navarrese and the *Flechas Negras* Brigades, making a total of about forty battalions; these forces also had some long-range guns which could lob shells on Bilbao.

The 4th Navarrese Brigade was also in contact with the 'Ring', but did not take part in the attack. The 3rd Navarrese Brigade and a few units from the 1st Castille Brigade and the CTV remained at the Orduña front.

The only battles in the air took place on the 4th and 5th June. On the 4th the Italian *La Cucaracha* group claimed to have shot down five Chatos; the Government bulletin claimed the destruction of two Fiats. The next day, during an attack on Bilbao aerodrome, they lost their 'ace' Guido Presel, who was posthumously awarded the Golden Medal for Valour. On the same day the He 51s shot down a Chato at Peña Lemona and the Fiáts destroyed another Chato at Somorrostro, and five others on the ground. These losses were acknowledged by the Government Air Force bulletin.

On May 8th, to reinforce the Biscay air force, the Government had decided to despatch a squadron of Chatos to Somorrostro, routed via Toulouse. Led by Jiménez they left Lérida, but within 24 hours they were turned back from Toulouse by the Control Committee, despite the fact that the French Government had given permission for the squadron to pass through the country.

On May 17th another attempt was made, this time led by Jover and accompanied by two DC-2s and Alonso Vega's Natachas. The weather was appalling, with snow over the Pyrenees, and when some of the Chatos and the DC-2s landed at Pau there were no refuelling facilities available. This gave the Control Committee time to intervene, and they disarmed the aircraft before allowing them to continue. Within five days they returned to Madrid and, finally, during the last days of May, they arrived in Santander on a direct flight from Algete. Even this flight was not without incident, for nine of the pilots lost their way and flew over San Sebastian, where one aircraft was shot down. Days later they moved to Somorrostro and on June 4th and 5th suffered the losses already mentioned. On June 11th, when the attack on the 'Ring' began, four Chatos led by Aguirre landed at Parma aerodrome (Biarritz), supposedly on their way from Bilbao; they, too, were disarmed and sent back.

In view of the difficult situation in Biscay, the Russians and Italians took great interest in events at Bilbao. The *Pravda* correspondent, Koltsov, arrived there on June 1st in a twin-engined Marcel Bloch piloted by Yanguas. He was forced to resort to military transport as, two days before, Nationalist fighters had shot down the Airspeed belonging to the Air Pyrénees line. On June 4th Nino Nanetti arrived in Bilbao and days later took over command of the 2nd Euzkadi Division (later 49th Division). Even before this, the Russian General Goriev and Enrique Castro Delgado were in Bilbao, although the latter returned with Koltsov to the Centre on June 10th after being nominated General Sub-Commissioner to replace Mije.

On June 11th General Dávila ordered the assault on the 'Ring', following the plan of attack devised by his predecessor, General Mola, despite the existence of two alternative plans, involving attacks at Valmaseda or Ramales. Striking from the Bizcargui, the 1st Navarrese Brigade broke through the first line of defence at Urcullu. This action was supported by a heavy barrage from all available artillery and with strikes made by the Air Force which dropped a total of 35 tons of bombs and, in the process, lost one Hs 123 dive bomber which was undergoing its first baptism of fire.

Early in the morning of June 12th the 1st Brigade had to fight off a violent counter-attack. Then, at 07.00hrs an intense artillery barrage began, which was maintained for five hours, backed up by seventy bombers which dropped one hundred tons of bombs. At 12.30hrs, shortly after the barrage ended, the 3rd Battalion (Commander Holguin), of the 5th Navarrese Brigade, made a rapid advance and broke through the famous fortifications. The 1st, 5th and 6th Brigades exploited the situation immediately, managing to get about half of their men through the gap and inside the 'Ring'. The rearguard of the 1st and 6th Brigades advanced parallel to the 'Ring' and succeeded in increasing the gap to the north and south, making a breach in the defences of some 3 miles (5km). The remainder of the 5th Brigade maintained its pressure and succeeded in penetrating 1¾ miles (3km) into the 'Ring'.

On June 13th the attacking troops expanded rapidly their footholds of the previous day. The 6th Brigade occupied an additional 3 miles (5km) of the 'Ring', despite determined counter-attack by the Basque Brigade (Cristóbal). The 1st and 5th Brigades crossed the Asúa valley and gained a line alongside the river Nervión, overcoming strong resistance from the Government 4th Brigade (Gorricho) and the 12th (Domenech). On the same day the *Flechas Negras* and 2nd Brigades began their advances, on each flank of the main attack.

Because of the catastrophic situation, Putz was brought in to take command of the 1st Basque Division, leaving Gómez as Chief of Staff.

On June 15th, the 1st Navarrese Brigade crossed the rivers Ibaizabal and Nervión, at a point just before their union south of Bilbao, and the *Flechas Negras* Brigade gained the coast at Plencia. The next day the 6th Brigade occupied Sondica aerodrome and the 1st Brigade, supported by the 2nd, continued their advance along the left bank of the Nervión; one Heinkel He 70 reconnaissance aircraft was shot down over Bilbao.

Mount Archanda, the last stronghold to the north-east of Bilbao was defended fiercely, but on June 17th this fell finally as a result of ceaseless pressure maintained by the 5th Navarrese Brigade. Meanwhile, the *Flechas Negras* Brigade occupied Las Arenas, at the estuary of the river Nervión. They waited there for one day before advancing on Bilbao, a day spent in occupying Pagasarri and other mountains to the south-east, and in making contact with the Navarrese forces. The capture of Lamiaco aerodrome yielded four aircraft; two of which had been burnt; thirty aero-engines (15 burnt); one hundred drums of oil and twenty-three cases of bombs.

On the morning of June 19th, two companies of tanks advanced close to Bilbao, and in the afternoon the 5th Brigade came down from Mount Aschanda and took up a new position in front of the town. The 1st and 2nd Brigades arrived at Bilbao by advancing along the left bank of the Nervión, and the *Flechas Negras* and 6th Brigades followed the river estuary upstream. Baracaldo, on the left bank of the Nervión, opposite Las Arenas, was still in Government hands.

On June 20th the *Flechas Negras* Brigade ferried themselves across the river in small boats and occupied Somorrostro. A different 'Iron Ring' now surrounded Bilbao, which was soon in Nationalist hands. Reports from Italian sources would suggest that they were the occupiers of Bilbao; but although the

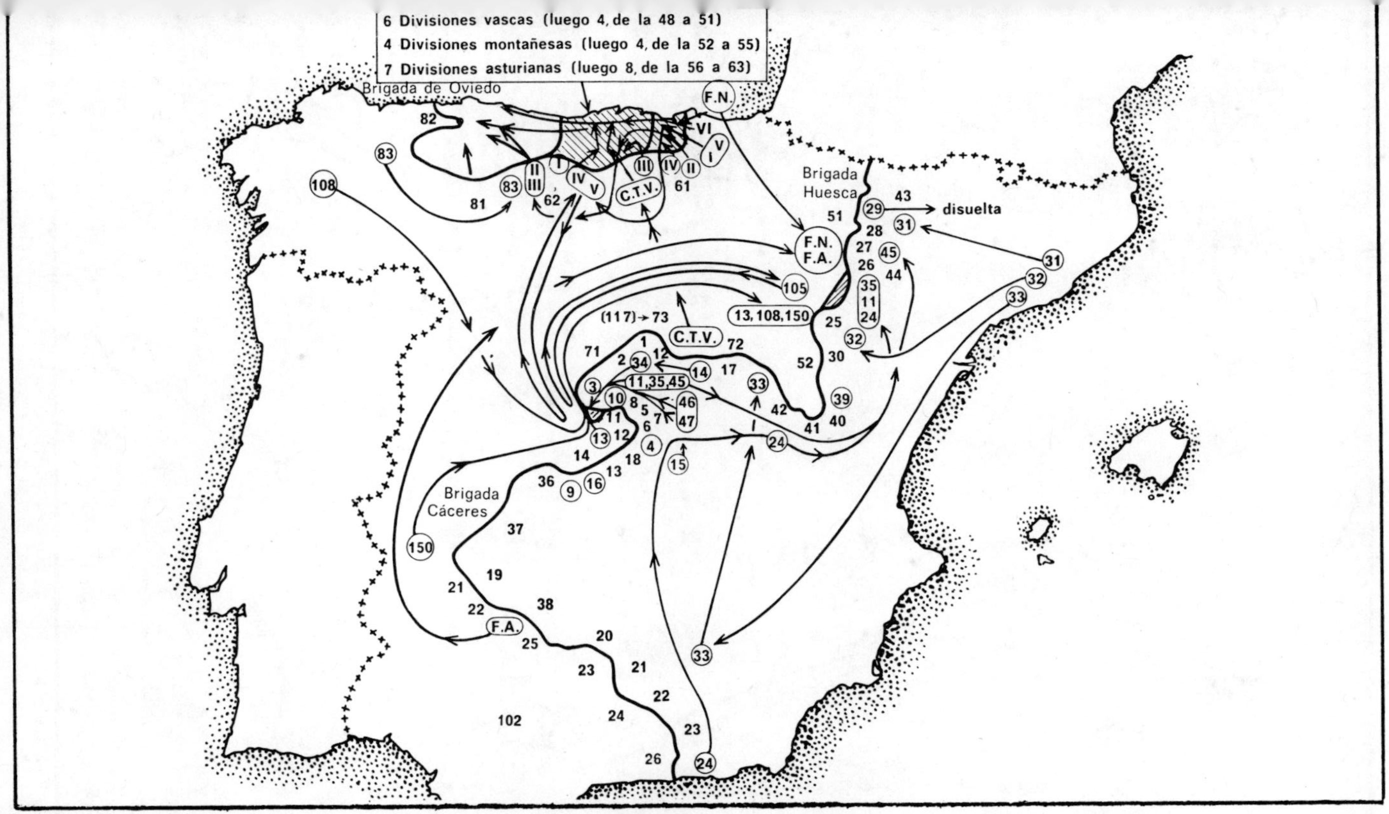

VIII. Position of the Divisions in the middle of 1937. The Roman numerals indicate Brigades from Navarre and the 1st Castilian Brigade. FN and FA are the Brigades from Flechas. Government forces occupy the area to the right of the black line extending from the French border in the north to the south coast at Motril.

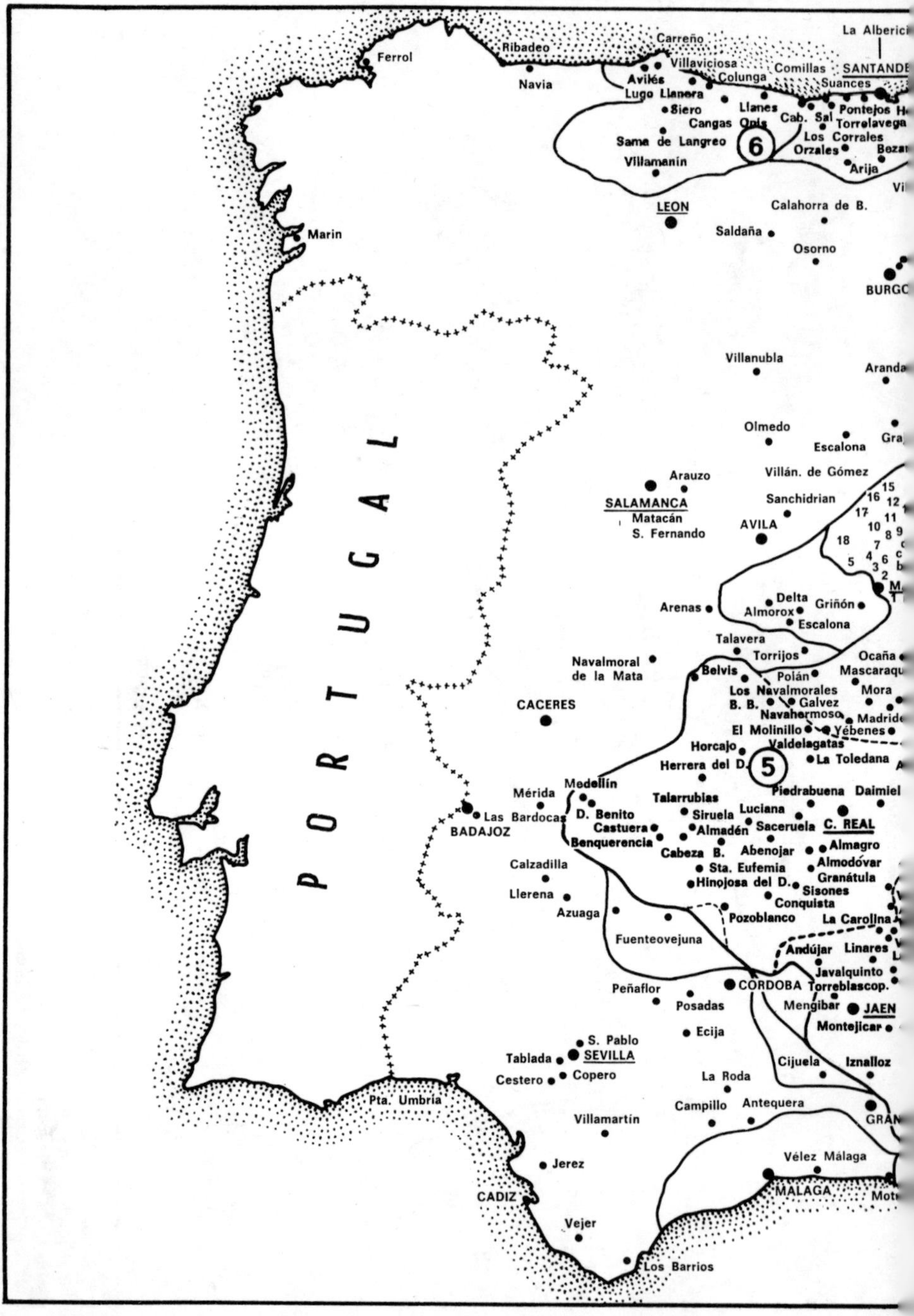

Ferrol
Ribadeo
Navia
Carreño
Villaviciosa
Colunga
Comillas
SANTANDE
La Alberici
Suances
Avilés
Lugo Llanera
Siero
Llanes
Cangas Onís
Cab.
Sal
Pontejos
Torrelavega
Los Corrales
Sama de Langreo
Orzales
Arija
Villamanín
6
LEON
Calahorra de B.
Saldaña
Osorno
BURGO
Marin
Villanubla
Aranda
Olmedo
Escalona
Villán. de Gómez
Arauzo
SALAMANCA
Matacán
S. Fernando
Sanchidrian
AVILA
P O R T U G A L
Delta
Almorox
Griñón
Escalona
Arenas
Talavera
Torrijos
Navalmoral de la Mata
Belvis
Polán
Los Navalmorales
B. B.
Galvez
Ocaña
Mascaraqu
Mora
CACERES
Navahermoso
Madride
El Molinillo
Yébenes
Horcajo
Valdelagatas
La Toledana
Herrera del D.
5
Mérida
Medellín
Piedrabuena
Daimiel
Las Bardocas
BADAJOZ
D. Benito
Talarrubias
Siruela
Luciana
Castuera
Almadén
Saceruela
C. REAL
Benquerencia
Cabeza B.
Abenojar
Almagro
Almodóvar
Calzadilla
Sta. Eufemia
Granátula
Llerena
Hinojosa del D.
Sisones
Conquista
Azuaga
Pozoblanco
La Carolina
Fuenteovejuna
Andújar
Linares
Javalquinto
CORDOBA
Torreblascop.
Peñaflor
Posadas
Mengibar
JAEN
Montejicar
Ecija
S. Pablo
Tablada
SEVILLA
Cestero
Copero
Cijuela
Iznalloz
La Roda
Pta. Umbria
Campillo
Antequera
Villamartín
GRAN
Jerez
Vélez Málaga
CADIZ
MALAGA
Mot
Vejer
Los Barrios

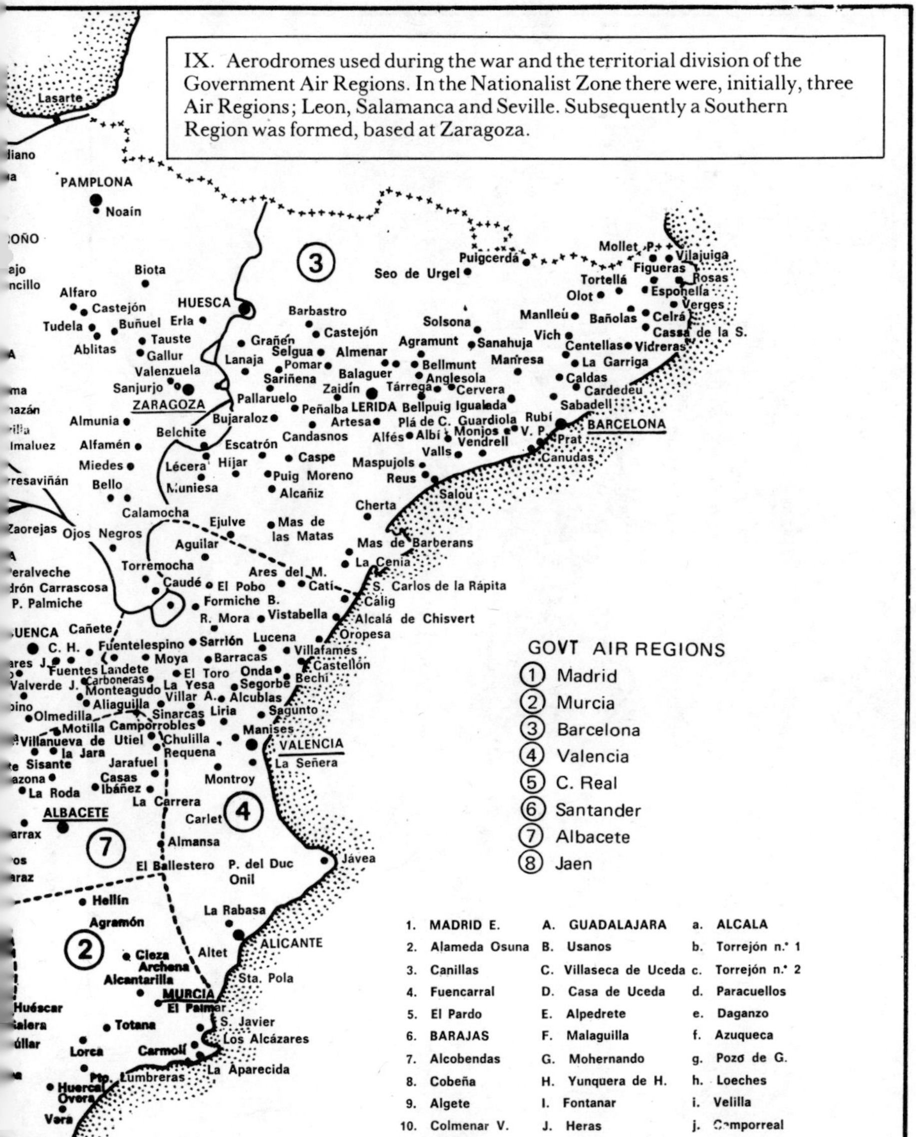

IX. Aerodromes used during the war and the territorial division of the Government Air Regions. In the Nationalist Zone there were, initially, three Air Regions; Leon, Salamanca and Seville. Subsequently a Southern Region was formed, based at Zaragoza.

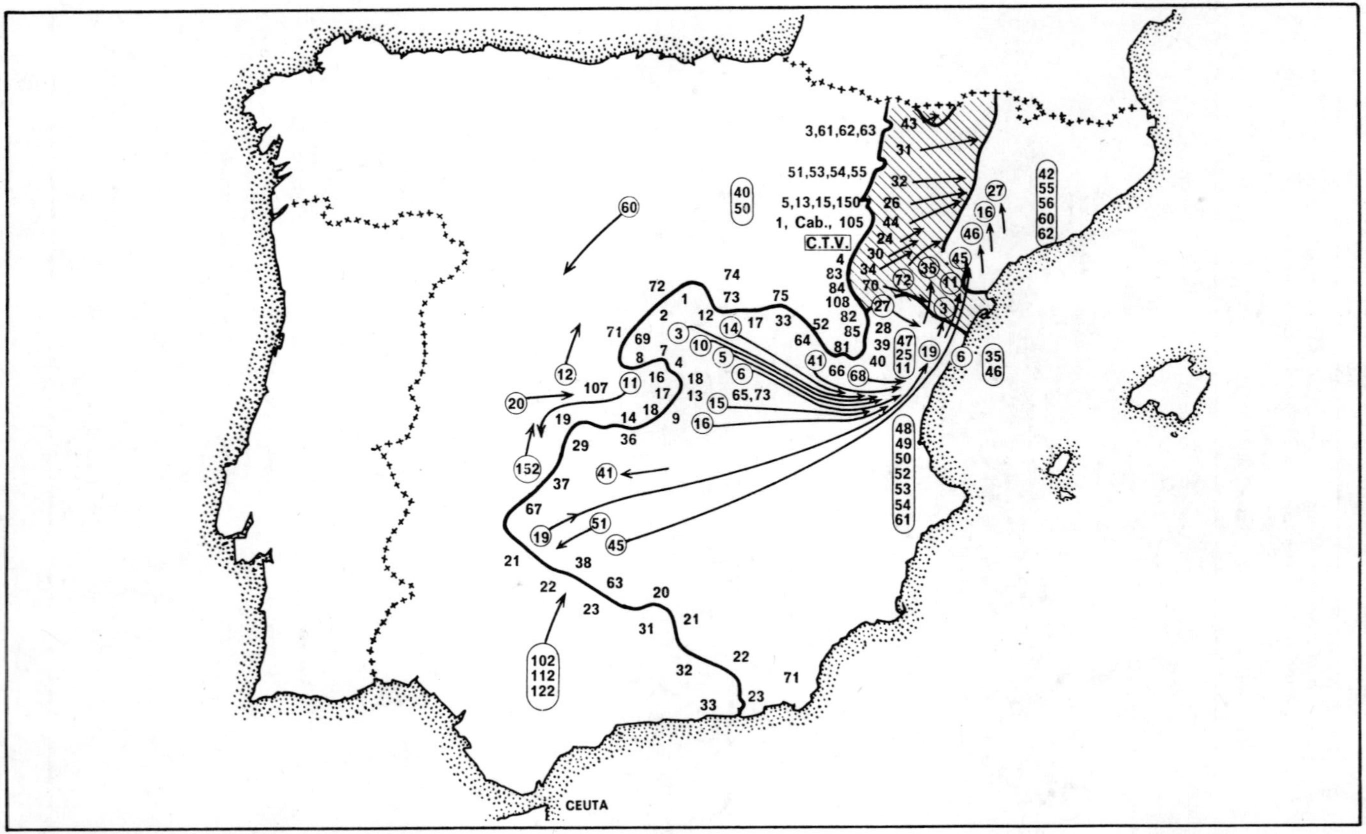

X. Position of the Divisions in the spring of 1938. Government forces are again to the right of the continuous black line.

Flechas Negras Brigade took a major role in the occupation of the town, this International Brigade consisted of about 95 per cent Spanish troops and half the officers were also Spaniards.

After the fall of Bilbao, Vidal assumed command of the Basque Corps and Nanetti replaced him as commander of the 2nd Division. When the Northern Army was re-formed under the overall command of Gamir Ulibarri, Prada left Madrid to become commander of the Basque Army Corps (later redesignated XIV Army Corps), and Vidal became responsible for Coastal Defence.

The Government's 4th Division and Liaison Division were disbanded and the 5th became redesignated 4th Division. The 5th and 6th Divisions were re-formed with new brigades, which had arrived from Santander and Asturias. Francisco Galan, San Juan and Barzana then became the commanders of these three divisions. Ibarrola was the only divisional commander to retain his command after the defeat, although Gómez was reinstated at a later date, when Putz returned to the Central Zone.

Six of the eighteen Basque brigades were lost in the battle. Only twelve remained (Nos 1–9 and 11–13), and shortly afterwards they received new numerical designations, namely Nos 154–165. The six expeditionary brigades were also greatly weakened and these returned to their former bases to rest and be re-organised.

The Biscay campaign lasted until July 5th, when the lines became stabilised in front of Castro Urdiales, in the Castro Alén mountains.

The Battle at Brunete

The battle at Brunete was begun by Government forces in their 10th Division's sector, which was the area between the Sierra sector (I Army Corps, Moriones) and the North Madrid sector (VI Army Corps, Prada, later Fernández Heredia).

For the Brunete offensive the 10th Division was joined by the 15th and 34th initially, and at a later date by the 3rd and 45th Divisions of the XVIII Army Corps, which was commanded, in succession, by Jurado, Casado and Fernández Heredia. To their right the V Army Corps (Modesto) was stationed, with the 1st, 35th and 46th Divisions, and they were later joined by the 14th, and 39th to 47th Divisions: their objective was to penetrate the defences of Brunete and Navalcarnero. To spearhead the attack, each of these Army Corps had 64 tanks. To the south of Madrid the II Army Corps (Romero), advanced towards Alcorcon, with one Corps of shock troops, which included the 4th and 24th Divisions, and attempted to make contact with the XVII Corps; the III Army Corps (Álvarez) attacked Cuesta de la Reina.

The Brunete sector was to the extreme left of the Nationalist Madrid Army Corps (Yagüe) which, from the beginning of the offensive, came under control of the neighbouring VII Army Corps (Varela). In turn, both of these army corps were controlled by the Central Army (Saliquet). The Nationalist air units in the central area, both in the Madrid and Ávila sectors, were under the overall control of Lieutenant-Colonel Lecea.

On July 5th, the sector under attack was guarded by half a brigade of the

2nd Division, commanded by Mancebo. To reinforce them on the western flank the 13th Division (Barrón) was called in, together with the 150th Division (A. Sáenz de Buruaga). This latter division had recently returned from Africa, and was then in Cáceres, finishing a course of instruction in preparation for the Santander offensive which was planned for the middle of July. A provisional Division was formed under Ascencio's command with battalions from the 11th, 12th and 14th Divisions, and they halted an advance being made towards the east by the XVIII Army Corps. Battalions from the 105th and 107th Divisions and reserves from Aragón and Castile were rushed to the area. Later, for the counter offensive, the 4th and 5th Navarrese Brigades (Vega and González) came down from Santander, and the 108th Division (Lafuente) from Galicia.

Nationalist air defence in this sector was provided by Ansaldo's Group of Romeo Ro 37s, which were based at Griñón aerodrome, and Cdr. Zotti's group of Fiat fighters at Torrijos aerodrome. Gallarza and Carrillo's groups of Ju 52s were flown in to provide reinforcement, and these operated from Delta, Olmedo and Cáceres aerodromes successively. They were followed by Cipriano Rodríguez's 'Cucufate' group of He 45s and Capt. Gregorio Gómez Martín's Aero 101 squadron, which were based initially at Ávila aerodrome and later at Delta (Casa Vieja). The light aircraft of the Condór Legion and Commander Casero's Fiat group were based at Ávila aerodrome. The Italian bombers operated from bases in Soria and those of the Condór Legion from Salamanca and Ávila; the latter force's fighter aircraft operated from Villa del Prado and Escalona.

At this period, the pilots that had formed Pardo's Ju 52 group were in Italy, where they had gone to take delivery of the first Savoia S-M.79s, with which they were to form Group 3-G-28. They did not return in time for the battle at Brunete, and their ground crews which had been waiting for them at Tablada set off immediately to provide any assistance possible to other units operating at Brunete.

The Government Air Force took part in great numbers. Squadrons from the No 11 Fighter Force, comprising No 21 Group Ratas and 26 Group Chatos, were based at the many aerodromes of the air sectors of Alcala, Barajas and Guadalajara.

Under Eriomenko's orders a night fighter squadron was created at about this time. Its pilots included the well-known Serov and Yakushin, as well as Antónov and Ribkin. Equipped with Chatos, the squadron also operated by day, when the pilots included two Austrians, two Americans, one Yugoslav and three Spaniards.

The Army Co-operation squadrons (Nos 20, 40 and 50, composed of Natachas) and three aircraft from No 30 Squadron, together with the Katiuska bombers of Nos 12 and 24 Groups, operated from various airfields in the Mancha. At this time the Rata squadrons were composed mainly of Russian personnel, although there were still a few Spanish pilots and some of other nationalities. The Americans Tinker and Baumler remained in a Rata squadron until the end of this battle. The Spanish Chato squadrons operated in the North from the month of May, led by Aguirre and Riverola, so that all

Government fighter aircraft taking part at Brunete were of foreign origin.

The first batch of Spanish pilots who had been trained in Russia (200 men) had been back in Spain for about six weeks, but very few took part in the battle of Brunete, although the majority of them were stationed at Santander and Belchite.

The Spanish groups of Natachas were led by Commander Moreno Miró and by Hernández Franch, and Arceaga was in command of 24 Group's Katiuskas, with Pereira and Leocadio Mendiola as leaders of the 2nd and 3rd squadrons. The 1st Squadron was Russian, but when its leader, Enrique Pereira Basanta, was promoted Commander in the Naval Air Force at the end of August, and took command of the group, Arceaga replaced him as leader of the 1st Squadron.

The battle began on the night of July 5th/6th. The orders given to the V Army Corps were to join up with the 46th Division 'Campesino' during the night and to encircle Quijorna, the 11th Division moving towards Brunete. The attacks on these points were to begin after a thirty-minute artillery barrage, at 17.30hrs and 18.30hrs respectively, and immediately the guns stopped firing they were to force bridgeheads across the Rivers Guadarrama and Perales and to occupy Sevilla la Nueva. The 35th Division (Walter), was to be held in reserve, behind the 46th Division, covering the right flank of the attack. The task of the XVIII Army Corps was to occupy Villanueva de la Cañada and Villanueva del Pardillo, then to press on across the river Guadarrama as far as Boadilla del Monte and to make contact with units of the II Army Corps.

This night attack was carried out successfully, but at Quijorna and Villanueva del Pardillo Nationalist resistence was much stronger than had been anticipated. To add to the problems, Lister failed to occupy Sevilla la Nueva, where General Varela immediately set up a Command Post to ensure that he was in the midst of what Franco realised was a critical battle.

On July 7th the Valdemorillo–Brunete road was clear of Nationalist troops, which should have allowed the 11th Division to continue their advance on Navalcarnero or, even better, on Villaviciosa de Odón, to support the XVIII Army Corps in its advance on Boadilla. But neither Líster, nor his adviser Rodimtsev (Captain Pablito), could make up their minds to proceed with this advance whilst Quijorna and Villanueva del Pardillo were still holding out. In fact these two points fell on the 9th and 11th respectively, but indecision had already proved costly.

Varela accumulated forces with great speed. As early as July 7th the 13th Division (Barrón) arrived and the Nationalist Air Force began to operate from its bases in the North. The following day Asensio began operations at the Guadarrama line and on the 10th the 150th Division (Buruaga) reached the western flank.

The Nationalist Air Force went into action on the 9th, but the Condór Legion's bombers were unable to take part because of the air superiority then held by the enemy fighters. Despite the enemy strength, the Spanish Ju 52s and He 45s began operations on July 9th.

By July 11th Asensio had succeeded not only in resisting four attacks on Boadilla, but managed also to recapture Villafranca del Castillo. The next day, with the arrival of two Navarrese brigades and the 108th Division, Nationalist forces began widespread counter-attacks.

During the first few days of the offensive Government air superiority was overwhelming. Troops fighting in the Las Rozas–Casa de Campo sector will never forget the large numbers of aircraft which passed over their heads to an unknown destination, presumably to attack their supply columns.

According to Tinker, on July 5th two squadrons of Ratas with Russian pilots arrived at Barajas and Alcalá de Henares; his own squadron was based at Manzanares de la Sierra. A squadron of Chatos with Russian pilots replaced La Calle's squadron at Airfield X (Azuqueca), and another Chato squadron flown by Russian pilots was based at Campo Soto. The American pilot, Harold Dahl, was also a member of this latter squadron. According to Government bulletins a total of thirteen of their fighter squadrons took part.

On July 6th and 7th respectively, a Rata flown by Jhosianov and a Katiuska by Chercasov were shot down. Tinker makes no mention of these losses, but recorded that on the 8th Beliekov's Rata was destroyed by anti-aircraft fire, and that his squadron leader, Lockiev, made a crash-landing the next day. Nationalist sources admitted the loss of three Fiats, those of Vercellio 'Vinci', Passeri and Mattei, and a fourth pilot, Commander Zotti, was injured. The Government's 1st Air Region bulletin claimed the destruction of three He 51s at Illescas, and three more fighters at Brunete on the 6th, and acknowledged the loss of one single-engined aircraft.

The Morato group was caught on the wrong foot at the beginning of the battle, with their Fiats being overhauled and most of the pilots on leave. However, by July 8th Tablada Park had five machines ready for service (3-52, 3-54, 3-56, 3-60 and 3-62). On July 9th, just prior to take-off, No 3-52 developed a fault and was replaced by 3-59, and these five aircraft were flown to Ávila by Bermudez de Castro, Guerrero, Jesús Rubio and Arístides, with García Pardo as leader. On the 10th Morato and Salvador joined them with aircraft Nos 3-57 and 3-58, but Guerrero had to return to Tablada with 3-54 which was giving some trouble.

On the 10th, during a sortie in which Bermúdez de Castro, Arístides García López and Jesus Rubio took part, the engine of Rubio's Fiat lost power and he was left to limp back to base. En route he was attacked by enemy fighters and, with his aircraft badly damaged, had to take to his parachute; his aircraft, 3-56, was completely destroyed when it crashed.

On July 12th, Morato, García Pardo and Bermúdez de Castro were in combat with three Ratas and fifteen Chatos. During this battle the Morato Group suffered their first fatal casualty when Captain Bermúdez de Castro lost his life, his aircraft (3-62) crashing near the Villanueva de la Cañada road. Morato related in his book that he was helpless to prevent his companion from being shot down as his machine-guns had jammed. García Pardo, however, managed to shoot down a Chato.

Tinker's squadron was not in action until the afternoon of that day, but he recorded that in the morning the two Alcala squadrons were in action and were confronted for the first time by a new German monoplane (new on the central front, that is). The Alcalá squadrons lost three fighters and destroyed eight Fiats and one Heinkel. The Italians claimed a total of nine victories, five Chatos and four Ratas.

On July 13th, during Tinker's third mission at this front, there was an aerial battle which was fought for nearly an hour. In this engagement two Ratas were shot down, as well as Harold Dahl's Chato, and he was taken prisoner. Tinker stated that Government aircraft shot down twelve of the enemy, including two Me 109s, one of the latter falling to his own guns (probably that of Höness). The Nationalist Air Force bulletin claimed the destruction of one Chato and admitted the loss of two Fiats which collided in the air.

The 1st Air Region's bulletin quoted four separate air battles on July 13th, one early in the morning and three in the afternoon. Their fighters were operating in a formation of twenty-six to thirty aircraft, and shot down nine enemy fighters, two Romeos and one twin-engined Junkers aircraft.

On July 14th, four of the Fiats were detailed for operations, piloted by Morato, Salvador, Arístides and Guerrero. The latter had returned from Seville on the previous day, flying Fiat No 3-61 which he had been given to replace No 3-54. This patrol encountered a squadron of Natachas, escorted by several Ratas, which were quickly scattered. Morato shot down two and the other three pilots one each. These losses were confirmed to me by several officials of the Government Air Force, although the 1st Air Region's bulletin admitted only that the Fiats destroyed three single-engined bombers near to Hoyo de Pinares.

Tinker recorded that on July 14th only three missions were carried out, and that because of strong cross winds they had to land at Alcalá and Barajas. On the following day they flew to Campo Real where their aircraft were readied for the day's operation, and they took off, accompanied by the Ratas from Alcala, to escort eighteen Rasantes. According to Tinker, in the air combats that ensued, no less than eleven Nationalist aircraft were destroyed, comprising a mixed bag of Fiats and Heinkels. Government losses totalled two Chatos and a Rata.

Morato claimed the destruction of two Ratas on that day, and Salas joined the group, arriving from Tablada with Fiat No 3-63.

On July 16th Lockiev, leader of Tinker's squadron, and two other men who had flown with the unit for some time, were replaced by new Russian pilots. On that day they were not called upon for any operations, which Tinker explained by saying that due to the excessive heat their aircraft needed a great deal of servicing, which seemed a not very convincing explanation. Also on July 16th, during an attack on Alcalá by Nationalist aircraft, the Russian Jose, formerly leader of a Chato squadron, and Agustin Sanz Sainz who was the station commander, were both wounded.

On July 17th Tinker recorded that a Junkers, two Heinkels and two Me 109s were shot down, one of the latter by himself, and he admitted the loss of one Russian Chato. The leader of the Me 109s claimed the destruction of one enemy fighter and did not report any losses.

July 18th proved to be the first day of the Nationalist counter-offensive, which was supported by sixty batteries of artillery. Activity in the air was intense and there were at least five major clashes. Tinker destroyed a Fiat, his eighth and last victory in the air, and one Me 109 was certainly destroyed, its pilot, Harbach, being taken prisoner. The Fiats claimed to have destroyed eight Natachas, one of which fell to Morato's guns, while they admitted only the loss of Lieutenant Mollo's machine.

The 1st Air Region's bulletin (Madrid) claimed that three fighters (one Fiat, one monoplane and one biplane) and one Ju 52 had been destroyed, and admitted the loss of two fighters and two Natachas.

Morato's Group did not find any further opportunity of taking part in this battle. Neither did Tinker, but he recorded the destruction of a Rata by anti-aircraft fire on the 19th, the loss of another on the 20th, and of one which crash-landed on the 22nd. Government anti-aircraft fire accounted for an He 51 on July 19th, and Lieutenant Reuter's He 51 and a Do 17 on the 24th.

It was on July 24th that prolonged resistance by the 11th Division came to an end, and the battle for Brunete was virtually over. The Government's 14th and 35th Divisions were ordered to recapture the town at all costs, but they were unable to achieve success. The 35th Division did manage to regain a foothold in Brunete cemetery, but a violent attack by Nationalist bombers on the 25th finally scattered the weary troops and the area was in Nationalist control.

On July 26th a Ju 52 flown by Captain Pardo Pimentel exploded in mid-air, and he and his crew of five were all killed. It was at first thought that the aircraft had been hit by anti-aircraft fire, but when an identical accident occurred at Santander in the following month in an area where no anti-aircraft guns were firing, a careful investigation of the accident was made. This revealed a fault in the electrical circuits which was claimed to be responsible for both accidents.

During the night of July 26th one of the Condór Legion's Ju 52s was shot down during a mission, an event which was repeated the following night. According to the Russian correspondent Koltsov, Carlos Castejón (The Russian, Serov), was promoted to the rank of Captain for these two victories. Yakushin also claimed the destruction of another Ju 52 on July 26th.

When the battle of Brunete ended, Serov was placed in command of the night fighter squadron which, in the days preceding, had lost the pilots Kárpov (killed) and Sheliganov (wounded). Replacement pilots sent to the squadron included Stepanov, who later became Serov's successor, Gorójov, Kustov and Popov.

In the air battles at Brunete, the Morato Group destroyed nine aircraft for the loss of two of their numbers. This was no mean achievement when one considers that, at the most, six war-weary Fiats were involved in combat with large formations of enemy fighters and bombers. Of the nine aircraft shot down, Morato personally claimed five, the others being destroyed by García Pardo, Salvador, Guerrero and Arístides. At the end of July the Group's aircraft were flown to Tablada for repairs and servicing and this task was completed on August 9th.

During the battle of Brunete the two Spanish He 51 squadrons had been stationed at Aragón and León until July 17th, when they were both sent to Calamocha in preparation for a Government attack at Albarracin.

The battle of Brunete marked a new level in the preparation and training of the Popular Army. For the first time they proved their ability to make a six-mile (10km) infiltration at night, without hitches. They were incapable, however, of maintaining this initial success when they met determined resistance and, even more strangely, were completely at a loss if they met no opposition at all. This cannot be blamed entirely on the lack of initiative displayed by their secondary leaders. In order to exploit a success it is vital to decentralise and the *Alto Mando* (High Command) failed to do this.

In the air over the battlefield the Government fighters had maintained superiority: by numbers during the day, by improvisation at night. This had made it almost impossible for the Nationalist Air Force to deploy their Ju 52s and S-M.81s to any real effect. They had even lost one of the fast Do 17s.

Santander, a Military Walkover

At the beginning of August 1937 the Popular Army in the North, under the command of Gamir Ulibarri, comprised four Army Corps: the XIV (Basque, led by Prado, 48th, 49th, 50th and 51st Divisions), the XV (from Santander, led by Garcia Vayas, 52nd, 53rd, 54th and 55th Divisions) and the XVI and XVII (Asturian, led by Gallego and Linares respectively, with Divisions 56 to 63). The 63rd Division was duplicated, this numerical identification being allocated also to another Division in Extremeño.

Of the eighteen Basque brigades, only twelve (Nos 154 to 165) were placed on a war footing in Santander, and fourteen other Brigades (Nos 166 to 178 and 181) were raised in the town. Asturias supplied for the defence of Santander five of the nineteen Brigades that were raised (Nos 179, 180, 183, 184 and 185), which brought the number of Brigades to 31, with a total of just over 100 battalions (43 from Santander, 45 Basque and 15 Asturian). The 5th and 6th Divisions of the Basque Army Corps (Santander and Asturian expeditionary) became Tactical Division Nos 55 (San Juan, later De Pablo) and 57 (Bárazana).

The attacking Nationalist forces were slightly superior in numbers, but their morale was much higher. The Basques, fighting outside their own region, did not show the same determination they had displayed in defending their own countryside. Only some of Ibarrola's battalions (three were deployed in Santoña) put up any serious resistance to the Nationalist attacks. In a short time the bulk of the defenders laid down their arms, and their leaders fled by air to France. Only the Asturian and Ibarrola's Brigades, supported by naval infantry, continued to fight on in Santander, but it was impossible for them to contain the Nationalist avalanche.

The Government had not neglected to bring in considerable reinforcements for its air units, which comprised originally the Chatos from Jiménez and Alonso Santamaría's squadrons which had moved North during the month of May. They were now joined by two squadrons of Ratas which flew from Madrid to Santander, and by some additional aircraft which arrived by ship at Gijón some days later.

Amongst the outstanding pilots of the Spanish Chatos were Comas and Zambudio, who later became group leaders, Morquillas who became a squadron leader, and Duarte and Castillo Puretas who joined the squadron shortly afterwards.

The leaders of the Rata squadrons and patrols were Russian, but the remainder of the pilots were Spanish. The Tarazona squadron, led by Pligunov and which had Mijailov and Querenco as patrol leaders, moved from Alcalá to La Albericia probably on August 7th, since Tarazona recorded that the aerodrome had been attacked shortly before they landed, and that some aircraft were still in flames. This links up with the Nationalist bulletin for that day, which quotes the destruction of twelve aircraft on the ground in Torrelavega. The other Rata squadron was later led by Boris Smirnov, who arrived from Aragón at the end of August.

Apart from these squadrons of Ratas and Chatos, there were still many obsolete types of aircraft flying (Bristol Bulldogs, Gourdou Lesseurres, Letovs, Koolhovens, Potez, Dragon Rapides, Nieuports and Breguets), which Tarazona called 'The Krone Circus'. The total number of aircraft available to the Government for operations in support of the defence of Santander was at least eighty landplanes, and a squadron of seaplanes commanded by Captain Beneito.

Almost the whole of the Nationalist Air Force was concentrated at the Santander front, which meant leaving the immense line from the Pyrenees to Málaga very weakly guarded. Only part of Pérez Pardo's Group of He 46s (3-G-11) and a squadron from Corsini's 1-G-2 were left in Aragón. Three squadrons of Fiat fighters and the Romeo group (4-G-12) remained in the central area, and in Andalucia there was the Baquera mixed Breguet-Aero group (designated 1-G-10 after the Breguet groups in the North had been disbanded) and two Romeo Ro 41s in Granada.

The Condór Legion had seventy aircraft available to support the attacks on Santander (one squadron of Me 109Bs, two of He 51s, two of Ju 52s and one of He 111s, all with reduced numbers of aircraft, one mixed squadron of He 70s and Do 17s and some He 123s and He 46s). The Legionary Air Force had five Fiat squadrons, one group of Ro 37s and a bomber squadron (comprising one group of S-M.79s and one of S-M.81s) making a total of about eighty machines. There were also Gallarza and Carrillo's groups of Ju 52s (1-G-22 and 2-G-22), the Morato group (2-G-3), Cipriano Rodriguez's group of He 45s (6-G-15), A. Llorente's Aero 101 group (5-G-17), some He 46s, Martín Campo's He 51 squadron, and the He 70 patrol, making a total of about sixty more landplanes, to which were added Enrique de la Puente's seaplane squadron.

Nationalist superiority in the air over the Santander area was overwhelming, almost three to one if all aircraft types are included. Their deployment in the air had only slightly more potential than at Brunete, but here there were only four squadrons in opposition instead of the thirteen squadrons that had contested the battle of Brunete.

Nationalist leaders knew that a quick victory at Santander was essential if they were to end the war in the north before the onset of winter. Their defensive success at Brunete made it possible to face this new offensive with confidence. Furthermore, the Santander manoeuvres were perhaps the most brilliant of the entire war. This was the first great battle in which each side deployed forces equivalent to three Army Corps. The initial risky move of the XV Army Corps made the manoeuvre easier; in fact, once this Army Corps had advanced from the east and occupied the south of Reinosa, on the southern slopes of the Cantabrian mountain range, the road to the coast was left clear.

General Solchaga attacked to the west of their target with the 1st, 4th and 5th Navarrese Brigades, and General Bastico was to the east with three Italian divisions (*Littorio, XXIII March* and *Llamas Negras*). The 1st Castille Brigade was also at the line, and in reserve were the 2nd, 3rd and 6th Navarrese Brigades and the Mixed Brigade *Flechas Negras*.

Solchaga broke through the 54th Division's front on August 14th; the Italians encountered strong resistance that day at mount Maza and the Magdalena mountain range, but on August 15th they managed to break the 53rd Division's front and advanced to Reinosa.

In the face of these events, the 50th, 55th and 57th Divisions were moved in to reinforce the Government positions. It was too little and too late: on August 16th Puerto del Escudo fell and on the 18th the battle was decided. On that day Francisco Galan took over command of the 54th Division, after their leader had fled by plane to France; command of Galán's 51st Division was taken over by Cristóbal.

Heavy storms between August 18th and 20th did not prevent Nationalist troops from improving their hold on Santander. On the 22nd, the Government ordered some units to be evacuated to Asturias, and the next day they moved the XIV Corps and 52nd Division to the eastern front along the line of the river Asón, to defend the capital. Large numbers of the XIV Army Corps refused to comply with this order, as it would take them away from their home towns.

At 04.00hrs on August 24th, the Government ordered the complete evacuation of Santander within twenty-four hours. This had to be effected at great speed and their only means of exit was over the Puente Barreda. At 09.00hrs the Army's Chief of Staff, Ángel Lamas, left for Santoña and Hernández del Castillo took over command. At 16.00hrs the Asturians were in retreat across the Puente Barreda, but at 18.00hrs the 1st Navarrese Brigade occupied Torrelavega and simultaneously destroyed the vital bridge. The Government's 52nd Division made an attempt to recapture Torrelavega, but without success. The remaining staff of the Army's Headquarters were evacuated from Santander by sea, under the cover of darkness.

On August 26th, General Dávila marched triumphantly into Santander at the head of his troops, meeting no resistance despite the fact that the town still held about forty Basque battalions as well as others from Santander and Asturias.

With regard to the activity in the air, the Morato Group arrived at Osorno aerodrome on August 11th, their Fiats having been thoroughly overhauled at Tablada.

The offensive, planned originally for August 8th, and delayed until the 12th, actually began on the 14th. During the first three days the Morato Group went out three or four times each day to protect groups of He 46s and Aero 101s, but they did not encounter any enemy opposition in the air. On August 14th and

16th their flight time averaged more than four hours; on the 15th it was almost five.

During the third sortie of the Ju 52s on August 14th, an aircraft from Haya's squadron, flown by Lieutenant Ercilla, exploded in mid-air. At the time of the explosion there were no enemy fighters nor any anti-aircraft fire, it was obvious that the explosion must have been caused by a fault in the aircraft itself. Subsequently an engineer, Ruiz Ayllón, discovered a fault in the electric system of other Ju 52s which could have been responsible for the accident.

Captain Martín Campos' squadron of He 51s was also in the North, this time operating initially from Calahorra de Boedo. The Condor Legion's two He 51 squadrons, under the leadership of Commander 'Hermann' Handrick, were also located at this same aerodrome, which Galland mistakenly referred to as Herrera de Pisuerga aerodrome, probably because the crews were billeted in this latter town.

In the middle of August on returning from a mission, 2nd Lieutenant Queipo de Llano managed to stand his aircraft on its nose. German pilots soon gathered in curiosity around the machine to discover that de Llano was very much a novice pilot who had only attended his first pilots' course three months before, although he had gained a brilliant record as a crew member before taking this course. The German commander, short of ground crews, left the aircraft in its undignified attitude, and the next day a Spanish pilot attempted to photograph the He 51; an action that was not exactly well received by the Germans.

The He 51 group was really the origin of the Fighter School, which was not established until 1938. In addition to Queipo de Llano, Carlos Bayo, Ignacio Alfaro and Antonio López Sert joined the squadrons following training in April—June 1937, and Jóse Larios, Francisco Dieguez and Andrés Robles were trained during May–July 1937. Progreso Núñez, from the first course, and Luis Herrero de Teresa who had recently changed his allegiance from Government to Nationalist cause, were sent to the squadron in Aragón. All these pilots were later to join the Fiat groups, along with Serra, Henricourt, Olivera, Careaga, Rafael Simón and I. Comas.

During these first days the Condor Legion's fighters were more fortunate than those of the Spanish Nationalist units, managing to make contact with the enemy's aircraft, of which they destroyed seven.

On August 18th violent rainstorms restricted flying, but the following day the storm was so bad that all flights were cancelled. August 20th proved a bad day for Martín Campos' squadron. The weather was still bad, and during one of the few missions that were carried out, two of his patrols took off for the front. The first was formed by Manrique Montero, José Larios and Antonio López Sert, the second by César Martín Campos, Manuel Ferreras and Rafael Simón. As they crossed the mountain range the second patrol entered very dense cloud: Simón saw the aircraft of Campos and Ferreras collide; Simón, in his turn, lost his way and had to force-land in a field. Nobody knew what had happened until nightfall, when Simón returned to the aerodrome. The next day the wreckage of the two aircraft and the bodies of the pilots were located.

When the threat to Santander was mounting, the Government decided to send all their fighter aircraft into the attack, and they suffered a heavy defeat. According to Nationalist bulletins issued for August 21st to the 23rd, thirty aircraft were destroyed, the majority by the *Gamba de Ferro* group. This group, which was taking part in an important action for the first time, lost four aircraft, and one of their pilots was seriously injured.

On August 22nd Group 2-G-3 moved to Orzales aerodrome (Reinosa), which had recently been captured, and from there they continued to support the advance of the Navarrese Brigades towards Torrelavega and Santander.

Three days later they received urgent orders to move to Saragossa, as the battle of Belchite had begun. On September 2nd, when the Santander campaign was over, the expeditionary squadron of He 51s were also transferred to Saragossa.

During the last few days of August there were four air battles, during which the Condor Legion destroyed four enemy aircraft. The story of two of these actions follows, as related by Tarazona in his book *Sangre en el Cielo* (*Blood in the Sky*).

"We were waiting for the order to take off: any moment now. Finally we climbed aboard the fighters.

"The decisive moment had arrived! That moment when the unknown factor which had been worrying me for some time would be cleared up. Would I make a suitable fighter pilot? I wanted to think so.

"Pligunov took off, followed by Eloy and Prada. Mijailov's aircraft roared alongside. It moved forward and up. Now it was my turn. A quick look at the instrument panel and all is ready. I raise my head and there, in front of me, the wet surface of the runway is shining through the rotating propeller blades.

"I open the throttle wide. The noise and vibration increase in the cockpit, my *Mosca* (fly) moves forward, slowly at first, but soon the speed increases. The green fields rush past. The engine roar becomes louder. The fighter raises its tail. I move the stick backwards. I am taking off. I'm in the air.

"I have not lost sight of Mijailov. The others were taking off behind me. I think of Elena, my fiancée. I seemed to catch a fleeting glimpse of her the moment I took off. Suddenly this is all erased from my memory. Mijailov is signalling to me to come nearer. Huerta is already behind me, quickly coming into formation. Soon the squadron is closely packed.

"As we climb, dense clouds of smoke and explosions tell me that we are now flying over the front, where violent battles are taking place. I suddenly remember the advice given to me by Orlov—my battle instructor—: 'Never for one moment forget to look behind! The enemy will hide on the ground! They will attack your tail, beware of your tail! Beware of the ground, they hide there!' My head is in a whirl, I try to look around but see nothing. Suddenly I turn my head and see that Mijailov is firing his machine-guns. At whom? Oh yes, there they are. I can see some planes, painted dark green, passing barely two hundred metres in front of me. They are strange, as if camouflaged, with a marking on the rudder, a black cross on a white background. Black cross on a white background! Enemy planes! Italians? Germans? Enemies!

"My nerves become tense, I squeeze the triggers, hoping to feel the vibration of my machine-guns, scent the smell of gunpowder, to see their traces in the air. But no, I see nothing, I hear nothing. Christ, what's going on! I'd forgotten to release the safety catch on the machine-guns. I try not to fly horizontally for a single minute. I dive, climb, turn sharply and do some half rolls. I remember Orlov's advice: 'Don't stay still for a single moment.' That series of manoeuvres caused me to lose sight of Mijailov.

"I look around me, above, below. Nothing. Not a sound! I am alone. Perhaps I should say we are alone, my fighter and myself. An hour has passed since we left La Albericia. Remembering the fuel consumption, I decide to return. I set my *Mosca* in a northerly direction, trying to use the coastline as a guide to locate the airfield. Unmistakable, Santander looms before me. I land. As soon as I am on the ground I jump from the cockpit and the mechanic helps me to take off my parachute, asking me at the same time:

"'How was the battle?'

"'Have all the others already landed?,' I ask, in turn.

"'Six. The leader and one other are missing.'

"'Pligunov!' I exclaim in astonishment. 'Never!'

"At that moment our attention is drawn to an aircraft which is approaching the airfield and several pilots turn to watch it. A *Mosca* with a dead engine is trying to reach the airfield. It is already close, almost on the boundary line, but it will not reach us. It tries to land on its belly, and suddenly the pilot pulls the stick back to clear a mound of earth. The *Mosca* jolts, nose dives and turns somersault, ending up on its back inside the airfield, and slides in this position for about one hundred metres. Finally it comes to a halt. We all rush to try and free the pilot from this predicament. It is Pligunov. Although he has no bullet wounds he is badly bruised and suffering from shock.

"In the command hut news is waiting for us that Prada has been shot down by anti-aircraft fire. He managed to jump from the plane, but his parachute failed to open. It is our first loss in battle. Mijaillov asked me what I thought of the battle. Rather confused, I asked what battle.

"He insisted and asked:

"'Didn't you see the planes which attacked you?'

"'No, I didn't see anything . . . I only saw some biplanes which crossed in front of us when we were still climbing. I saw that they had the markings which the other side use. I thought they could be Fiats. But a battle? Never! I shot at them out of nervousness, but I thought they were a long way off, quite a long way off.'

"We took off again, six *Moscas*. In one patrol were Pligunov, Huerta and myself. In the other Mijailov, Eloy and Saladrigas.

"6 am. We are flying at a height of 3,000 metres. A thick blanket of fog spreads over the rivers and fords. The Europa Peaks rise up from that impalpable sea.

"Pligunov, who had now recovered from his experience of the day before, turned like an arrow towards the south east, looking for the Chatos we had come to protect. To our right, the pilots of the second *Moscas* squadron are flying, on the look-out, moving from one side to another like waves, guarding our flanks. They are a thousand metres higher than us.

"A sudden movement from Mijailov interrupts our calm flight, and as we draw near to his plane he stretches out his arm to point at a speck in front and below us. I manage to distinguish about fourteen little dots moving around, then eighteen, twenty, until there were finally twenty-two Chatos coming out of the sea of cotton wool, looking for friendly fighters.

"To one side the 'Krone Circus', with the courage of brave men, were forming a solid wedge. With more faith than weapons we go towards the front. We fly on a fixed course and, suddenly, on rounding a mountain, we see the objective: the main road.

"The enemy are marching in perfect formation. On noticing our approach the lorries stop, their occupants jump out and take refuge on both sides of the road. The Chatos begin to fire. Soon several lorries are burning. Many soldiers lie dead and wounded on the ground. The enemy quickly recover from the surprise caused by our attack and, using several machine-guns, they reply to our attack with vigorous fire.

"High above us the second squadron is involved in a furious combat with Italian fighters. Higher and above them are some small white dots. I make signs to Mijailov, but he is already aware of approaching German fighters and seems to be waiting for the Chatos and the 'Krone Circus' to finish their mission before starting battle with the enemy; time permitting. But it is impossible to wait that long.

"The Fiats come down quickly and are threatening us from behind. Mijailov dives to warn the Chatos and then zooms to gain height for the battle. Within seconds a great battle has begun in the air. The thing that worries me most is that our adversaries may make contact with our 'Krone Circus', when our hopes of saving any of them would be slight. Fortunately these companions had fled from the danger zone.

"I then found myself alone. I tried to take account of everything, to place myself within the confines of the battle, and at the same time to make sure I was not in any immediate danger. The first thing is to look behind, at my tail. There is nobody. All the fighters seem to be below.

"I look for an objective. There it is! There is one in front and below me. My intended victim. I make a concerted effort to keep calm and then I dive, placing myself very close behind him, almost on his tail. How enormous it seems! I almost cut off his tail with my propeller. I feel a strange emotion. A whole Fiat within range of my guns! I must fire. I tense my nerves and squeeze the triggers, and a new feeling of power and confidence comes over me as I see the bullets pierce the Fiat's body. 1,600 rounds per minute, soft-nosed, armour-piercing, explosive. All for the intruder! The Fiat, wounded, gives a half roll and tries to escape death. But his engine is damaged. Volumes of black smoke are pouring from it. I follow it. We are very low and I must soon correct my flight. On doing so I see a shadow come out of the cockpit, then straight-away the Italian fighter goes out of control and zigzags through the air.

"The shadow I saw jumping out, I presumed to be the pilot, but he was so low that he would not have time for the parachute to open. There could be no other end. Dashed to pieces on the ground. All this had happened within the space of a few moments. I felt great satisfaction, because this was my first victory. The first enemy plane I had shot down!

"However, on reconsidering the episode, I realised that I had made several silly mistakes, the result of my lack of experience and nervousness. I had gone too close to the Fiat. I did not look behind, to protect my rear. Afterwards I had watched the trajectory of his fall. These stupid errors could have cost me my life. I promised myself solemnly that I would not make the same mistakes again for the rest of the war. After the first few intoxicating moments had passed, I went to look for my companions in the hope of joining them. Some were involved in a large battle against the Fiats and in the meantime the others were still firing at the main road . . .

"A glance at my watch told me that I had been flying for nearly an hour and forty minutes. I had little fuel left, but I landed without incident.

"When they told me on landing that Pligunov had been shot down I am amazed. It was not possible!

"When they brought Pligunov back to the squadron's quarters, we went to see him. His right arm and leg were broken, his eyes bloodshot. He had had to take to his parachute at great speed, and the jolt of this, as it opened, had been vicious.

"(Orders had arrived to evacuate La Albericia. The enemy were pouring over the shattered defences at Santoña and were rushing towards Santander).

"'We will go to Colunga' said Mijailov.

"The armourers were taking the pins out of the bombs as fast as possible. All the ground staff, mechanics, armourers etc, were walking towards the road. They will take a westerly route to Llanes, then to Colunga and, finally to Gijón."

The Battle of Belchite

This battle is perhaps the most difficult to understand of the whole war. The overall superiority of the Government forces that mounted the attack on Belchite was so great that it seems incredible so little was achieved.

At Brunete the initial disproportion of strength had been overwhelming in favour of the attackers, and the Nationalist 13th and 150th Divisions had been rushed in to strengthen the defences. At Belchite it was these same two divisions which were brought in to stiffen the defence, transferred from Albarracín and the central front, since the entire Aragón front was guarded by only the 51st and 52nd Divisions. The only reserve Division on the Aragon front, the 105th, also sent battalions to Brunete. The *Flechas Azules* (Blue Arrows) International Brigade, which arrived from the South in September, took only a small part in the battle.

When the offensive began, all the Nationalist fighter units were in the North, apart from Zotti's group which was still in the Central area. In the sector under attack there was only Commander Pardo's group of He 46s and one squadron of He 51s from Corsini's group.

The Government Air Force was concentrated in Aragón. Although they had lost almost all of the four fighter squadrons sent to Santander (two of Ratas and two of Chatos), and their losses at Brunete had also been significant, it was still a powerful force. It not only had adequate supplies of aircraft, but there was also an abundance of pilots. There were the two hundred available from the first training course in Russia, more than fifty trained in France, about two hundred trained in the Government's own flying schools in Spain, as well as the Russian pilots, which at this time numbered about two hundred. As a result, Lister was able to report that: ". . . the activity of our air force was of the greatest importance. Especially during the first few days . . ."

In the battle of Belchite many of the pilots from the first Russian training course took part. In Boris Smirnov's Rata squadron were Claudín, Arias José Alarcón, Bravo, Marañón and Saavedra. Manuel Aguirre, Mariano Palacios and Gandia were patrol leaders. This squadron and one composed entirely of Russian personnel operated from Caspe, and another Russian Rata squadron operated from Escatrón. The group of Ratas was under the command of Ujov at this time.

Amongst the outstanding Chato pilots were Chindasvinto, González García and José Redondo. Another Russian Chato squadron was operating in Hijar and Serov's squadron was at Candasnos. For the first time the Katiuskas had a Spanish Commander, Arcega: its No 1 Squadron was led by a Russian, the 2nd Squadron by Pereira (later Cremades), and the 3rd Squadron, which was operating from Reus, was led by Leocadio Mendiola.

The Belchite operation was planned as a double offensive, to the north and south of the Ebro. The main action was that to the south of the Ebro, directed against the Nationalist troops in Quinto and Belchite.

'D' Group, whose nucleus was the V Army Corps (Modesto), was given the task of breaking through the Nationalist lines between Quinto and Belchite at 21.00hrs on August 23rd. It was planned that the 11th and 15th brigades of the 35th Division (Walter) were to wheel to the right to surround Quinto, and the 32nd and 116th Brigades under Toral's command were to wheel left to attack Codo and Belchite. A motorised brigade from the 11th Division (Líster) and the 4th Cavalry Brigade were to be sent to the Fuentes de Ebro–Mediana line; this latter brigade was then to continue to El Burgo and finally to the Saragossa–Cadrete line. The other two brigades of the 11th Division were given the task of attacking Saragossa.

To complete the siege of Belchite, the XII Army Corps (Sánchez Plaza), was to attack from Azuara to Puebla de Albortón and then to turn south-east to join up with the V Army Corps. This manoeuvre was carried out "with magnificent precision", according to Vicente Rojo, by the 25th Division (Ortiz, later García Vivancos) reinforced by a brigade from the 30th Division.

The siege of Quinto was assured once the Ebro had been crossed from north to south, at a high spot near Pina, between Quinto and Fuentes de Ebro, thus blocking the only road which could be used by the Nationalists to bring reinforcements from Saragossa.

The manoeuvre to the north of the Ebro was intended to make it difficult to bring in reinforcements, to prevent the arrival of troops from Huesca and to assist the advance towards Saragossa from the north. 'A' Group, formed by the 27th Division (Trueba, later del Barrio) reinforced by the 127th Brigade from the 28th Division was to set out from the south of Tardienta, cross the Gállego at Zuera and to occupy this area. They were then to continue along the Zuera –Villanueva road from Gállego–Saragossa to the district of Arrabal. 'B' Group, (45th Division, Kleber), setting out from Farlete, in the los Monegros zone, was to support the 27th Division's advance by sending one column towards Villanueva de Gállego, and to enter Saragossa from the north east.

The 24th Division (Gallo), and the 119th, 134th, 141st, 143rd and 153rd Brigades remained in reserve. From these details of the deployment of their forces it can be seen that the Government had overwhelming superiority. The total number of brigades taking part in the battle was 32, of which 18 belonged to the Eastern Army; with 14 Brigades in reserve, the majority from Madrid.

In the General Order for Attack No 1 for 'D' Group, issued on August 22nd at 13.00hrs, it was said that the Zuera–Quinto–Belchite line "was guarded by few troops of poor calibre", that "in Saragossa there were few reserves", and that "the leaders propose that you should march on Saragossa with courage and decision". Later on it insisted that the enemy had "a mediocre defensive organisation, reduced to occupying small positions, leaving wide gaps without defence," and that "the density of their effective strength in Codo is poor, but slightly better in Belchite and Quinto." Modesto reserved the final success for the 4th Column (Lister) and carefully detailed their route to enter Saragossa and the important points inside the town that they were to occupy. However, they were only to launch their offensive when he himself had given the order. This column was also assigned twenty-four of the thirty-four tanks from 'D' Group, and twenty-seven armoured vehicles.

On August 25th the Morato group had flown urgently to Saragossa from Orzales aerodrome (Reinosa). Shortly before this the *As de Bastos* group had arrived from their usual base at Torrijos, and during the afternoon of the 25th they were in combat over Osera.

On August 26th another air combat took place over Osera. The He 46 group and the He 51 squadron were involved, and in this action the aircraft of Commander Pérez Pardo and Second Lieutenant Salvador Blasco were both shot down. Pardo crash-landed in enemy territory and was seriously injured: he was taken to Fraga hospital and was interrogated there before his death. Salvador Blasco had only just joined Group 1-G-2, straight from the training school at Copero. The subsequent Government bulletin claimed the destruction of four Fiats and one Romeo, and added that an Italian Commander had been taken prisoner.

In the V Army Corps General Order for Operations, No 2 (dated August 26th at 21.50hrs) it was planned that once Codo and Quinto had been occupied, Mediana and Fuentes de Ebro should be attacked. The advance was then to continue towards Saragossa. On August 27th Zuera, Villamayor de Gállego and Mediana were occupied, but with this effort the offensive fizzled out.

In the afternoon of August 30th ten Junkers Ju 52s escorted by twenty-one fighters were operating in support of those defending Belchite. These operations were so effective that the attacking divisions complained bitterly of the lethal activities of the Nationalist Air Force. On September 1st Walter assumed command of the Belchite sector and the Nationalists began their counter-offensive at Zuera.

The Fiats and Spanish He 51s were concentrating their efforts to support the land forces, but on September 2nd, Group 2-G-3 surprised a formation of about fifteen Chatos, of which they destroyed seven. These victories were scored by Salas and Salvador, two each, and by Morato, Allende and Careaga.

On the 4th, the other squadron from group 1-G-2 flew from Orzales to Saragossa.

On September 4th the 13th Division (Barrón) recaptured Mediana and Vértice Sillero, where earlier the 11th Division (Lister) had had to fall back in face of the heavy attacks mounted by the Nationalist Air Force.

On September 6th, the defenders of Belchite surrendered, on Franco's orders. This action was taken to bring to an end the Santander campaign so that the Nationalist forces could be concentrated on the offensive in Asturias. In fact, by September 6th the Navarrese Brigades had already advanced to Llanes. The renewal of the offensive in the North had been decided at a meeting held in Alfaro during August. Franco, who presided at this Nationalist Council, was convinced that victory in the North was the key to overall Nationalist success.

During the battle of Belchite, the Savoia S-M.79 Group 2-G-28 made their debut, led by Luis Pardo Prieto, operating alongside Gallarza and Carrillo's Ju 52 groups. Haya, a squadron leader of Carrillo's group, was outstandingly successful in dropping supplies to the besieged defenders of Belchite.

When the battle of Belchite ended, Morato was sent on a commission to Italy and Captain Salas took command of Group 2-G-3, Captain García Pardo replacing him as leader of the 2nd squadron.

At that time, the Morato group, had destroyed a total of forty-two enemy aircraft: Morato nine, Salvador eight, Arístides and Vázquez Sagastizábal five each, Guerreo and García Pardo three, Salas and Jesús Rubio two, and Bermúdez de Castro, Murcia, Senra, Allende and Careaga one each. Individual scores of victories, including those aircraft destroyed before formation of the group, were as follows: Morato twenty-seven, Salvador fourteen, Salas nine, Guerrero seven, Arístides six, Vázquez Sagastizábal and García Pardo five each.

Asturias

After the collapse of Santander, Prada was named as leader of the Popular Army in the North, and Francisco Galán took command of the XIV Army Corps (the XV was disbanded). Gallego and Linares remained in command of the XVI and XVII Army Corps respectively. A little later, Ibarrola, who together with Galán had controlled the retreat from Santander, replaced Gallego in command of the XVI Army Corps, which reverted to its old name *Agrupación de los Puertos*. These three Army Corps had a total of eleven Divisions, Nos 50 and 54 to 63, which included the nineteen Asturian brigades, four Basque brigades and two from Santander, totalling in all about ninety battalions.

The Nationalist Army in the North continued to be commanded by General Dávila, who had at his disposal Nos 1, 4, 5 and 6 Navarre Brigades and half the Castille Brigade (General Solchaga), the 81st, 82nd and 83rd Divisions from

Galicia, Nos 2 and 3 Navarre Brigades and the other half of the Castille Brigade (General Aranda) comprising about 120 battalions, with the CTV in reserve.

So far as the Nationalist Air Force was concerned the following units were available for action at the Asturian front: Fiat group (Morato), He 45 group (Cipriano Rodriguez), Antonio Llorente's Aero 101s (then commanded temporarily by Captain Gregorio Gomez Martin), Enrique de la Puente's squadron of Do-Wal seaplanes and the Condor Legion, making a total of more than one hundred aircraft.

The Government Air Force in the North, from which the Russian pilots and nearly all the Spanish veterans had disappeared, was reduced to two patrols of Ratas (led by Eloy Gonzalo Obarro and Andrés Rodríguez Panadero, until they were killed in action) and a few Chatos.

The Morato group, then led by Salas, moved to Leon aerodrome on September 10th to support the offensive which General Aranda had begun on the 9th. Later the He 45s, Aero 101s, and Gallarza's Ju 52s operated from this same airfield. The seaplane squadron operated from bases at Santander, Ribadeo and Ferrol. The Condor Legion, which had the task of supporting Solchaga's advance, based their fighters at Calahorra de Boedo and Llanes.

By September 18th Solchaga had only managed to advance a short distance along the coast, from Llanes to Posada, and from Panes to Arenas de Cabrales towards the interior. This advance of only 7½ miles (12km) had taken seventeen days, but it should be appreciated that the terrain was extremely rugged and, in places, troops were advancing over mountain ranges that were almost 6,000ft (1,800m) in height. The most fierce fighting was at Mazuco, which was defended strongly by the 156th Brigade (Arriaga), 184th Brigade (Manolín Álvarez) and the Navy's infantry.

General Aranda advanced to Peña Ubiña, Sierra de Calleros and Puerto de Pajares and halted facing the enemy positions at Piedrafita and Vegarada. Here there were no roads, making movement almost impossible, and at Peña Lasa there were fierce battles which lasted from the 19th to the 24th.

The Fiat group devoted their efforts to close support of their infantry, strafing the enemy positions, and escorting the He 45s, especially to the north of La Robla, in Pola de Gordón, Viadangos, Buiza, Santa Lucía and Villamanín. On September 21st their courageous support of the infantry at Pico Gallo, involving low-level attacks on enemy positions in a most hazardous environment, brought the following congratulations from Colonel Muñoz Grandes, then commander of the 2nd and 3rd Navarre Brigades: "During my long military career, I have seen many heroic acts achieved by our soldiers; but I have never seen courage to equal that shown by your pilots over the Espandes peaks."

In the middle of September, with the onset of bad weather imminent, the Nationalists leaders decided that it was vital to speed up the advance if they were to make sure of liquidating the Northern front before the winter. As a result, General Aranda was ordered to abandon the operations in Pajares, and to begin a new offensive on the eastern side of the sector, from Riano to Lillo, towards the ports of Tarna and San Justo. This move was aimed at approaching the Europa Peaks from the south and assisting the advance of Solchaga's troops. Support from the air was provided by groups 2-G-3 (Salas), 6-G-15 (Cipriano Rodriguez later Elviro) and 1-G-22 (Gallarza).

Aranda's new offensive began on September 25th, and by the 27th Munoz Grandes had advanced to Tarna. On the same day Solchaga's 1st and 4th Brigades broke through the line at Nueva, arrived at the fortified line along the river Sella, and occupied the estuary at the port of Ribadesella. Farther inland, Covadonga was occupied on October 1st, by the 5th and 6th Brigades. During these operations two He 45s were shot down, one crewed by Crespi and Ángel Hernández on the 27th September, and that of Olivear and Willy Wackonig on the 30th. All four crew members escaped unharmed, but for Olivear and Wackonig it was the second time they had been shot down within the month.

In October a fierce struggle developed, and this was decided about the 11th of the month with the crossing of the Sella and the occupation of Cangas de Onis by Solchaga's two columns, and by an advance into the port of Tarna and towards Campo de Caso by Aranda.

The Fiat group collaborated brilliantly in this last advance, blasting the enemy positions at San Justo on the 6th, and especially those at Tarna on the 9th and 10th, for which they received congratulations from the commander of the 81st Division and the commander of the Condor Legion (at this date still General Sperrle, but, who handed over command to his successor Volkmann only days later). During these last two days Group 2-G-3 flew 3hrs 30min and 3hrs 20min respectively.

From this moment onwards the pace of the advance increased. Solchaga's battalions occupied Arriondas on the 14th and those of Aranda broke through the front at Pena Lasa. On October 17th Colunga fell, and three days later the troops of both Generals joined forces at Infiesto. On October 21st Gijón was occupied without a struggle, which signalled the end of Government resistance on the Northern front.

As the territory available to the enemy was being reduced daily, so the situation of the Government fighters was becoming more distressing, as can be appreciated by these two extracts from Tarazona:

"We are still at Carreño. We fly to the front in a squadron formed by Eloy, Frutos, Huerta and myself. In the other squadron are Panadero, Ortiz, Riverola and Sardina. Two squadrons, which theoretically should consist of eighteen planes, now have a total of 8 Moscas. Eloy is flying as group leader and Panadero and I are leaders of the two squadrons. That's not really the right word for them, but they have to be given some name. The front is a little beyond Villaviciosa; Colunga has already been shelled by heavy artillery.

"The mission is to do 'a little bit of everything'. Firstly to escort the Chatos, which we hope to meet at Siero. When the Chatos have finished their machine-gun attacks they will return to their lines, and we will remain to support a counter-attack to rescue a nearby unit. Then events will dictate what we should do.

"We cross over Siero. The Chatos are forming a thousand metres away. They have just taken off. The graceful silhouette of this combat plane makes it look more like an inoffensive toy rather than a war weapon. There are seven altogether.

"Beneath my wings I can see plumes of white cotton-wool rising slowly from the cold mountain peaks.

"The countryside is quiet and sad. To our right the great mountain range; to our left the violent Biscay sea. Our assigned height above the Chatos is five hundred metres. Our two squadrons cross above them to protect their flanks. I am beginning to suffer from nerves which usually precedes any action, but which disappears as soon as one is involved. The objective is below us. The Chatos begin their task whilst we begin to turn in large figure eights, trying to quarter a maximum expanse of sky.

"I note that the sun is on the opposite side; if they attack us the Fascists will make use of this advantage. The fire from the anti-aircraft guns is very heavy; the Chatos are not doing too well. The wise advice of Orlov—my battle instructor—comes to mind: 'Don't only *look at* things; you must see, you have to see.'

"I start to see. My neck turns slowly from one side to the other. On one of these turns, when I am staring into space, I manage to distinguish some small dots in the distance, about two thousand metres above us. I warn the rest of the Moscas. Those little dots, at that height, have to be Messerschmitts or Heinkels—they are manoeuvring to attack us.

"We form into a large circle, one behind the other and maintain a safe distance, so that we can guard each other's tail. If they want to attack us they will have to cross over into our zone and then they will become the attacked.

"This manoeuvre had hardly begun when two Messerschmitts dive over to one side of our group, whilst the others stay above. Panadero and Ortiz rush after them. Then another of our Moscas joins the chase. I cannot remember who it was. His engine begins to leave a long trial of white smoke. Straightaway three Heinkel fighters dive after him. The Mosca seems to be damaged. Sardina and Riverola go to protect it.

"The battle begins in earnest. The Messerschmitts attack Eloy and myself. Another is already behind Frutos. Looking ahead I can see two white trails which serve as a guide. Suddenly I feel my aircraft shudder violently, on turning my head I am nearly face to face with a yellow painted Messerschmitt, about 200ft (60m) from my tail. I flick into a sharp turn and push the stick right forward, diving as steeply as possible to avoid him. I manage to escape.

"I look for my companions, to see a Mosca being chased by two Heinkels which are already breathing down his neck. I make for the nearest one and open fire. On seeing my first shots he abandons his attack. I try to follow him, but lose him as he dives.

"I have very little fuel left, largely because of the full engine power used in combat. I decide to make for home and look for someone to accompany me. I make contact finally with six other machines, a mixture of Chatos and Moscas. The Moscas are flown by Frutos, Huerta and Sardina; Llorente, Cayo and Castillo are in the Chatos. The others are not to be seen anywhere. As we pass over Siero we see that the airfield has been bombed. We continue towards Carreño, and when we can see the port I gain height so that, in case the fuel runs out, I can glide into the airfield. The others follow suit. I do not think it will be necessary to glide, because I can already see the aerodrome. I keep my height just in case. In vain. As I approach the airfield I can see that it is impossible to land there. The ground is completely riddled with bomb craters. They have attacked it on three sides. Where can we go? Siero has also been bombed. Besides, it is too small to land the Mosca there.

"The fuel gauge tells me that we have barely enough fuel to fly for fifteen minutes. Although seemingly out of the question, I have no option but to decide to go to Colunga. I turn my Mosca and the others follow. Huerta overtakes and points behind to where Sardina is trying to land on the road. We continue. I notice that Frutos is no longer accompanying us either. Only Huerta and myself land at Colunga, together with a Chato flown by Llorente.

"Llorente told us that he was unable to land at Siero because a Kolhoven had crashed and was blocking the only damage-free runway. Two of his squadron of Chatos were left behind at the front; one shot down, while the other had to make a forced-landing in a ploughed field behind our own lines; he had no news of the remainder of the Chatos. He also saw two parachutes drop, but did not know if they were those of friends or enemies.

"Of the Moscas which took off, Frutos was possibly in Carreño; Sardina, if he was lucky, on the road. We knew absolutely nothing about the others.

"The three of us started to try and find a solution to our immediate problems. We left a few soldiers to guard our aircraft, with orders to shoot anyone who came near. We then tried to locate a telephone to communicate with Carreno, Siero or with somebody from the Air Force. Huerta, Llorente and I set out with our parachutes on our backs, since there was nowhere to leave them at the airfield. We went towards the town, which was two or three miles (4–5km) away. We carried our revolvers, to be ready for anything that might happen, as we did not know whether anyone might attempt to ambush us.

"October 9th. I have not touched this diary for three days. One lives with one's companions; and dies with them. Eloy Gonzalo Obarro is dead. The day they shot him down low clouds were covering the mountains. Some people are presentient, others are not. Perhaps it was because of the oppressive atmosphere; or the small glimmer of light filtering through, that the clouds seemed grey and sad; because the wind was cold, or because we did not look at one another and were silent. I don't know why; but we could sense tragedy.

"I was dozing in the cockpit of my Mosca when the noise of a car engine awoke me. It was Eloy, bringing a message from the Chief of Staff. Enemy aircraft were reported flying towards the airfield. Commander Luna was anxious that we get our fighters into the air before they attacked. We could not afford to lose any more planes.

"I was beginning to start my engine, its propeller turning slowly, when Eloy opened the throttle of his Mosca and raised the tail of the aircraft; he raced down the runway and passed over me at full speed. I soon followed Eloy, who was already turning in the direction of the port. As we passed over the airfield, we saw Fruto's plane taking off. The clouds were then very low, little more than 300ft (100m) between them and the ground.

"Almost as soon as I was in the air I had to fly by instruments, something I had not been taught in Russia. Eloy was lost to sight. I looked around me for Frutos. I saw nobody. I imagined that they had already entered the bank of clouds that was fast approaching. I entered the cloud and could see nothing at all. I had to gain height, to get above the clouds. I pulled back on the stick and immediately the Mosca started to climb. The cabin filled with microscopic beads of moisture, rather like smoke. I stared at my instruments and tried to keep the wings as level as possible. The air speed indicator was unsteady: only the altimeter convinced me that I was climbing.

"As I gained height I entered zones of greater condensation and the rain increased. Fortunately there was little turbulence and I was able to hold the plane steady. I slipped my helmet over my head and shut the cockpit; at the speed I was travelling the raindrops really hurt as they hit one's face. Then, suddenly, I rose above the bank of cloud; I found myself flying over a bed of cotton wool which stretched as far as the eye could see. I was now flying at more than 6,500ft (2,000m). I opened the cockpit so I could keep a sharp look out for the enemy. I also searched the sky anxiously for my companions.They were nowhere to be seen. I took my Mosca up to nearly 10,000ft (3,000m) and then to 12,000ft (4,000m). Nothing. Complete solitude.

"I tried to get my bearings and I circled over a zone which I thought to be Gijón. My only point of reference was the Pyrenees and these stretched as far as France. I managed finally to see something which was different from the clouds. It was smoke, which was probably coming from Gijon, which must be burning. I wanted to cross the clouds but I did not know where I was. I was possibly over a mountainous area and then . . .

"I decided to fly towards the sea. From what I considered to be the position of Gijon I turned northwards and flew for five long minutes. When I I thought I was over the Cantabrian sea, I probed down cautiously through the clouds. Within a few seconds I found myself below them and over the sea. I was compelled to fly close to the waves. The clouds seemed glued to the water.

"From time to time I went through heavy showers. I approached the coast and was happy to see a landfall I knew well. I was between el Musel and the airfield at Carreno. I tried not to lose visual contact with the ground; there were times when I was flying blind, and soaking in sweat! When I finally saw the airfield I could hardly believe my eyes. As the wheels rumbled along the ground I started to breathe again.

"As I climbed down from the aircraft I could see only Fruto's plane. He had landed shortly before me. He had come into contact with enemy bombers, spotting them as they broke from cloud cover. When he saw they were unaccompanied by fighters he followed. He caught them up over Colunga and fired at one of them. He did not know if it fell, but he saw it separate from the formation and lose height.

"He decided to follow it down and found himself surrounded by fighters. They did not open fire at him: it seemed rather that they were trying to capture him and his plane intact. When he tried to escape they opened fire at his machine. His engine was hit and lost power and the aircraft began to lose height. Choosing his moment he headed his Mosca down through the clouds. He came out over the sea, close to the little town of Tazones.

"I asked him about Eloy. He knew nothing. I asked the Chief of Staff the same question, and it seemed that he was trying to hide something from me. He only knew that, once again, Gijón had taken serious punishment. Bombs had fallen on the church, which was being used as a hospital.

"I was convinced that Eloy was dead or injured and began to search for him. At the Gijón hospital a nurse showed me a young body. It was naked. There were some small holes in his skin. They were bullet wounds. He was lying with his face downwards. I went up to him.

"I was afraid. This must be Eloy. I took him by the shoulder and tried to turn the body over. He slipped from my grasp, but not before I had seen part of his face. My heart began to beat quickly. The nurse helped me to support the man. Between us we managed to turn the body face upwards. Eloy's eyes were open. His mouth was gaping and one could see that his teeth had almost been pushed out. A bullet had exploded in the middle of his chest and his heart was near the surface of his skin.

"'Is this your friend?' the nurse asked in a quiet voice. I could not answer. The screams of the injured and the shouts of their relatives were not loud enough to penetrate the blank that filled my heart, mind and soul. Eloy—my friend—was dead."

In fact, Nicolás Sardina Pérez died on the 2nd September, Eloy Gonzalo Obarro on the 19th and Andrés Rodríguez Panadero, Daniel Ranz and Díez de Artazcoz on the 30th, according to the official Diaries of the Ministry of Defence.

On October 22nd the eleven surviving Fiats were sent to the Southern Regional Park for repairs, and the pilots managed to have a well earned rest after battling almost continually for six months at Pozoblanco, La Granja, Huesca, Brunete, Santander, Belchite and Asturias.

The activities of Morato's Group 2-G-3 in the last fifteen and a half months is truly amazing. With only thirteen aircraft they managed to destroy fourty-two enemy machines, losing only two of their own and one pilot. The pilots carried out between 80 and 140 war missions totalling 150 to 225 flying hours.

The aircraft had flown for longer than this, because there were more pilots than machines. Furthermore, they had always been operating at fronts that were more than 300 miles (500km) from their headquarters at the Southern Regional Park. The rugged construction of the Fiat was primarily responsible for the part played by these aircraft, but one must not forget the untiring efforts of the mechanics, who, often isolated and without the invaluable technical manuals that are commonplace today, managed to keep the aircraft flying constantly. To carry out all the 'in situ' repairs on the Fiats when the group was attached to a distant front, there was only one engineer and a small mobile workshop.

The Condor Legion contributed in an important way towards the outcome of the Asturian campaign. This was due to their attack upon the port of Gijon, where they managed to sink the destroyer *Císcar* as it was preparing to evacuate the Government high command. Their fighters were the only ones to enter into combat with the few Government fighters that were attacking the strategic bombers. Harder, flying a Me 109, managed to destroy seven enemy machines and Bodden and Woitke claimed two each.

The Condor Legion also paid their share of blood. The most notable loss was that of First Lieutenant Kessel, leader of the reconnaissance squadron. General Dávila personally placed the Military Medal on his body. This same squadron had previously lost Lieutenants von Poser and Gottanka.

Of the entire Government fighter force the only ones to escape to France were three Chatos and one Rata. The latter machine was piloted by Luis de Frutos, as one can deduce by this passage from Tarazona's book:

"I came to on the deck of a ship. My arms and legs were extremely painful. The bandage covering my head served as some reminder of what had happened. I was surrounded by unknown people, apart from Amparo, one of the people employed by the squadron. I felt very relieved to know that she was near.

"I raised my head slowly. The first thing I saw was Gijón in flames and dense columns of smoke rising from the town. We had been evacuated (so they told me) after a dreadful struggle when there were thousands and thousands of people trying to escape.

"We were on board an English ship named the *Stanley Wood*, or something like that. The majority of the passengers were Air Force or Artillery officers; and their inevitable 'friends' who tried to pass unnoticed, but were obvious from a mile way. My companions hardly replied to my questions. They, too, were deeply affected by the events of that particular moment. The Bay of Biscay was a factious sea: and neither would our route to Bordeaux be free of ships flying the enemy flag . . .

". . . About two hours after dawn the engines of the *Stanley Wood* stopped. We were all lying on the deck and could not see what was happening. Anyone who attempted to stand up was quickly dragged down again. The ship's Captain did not want the Fascists to discover that Republican soldiers, evacuated from Gijon, were on board his ship. I did not know what laws could protect us, and nor did the others.

"Between cracks in the woodwork we watched the grey masses of Fascist ships approaching across the waves. The imposing silhouette of the cruiser *Almirante Cervera* passed close to us, followed by those of the armed fishing trawlers *Ciriza* and *Alcázar de Toledo*.

"The Captain of our ship was ordered to stop, and he and the Nationalist Captains talked for a long time. We expected, any moment, to be taken to Ribadeo as prisoners. We wrote hurried notes for our families, which we gave to the women who were to be allowed to continue the journey. I tlooked as if the war was going to end for me.

"But high politics suddenly changed everything for the Fascists. The British Home Fleet appeared and the cruiser *Exeter* freed us from our hungry captors. I had something to thank the English for now. After several days of uncertainty we reached Bordeaux.

"Of the Moscas which fought at the Northern front, only one, flown by Frutos, left Carreño. The others remained on Asturian ground as a reminder of the unequal battle. Only three Chatos survived from the three squadrons which had been sent to the Northern front. The 'Krone Circus' perished in the sea or on the mountains, together with its brave pilots. On the ship were Huerta, Toquero, Saladrigas, Otaño, the Chief of Staff, some mechanics and armourers. Left behind were Pradas, Panadero, Ranz, Eloy . . . for these the war had ended. May they rest in peace! There are no more tears. Now . . . we who are left, have to continue this battle which we started together."

Seventeen Government aircraft were abandoned in Asturias, comprising four Ratas, four Chatos, three Loire-Gourdous, one Letov fighter, one Koolhoven, one single-engined Potez—probably a Po 25—one Nieuport 52 and two Breguet 19s. Also left behind were twenty-five aero-engines: twenty American-built Wright Cyclones and five French-built Gnóme-Rhônes. Five more aircraft had been abandoned in Santander, these including one Dragon Rapide, two Breguet 19s, one single-engined Potez and one Monospar. There were also fifty-two engines, mainly Gnôme-Rhônes, Walter Mercurys and Pratt & Whitneys. Apart from these aircraft and engines, the Nationalists also gained large quantities of spares, arms, ammunition, radio components and reserve dumps of fuel and oil.

Balance of the Northern Campaign

The victorious end to the Northern campaign in the autumn of 1937, assured the Nationalists of final triumph, based on three fundamentals: industrial equilibrium, numerical superiority in men and materials, and qualitative superiority.

It is not necessary to stress the economic importance of the Cantabrian area to the Nationalists, who had lacked the support of an industrial zone. Industrial production in the North represented about half of Spain's total, so that its incorporation into the Nationalist zone gave both sides an equal industrial footing. So far as war industries were concerned, the most important were the ordnance factories at Trubia and Reinosa, the factory at Mondragon which produced field mortars, and those at Moreda and Gíjon which specialised in grenades and aircraft bombs.

The Northern Campaign also caused the Government to lose twenty-five per cent of their forces: 192 infantry battalions, at least 350 field guns, more than 100 aircraft, the submarines B-6, C-5 and C-6 and the destroyer *el Císcar*. Another destroyer, the *José Luis Díez* and the submarines C-2 and C-4 fled to France.

Of the 150,000 to 180,000 men involved, only 10,000 were evacuated, leaving 30,000 dead and more than 100,000 prisoners. The number of men injured during the campaign was about 105,000, so that the number of casualties amounted to more than seventy-five per cent of the troops involved.

To compensate for these tremendous losses of manpower, the Valencian Government (which shortly afterwards moved to Barcelona) mobilised four new groups of militia, between August and October, comprising those men who registered in 1930 and between 1937 and 1939. But this was not sufficient to restore the balance of manpower, because the Nationalists incorporated into their ranks half the prisoners taken in the North.

At the end of October 1937 the Government had slightly more than 600,000 under arms, compared with the Nationalist total of approximately 700,000. Within a short time they managed to organise a number of new divisions and Army Corps. These divisions were numbered 63 to 70, and the five new Army Corps comprised the XIV, which formed the Mediterranean army in conjunction with the XIII, the XX, XXI and XXII, which swelled the numbers of the Army of Manoeuvre, and the XXIII, which formed the Andalucian Army with the IX. Despite these changes, they now had only fifty-five Divisions (Nos 1 to 47 and 63 to 70), by comparison with their previous total of sixty-three. The number of brigades totalled one hundred and seventy, numbered from 1 to 153 and from 209 to 225, with a total of six hundred and eighty Infantry battalions.

It was more difficult to replace the material they had lost. In October of the preceding year they had been successful in organising 25 new brigades because vast quantities of supplies were arriving in Spain, unhindered by the Nationalist Fleet who were unable to prevent supply ships from reaching the Mediterranean ports. But now, coinciding with the end of the Northern Campaign, the Headquarters for the Land, Sea and Air blockade were set up in Palma de Mallorca, under Admiral Francisco Moreno.

The destroyer *Velasco* came down from the Cantabrian coast and, together with the *Velasco-Ceuta, Velasco-Melilla, Huesca* and *Teruel*, which were bought from Italy, they were able to provide some protection for the Nationalist cruisers which, up until this time, had to operate without escort. Lack of support had not prevented these cruisers from taking aggressive action, such as the battle of Cape Cherchel and the destruction of the Valencia–Barcelona–Mahón convoy. This latter action was responsible for Buiza losing command of the Government Fleet and Monreal the command of the Destroyers.

They also had to contend with the submarines *General Mola* and *General Sanjurjo* (previously *Torricelli* and *Archimede*), which had been operating under the command of Pablo Suanzes and Rafael Fernandez de Bobadilla since the month of May. The battleship *España* had been lost in the Cantabrian sea on April 30th, but this loss was compensated by an explosion aboard the *Jaime I* at Cartagena, where the battleship was undergoing repairs of damage caused during an air raid.

The seaplanes from the North and from Cadiz (Group 1-G-70, with Alemán replacing Martínez Merino in command) went to the Balearics, where they operated alongside the Noreña group. Their squadron leaders were Soriano and Álvarez Pardo in the Cant 2s and P. Bazán and E. de la Puente in the Do-Wals. The He 60 squadron (Boyano, later Barrera) had its base in Melilla.

Another problem which added to the difficulties of replacing this vast quantity of captured material was the fall of Léon Blum's Government in France and the rise of Camille Chautemps. Even though Blum persuaded the new cabinet to continue to give all possible aid to the Spanish Government, this help was considerably reduced, especially when Chautemps formed his second government at the end of the year.

So far as the air force was concerned, it was not so difficult to replace this material, since the majority of aircraft lost in the North were fighters and at this stage the Sabadell-Reus factory was mass-producing aircraft. In 1938 they attained a production rate of one Chato per working day. At this time there was an abundance of Katiuskas, since a third consignment of thirty-one machines had arrived. Some Ratas were also received at the end of 1937 (Nos 143 to 157), and the 6th squadron was formed, again with Russian pilots. But these Ratas did not compensate for the two complete squadrons which had been lost in the North. Russia now had to send Ratas to China, for defence against the Japanese, and could no longer maintain the generous supplies to Spain.

The loss of at least 350 field guns in the North was also of great significance for the future. It should be remembered that to break through the 'Iron Ring' the Nationalists used only 144 field guns, and that at Santander, reinforced by the entire Italian Artillery, only 61 batteries had been used.

Apart from the foregoing points, there were other qualitative matters which should not be overlooked. Seven months of continual, hard fought battles had produced some very tough troops, and three army shock corps were formed, one in Navarre, one in Castille and one in Galicia. These, together with the veteran Moroccan Army Corps and the CTV constituted a formidable manoeuvrable force, which had no equal on the Government side, since the best units from the Basque and Asturian corps disappeared at the end of the Northern campaigns. The only comparable Government unit was the V Army Corps, which had opposed the Moroccan Army Corps at Brunete and Belchite. The V Corps, the main participant in the unsuccessful Government offensives, could not be expected to have the same morale as troops which had been victorious in three Northern Campaigns.

The Navarre Army Corps was formed basically from the six Navarre Brigades, of which the 1st, 3rd, 4th and 5th were turned into Divisions, retaining the same numbers. The 2nd and 6th Brigade were disbanded and their troops joined the two Castille Brigades, becoming the 61st Division (García Navarro) 62nd (Sagardía), and 63rd (Tella) which were incorporated into the new Castille Army Corps. Varela was named as its commander. The old VI Army Corps became the VI Military Region, retaining López Pinto as its commander. The VIII Army Corps similarly became the VIII Military Region and General Lombarte (who later became under secretary for Air) was appointed its commander.

Three divisions from the old Asturias-León front, the 81st (Múgica), 82nd (Ceano) and 83rd (Martín Alonso), together with the reserve division 108th (Lafuente, later Amado), formed the new Galician Army Corps, with General Aranda being retained as its commander. The Moroccan Army Corps (Yagüe) was formed from Divisions 13 (Barrón) and 150 (Sáez de Buruaga), which had helped stabilise the Brunete and Belchite fronts, and which had been joined by the 5th, 54th, 74th, 82nd and 108th Divisions when they were based in Guadalajara.

Ponte replaced Yagüe in command of the 1st Army Corps. General Moscardó replaced Ponte in Aragón (V Army Corps which was later called the

Aragón Army Corps) and had under his command the 51st Division (Urrutia), 52nd (Munoz Castellanos) and 105th (Santiago), and three others which were in the process of formation, the 53rd, 54th and 55th (Sueiro, Marzo and Adrados). In reserve on this front, and controlled by the Northern Army (Dávila), were the Navarre and Galician Army Corps. Those from Castille and Morocco, as well as the CTV (Berti) remained on general reserve.

Ferrer replaced Varela in the VII Army Corps; with his forces a re-grouping of the Ávila-Segovia Divisions (Serrador) was organised with the 71st Division (Palenzuela) and 72nd (Valverde) and also of the Soria-Somosierra Divisions (Cebrián), with the 73rd Division (Abriat), 74th (Arias) and 75th (Los Arcos).

Division 15 (García Escámez) and 107 (March, later Santa Pau) remained in reserve at the Madrid front, which was defended by the I Army Corps, with the following divisions: 11th (Delgado Serrano, later Bartomeu), 12th (Asensio) and 14th (Carroquino). The Caceres front was covered by the 153rd Division (Rada). All these forces were controlled by the Central Army (Saliquet).

The Southern Army (Queipo de Llano) comprised the II and III Army Corps. The II Army Corps then consisted of the 21st Division (Rubio Oliver), 22nd (Álvarez Rementería, later Redondo) and 23rd (Borbon, later Munoz Castellanos). The III Army Corps comprised the 31st Division (Martín Prats), 32nd (González Espinosa, later Tamayo) and 33rd (Rosaleny), and the divisions in reserve, of which there were two at the time, 102nd (Castejón) and 112th (Baturone).

Apart from the divisions mentioned, there was also the 151st (Fuentes) guarding Morocco, and 154th (Iruretagoyena).

At the end of 1937 the Nationalist Army had 44 divisions organised: Nos 1, 3, 4, 5, 11 to 15, 21 to 23, 31 to 33, 51 to 54, 61 to 63, 71 to 75, 81 to 84, 102, 105, 107, 108, 112, 150, 151, 152 and 154, and the *Littorio*, *XXIII March* and *Flechas* (formed the union of the Mixed Brigades), but some of these, especially those from Madrid, had more than the theoretical twelve battalions.

During the first part of 1938, eight more divisions were formed, 16 to 18 (by splitting the Madrid divisions), 19, and 24 (split from 22), 55, 85 and 122, as well as the 1st Cavalry. So far as the number of divisions was concerned, the Nationalists still had an inferior number, but it must be remembered that they were of superior quality to those supporting the Government.

There is another point worth mention; from April 1937 the Nationalist Army frequently left their secondary fronts practically unguarded, sometimes dangerously so, and this allowed them to have local superiority at vital points. This applied to their infantry, but more especially to the artillery, armoured vehicles and air force. This attitude contrasts sharply with that of the Government, who maintained an inexplicable abundance of troops in the Madrid sector until well after March 1938. One cannot help wondering if this obsession regarding the defence of Madrid was what made the Popular Army lose the war.

In 1937, with the centre of gravity for battles in the North, Madrid and Aragon, the advantageous position of the Nationalist Armies, who could move along interior lines, favoured the policy of economising on forces. For this reason, attacks on Extremadura and Andalucia would have seemed more advisable than those which took place in La Granja, Brunete, Huesca, Saragossa and Teruel.

In 1938, the Popular Army of the Central-Southern zone was the one with the advantage of being able to operate along interior lines, but they did not take advantage of this until January 1939, when it was already much too late.

CHAPTER FIVE

The War is Decided

The Air Force in Aragón in the Autumn of 1937

As we have seen in the previous chapter, during the Asturian campaign only the Fiat group (Salas), the Heinkel He 45s (Cipriano Rodríguez), Aeros (Gómez Martín), the Ju 52 day operations group (Gallarza) and the Condor Legion took part. The Ju 52 night operations group (Carrillo) operated sporadically from León.

The Heinkel He 51 group (Manrique Montero), He 46s (Castro Carrasco), the Ju 52 night operations group (Carrillo) and the majority of the Legionary Air Force remained in Aragón.

With the end of the battle of Belchite, the Government forces maintained pressure on various sectors of the Aragón front and in the middle of September the Nationalist leaders decided to organise night bombing raids on the enemy aerodromes. At this time the two Ju 52 groups were still based in Saragossa and these were assigned to attack the aerodromes of Sariñena and Bujaraloz. On the night of September 14th/15th two aircraft bombed Sariñena aerodrome, the first crewed by the group leaders Gallarza and Haya and the second by Muntadas and Marchenko. This second aircraft, 22-61, was shot down by a night fighter (a victory attributed to Eriomenko) and the crew were killed, with the exception of the machine-gunner, Corporal José Ramón Blasco Lavín. He was uninjured and managed to make his way back to the Nationalist lines, travelling on foot by night. Despite the loss of this machine, Haya attacked Bujaradoz aerodrome the following night.

At the end of the month the two groups of Junkers were moved to León, but shortly afterwards Group 1-G-22 (Carrillo) returned to Saragossa.

On October 7th an Order for Operations was published. Beginning on November 5th, these were to be mounted to the north of the Alcubierre mountains, with the objective of reaching the Cinca or the Segre. Prior to the start of these operations the Air Force was required to soften up the defences by a series of systematic attacks. These were scheduled to begin on October 20th and the targets included aerodromes in Aragón and Catalonia, lines of communications, ports, electricity power stations, military centres and supply dumps. The Air Force order quoted as objectives the aerodromes at Sariñena, Bujaraloz, Puebla de Híjar, Selgua, Lérida and Balaguer, which were to be attacked from Aragón, and Reus, Sabadell, Figueras, Celrá and Los Alcázares to be attacked from the Balearics.

Designated for use by the Spanish Nationalist Air Force were the aerodromes at Alfamén, Almunia, Sanjurjo and Palomar; the Legionary Air Force would operate from Valenzuela, Sanjurjo, Ablitas and Logroño; and the Condor Legion from Erla, Berdún, Buñuel, Tudela, Alfaro and Soria.

On October 13th the attack on the aerodromes of Selgua and Balaguer, which had been planned originally for attack by the Condor Legion, was assigned to the Nationalist and Legionary Air Forces respectively.

By this time, however, the Government had taken the initiative, and Saragossa was attacked by the XXI Army Corps (Casado), which had been formed from the 27th and 28th Divisions only a short time before, and nearly all available air units took part. The land offensive was a complete failure, but there were some important events in the air.

On October 12th five Fiats from the *Gamba de Ferro* group were shot down during a battle with Government fighters. Then, on the morning of the 15th, Government Chatos and Katiuskas made a surprise attack on Sanjurjo aerodrome (Saragossa), escorted by the Ratas. This aerodrome was 10 miles (16km) from the front and was dominated by observation posts on the Alcubierre mountains. Despite this drawback, a large number of bomber and fighter aircraft were based there, which made it an attractive target for the enemy air force. The attacking aircraft approached from the north east and left the area in the direction of Belchite.

The ground crews of the Nationalist Ju 52s were making their way to their aircraft to carry out daily inspections when the enemy came sweeping in to the attack. They quickly took cover in the ditches alongside the road as bombs and machine-gun bullets began to take their toll. Planes 22-49, 22-54 and 22-62 caught fire and exploded, flaming debris setting fire to three more Heinkel He 46s. As the enemy machines raced away ground crews ran to use fire extinguishers on burning aircraft, but despite the most courageous efforts several Heinkels were badly damaged and six Fiats completely destroyed.

At about this date the Northern Campaign ended and Group 1-G-22 was re-equipped with Junkers Ju 52s supplied to them by the Condor Legion. Then based at Pontejos, the Condor Legion had itself been re-equipped with Heinkel He 111s, with which they formed three bomber squadrons. The remainder of the Ju 52s were retained for daytime operations although, occasionally, they were used for night attacks.

To ensure, so far as possible, that their own air units were not subjected to a surprise attack as damaging as that which they had inflicted on Sanjurjo, the Government Air Force began to disperse their aircraft over a maximum number of aerodromes. The fighter squadrons picketed their aircraft around the perimeter of the airfield and experimented with a system of taking off from different points. They also began to site dummy aircraft at aerodromes which were not in use.

At this time the Katiuska squadrons were operating from Lérida, Balaguer and Reus, the Ratas from Caspe, Alcañiz, Escatrón, Puig Moreno, Candasnos, Castejón del Puente, Reus, Sagunto and La Señera, and the Chatos from Figueras, Reus, Sariñena and Almenar. They also used more remote airfields at Grañen (Almuriente) and La Naja (Pallaruelo).

After the losses suffered by the squadrons in the North, the 6th Squadron was replenished with Ratas and, once again, they were flown by Russian pilots. Gussaiev was appointed commander, and the three patrols were led by Panfilov, 'Victor' and 'Juanito'. The twelve new Ratas for the 6th Squadron were supplied from Archena, out of a total of fifteen that were held there (Nos 143 to 157). This squadron made its first operations from Cabeza de Buey aerodrome in Extremadura. Later, they returned to La Señera, and then moved to Reus, from where they operated in October.

At the end of October the few pilots that had survived the bitter campaign in the North arrived back in Catalonia. They consisted of Frutos (who had flown the only surviving Rata into France), and Tarazona, Toquero, Huerta and Saladrigas who had escaped from Santander in the British merchant ship *Stanley Wood*.

Comas, who had been transferred from the North at the end of August, was promoted to Lieutenant on September 19th and given command of the 3rd Squadron (Chatos). Riverola had been promoted to Captain and was sent first to Manises and later to Rosas, to the 7th Squadron, commanded by Rafael Pena. Zambudio and Duarte were also promoted to Lieutenant. All these men eventually became leaders of squadrons. Aguirre was promoted to Captain on October 12th and was given command of a Ratas squadron, the first Spaniard to hold such a position.

The month of November was relatively quiet, but both Government and Nationalist Air Forces concentrated their efforts on attacking aerodromes. In fact, both sides were preparing for a battle which seemed likely to erupt at any moment, one which threatened to be decisive.

At the beginning of the month the Nationalists decided to put into action their plan to attack between the Pyrenees and Saragossa. However, during the last ten days of November Franco changed his mind and decided instead to attack from Guadalajara, between the Jarama and the Tagus. To deceive the enemy, massive air attacks in Aragón were planned for the period December 10th–12th.

Before going to Aragón, Group 2-G-3 spent a large part of the month of November practising combat tactics as a group. On November 20th they moved from Seville to Villanueva de Gámez, on the 24th to Saragossa and on the 28th to Buñuel. On December 1st they made two reconnaissance sorties, one along the Belchite Fuendetodos road, the other over the Monegrillos zone, with the objective of preparing for the attacks which were planned to begin on December 10th. The action planned for that day had several aims: revenge for the attack on Saragossa aerodrome in the middle of October; to deceive the enemy of their intention of attacking towards Madrid, via Guadalajara; and to destroy the largest possible number of enemy aircraft before the beginning of the main offensive, which was scheduled to begin on December 18th.

About half of the Nationalist Air Force took part in this operation, involving some two hundred aircraft, of which one hundred were fighters. The slower bombers (S-M.81s and Ju 52s) were to attack the nearby aerodromes in the Barbastro zone; the fast machines (S-M.79s, Breguet 20s, He 111s and Do 17s) those at Sariñena, Bujaraloz, Candasnos, Puebla de Híjar, Selgua, Pomar, Lérida and Balaguer. The Condor Legion's bombers, which had to operate from more distant bases, would require re-fuelling before making their return flight, and facilities were provided at Sanjurjo.

As a preparatory move, the He 111s dropped almost thirty tons of bombs at Bujaraloz on December 4th; during the ensuing combats over the aerodrome an Me 109 escorting the bombers was shot down (Second Lieutenant Polenz). The reconnaissance squadron was given the task of photographing enemy aerodromes in the central region (Tembleque, Quintanar de la Orden, Fuentes de Pedro Naharro, Pozorrubio, Villamayor de Santiago) and the station at Alcazar de San Juan. On the appointed day the aerodromes were empty, their seventy odd fighters airborne, so the results, so far as determining the deployment of these aircraft, were disappointing.

Between Alcubierre and Lanaja the Italian *Gamba de Ferro* group were in combat with the enemy's Chatos. Group 2-G-3, which was flying below the Italians, climbed to their assistance and achieved a great victory, destroying seven of the Chatos without loss. Morato, who was leading the group, later destroyed an eighth Chato. The Italians claimed the destruction of six Chatos, losing one of their machines piloted by Barberis. It seems likely that there was a duplication of claims in this engagement, since this appears to be a large number of victories for a single action at that time. However, the Nationalist bulletin reported twenty victories, a figure presumably calculated by adding probables.

Apart from this success, the operation failed to produce the rewards anticipated for so much preparation. The fact was that, apart from the clutch of enemy Chatos destroyed by the two Fiat groups, the Nationalists failed to eliminate any significant proportion of the Government Air Force.

On the second day of the operation they failed to lure the enemy fighters into battle. On the third day they despatched the light bombers without fighter escort. These, too, were ignored, and they next planned an intruder operation, to attack enemy fighters as they returned to their home airfields. Fog and snow contributed to the failure of this plan, but it seemed that the enemy were fully aware of Nationalist intentions, although there is no evidence that this was the case.

On December 14th, Group 2-G-3 moved to La Ventosilla aerodrome (Aranda) and the following day Group 6-G-15 arrived at Olmedo. According to the plan of operations, the Hispana Air Brigade (Apolinar Sáez de Buruaga) was to support the Moroccan Army Corps (Yagüe) on the right flank of the offensive. The main thrust in the centre would be made by the Corps of Voluntary Troops (Berti), supported by the Legionary Air Force (Bernasconi). On the left flank the Castille Army Corps (Varela) would have the support of the Condor Legion (Volkmann).

The Air Headquarters for these three air support groups were set up in Burgos, at Aranda, Almazán and Saragossa. In reserve were the Galician and Navarre Army Corps, and once again Yagüe and Varela were poised to enter Madrid.

Reorganisation of the Air Forces

Once the Northern Campaign had ended, and preparations for the next offensive had been finalised, the 1st Hispana Air Brigade was organised, with

Colonel Apolinar Sáez de Buruaga in command. Initially, the following groups made up this 1st Air Brigade: Gallarza's No 1 Squadron (Junkers Ju 52s; Groups 1-G-22 and 2-G-22); Lacalle's No 2 Squadron (Savoia S-M.79s; Groups 3-G-28 and 4-G-28); Alfonso de Oreleans' No 3 Squadron (Savoia S-M.79s; Group 5-G-28 and Heinkel He 70s; Group 7-G-14); and the Fiat Group 2-G-3. García Morato was nominated operational commander of the 1st Air Brigade, and Salas replaced him as Commander of Group 2-G-3.

Groups 4-G-28 (Navarro Garnica), 5-G-28 (Goma) and 7-G-14 (Carlos Soler) had only recently been formed. Groups 1-G-22, 2-G-22 and 3-G-28 were then commanded by Gallego, Luis Roa and Juan Antonio Ansaldo respectively. The twelve squadrons of these six groups were led by Micheo, Presa, Pérez y Martínez de la Victoria, Penche, Rute, Larrauri, Jiménez Ugarte, Ureña, Gómez Martín, Manuel Ugarte, Martínez Mejías and Barrera (later Alonso Pimentel when Barrera was transferred to seaplanes).

Group 2-G-3 was increased to two squadrons, each with nine aircraft. At the end of October they had received fourteen new machines, numbered from 3-64 to 3-77 (factory Nos 748 to 760 and 765), and in November ten of the thirteen original Fiats were returned to the Group after being completely overhauled. (Of the remaining three, two had been destroyed at Brunete and 3-55, with factory No 603, was not repaired until later).

In December 1937 twenty-three more Fiats were received from Italy and the 3rd and 4th Spanish Fiat squadrons were formed. The 3rd Squadron, 3-E-3, was led by Capt. Murcia, the 4th Squadron, 4-E-3, by Manrique Montero Mera. These new aircraft were numbered from 3-78 to 3-100 (Factory Nos 766 to 790, except 769 and 777).

In January 1938 Squadron 3-E-3 was split from Salas' group and, together with Squadron 4-E-3, formed a new Fiat group, 3-G-3, under the command of José Ibarra Montís. Montís had only recently joined the Nationalist Air Force, but was a well-known pilot and had been Morato's principal rival in pre-war aerobatic competitions. It was soon proved, however, that he was not the ideal leader of a fighter group. During one of his first missions over Teruel he spent much of his time flying aimlessly back and forth: ". . . because he was overcome by the marvellous sunset". In July he handed over command of Group 3-G-3 to Morato when posted on an advanced pilots' course and subsequently he led the Dornier Do 17 Group. Coincidentally, he died on the same day as Morato.

At the end of 1937 the Spanish Air Force had a total of about 150 aircraft, 75 of them in the Hispana Air Brigade. The Condor Legion had maintained its strength at 100 machines, but due to its recent growth the Legionary Air Force had slightly increased its numbers.

When the new Fiat group was formed, the old Heinkel He 52 fighter group became redesignated as the *Cadena* (Link) Group, retaining the numerical designation 1-G-2, and Captain José Muñoz Jiménez remained in command.

The close-support groups remained under individual Commanders who, at that period, were as follows: 1-G-2 (He 52s; Jiménez); 3-G-11 (He 46s; Carrasco); 4-G-12 (Ro 37s; de las Cuevas); 6-G-15 (He 45s; de Castro); and

5-G-17 (Aero 101s; Alvarez). The He 70 reconnaissance Squadrons also were under individual command: 3-E-14 (de Mendoza) and 4-E-14 (Ureta). The Pollensa seaplane group remained under the leadership of Federico Noreña Echevarría. The Cadiz seaplane group was moved to Pollensa and Alcudia and the squadron of He 60 seaplanes commanded by Moyano, (later Barrera), was transferred from Melilla to Cadiz.

The Legionary Air Force was also reorganised in the autumn of 1937. The three fighter groups, each of which was composed of three squadrons, were integrated into a single fighter squadron, under the command of Colonel Casinelli 'Canaveri'. Zotti, Casero and Leotta continued as group commanders, and the nine squadrons were led by Nobili, Foschini, Calosso, Bianchi, Fassi, Francois, Ippodrino, Criscione and Vizotto.

The Mixed Bomber Squadron became divided into three, consisting of a squadron of fast bombers (S-M.79s led by Lieutenant Colonel Cupini), a squadron of heavy bombers (S-M.81s, led by Colonel Barba) and an autonomous group of fast bombers (Fiat B.R.20s, led by Commander Sergio Lalatta). Army co-operation was still the task of the Ro 37 group, which was led by Lieutenant Colonel Franciosa until he was killed in an accident in Vitoria, and then by Lieutenant Colonel Achenza. This group later received a number of Breda Ba 65s which were used for reconnaissance. General Bernasconi 'Garda' remained in overall command of the Legionary Air Force, with Colonel Velardi as leader of the air forces in the Balearics. Lieutenant Colonel Appignani 'Aprille' returned to Italy at the end of 1937.

The organisation of the Condor Legion was unchanged, but their equipment was brought more up to date. The combat group (Handrick) consisted of four squadrons, two equipped with Me 109Bs (Schellman and Schlichting) and two with He 51s (Galland and Roth). The bomber group (Wehnert) handed over its Ju 52s to the Spanish Air Force, and these were replaced by He 111s. The reconnaissance squadron retained its three patrols of Do 17s, but one patrol of He 45s also went to the Spanish Air Force; the seaplane squadron continued to operate with its He 59s. Maintenance of the Condor Legion's aircraft was carried out in the Northern Regional Park, at León. Volkmann replaced Sperrle as Commander of the Condor Legion in October, and shortly afterwards Plocher replaced Richthofen as Chief of Staff.

A Spanish patrol of He 111s was also formed, and this was initially led by Luis Ureta Zabala and, after February 1938, by Luis Rambaud.

In 1937, for the first time, the Nationalist fighter force held slight numerical superiority with a force of 15 fighter squadrons (13 Fiat and 2 Me 109B) totalling 141 aircraft. The Government fighter force then totalled 12 squadrons, with a strength of 120 aircraft. This was the moment when the loss of four Government Squadrons in the Northern Campaign was critical. Without this loss they would have retained numerical superiority.

In fact, by the end of 1937, the Nationalist Army had received about 300 modern fighters (some 250 Fiats and 50 Me 109B), by comparison with approximately 400 supplied to the Government (157 Ratas, at least 147 Chatos and 34 Super-Chatos from Russia, and 40 Chatos manufactured at Sabadell-Reus).

So far as modern bombers were concerned, Nationalist superiority was even greater, with about 50 He 111s and Do 17s, and a similar number of Savoia S-M.79s, compared with the 50 Katiuskas which were then flying.

In 1937 Russia had sent to Spain about thirty-one more machines of this type, but this delivery exhausted the available supplies. France had no modern bombers in service, and in the United States production of the Martin 139 bomber in its various versions had ended and, at that time, no other bomber had gone into large scale production. The Boeing B-17 prototype had been enthusiastically received by the US Army Air Corps, but there were no funds available for its manufacture in quantity. Instead, since 1936, they had been forced to make the best possible use of adaptations of the fast and reliable civil aircraft that were being produced by the American aircraft industry.

In 1937 the Valencian Government ordered 40 carrier-based fighters from the Canadian Car & Foundry Co, which had obtained a licence from the American Grumman Aircraft Engineering Corporation to build its highly successful FF-1. According to Spanish sources only twenty-seven of these aircraft were received, but information from England indicates that all forty, theoretically destined for Turkey, were handed over to the Spaniards.

A licence to build the Fokker C.X. was obtained from the Netherlands, but little use was made of this, since only one example was built and flown in Spain.

Not only were Russian aircraft becoming scarce at this time, but the Russian pilots were disappearing too as they became absorbed into the Sino-Japanese War, which was of more direct interest to Russia than events in Spain. The replacement of these pilots did not cause the Valencian Government too many headaches, even though Chautemps' second Government had stopped the training of Spanish pilots in French flying schools. The fact was that the first two hundred pilots who had been trained in Russia had returned to Spain two months earlier, and four hundred more from the second and third pilots' courses were due to return during 1938.

The Nationalist Air Force was not so dependent upon other nations for pilot training, although during the war eighty were trained in Italy and forty in Germany. Almost five hundred came from their own flying schools in Spain, as well as 242 other crew members and approximately 70 air-gunners/bomb aimers.

At the beginning of 1938 (Decree of the 4th January, 1938) the Air Force Arm was reorganised, and was then formed into a number of Corps, comprising General, Mechanics, Radio Telegraphists and Meteorologists, Armourers, Aeronautical Engineers, Specialist Aero-Engine, Medical, Troops and Services, Automobile Drivers, and the Air Force Arsenal.

The registration marks issued to aircraft in Government service in 1938, which are shown in Appendix 9, date from this time. Similarly, those issued to Nationalist aircraft are shown in Appendix 10.

In the Autumn, in preparation for possible operations in Aragon or Madrid, the Nationalist leaders ordered the construction of two networks of aerodromes in the valleys of the Ebro and Duero. The distribution of aviation fuel to Nationalist airfields was made by rail, and throughout the war some 60 million litres was supplied by this means without accident. Following the occupation of Biscay and the industrial areas of the North, the manufacture of aircraft bombs of 10, 50, 100 and 250kg was initiated. The explosive charge of these weapons consisted mainly of Amonal, an explosive invented by a Captain of the Blanco Artillery.

At this time Nationalist forces acquired a large number of 75mm anti-aircraft guns and with these the Anti-aircraft Artillery Regiment was formed at the beginning of 1938. This Regiment was attached to the Air Headquarters, which provided transport to make them mobile. The 1st Air Brigade was assigned one group of 75mm guns and three sections of anti-aircraft machine-guns, consisting of sixty 20mm weapons mounted in pairs. The Air Headquarters reserved three groups for aerodrome defence, and distributed the remainder amongst the Army Corps.

Teruel

The Central Chief of Staff for the Popular Army, Vicente Rojo, was aware of Nationalist intentions to attack Madrid via Guadalajara. In fact, he had already planned an offensive in Extremadura, with the object of splitting the Nationalist Zone. For this he had organised Army Corps XX, XXI and XXII which, together with the old Army Corps V and XVIII, formed an offensive force of thirteen divisions, similar to that prepared by Franco for the attack upon Madrid.

Rojo realised that he could not continue with his plan and, as an alternative, proposed a diversionary manoeuvre on the Teruel front, which was approved by the Valencian Government. At the same time, he ordered each of the Army Corps I to IV to organise a reserve division, initially to be numbered 101 to 104, and these were to serve as a basis for the creation of Army Corps XVI and XVII, intended to replace those lost in the North.

Government forces taking part in the Teruel offensive included the XVIII Army Corps (Fernández Heredia), XX (Leopoldo Menédez) and XXII (Ibarrola) from the Army of Manoeuvre, and the XIII (Balibrea, later Salavera) and XIX (Vidal), from the Mediterranean Army, all under the command of Juan Hernández Sarabia. The Vth Army Corps (Modesto) and XXI (Perea) were held in reserve.

Initially, five divisions of the Army of Manoeuvre were in action at Teruel: 11th (Líster), 25th (García Vivancos), 34th (E. Vega), 68th (Triguero) and 70th (H. Toral), and five divisions from the Mediterranean Army: 39th (Alba), 40th (Nieto), 41st (Luis Menéndez), 42nd (Naira) and 64th (Martínez Cartón). Of the remaining divisions in the Army of Manoeuvre the 35th (Walter) and 47th (J. Durán) were held in reserve at Teruel; the 66th (González Gómez), 67th (Fernán) and 45th (Hans) remained in Extremadura; the 46th ('Campesino') in Tarancón, and the 27th (del Barrio) and 28th (Jover) in Aragón. At a later stage the 27th, 28th, 45th and 46th Divisions were sent to Teruel.

It is interesting to record the total deployment of the Government Army at this time, when the end of the war was drawing near. The Eastern Army still had seven divisions: 24th (Yoldi), 26th (Sanz), 30th (J. Pérez Salas), 31st (Navarro), 32nd (Gancedo), 43rd (Escassi) and 44th (Peire). The Central Army comprised twenty divisions: 1st (Hortelano), 2nd (Barceló), 3rd (Tagüeña), 4th (Bueno), 5th (Palacios), 6th (Melero), 7th (Zulueta), 8th (Ascanio), 9th (Rubert, later Guerrero), 10th (Enciso), 12th (Jiménez Durán), 13th (Berenguer), 14th (Gutiérrez Caro), 15th (del Castillo), 16th (Fresno), 17th (Rovira), 18th (Márquez), 33rd (Medrano), 65th (Fernández Ordóñez) and 69th (Gallego). The Extremadura Army totalled six divisions: 19th (Juan Bautista Gomez), 29th (Rubert), 36th (Gómez Palacios), 37th (Ruiz Farrona), 38th (Blanco Pedraza) and 63rd (Morandi). The Andalusian Army then had five divisions, 20th (Orad de la Torre), 21st (Martín Calvo), 22nd (Menoyo), 23rd (Jiménez Canito).and 71st (Muntaner). Divisions 48 to 62 had been lost in the North and had not then been replaced.

The line up of the Nationalist Army at the same period consisted of three divisions in Aragón (51, 52 and 53), five in reserve in Aragón (3, 63, 83, 84, 105), sixteen prepared for the Guadalajara offensive (1, 4, 5, 13, 54, 61, 62, 74, 75, 81, 82, 108, 150 and those from the CTU), three in the Sierra (71, 72 and 73), five in Madrid (11, 12, 14, 15 and 107), one in Caceres (152), and eight in the South (21, 22, 23, 31, 32, 33, 102 and 112). The majority of their air force was concentrated in the Provinces of Burgos and Soria and the Ebro valley.

The Government Air Force, which had been based mainly in Aragon, moved to Valencia and Castellón aerodromes. The 1st and 4th Spanish Rata squadrons, led by Claudín and Zarauza, moved to Caspe and Villar del Arzobispo. The four Russian Rata squadrons were maintained in a state of readiness at Sagunto, Reus, Villar and Sarrión. The 2nd and 3rd Squadrons of Chatos from Group 26, led by Gonzalez and Comas respectively, were moved to El Toro. The 1st Squadron, led by Stepanov, remained at Barracas aerodrome, and the 4th Squadron (Duarte) was still under training at Sabadell. Three squadrons of Katiuskas were based at Villar del Arzobispo and Liria; during the battle the 4th Squadron was formed.

Four squadrons of Natachas from group 30, and commanded by Juan Alonso Vega, were also based on the Valencian aerodromes, and Nos 1 to 4 were led respectively by Vargas, Sánchez Calvo, Montalbán and Pelayo.

On December 15th the XVIII and XXII Army Corps attacked towards Campillo and Concud, on both sides of the Teruel corridor and some 9 miles (15km) apart, but on the 16th they met up in San Blas, on the river Turia.

The 11th Division had reached San Blas during the night of December 14th/15th, and this town was occupied without fighting on the morning of the 15th. Concud, which was nearer to the front, and whose defenders were on the alert, managed to resist until the afternoon. The XVIII Corps reached the outskirts of San Blas before nightfall, but did not join up with the 11th Division until the following day.

Nationalist leaders hesitated initially: should they continue with the carefully laid plans of their own offensive; or should they hurry to the defence of Teruel. On the 16th Franco ended any indecision: he ordered Aranda to counter-attack with seventeen battalions from the 52nd, 53rd and 84th Divisions, and told Dávila to move the 81st Division from its position on the upper Tagus;

he also sent some artillery and two anti-aircraft batteries to the Teruel front.

The weather favoured the attackers: when the Nationalist Air Force despatched eighteen Italian Fiats into operations over Teruel, eleven landed in Calamocha, six in Molina de Aragón and the eighteenth had to rely upon his parachute to offer a chance of landing in one piece. The next day, despite continuing bad weather, twenty-three He 111s took off from their base at Burgo de Osma to support the defenders of Teruel; six of these landed in aerodromes as far away as Salamanca, Ávila, Escalona and Talavera, and one force-landed in enemy territory.

The order for Group 2-G-3 to move to Alfamen was not given until December 19th, and Group 5-G-15 remained at Olmedo until the 21st, from which date they began to operate from the nearby aerodrome at La Almunia de Doña Godina. The Spanish Savoia S-M.79s and Ju 52s remained weather-bound at their airfields in Burgos and Soria. The Italian bombers in the Ebro valley started operating from the 19th. Group 4-G-12's Romeos did not arrive in Ojos Negros until the 27th, and at the same time the He 52s of 1-G-2 began operating from Calamocho, where the He 46s had been for some days.

Group 2-G-3 began its reconnaissance sorties over Teruel on December 20th, the day after their arrival at Alfamén. On the 21st their five available He 46s, accompanied by ten He 45s newly-arrived from Olmedo, were provided with an escort of seventeen Fiats. The only enemy encountered was, once again, the weather and this force had to land in Saragossa because, by the time of their return, Alfamén was deep in snow.

On December 22nd Franco called a meeting of his Generals to discuss the overall situation: the unanimous decision was to mount a strong counter-attack utilising two Army Corps. On that day the weather prevented any attempt at reconnaissance from the air, but the next day Salas twice flew through snow flurries in an attempt to discover vital information of enemy strength and intentions. The same day the Fiats of 2-G-3, which had been diverted to Saragossa on the 21st, were able to return to Alfamén where snow had been cleared from the airstrip.

Early on the morning of December 23rd, Instruction No 1 was distributed, this detailing the constitution of the Nationalist Teruel Operations Army, its two Army Corps to be known as *Norte del Turia* and *Sur del Turia* (North of the Turia and South of the Turia). These two Army Corps were composed of elements from the Army Corps in Galicia and Castille, artillery from the Northern Army and from the eight motorised legionary groups, and these troops were moved by train as far as Cella.

On December 25th the re-arrangements of the Nationalist forces were well advanced: the two Army Corps had been formed, the 84th Division had arrived from Aragon, and the 1st, 54th, 61st, 62nd, 81st and 82nd Divisions had come from Guadalajara. As soon as the 82nd Division arrived its Commander (Ceano) received serious head injuries during an artillery barrage directed on his Headquarters, and Revilla took over his command.

During following days the 5th, 13th and 150th Divisions arrived from Guadalajara, this making a total of ten divisions, which was the same number as deployed by the Government.

On Christmas Day sixteen Fiats, led by Salas, were detailed to escort six He 46s and nine He 45s sent to attack La Pedriza, where they encountered strong anti-aircraft defence. On the 26th they carried out a similar mission at San Blas, as well as two reconnaissance sorties over the Saragossa front from Tardienta to Belchite. The next day Group 2-G-3, eighteen strong, accompanied five Ro 37s and ten He 45s to the junction of the Albarracín road with the main road, where they located a large number of lorries and tanks and two anti-aircraft batteries, one of which opened fire at them. In the afternoon a reconnaissance was made over the Huesca front, since it was in this area that an attack seemed most likely.

In accordance with Instruction No 2, distributed on the morning of December 26th, the Nationalist counter offensive began on December 29th. This was preceded by the greatest artillery barrage mounted up to that time and which, backed by Air Force bombing attacks, blasted the enemy lines for about two hours.

To support the counter-offensive, the Condor Legion was assigned to the *Norte del Turia*, and the Legionary Air Force to the *Sur del Turia*. The 1st Hispana Air Brigade and the army co-operation groups were retained for deployment as needed under Franco's orders. Air Headquarters was set up in Daroca, adjacent to the Northern Army's Headquarters at Caminreal, and not far from the Generalissimo's Headquarters at Fuentes de Jiloca. The Condor Legion set up their Headquarters in Bronchales, basing their fighters at Calamocha and leaving the heavy aircraft at Burgo de Osma.

On the eve of the counter-offensive Group 2-G-3 returned to the crossroads at Albarracín, in company with five He 46s and ten He 45s, intending to attack the enemy transport and armour that had been massed there on the previous day. The enemy was equally interested in preventing such an attack, and had provided protection for their mobile columns. On this occasion it took the form of six Chatos with an umbrella of fifteen Ratas. The 1st squadron of 2-G-3 immediately began a dogfight with the Chatos, while the 2nd Squadron, which had been flying cover at higher altitude, intercepted the much larger flock of Ratas.

The sky seemed packed with military aircraft, and within seconds Lieutenant Allende of the 1st Squadron opened the scoring with a Chato, which burst into flames shortly before hitting the ground, and within minutes he could claim a second victim. Lieutenant Bayo attacked a Chato head-on, scoring some hits, but had to make a second attack from astern before it, too, began to lose height, painting the track of its last flight in a pall of smoke that terminated with a burst of flames as it crashed behind Government lines. Lieutenant Muntadas put flames to a third Chato while Lieutenant Vázquez, plagued by machine-guns which kept failing, eventually managed to destroy a Rata, which crashed in a pine forest several kilometres to the south west of Teruel. López Sert of the 1st Squadron did not return to base and was thought to be dead, since Muntadas reported seeing a Fiat crash over the line of the Turia.

In this initial clash 2-G-3 had destroyed five enemy machines at a cost of some damage to their own aircraft and the loss of one Fiat, confirmed as that of López Sert, who had been killed when his machine crashed. Strangely, a close examination of the wreckage failed to reveal any trace of damage caused by machine-gun bullets, which confirmed the belief of Juan Coma—who had been in combat with Sert—that he lost control in attempting to avoid a head-on collision.

On December 29th seventeen Fiats, ten He 45s and eight Ro 37s returned to the Albarracín crossroads hoping to repeat their success. This time they were limited to ground targets but later, over Teruel, they encountered twelve Ratas, which the Fiats attacked with blazing machine-guns. The enemy could not be enticed into combat, however, and quickly scattered over their own lines.

On the same day eight aircraft of 2-G-3's third Squadron, led by Captain Murcia, arrived at Alfamén from Seville which enabled the group to operate with three squadrons for the first time on December 30th. On this occasion they were escorting units of Romeos and He 45s in an attack on enemy positions, and were soon in combat with a force of Ratas shepherding Katiuska bombers. Lieutenant Arístides destroyed a Rata over Escandon, as well as a Katiuska; Captain Murcia got another Rata to the north of Teruel. Guerrero and Simón each claimed probables, but the final result of the battle was three confirmed victories and no losses. On that day, a dry one with better visibility, Nationalist aircraft dropped more than a hundred tons of bombs on enemy positions.

On the 31st a very heavy snowstorm and the lowest recorded temperature of the century (18°C below zero) put a stop to air activity. At 16.00hrs on that day, Vicente Rojo reported to Valencia that: ". . . there has been considerable panic amongst the troops in La Muela", which had been attacked by the 61st Division (García Navarro), to which Prieto replied: "I appreciate that they have hardly fought at all. It is to be feared that, as the day advances, there may be no hope of reacting with the necessary vigour after the wave of panic which has struck the troops".

On New Year's Day 1938, General Rojo confirmed the loss of San Blas, the town where the XVIII and XXII Army Corps had joined forces and this passed into the hands of the Norte del Turia Corps. The Nationalist Air Force carried out intensive bombing raids on Concud, which was soon occupied, but Aranda was unable to take el Muletón by storm. The bitter weather had made air operations a nightmare for ground crews: it was bad enough having to warm engine cylinders by blowlamp before engines could be started, but the task of removing ice from flying and control surfaces without proper equipment was almost impossible. Further falls of snow meant that air support could not be used to exploit the early success of the Nationalist Army. Thus, the forces which had occupied la Muela and Concud, and had been poised to make contact with the besieged troops in Teruel, were unable to advance and the link-up did not materialise. During the first few days of January the V Army Corps (Modesto) made a furious counter-attack against Aranda's troops and on January 6th the remaining defenders of Teruel were forced to surrender.

The battle in the air continued, but with the limitations imposed by weather and terrain. On January 2nd, while the Fiats were escorting nine He 45s and eight Ro 37s to Alto de Celadas, they were met by a vicious barrage of fire from anti-aircraft batteries and heavy machine-guns, in which Fiat 3-77 flown by Lieutenant Careaga was hit and destroyed. Careaga escaped without injury, but was imprisoned in Montjuich until the end of the Catalan Campaign.

The Government anti-aircraft batteries at le Celdas were particularly efficient: on January 5th three more Fiats were caught by their fire. Muntadas had to make a forced-landing at Calamocha aerodrome, whilst Ansaldo and Muerza, the latter wounded in his left leg, managed to reach their base.

On the morning of January 6th there was a fleeting battle with eleven Ratas directly over Teruel. In the afternoon, at Santa Eulalia, 2-G-3 again met concentrated anti-aircraft fire, apart from Lieutenants Vázquez and Bayo, who went to the defence of a unit of He 111s that was being attacked by enemy fighters. Vázquez attacked the lower group, gunning a Chato which fell in flames to the East of Teruel, while Bayo was successful in destroying a second Chato.

It was on this same day that Teruel fell to Government troops, explained in part by the weather conditions and terrain. Primarily, however, it was a repetition of earlier mistakes, with too much reliance upon a single frontal attack. Lieutenant Beumelburg has written that the advance of troops along a single road reminded him of battles in the Middle Ages. The fact is that the weather conditions at the time of the attack made it virtually impossible to adopt other measures. Perhaps the greatest mistake was to initiate a campaign at Teruel during the month of December. Surrounded by high mountains, it lies in inhospitable country, bitterly cold and snowbound in winter. Not only did terrain and weather combine to limit the movement of ground forces to a minimum, but imposed almost unacceptable hazards to the all-essential air support. Added to problems of cold-weather operation that plagued ground and flying crews alike, air combats were fought in poor visibility between and around mountain peaks that towered over 6,500ft (2,130m).

With this unsatisfactory termination of the first phase of the campaign, General Volkmann was in favour of a reversion to the original plan of an attack in Guadalajara. His proposal was unacceptable to other Nationalist leaders, but it was agreed mutually to reinforce the left-flank for operations against Alfambra.

Between January 6th and 17th aerial activity was restricted considerably, but this period was used by the Nationalist Air Force to change the deployment of some of their units. On the 13th Group 6-G-15 was transferred from Almunia to Bello. The Ju 52s moved to Aranda and the S-M.79s to Burgos, the He 111s remaining in Burgo de Osma. The Italian bombers were stationed in the Ebro valley and the Fiat fighters were deployed at Sanjurjo, Bello and Alfamén. The Me 109B were based at Calamocha, from where Group 1-G-2 also continued to operate.

Captain Schellmann, leader of the 1st Me 109 Squadron, shot down a Rata on the 18th and on the same day Woitke destroyed a Chato. The previous day, in three combats, ten Government aircraft were shot down and one Russian pilot was taken prisoner.

There were movements of Government aircraft units at about the same time. The 1st and 4th Squadrons of Ratas went to Sarrión. The 5th Squadron remained in Villar del Arzobispo and the 6th returned to La Señera. The 2nd Squadron moved to Villar with the remains of the 3rd. A few days later Luis de Frutas, pilot of the only surviving Rata from the North, was killed in combat. The Chatos returned to aerodromes at Barracas and El Toro, after a short stay at Villar, and their 4th Squadron (Duarte) went to Sagunto.

Group 2-G-3 was operating normally at this time, with three squadrons and a maximum total of eighteen planes. For the attack on Muletón and Celadas they had been joined by the 4th Fiat Squadron (4-E-3), which had been formed in Seville on December 20th with aircraft numbered 3-92 to 3-100, and six of these machines arrived at Alfamén on the 18th. Group 2-G-3 was then reduced to two squadrons, and with the 3rd and 4th squadrons the new group 3-G-3 was formed. On January 19th both groups operated together for the first time, each with twelve aircraft, and joint missions were repeated on the 20th, 21st, 22nd and 23rd.

During the morning of January 24th, 2-G-3 and 3-G-3 were escorting a Ju 52 Squadron (Gallarza) which was attacking Perales. When their escort duty was over the Fiats continued to Teruel and the Fiat of 3-G-3's leader, Commander Ibarra, was shot down by their own anti-aircraft fire. He had to escape from the aircraft by parachute, the wind carrying him towards his own lines: throughout his descent he was protected by both groups of Fiats. No sooner was he safe than twelve Ratas were sighted to the south of Teruel, their formation ragged as they jinked to avoid Nationalist anti-aircraft fire.

Vazquez pushed his Fiat into a climb to get above the enemy, manoeuvring to put the sun behind him. His machine dropped like a hawk as he made a head-on attack, pulling up into a loop and rolling off the top to rake the Ratas in a second attack from behind. Within seconds one of the enemy was diving steeply to the ground. García Pardo attacked another Rata from behind and it, too, crashed to the ground. Barely were the flames of its disintegration lit than a third machine went into an uncontrollable dive.

The pace was hotting up and Ratas were scattering all over the sky. Guerrero destroyed the straggler of a formation of seven; it joined the other three on the ground. The Fiat pilots felt invincible: Arístides even had the audacity to take on three Ratas and sixteen Chatos unaided, attacking at close range. Allende confirmed that one of the Chatos fell in flames. Comas machine-gunned two Ratas, one of which was destroyed, and within seconds Herrera claimed the group's seventh victory.

This battle ended 12 miles (20km) inside the Government Zone, but all the Nationalist fighters were successful in evading the curtain of steel thrown up by Government anti-aircraft batteries. Apart from Guerrero's machine, which had collected three bullet holes, the Fiats were undamaged.

January 24th also marked the beginning of the Government attack on Singra, led by the 27th Division (del Barrio) reinforced by a mixed brigade and a tank company: the aim was to dominate the Saragossa–Teruel road, the only supply route for the Nationalist front.

This attack was unexpected, although at the last minute knowledge of its imminence was gained from a deserter, permitting a hurried deployment of three Nationalist battalions near Singra in preparation for the attack.

Nevertheless, both Vigón and Aranda realised that the active support of the air force would be essential if they were to defend successfully the 1¼ miles (2km) of flat land between the Sierra and Singra.

On January 25th the two Fiat groups were once again in joint action at the front, but failed to encounter any enemy planes. On succeeding days even the reconnaissance aircraft could find few signs of enemy activity, until the 29th. On that day, at 08.00hrs, García Pardo and Bayo spotted Russian tanks moving to attack Nationalist positions at Cabezón, in the Singra sector. They attacked these at low-level with machine-gun fire, and shortly after found eleven more tanks attacking to the east of Celadas. Returning to base, their ammunition exhausted, they located five tanks on the plain near Singra, with five more behind them.

At this same time Salvador and Vázquez were making a reconnaissance of the sector south of the Ebro, where they found no activity. However, near Quinto, they spotted three tanks indifferently camouflaged by canvas and, as they were returning to base, they surprised twenty lorries at Azuara which they raked with machine-gun fire. At midday the group made a sortie with nine aircraft, led by Garcia Pardo. Reaching Singra they found the attack was already over, but at Celadas there were six tanks facing the Nationalist positions, most of them out of action. However, five more were discovered in a narrow gulley, moving forward slowly to attack. Before take-off they had decided upon a plan of attack, and one of the squadrons dived to machine-gun tanks and enemy trenches, whilst the other squadron maintained patrol above them. Once the first squadron had made their attack the positions were reversed and within minutes the tanks in front of the Nationalist positions were put out of action and the enemy was forced to evacuate one line of trenches, suffering heavy casualties in the process. In this action Fiat No 3-64, flown by Luis Herrero de Teresa, crashed into the ground. The machines flown by Muntadas and Comas were both hit by fire from the ground, that of Comas losing fuel and being forced to make an emergency landing at Calamocha.

At this time Franco left the Teruel front, journeying to Burgos, where on January 30th the first Nationalist Government was constituted (Official Bulletin No 468, of February 1st, 1938). On his return he ordered the start of the Alfambra operations, an extension of the left flank, which were to prove decisive for the final result of this battle.

Volkmann then insisted that all operations in the Teruel region should be abandoned. Berti, whose Italian troops had remained inactive since Santander, went to Rome to receive instructions. It is not surprising that the German and Italian leaders were worried, since the agitation in Austria was then at its height preparatory to its annexation by Germany. Under these circumstances neither Germany nor Italy wanted senior military leaders out of their own country.

On February 4th Hitler dismissed the War Minister (Von Blomberg), the Commander in Chief of the Army (von Fritsch), and the Ministers for Foreign Affairs (von Neurath) and Economy (Schacht), all of whom opposed his dangerous plans put forward at a meeting on November 5th, 1937. It seems certain that it was at this meeting when Hitler said: ". . . from the German point of view we are not one hundred per cent interested in a Franco victory. What does interest us is a prolongation of the war in Spain, so that tension in the Mediterranean is increased."

Spanish Government leaders now made their first serious mistake at the battle of Teruel. Until this time they had succeeded in forestalling a major Nationalist attack for almost two months, but in so doing they had carried the battle to a point that led nowhere. Logically they should not have committed new troops, and ought to have gone to any lengths to avoid serious losses of manpower, since they no longer had numerical superiority. Neither did they have available a significant hardcore of select troops and their external supply routes were beginning to dwindle. However, they insisted on defending the territory they occupied, even risking their best reserves to this end, a decision that was to prove fatal. It is probable that the International situation at that particular moment had influence on Government plans: they may well have believed that by gaining time there was a possibility of receiving more positive assistance from Italy or Russia.

In the earlier Government action at Teruel, five Army Corps had taken part, three from the Army of Manoeuvre (XVIII, XX and XXII) and two from the Mediterranean Army (XIII and XIX), a total of ten divisions, with two more in reserve. At the beginning of January the V Army Corps (Modesto) was brought into the battle and the XXI (Perea) was placed on the right flank, behind the zone where the Mediterranean and Eastern armies met.

Until this moment the Nationalist forces in this sector had comprised the *Norte del Turia* and *Sur del Turia* Army Corps. These were now reinforced by Divisions 4, 83, 85, 105, 108 and a cavalry division. The new Nationalist attack took place in precisely that sector where the Government's Mediterranean and Eastern armies met. The Army Corps in the Sector (Galicia) was reinforced by the Moroccan Army Corps (Yagüe) and by a Joint Group formed by the Cavalry Division (Monasterio) and the 5th Navarre Division. Divisions 3 and 63 from the Navarre Army Corps (Solchaga) and the CTV were held in reserve.

The action had been well planned and was carried out with precision. The Moroccan Army Corps, then consisting of Divisions 1 and 4 from Navarre, 82 and 108 from Galicia and 105 from Aragon, attacked towards Rillo on the north flank, whilst the Galician Army Corps (with its own 83rd, 84th and 85th Divisions plus the Moroccan 13th and 150th) attacked the southern flank from Celadas to Alfambra. It was also planned that the Sierra Palomera was to be occupied by the Reserves (Joint Group), whose mission was to establish a strong point.

Heavy snow prevented the attack from being launched on February 4th, and this delay gave time for some deserters to alert the enemy. This advance information of Nationalist plans proved inadequate defence: when the attack was made, on February 7th, several thousand prisoners were taken by the Nationalist forces, as well as sixty machine-guns and three artillery batteries.

On February 5th eleven aircraft from Group 2-G-3 were patrolling the area of operations but did not encounter enemy aircraft. On the 6th fifteen Fiats led by Salas took off on patrol at 10.30hrs. An hour later they witnessed the occupation of Argente by the Cavalry Division, and shortly afterwards caught sight of thirteen tanks moving from Perales to Visiedo to attack the cavalry. On three consecutive occasions they forced them to turn back, making repeated low-level machine-gun attacks. This treatment was too much for the tanks for they withdrew finally leaving one overturned and two more damaged. This action brought 2-G-3 the congratulations of Colonel Sáez de Buruaga, leader of the Hispana Air Brigade. The next day it was 1-G-2's turn to attack the tanks opposing the 13th and 84th Division.

On that day, February 7th, the German Lieutenant Balthasar flying an Me 109 created a record by destroying three Katiuskas and one fighter in a single sortie. This achievement, equalled by Salas on September 2nd of the same year, gave Balthasar his seventh and final victory in the skies over Spain.

On the previous day Nationalist bombers had dropped a total of 120 tons of bombs on enemy positions, a record for this battle and exceeding the tonnage dropped when they broke through the 'Iron Ring' at Bilbao. But the relative importance of air bombardment by comparison with an artillery barrage had decreased from Biscay to Teruel. At the end of December the Nationalists had nearly 400 artillery weapons: by February, there were almost 600 that could put up a barrage totalling 150 tons per day.

From February 16th to the 22nd there were daily sorties by the Fiat groups, in addition to the regular flights made by pairs of aircraft. These sorties usually lasted for two hours, but on the 20th it stretched to 2hrs 20mins and three machines had to make emergency landings at Calamocha, their fuel supply exhausted. On February 17th the Condor Legion's Ju 87As flew on operations for the first time, replacing the 'Angelitos', which had been returned to the south.

On February 21st García Pardo and Allende took off at 10.20hrs on a routine reconnaissance flight over the Teruel front. There they discovered twenty Chatos and a similar number of Ratas in combat with a few Me 109Bs. When Pardo and Allende went to the assistance of the Messerschmitts, the German pilots failed to recognise them as allies and opened fire on them. They beat a hasty retreat, calling into battle another formation of Fiats before continuing with their reconnaissance.

This new formation comprised twenty-four Fiats of the *As de Bastos* Group, the pilots including Captain Haya who, after attending his mother's funeral, arrived by car in Bilbao just as the group was about to take off. Despite Commander Zotti's opposition, he insisted on taking his place in the formation. At 11.04hrs over Puebla de Valverde they encountered about forty enemy fighters already in combat with seventeen Me 109s. The leading pilots of the *As de Bastos* Group attacked two formations of Chatos which were flying at about 11,500ft (3,500m), whilst the remainder repelled a rather timid attack by a squadron of Ratas which were flying above the Fiats at 14,700ft (4,500m). In attempting to destroy a Chato that was attacking another machine of his squadron, Haya approached too close and collided with the Chato, falling to his death.

General Rojo advised Prieto, the Minister of Defence, that the Air Force had carried out three operations on that day (February 21st), and that during the last of these they had been involved in a large-scale combat with the Nationalist Air Force. He later advised Prieto that according to information from Jerica (the Air Force's command centre) five German aircraft —later stated to be five Me 109s—seven Fiats and one twin engined machine had been destroyed. This message included the information that the ace pilot, Carlos Haya, who was reputed to have carried out the night attack on the War Ministry in Madrid, had been killed in this engagement. Their own losses were quoted as two Ratas which failed to return to base and two others which were damaged and whose pilots were injured. Hidalgo de Cisneros recommended that Sergeant Orozco, who managed to fly his aircraft back to base after its tail had been destroyed in a collision with a monoplane, should be granted an award for outstanding bravery and skill.

In the afternoon of February 21st, Group 2-G-3 was operating with fifteen Fiats, providing escort for six Ju 52s which they met over Bello and accompanied to Cascalde. When the Junkers aircraft had dropped their bombs, 2-G-3 saw them safely back to base, and then accompanied five Ro 37s from Santa Eulalia to the north of Villaescusa. On their return flight they spotted enemy tanks attacking to the east of Valdehechos, and strafed them with machine-gun fire until they were forced to retreat. The majority of the Group were able to return to Bello, but due to shortage of fuel some were forced to land at the Me 109 airfield at Calamocha.

On February 22nd 2-G-3 operated as a complete group for the last time during the battle of Teruel, but patrols in pairs continued until the 25th, when aerial activity ceased.

During the last phase of the battle the 1st and 5th Rata squadrons operated from Alcublas, an aerodrome offering a short take-off run for this type of machine: in addition, it had a road running across the centre of the airfield, and these factors help to explain the large number of accidents which were reported there. The 6th and 2nd Rata squadrons returned to Villar del Arzobispo, and the 4th operated from Alcalá de Henares and Villar. At the end of the battle the 3rd squadron was disbanded, and on March 2nd the 6th squadron suffered the same fate. The 2nd and 5th squadrons were then re-equipped with the latest Ratas, which were armed with four machine-guns (Ratas from Nos CM-158 onwards), and these squadrons then became led by Vijrov and Susekalov. The aircraft which had equipped the 2nd and 5th Squadrons were then used to equip the 3rd Squadron, which was being reorganised under Bravo's command. One month later a new consignment of Ratas and Katiuskas entered Spain via the French frontier, and these brought up to strength those squadrons which had become depleted during operations at Teruel.

With the end of the battle of Teruel, General Kindelán issued the following General Order to the Air Army, on February 23rd:

"With the conquest of Teruel and the surrounding area a long and bloody battle has ended in a wholly triumphant manner for us, and in a disastrous way for the enemy. All the forces under my command have acted in a brilliant and courageous way, saving countless lives amongst the Land Army's forces and making it easier for them to capture vital positions. This fact is recognised unanimously by all, from the Generalissimo down to the last soldier. You may be proud of having fulfilled your military duty in this campaign. Our triumph has not cost many lives, but there were certainly some sad losses: magnificent leaders like Commander Negrón and Captain Haya, as well as courageous officers such as López Sert, Luis Herrero and Luis Martínez Amoedo, represent the appreciable tribute paid by the Air Army to achieve victory. The Hispana Brigade in its brilliant military debut, the Heinkel He 45s, Heinkel He 51s and Romeo and Heinkel He 70 reconnaissance units, and the various advisory organisations and liaisons between commands, can rest assured that their efforts, given tirelessly and beyond measure, have been valuable and productive. Seventy five per cent of the victory deservedly belongs to the Nationalist Air Force. Teruel was recovered as soon as the weather allowed the air force to operate, and it would never have been lost if it had not been for the deplorable conditions at the beginning of January. The Nationalist Air Force had always been triumphant; victory is our faithful companion. With God's help we will soon conquer."

During the battle of Teruel eleven Nationalist pilots were killed in action, but considerably more than this number lost their lives in accidents that, in the main, were caused by the very adverse weather conditions suffered during January. The Condor Legion also lost Lieutenant Runze, one of the veteran patrol leaders of their reconnaissance squadron.

When the battle of Teruel ended, the front became stabilised at a short distance from the town, in much the same position as in December, although Puerto Escandón was not recaptured. However, with the occupation of Sierra Palomera, the access route to Teruel was widened considerably. Initially about 19sq miles (50km^2) of territory was lost to the Government, but by the end of the battle Nationalist gains in the area totalled no less than 463sq miles (1,200km^2).

It was difficult for foreign observers to appreciate why Nationalist forces had taken two months to fight a battle that had merely restored the front to its position in December. Thus, they arrived at the conclusion that the Popular Army had equalled the skill and efficiency of their Nationalist adversaries. Even Nationalist leaders began to wonder if, in fact, they faced a more powerful enemy than they had appreciated, and gave to General Kindelán the task of assessing their potential. Kindelán's report was reassuring: numerically the enemy was similar (half a million men and about 650 battalions on each side) but their air force and artillery, especially the latter, were inferior. The infantry had not mastered the technique of advancing behind a spearhead of tanks and seemed to have lost the drive displayed at el Jarama: the artillery had made little progress, the accuracy of their barrage leaving much to be desired and, in general, they had not advanced technically since Brunete.

Despite this report, it was obvious that at Teruel the Popular Army had achieved success of a kind previously unknown to them. This can be explained by the circumstances, for the siege of Teruel was the simplest operation undertaken by them, with an advance of only 6 miles (10km) on each flank. At Brunete and Belchite they had penetrated farther on the first day of the attack but had failed to make further progress in later operations. They had always achieved notable successes on the first day (this pattern was to be repeated at the Ebro and Pozoblanco) but they failed to press home this initial advantage. But at Teruel there were no objectives other than those of the first day. The Belchite stronghold resisted for sixteen days: Teruel for twenty-three days; the former in overwhelming heat and the latter during the coldest days of the worst winter of the century. There was little difference between the two objectives, except that the Teruel stronghold was larger and the external fortifications were much stronger.

The first Nationalist counter-attack on the 23rd, with only the 84th Division to the north of the Turia and the 81st to the South, failed in the same way as the first counter-attack at Brunete had failed. The counter-offensive on the 29th was successful to the south of the Turia and arrived within sight of Teruel, but the link-up of the two divisions had failed as had happened at Belchite. The counter-offensive to the north of the Turia achieved only the occupation of Concud and San Blas, without succeeding in recovering the strong left flank positions of El Muletón and Celadas, which brought an end to the advance. This is not surprising, however, since the Generalissimo's Instruction of the 27th gave priority to the attack south of the Turia, a priority probably dictated by the proximity of the Castille Army Corps which could have used its divisions to close the Albarracíon road.

When, in the middle of January, El Muletón and Celadas were occupied, the fall of Teruel was inevitable. The second month of the battle proved disastrous for the Government troops and ended in the inevitable loss of the provincial capital. Líster pretended that the hard fought battle in Teruel had favoured the Government side, but this made little sense, for the Nationalist Army had adequate forces to provide a mass of manoeuvre in Aragón, supported by air and artillery forces of superior quality. Furthermore, they were better placed to mobilise additional forces and replenish materials. The logical Government move would have been to abandon the struggle at Teruel and to try and gain time by a new attack, such as the one planned in Extremadura, for which they had the great advantage of being able to move their troops along interior lines.

At the beginning of the war the population in the Nationalist zone was somewhere in the order of 39 per cent of the national total, (about 25 million inhabitants in 1936), with a distribution of 27 per cent in the North, 8 per cent in the South and 4 per cent in the Islands. The population controlled by the Government (61 per cent) was mainly in the Central Zone (53 per cent), leaving 8 per cent in the Cantabrian region. On October 1st, 1936 these percentages had changed so that 46 per cent were in the Nationalist Zone (42 per cent in the Peninsular and 4 per cent in the Islands) and 54 per cent in the Government Zone (47·5 in the Centre and 6·5 in the Cantabrian region). One year later, in October 1937, the population in the Government Zone totalled only 42 per cent, which suggest that 5 million people had changed sides. At that time the Popular Army could mobilise theoretically up to 10 per cent of the maximum, i.e. one million soldiers. Burgos was able to recruit one and a half million, which was the equivalent of having inverted the proportion that existed at the beginning of the war.*

Fifteen Days' Truce in Land Operations

By February 24th the air groups had already begun to leave the Teruel sector, with Group 6-G-15 moving from Bello to Sanjurjo and 2-G-3 from Alfamen to Tauste. During the days which followed Group 1-G-2 moved to the new Logrono Park, which had been built to avoid the long trips from Seville to León, and Group 7-G-15 from Bunuel to the Seville Park. The few surviving He 46s were transferred to the Crew Training School, which had then moved to Malaga, and this meant the end of Group 3-G-11. The two Angelitos which had been moved to the south on December 30th, operated successively from Almunia, Alfamen and Bello before returning to Seville at the end of January.

Taking advantage of the pause in operations, Commander García Morato, who was married to the sister of Carlos Haya's widow, wrote the following letter:

28th February 1938

Open letter to the leaders of the Republican Air Force, Colonels don Ignacio Hidalgo de Cisneros and don Antonio Camacho Benítez.

On the Teruel front, in the vicinity of Puerto de Escandón, Captain Haya fell during the battle.

I am not addressing friends of yesterday nor enemies of today; I am addressing you because you are companions in the same Arm as the deceased.

His wife requests his body. I am making her plea my own, and if we should meet in the air one day, before the battle begins I will salute you in recognition of this.

Commander of the Nationalist Air Force

Joaquín García Morato.

Morato decided to deliver this letter personally, without involving any other pilots, and the following words are his own:

"I assumed the entire responsibility of delivering the letter in a place where I could be absolutely certain that it would reach the hands of the leaders to whom it was addressed. And on February 28th, alone in my Fiat, I set out towards the Red Zone in search of Almuriente aerodrome. I did not encounter any enemy aircraft on the way and nothing hindered my journey. Finally, once over the aerodrome, I dived low, almost touching the ground, and dropped the message in the centre of the aerodrome. During these few seconds I noticed three camouflaged Ratas, but before they could react and take-off to punish my audacity I had already begun the return flight towards my base, having fulfilled my mission. A few moments later and I was back amongst my companions, waiting for the result of my gesture. The message was certainly received, because it was printed in the Red press and announced over their radio stations, but I never received an answer to my letter of any kind. The

* All these calculations have been based on the General Census of the Population dated December 31st, 1950, a time when the distribution of the population had changed little from the 1936–1939 period.

remains of our hero stayed in the Red Zone because of the inertia of his former companions who, even after his wife's plea, failed to make this chivalrous gesture."

Information collected from members of the Popular Army confirms the truth of this story, which had wide repercussions in the Air Force. It also made it clear that the three camouflaged Ratas at Almuriente (Grañén) were in fact dummies to deter the Nationalist Air Force. Haya's body remained in the area where his aircraft had crashed until, at a much later date, it was moved to Santuario de la Cabeza, where it lies alongside that of Captain Cortés.

At the beginning of March various reports were published about the material and morale boosting effects of Nationalist Air Force operations at the Teruel front. A joint report by the engineer Ruiz Ayllón and López Carrizosa said that to fight an enemy of low morale it was sufficient to use a large delayed-action bomb, but that to have any real effect on troops of strong morale it was better to make concentrated attacks with small calibre delayed-action bombs. In both cases the material effect was far less than the effect on morale.

A report by Lieutenant Colonel Palacios said that in a fortified zone the 10kg bomb produced results only if it fell in a trench. It added that, according to Lieutenant Colonel Plocher, Chief of Staff of the Condor Legion the average bombing error achieved by the new Ju 87s amounted to only 16ft (5m). Palacios considered it effective to machine-gun troops and to bomb towns with 50 and 250kg bombs. Like Ruiz Ayllón, he considered that the effects on morale were greater than the material effects, attacks with less than three aeroplanes failed to make any impression.

On the morning of March 6th the most important naval battle of the entire war took place. This involved the cruisers *Baleares* (Fontenla), *Canarias* (Estrada) and *Almirante Cervera* (Agacino) which had sailed from the Balearics with the destroyers *Velasco, Huesca* and *Teruel*, together with the mine-layers *Jupiter* and *Neptuno*. Government forces comprised a Squadron which had left Cartagena on a mission to protect a number of torpedo boats which were to attack the Nationalist Fleet at their bases in the Balearics. Flagship of this Squadron was the cruiser *Libertad*, which was accompanied by the cruiser *Méndez Núñez* and the destroyers *Sánchez Barcáiztegui, Almirante Antequera, Lepanto, Gravina* and *Lazaga*. The 2nd flotilla of destroyers, *Jorge Juan, Escaño, Almirante Valdés* and *Ulloa*, was providing direct protection for the torpedo boats.

At 00.40hrs on the 6th the Nationalist fleet sighted a cruiser and four destroyers. At much the same time the destroyer *Sánchez Barcáiztegui* came within range of a cruiser of the *Baleares* class at which it discharged two torpedoes.

Admiral Vierna, commanding the Nationalist fleet, ordered a change of course with the idea of engaging the Government Squadron. At 02.15hrs the *Sánchez Barcáiztegui*, which was in the vanguard and to port of the *Libertad*, sighted a cruiser which was recognised as the *Baleares*, and immediately attacked her with four torpedoes. The destroyers *Almirante Antequera* and *Lepanto*, which were following the *Sánchez Barcáiztegui*, each discharged a salvo of torpedoes at the Nationalist cruiser. Three, of the twelve or thirteen torpedoes deployed, hit their target, and the *Baleares* sank within a short space of time.

Command of the Nationalist formation was then assumed by the Captain of the *Canarias*, who ordered a withdrawal under the cover of darkness, intending to resume the engagement at dawn. This was not to be for Ubieta, commanding the Government Squadron, was satisfied with the results already achieved and ordered all vessels under his command to return to Cartagena.

At first light a squadron of Katiuskas and one of Ratas flew from Carmolí to finish off the *Baleares*, only to discover that it had already sunk. Instead, they attacked two destroyers which were attempting to save the survivors numbering about three hundred. Amongst the 726 dead were Admiral Manuel de Vierna, his Chief of Staff, Gabriel Fernández de Bobadilla and the Commander of the *Baleares*, Isidro Fontenla.

On March 7th the Nationalist Air Force bombed the port of Cartagena, claiming that they had hit the *Libertad* and one destroyer.

The loss of the *Baleares* was due primarily to overconfidence caused by an underestimation of the enemy fleet and the belief that it would not take offensive action. Despite this, the Nationalist Fleet continued to operate freely in the Mediterranean. When the next offensive sortie was made on March 12th, Admiral Francisco Moreno was in command, with the cruiser *Canarias* as his flagship. With the lesson of the *Baleares* in mind he ensured that his flanks were protected by destroyers and made full use of reconnaissance aircraft. Shortly afterwards re-construction of the old cruiser *República* was finished and this vessel, re-named *Navarra,* brought the fleet back to its former strength.

During the interval between the battles of Teruel and Aragón, Groups 2-G-3 and 3-G-3 were reorganised. Two new Fiat squadrons—5-E-3 (Miguel Guerrero) and 6-E-3 (José Barranco)—were formed, providing a third squadron for each group. These had a total of fifteen new aircraft, numbered from 3-101 to 3-115, but they did nothing more than compensate for the losses of the winter. During the battles at Teruel they had lost one machine destroyed in combat (López Sert), three aircraft to anti-aircraft fire (Herrero, Careaga and Ibarra) and seven in accidents (Mazarredo, Olivera, Varona, Núñez and Gil Escoaín one each; Giménez Garrido two). This high proportion of accidents, never repeated during the war, was due mainly to the large number of novice Fiat pilots.

The proper establishment for each group was twenty-seven machines (three squadrons of nine aircraft), but in fact there were only fifty-two between both groups: the sixty-five which had been received (numbers 3-51 to 3-115) minus the thirteen which had been lost up to that date (two at Brunete and eleven at Teruel).

The Legionary Air Force was once more increased and attained its maximum strength; later, in the summer, one fighter group and the S-M.81 groups were disbanded. The Bomber Group was divided into the Fast Bomber Squadron (S-M.79s), the Heavy Bomber Squadron (S-M.81s) and the autonomous group of fast Fiat B.R.20 bombers, its two squadrons led by Martire (later Gaeta), and del Lupo y Lalatta (later Cigersa). They also formed two close-support squadrons, one with Breda Ba 65s (Miotto) and the other with Fiats (Captain Vossilla). The fighter groups were then under the command of Rossi and Aiello, and the veteran François who had just been promoted to Commander.

In the Government Air Force, Claudín, Zarauza, Duarte, Morquillas and Comas wer given the rank of Captain, heading a string of promotions resulting from operations in the battle of Teruel. The bomber pilots who were promoted included Armario and Pelayo, who became leaders of the Chatos Group 26 and Natachas Group 30 respectively.

The Great Offensive in Aragón

On March 9th the most brilliant offensive of the whole war began. Although expected by the enemy, they were still taken by surprise because of the speed with which it was initiated, and the sector chosen for the breakthrough.

The Central Chief of Staff for the Popular Army, in a study made some months before this battle, appreciated the advantages of an attack to the south of the Ebro, but rejected this plan since this area was really a dead end. As we will see later this reasoning was correct, but it led Vicente Rojo to a great disaster.

The principal cause of this disaster was the speed of Nationalist preparations. On February 22nd Teruel was occupied: only fourteen days later four Army Corps were beginning the new offensive. The Galician Army Corps (Aranda) hardly had to change their position; the 1st Mobile Navarre Division (García Valiño) and the Moroccan Army Corps (Yagüe) moved from the Alfambra to the Belchite Sector, and the CTV (Berti) came directly behind them, between García Valiño and Aranda. The Air Force did not need to change their bases, since they were mainly in Aragón, over the line of the Ebro.

To the north of the Ebro the Government had the X (Gallo) and XI (Gil Otero) Army Corps of the Eastern Army (Pozas) face to face with the Nationalist Navarre (Solchaga) and Aragón (Moscardó) Army Corps. The Popular Army had its third Army Corps, the XII (Sánchez Plaza), to the south of the river, in the sector under attack. Between the Eastern Army and the Mediterranean Army (which were defending the Teruel front, with Army Corps XIII and XIX commanded by Salavero and Vidal respectively), was the Army of Manoeuvre. This Army had lined up, from north to south, the XVIII Army Corps (Fernández-Heredia), XXI (Perea) and XXII (Ibarrola). At the time of the offensive, Division 30 of the XVIII Army Corps had become dependent on the XIII Army Corps, and together with Divisions 34 (Etelvino Vega) and 70 (Toral) they had formed the Perea Group. The XXI Army Corps, plus some other divisions, then came under Cristóbal's command, and the XVII moved to the rear to be reorganised.

In the zones controlled by the XXI and XXII Army Corps were Divisions 27 (Del Barrio), 28 (Jover), 11 (Líster) and 25 (Eusebio Sanz), as well as Division 45 (Hans Kahle), which had arrived from Extremadura. The V Army Corps (Modesto), with Divisions 35 (Walter), 46 ('Campesino') and 47 (Durán), remained in reserve. The XX Army Corps (Menéndez) kept Division 67 in Extremadura and 66 (Bravo) and 68 (Trigueros) in Teruel.

The Nationalist offensive had been planned in three phases. The first move was an attack to the south of the Ebro, advancing to the Caspe-Alcañiz line. In the second phase the attack would be to the north of the Ebro, to protect the left flank of the Moroccan Army Corps. The third drive was to bring the Nationalists to the sea, between Tortosa and Amposta, so cutting Government territory in two. Plans for the second phase were changed several times, Nationalist leaders finding it difficult to arrive at a decision as to whether they should advance to the river Cinca or Segre.

The first phase of the offensive, which began on March 9th, went according to plan. The Moroccan Army Corps, supported by light tanks, routed the 44th Division (Muntané) and, by a rapid advance of some 22 miles (36km) from Belchite to Escatrón, cut off their retreat route towards Caspe. The Moroccan Army Corps had been in contact with the 44th Division earlier, when they had offered some resistance at Belchite, which was occupied on March 10th. Divisions 24 (Yoldi) and 30 (Arrando) were harried by García Valiño and Berti's forces, which drove them back as far as Hijar and Andorra respectively. Thus, the XII Army Corps virtually ceased to exist, and Fernández Heredia was instructed to reorganise the remaining units, but was unable to do this.

On March 12th Yagüe led the memorable advance of 22 miles (36km) to Escatron, utilising two companies of German and Russian tanks (the latter captured) and the 5th Navarre Division transported in lorries. The anti-aircraft batteries intended to defend his headquarters had to change their position three times in a single day. Farther to the south, the 35th Division (Walter) arrived in Híjar, and together with the 72nd Division attempted to hold the gap formed by the river valley. In Caspe the Reyes Group was formed, but they were unable to stabilise the front and soon crossed the Ebro towards the north.

On the 17th the Nationalist forces reached a line formed by Caspe, Alcañiz, Calanda, Alcoriza and Montalbán. In eight days they had occupied 2,700sq miles (7,000km^2) an area larger than the province of Santander.

On this line the 45th Division was reinforced by the 35th and together they formed the Walter Group, and the XII Corps was joined by Divisions 11 and 47 from the V Corps. Divisions 24, 30, 34, 44 and 72 all crossed the Ebro towards the North. The 70th Division withdrew towards el Maestrazgo and served as a basis for the new XXI Army Corps (Cristóbal), which was joined by Division 19 (Recalde), brought from Extremadura. Divisions 25 and 28 remained between Army Corps XXI and XIII. Divisions 24 and 46 were held in reserve.

The Galacian Army Corps was the only Nationalist Corps to meet strong resistance from the beginning, having to fight against Division 27, 34 and 70 of the Perea Group.*

As a result of the rapid retreats made during these eight days, the Government fighters lost their operational bases. The 1st and 4th Spanish squadrons, which had been operating from Caspe and Escatrón, moved to Candasnos, Lérida, Bell-Puig and later to Reus. The 2nd and 5th moved from Puig Moreno to Bell-Puig, and later to Castellar and Valls. The 3rd Squadron consisted of only two patrols, until it was re-organised at Salou with Spanish

* This Group was disbanded when their leader took command of the Eastern Army, replacing Pozas. The XX Army Corps was also disbanded temporarily when their leader, Menédez, assumed command of the Army of Manoeuvre.

crews, and led by Bravo. The two patrols in Celrá and Barcelona formed a basis for the new 6th Squadron. The three Spanish Squadrons of Chatos (Comas, Duarte and Morquillas) operated from Bujaraloz, Candasnos, Escatrón, Pomar and Balaguer.

On March 22nd the second phase of the offensive began. The main action had been assigned to the Aragón Army Corps (Moscardó), which was to advance from Saragossa towards Lérida. Their flanks were to be protected on the left by the Navarre Army Corps (Solchaga), which was to advance from Huesca towards Tremp, and on the right by the Moroccan Army Corps (Yagüe), which had crossed the Ebro between Pina and Quinto on the second day of the offensive, and which was to continue towards Bujaraloz and Fraga.

In fact, the advance made by Yagüe's Corps was so vigorous that the commander of the Northern Army (Dávila) changed the plan of campaign and assigned the main action to them. His faith was justified: the 5th Division (Juan Bautista Sánchez), 13th (Barrón) and 150th (Muñoz Grandes), using motor transport, made a spectacular advance of almost 25 miles (40km) on March 25th. On the 26th they continued to Candasnos and the hills which dominate Fraga—another 28 miles (45km). By the 30th they held a line along the river Cinca, stretching from Barbastro as far as Monzon and had established three bridgeheads across the river. One was at Barbastro, another at Bellver and the third and deepest at Fraga, where a large wedge had been pushed in as far as the outskirts of Lérida.

The Government immediately began to rally their defences. Divisions 27 (Del Barrio), 46 ('Campesino') and 16 (Fresno), were rushed to Catalonia to strengthen the defence of Lérida. The remains of Divisions 26 (Sanz), 44 (Liberal), 24 (Ortiz, later García Vivancos), 30 (Nicanor Felipe), 34 (Etelvino Vega) and 72 (Enciso) were all pouring into the same area from the north of the Ebro. With all these forces available the Southern Group was organised, and this was later split into Army Corps 'A' (Del Barrio) and 'B' (Claudio Martín Barco), which were eventually called Army Corps XII and XVIII. Farther to the north, Divisions 31 (Navarro) and 32 (Gancedo) retreated, and Division 43 (Escassi, later Beltrán) remained in Boltaña.

To the north of the Ebro, apart from the Moroccan Army Corps, other Nationalist Divisions involved included the 3rd (Iruretagoyena), 61st (García Navarro), 62nd (Sagardía), 63rd (Tella), 51st (Irrutia), 53rd (Suerio), 54th (Marzo) and, for a short time, 55th (Adrados).

On March 24th the third phase offensive began to the south of the Ebro. The enemy had improvised a defensive line between the rivers Guadalope and Matarrana, where they had concentrated the best units of the Popular Army: Divisions 45 (Hans), 35 (Walter), 11 (Lister), 3 (Tagüeña, later Cabezas) and 41 (Cortina), which were combined to form Líster and Tagüeña's Groups within the Vth Army Corps (Modesto). In this sector Nationalist attacking forces then comprised two Army Corps instead of three: García Valiño's Group and the CTU, which were joined on March 30th by Division 55 (Adrados).

Government Divisions 47 (Duran), 70 (Toral), 19 (Recalde) and 25 (Sanz, later Trueba) operated in the XXI and XXII Army Corps' zone, where they were in confrontation with the Galician Army Corps (Aranda) and with Brigades which had arrived from the Central Zone and had been organised into the provisional Divisions 'Centro', 'Extremadura' and 'Andalucia'. At this time the Coastal Defence Group was also organised (García Vallejo), and this was situated at the mouth of the Ebro.

The struggle to cross the defensive line between the rivers Guadalope and Matarrana was prolonged dramatically for four days, from March 26th to 29th, and the Air Force had to be called in to help break the enemy's resistance. On March 30th, the 15th Division (García Escámez) and García Valiño's Groups succeeded in advancing on both flanks of the attack. García Valiño, making a risky night advance of 12 miles (20km), led the 1st Navarre Division from Maella to Gandesa and the Caballs mountains. In Gandesa, on April 3rd, García Valiño and the CTV joined forces. But once again Lísters 11th Division barred the way to the motorised troops of the CTV, despite the fact that Divisions 35 and 45, commanded by Walter and Hans respectively, had already surrendered at the Ebro.

The battles fought at Paúls and Vértice Rey were particularly fierce, and farther to the south there was a hard struggle between the 15th Nationalist Division and the 3rd Government Division for possession of the port of Beceite. Under these conditions it was impossible to continue the advance to Tortosa.

The Northern Army once more changed its plans; they took Divisions I (García Valiño) and 55 (Adrados), and one Brigade of the 105th Division from the left flank of the advance. The remainder of the 105th Division and the cavalry (Monasterio) stayed on the left, while the above-mentioned forces moved to the right flank, enabling Aranda to occupy Morella on April 4th and to advance almost to the coast. The final assault began on April 12th and was carried out with extraordinary precision. On the 14th San Mateo and la Jana were occupied, and on the 15th (Good Friday), Divisions 4 (Camilo Alonso Vega), 1 (García Valiño) and 38 (Martin Alonso) reached the coast at Vinaroz, Ulldecona-Alcanar and Benicarló respectively.

This setback for the Government brought formation of the Autonomous Ebro Group on April 15th, under Modesto's command, with Headquarters at the Rusiñol Palace in Reus. Líster replaced Modesto in command of the 5th Army Corps, which initially included Divisions 11 (Rodríguez) and 3 (Cabezas) and Brigades 53, 68 and 124, and which was later re-formed from Division 11, 45 and 46. Tagüeña was given the command of the new XV Army Corps, initially with Divisions 35 and 45, and later with Divisions 3, 35 and 42.

On April 19th García Valiño's Group arrived at the Ebro line, in a position stretching from Tortosa to the estuary, where they joined up with the CTV and Division 15 (García Escámez).

Divisions 4, 83 and 84 (Galera) widened the sector towards the south, crossing Peniscola to the Albocácer–Cuevas de Vinromá–Alcalá de Chivert line. Opposing them were the XXI and XXII Army Corps and García Vallejo's forces, which then became known as the XVIII Army Corps. Romero and Güemes came from Madrid with the reserves from the II and III Army Corps and those of the disbanded VI, (Divisions 5, 6, 10 and 15), and with these reserves the 'A' and 'B' Army Corps were formed to act as a rearguard to the

XIII and XXI. The reserve Divisions from Army Corps I and VI (Nos 3 and 16), which had been led by Tagüeña and Fresno, were used to strengthen the gaps between Tortosa and Lérida.

Meanwhile, to the north of the Ebro, Almenar aerodrome had been occupied on April 3rd and Lérida on the 4th by the Moroccan Army Corps. Balaguer fell on the 6th to the 54th Division; Tremp on the 7th to the 63rd Division, and Sort on the 11th. The port of Bonaigua was gained on the 17th, Viella fell on the 18th and Nationalist forces reached the French frontier on the 20th. This left the Government's Division 43 cut off in Bielsa, surrounded by the 3rd and 62nd Divisions, both from the Navarre Army Corps.

At the end of the offensive the front was at the line of the Noguera Pallaresa (with three bridgeheads at Sort, Tremp and Balaguer) until it opened out into the Segre, from where it followed this river until it joined the Ebro, and finally followed the Ebro to the sea.

For this offensive Group 2-G-3 was centred at Tauste and 3-G-3 at Alfamen. On March 1st twelve aircraft of 2-G-3, led by Salvador, escorted the He 45s and He 70s during a photographic reconnaissance. On the 8th, the eve of the attack, two machines made a reconnaissance of the Montalbán–Utrilla sector, which was assigned to the Galician Army Corps and the Hispana Air Brigade. The Moroccan Army Corps operated in collaboration with the Condor Legion, and the Legionary Air Force supported the CTV.

On March 9th 2-G-3 carried out two missions, the first with the entire group (eighteen aircraft) when they escorted the Ju 52 bomber squadron, and the second with six machines from the 2nd squadron, under Salas' command, when they reconnoitred the Galician Army Corps advance and the southern wing of the CTV. On this day Nationalist bombers dropped a total of 210 tons of bombs of mixed calibres, a record figure for the whole war.

The next day, during a joint mission by the Ju 52 squadron (Gallarza) and the He 45 group, escorted by the Fiats, an He 45 crewed by Saracho and Laffite was hit and fell to the ground in flames, both of its occupants being killed. On April 1st a Heinkel He 111 and an Me 109 were destroyed and five more He 111s were badly damaged during attacks on the aerodromes of Bujaraloz, Candasnos and Caspe and the area around Belchite. In these raids the He 111s destroyed many aircraft on the ground.

Commander Aiello, who had recently replaced Zotti as leader of the *As de Bastos* Group, was shot down, and Zotti returned as Group leader. His squadrons were then led by Larcher, Foschini and Calosso. The *Gamba de Ferro* group also had a new leader, Commander Rossi, but retained the same squadron leaders as at Teruel. At this time the Italian group achieving the best results was *La Cucaracha*, with its veteran captains Bianchi, Fassi and François, the latter having recently been promoted to Commander and becoming group leader.

The offensive on the ground was assisted by attacks on the Catalonian ports, carried out by Savoias from the Balearics. Barcelona suffered some fierce attacks, which forced the Generalissimo to repeat his prohibition of bombing urban areas.

On March 12th 2-G-3 at last encountered enemy aircraft attempting to stop the sweeping advance. During the afternoon eighteen Fiats, led by Salas, escorted the Ju 52s on a raid, and having completed this task made a sweep of the front as far as Híjar, where they encountered twenty Chatos. In the ensuing dogfights, Salas claimed one probable, while García Pardo destroyed one Chato which fell near Híjar. The wreckage of this machine was recovered subsequently, and a piece of it was retained, on which ensuing victories of 2-G-3 were recorded, as well as the names of all those in the group who were killed. Guerrero set fire to another Chato, whose pilot took to his parachute from a very low height. Salvador attacked another machine, which began to trail smoke, but he was unable to continue his attack as his Fiat was almost out of fuel: unable to return to his base at Tauste, he had to land at Saragossa. Carlos Serra, Bayo and Henricourt each were successful in shooting down an enemy machine.

At the beginning of this air battle Vázquez spotted a Katiuska attempting to cross Nationalist lines and he attacked head on. It jettisoned its bombs immediately and banked steeply to gain the safety of its own lines. At that moment two more Katiuskas appeared. Vázquez was well above them and again made a head on attack: they turned in an attempt to escape, but Vázquez's Fiat had gained speed in the dive and he was able to make a second attack from the rear, firing at both machines which, considerately, kept close together. One of the Katiuskas began to trail smoke, but when Vázquez tried to finish it off he was attacked by no less than twelve Chatos. He was now fighting for his life, and at the critical moment his machine-guns jammed. He reacted quickly, putting his machine into a near vertical dive which must have fooled his attackers into believing that he was their victim. Pulling out of the dive close to the ground, Vázquez rejoined his companions near Hijar. His destruction of the Katiuska was confirmed later, for a commander of a ground unit had seen it crash near Escatrón.

In this engagement the group claimed the destruction of five Chatos (García Pardo, Guerrero, Carlos Serra, Bayo and Henricourt) and one Katiuska (Vázquez), without suffering any losses. According to information from Government sources their losses on that day amounted to destruction of the Chatos CA-034 and 057, piloted by Llorente and Aradín, and CA-040 and 018 force-landed at Flix and Caspe respectively. The formation consisted of 20 Ratas and 19 Chatos, escorting a number of Katiuskas, and they claimed to have fought against 25 Fiats of which they destroyed three.

On March 12th German troops entered Vienna and Austria was annexed by Germany. In France, as a reaction to this event, Chautemp's second Government fell and León Blum returned to power. He immediately received Negrin in Paris. In England Anthony Eden resigned his position as Minister for Foreign Affairs, being replaced by Lord Halifax. Italy, who had viewed with some apprehension a union of Germany and Austria, was forced to accept the situation but immediately entered into negotiations with England covering the withdrawal of Italian troops from Spain. It was agreed that this should take place on April 16th, but for various reasons it did not happen until October.

On March 13th the Condor Legion's fighters, which were still based at Gallur, destroyed two Chatos, and on the following day, during a large scale battle between forty-five Fiats and fifty enemy planes, two Ratas, five Chatos and four Fiats were shot down at Alcañiz. On March 15th Claudín shot down a Fiat.

Whilst waiting for reinforcements which were already coming across the French frontier (which had been closed during the three months of Chautemp's second Government) Government fighters suspended all operations for a period.

Because of this, and the ease of the advance at that time, Nationalist aerial activity was greatly reduced from April 15th. This enabled Captain Joaquin García Morato to attend a ceremony held at Castejón on March 18th, when General Kindelán presented him with the Laureate Cross of San Fernando. This solemn award to their hero was witnessed by the entire Group and by representatives from other air units.

On March 19th in order to operate nearer the front, 2-G-3 moved to the aerodrome at newly-occupied Belchite.

After a short pause the attack to the north of the River Ebro was resumed on the 22nd. Eighteen Fiats from 2-G-3 supported the Navarre Army Corps as they entered the Huesca sector. On the 23rd the Moroccan Army Corps began to cross the Ebro at Quinto. Group 2-G-3 carried out five sorties in this sector, two by the entire group, one with two squadrons and two with patrols. At 13.15hrs Salas and Vázquez took off to locate a battery which was firing at the pontoon bridge in Quinto. During the course of this patrol they spotted twelve Chatos flying above them and immediately climbed to attack. Salas and Vázquez both made a number of passes at the enemy without registering any vital hits, and just before the Chatos withdrew Vázquez's machine-guns jammed. Salas returned to base and Vázquez continued a reconnaissance on his own. He spotted a battery of three guns which were being dismantled and loaded on to lorries. When he returned to the airfield the group had already taken off, under Pardo's leadership, which meant that only Salas, Salvador and Vázquez were available to mount an attack against the enemy battery. Only minutes elapsed before all three were in the air, and so fast had been their reaction that the battery was still in the same position. Low-level attacks soon had five lorries in flames, one of which carried the battery's ammunition, and which exploded spectacularly.

On March 24th eighteen Fiats led by Salas provided escort for the He 51s and S-M.79s attacking Quinto, over which town they encountered eleven Ratas and 30 Chatos. In the ensuing combats four Chatos were destroyed, Salas, Arístides, Senra and Rúiz Jiménez each claiming one. Lieutenant Jurado, flying Fiat No 3-104, was killed in action. At the termination of this air battle, Salas almost succeeded in capturing a Chato. He had attacked one of the enemy and, although unable to destroy the machine, he so clearly held the upper hand that the Chato pilot descended to a low altitude and was making for Nationalist lines, with Salas in close attendance. Just as the Chato was about to land it was attacked by an Me 109B (No 51) and destroyed.

In this battle Government aircraft Nos CA-006, CA-032, CA-037 and CA-052, piloted respectively by Antonio Sánchez, Benigno Hueso, Jesús Pérez and Villins, were destroyed; Viñals and Elías Hernández flying machines Nos CC-030 and CC-027 collided; and Alfredo Dealbert, aircraft No CA-038 force-landed outside the airfield. The Government Air Force had not previously lost so many aircraft in a single battle.

During a second sortie on the 24th, Group 2-G-3, operating in its normal sector in support of the Galician Army Corps, set fire to four more lorries transporting an anti-aircraft battery at Mas de las Matas. On the 25th the same group destroyed five more lorries in the morning and a similar number in the afternoon. As this second sortie was ending, Captain Salas saw three Government light aircraft landing on the aerodrome at Mas de las Matas, which was about to be occupied by the land forces. Salas landed alongside these light aircraft, while his group maintained air cover. The enemy aircraft were soon captured, but the land forces tried to include Salas among the prisoners. These aircraft, which belonged to the School at Reus, were *en route* from Celrá to Valencia, under the leadership of Lieutenant Momblona; the pilot of a fourth machine, which was still airborne, realised what had happened and made good his escape.

On March 26th Group 3-G-3, which was also operating from Belchite, had the task of escorting the Ju 52s to Caspe and Gandesa. With this mission completed the group strafed enemy trenches and their access roads, and during this action the Fiat flown by García Díez (who had recently joined the unit) was destroyed and that of Antonio Figueroa, the Count of Romanones' nephew, was hit by anti-aircraft fire. He died subsequently in Caspe hospital.

Group 1-G-2 had a hectic period during this battle, and was operating from Alfamén during the first few days, supporting the Galician Army Corps. On the 20th to 22nd they were seconded to the Aragón Army Corps, operating from Saragossa, and on the 23rd they received orders to move to Alcaniz (La Salada aerodrome). From there they co-operated with the Moroccan Army Corps during their lightning advance across los Monegros. On the 26th nearly all the Nationalist Air Force was sent to the River Guadalope sector, where their support was essential to enable the ground forces to break through the enemy's defences.

Group 1-G-2 carried out two consecutive sorties, making a number of low-level attacks on enemy positions during each. At every pass one of the machines was hit, but the remainder continued to press home their attacks. Finally, only one machine was left undamaged, that of the Group leader José Muñoz Jiménez, nicknamed El Corto, 'The Short One' (short in stature, but a giant in spirit). So keen was the attitude of this group that two pilots who had received head injuries demanded to be allowed to fly alongside Jiménez, and it is not surprising that the group was recommended collectively to receive an award of the Laureate.

The Condor Legion moved their combat group forward, the He 51s going to Sariñena and the Me 109s to Escatrón. From these bases they attacked Lerida aerodrome on March 27th, and were successful in destroying several Ratas on the ground.

According to General Líster, two Nationalist fighters were destroyed by light machine-gun fire from the ground, and the anti-aircraft artillery attached to his Division shot down three bombers. This may refer to two S-M.81s lost on the 28th and one Ro 37 destroyed on the same day, or possibly a Ba 65 which fell on the 30th. On March 26th three S-M.81s and one S-M.79 were damaged by anti-aircraft fire, but they were able to return to their bases.

During this same period Group 2-G-3 enjoyed considerable success in low-level attacks on enemy supply columns, destroying many transport vehicles in the Zorita sector.

On April 8th, after escorting Ju 52s and He 45s to the Morella front, Captain Salas' Fiat was hit while he was strafing enemy troops. The bullet had severed an oil pipe, and with oil pressure falling rapidly he had only seconds to choose a suitable area for the inevitable forced-landing.

The terrain to the North of Morella was all hill country, an extremely difficult area for a landing. Salas was preparing to bale out when he caught sight of a clear patch of ground that seemed to offer a fair chance of getting his aircraft down safely, and immediately he circled to make an approach, putting the Fiat down with such skill that only the landing gear and the under surface of the port wing was damaged. The site of this manoeuvre was within half a mile (1km) of General Aranda's Command Post. Aranda watched the landing with great interest, and lost no time in recovering both pilot and aircraft.

This aircraft was No 3-61 (Factory No 111), which was flown by Salas throughout the war. He had first flown this Fiat in 1937, in the Dequal Squadron; he retained it when Squadron 2-E-3 was formed and flew it until his forced-landing at Morella on April 8th, 1938. He regained possession of 3-61 on July 3rd, 1938, following repairs, and continued with it until November 12th, when he suffered a serious accident. After being repaired again the Fiat came back into the possession of Salas in January 1939, remaining with him until the end of the war. He continued to fly this machine from Getafe for a considerable time after the war's end, until it was completely destroyed in an accident. This aircraft, like Morato's Fiat (3-51), retained the two Breda-Safat 7·7mm machine-guns throughout its service life. Later machines of this type had two 12·7mm machine-guns of the same make, but the Spanish pilots normally preferred a combination of one 7·7mm and one 12·7mm machine-gun. The Italians had experimented with four machine-guns in Fiats, nicknamed *Cuatriarmi*, but their evaluation of this armament was inconclusive.

During a second sortie on April 8th seventeen Fiats took off under the leadership of García Pardo. They were joined by Morato who was flying Commander Gomá's S-M.79, with which he made a reconnaissance of La Cenia aerodrome. Despite the strength of the 'escort', Morato's machine was hit by anti-aircraft fire.

On April 11th Salas, in company with the entire Group, was able to celebrate a double event: his escape unharmed from the difficult forced-landing near Morella, and his promotion to Commander, which had been authorised on April 4th. The news of this did not reach him until April 11th, hence the date of the Group's celebration in Saragossa.

On April 9th the Government Air Force had made a show of strength over Barcelona, using a total of sixty aircraft to demonstrate their support for Negrín and his new Government, in which he assumed responsibility for Defence. The following day Daladier replaced León Blum as leader of the French Government.

On April 14th seventeen Fiats took off at 08.30hrs under the leadership of Salas, accompanying Muñoz, that were to strafe the enemy in the San Mateo sector. Group 1-G-2 had just arrived at the aerodrome of Mas de Las Matas, after spending two weeks in Logrono for repair and service of their aircraft. At 13.30hrs Salas again led a group of Fiats escorting the He 51s which were attacking La Jana. During this sortie they spotted nine Katiuskas escorted by twelve Ratas, bombing Nationalist lines from a much higher altitude. Vázquez, who knew that because of the difference in height and speed he would be unable to attack the Katiuskas, turned towards the sea, gaining height, with the idea of attacking them as they returned in the direction of Barcelona. Near to Tortosa, however, he spotted another formation of eighteen Katiuskas escorted by fifteen Ratas. This time he had the advantage of height and attacked a formation of three bombers. He was soon involved in a running fight with the Ratas, managing to damage one machine, but lack of fuel forced him to withdraw from the combat and he made an emergency landing at Mas de las Matas.

Meanwhile, the remainder of the group had become involved with the Ratas. Carlos Serra destroyed one which crashed in the sea in the port of Los Alfaques. Matamoros attacked another Rata which burst into flames and crashed, and Salvador Serra destroyed a third which spun into the sea. Salvador Serra and Comas were injured in this engagement.

The next day Group 2-G-3 made two sorties over the sea. During the first they attacked the Government vessel *Cala Morlanda* and another small ship, forcing them to return to port where they were captured. During the second they sank one vessel, put others out of action and forced the remainder to retreat. Morato recorded these events:

"During the twenty minutes of our attack, ten small boats were holed by our machine-gun fire and sank. Two small motorboats ran aground on the coast at Mansiat, and the *Cala Morlanda* was temporarily put out of control as a result of concentrated fire directed at the bridge. Soon after the attack ended the ship was got under control, but when it was off Benicarlo repeated attacks from the fighters forced it to take refuge in the port, where it dropped anchor and disembarked its occupants, who escaped in cars and lorries only moments before our forces arrived.

"When inspected the *Cala Morlanda* was found to have received more than 500 hits from machine-gun bullets; the bridge suffered considerable damage and the compass was destroyed. In the cabins, first aid kits were in a state of disarray, showing the extent to which they had been used to tend the wounded; one man had been so badly injured that he was left behind.

"On the deck a picket of airmen confirmed that the *Cala Morlanda* was the legitimate prize of 2-G-3. . . ."

The last sorties in this theatre of operations were carried out on April 16th and 18th, following which the Condor Legion was stationed at La Cenia, the former base of the Katiuskas. The Spanish fighter groups were sent to Bello to support the Castille Army Corps at Teruel.

Top: Aerial view of Barajas aerodrome, with the Air Force drawn up for review by General Franco in May 1939.

Above: Malaga aerodrome photographed during a bombing attack./*Sanchez Gallicher*

C. de M.

92

Top left: Aerial photograph of the bombing of the Cinca fortifications./ *Sanchez Gallicher*

Centre left: Mobile field gun destroyed by air attack./*Guereta*

Bottom left: 250 and 50 kg aviation bombs./*Guereta*

Morato (*top right*) and Vara de Rey (*right*), the only members of the Nationalist Air Force to be decorated before the war's end./*Región Aérea del Estrecho*

Left: Carlos Haya./*Región Aérea del Estrecho*

Bottom left: José Muñoz./*Balaguer*

Top right: A group of outstanding officers, photographed at the end of the war: Cuadra, Sirvent, Murcia, del Río, Salvador, Planell, Salas, Guerrero, Llop, Vierna and Muñoz)./*Balaguer*

Right: Isidoro Giménez, José Ma Bravo and Manuel Aguirre in the summer of 1938./*Tarazona.*

Left: Comas (with crutches), Bastida and Zambudio, at Gers concentration camp in France.

Bottom left: Pilots of the 3rd 'Chato' squadron during the Teruel offensive: Comas, Zambudio, Redondo, Ortega, Perez, Britz, Montagut, X, X, Nieto, Puig, Hueso and Elías.

Right: Andrés García La Calle, the official hero of the Government fighter force./*Tarazona*

Below: Group of pilots from the first training course in Russia, including Arias, Tarazona, Eloy Gonzalo Obarro and Frutos./*Tarazona*

Leocadio Mendiola, the only pilot of the Government Air Force to receive a decoration./*Jaime Mata*

The Condor Legion's bomber squadrons carried out a notable operation between April 16th and 18th, (Operation Neptune). Forty He 111s took off from Sanjurjo *en route* to Granada, and some of these landed at Avila and others at Salamanca. The weather forecast for the south had predicted clouds at 1,600ft (500m), but in fact they proved to be much lower. They were encountered first at Seville, and almost immediately caused the loss of one machine, which crashed at Cabeza de Vaca. Another machine made an emergency landing and two others turned back to their base. With worsening weather the squadrons were recalled, but nine pilots did not hear the radio message and completed the trip to Granada despite the weather.

On April 17th twenty-five more He 111s arrived in Granada and, at midday, these thirty-four bombers crossed the Sierra Nevada at a height of 19,700ft (6,000m), making for Cartagena. Half of the formation attacked the south eastern area of the port, the other half the north west. Twenty-five ships, railway sidings and port facilities felt the weight of their bombs, initiating heavy anti-aircraft fire from the ground batteries, as well as vessels of the Government Fleet, their efforts being supported by three Chatos which climbed to attack. At 17.45hrs twenty-five He 111s took off to make a second attack on the port. Direct hits were scored on port installations and the railway, and a torpedo boat was sunk; other bombs hit the *Jaime I*. This time the anti-aircraft fire was even more intense and aircraft No 25-27 was hit, putting both engines out of action. The crew managed to re-start one of the engines and attempted to regain their base. Over Almería, which had by then been attacked by the second squadron, the anti-aircraft fire was concentrated on the single slow-flying aircraft, which was hit again and crashed at Motril. The He 111 No 25-15 was damaged by machine-gun fire from an enemy fighter, but of the twenty-five aircraft involved twenty-one landed at Granada and three at Málaga.

On April 18th, twenty-seven He 111s returned to Saragossa and eight more arrived some days later. Of the five that were missing from the forty that set out, two had been destroyed and three damaged.

From December 1937 to April 1938 Group 2-G-3 destroyed 40 Government aircraft, which together with those shot down previously, made a total of eighty-two victories. The victorious pilots of this period were Vázquez Sagastizábal with four, followed by Morato, García Pardo, Guerrero, Arístides García López, Allende and Bayo with three each, Rubio, Senra and Carlos Serra each with two. Salas, Salvador, Murica, Mazarredo, Muntadas, Comas, Herrero, Henricourt, Matamoros, Ruiz Jiménez and Salvador Serra gained one victory each.

The list of aircraft destroyed by Nationalist pilots since the beginning of the war was headed by Morato with thirty, followed by Salvador with fifteen; Salas and Guerrero with ten; Arístides and Vázquez Sagastizábal with nine, García Pardo with eight, Allende five and Rubio and Senra with four each.

In the battle of Aragon Groups 2-G-3 and 3-G-3 suffered only a single loss; that of Jurado. The Italians lost at least seven Fiats and the Germans one Messerschmitt.

The Condor Legion had also lost one Ju 87 at Bujaraloz before the offensive began, two He 111s in Operation Neptune and one seaplane at Tarragona.

The Legionary Air Force lost two Savoia S-M.79s, one Romeo Ro 37 and one Breda Ba 65.

According to Nationalist bulletins the Government Air Force had lost thirty-three Chatos, twelve Ratas, four Katiuskas and nine miscellaneous aircraft in the Aragón campaign, plus five more destroyed on the ground. Direct information suggests that more Ratas were lost on the ground than in the air.

The very small number of losses in combat suffered by the Nationalist Air Force should not be attributed to reduced activity in the air. On the contrary in March and April they broke all previous records as regards the number of hours flown on operations. But in fairness it should be remembered that the Government fighter force had been considerably weakened in the earlier battle of Teruel.

CHAPTER SIX

The Pause in the Middle of 1938

The Popular Army's Great Attempt at Reorganisation

Negrín had formed a new Government on April 7th, reserving for himself the portfolio for Defence. He mobilised immediately the 1927 and 1928 reserves, and the 1941 call-up and, during the month of May, added the 1925 and 1926 reserves, with the object of replacing most divisions lost in the North (Nos 48 to 63) and those which were far below strength as a result of the recent battle of Aragón. A little earlier Prieto had mobilised the 1929 reserves and 1940 call-up.

With these men and other forces taken from the Centre they created in Levante these new Army Corps: XVI (Palacios), XVII (Garcia Vallegjo), 'A' (Güemes) and 'B' (Romero), which joined the old XIII (Gallego) and XIX (Vidal), and those from the Army of Manoeuvre which remained south of Vinaroz, the XXI (Cristóbal) and XXII (Ibarrola); the XX Corps (Durán) was also reconstituted.

In Catalonia during mid-April the Autonomous Ebro Group was formed, comprising the forces which were defending the line from Mequinenza to the sea. These forces were then organised into two Army Corps: the V, whose command was assigned to Líster, and the XV, under Tagüeña's command.

Initially the V remained at the line, with the veteran Divisions 2 and 11, independent brigades from the sector (53, 56, 68 and 124) and scattered troops from Brigades 49, 73 and 74. On April 16th Divisions 11 (Rodríguez), 45 (Hans) and 46 ('Campesino') were assigned to the V Corps, and 3 (Cabezas), 35 (Walter, later Merino) and 42 (Manuel Álvarez) to the XV Corps. This last Division had been disbanded after the battle of Alfambra, and was then reformed from the 56th Brigade and men gathered from other units; these were then organised into the new Brigades 226 and 227.

The Eastern Army (Perea) was reorganised from April 19th, 1938, becoming subdivided into North and South Groups, the former consisting of Army Corps 'H' (later X) and XI; the latter of Corps 'A' (later XVIII) and 'B' (later XII). The Army Corps 'H' consisted of Divisions 'X' (later 31), 'Y' (later 24) and 34. In the XI Corps, the only one in the Eastern Army which had not become disorganised in the Aragon campaign, were Divisions 26, 30 and 32. The Southern Group was formed basically from Division 16, which was itself the main stem for Corps 'B', and from Division 27 of the Army of Manoeuvre which served as the basis for Army Corps 'A'. This Corps was completed by Division 27A (later 60), and 72. Division 44 and the one from Bellvís (later 56) went to Army Corps 'B'.

On May 29th the Forces of the Catalan Region were reorganised, becoming divided into the Eastern Army, with Corps X, XI and XVIII; and the Ebro Army, with Corps XII, V and XV, and a minimum reserve of three divisions per Army. From these reserves the Army Corps XXIV (with Divisions 43, 55 and 62) was formed at a later date.

In Levante, the XXI and XXII Army Corps continued to operate with the 47th, 67th and 70th Divisions from the Army of Manoeuvre, these being joined by Division 19 which arrived from Extremadura. The Army Corps 'A' was formed from Division 15 (Del Castillo), Division 10 (Víctor de Frutos) from the VI Corps, and 50, which had been newly formed.

The XX Corps was reorganised from Division 6 (Melero), and was completed with the new divisions Nos 49 and 53. Romero took command of Army Corps 'B', which consisted of Division 28 (Jover) from the Army of Manoeuvre and the new 54th and 61st Divisions.

The new Army Corps XVI and XVII were formed from the former Levante Army Divisions 39 and 40, number 25 from the Army of Manoeuvre and the new 48th and 59th Divisions. They were joined later by the 19th Division, when the XXI Army Corps became embodied in Corps 'A'.

Finally, the XIX Corps retained its 64th Division (Calderón, later Sáez de San Pedro) and received 66 (González Gómez) from the Army of Manoeuvre and 5, which they sent as reinforcement for the VI Corps.

To sum up, by these changes twelve new divisions were created: four in Catalonia (Nos 55, 56, 60 and 62), seven in Levante (Nos 48, 49, 50, 52, 53, 54 and 61) and one which remained in Extremadura (No 51).

This enormous effort made by the Government to gain numerical superiority was counteracted by the creation of twelve new divisions in the Nationalist Zone: Nos 16 to 20, 24, 40, 50, 55, 60, 85 and 122. This was achieved by mobilising the 1940 call-up in February 1938, and by recalling all the troops who had been mobilised in the Cantabrian Region and those who had been wounded in the Northern Campaign. Of these twelve new divisions only five were assigned to the Northern Army, five remaining in the Centre and two in the South.

In the middle of 1938 the opposing forces were numerically equal, with about 800 to 900 battalions on each side. The Government Army had 70 Divisions (Nos 1 to 56 and 60 to 73), each comprising 12 infantry battalions and one machine-gun battalion, facing the 50 divisions each of 12 battalions in the Nationalist Army. The Nationalist battalions each contained more men, and this compensated for their fewer numbers.

The Offensive Against Valencia

This offensive, in its various phases, lasted from April 23rd until July 25th, 1938. It is not easy to appreciate the motives which led to this campaign. It was difficult terrain for any land operations, which was the reason why Vicente Rojo had not anticipated any serious Nationalist attack south of the Ebro. The forces from the Levante (Menédez), Centre (Cardenal, later Casado), Extremadura (Burillo) and Andalucian Armies (Casado, later Moriones), which were now integrated in the Central Army Group under command of Miaja, were fresh and previously unbeaten. Furthermore, Government potential of reinforcement from the Central Zone was very good. It was easy also to deploy the Government Air Force to provide air support: Nationalist aircraft would have to operate from more distant bases.

Added difficulties for this campaign were the lack of suitable maps and supply routes. Fuel was brought as far as Vinaroz, carried from Mallorca in the small tanker *Ophir* (500 tons displacement), which had been captured at Málaga.

The offensive on Valencia was carried out with very few forces (until July only the Castille and Galician Army Corps and the Liaison Group took part), and because of the difficult terrain it progressed very slowly. On the other hand, the Barcelona Government made a tremendous effort with seven new Army Corps, Nos XXIV and XV in Catalonia, Nos XVI, XVII, 'A' and 'B' in the Central Zone, as well as the XIV Army Corps of guerillas (Hungría).

When the Nationalists came to the final assault on Valencia, on July 13th, the five attacking Army Corps, 'Castilla' (Varela), 'CTV' (Berti), 'Turia' (Solchaga), Liaison Group (García Valiño) and 'Galicia' (Aranda), faced seven Government Army Corps lined up in defence. Here, as earlier in Madrid, the defenders had massed numerical superiority at the right moment in time.

During the first phase of the offensive the Castille Army Corps operated with Divisions 108 (Lafuente), 82 (Delgado Serrano) and 5 (Juan Bautista Sánchez González), occupying Aliaga on April 23rd, and were poised to attack Allepuz and Villarroya on the 27th when operations were suspended because of bad weather.

The attack was resumed on May 4th, with the Castille Army Corps operating from north to south (Divisions 82 and 5) from the Allepuz-Villarroya sector towards Alcalá de la Selva and Cedrillas and, from west to east, from Teruel to Corbalán and Escriche, with Divisions 85 (Cuervo), 15 (García Escámez) and 81 (Ollo). The Liaison Group, with Divisions 55 (Adrados) and I (García Valiño) attacked from Morella towards the west, in the direction of Mosqueruela. This second phase was virtually ended by May 17th, although Varela continued operations until the end of the month, near to Teruel, until he occupied Formiche Alto, Formiche Bajo, La Puebla de Valverde and Puerto Escandón.

The third phase began on May 26th in the Liaison Group's zone. This group now turned the direction of their advance through ninety degrees and followed the routes Mosqueruela-Lucena-Castellón (Division I) and Villafranca-Culla-Villafamés-Castellón (Division 55), trying to cut off and capture the forces which Divisions 83 (Martín Alonso) and 84 (Galera) were still containing on the coast at Vinromá and Alcalá de Chivert. Division 4 (Alonso Vega) from this Army Corps acted as a form of liaison between both manoeuvring groups and joined Division 55 in the Culla zone, before continuing towards Castellón. On June 13th, with the occupation of this capital, the third phase was considered as ended, although García Valiño continued as far as Onda (22nd), Arlanda (30th) and the foothills of the Sierra de Espadán.

García Valiño and Aranda received orders to attack towards this sierra and to the south of the River Mijares, although Valiño thought that it would have been more logical to set up fortifications lower down on the Mijares and to advance up-stream along the river. Aranda succeeded in occupying Burriana and Nules, on the plain, but García Valiño failed at Espadán, which prevented him from reaching the Segorbe–Sagunto line.

The fourth phase began on July 13th, with the Army Corps del Turia (Solchaga), CTV (Berti) and Castille (Varela) attacking in the Teruel-Sarrión-Segorbe-Valencia direction, and the Liaison Group and the Galician Army Corps attacking from north to south, parallel to the coast. This phase ended indecisively on July 25th, (when the Popular Army began their offensive on the Ebro), as Nationalist leaders did not reinforce their right wing adequately (Terruel sector) and insisted on trying to gain the Segorbe-Sagunto line with a weakened left flank.

For most of this offensive there were three squadrons of Ratas operating in Levante: the 1st at Liria, the 3rd at Sagunto and the 4th at Camporrobles. Squadrons 2, 5 and 6 remained in Catalonia, although they were occasionally moved into Levante, operating from Casino aerodrome. The 3rd Chato squadron remained at Barracas until May, when it went to Alcublas.

Nationalist Groups 2-G-3 and 3-G-3 operated from Bello during all the phases, supporting the Castille Army Corps. General Vaerla's troops were also supported by Groups 1-G-2 and 6-G-15, based at Caudé, although 6-G-15 moved to Castejón del Puente to operate at Bielsa, remaining there from the middle of May until June 20th.

During the first phase there were no clashes in the air. Ground attacks were carried out from April 23rd to 27th.

The bad weather caused a pause until May 11th, although odd reconnaissance sorties were made in this period. On April 29th an He 45 crewed by Second Lieutenants Puig and Campos was shot down by ground fire, but the crew were uninjured and managed to gain safety on foot.

Group 2-G-3 made two sorties, on May 2nd and 4th, but their luck was out. On the 2nd Second Lieutenant Mesía had to force-land when his Fiat (3-58) was damaged, and on the 4th Commander Salas had his fuel and water tanks holed by machine-gun fire from the ground, forcing him to make an emergency landing at Aguilar aerodrome, which had been occupied only days before. During the same sortie the Fiats flown by Bayo, Muntadas and Henricourt all received damage from ground fire.

On May 11th normal aerial activity was resumed, and eighteen Fiats from 2-G-3 took off to escort twelve Ju 52s and He 45s over the El Pobo sector. Six Fiats were damaged (Nos 3-67, 3-105, 3-106, 3-108, 3-109 and 3-112) and one of them had to force-land at Teruel aerodrome.

On May 12th 2-G-3 made four sorties, two of them in collaboration with 3-G-3, without meeting any enemy fighters. On that day Bermúdez de Castro and Delgado Valle were injured and Cuadra was shot down. On the 13th both fighter groups made three joint sorties. During the second 2-G-3 was accompanied by a single squadron from 3-G-3 (a total of seventeen machines) to escort twelve Ju 52s and He 51s over the Corbalán sector. Enemy aircraft appeared but declined to enter into combat.

In the afternoon of the same day, Montero and Barranco's squadrons from 3-G-3 were operating with squadron 5-E-3 (Guerrero), escorting Ju 52s over the Allepuz sector. They encountered fifty enemy fighters in two formations: the Ratas at the same height as the Fiats and the Chatos below them. The Ju 52s, which were well below the altitude of the Chatos, immediately sought cover in the clouds.

In the ensuing dogfights, four pilots of 3-G-3 gained their first victories: Manrique Montero, Larios, Velasco and O'Connor, who each claimed one Rata.

In the accompanying 5-E-3 squadron, Aristides shot down one Chato near Aguilar aerodrome; Ibarreche battled with a Rata until it crashed between Valdelinares and the Tarancon mountains, and Ruiz Jiménez was successful in destroying two Ratas, both of which were seen to crash. On that day Morato was slightly injured by machine-gun fire from the ground.

On May 14th anti-aircraft fire accounted for three Nationalist aircraft. Two He 51s were shot down, but the pilot of one was able to make a successful landing behind his own lines. An He 45 was also hit, and Second Lieutenants Serafín Serra and Feliciano Rodríguez were killed when it crashed. The pilot of another He 51 escaped by parachute and managed to reach his own lines.

At this period Tarazona and his 3rd Squadron of Ratas, as well as the 1st squadron, were usually operating along the coast. They were opposing the Nationalist fighters from La Cenia, but there were no important battles in this sector. The Spanish Fiat groups must have been opposed by the 4th Squadron, or the Russian squadrons which had come down from Catalonia.

On May 15th the leader of the 3rd Chatos Squadron, Captain Juan Comas Borrás, was injured when making a forced-landing at El Toro. He was replaced by Lieutenant Zambudio, and at about the same time Captain Ladislao Duarte Espés also had a serious accident.

On May 18th, in 2-G-3's first sortie of the day, five Fiats were damaged and of these Martínez de Irujo had to land at Aguilar, and Serra and Allende at Teruel. On the previous day Second Lieutenant Francisco Encinas, a pilot of 1-G-2, had been killed.

On the 23rd, Groups 2-G-3 and 3-G-3 made three joint sorties over the Teruel front, each lasting about two hours. On that day the Eastern Army began their fierce attacks on the bridgeheads at Tremp and Balaguer.

On the 24th and 25th both groups were detailed to the Tremp sector to help in repelling the enemy attack. On these two days they made five joint sorties, in addition to the trip from Belchite to Castejón del Puente (near Barbastro) and back.

To assist the Government attacks on Tremp and Balaguer, the three Rata Squadrons in Levante were moved to that area. The 1st Squadron was based at Reus, the 3rd at Vendrell, and the 4th at Monjos, between Vilafranca del Panadés and Vendrell. When the offensive ended, these squadrons returned to Liria, Sagunto and Camporrobles.

On May 23rd there was a large-scale air battle, following which the 2nd, 3rd and 5th Rata squadrons claimed twenty-two victories, amongst which were two Savoia S-M.79s and seventeen Fiats.

A Government leader, one of whose sons was a fighter pilot, arrived at his aerodrome and insisted on seeing the wreckage of the Fiats that had been shot down. He was unlucky for, in fact, only three Fiats were lost: Boschelli, who was missing, and two others who were in collision over the enemy's lines, both pilots escaping by parachute. The Fiats had come from the *As de Bastos* and *La Cucaracha* groups, and they claimed the destruction of five Ratas and six Chatos (the Nationalist bulletin quoted five Ratas plus seven Chatos). According to Tarazona the Government forces lost one Katiuska and three Ratas.

In attempting to make sense of these claims and counter-claims, it should be remembered that during the Spanish War any aircraft which was forced to land outside its own airfield was classified as being shot down. Conversely, the loss of an aircraft was only admitted if it had been destroyed. This explains the great difference between claims and losses, and we have seen in earlier pages that Cuadra, for example, was shot down three times without any aircraft being lost. To confirm this point, Hispano-Suiza rebuilt only forty-nine Fiats in Seville during the entire war, and a similar number of Ratas were rebuilt at Alicante.

On May 26th, the beginning of the third phase of the Levante offensive, both Fiat groups were again operating in Teruel. During their first sortie on May 28th four lorries were set on fire, and during the first sortie on May 30th, Salas, García Pardo and Carlos Serra all received damage to their aircraft.

On May 31st 2-G-3 took off with a total of eight machines, in company with Captain Murcia's squadron. Their task was to escort a number of Ju 52s and Ro 37s over the Puebla de Valverde sector. On arrival at the front they encountered about twenty-five Chatos and ten Ratas. Combat began immediately, but the Nationalist crews were successful in protecting the bombers which, their task completed, made good their escape.

In the air battle which resulted, Salvador gained his best personal score for a single sortie, and one which was the most notable of the group until that date. Throwing his machine around the sky he managed to shoot down three bombers: the first dived into the ground, the pilot of the second machine took to his parachute, and Salvador pursued the third as far as Sarrión aerodrome, where it crashed and burst into flames. Henricourt and Simon each shot down one Chato, and Salvador destroyed a Rata. Vázquez also shot down a Chato, which crashed to the north of the Puebla de Valverde road, and attacked the Rata which Salvador eventually destroyed at Sarrion. Whilst Salas was attacking another Chato he, in turn, was attacked by three enemy machines. His Fiat was hit several times before he managed to break away from the attack, but his machine was vibrating so badly that he had to return to base.

In Group 3-G-3 Murcia destroyed one Chato and Meurza a Rata. A second Chato, which Murcia claimed as a probable, was later confirmed as having been destroyed.

In the first half of June, the third phase of the offensive, aerial activity in the Teruel sector decreased. This was due mainly to the fact that supplies and spares for the Fiat groups were becoming exhausted, as a result of almost continuous operations since December. By June they rarely managed to take off with more than ten or eleven Fiats per group.

The main operations then moved to the coastal sector, where the Galician Army Corps and the Liaison Group were operating. Aerial support in these sectors was provided by the Condor Legion, which had not received any supplies since Germany began preparations for the annexation of Austria. As a result, the number of aircraft available for operations was diminishing at an alarming rate. Of the thirty fighters which had been at their disposal in the winter, only sixteen were available for active service.

The Government fighters had suffered similar problems in February and March, but this had been overcome with the receipt of new supplies which arrived across the French frontier in the Spring. At the end of June and in July, when León Blum's second Government had collapsed, the Ratas also went through a period of shortages, but by August there was an abundance of aircraft, their numbers reaching the maximum of the entire war, allowing the formation of a seventh Squadron, as we shall see later.

The Chatos squadrons suffered less ups and downs as, by this stage, the Sabadell and Reus factories were in full production, assembling one Chato per day. The factory at Alicante, where it was intended to assemble a series of one hundred Chatos, had not then started production.

In the Nationalist Zone the only aviation factory was CASA, in Cádiz, which was devoted to seaplane production. Servicing and repair of landplanes was carried out in the Southern and Northern Regional Parks (Tablada and León), and later in the one built at Logroño. For major repairs Hispano-Suiza erected a new factory in Seville in the summer of 1937, but this was devoted initially to the repair of the Fiat liquid-cooled in-line engines which powered the Fiat C.R.32s. It was not until 1938 that this factory handed over the first aircraft which had been rebuilt there. By the time the war ended it had rebuilt 49 Fiats and was preparing for the production of one hundred new units. (This series of one hundred machines was handed over in 1940). There were no facilities for flight testing at Hispano-Suiza's Seville factory, which meant that the Fiats had to be taken to Tablada before they could be flown.

On June 2nd Government Katiuskas attacked La Cenia aerodrome, the German fighter base, suffering heavy losses: two of these were destroyed by anti-aircraft fire and three by fighters. The anti-aircraft batteries continued to demonstrate their efficiency throughout the month, during which they shot down a total of ten aircraft (seven Katiuskas, two Natachas and one Chato).

During the first fortnight of June there were four important aerial combats, on the 8th, 10th, 13th and 14th. In the first, the *Gamba de Ferro* group claimed 11 victories (ten Chatos and one Katiuska), without losing any of their number. Perhaps these victories brought a little compensation for the loss of one of their pilots on June 4th who, having taken to his parachute, was raked with machine-gun fire and killed. The Condor Legion had lost an He 51 at the beginning of the month, a second on June 4th and the third on June 9th. It was also to be the last, for very soon afterwards the 3rd Squadron (assault) was withdrawn from the front to be re-equipped with Me 109s.

The Messerschmitts were involved in the other three battles. On the 10th, at Adzaneta, the 2nd Squadron shot down two Ratas and one Katiuska without loss; Tarazona admitted the loss of the two Ratas, but claimed the destruction of an Me 109. On June 13th, the Me 109s claimed two Ratas and five Chatos over Castellón. But on the 14th the tables were turned. Lieutenant Plieber was wounded, and Lieutenant Henz was shot down to the north of the River Mijares. According to German sources Henz set fire to his aircraft before attempting to escape, but according to Tarazona's diary, from which an extract is given below, it would appear that the Me 109 was recovered intact, and that it was set on fire subsequently by attack from the air.

". . . 14th June. Today we were returning, the first and third squadrons, from Castellón front. Nules had been bombed brutally. We had had a tremendous battle with Heinkel bombers and Me 109 fighters. During the battle I had teamed up with Claudín. Yuste was at my side.

"Whilst looking at the destruction caused by the Fascists at Nules, something down there, near the beach, caught my eye.

"A plane, leaving a trail of white smoke, was turning towards the north. I pointed this out to Claudín. We dived. We discovered that it was an Me 109. It had been hit. We swooped over it, without firing, where it had landed on the beach, on the right bank of the River Mijares . . .

". . . On reaching Sagunto I received orders to go out and bring back the Me 109. We went in a lorry, various mechanics, armourers and myself . . .

". . . 'There is the ugly bird', said one of them. 'The pilot is nearby, in a gully at Villareal. He has been detained; he is only a lad of about 18 years'.

"I am enthralled with the beauty of this fine piece of German aeronautical engineering. I admire it from outside for a long time. Then, with aplomb, I sit in the cockpit. The oxygen, the radiotelephone, the fuel tank which serves as the pilot's seat . . .

". . . We need to fly in it; to study its characteristics, to compare it more closely with our own fighters. It is intact. As we are talking, the rattle of friendly machine-guns and the hollow sound of cannons from both sides serve as a background. The enemy is barely fifteen kilometres from us; within sight of Castellón . . .

". . . The rumble of aeroplane engines makes us look up. The noise increases; it seems as if they are coming along the road, but they are not yet visible.

"There they are!

"Six Me 109s appear over the sea, skimming the water. When they reach the Mijares estuary they make a gentle bank to starboard.

"They are coming towards us. . . .

"Get out quickly!

"The monoplanes form a circle around the Me 109 on the ground. They fire at it. At their second attack it bursts into flames. . . ."

On June 13th the Galician Army Corps, with the Drohne Group leading, had penetrated as far as Castellón: the 4th Navarre Division occupied Almazora and Villareal. But they had lost the opportunity of isolating and capturing two enemy divisions, and this prevented them from gaining the final objective, Segorbe and Sagunto.

When the third phase of the offensive was over, Claudín assumed command of Group 21, and left Merono in charge of the 1st Squadron of Ratas, which began to operate in the Teruel sector. The 3rd Squadron was transferred from Sagunto to Liria, and later to Alicante.

In the middle of the month flights in the Castille Army Corps Sector were resumed. On the 14th, 2-G-3 made three sorties, the second of which was led by Morato from Teruel aerodrome. Morato had been in the South for a few days and returned, much to his delight, to assume command of 3-G-3. He celebrated his arrival at Teruel in typical Morato style, skimming the surface of the airfield—in inverted flight!

The next day the pilots of 3-G-3 were complaining of bad luck. Apparently, after patrolling for two hours over Puebla de Valverde, they were returning to base when they spotted a formation of 17 enemy bombers accompanied by 'only' thirty fighters. The complaint was that lack of fuel prevented them from catching this easy prey.

June 16th, 1938, was graduation day for the pilots of the first fighter course held in the Nationalist zone. The large number of accidents caused by new and inexperienced Fiat pilots in December and January had showed that it was essential to set up a school of this type.

Gallur was chosen as the aerodrome and Captain Nobili, the veteran squadron leader of the *As de Bastos* Group, and Lieutenant Senra, from Group 2-G-3, were posted there as instructors. Senra, who had been flying fighters since July 1936, was a founder member of 2-G-3 and had shot down the first enemy machine destroyed in Aragón.

This first fighter course lasted for two months and was attended by twenty-three pupils. Of these, six were sent to 2-G-3 (Bernal, Etayo, Alcocer, Manrique, Cesteros and Diego Vigueras), nine to 3-G-3 (Gautier, Munaiz, Arrechea, Carracido, Acuña, Alonso, Fariñas, Téllez and Epelde), and of the remainder four were posted to fly He 51s, three to the He 45s and one to the Aero 101s.

On June 18th ten Fiats from 2-G-3 became involved in a satisfying little mission when they rescued the pilot of an He 51 who had fallen between the lines. This pilot, Alegría, a former member of 3-G-3, was shot down by fire from the ground when his group (1-G-2) was harassing enemy forces on the Crementala slopes. Salas wrote in his book:

"When I saw the pilot of an He 51 take to his parachute and land between the lines, I went down low to prevent his capture. After watching the situation for a while, I fired at the Red trenches, forcing the enemy to flee. At that moment two or three of our own men came out and picked up the pilot."

During 2-G-3's second sortie, at 18.00hrs on the 19th, ten Fiats took off, led by Salas, to escort Ju 52s bombing Puebla de Valverde. They encountered a formation of eighteen Chatos, which they chased as far as Alcublas, where nine Ratas joined the fray. Salas dived over the Chatos to attack, but was unable to fire his guns because a leak had emptied his compressed air bottle; despite this he continued to make dummy attacks during a battle which ranged as far as

Alcublas, being hit five times by the Ratas, one bullet puncturing the coolant radiator. Salvador enjoyed better luck, destroying two Chatos, one of which exploded in the air, the other following in flames; but he then had to retire because his engine was overheating. García Pardo effectively removed a Rata from the tail of Aristides' Fiat by shooting it down. Henricourt downed a Chato near Alcublas, then a Rata to the north of Villar del Arzobispo, and saw a Chato turn somersault as it attempted to land at its aerodrome. Ibarreche fired at a Chato close to the ground, and this separated from the rest of the formation and fell near to Higueruela. Ansaldo had to return to base when an engine cowling parted company from his Fiat.

At about this time Group 6-G-15, which had been operating at Bielsa throughout the month of June, returned to Caudé aerodrome.

On June 22nd a selection and training course for squadron leaders was held at Logroño, Commanders Mata and Ricardo Guerrero acting as instructors. Fifteen pilots were selected to attend the one-month course. Vázquez Sagastizábal from 2-G-3 and Queipo de Llano and Larios from 3-G-3 were included in this number, of which twelve completed the training satisfactorily.

On June 25th, Morato took off alone to make a reconnaissance flight, although it was more usual for the Fiats to go out in pairs. He spotted about fifty enemy machines, which failed to see him, and which allowed him to take them by surprise. By the time they were aware of the Fiat in their midst, two machines were falling in flames. But let Morato relate the event in his own words:

"It was during the month of June, on the 25th to be exact, that I carried out a sortie which I will remember for the rest of my life.

"I was flying my faithful 3-51, completely alone, making a reconnaissance sortie over the front. Nothing in particular had happened when, suddenly, I saw the enemy air force appear: sweeping towards our lines was a mass of more than fifty aircraft, a mixture of fighters and bombers.

"I quickly made up my mind. It was obviously an unequal battle which I had every chance of losing, but I couldn't just sit back and let them attack our troops without trying to do something to stop it. Tactically speaking I should have avoided combat, since I was at a lower altitude than my adversaries, but this was impossible.

"In fact, the speed with which I acted allowed me to profit by the tactical disadvantage of lower altitude for, choosing a favourable moment, I attacked the bombers from below, so that they screened my aircraft from the higher flying fighters. Before they or the bomber pilots were aware of an enemy in their midst two aircraft were falling in flames. The remaining machines, thinking they were being attacked by a large number of aircraft, scattered all over the sky, and by the time the Ratas reacted it was too late. The invisible enemy, of which they had seen neither the arrival nor departure, had already gone.

"I felt immense satisfaction at being able to deceive and punish such a large group of enemy aircraft."

It was at about this time that Morato went to La Cenia to try out the Heinkel

He 112 fighter. Only a small number of these aircraft were built, and Harder had brought one back from Germany. Ernst Heinkel had evolved the He 112 as a competitor to the Me 109, but despite favourable test reports it had been rejected by the *Luftwaffe*. Hence, the Heinkel Company were seeking to find a market for these machines and, in fact, a total of 17 He 112B-Os served in the Nationalist Air Force.

Shortly afterwards, Morato took command officially of Group 3-G-3. Ibarra went to the Pilots' School, and Manrique Montero, who was older than Morato, was sent on a conversion course. Morato named Murcia and Barranco as squadron leaders, despite having more senior Captains. It was not the first time that he had acted in this way. He believed that ability, alone, was the criterion for leadership, and this had sometimes brought unrest, causing pilots to leave the group.

Group 3-G-3 then consisted of the following pilots: Murcia, Ignacio Alfaro, Queipo, Robles, Chapaprieta, Ruibal and García de Juan in the 1st Squadron (3-E-3, later 5-E-3); Gautier, Velasco, O'Connor, Acuña, Arrechea, Munaiz and Alonso Farina in the 2nd (4-E-3, later 7-E-3), and Barranco, Larios, Muerza, Lacour, Bartolomé, Kindelán, Carracido and Téllez in the 3rd (6-G-3). It was not until July 3rd that Morato led the group into action for the first time.

Also, at the end of June the Condor Legion received new equipment and supplies, enabling them to re-organise their fighter group, which was then formed with three squadrons of Me 109s. This 3rd fighter Squadron (Mölders') was equipped with the Me 109C version, which was generally similar to the Me 109B, but with improved armament of four MG 17 machine-guns. The Spanish pilots José Muñoz, Miguel García Pardo and Javier Murcia joined this squadron at a later date.

With the remaining He 51s from the Condor Legion a new Spanish group was formed: this was 4-G-2, commanded by Fernández Pérez.

On July 5th a patrol formed by Salas, Comas and Cesteros took off to seek out enemy aircraft operating over the Villel front, to the south of Teruel. Anti-aircraft fire indicated the position of an enemy formation and, closing gradually, Comas and Cesteros each were successful in destroying a Rata.

One of these Ratas was flown by Claudín, leader of Group 21 since June 15th, and previously the leader of the 1st Rata Squadron. Claudín had been an aeronautical engineering student, and received his training as a pilot at the first course held in Russia, along with Herrera, Eloy Gonzalo, Bravo, Arias, Meroño, Tarazona. They were in Russia from November 1936 to May 1937, returning by ship to Le Havre and arrived in Catalonia via the French frontier. They joined the Rata squadrons at the end of the battle of Brunete; Eloy Gonzalo, Frutos and Tarazona at Santander, Herrera, Claudín, Gandía, Arias and Bravo at Belchite. The first of these to lead Rata patrols were Gandía, and Eloy Gonzalo who was killed in Asturias.

At Teruel the 1st Rata Squadron had been led by Claudín (Aguirre had become group leader) and the 4th by Zarauza. The 2nd, 3rd, 5th and 6th Rata Squadrons had Russian crews until, in April, the 3rd Squadron was reorganised with Spaniards, led by Bravo. The first Spanish leader of Group 21 was Aguirre, who was replaced by Claudín on June 15th and, after his death, by Zarauza. Arias then took over command of the 4th Squadron and Meroño the 1st. Redondo had been the leader of a Chatos squadron until he attended a Rata conversion course at El Carmolí, and subsequently went on to lead the 1st Squadron.

One should not confuse Isidro Comas Altadill, of the 1st Fiat Squadron, with his opponent Juan Comas Borrás, leader of the 3rd Chato Squadron until becoming wounded on May 15th, 1938, and later leader of the Group 26 from September 13th to November 5th, 1938, at which date he lost a leg during an attack on Monjos aerodrome.

Groups 21 and 26 formed fighter Squadron 11, whose first Spanish Commander had been Puparelli, a non-flying officer, and who was replaced in turn by Alonso Vega, Giménez and García La Calle. The first leaders of the groups were the Russian Colonels 'Julio', Maroxo and 'Pablo'. At the time of the battle of Brunete the Russian 'José' was one of the leaders; he had previously been a Chato leader at Alcalá, and was wounded in one leg in the bomb attack on that aerodrome.

By the middle of 1938 the number of foreign pilots flying the fighter aircraft of both sides had decreased considerably, to a point where they no longer predominated. Since April three of the six Rata squadrons were led by Spaniards; half way through the battle of the Ebro the 6th Squadron was given a Spanish leader and the 7th, which was formed in September, was also led by a Spaniard.

In the Nationalist zone a 7th Spanish Fiat squadron was formed, which was designated 8-E-3. To avoid any confusion, it should be explained that Squadron 5-E-3 became re-designated 3-E-3, since it was the 3rd in group 2-G-3; the original 3-E-3 became 5-E-3, the designation of Squadron 6-E-3 was unchanged, and 4-E-3 became 7-E-3. Squadron 8-E-3 was attached to group 2-G-3 at the end of the war, then becoming re-designated 4-E-3.

On July 7th the 3rd Rata Squadron was given a short period of rest at el Carmolí. From there they were sent to Camporrobles, where they found an excess of new pilots to vie for the comparatively small number of fighters remaining to them.

On July 13th, five Nationalist Army Corps began what they thought was the final attack on Valencia, despite the fact that aerial reconnaissance and intelligence reports confirmed the deployment of six select Government divisions near Tortosa. In addition, there was considerable movement in Barcelona, and an accumulation of materials that appeared to be intended for bridging, which suggested the imminence of a serious attack across the Ebro.

On the first day of the offensive Spanish Nationalist fighter groups made two sorties without meeting any enemy aircraft. The Legionary Fiats were more successful, destroying four Chatos and one Katiuska, at the cost of one of their number. Three He 51s were damaged during the second sortie and one was destroyed in a fourth attack, its pilot, Lieutenant Rafael Serra, being killed.

During the period July 10th to 18th the two Spanish Fiat groups operated jointly under Morato's command, as Salas took advantage of the arrival of his old friend and leader to make a short break from operations.

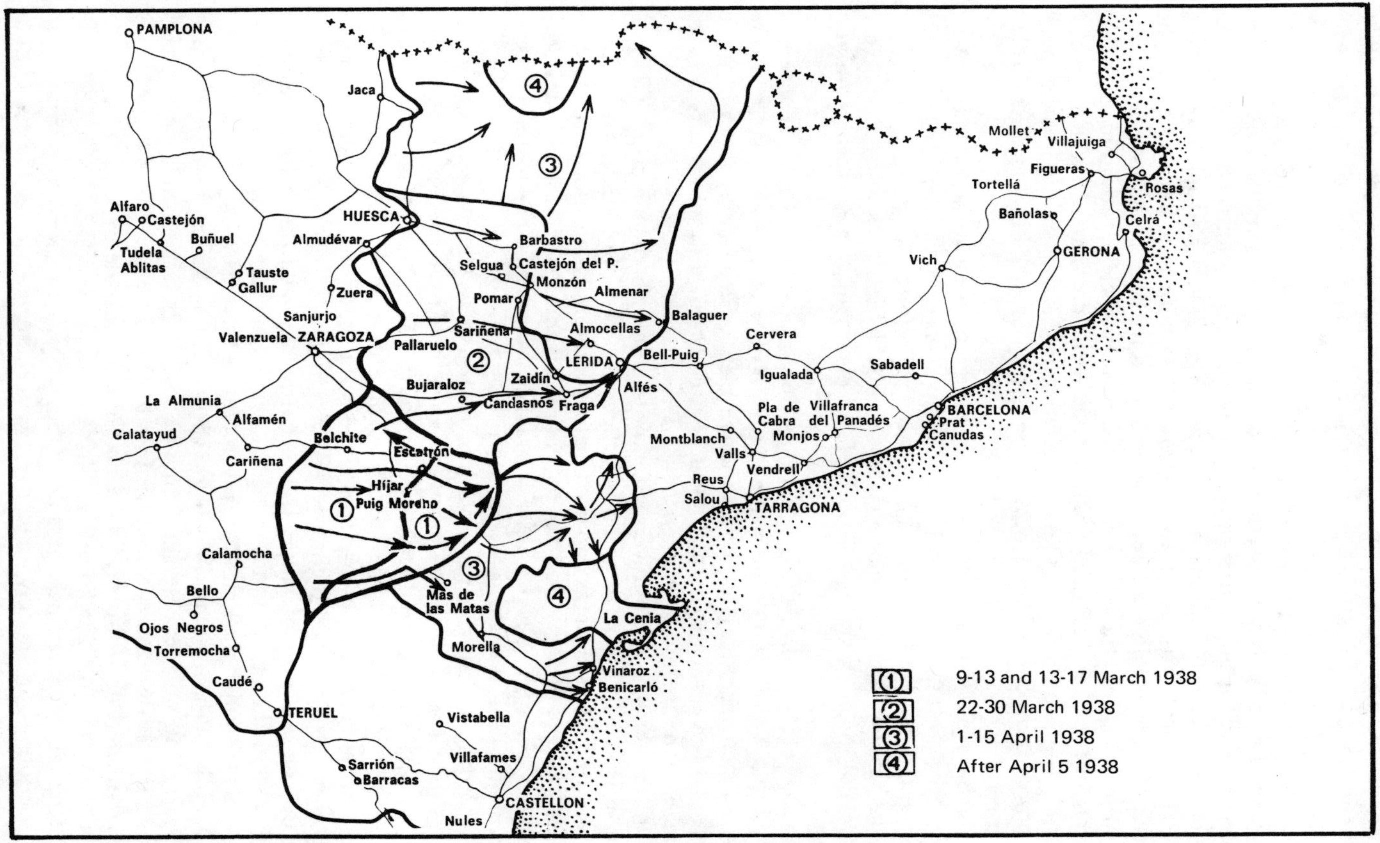

XI. The great offensive in Aragón.

The Spanish Savoia S-M.79s also supported the offensive from the first day although at one period they were transferred temporarily to Palma to make an attack on the port of Valencia.

During 2-G-3's second sortie on July 14th, when they were escorting a number of Ju 52s over the Sarríon sector, García Pardo and Henricourt split away from the group, attempting to pinpoint enemy anti-aircraft batteries which had been troublesome. Seeing that the Ju 52s then had only six escorting fighters (flown by the veterans Salvador, Guerrero and Ibarreche and the novices Cesteros, Bernal and Estayo), a squadron of high-flying Ratas attempted to jump the bombers. The Fiats, nevertheless, proved more than a match for them, and all the Ju 52s escaped without damage, but in the mêlée Bernal disappeared. It is not known whether he was shot down, or if the speed of combat proved too much for his inexperience, causing him to lose control of the aircraft.

The Spanish Fiat fighter groups continued operating at the Teruel front on July 15th and 16th, but on the 17th they were transferred from Bello to Mérida (Extremadura), making a direct flight which took 2hrs 20mins.

The Mölders squadron made its debut with the Me 109Cs, and this was very successful. Mölders destroyed his first two enemy machines on the 15th and 17th.

In view of the strong resistance of the Government Army Corps, it was proposed that Valiño should be reinforced with all available artillery to enable him to reach Segorbe. However, Nationalist leaders felt that by continuing the Sarrión-Viver attack they might still be able to cut off and capture a large number of the enemy.

On July 18th, second anniversary of the beginning of the Spanish Civil War, there was a costly air battle in the Segorbe zone, when Me 109s destroyed three Ratas; the Fiats two Ratas and five Chatos; and three Fiats, flown by Captain Raffi (leader of the *As de Bastos* Group), Frattini and Vestrini, were lost. In the Barracas sector a Savoia S-M.79 crashed some 2,000ft (600m) outside Nationalist lines after being hit by anti-aircraft fire.

According to Tarazona, this clash involved twelve Chatos and twenty-five Ratas (five from the 3rd Squadron and the others from the 2nd, 4th and 5th Squadrons). He claimed that they destroyed two Me 109s and eight Fiats.

On July 19th the 3rd Me 109 squadron encountered eighteen Katiuskas over the Sagunto zone, escorted by three Rata squadrons. Mölders achieved his third victory and Ebbighausen, Hein and Tietzen each claimed the destruction of an enemy machine. In this battle Casola of the 3rd Rata Squadron was killed, according to Tarazona, who wrote that they had destroyed five Fiats, although the Fiats were not operating on that day.

On July 20th Schellmann shot down two Ratas, his seventh and eighth victories, and on the 21st one Fiat was lost. July 22nd was a costly day, during which three Fiats were lost. In addition, four Ro 37s and one He 45 were damaged, and Olivera and García Gil were wounded.

At Viver, on July 23rd, the three Me 109 squadrons fought against about forty fighters, comprising Ratas and Chatos. No losses were confirmed, but destruction of six enemy machines was claimed by the Messerschmitt

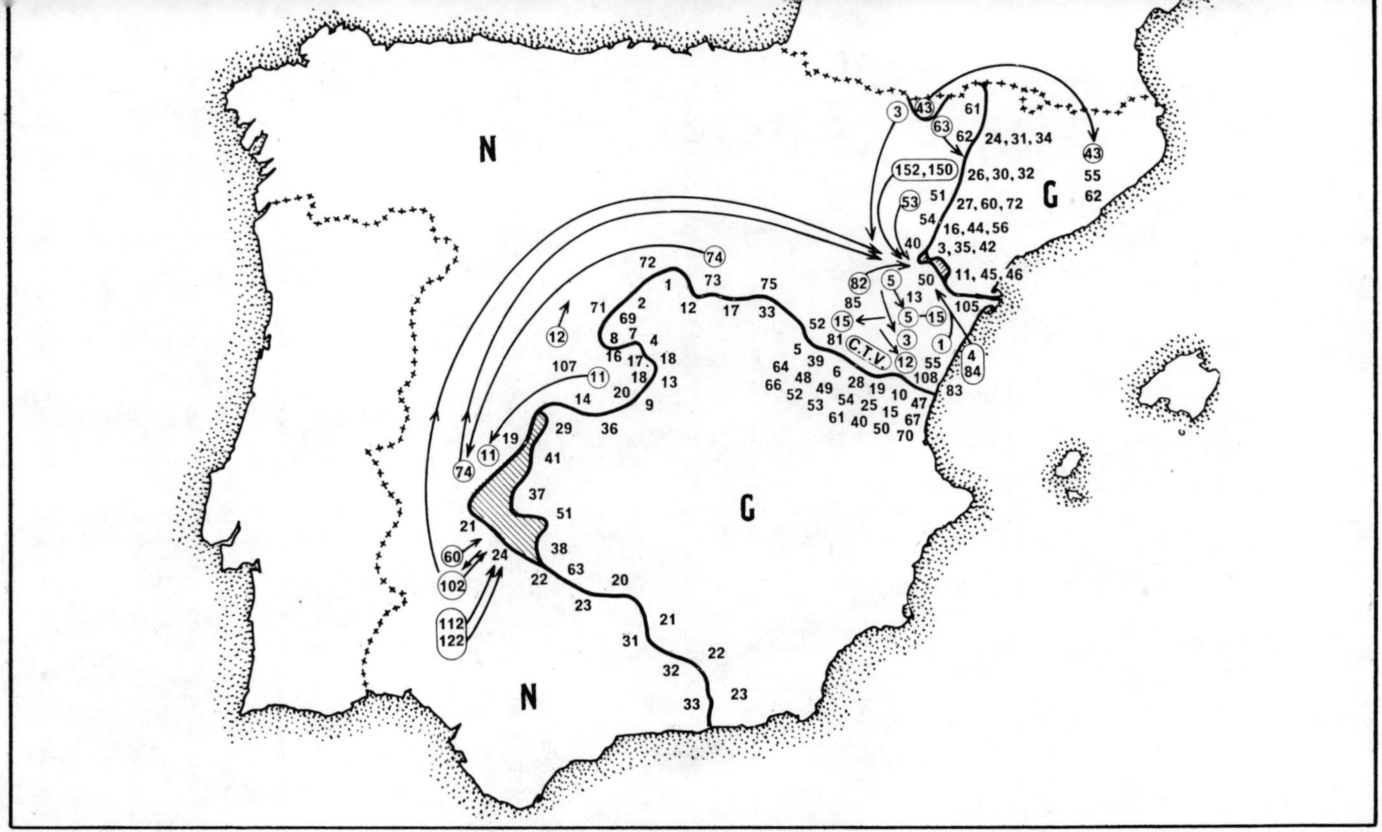

XII. Position of the Divisions in the summer of 1938. N indicates areas under control of the Nationalist forces, G the diminishing areas held by Government forces.

squadrons. They suffered no losses, but Boer wrecked his machine when landing.

On July 25th the Popular Army crossed the Ebro, which brought an end to aerial activity on the Levante front.

Operations in Extremadura During the Summer of 1938

The Southern fronts had remained stable from May 1937 until June 1938. In this latter month General Queipo de Llano began a local offensive against the Blázquez sector, which was defended by the Extremadura Army (Burillo). Divisions 21 and 24 from the sector, together with Nos 102, 112 and 122 from the Andalucian reserves, took part in this Nationalist offensive. They were opposed by Divisions 29, 36 and 37 (VII Army Corps, led by Rubert) and 38, 63 and 67 (VIII Army Corps, Márquez) from the Popular Army.

These operations proved very successful and allowed them to mount an offensive in co-ordination with the Central and Southern Armies, with the object of capturing the La Serena valley. This joint offensive was planned to take place simultaneously with the final attack on Valencia. In the Southern Army's zone the forces participating were the same as those which had been involved in the attack on the interior. In the Central Army's zone Division 19 from that sector, together with No 11, the reserve from the Madrid front, and No 74, which had been held in reserve at the Guadalajara front, all took part. In the Popular Army Division 67 had been replaced by 68, which was a reserve Division for the Extremadura Army. Three of the Government Army Corps participating originated from the Extremadura Army, which was commanded by Burillo.

Operations began on June 20th at Sierra Trapera and Madrigalejo, and on the fifth day of the offensive the Central and Southern Armies joined up at Campanario. On the following day the battle of the Ebro began, and Divisions 74 and 102 were ordered to move immediately to Catalonia. At 18.00hrs on the 25th, Division 74 set out in lorries towards Cáceres where, on the morning of the 26th they entrained to Plasencia: there they learned news of the crossing of the Ebro. When they reached Bot they were strafed by enemy aircraft before they left the station.

Despite the transfer of Divisions 74 and 102 from Campanario, the occupation of the Serena basin continued as planned. But the enemy were not idle. On August 1st Prada arrived to take command of the Extremadura Army, whose morale was then very low.

It was not surprising: their losses had already been significant. De Blas, Cano's successor in the 37th Division, had been taken prisoner. Commander Diego Martín Montilla, leader of the 91st Brigade, was another prisoner. At Campanario two large batteries of artillery had been captured, one of 107 and the other of 44 guns, as well as another battery at Castuero, and these represented an important proportion of Corps VII and VIII's artillery. Prior to this, at Los Bláquez and Monterrubio, they had lost three other batteries.

To close the gap left in Division 37's sector, a new Division from Zújar (comprising Brigades 21, 66 and 81) and one from Melalcazar (Brigades 88, 189 and 191) were brought in. Later, on August 12th, the Extremadura Army's forces were divided into three Army Corps: the VI (Divisions 29 and 36) under Gallego's command; the VII (Divisions 37, 41 and 51) which Marquez commanded for some time, being replaced later by Martín Calvo; and the VIII (Divisions 38, 63 and 68) with Castillo in command. José Sabín took over the unfortunate 37th Division and Copérnico Ballester the 91st Brigade. The leader of the 5th Air Region was still Enrique Pereira Basanta, who had been a Katiuska pilot from the beginning of the war.

On August 9th the Central Army resumed its advance to the north of the Guadiana, and in the bend of the river Zújar the Southern Army became active again. On the Ebro they launched an attack on the Sierra de Pándols. Queipo followed the line of the railway to Ciudad Real, occupied the crossing at Almorchón on the 10th, the town of Cabeza de Buey on the 12th and reached the river Zújar and the town of Zarza-Capilla on the 15th. He could not, however, manage to occupy the whole of the bend of the Zújar. The Extremadura Army, seeing that the advance was threatening their headquarters at Almadén, began to counter-attack fiercely.

The Central Army, which had reached the River Guadalopejo on August 3rd, was holding a sector from Guadalupe to where it opened out into Guadiana. On the 21st they began a new attack, between Guadalupe and the Tagus, reaching the line Belvis de la Jara–La Nava de Ricomalillo (Headquarters of the 37th Division)—El Puerto de San Vicente–Alía on the 26th.

To support these operations the local air units were deployed, comprising Group 5-G-17 (Baquera) and Squadron 4-E-14 (Rueda, later Martínez Mejías) in the South; Squadron 3-E-14 (Sartorius) in the Centre; and part of the 1st Hispana Air Brigade in Aragón. The two Ju 86s and the two 'Angelitos' also took part. With these machines and the He 70s they later formed the Mixed Group 86-70 (Martínez Mejías).

The fighter Groups 2-G-3 (Salas) and 3-G-3 (Morato) moved to Mérida on July 18th and remained there, in oppressive heat, until the 28th. The Squadron of Ju 52s (Eduardo Gallaraza) also went to Extremadura, as well as the new He 51 group, which was led by Gerardo Fernández Pérez and designated 4-G-2. On July 28th the fighter groups flew back to Escatrón, leaving Captain Guerrero's squadron at Mérida where, on August 11th, it was joined by the new Fiat Squadron 8-E-3 (Pazó). On August 25th, to contain the Government counter-offensive in the bend of the Zújar, fighter Groups 2-G-3 and 3-G-3 returned to Mérida, where they remained until September 18th.

During the first stage of their activities in Extremadura, between July 18th and 28th, there were few aerial combats. Salvador and Vázquez, making a reconnaissance patrol on the 24th, sighted six Katiuskas which they were unable to attack as they were too far above them. Vázquez penetrated towards Almadén alone and attacked a small flight of enemy aircraft; he was successful in damaging one machine which he last saw diving steeply. During his return flight to base he attacked three Katiuskas, damaging one. Vázquez landed at Benquerencia aerodrome, only recently occupied by Nationalist forces, with fuel and ammunition exhausted.

The day after the Fiat groups returned to Escatrón, Captain Guerrero's squadron was involved with six Papagayos and nine Chatos, destroying one

Papagayo (Simón) and four Chatos (Guerrero, Arístides, Ibarreche and Cesteros).

On August 9th, when the second phase of the offensive began, Guerrero's squadron was in combat with nine Papagayos and 35 Chatos over Monterrubio, during which Salvador Serra shot down one Chato. On the same day two He 51s were damaged by anti-aircraft fire, one of which force-landed at Castuera.

On August 11th Squadron 8-E-3 arrived at Mérida, and on the following day Squadrons 3-E-3 and 8-E-3 operated together for the first time. They were soon engaged against 25 Chatos. Guerrero, Arístides, Ibarreche and Cesteros each destroyed one enemy machine and Pazó, leader of 8-E-3, claimed one probable.

On August 23rd, over the Zarza-Capilla sector, there was an inconclusive battle between eight Fiats (five from the 3-E-3 and three from the 8-E-3) and 18 Chatos. On the following day Groups 2-G-3 and 3-G-3 were involved in a fierce battle over the Ebro, but on the 25th they were sent back to Extremadura.

This marked the beginning of a series of fierce combats to gain local air superiority, these taking place during the period between August 25th and September 4th, all in the River Zújar–Cabeza de Buey sector.

On the 25th, 2-G-3 shot down two Chatos (Salas and Salvador) and lost Etayo, who died of injuries after trying to land his burning Fiat. On the 26th 3-G-3 claimed two Ratas (Alfaro and Robles) and one Chato (Muerza). In combats fought on the 27th, 28th and 30th no enemy aircraft were destroyed, but on the 31st Squadron 8-E-3 achieved its first real success, with three Ratas destroyed, one each by Muntadas, Vázquez and Ansaldo. On the same day Francisco Gomez Trenor, one of 8-E-3's pilots, was killed by anti-aircraft fire.

On September 1st García Pardo and Henricourt surprised a squadron of Delfins and managed to destroy one each. But it was on the 2nd when the Nationalists gained air supremacy.

On that day, in a single attack, Salas destroyed three Katiuskas, then capped this by damaging the aircraft flown by the leader of the Ratas squadron that was escorting them. This pilot, Redondo, took to his parachute and was guarded by Salas until he had almost reached the ground. Salas, before flying away, raised an arm in salute, and Redondo responded in a similar manner.

This event must have been well-known in the Government zone, as it was reported from several sources. Generalissimo Franco, in his introduction to the book *Guerra en el Aire*, referred to this event in the following paragraph:

"The combats in the air recalled battles of olden days, warrior seeking warrior, eyes and arms ready to strike the weak rearguard. Assistance given to companions in trouble, one against several; serious attacks, preparation to renew the attack; fallen warriors, broken wings, chivalrous gestures when the warrior shot down is saluted by his conqueror, who shows his respect as he falls. . . ."

In the battle of September 2nd, referred to above, 2-G-3 rounded off the

Nationalist triumph by shooting down four more Ratas (Vázquez, Alcocer, Bayo and Ibarreche) and one more Katiuska (Salvador Serra)*

When Salas landed at Mérida he received news that his brother, Ignacio, had just been killed in the Ebro sector, during an attack on Bot by another Katiuska squadron.

The Colonel in Charge of the 1st Air Brigade sent the following congratulations to Salas:

"The part played by the group under your command in today's operation has filled me with pride and it gives me great satisfaction to have people under my command who know how to make the best use of prevailing circumstances. It gives me great pleasure to congratulate you personally, and the whole of your unit, to whom I hope you will convey this message."

García Pardo was in temporary command of the group until Salas arrived back on September 7th. On the 4th, twelve Fiats had taken off under the leadership of Salvador. At Cabeza de Buey they were surprised by a formation of fifteen Ratas which, shaken by the violent reception received from the Fiats, turned tail and fled. Salvador and Vázquez pursued them, but were unsuccessful in destroying any of the enemy.

These operations continued in Extremadura until September 15th, and on the 18th the fighter groups returned to Escatrón, stopping at Ávila *en route*.

Between the middle of July and the middle of September, Group 2-G-3 had destroyed 34 aircraft and 3-G-3 ten more. Individual scores were topped by Salas with five victories, followed by Vázquez Sagastizábal with four, Ibarreche with three, Morato, Salvador, Guerrero, Arístides, García Pardo, Bayo, Henricourt, Salvador Serra, Cesteros, Manrique and O'Connor, each with two, and Muntadas, Allende, Ansaldo, Alcocer, Velasco, Simón, Lacour, Alfaro, Robles and Muerza, one each.

In total, Group 2-G-3 had by them accounted for 133 enemy machines and 3-G-3 19 more. Individually, Morato had a total of 34 victories, Salvador 22, Salas 15, Vázquez Sagastizábal 14, Guerrero and Arístides 12, García Pardo 11, Allende and Henricourt 6, and Bayo and Ibarreche 5. These last three pilots, who did not belong to the original group, were the first to join the aces. Bayo had been a machine-gunner/bomb aimer in the Cordoba Breguets until the Spring 1937, when he went to the Pilots' School; from there he was posted to the He 51 group, joining the Fiats in November 1937. Ibarreche joined the Nationalist Army at the end of the Biscay campaign, and completed his pilot's course in January 1938, from where he was posted direct to group 2-G-3. Henricourt was a Belgian volunteer who flew He 51s throughout 1937 and, after a conversion course, was transferred to 2-G-3.

On August 22nd, when the operations in Extremadura had ended, Commander Pazó returned to his former post at the Southern Regional Park, being replaced as leader of Squadron 8-E-3 by Arístides García López, who arrived at Posadas on October 7th.

* The Katiuskas flown by Blas, Monzõnis and Pavía were shot down; all from the 4th Squadron led by Ricote.

Pazó has made the most of his short period with the fighter squadron. In August he made 39 operational sorties and accumulated a total of 71½ flying hours. Thirteen more operational sorties in September brought his total flying hours to 99, and in which period he gained one probable victory, that of a Chato during combat on August 12th. The other pilots in the squadron, while not equalling Pazó's record, had all flown for more than 50 hours during August.

The Battle of the Ebro

On July 25th, 1938, the V Army Corps (Líster), XV (Tagüeña) and part of the XII (Vega), from the Ebro Army (Modesto), crossed the Ebro north and south of the large bend in the river between Fayón and Benifallet, and also near to its estuary.

The sector under attack was defended by the Moroccan Army Corps (Yagüe), which had its headquarters at Caspe. Yagüe had known for some time, from intelligence reports and aerial reconnaissance, that this offensive was imminent and succeeded in persuading high command to reduce his line of defence. This was accomplished by handing over the Segre sector to the Aragón Army Corps, although this meant losing the 40th Division. With only three Divisions at his disposal, Yagüe placed No 13 (Barrón) in reserve. The recently-formed 50th Division (Campos Guereta), was to hold the 50 miles (80km) from Mequinenza to Cherta and the 105th Division (Lopez Bravo) from Cherta to the sea.

One of the writer's brothers was, at that time, stationed at Caspe aerodrome, and had occasion to talk with Yagüe the day before the attack. He found him worried about the great inequality of equipment, and uncertainty of the main point of action. He was confident, however, that when the moment came to deploy his reserves, the 13th Division would not fail to contain the enemy.

The Government plan of attack was very ambitious, aimed firstly at a union of the two Army Corps at Gandesa and continuation of the advance towards Batea and Bot, which was the first objective. This was to be followed by an advance towards Valderrobles and Morella, combined with an attack by the Levante Army (Leopoldo Menedez). The attacks in the Mequinenza-Fayon and Amposta sectors were secondary. If successful they would make it possible to advance towards Caspe, so cutting the route needed to bring up Nationalist reinforcement and would, at the same time, allow them to bring troops to the coast and continue towards Vinaroz.

At the beginning the attack was a complete success in the zone of the main action, a partial success in the Auts and a failure at Amposta. Here they succeeded in crossing the river, but not the canal which ran parallel. During the afternoon of the same day, July 25th, four divisions had crossed the river, but had not been able to get their heavy supplies across.

General Volkmann, leader of the Condor Legion, left his command post at Benicarlo to visit Yagüe and appraise him of this move. He found him very calm and assured, despite the critical situation. Franco was taking no chances, and ordered five Divisions to be brought in to strengthen the defence, these coming from Fraga, Castellón, Teruel, the Central Army and Southern Army. He also ordered that the sluice gates of the hydro-electric stations in the Segre valley be opened, so that the increased level of the Ebro would wash away the bridges being used by the enemy, both temporary and permanent. The whole of the Nationalist Air Force was also concentrated on destruction of the bridges.

On the second day of the offensive both attacking Army Corps arrived outside Gandesa, but due to the bitter resistance of the 13th Division they were unable to occupy the city. By then the rapid Government advances had ended. Attacks made on the 30th and 31st at Villalba and Gandesa, with support from tanks and artillery, failed.

It was at this stage in the battle that Nationalist reinforcements began to arrive, comprising Division 4 (Alonso Vega) and 84 (Galera) from Castellón, 82 (Delgado Serrano) from Teruel and 74 (Arias) from the Central Army. Later, 53 (Sueiro) arrived from the Segre, 150 (Siro Alonso) and 152 (Rada) from Noguera Pallaresa, and 102 (Castejón) from the Southern Army.

On the Government side Divisions 11 (Rodríguez), 46 ('Campesino', later Domiciano Leal), 45 (Hans Kahle, later Luis Rivas and Ramón Soliva), 3 (Cabeza), 35 (Walter, later Merino), 42 (Manolín Álvarez), 16 (Zamora), 44 (Pastor), 27 (Usatorre), 60 (Ferrándiz) and 43 (Beltrán) were brought into the battle, as well as the 2nd Cavalry Brigade and the 2nd Regiment from that arm.

On the morning of August 6th a Nationalist counter-attack made by Divisions 81 and 102, brought elimination of the Auts basin on their left flank. On August 9th, when the situation in the Ebro was under control, the Extremadura offensive was renewed, with Nationalist strength at that front reduced by two Divisions. On the same day the Popular Army attacked along the Segre line.

Between August 1st and 14th, Nationalist Divisions 4 and 84 tried to recapture the Pándols mountain sector on the Nationalist right flank. On the 19th Yagüe attacked in the centre and three days later he succeeded in occupying the hilltops at Gaeta, between Corbera and Fatarella.

On August 25th the Government counter-offensive began in Extremadura, lasting until the beginning of September. It achieved a few land gains, but not the significant requirement of the recapture of Cabeza de Buey.

The proposal to use five Divisions for a two-pronged attack on Lerida dates from this time. However, the Nationalist Command was not prepared to approve this plan, as they did not want to risk such an operation while strong enemy forces were holding dominant positions on the right bank of the Ebro. Instead, they elected to bring in new forces to speed victory in the Ebro sector.

Thus, at the end of August, General García Valiño moved his 1st Navarre Division from the Espadán sierra into the Ebro sector, and this Division served as a basis for the creation of the Maestrazgo Army Corps. This Corps, commanded by Valiño, consisted of Divisions I (Mizzian), 82 (Delgado Serrano), 74 (Arias) and 84 (Galera).

On September 3rd the Maestrazgo Army Corps launched its attack on the right of the road from Gandesa to Venta de Camposines. On the left, Yagüe attacked on the left of this road, with Divisions 4 (Alonso Vega), 13 (Barrón), 50 (Coco) and 152 (Rada). Corbera was soon occupied, as were some of the foothills of the Caballs mountains, but they were unable to bring about a major breakdown of the enemy's resistance in this sector.

On September 13th a new attack broke through the Government lines at Villalba de los Arcos, near Fatarella. Before these gains could be consolidated, ten successive days of very heavy rain brought a suspension of operations in this sector. On the 18th the Levante Army attacked at Javalambre (Teruel) and there was also activity in the south, at Sierra Morena.

This was the period of the Munich Crisis, a time when both sides were extended to the utmost. The Nationalists were determined to end the war with a resounding victory, before events in Spain were forgotten in the holocaust of a new war in Europe: the Government was equally determined to prolong the conflict in the hope that a large scale war in Europe might enable them to avert defeat.

But in the month of October both sides were forced to accept a reduction in the intensity of activity. This came as a result of the withdrawal of several thousand foreign combatants from each side. On the 15th ten thousand Italians embarked at Cadiz and on the 28th some three thousand five hundred foreigners who had fought for the Government boarded ships at Barcelona. As a gesture of farewell to the latter, one hundred Government fighters flew over Ciudad Condal, to protect them from Nationalist attack. Mussolini, who was very indignant at the promise of neutrality given to France and England by Franco, withdrew one of the two Infantry Divisions, one fighter group and the Savoia S-M.81 crews, a move which did not please Berti, who was replaced by Gambara.

Nationalist leaders ordered that maximum pressure should be maintained in the Ebro sector, and assigned the principal task to the right flank, for which they reinforced the Maestrazgo Army Corps with one Division, two groups of vehicles and the anti-aircraft guns of the Condor Legion.

On October 30th a final attack on the V Army Corps was made by the Maestrazgo Army Corps, in the Caballs mountains sector, and on the following day the 1st Division gained the dominating heights of the Pándols.

On November 3rd the 4th Navarre Division occupied Pinell and reached the river, after which the battle of the Ebro could be considered as ended. On November 7th the V Army Corps retreated across the Ebro. On November 11th the offensive began against the XV Army Corps positions, from Venta de Camposines towards the north. The end was a foregone conclusion and on the 16th, at Flix, the withdrawal of the Ebro Army ended.

When the battle of the Ebro began the two Spanish Fiat fighter groups, the 1st Ju 52 Squadron (Eduardo González Gallarza), and the He 70 Group 7-G-14 (Soler, later Sartorius), were stationed in Extremadura. The Savoia S-M.79 bomber squadron No 2 (Lacalle) and No 3 (don Alfonso de Orléans) remained at their base in Alfamén, and Groups 1-G-2 (José Muñoz), 4-G-12 (Rafael Martínez de Pisón) and 6-G-15 (Félix Bermúdez de Castro) were stationed at Logroño, Castejón del Puente and Calamocha respectively. The new Heinkel He 52 Group 4-G-2 (Gerardo Fernández Pérez) had recently arrived at Trujillo, with Mariano Uriarte and Manuel Lapuente as squadron leaders. Group 5-G-17 (Baquera) and Squadrons 3-E-14 (Sartorius) and 4-E-14 (Rueda) were based in the Centre and the South, Group 2-G-10 (J. Simón) in Africa and the seaplanes (Noreña) in the Balearics.

The Condor Legion had their fighter group (Handrick) at La Cenia, their bomber group (Wehnert) at Sanjurjo and their reconnaissance squadrons at Buñuel and Tauste. One-third of the crew members of the bomber group were Spaniards and their two squadrons were still led by Commander Luis Rambaud Gomá and Captain Ureta Zabala. Mid-way through the war Spanish pilots began to join the fighter group, and especially in the 3rd Squadron.

The Legionary Air Force had two fighter groups at the Teruel front, and another at Caspe; the Savoia S-M.79 Squadron (Gaeta) at Valenzuela; the BR 20 group (Cigersa) at Puig Moreno, the Ro 37 group (Achenza) at La Salada and the Breda Ba 65 squadron (Miotto) at Puig Moreno. The fighter group *As de Bastos* (Remondino) and *Gamba de Ferro* (Rossi), moved to Escatrón and Sariñena on July 28th and August 2nd respectively. Group 3-G-3 had returned to Extremadura on August 1st, Group 2-G-3 on the following day, and both were based at Escatrón. The *Gamba de Ferro* group moved to Bello and then to Puig Moreno, from where it was disbanded. The *Cucaracha* Group (Tessari) remained in Caspe.

When the battle of the Ebro Region began nearly all of the Government Rata squadrons were in Levante. The 3rd Squadron (Bravo) moved from Camporrobles to Liria, and on July 30th to Vendrell. On August 3rd pilots of this squadron were sent to Figueras to collect twelve Super-Ratas. At this time, according to Tarazona, fairly generous supplies of new Russian aircraft reached the Government across the French frontier. These comprised fifty Ratas, fifty Chatos and twenty-four Katiuskas. Tarazona collected Rata No 193 and at the end of the autumn No 249 was being flown by Bravo. From this latter figure it can be deduced that, in 1938, they received approximately one hundred Ratas, bringing the total supplied by Russia to about 250 machines.

At the beginning of August the 3rd Rata Squadron (Bravo) was at Pla de Cabra, the 1st (Meroño) at El Vendrell and the 4th (Arias) at Valls. At that time the 2nd and 5th Squadrons were still composed of Russian pilots. A little later the 2nd (led by Pereiro), the 6th (Meroño) and the 7th (Cano), the two latter squadrons formed half way through the battle, were all operating in the Ebro sector.

The Chato Group 26 had its squadrons based at Borjas Blancas, Vilafranca del Panadés, Monjos and Cervera, with emergency airfields at Reus and Salou. Zambudio and Castillo ('El Valenciano') were squadron leaders as were, later on, Castillo ('El Andaluz') and Nieto. Comas took over command of the group in the middle of September.

During the last few days of July, Nationalist aerial activity was concentrated on destroying bridges over the Ebro: the task of the Government Air Force was to harry all concentrations of troops.

In operations against the Ebro bridges on July 25th several aircraft were damaged, but these were considered an insignificant cost for the bridges that were destroyed. Unfortunately for the Nationalists, they were rebuilt almost immediately. On July 26th tanks were crossing the river over a temporary metal bridge at Flix and heavy transports over a wooden bridge at Gandesa. However, both were destroyed later on the same day. On July 28th the bridge at Ascó was rendered useless, but at Flix the metal bridge was back in service again on the morning of the 30th.

Group 3-G-3 made its first sortie in the Ebro battle on July 28th, during which Captain Gautier, leader of Squadron 7-E-3, was killed. He had taken off in company with another Fiat on a low-level reconnaissance sortie, and was hit by small arms fire from the ground, a bullet penetrating his chest. Queipo de Llano succeeded him as leader of Squadron 7-E-3, becoming the first temporary officer to lead a squadron in the Nationalist Air Force.

The first aerial combat took place on August 1st, when Group 3-G-3 (Morato) and one squadron of 2-G-3 (Salvador) fought against a formation of between nine and twelve Chatos. Three of these were destroyed by 3-G-3 (Morato, O'Connor and Velasco) and the squadron from 2-G-3 claimed four more victories (Salvador and Vázquez one each, Manrique two).

Also on August 1st Captain Cuadra's He 51 was shot down, and several days later Lieutenant Gonzalez del Valle was killed in another He 51. On August 3rd no less than seven Nationalist machines were hit by anti-aircraft fire, stressing the strong defence provided for the all-important bridges.

On August 5th the *Cucaracha* Group destroyed one Rata and a Katiuska, and the Condor Legion lost a Dornier Do 17 to anti-aircraft fire. On August 12th and 13th the Me 109s joined in the operations, claiming seven Ratas and three Katiuskas.

In operations on the 13th the Super-Ratas of the 3rd Squadron were used for the first time, operating in conjunction with the 1st and 4th Squadrons. Opposing them were the two veteran Me 109B squadrons, Mölders 3rd Squadron, with its new four-gun Me 109Cs. Thus, there were more than thirty of the most modern fighters involved in this battle which, adding on the biplanes, gave a total of about one hundred aircraft in combat.

The following is an extract from Tarazona's account of this engagement:

"August 13th. It was a splendid day. From the hills at Reus we could see the 'Messers' take off from La Cenia. Several groups of dots could be distinguished in the distance, which were the Fiats from Alcañiz, Caspe and Etra. The whole squadron was at the ready for the enemy planes.

"I was waiting for Bravo's order to take off. The sun was to our left; the favourite hiding place for the German monoplanes, but as we were only just taking off there was time to manoeuvre. Bravo did not see it like this, and took us in a direct line to a point where we would all converge, Fiats, 'Messers', 'Moscas', Chatos and the Fascist bombers.

"Before reaching the Ebro we encountered a wall of steel, rising from 3,300–23,000ft (1,000–7,000m). Fortunately, there were some gaps in that anti-aircraft screen, but as soon as we tried to use them they seemed to close relentlessly. Nonetheless, we crossed the river without any losses.

"As we passed beyond the Ebro I saw the reasoning behind Bravo's decision; at about 11,500ft (3,500m) there were three compact formations of He

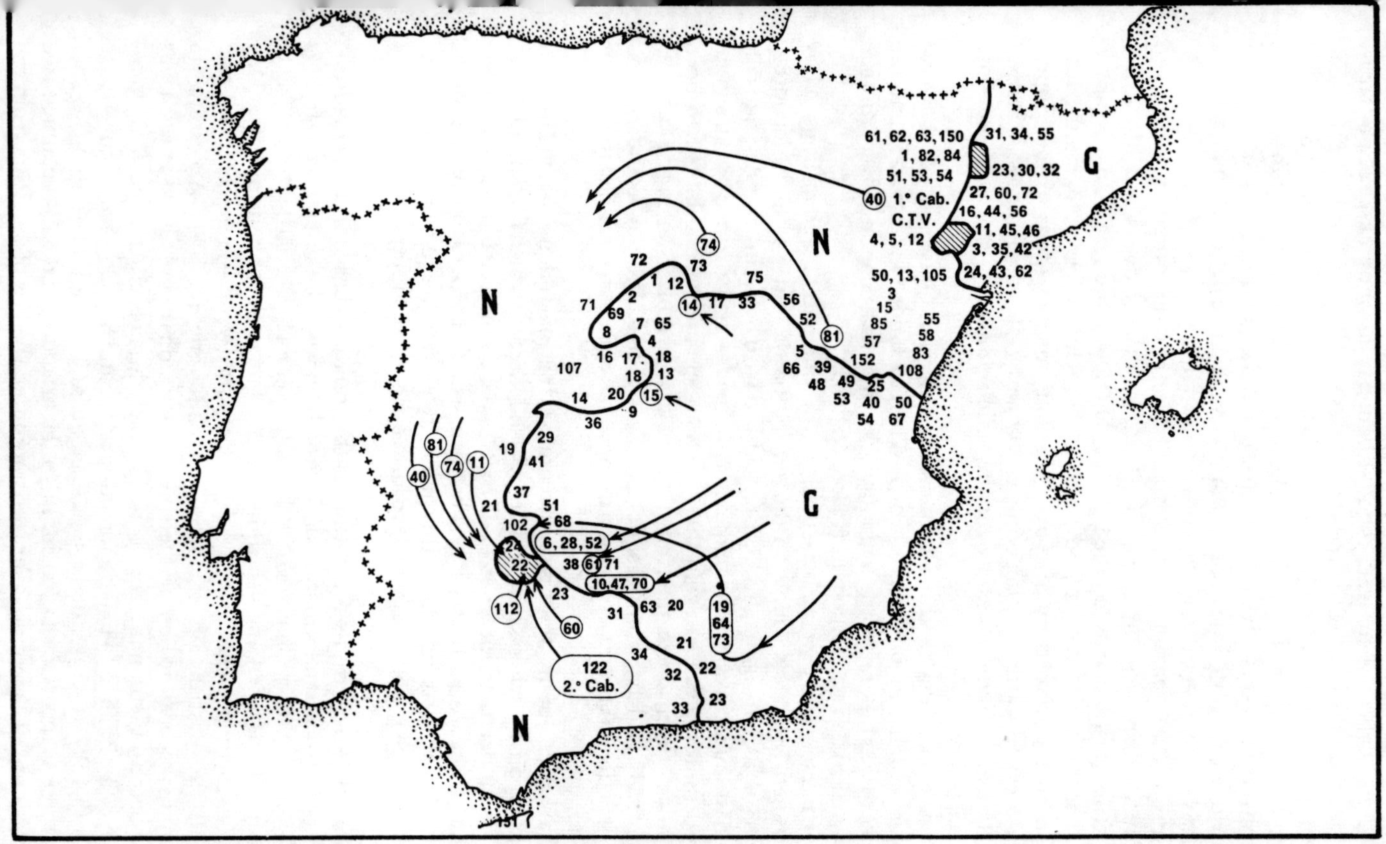

XIII. Positions of the Divisions between January 5th and 7th, 1939. N and G denote Nationalist and Government forces respectively.

111s. Slightly above them were the Fiat fighters, flown by Fascist Spaniards, and higher still the Fiats with their Italian crews.

We immediately dived on the German bombers so that we could dominate the first few moments of combat, thanks to a surprise attack. Within seconds I had to avoid collision with a Fiat which crossed ahead of me; I was so surprised that I did not react in time to fire at him. When I came out of the manoeuvre I found myself surrounded by a cloud of enemy fighters.

"The other 'Moscas' of the third were like me, and the formation had broken up. The bombers were dropping their loads over the bridges across the Ebro. The battle was now between the fighters. There were no less than a hundred aircraft in the air, twisting and turning. Parachutes were blossoming and hanging in the immensity of space. The four machine-guns of the 'Super-Mosca' were furiously spitting out fire. My new 7-16 was doing well. Several times its armour plate came between the bullets and me. I wonder whose those parachutes were?

"Once back at Pla de Cabra I counted the aircraft. Only eight of the twelve 'Moscas' which went out had returned. When we landed I went straight to the hut. Bravo was talking on the telephone. When he finished the conversation he sat down heavily in an armchair. He looked tired.

"Fortunately there were no casualties. Montilla had to land at Reus. Margalef joined Meroño's squadron during the battle and was at El Vendrell. Pitarch was at Tarragona, his 'Mosca' riddled with holes, and Sirvent had collided in the air with an enemy plane. Fortunately he had escaped by parachute and was unharmed. I was told that two bombers and several Fiats had been shot down. From our Squadron nobody was certain of having shot down anything. It had been impossible to follow a machine down and confirm its destruction, as there were far too many of the enemy determined to finish us off.

"I have tried out my new fighter in combat. It is marvellous. When I am in it I feel as if I am wearing a pair of shoes which I like and which do not hurt me. I want it to understand me when I talk to it, and it seems as if it does, sensing the direction I want to go. It does it gently; then, when it receives the force from the controls, it imparts power to the manoeuvre. We already have an understanding which is well, for we have to form an indestructible pair".

On August 14th, Groups 2-G-3 (minus the squadron based in Extremadura) and 3-G-3 attacked a formation of Ratas which were pursuing some He 111s over Gandesa. Other Chatos and Ratas later joined in the battle. According to Tarazona the 1st, 3rd and 4th squadrons fought against about ninety enemy machines, which included seven Me 109s and twenty-seven He 111s, and claimed the destruction of three Fiats and one He 111. According to Nationalist records no bombers fell on that day, and the only Fiat to be lost was that of Second Lieutenant Mesía (3-75) which did not return to base. Lieutenant Bayo (3-127) had to make a forced-landing and Second Lieutenant Alonso Fariña (3-139) was wounded and landed at Puig Moreno. Group 2-G-3 shot down three Ratas (García Pardo, Bayo, Henricourt) and 3-G-3 claimed two more (Morato, O'Connor). Tarazona admitted the loss of one Rata from the

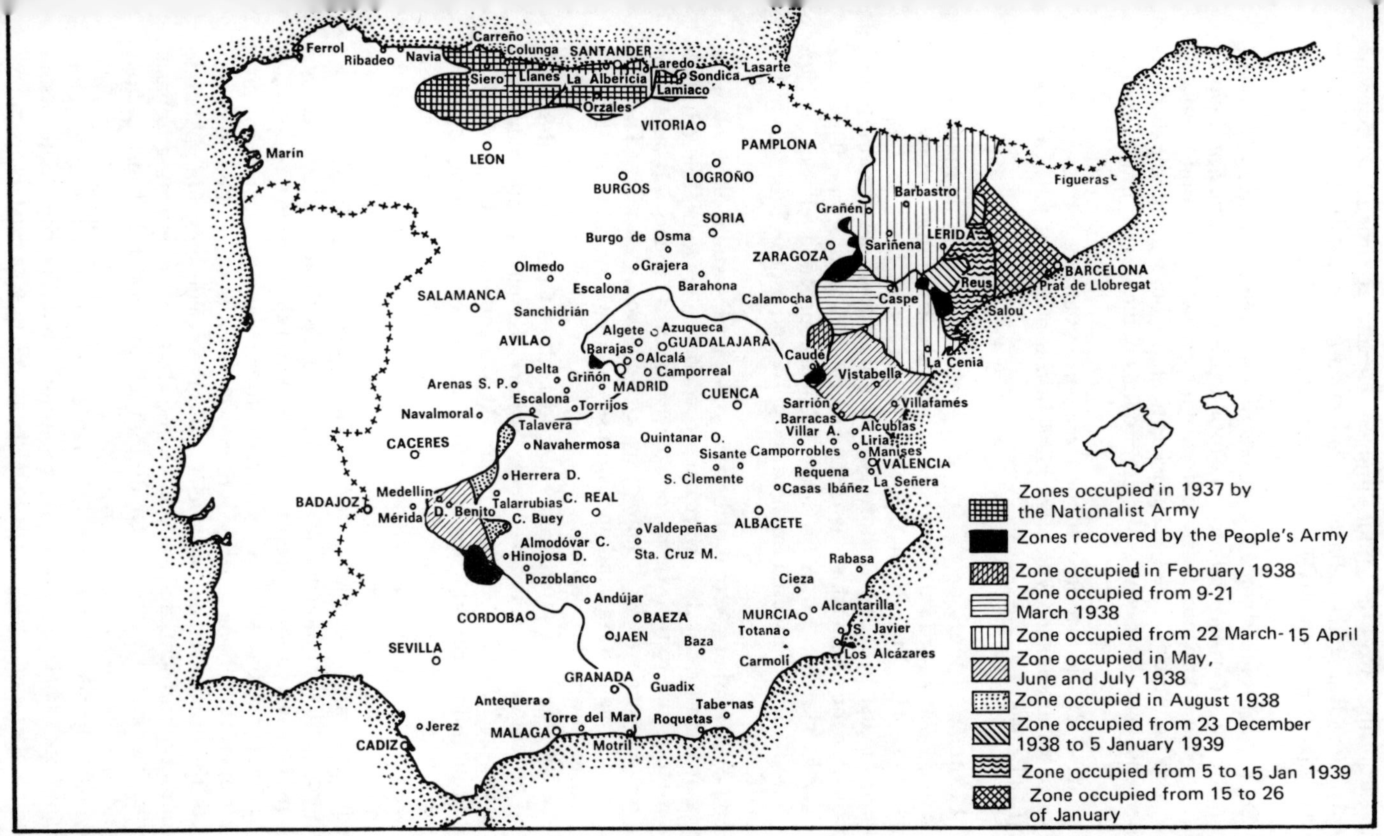

XIV. Zones occupied from April 1937 until the end of the war. The established aerodromes are shown, but more recent aerodromes and airfields are shown on map IX.

4th Squadron and two other pilots injured. He also recorded that Meroño managed to get a Rata back to base with half of the elevator shot away.

The record of operations of 2-G-3 described the group's victories as follows:

"García Pardo attacked some Ratas which were pursuing an He 111, shooting down one of them which fell near to Mora de Ebro . . . Lieutenant Bayo attacked three Ratas and succeeded in destroying one which fell on the edge of the Blanerías mountains. Later he attacked a Chato, but was unable to ascertain whether it was destroyed as damage to his engine forced him to land at Horte . . .

"Lieutenant Henricourt fired at one Rata without any result; and then attacked some Ratas engaged with other Fiats, hitting one which fell in a wood to the north of Reus . . ."

Second Lieutenant Manrique's Fiat was hit thirty times, but he managed to get back to base at Escatrón. Krug's He 51 was also badly mauled by enemy fire, but he too got back to base at Mas de las Matas.

Between August 15th and 20th the Me 109s shot down seven more Ratas, and on the 21st one Katiuska was destroyed by anti-aircraft fire. Tarazona claimed one Fiat on the 15th and in the same battle four Ratas fell. On the 19th an He 45 and an He 51 were damaged severely, and on the 20th an He 111 crashed at Reus.

On August 23rd there were four battles in which Fiats and Me 109s were ranged against Ratas, but these were not recorded by Tarazona. Three Italian Fiats failed to return to their bases, one of which crash-landed and burst into flames, and another was force-landed by a badly wounded pilot. The Fiat groups claimed eight Ratas and one Katiuska on that day, and the Me 109s another Katiuska and three Ratas.

At about this date the pilots from the 2nd Fighter Course at Gallur were posted to Squadrons. Jesús Saiz, Illera, Araluce, Romagosa and Barañano were sent to 2-G-3, and Mendizábel, Prieto, Arvizu and Alonso Calleja to 3-G-3. In addition, pilots from the 3rd Russian Course were beginning to arrive. Earlier, during the month of June, a number of Rata pilots had been sent to the High Speed School at El Carmolí. Towards the end of August they began to return to the squadrons. Amongst them was Redondo, formerly leader of a Chato squadron, and Aresti, who used the name 'Joseba Koldobika'.

On August 24th the Spanish Fiats were in combat with the 3rd and 4th Rata Squadrons. Five machines from Squadron 2-E-3 and eleven from Group 3-G-3 had taken off, led by Salas, to escort bombers to the Gandesa front. According to 2-G-3's operations book, enemy fighters were seen towards the end of this sortie, but they remained circling well within their own lines. Only Allende made contact with them, and shot down one Rata before returning to base. Group 3-G-3 gained a victory, a Chato that fell to Lacour, but lost Chapaprieta and Arrechea, who were taken prisoner.

Tarazona recorded that before this battle the Ratas of two new pilots Gascón and Badía were in collision; which induced him to write: "There is no school for combat pilots: they are produced only by the war itself. How can we dispense with novices?" In fact, Badía was a member of the 1st Squadron and was taken prisoner when he force-landed near Saragossa. At a later date he was exchanged, together with Fierro, Molinet, Pazos and other bomber pilots. It is probable that Gascón was shot down by Allende. In Tarazona's account, extract from which are given below, it seems to suggest that he shot down Arrechea, who was wounded, and that Bravo shot down Chapaprieta.

"August 25th. Today we are resting; the mechanics are checking squadron equipment. Nevertheless, I went to the airfield, sat down near the runway and began to update my diary.

"After Badía and Gascón's collision yesterday we took off. Near the front a large battle was being fought, and the Ebro army had asked for air support. Our squadron joined with the 4th at Valls, and they told us that the enemy was attacking the bridges over the Ebro with a large number of bombers, which were protected by even larger formations of fighters. We were soon within sight of the front, and turned to put the sun behind us before we made out initial attack. We could not then see the bombers, but we could certainly see the explosions of the bombs as they were dropping on the bridges.

"As we drew nearer to the zone the bombers were spotted, and our fighters raced towards the coast to cut off their retreat. A cloud of enemy machines suddenly blocked our way. Everywhere the sky seemed to be filled with aircraft, cleaving the air at fantastic speeds as they searched for an opponent, machine-guns ready to release a hail of fire. Everyone was concentrating on his own particular section of the battle.

"I saw a 'Mosca' with a pair of Fiats close on his tail and went to his aid. I managed to drive them off and then came in behind another Fiat. I was so intent on liquidating this machine that I forgot to check my tail for a second or so; bullets passed close to my ears, shattering the windscreen. I turned to find a Fiat some fifty metres from my tail. I dived at full throttle, and when my air-speed indicator showed 650km/h I climbed steeply and managed to escape. I had had a fright and gained some holes in the starboard wing.

"As I levelled off I spotted a Fiat which had been hit; it was leaving a trail of smoke, and losing height as it flew towards the sea. Its pilot was obviously trying to reach the coast and make some sort of landing at his own base. I stalked him as quietly as possible, and had to almost close the throttle to avoid hitting the tail unit of the Fiat. I did not need to use the gun-sight for this one; he looked immense through my own eyes. I squeezed the triggers . . . but not a single shot came from my guns.

"By this time I had lost so much airspeed that my aircraft was on the point of stalling: I rammed open the throttle and rocketed over the biplane, at the same time I tried frantically to clear the machine-guns, all the time fearing that he might take advantage of the situation to attack me at point blank range: he did not!

"My machine-guns were ready. This time I attacked head on: the Fiat went into a dive and my bullets pierced the pilot's cockpit. A moment later, out of control, it hurtled to the ground. It was another victory. I turned towards the coast and, skimming the wavetops, returned to the airfield. Bravo had also shot down a Fiat over the Caballs mountains. Nevertheless the enemy bombers had destroyed two important bridges over the Ebro.

"They had ordered us not to engage in combat with other fighters. I had heard all this before. We were only to attack the enemy bombers, but with the fighters at our disposal this was impossible. The high command was right, but they were spoiling our fiesta.

"August 27th. Bravo knew how to keep a secret well! I had been named as leader of the third squadron! The Squadron was at readiness and I was day-dreaming inside the cockpit of my fighter when the leader of Group 21 arrived at Pla de Cabra. He told me the news."

On August 25th Group 2-G-3 (Salas) moved to Extremadura, leaving 3-G-3 (Morato) at Escatrón, where they remained until the 27th. This latter group fought on the 26th and destroyed three aircraft (Alfaro and Robles one Rata each, and Muerza a Chato). On the same day Romeo No 12-42 was hit over Corbera, a bullet passing completely through the body of the pilot, Suárez Oviedo. Despite his grievous injury he managed to land his aircraft safely on the outskirts of Sástago, an achievement which won him the Military Medal, and his name was put forward for the award of the Laureate.

On August 30th, in rapidly deteriorating weather, Mölders landed his squadron at Pomar aerodrome. During the night violent winds overturned a Ju 52 and an He 45.

In the Ebro sector there were no important air battles until September 13th, when the Condor Legion destroyed four Ratas. In the interim period several aircraft were destroyed by ground fire. On the 9th Captain José Ugarte won the San Fernando Laureate when, fatally injured, he landed safely.

From September 13th to the 20th there was little air activity, and both air forces used this period for re-organisation. It was only days to the Munich Crisis and there was great diplomatic activity. The Condor Legion replaced a large number of their experienced pilots, amongst them the veteran leader of the fighter group, Handrick, who had been in Spain since the battle of Brunete, and the bomber leader, Wehnert. Their commands were filled by Grabmann and Härle. The three fighter squadrons were then led by Reents (Schellmann's successor), Krök and Mölders, with Oesau as the group adjutant.

Groups 2-G-3 and 3-G-3 returned to Escatron on September 18th, taking over the equipment which had belonged to the Italian group *Gamba de Ferro*, which had then been disbanded. The Italians had also handed over to the Spaniards all their old Savoia S-M.81s, apart from those in the Balearics. These aircraft formed Groups 15-G-21 (Cipriano Rodríguez, later Orduna), 16-G-21 (Ricardo Guerrero), 17-G-21 (Gil Mandizábal) and 18-G-21 (Carrillo), each group having six aircraft.

Félix Bermúdez de Casto (el 'Chili') and Rafael Martínez de Pisón left the command of their old groups and went to organise the two new Caproni Ca 310 groups, which were assigned initially to the Central Army and operated from Talavera as part of the 6th Squadron (Arranz). Group 4-G-12 was first taken over by Jesús Camacho ('Don Brito'), then by Cipriano Rodriguez

('Cucufate') who was killed in action on the 2nd October, and finally by Teodoro Vives. Llop took command of 6-G-15, which was sent to Posadas on September 22nd, and Eyaralar replaced José Muñoz as leader of 1-G-2. Fernández Pérez and Baquera continued to lead groups 4-G-2 and 5-G-17.

In the Balearics a squadron of four Cant Z. 506 seaplanes were received, numbered from 73-1 to 73-4, and these joined the old Cant Z. 501 squadron to form a new Mixed Group 62/73 (Noreña). The Mixed Group 62/70, which had been formed in April 1938, was then disbanded. Group 1-G-70 was reformed in Cadiz and the He 60 squadron (Barrera) moved to the Balearics.

On the Government side Comas, who was now a Captain and had recovered from his injuries, took command of the Chato group. Bravo became second-in-command of the Rata group and Tarazona was named as leader of the 3rd Squadron in this group. The 6th Squadron and the newly-formed 7th Squadron had Spanish leaders. The aircraft of the 4th Rata Squadron (Arias) were equipped with Wright supercharged engines and had an oxygen supply for the pilot, allowing them to be operated at altitudes up to 23,000ft (7,000m), as high as the Me 109s, although they still had an open cockpit and no heating. Tarazona was always complaining that the Me 109s could operate at a greater height than their Ratas, but he overlooked the fact that these machines were in a minority. The widely used Fiats, more usually encountered by the Ratas, had an inferior ceiling and rate of climb.

On September 20th a series of daily battles began, culminating in fierce combats on October 2nd and 3rd. Groups 2-G-3 and 3-G-3 fought jointly in all these battles, achieving a total of twenty-five victories. Martínez de Irujo was killed on September 22nd and Oliveras on October 2nd; Romagosa was shot down on September 21st, and Morato and Salvador on October 3rd.

During this period Bayo shot down four machines, Vázquez, Salvador, Simón, Henricourt and Ibarreche two each, and Salas, Arístides and Cesteros one each, making a total of seventeen victories for 2-G-3. In 3-G-3 Morato achieved two victories, O'Connor, Mendizábal and Larios one each, making a total of five.

For details of the battles at that time I have had to rely upon the records of Tarazona and José Larios. In his book, *Combat over Spain*, the latter wrote:

"On September 22nd I fought my toughest air battle. It took place across the Ebro, deep in Red territory. We were never lucky enough to fight over our own ground, which would have been far more comfortable from every point of view. That morning we had been briefed to escort 'Cadenas' and Romeos, whose mission it was to strafe the enemy positions between Gandesa and the Ebro River, where a fierce battle was raging. Both sides were fighting with great courage and determination. The Reds were on the defensive and the Nationalists on the offensive.

"The Red fighters were now appearing daily in great strength and had become more aggressive. We soon sighted two large formations of Ratas above and Chatos below, stepped up to over 4,000 metres. They were making a bee-line to intercept our bombers. Our whole group swung across their path to cut them off, and we clashed over the river.

"I made my first move when a Rata came flashing beneath me, fleeing from a Fiat. I banked over hard and came down on her tail, with my engine at full throttle and the whole machine vibrating from nose to tail. The Rata, which had not seen me closing in, eased out of the dive and zoomed up, giving me the chance to take a shortcut and rapidly close the distance. I held my fire until I was at close range and then gave her the works. Thin tracers went slamming into her fuselage; it was as if we were strung together by long white ribbons. I eased the throttle back and fired relentlessly; she began to roll and swing drunkenly, then suddenly rolled over and went down spinning. I followed her a few hundred metres, still firing, but I was jumped on by two Ratas who came in smack on my tail. I could hear the tattoo of their guns and sense the impact going home. I got one glimpse of them and violently rammed the stick forward and over and threw my Fiat into a spiral, kicking fiercely at the rudder to keep it on a crooked course. At least I would not give them an easy target. One of our Fiats must have intercepted, for they soon gave up the hunt, but I still kept going down, bucking and twisting, to be on the safe side. I then pulled hard back on the stick, blacked out, and came screaming up in a high-pitched whine, reaching for altitude.

"I checked over my dials. Everything seemed to be in working order, so I climbed up to a safe altitude to get my bearings. By then the battle had drifted still farther away from our lines. I soon discovered tiny black specks milling around in the distance at my level, and I recognised them as Fiats and Chatos, going all out at each other. I gained more altitude and came in over the top of them with the sun behind me. I jumped on the first Chato which came within range, taking her completely by surprise, and remained stuck to her tail. She soon began to lurch, then slowly rolled over and went down inert and lifeless. There had been no sharp evasive action. I was about to follow her down, but had to pull out quickly as another Chato streaked up beneath my starboard wing, meaning business. I had the extra speed and pulled my nose up, banked over the top of her in a half loop, and came in on her tail as she tried to break away. She was at my mercy and I stuck fast, firing as she turned and twisted desperately to get away. I was at very close quarters and every shell went home. She suddenly gave up the struggle and became uncontrolled as her nose slowly rose and she stalled; she rolled over on her back and went down spinning. She looked in very bad shape. But I had again made the all-too-common mistake of hanging on just too long, which nearly sent me spinning into the land of no return.

"Three Chatos swooped in behind me and I heard for the second time within only a few minutes the death rattle of machine-gun fire close on my tail —a sound never to be forgotten. My head snapped round on hearing the first burst, and in a frenzy I threw my machine into a vertical dive, using every trick I had ever learned for cases like this. But it seemed hopeless. I was convinced that this time it was the end. I could not wish my worst enemies that icy impact down one's spine and the hollow tightness in one's stomach that came with the continuous drilling of death at one's back. I felt trapped and powerless.

"The Chatos stuck to me like leeches and the din they were making sent my heart leaping in my throat. There was nothing I could do but keep going down and down in a spiral, first one way, then the other, expecting the knockout blow to come at any moment or my engine to burst into flames. The ground came rushing up in a dizzy whirl, waiting to embrace me. To my great relief I suddenly noticed a thick cloud layer lying low over the river at 45° to my dive. To reach it I had to ease my machine out of the vertical dive, which I did; it was my only hope. I had gained slightly on my pursuers, but they still stuck behind doggedly, keeping up a barrage of fire.

"Seconds later I shot into thick clouds, levelled out, and pointed towards our distance lines. I have never in my life loved a cloud so much. On breaking out I found myself low over the Ebro, and the Caballs mountains loomed up between me and my lines. To my great relief I saw only one Chato straggling 500 metres behind. I had outdived and outmanoeuvred them, and I blessed that cloud with all my heart. My immediate reaction, however, was one of blind rage. I swung my Fiat round on the tip of her wing and made a beeline for the Chato, clamouring for vengeance. He saw me coming, veered sharply, and dived. I managed to get a fleeting glimpse of the Red machine in my sights and pressed the trigger viciously. It was a long shot and only one of my guns was working, so I gave up and turned for Escatrón, licking my wounds, but very happy. I could not tell how much damage I had received, and to be on the safe side I gained as much altitude as possible in case I had to bale out. I nursed my Fiat all the way home.

"There was no question this time of buzzing the airfield, which was the usual habit with us and I think with all fighter pilots the world over after a fight. Instead, I let my machine down very gingerly, and as I touched down I felt the jar of flat tyres rolling along the hard ground. Rossi (Larios' mechanic) looked very worried as I taxied up to the line. I was the last to get back and long overdue.

"We inspected the damage which was considerable. There were about thirty bullet holes, the wing struts had been nearly severed, there were two flat tyres, the fuselage and tail had been riddled, and one shell must have shaved my head on its way through the engine cowling, only a few inches in front of my windshield, lodging deep inside the motor. Rossi probed around until he found it and kept it for luck. The next day my aircraft was dismantled, loaded on a truck, and sent to Seville. I was allotted a spare one.

"I reported to Morato three damaged fighters, one Rata and two Chatos, unconfirmed, which was most disheartening. Still, I had no right to complain. Matters might have been far worse under the circumstances. Morato had shot down a Chato."

By way of contrast, Tarazona's description of the same battle is given below:

"September 22nd. This morning, when I got in touch with the squadron, I learned that the pilot of the 6th Squadron who escaped by parachute was fired at in the air during his descent. The same thing happened to Ruiz, at Nules. What can be in the mind of these Fascists: firing at and damaging a plane is one thing; but killing a pilot who takes to his parachute is something quite different. I don't know. It must be a question of one's stomach or spiritual education. I cannot believe that the Spanish Fascists did it. They may be ideologically different from us, because of their upbringing, but they are still Spaniards.

"The machines of Arias' fourth squadron, those equipped for high altitude operations against the 'Messers', gave us some real frights. The blue belly of these machines, flying two or three thousand metres above us, looked like the German monoplanes, even though the line was different. We could only differentiate between them by the formation in which they flew. Whereas the Germans flew in pairs, wing to wing, Arias' 'Moscas' flew in spearhead formation. Sometimes, during the course of a battle, we saw the Germans diving steeply, often in flames and pursued by the 'Moscas'. Whenever we were joined by a member of the fourth squadron, the appearance of these machines always created a great impression.

"Today my squadron took off for the front with only seven 'Moscas', Pallarés and Vallecas' planes were being repaired. We were detailed to protect the lines in the Corbera sector. We were accompanied by the Galician Pereiro's squadron, comprising eight machines. I was not very pleased about their company, because small people usually display excessive courage and lack brains.

"Pereiro's squadron weaved from one side to the other, as if they expected to come across the enemy at any moment. 'Stay still!', I commanded in my mind. My neck was extremely painful. The constant turning to look behind for the enemy had caused a sore spot. The Galician's undulations were driving me mad. When we reached the front, via Falset, Fiats and bombers could be seen on all sides. I thought that now Pereiro would have to move.

"There were at least sixty fighters and three squadrons with some Savoia S-M.79s and He 111s. Montilla came up close alongside and signalled with his eyes, to draw my attention to the enemy. Pereiro also came alongside and did the same thing. His small face was a mixture of happiness and surprise. I felt calm although fear was all around me. I have always felt like this in the moments just before a battle. Once it has started things change.

"Banking steeply, I dived down over a formation of twin-engined machines which were coming from the Gandesa-Corbera zone. Before we reached them shots were fired ahead of our track. I squeezed the trigger as a silhouette passed barely twenty metres in front of my nose. The Fiat's belly looked like a shark's; I followed him for a moment with my fingers glued to the trigger, and the shots from my guns buried themselves in the Italian's machine. A crescendo of noise behind made me turn round: a Fiat was close on my tail. Montilla, on my right, tried to get rid of him; he closed in and they almost collided. The biplane dived away.

"The Fiats were now surrounding their bombers and it was almost impossible to reach the twin-engined machines. As they began to turn towards their own lines, exactly over Corbera, I saw a pair of 'Moscas' come out from below and in the middle of the bombers. They raced through the air and made a half turn before diving over the Heinkels. When they came out several Fiats were waiting for them. The 'Moscas' tried to regain height, and were successful as several of us rushed to their aid, preventing the Fiats from reaching them.

Nevertheless, the most distant one seemed to have been hit. He dived, and immediately a pair of Fiats followed him down. Calvo, Montilla, Margalef and I all rushed after them, the pursuers becoming the pursued. They abandoned their prey and tried to escape, but for one of them it was already too late: as he made a half turn Montilla and I both fired at him and down he went.

"The Fiats were now trying to cordon us within the area, maintaining a guard over the line of the Ebro. Their bombers had all left the front. I was in a formation with five 'Moscas', three of Pereiro's and two of mine: Montilla and Calvo. Far below us there were three 'Moscas', with two more straggling behind them. The rest of the sky was filled with Italian Fiats.

"We had been out now for an hour and forty minutes, and our fuel was running low. I gave the signal for our return. We formed wing to wing and dived from four thousand metres almost to ground level. The Fiats were taken by surprise. By the time they reacted the speed and distance separating us were too great for them to follow.

"As we flew over Valls I counted the numbers in my squadron. Sirvent was missing. When I landed the first thing I saw was a 'Mosca' slewed round on one wheel, a wingtip buried in the ground. It carried Sirvent's number. Happily he was uninjured, but his machine was riddled; there were 58 bullet holes. How lucky he had been! He was already in the dispersal hut. I spoke to him but there was no answer; he was fast asleep!"

Larios refers to the battles on September 23rd as follows:

"The following day we patrolled the Corbera sector, guarding the Cadenas, which were hard at work, as usual, carrying out their routine and dangerous missions over broken, mountainous country. We escorted them back as far as our lines and then swept over the Ebro and Falset, which lies halfway to Reus, the chief Red fighter base. We were waiting to intercept, pounce on them and force them to fight on their way to the front. The plan worked well, for we soon sighted a wing of Chatos climbing towards the Ebro. We were on them before they could make a getaway.

"They quickly broke up and began milling round in circles, in sections of twos and threes, Indian style. I led my section into battle, made my choice, and stuck fast, diving down on a Chato's tail. She saw me coming and wheeled up in a tight turn to come in beneath me. She was too late. Like a flash I was over and beyond her. I dived down, reaching for her tail, levelling out for the kill. Bullets slammed home as I closed in to point-blank range. She made a desperate attempt to get away by wheeling around on a vertical turn and trying to reach my tail, but I stuck fast, following her every movement, firing burst after burst. She suddenly gave up, rolled over, and spun slowly down out of control. White fuel vapour streamed from her pierced tank. I lifted my Fiat's nose and climbed. I did not want to be caught napping again—once bitten, twice shy. I had already had my full share of bites. But the sky was emptied of friend and foe alike. I turned for our distant lines and home, and reported one damaged Chato. The chances were that she would never reach her base.

"A very young pilot, Perico Martínez de Irujo, a friend of mine, a grand person, and son of the Duke of Soto Mayor, was killed during this fight. He had only just recently joined the group.

"Air battle is one of the most individualistic, thrilling and great tests man has in war. It can bring out the best and the worst in him.

"The opening rounds of a fight, playing for a lead, are tense and packed with emotion, and one's nerves are strung taut to the breaking point. Then, bang! the fireworks start and a mad fight for supremacy begins. The sky becomes black with machines, turning, twisting and diving in a vicious life and death struggle, where no quarter is given and no wounded are picked up. The battle spreads out in an ever-increasing arc, and the blue heaven is criss-crossed by white vapour ribbons forming great loops—a beautiful sight. In the heat of the battle one loses all sense of time and space, and the earth rocks around one's head in a whirling dance. Blackouts come swiftly and suddenly, blood is drawn from head to feet, and life fades out for what seems eternity. Then, suddenly, you find yourself deserted and alone in the vast circumference of the sky. A feeling of utter peace and solitude creeps through your senses and your body relaxes. You sit snugly in your warm cockpit, high above the world, and the biting, crisp air is like champagne. For a short spell you seem not to have a worry in the world. The only sign of life is the steady and comforting drone of your engine, your close friend. She often complained when I pressed her too hard in battle and gave out a high-pitched, painful whine, but I learned to nurse her whenever possible. It paid off in the long run."

In this battle the Italian *Gamba de Ferro* Group and the Russian squadrons (Nos 2 and 5) took part for the last time. The two Spanish Fiat groups, the Me 109s, the Rata squadrons 3, 6 and 7 and some Chato squadrons also participated.

The *Gamba de Ferro* Group claimed to have shot down two Ratas and one Katiuska, the Me 109s one Rata and two Katiuskas, Group 2-G-3 two Chatos and three more Ratas, and 3-G-3 another Chato, making a total of six Ratas, three Chatos and three Katiuskas. The bulletin raised the total number to fourteen, giving the number of Ratas shot down as eight. I have been able to confirm that three Ratas were destroyed, those flown by Catalá, Margalef and a Russian, from Squadrons 2, 3 and 5 respectively. The Nationalist Air Force bulletin did not record any losses. (Martínez de Irujo was shot down on the 22nd).

Of these events Tarazona wrote:

"September 23rd. Today they shot down Margalef. He was hardly eighteen years old. The soldiers in the Camposines–Pinell sector saw the battle. We had gone out to protect a group of 'Kats', seven of us from the third squadron. Dust and mist in the atmosphere was reducing visibility. The Republican bombers could hardly be seen. The sun, which was facing us made it difficult to see what was in the distance. Meroño's sixth squadron was flying to the left of the twin-engined planes, the seventh squadron to the right and below. We were above, at about five thousand metres.

"The fighter force consisted of twenty-three aircraft. Our mission was to go in with the 'Kats' and to stay at the front to protect them; the seventh squadron would go with the others and Meroño was to stay with me. The anti-aircraft seemed to have the 'Kats' in range, but this time they did not fire at them. When they arrived at the front and found their objective they dropped their bombs and turned back to base.

"Once the bombers had left the Ebro, Meroño went down to attack some He 51 biplanes which were firing at our lines. I waited in readiness. Suddenly, to the left of Montilla, twelve Fiats appeared, above them a bunch of German 'Messers'. I tried to gain more height and position the squadron backs to the sun, but another Fiat squadron came to attack, firing their machine-guns. I signalled my squadron to dive steeply. There were so many Fiats following us that I could not see any way of climbing to get above them, and was afraid of colliding with them. I changed the direction of the dive and headed the 'Moscas' towards our own lines, eluding our pursuers for a moment, giving time for us to climb at full power and re-form at five thousand metres.

"One plane was still down below. At first I did not know who it was. The German monoplanes were looking for us, waiting an opportunity to attack. I looked for Meroño, but could not find him. I felt sure that the solitary 'Mosca' would soon be in serious trouble. I searched the sky for someone to attack. Spotting a squadron of Fiats below I led the squadron towards them, in a steep dive, but before we could get within range I discovered the 'Messers' were above. We sprayed one Fiat patrol with bullets and banked hard to our right, to prevent the Germans from firing at us. When they saw that we were giving them the slip they took up their original position, waiting for any unwary pilots.

"The sun was beginning to set. Our adversaries were tired of watching over us and we were tired of being watched. I ordered the squadron to return to base. There I learned that a telephone call from the front reported that Margalef had been shot down by three Fiats. The engine of his 'Mosca' must have been hit earlier, for it had been emitting large quantities of black smoke when he tried to open the throttle. He was defenceless, and they riddled his machine with bullets until the young lad crashed into the side of the Caballs mountains.

"What can I say? Merely that he was an immature lad whose life was taken away by a war he did not begin."

During these two days of strong aerial activity one of the Condor Legion's He 45s crashed after being attacked by a fighter, as did a Romeo flown by Saracho and Corporal Luján, and Borrás was injured in another Romeo.

Towards the end of September Queipo decided to give O'Connor's Fiat an air test, as there had been some trouble with this machine, its engine cutting on take off. He climbed to a fair altitude and then put the Fiat's nose down in a power dive: without any warning the port upper wing was torn away, and Queipo needed all his skill to pull out of the dive and escape with injuries which kept him in hospital for ten days. In his absence the squadron was led by Mendizábal, but ill-luck continued, and several people were injured when a machine-gun was accidentally discharged on the ground.

There was a slight pause in aerial activity until October 2nd, when 2-G-3 were involved in a fierce battle. Arístides and Henricourt each destroyed a

Rata and Salvador added a Chato to his score. Murcia of 3-G-3 achieved his fifth victory, the first pilot in this Group to do so, and they also lost Sergeant Olivera. Here is Larios' version:

"On October 2nd, while escorting Romeos beyond Gandesa, we again came to grips with a large pack of Ratas. They swept down from a great height straight on top of us. I lifted my nose to one Rata which dived on me in a frontal attack, her four guns viciously spitting like small jabbing red tongues, never a pleasant sight. I held my ground, firing back, and managed to get one quick burst into her belly as she swept over my head and up at a great speed and came around to reach my tail. But I had her beat there; the Fiat could out-turn the Rata. The moment I began to gain on her, she gave up and dived away. I was about to follow when I spotted a Fiat being hotly chased by two Ratas. They were closing in fast and there was not a second to waste. I jammed the stick forward and went down with my engine roaring, firing at each in turn, hoping that the sight of my tracers would scare them off before it was too late. It worked, for they laid off their victim and dived away. The Fiat pilot turned out to be Ibarreche, one of our best.

"The battle by then had spread far and wide. I climbed towards the sun and levelled out at 6,000 metres, the Fiat's limit, and the altitude at which she became sluggish. Breathing at that altitude was an effort. If one remained up there for any length of time head and arm movements became difficult because of the lack of oxygen in the thin air. But the advantages of altitude were well worth it. It was a brilliantly clear day and the beauty of the vast panorama spreading away beneath me was breathtaking. To the north rose the towering snow-capped Pyrenees . . .

"I was briskly awakened from my daydreams by the sight of a homing Rata a few hundred metres north of me, pointing straight for her Reus base. She had been in my blind spot while I climbed, and I spotted her only on levelling out. She was cruising along quite unconcerned, which seemed odd. Possibly her pilot (a green one maybe) thought he was well beyond the danger zone and above the Fiat's ceiling. He was partly right there. However, he was to get a rude awakening a few minutes later. I had the sun behind me and if I could creep up without being seen, I had a good chance of making a kill. The Rata had poor visibility to the rear, which added to my chances of surprising her. I kept my machine slightly below the level of her tail as I pushed my Fiat at full power and slowly began to gain ground. A shadow flicked across the sun, startling me, but it turned out to be another Fiat, hot on the same scent. If the Rata did not change course, I would reach her first . . .

"I held my fire until I was within 30-metre range, although the temptation to press the trigger long before had been overpowering . . . Above the roar of my engine sounded the high nervous chatter of my machine-guns, and bullets ripped home, burst after burst. But to my amazement she continued to fly on. I could not believe my eyes. Her pilot must have been mad, or dead, or both. I had been prepared for lightning evasive action after the first burst.

"She soon began to swing from side to side; her nose came up slowly till she hung suspended from the sky, then she rolled over and went down . . . I followed her until smoke streaked back. A minute later she crashed into the ground.

"Meanwhile, the Fiat trailing behind, whose pilot turned out to be Ibarreche again, had been a silent but watchful spectator of the dramatic action . . ."

Tarazona, who was not in action that day, wrote in his diary that, after several days of bad weather, his squadron had re-formed at Valls, with twelve Ratas and some new pilots.

On the 3rd there was a tense situation. Neither Morato nor Salvador, leading aces of the Nationalist Air Force, returned to their base. This came only a day after the deaths of Oliveras—leader of the Romeo group—and Cipriano Rodríguez.

Guerra en el Aire describes these events as follows:

"Whilst over Corbera, on a flight to escort a squadron of Romeos, enemy fighters made their appearance. Commander Morato opened the battle by attacking some Chatos flying at low altitude, followed by half of the twenty-four strong Fiat formation. The other twelve attacked the Ratas, which were providing top cover for the Chatos.

"As usual, the Reds withdrew deep within their own lines, gradually dispersing as they were followed many kilometres from the front. When there were no longer any signs of enemy planes, the Nationalist fighters began re-assembling over the front, watching for their leader's Fiat: it did not appear.

"Aircraft were milling around the sky as the pilots of 3-G-3 examined and re-examined every Fiat in sight, hoping to see the characteristic rocking movement by which Morato communicated his identity. Finally, when they were convinced that it was useless circling any longer, they returned to base. But the commander was not there either. Their concern increased. Not only was he missing but Captain Salvador, the other supreme pilot, who had fought alongside Morato throughout the war, had not returned either. It was inconceivable. Morato and Salvador both shot down?

"Soon after, information came that a Fiat had landed without incident near Corbera. Who could it be? It was not long afterwards that Morato got in touch with us, from the Northern Army's command post, saying that he would soon be arriving by car at the airfield. His plane had to be dismantled, but he would explain later.

"It was also learned later that Salvador's aircraft had gone into a dive and crashed, but that he had escaped by parachute. The Red radio announced subsequently that he had been taken prisoner, but fortunately he was set free at the end of the Catalonian campaign.

"Meanwhile, at Escatron, the pilots of 3-G-3 were giving details of the action. One of them related how he had fired a deflection burst at a Rata and had seen it catch fire, but at that point he had noticed another Fiat alongside and was not sure whether he had fired as well. Questions were asked about this, and since nobody had any recollection of firing under the circumstances the Rata was counted as a victory for that pilot; his first.

"Soon afterwards Commander Morato arrived back at Escatron, wanting to know, in no uncertain terms, who was the pilot of the Fiat that had fired a burst into the engine of his machine when he was hot-foot after a Rata.

"At once all eyes turned towards the pilot who was celebrating his first 'victory'. Soon all the details were known. In attacking another aircraft from above, allowance has to be made for its speed and range. With a fast target a large correction factor is necessary, the aiming point being well ahead of the aircraft in order to hit it. In this case the correction factor had been too small and the bullets passed harmlessly, well behind the Rata. They were not completely harmless: hidden from view by the Fiat's lower wings was a second Fiat—Morato's—and one of these bullets shattered an oil pipe in the engine.

"Fortunately he had enough height to glide to the safety of his own lines, twenty kilometres away. Here, close to the front, there was no airfield and Morato made an incredible and perfect landing, in a tiny and very rough field. So small, indeed, that it would have been quite impossible to have flown the Fiat out of it, so it was dismantled and returned to Escatron for re-assembly. A 12·7mm bullet recovered from the engine left no doubt that reconstruction of the incident was correct, for ammunition of this calibre was not used by the enemy.

"During the entire war, Morato was shot down only on this one occasion. How ironical that he should fall victim to a pilot of his own group!"

On October 3rd the Rata group lost three machines, two from the 3rd Squadron whose pilots, Sirvent and Pitarch, escaped uninjured, and one from the 7th Squadron flown by Gutiérrez Chiclana. According to Tarazona, Merono was the person who gained the victory over Salvador.

On October 4th Mölders shot down a Rata (probably Tébar), which made his eighth victory, and lost the Me 109 flown by Otto Bertram. At this time the Condor Legion used as their regular tactical formation a patrol of four machines, which could split up into two pairs, but never employed closed formations or single aircraft. This formation was used later, at the beginning of World War II, by both German and English fighters. The patrol leader's job was to attack the enemy, the 'dogs' protecting their master.

It is clear from the accounts of Larios and Tarazona, that the Ratas and Fiats fought as individuals once battle had been joined. They had found large formations—thirty plus—an embarrassment, with the emphasis on collision avoidance rather than destroying the enemy. Italian reports claimed that, during the battle of Catalonia, Remondino led his group into battle without breaking their formation, but this was at a period when the enemy fighters were not at full strength.

At about this time, García Pardo and Murcia were attached to the Condor Legion, under Muñoz's orders, to gain experience with Me 109s before the changeover to Spanish crews. They were replaced in 2-G-3 and 3-G-3 by Cuadra (who had spent a few days at the Fighter School) and Queipo de Llano, then recovered from his injuries.

On October 15th four squadrons of Fiats made a combined sortie, three from 2-G-3, and one from 3-G-3. They succeeded in destroying two more

Ratas (Bayo and González Guzmán), one for each group. Salas, Vázquez and Bayo each damaged another, adding three probables to the day's score. In the Condor Legion Mölders shot down two Ratas, a double which he repeated on October 31st, bringing his total of confirmed victories to thirteen.

On October 16th Tarazona, leader of the 3rd Rata Squadron, and his three patrol leaders Paredes, Beltrán and Sirvent (the four founder members of the 3rd Squadron) were promoted to the rank of Lieutenant. Bravo, who was then second-in-command of the Group, had been a Captain since May 31st: on November 11th, 1938, Redondo, Arias and Meroño, leaders of the 1st, 4th and 6th Squadrons, were also promoted to this rank.

On October 18th came a spell of bad weather, during which La Cenia aerodrome, the Me 109 base, became flooded. However, airfields in the west remained dry.

In operations over a comparatively small area, one well patrolled by enemy fighters and defended by a mass of anti-aircraft guns, it proved impossible to use the Cadenas. Consequently, it was decided to send Groups 1-G-2 (Eyaralar) and 6-G-15 (Llop) to the South. Their opening operations there were far from successful: on September 27th M. Moro was injured and on October 10th Gascón and Gorostiza's Pavo crashed. The Romeos, because of their greater speed, were retained at Castejón del Puente, but had one group leader killed (Cipriano Rodríguez), another wounded (Jesús Camacho) and one squadron leader wounded (Juan Díaz Criado). The new Heinkel He 51 group (4-G-2), operated from Calzadilla de los Barros and Benquerencia aerodromes in Extremadura throughout the Summer, moving to Escatrón on September 14th.

The Balearic Air Force continued its systematic action against ports and coastal traffic. During a routine patrol over Valencia on October 28th, (when the International Brigades left) the Cant Z.506 seaplane No 73-1 was lost. Its pilot was Lieutenant Colonel Ramón Franco, leader of the Balearic Air Forces and, despite a sea rescue operation, he and his crew perished. This was the only seaplane of this type to be lost in action throughout the war, although another Cant, No 73-4, was destroyed whilst being towed at night.

On October 29th, a Dornier Do 17 was lost near Salas de los Infantes. Flown by Luis Rambaud, it was *en route* from León, and subsequent enquiries proved that the loss was due to sabotage. Several other cases occurred until the cause was traced to the Parque workshops. Rambaud and three crew members were killed, the wireless operator escaping without injury.

At this time Madrid was becoming desperately short of food. The Nationalist Air Force seized the opportunity, for both propaganda and humanitarian reasons, to drop sacks of bread to the population. This was galling for the Government, who used press and radio to warn that the bread was poisoned: not surprisingly, no one took notice of this false alarm.

Those who took part in the operation long remembered the difficulties with which they were faced. Aircraft for dropping supplies from the air were not available: when loading hatches of the bombers were opened it proved a near-impossible task to heave the sacks of bread out against the pressure of the slipstream. Not long after this, seaplanes from Pollensa dropped roses over Alicante gaol, in remembrance of Prima de Rivera, who had died two years earlier.

In the second fortnight of October there was another pause in aerial activity; this was broken by a series of violent battles which took place between October 30th and November 3rd. There were six in all, during which 2-G-3 and 3-G-3 destroyed thirty more aircraft (17 and 13 respectively), without suffering any losses. Most outstanding pilots in this period were Velasco and Larios of 3-G-3, with seven and three victories respectively, not forgetting the inevitable Vázquez Sagastizábal of 2-G-3 who shot down three fighters. Also in 2-G-3 were two promising young pilots, Alcocer and Illera, who each gained two victories.

The fact that the Fiat groups had suffered no losses in these battles would suggest a weak Government fighter force. This was not the case, numerically speaking, for one hundred fighters had flown over Barcelona on October 28th to pay their respects to the departing International brigades, and in a single operational sortie on October 31st no less than fifty Ratas and thirty Chatos were deployed.

Larios described the battle on October 30th as follows:

"... on a routine mission over Gandesa and the Ebro, escorting Savoia 79s and 81s, followed by Junkers 52s and He 70s, around twenty Ratas streaked down through broken clouds and jumped on us. I was on top and received the first impact. A Rata dived straight down on me. I had a split second in which to jerk the stick back and lift my nose to receive the shock and simultaneously fire a short burst as the Red machine roared over my head and dived. The result was a neat round hole in the centre of my front windshield panel ...

"Thoughtful Rossi kept the panel for me. After the war I had it mounted in a wooden frame, a souvenir which I cherish highly."

This version of the battle is confirmed by Tarazona, whose account follows:

"October 30th. We were flying over Pinell when two squadrons of Fiats appeared: they were in close formation well below and coming towards out third squadron. The sun behind us and the height at which we were patrolling provided ideal conditions for a surprise attack. They were coming from their own lines, and it was unlikely they could see us. The closing speeds of the adversaries were enormous; in an instant they were beneath us. We must have been spotted for suddenly, as if someone had pulled the string of a mechanical toy, the formation of twenty-four biplanes opened out. One squadron veered right, the other left.

"Merono's sixth squadron could be seen in the distance, fighting against the 'Messers' which had attacked Arias' fourth squadron. We turned and dived to attack the squadron which was flying towards the sea. As we approached them, from behind, we discovered in front and above us three more Fiat squadrons: these were, without a doubt, Italian.

"I went straight for the leader of the squadron we had selected for our target, with Paredes guarding my tail. Montilla and Calvo were close behind. The

Fiats suddenly became aware of the attack and banked steeply. We flew over them like fireballs our machine-guns beating a tattoo. We turned for a head-on attack, the two squadrons racing towards each other with a closing speed of a thousand kilometres an hour. Neither squadron would give way. Bullets from the Fiats were hitting the 'Mosca's' engines, our windscreens shattering into tiny pieces.

"I felt that I had lost all control of my actions; my fingers were as if glued to the trigger of the machine-guns. The smell of gunpowder had inflamed me. The nose of the Fiat I was attacking grew bigger and bigger. I saw my shots plunging into its fuselage which was there, immense, just in front of me, spitting fire. I waited and so did he. I imagined the impact, shattered bones, blood and death. A moment later, blackout . . .

"The slamming impact of bullets on the armour plate behind me was the first thing to register as I recovered consciousness. I quickly glanced behind, to discover a Fiat firing from scarcely fifty metres. I nose dived through a cloud, the biplane close behind, but my speed was greater. I pulled back on the stick and my 'Mosca', like a piece of wood, swept up over the sea of foam and floated on top. I looked around me. We were alone, my fighter and me. Her nose was dripping black blood, but her wings were undamaged: she had not let me down, and once more had brought me to safety.

"I dropped through the clouds again, back to the battle area. A 'Mosca', trying to reach its lines, was being attacked by a Fiat. In his concentration on a 'kill' he failed to see me. I went closer and closer, then fired two long bursts from my machine-guns. A ball of fire enveloped me, and I had to pull the 'Mosca' upwards quickly to avoid a collision. The Fiat's pilot went over the side in his parachute.

"I moved alongside a damaged 'Mosca'. The whole of the starboard side of the fuselage was soaked in oil; part of the windscreen had been shot away. I signalled to the pilot to return to base: I went up closer and saw the pallor of his face: he was badly wounded. I indicated that he should follow me. Sanz, from the third squadron, joined us. We accompanied him as far as the sea, near Salou, where he made a landing on the beach. We could see people running up to his plane.

"I wanted to return to the front but my engine began to lose power. It was low on oil; the pressure dropping. I gained height slowly. When I was over Reus a sudden doubt came to my mind. Should I land there or continue to Valls? I decided to carry on. Near the airfield the engine seized.

"Sanz, on my right, was watching me closely. I was losing height rapidly and the airfield seemed to be slipping farther and farther away. I considered landing in a field, but this seemed an easy way out. I had to get home, and in one piece. After all, I was the squadron leader and Sanz was watching me all the time.

"When, at last, I felt sure of reaching the airfield, new doubts assailed me. Should I land with my wheels up? This seemed the safest course, but it would cause serious damage to the aircraft. What if I put the wheels down and, with the dead engine, misjudged my landing and turned somersault? Then there would be even more damage and I might end up badly injured.

"I banked gently. With no engine, I could hear the whistle of the slipstream, which was strangely comforting. I put the wheels down and passed high over the airfield boundary. I pushed the 'Mosca's' nose down, then levelled off and began to float. The trees in front of me grew larger. I landed heavily, put the wheel brakes on and pulled the stick back hard against my chest: the 'Mosca' was still going towards the trees at great speed. I released the left brake, the game little fighter docilely began to turn towards the right. It stopped a few metres from the squadron's hut.

"When Commander Giménez came up to me my first request was for a glass of wine. This was provided quickly and I drank a long draught. Rodríguez examined the damage. I jumped down from the cockpit. As at Llanes, I could not stop my legs from trembling."

On October 31st the 2nd, 3rd, 4th, 6th and 7th Rata Squadrons took off in company with two Chato squadrons. It was a quiet day, but Tarazona's squadron shot down an He 111.

On November 2nd Groups 2-G-3 and 3-G-3 had a resounding victory. Larios' tone was triumphant, as can be seen in the following extract:

"November 2nd was my *Red*-letter day. On crossing the Red lines, as we swept over Gandes and the Pandols mountains, we sighted compact formations of Ratas and Chatos putting on a big show of air power: Ratas above, Chatos below, as usual. They were milling around, waiting to pounce on us. Both our groups were out in strength that day. Contact was immediate, there was no dilly-dallying, and the clash came with its usual violence. Formations rapidly disintegrated as each one sought out his victim.

"A Rata shot across my nose. I swung in behind her and got in a fleeting burst as she dived away. Another one streaked by with a Fiat two hundred metres behind. I gave her a burst of cross-fire to keep her going and climbed rapidly to where the battle seemed thickest, resembling a swarm of angry bees. A Chato came at me, head-on, and we both opened fire simultaneously, shot past each other, and banked over hard to reach each other's tail. The circle tightened rapidly. After the second round the Red pilot gave up and dived. This was the opening I was waiting for. Down I went after him in a vertical dive, and closed up fast, pouring in bullets. Dense black smoke streamed back, and the stricken machine began to spin; it hit the ground close to the Ebro River. That day I claimed one confirmed Chato.

"On our next patrol, that same day, escorting Junkers and Savoias over the same sector, we came across a wing of Ratas. The alarm was given, and eager as a pack of hounds at full cry we ripped into them. A Fiat streaked by me, chased by a couple of Ratas hot on her tail. She looked desperate. I dived in behind them, raked one, then the other, and scared them off. My good deed for the day had been done. I came up for air and climbed fast. The battle had spread out and was less concentrated. Two Chatos, flying wing to wing, swept in 300 metres beneath me. They looked happy and unconcerned, and I decided to give them something to think about. I threw my Fiat over and came in behind them in a fast shallow dive. The first news they got of my presence was of my bullets going home. The leader dived away but the other one kept going straight.

"I throttled back and gave her my full concentration. The Red machine loomed up big in front of me as I closed in with my fingers pressed on the trigger. She began to rock, then rolled over and spun down; smoke and flames shot back as she streaked to the ground. I reached for the sky for the third time in fifteen minutes. I was still climbing, with my nose straight up when a Chato jumped on me. I wheeled, trying desperately to bring my machine beneath her belly and away from her line of fire, but failed. She had me cornered and at her mercy. With the extra altitude she could outmanoeuvre me, which she did by coming round to my tail. At that crucial moment, a Fiat came to my rescue and shot hell out of the Red machine. My good deed had been fully repaid. I never discovered who the pilot was.

"Minutes later I came across a Fiat in an identical predicament, with a Chato glued to her tail. She was trying every trick in the trade to get away, but was cornered. I struck fast and just in time. I dived on them and began firing from a distance to get the Red pilot off his victim quickly. The effect was instantaneous. He broke away and dived to the ground. I followed him down with the full advantage of superior altitude and closed up rapidly, giving him short, sharp bursts at point-blank range. Seconds later, smoke poured out as the Chato shot into thick cloud and vanished. I pulled out and climbed, but finding myself alone, I turned for Escatrón.

"When I got back to base, the last machine was confirmed as my third kill by Patino Vázquez, one of our top fighter pilots . . . Vázquez was beneath the cloud layer when the Chato broke through and dived to the ground in flames. The pilot never baled out, poor devil, but the chances are that he was already dead. I was overjoyed with the results . . .

"The total record score had been seven in the morning and ten in the evening!"

In Tarazona's description one can sense the growing anguish in the North as they began to appreciate that victory was impossible:

"November 2nd. The blow today was much nearer . . .

"I sleep alone in my room. Paredes' bed is empty. Today they shot him down. He crashed in the mountains, near the little town of Garcia. Some peasants recovered his body and a Land Army vehicle took him to hospital. He has a fracture at the base of his skull. They have carried out a very delicate operation on him. Let us pray to God that he will be saved.

"The battle was tremendous. We tried to carry out the orders from high command: to avoid combat with Nationalist fighters. But that is not easy. We were patrolling the zone between Pinell and Camposines when two Fiat Squadrons arrived on the scene. We withdrew, wanting to see if they were going to protect a bombing operation or to fire at our lines. They followed us. We saw that behind them there were no less than three squadrons of bombers, which were slowly but surely going towards the zone we should have been patrolling. Above them were the Italian Fiats, and even higher the Me 109s. Twenty-four Moscas—the third and sixth squadrons—would have to face up to that avalanche of fighters.

"Without daring to give the matter too much thought, I launched an attack on the twin-engined machines. As we passed the protective umbrella of Fiats we found ourselves surrounded by bullets. The squadrons of bombers were slipping, one after the other, through the theoretical protection that we were supposed to be providing. Fighters from all the enemy patrols wanted to take part in the day's carnage, all anxious to return to their airfield and boast the destruction of a Red Rata.

"In wing to wing formation, and scorning the Fiats, we attacked a squadron of He 111s. As we fired, our shots became mingled with those of the Me 109s firing at us. The yellow noses of these machines were now close to our tails.

"The forward fuselage of a bomber disintegrated, hit by an anti-aircraft shell intended for us. We took advantage of the temporary confusion caused by this, and made a determined attack on the twin-engined machines, which broke up their formation.

"The first patrol, under my command, managed to position themselves amongst the German bombers, shielded by them from the guns of the Fiats and 'Messers'. We opened fire on them, but without any plan of attack. We had an enemy fighter force above us; below us there were not even two thousand metres of altitude to provide an escape route.

"Paredes' patrol attacked a Savoia 79 which they set on fire, curiosity making me follow its fatal trajectory. It crashed among the Caballs mountains. When the Fiats saw this they came diving down to wipe me out. They flashed down between the bombers, their guns spitting a hail of death.

"My neck was raw with constantly turning round to look behind, and trickles of blood were running down below my silk handkerchief. But what I was defending at that moment was my life: at times it seemed as if it was about to slip away from me.

"I dived in desperation, then pulled back hard on the stick, slipping between the formations of Fascist biplanes as I rocketed up into the sky. There the Me 109s were waiting. I dived again, straight down, with those bandits on my tail. When the air speed indicator showed 700km/h, I grasped the control column firmly with my right hand, steeled my body, fixed my eyes on a point on the ground and, thinking again of my life, pulled the stick back.

"I felt a brutal jolt, the tips of the wings shuddered for a few seconds, and the sight left my eyes. Instinctively I must have eased the stick forward, for once more I could see the sun's brightness. My blood was still providing vision, and life.

"Red streaks came flashing past. I twisted my head round, soreness forgotten: a Fiat was sitting on my tail. I dived once again, but could not lose him. His guns were boring holes in my 'Mosca'. I climbed vertically, but still the devil was behind me. I could feel the bullets from his guns hammering the steel armour plate behind me. As the 'Mosca' went higher and higher, speed was draining away. Within seconds she would stall, and I would be at the mercy of the Fascist who, already, must surely have added me to his list of victories. I could imagine his triumphant return to base: 'I have shot down a squadron leader. I saw the white number on his fuselage'.

"I was about to make a final desperate attempt to escape by diving when a 'Mosca' came tearing in to my aid, all four guns blazing. I looked behind. The Fiat was already dropping towards the ground: the hunter was now the hunted. I formed on this 'Mosca', which belonged to Paredes, and together we followed the Fiat. It was still going down fast, and as its pilot attempted to level out, he collided with another Fiat. Both machines exploded. Paredes gave me a sad little smile; rather like that of someone who inadvertently kills an insect, and then feels guilty for its death.

"The battle was still raging. No less than six parachutes were descending. Heaven only knows who were the little dolls hanging beneath them. We spotted a 'Mosca' being chased by three Fiats. Paredes and I raced over and ended up by dispersing them. One Fiat came out of the encounter in flames, its pilot joining those who had finished their mortal task on that day.

"I was exhausted by now, and looked to see if we could return to base. No such luck, for I immediately spotted two 'Moscas' making frantic endeavours to shake some German monoplanes from their tails. They had descended from their higher levels to join the feast of Red machines.

"I tried to form a line so that we could defend ourselves, but this was impossible. We had no choice but to fight, as the Fiats were already there, waiting to attack us. We were then at three thousand metres, an ideal height for them. A sideways glance at my fuel gauge almost gave me a heart attack: its needle was barely registering.

"I dived towards our lines, using very little throttle. Several Fiats followed me, but I finally levelled out about two metres from the ground. Some other 'Moscas' joined me, most of them bearing the scars of battle. Paredes was not among them.

"After what seemed an eternity we crossed our own lines. I looked behind and saw the Fiats turning tightly through 180 degrees. I was astonished. One of Meroño's 'Moscas' drew close to me, its pilot pointing ahead excitedly. Above us was another squadron of 'Moscas'. Arias' fourth squadron had come to our aid! How I blessed them.

"Paredes, my companion of the battle, was not at the airfield. Meroño told me over the telephone that he escorted him until he attempted to force-land near Mora. His engine, starved of fuel, was no longer turning, and gallant Paredes crashed among the mountains. . . ."

With the death of Paredes, the 3rd Rata Squadron had lost its three patrol leaders, Sirvent on October 3rd, Beltrán on the 31st and Paredes on November 2nd. Calvo, Montilla Pitarch and Díaz were sent as replacements.

On November 1st the Government fighter squadrons had received orders not to enter into combat with enemy fighters. Because of this, the Nationalist Air Force concentrated their attacks on the aerodromes in Catalonia. In a raid on Monjos, made by the Spanish Savoia S-M.79s on November 5th, Captain Comas, leader of the Chato group, was injured by falling bombs and had to have a leg amputated. Zambudio replaced him in command.

On November 7th the attack on the aerodromes was intensified, and Valls, El Vendrell, Monjos, Cervera and Vilafranca del Panadés were all bombed. On the same day, near to Aytona, in the Segre sector, Morato discovered three tanks which he attacked, in company with Salas and Vázquez. After repeated attacks they were successful in setting all three on fire. When they landed at base, Morato commented that: "They were different from usual; they seemed larger and I could not see their turrets. They must have had something covering them." Vázquez was amazed by the fact that once they had burned there seemed to be little débris.

It was discovered later that they had been 'taken in', and had mistaken three haystacks for three tanks. This was not really surprising for it was usual to camouflage these vehicles with branches and straw. Two days later the same patrol fired at two authentic tanks, which were attacking the bridgehead at Serós, but had to withdraw in face of a tremendous anti-aircraft barrage. By the 7th, the V Army Corps had re-crossed the Ebro, whilst the Eastern Army was staging a diversionary attack in the Segre.

During the last few days of the Battle of the Ebro, Tarazona's squadron received even more punishment. On the 8th, in combat with the Me 109s, Pallarés was wounded, and Pitarch had to land at Reus; on the 10th, anti-aircraft fire shot away one of the wings of Montilla's machine, and on the 11th, Ucar was seriously injured when he attempted a forced-landing at dusk. On November 16th these losses were replaced, with the arrival of four Ratas and two novice pilots, Arrés and Francés. The first of these was killed in a combat exercise, before making an operational flight.

On November 12th eighteen Fiats of 2-G-3 and six from 3-G-3 took off under the leadership of Salas, to escort Ju 52s and He 70s in the Segre sector. Six Katiuskas were encountered, escorted by two formations of Ratas. Henricourt succeeded in destroying one Rata, and one Katiuska was shot down by the combined attack of about five machines. This combat marked the end of air operations in support of the battle of the Ebro, which ended on November 16th with the retreat of the XV Army Corps.

As the Fiats landed back at base from this final sortie—one, which had been damaged in combat, collided with machine No 3-61, Salas' plane, damaging the lower wings. This latter machine, one of the first to serve with the group, was repaired by the middle of January and Salas finished the war in it.

During the three and a half months of the battle of the Ebro, Group 2-G-3 had destroyed seventy aircraft, bringing their total to one hundred and seventy. In the same period 3-G-3 achieved twenty-eight victories, bringing their total up to thirty-seven.

Group 2-G-3's victories over this period were achieved as follows: ten (plus one in collaboration) by Vázquez; eight by Bayo; six (plus one in collaboration) by Salas; five each by Henricourt and Ibarreche; four by Salvador; three each by Guerrero, Arístides, Simón, Cesteros, Manrique and Alcocer; two each by S. Serra, García Pardo, Allende and Illera; and one (plus one in collaboration) by Carlos Serra, Ansaldo, Comas, Romagosa and one not allocated to a specific pilot.

In 3-G-3, Velasco achieved eight victories; Morato, O'Connor and Larios four each; Ignacio Alfaro two, and Murcia, Lacour, Robles, Muerza, González Guzmán and Mendizábal one each; another two were probably destroyed by Velasco as, totalling his victories in 7-E-3 Squadron, one arrives at eleven, and not thirteen, as recorded by the group.

The general list of aces was then as follows: Morato, thirty-six; Salvador, twenty-four; Vázquez, twenty and one in collaboration; Salas, sixteen and one in collaboration; Arístides and Guerrero, thirteen; Bayo and García Pardo, eleven; Velasco at least nine; Henricourt, nine; Allende and Ibarreche, seven; Murcia, O'Connor and Larios, five. Four pilots from 3-G-3 had entered this list of aces Murcia, Velasco, O'Connor and Larios, the second of these with a meteoric rise, similar to that of Vázquez and Bayo. Amongst the foreigners, Mölders had reached fourteen victories and Schellmann eight.

On the Government side nobody had exceeded Garcia La Calle and Aguirre's totals; Zarauza, Bravo, Comas and Zambudio reached a figure of about ten victories, and Tarazona destroyed more than five machines. On November 11th Zambudio, Redondo, Arias, Meroño and Vicente Castillo were promoted on merit to the rank of Captain: in the following month Zarauza was promoted to Major.

When the battle of the Ebro ended, and while making a routine patrol on November 27th, Salas suffered a sudden hernia and was taken immediately to hospital for an operation. He was discharged in the middle of January, and returned to lead 2-G-3. Strangely, he was absent from his unit for the same time as his faithful Fiat 3-61.

There were also considerable losses during these three months, as has been recorded in these chapters. Group 2-G-3 and 3-G-3 lost twelve Fiats, and five of their pilots were killed (Gautier, Munaiz, Etayo, Martinez de Irujo and Olivera) and three wounded (Téllez, Alonso Fariña and Queipo). Squadron 8-E-3 added one more death, that of Francisco Gómez Trenor.

The 'Cadenas' suffered ten deaths: Porto, Allepuz, José Ugarte, Gascón and Gorostiza in He 45s; González del Valle, Soares de Oliveira and Macías in He 51s; and Suárez Oviedo and Cipriano Rodríguez in Ro 37s.

The bombers lost Rambaud's Do 17 and Ramón Franco's seaplane. Apart from these, Vilar, second-pilot of an He 111, was killed on November 5th.

Juan Ansaldo, Sánchez Vidal, Güerbós, Manrique Montero, Eduardo Bermejo and José Luis Calleja were killed in accidents at flying schools.

The Ebro offensive was the most difficult launched by the Government. As in earlier battles, they achieved great success during the early days but seemed to lose the initiative as soon as the action became more static. They managed to prolong the defensive phase of three months by using up all the reserves in Catalonia. But when communications with other zones became difficult, they found it practically impossible to bring in sufficient quantities of reinforcements. On the other hand, facilities for the arrival of supplies, across the Pyrenees and via the Gerona ports, were some of the best they had enjoyed. The losses and wastage of material on both sides were very great.

CHAPTER SEVEN

The Denouement

The Fighters in the Last Struggles

Once the battle of the Ebro was over, all aerial combat ended until the middle of December.

At this time, Muñoz, Murcia and García Pardo left the Condor Legion and were given the task of organising the new 5-G-5 group, which consisted of a squadron of Me 109Bs (Murcia) and another of He 112s (García Pardo). This second squadron took part in the Catalonian Campaign, their leader destroying an enemy machine at Igualada on January 19th, 1939. Formation of the Me 109B squadron was completed in March 1939, when the Condor Legion received their new Me 109Es, handing over to the Spaniards the outdated Me 109Bs.

When the new Group 5-G-5 was formed this, together with 2-G-3 and 3-G-3, became the 7th Squadron (Fighter), and Morato was appointed its Commander, Barranco replacing him in 3-G-3. Group 2-G-3 had been led temporarily by Guerrero until January 15th, when Salas returned from hospital.

At the end of December, in view of information regarding impending operations received from the South, a temporary Fiat Squadron was formed, led by Lieutenant Simón, with Alcocer, Arango, Acuña, Arvizu and Saiz, and occasionally Salvador Serra and Diego Vigueras, as its pilots. This squadron operated from Posadas aerodrome, in Córdoba, between December 30th and January 12th, 1937.

On January 12th five more Fiats, led by Guerrero and Vázquez Sagastizábal, were transferred from Catalonia to Posadas. With these machines and those of the temporary squadron, the 1st and 3rd Squadrons of 3-G-3 were reformed. Squadron 8-E-3, now led by Arístides García López, operated in conjunction with them.

The 2nd Squadron (Cuadra) and the Group leader (Salas), remained in Escatron until January 17th when they moved, together with 3-G-3, to Balaguer aerodrome (Lérida). There they were joined by the former leader of the 2nd Squadron, García Pardo, with his new Heinkel He 112s, and Group 5-G-5 (Muñoz).

When the Catalonian campaign ended, all of Group 2-G-3 (Salas) were based at Posadas: there they were joined by 8-E-3, which became a 4th Squadron. Group 3-G-3, with Morato, moved to Griñon (Madrid) and 5-G-5 (Muñoz) to Almaluez (Soria).

The Italian groups and the German group were led until the end of the war by Remondino, Tessari and Grabmann respectively. In the closing stages, as an experiment, the Italians sent fifteen Fiat G.50 monoplanes to Spain, under the leadership of Captain Bonzano, former leader of the *As de Bastos* Group. Bonzano ordered that his previous emblem should be used to identify these aircraft although they did not belong to that group. Despite a keen desire to evaluate these machines in Spain, they were never actually in combat.

In the autumn of 1938 the Nationalist fighters held a clear numerical superiority, due primarily to the fact that they had lost less machines in combat. The Government Air Force had received larger numbers of fighters (see appendices 7 and 8).

In the Spring of 1938 the Nationalist superiority in bombers had been manifest, but the Government fighter force was then almost as strong as their opponents. By the end of 1938, the Government found it difficult to maintain a total of one hundred and forty fighters in the air, a mixture of Ratas and Chatos. The Nationalists, on the other hand, had fourteen squadrons of Fiats, each with nine aircraft, and three squadrons of monoplanes. Counting the Fiats stationed in the Balearics, this gave them a total of about two hundred fighters.

In the battle of the Ebro the Ratas, which were abundant and consisted mainly of the later four-gun type, had proved more formidable than the Chatos. In Catalonia the situation was reversed, since the majority of the fighters lost were replaced by Chatos produced at the Sabadell-Reus factory (set up by using machinery from Construcciones Aeronáuticas in Getafe, and other machinery imported from the United States and Russia) and which at this time was reputed to be producing one aeroplane per day. So far as the Ratas were concerned, their replacement depended exclusively on supplies from Russia. These were not as numerous as the Government could have wished, since from 1937 they were also being supplied to the Chinese for use in the war against Japan, a conflict in which Russia had a direct interest. The Alicante factory (set up using machinery from Hispano-Suiza in Guadalajara and from Loring at Cuatro Vientos) re-built a large number of Ratas and began, without a licence or official plans, the manufacture of one hundred of these machines. However, only twelve were handed over to the Government Air Force.

Many of these Ratas were assembled after the war at Jérez, in the Talleres Experimentales del Aire, and were still flying from Tablada in the 1950s.

In Andalucia (the Pozoblanco–Peñarroya offensive) the Chatos were practically the only Government aircraft used on operations.

So far as pilots were concerned, the position on the Nationalist side had also improved considerably. By the end of 1938 almost four hundred pilots had been passed out of the Spanish schools, and to these must be added the eighty from Italy and twenty from Germany. However, these were still small numbers by comparison with approximately a thousand pilots in the Government Zone, of which about six hundred were trained in Russia, one hundred in France and the remainder in the Levante Schools (Los Alcazares, La Ribera, El Palmar, Alcantarilla, El Carmoli, La Costera, Lorca, Archena, Totana, Rabasa . . .). It must be remembered that the number of pilots lost on the Government side was considerably higher. The number of aircraft available was roughly the same on both sides: about three hundred first line machines, plus approximately one hundred and fifty school, transport and other types.

With regard to fighter pilots, in the Nationalist Zone the 3rd Course, the last of those held at Gallur had just ended, and the 4th Course was beginning at Villanubla. A large proportion of the crews in the squadrons were new. Of the fifteen initial members of 2-G-3, Salas, Guerrero and Vázquez Sagastizábal were still in the group; Morato was commanding 3-G-3. Murcia, had gone to 3-G-3 but was now in 5-G-5, together with García Pardo and Ansaldo. Allende went to replace Mendizábal in 3-G-3, when the latter was shot down on the first day of the Catalonia offensive; Arístides went to lead squadron 8-E-3, which also included Muntadas. Bermudez de Casto was killed in battle and Mazarredo in an accident. Salvador was a prisoner in Barcelona; Senra went to the Fighter School and Jesús Rubio was found to be flying a Katiuska that was captured. Of those who formed the first batch of replacements, Carlos Serra, Henricourt, Simón and Comas were still there; López Sert and Herrero were dead, Matamoros crippled and Careaga a prisoner. Bayo had gone to 5-G-5, Ibarreche, Salvador Serra and Mendoza were still active but Martínez Irujo had died and Mesía was wounded.

From the first fighter promotion, Alcocer, Manrique, Cesteros and Diego Vigueras were still flying, but Etayo and Bernal had been killed. From the second there was Saiz, Illera, Araluce and Barañano; Romagosa was dead. Cuadra, Frutos, Llovet, Alonso Allende, Alonso Calleja, Ferrer, Ruiz Hermosilla, Azqueta and Recasens had recently joined.

In Group 3-G-3, of the original members Barranco, Queipo, Ignacio Alfaro, Larios, Muerza and Robles were still flying. Mazarredo, Núñez, Gil Escoain, Montero and Figueroa were dead. Ibarra, Vela de Almazán, Alberto Santamaria, Velaz de Medrano, Murcia, Noguera and Giménez Garrido had left the group. Chapaprieta was a prisoner. Velasco, O'Connor, Bartolomé, Lacourt, Varona and Vierna were still operational. Beiztegui, Ruibal and García de Juan and Algería had left the fighters, Jurado and García Diez were killed.

From the first fighter promotion, Kindelán, García Rodríguez Carracido and Acuña were still flying; Gautier and Munaiz were killed, Alonso Fariñas and Téllez were wounded, Arrechea was shot down and taken prisoner and Epelde was another casualty. From the second fighter course Prieto, Aruizu, Calleja, González Guzmán and Ripollés were still flying. Ozores, D. Arango, Maura, Pedrosa, Pallejá, Chávarri and Marquést Maristany were recently joined. Mendizábal was taken prisoner on December 24th, 1938, and later assassinated.

Squadron 8-E-3 consisted of Arístides García López and Muntadas (veterans from 2-G-3), Mendía, Pedro Lacalle, Zorita and Garret (all from the Pilots' Course in Germany). Gómez Trenor was dead and Pazó had returned to the Parque in Seville.

The veteran fighter pilots Murcia, García Pardo and Ansaldo (founders of 2-G-3), Bayo, Ruibal and García de Juan (from the 1st, 5th and 4th Pilots' Courses) had joined 5-G-5. Muñoz had brought with him from 1-G-2 Escude (previously with the Romeos), Llovet (from the 3rd Fighter Course), Ozores and Ripollés (who had been in 3-G-3 for some time) and García Martin, Diéguez, Jiménez Millas and Rey-Stolle, who were new to fighters.

In the Government Zone the changes were far worse. Of the veterans in the fighter force, Giménez, leader of the Fighter Squadron, and Aguirre and García La Calle, who followed one another as his Chief of Staff, were still active. Castañeda, Gerrardo Gil, Justo Fernández, Francisco Alarcón, Mariano Palacios and others were instructing at the Fighter School. Cascón, a Colonel since the middle of November, was Commander of the 2nd Air Region; Puparelli was Commander of the 4th Region and, after his promotion to Lieutenant Colonel, Commander of the operations section for the Chief of Staff of the Air Forces. Alonso Vega was in the Headquarters for Air Forces (Centre); Pena and Riverola in the 7th Squadron, etc.

In the Ratas group there was still Zarauza (promoted to Major in December 19th, at the same time as Aguirre, Duarte and Morquillas), Bravo, Arias, Merono and Redondo (all Captains), Pereiro, Cano and Tarazona. At the beginning of January, the latter was rested from operations and sent to Valencia, and Calvo assumed leadership of the 3rd Squadron.

In this 3rd Squadron, since June 1938, Utrilla, Diaz, Yuste, Casola, Fernandez Prada, Gascon, Margalef, Tebar and Arres had been killed, and twelve pilots had been seriously injured. Five others had left the squadron. Altogether, thirty-four pilots had passed through this squadron, which had a complement of only twelve aircraft.

Of the fourteen original members only Tarazona was left, and of the four who had joined in June, only Calvo remained. The two who had joined in July, Pitarch and Montilla, had enjoyed better luck. Of the seven who joined in August, only Diaz was left. Of the seven who were sent there in the autumn, Sanz and Balsa remained. A really terrifying balance sheet.

In the Chatos Group, Captain Zambudio was now the leader, replacing the crippled Comas, who was promoted to Commander after losing his leg. The two Castillos (one from Andalucia and one from Valencia), Nieto, etc., were leading Squadrons.

The foreign contingents had also changed their crews. The last Italian Fiat Squadrons were led by Mezzetti, Crosara, Favini, Gasperi, Meille, Valerio and Jannicelli. The Me 109s now had as leaders Reents, Lojewsky and Von Bonin.

The Russians had abandoned Spain. There were the days after Munich, when the Russo-German pact was brewing. Apart from this, the tremendous purge of 1937 (when more than half of the Russian officers were eliminated) had made it inadvisable to travel abroad. There was also a third reason: the fact that they considered the war as lost, and it did not seem reasonable to let their men be taken prisoner. They had already used these tactics in the North when they saw that all was lost.

The Catalonian Campaign

On November 26th, ten days after the end of the battle of the Ebro, Franco ordered an attack in Catalonia, to begin on December 10th. The idea of operations against Madrid had been abandoned, since this would have needed the transfer of many more troops, with a consequent loss of time. Apart from this, they were anxious to prevent Catalonia from declaring itself independent.

Franco divided the Northern Army into two: one half retaining the same name, and still commanded by Dávila, the other designated as the Levante Army, commanded by General Orgaz. The Northern Army retained the Army Corps from Urgel (Muñoz Grandes), Maestrazgo (García Valiño), Aragón (Moscardó), CTV (Gambara), Navarre (Solchaga) and Morocco (Yagüe), which were deployed between the Pyrenees and the mouth of the Ebro, in that order.

The main action was entrusted to the Navarre and CTV Army Corps, which were to advance from the bridgehead at Serós, towards Mountblanc and Valls. The Urgel and Maestrazgo Army Corps were assigned the task of breaking through the left wing of the front, south of Tremp and upstream from the confluence of the Noguera Pallaresa with the Segre, then to advance towards Artesa de Segre and Cervera. The Aragón Army Corps, together with Division 40, (González Badia) and the Cavalry division (Monasterio), were to maintain liaison between both attacking flanks. The Moroccan Army Corps was to cross the Ebro when the Navarrese had forced the opposing XXIV Army Corps to retreat, and then to advance towards Tarragona.

The Condor Legion, with their fighters at La Cenia, the bombers at Sanjurjo (Saragossa), and their reconnaissance aircraft at Tauste and Buñuel, were given the task of supporting the Moroccan and Navarre Army Corps; they also used the auxiliary aerodrome at Zaidín. The Legionary Air Force, with fighters in Sariñena and Caspe, bombers in Valezuela (Saragossa) and Puig Moreno, and assault aircraft at Candasnos, was to support the CTV. The Spanish Air Force, which was then divided into two Brigades (Joaquín González Gallarza) at Alfamén, later at Lanaja; the Savoia S-M.81 Squadrons Army Corps. The 1st Brigade had the No 1 Ju 52 Squadron (Eduardo González Gallarza) at Alfamén, later at Lanaja; the Savoia S.M.81 Squadrons Nos 4 and 5 (Julián Rubio and Manzaneque) at Ablitas, later in Huesca; and group 7-G-4 (Sartorius) at Alfamén, later at Castejón del Puente. The new No 6 Squadron, (J. Ansaldo), formed from groups 8-G-18 (Bermúdez de Castro) and 9-G-18 (Martínez de Pisón), operated from Candasnos, later Albarratex and Bell-Puig.

The four independent groups (1-G-2 and 4-G-2 with Heinkel He 51s, 6-G-15 with Heinkel He 45s and 4-G-12 with Romeo Ro 37s), were based in Castejón del Puente and Pomar, moving later to Albatarrex, Araño, Bell-Puig and Prat de Llobregat. The leaders of these groups were now Eyaralar, Fernández Pérez, Llop and Teodoro Vives.

The two fighter groups from No 7 Squadron (Morato) remained at Escatrón.

In León the 3rd Fighter Group (5-G-5) was being formed. For a while it consisted of only one squadron of Heinkel He 112s, but this was joined later by a second squadron of Me 109Bs. These latter aircraft were received at the end of the Catalonian Campaign, when Me 109Es were arriving to equip the Condor Legion's three squadrons. Two or three Me 109Es arrived in La Cenia, on trial, during the last few days of December.

The total deployment of the Nationalist Air Force on December 23rd is shown in Appendix 12.

On the Government side Vicente Rojo was preparing an offensive in the Pozoblanco sector, which was to be combined with a diversionary attack in Jaén and a disembarkation on the beaches of Motril. For this he took the Army Corps XVII (García Vallejo) and XII (Ibarrola) and Divisions 6 (Marquina), 28 (Mayordomo) and 52 (Torruz) from Levante, with which he formed the Agrupación Toral. Agrupacón 'C' was later formed with divisions 38 (Fernández Sánchez), 62 (Hortelano) and 71 (Cuerda) from the same sector. The Army Corps XXII and the Agrupaciones Toral and 'C' were centred in Pozoblanco, and this left the Army Corps XVII in Jaén, where it was a threat both to Córdoba and to Granada. The disembarkation in Motril was to have been carried out by a reinforced brigade, but there were difficulties.

Preparations advanced much more slowly on the Government side, and they were not able to begin their plan of campaign until January 4th. Because of bad weather Franco had to delay his offensive in Catalonia until December 23rd. But despite the bad weather Katiuskas bombed La Cenia on December 16th, when two Me 109s were destroyed on the ground, and the Katiuskas of Gomez and Ricondo (from the 1st Squadron) were lost, and their crew members killed.

On December 23rd 1938, the attack began, amidst fog and a snowstorm; in the Urgel Army Corps sector (Tremp) the snowfall was especially heavy. After the enemy's defences had been saturated by a two-hour artillery barrage, the Nationalist Air Force followed with an attack which lasted for a further forty-five minutes. No enemy aircraft were sighted, but they did make an appearance during a second Nationalist sortie.

The results of the first day of the offensive were not very encouraging. The only advances were those made by the Navarre Army Corps and the CTV; furthermore, the latter had their left flank unprotected. On the Noguera Pallaresa line no progress was made during the ensuing three days.

Vigón, the Northern Army's Chief of Staff, ordered the Aragon Army Corps to break through the front at Balaguer; simultaneously, two Divisions of the Maestrazgo Army Corps were to attempt an advance along the southern bank of the Serge. These forces were assigned large quantities of artillery, all available tanks and three anti-tank guns loaned by the Condor Legion. These attacks began on December 28th, without much initial success.

The air force and the tanks defended the exposed left flank of the CTV, whilst the Navarre Army Corps reached the outskirts of Granadella. The Moroccan Army Corps failed to cross the river because of floodwater and snowstorms. It became clear that the only decisive move must come from the Navarre troops' sector, but the enemy was also aware of this and concentrated all the reserves from the XV Corps in Granadella.

The Government high command had planned to allow the enemy to advance for a period of 10 or 12 days, by which time they anticipated they would have made an incursion of some 9–12 miles (15–20km) on a narrow front. It was then intended to counter-attack from the rear, with Army Corps V and XV, trapping them in a pocket.

As in previous months, during the attack south of the Ebro, the headquarters of the Popular Army was in Castelldans. In view of the situation on December 24th, the Central Chief of Staff ordered an immediate counterattack. On the afternoon of the 24th, the leader of the Ebro Army gave a verbal appraisal of the situation to the leaders of the V and XV Army Corps. The V Corps, reinforced by two companies of armoured vehicles, was to attack in the direction of Borjas Blancas–Sarroca; the XV Corps, reinforced by two battalions of armoured vehicles, was to cross from Granadella to Mayals.

On December 24th, 3-G-3 achieved a notable victory, destroying nine of a squadron of eleven Natachas. According to Larios, they were flying over Cap de la Serra, escorting Junkers and Savoia bombers, when they sighted about 1,600ft (500m) below them eleven Natachas with a strong escort of Ratas. It is probable that the Rata pilots saw the Fiats too late to intervene, but Larios considered that they acted completely irresponsibly. He commented: ". . . as soon as the bombers saw the Fiats bearing down on them, and realised that their escort was not fulfilling its task, they lost confidence, diving like madmen, hurtling towards the shelter of the Sierra, which was their best defence under these circumstances, when conditions were so unequal."

As before, at Brunete, Morato's group had almost completely destroyed a squadron of Natachas. In this engagement Captain Mendizábal, the leader of Squadron 7-E-3, was lost because of a stupid mistake; he was later replaced by Allende. Mendizábal escaped from his damaged aircraft by parachute and, landing in the enemy zone, was taken prisoner; he was later assassinated. In this combat Morato shot down three Natachas, Velasco two, and Lacour, Larios, Ruibal and Recasens one each.

Also on December 24th, the 3rd Rata Squadron was moved to this sector, their task of defending the port at Barcelona being ended. The next day Zarauza and Bravo arrived from Paris, bringing news of proposals to obtain new and very fast monoplanes from the United States.

On the morning of December 25th, the CTV's advance was halted by the 9th Brigade (Montalvo) of the 11th Division, and was later forced to withdraw when two brigades from the same Division were brought in to strengthen the Government defences. During the day Divisions 45 (Ramón Soliva) and 46 (Leal) also arrived, and they were able to contain the advance towards Castelldans until January 3rd. On that day the Navarre Army Corps reached the Borjas Blancas–Montblanc road, near to Vinaixa. This new threat made it necessary to move the V Corps command post from Castelldans to Borjas Blancas.

In this period the Spanish Fiats destroyed five Ratas, two on December 29th (Alfaro and Prieto), one on January 2nd (Henricourt) and two on the 3rd (Vázquez, and O'Connor). Tarazona recorded that from his squadron alone Balsa had to force-land at Borjas Blancas on the 27th; Díaz made a wheels-up landing on the 29th and three Ratas were damaged on the 30th. Tarazona claimed that his squadron shot down one Fiat on December 26th, one Me 109 on the 29th and two Fiats on the 30th.

The *As de Bastos* Group had their greatest success on December 28th, destroying 14 Chatos for the loss of one Fiat, and on the 30th *La Cucaracha* Group claimed the destruction of ten machines, again for the loss of a single Fiat.

In January the new leader of the Government Fighter Squadron, La Calle, ordered that the senior pilots who had been involved in almost continuous operations for months on end should now be rested, their place being taken by the abundance of new pilots.

Tarazona's Rata, No 193, which had carried him safely through so many combats, was badly damaged in operations on January 3rd. The next day he collected a new machine from Valls, which he flew to La Señera, an aerodrome situated on the main road from Valencia to Chiva. During the first few days of January the 4th Rata Squadron lost two of its patrol leaders.

On January 3rd the entire front was in a state of flux: Artesa de Segre was surrounded and fell on the 4th. In the south the Ebro was crossed and a bridgehead established at Ascó. A successful advance was made at Lérida, which finally relieved the left flank of the CTV, allowing Alfés and Castelldans to be occupied on the following day.

On January 4th the Popular Army began its offensive in the Pozoblanco sector, initially with some success. But the developments in Catalonia meant that it was already too late. Receiving news of this new Government Campaign, Franco ordered one Division to be transferred from Catalonia, but the other 21 Divisions in the Pozoblanco Sector (20 Infantry and 1 Cavalry) were sufficient to bring the offensive to an end. The Division which was transferred, No 40 (González Badía), had been intended to become the nucleus of a new Catalonian Army Corps, but in view of these circumstances it was never formed.

On January 5th, Borjas Blancas fell and on the 6th the Navarre forces entered Vinaixa. Once Borjas Blancas and Artesa de Segre were occupied the entire front, from Balguer to Lerida, was pushed back. On January 9th the Aragon Army Corps and the CTV joined forces in Mollerusa.

By that time the Popular Army had suffered 70,000 casualties and the Nationalists 40,000, according to Líster. Information of Nationalist origin speaks of 23,000 prisoners and 5,000 left dead on the battlefield, which also agrees with Líster's figures. Thus the battle was virtually over, since these losses could not be replaced from sources in Catalonia, and there was no time to bring in reinforcements from the Central region. Territory occupied by the Nationalists in this campaign amounted to about 1,158sq miles (3,000km^2). There was considerable talk, most of it Government propaganda, regarding establishment of a new line of resistance, but this proved wishful thinking.

On January 8th the second phase of the Catalonian offensive began with a bombing attack on Montsant. The Condor Legion was sent to provide support in the Navarre Army Corps' sector, and tanks and anti-aircraft guns were also assigned to this Corps. On January 9th, despite thick fog, aerial reconnaissance sorties were made. On the 11th the infantry was getting closer to Montblanc, although their right flank was exposed and vulnerable. However, on the 12th Montblanc fell and the march to Valls began. On the same day the Condor Legion's Me 109s attacked the aerodromes at Valls, El Vendrell and Vilafranca del Panadés, and the Fiats from *La Cucaracha* Group shot down four Chatos for the loss of two of their number.

On January 13th Angel Salas, in his new rank of Commander, returned from hospital to reassume leadership of Group 2-G-3, which was still based at Escatrón.

On January 14th, Valls fell. Solchaga, after discussions with the Condor Legion, decided to advance from there to Tarragona, perhaps one of the boldest decisions of the war. The march began on January 15th, with the heavy anti-aircraft batteries in the rear, and with an air umbrella provided by the Condor Legion. As part of the softening-up process, the port of Tarragona was bombed by the Condor Legion, supported by aircraft from the Balearics, and during this attack three ships were sunk.

The heavy anti-aircraft batteries, travelling narrow roads, were unable to maintain the pace of the march; a pace that, at the end of the day, saw the Moroccan Army Corps at Tarragona, having covered a distance of 31 miles (50km), in another of this Corps' prodigious marches. On arrival, they were surprised to find the Navarre troops already there, amongst them their old companions of the 12th Division (Asensio). Two other Divisions of the Navarre Army Corps were also well known to them; the 4th (Alonso Vega) and the 5th (Bautista Sánchez). They had fought alongside these Divisions at Brunete and now, as then, they were all under Yagüe's command.

On January 17th, advancing from Tarragona, they reached the river Gayá. The CTV was occupying Santa Coloma de Queralt; the Aragón and Maestrazgo Army Corps were at Cervera; and the Urgel Army Corps was approaching Pons, which it occupied the next day. On this same day, the Spanish fighter groups, including the 1st Squadron of Group 5-G-5, were transferred to Balaguer to simplify the task of providing close support.

General Vicente Rojo, commanding all Government forces in Catalonia, hoped to stabilise the front on the line as it stood on January 17th. For this, he counted on a breathing space of several days, which he thought the enemy would need to regroup their forces after such a long advance.

Franco, however, was not prepared to give his adversaries any respite: on January 19th the attack was renewed. By the 26th Solchaga and Yagüe were advancing parallel to the coast and Gambara was moving towards Sabadell. García Valiño and Moscardo were not long delayed at Barcelona, for no resistance was offered, and at Manresa y Cardona, on the river Llobregat, they turned towards the north.

On the first day of this third phase of the offensive, the Spanish Fiats had their last battle in Catalonia, and the He 112s were involved in their first and only combat. Morato shot down one Chato, and García Pardo a Rata; this latter victory representing the only one recorded by the He 112 group. Shortly before the capitulation of Barcelona, the *La Cucaracha* Group destroyed four Ratas for the loss of one Fiat. According to Tarazona, Pitarch was killed, Calvo force-landed on a road, and Díaz and Montilla managed to reach Villajuiga and Celra respectively.

At this point in the campaign, principal concern of Nationalist leaders was to prevent enemy aircraft from crossing to the central zone. To this end, the Condor Legion was moved to Lérida and Sabadell within twenty-four hours; the Me 109s which had been operating from Valls since the 21st also went to

Sabadell. The Italian fighter groups also moved their bases forward to Vendrell and Reus.

On February 1st a formation of Ratas attempted to reach Levante, but were intercepted by the *As de Bastos* Group, which destroyed two of them near to Palamós. The 3rd Rata Squadron, which had only five machines airworthy, was moved to Figueras.

On February 5th this aerodrome was attacked by the Fiats and Me 109s: when they turned for home they left behind a shambles of flaming wreckage. The most vivid account of this action is that recorded by Tarazona:

"February 5th. In the airfield hut at Figueras complete chaos reigned. All telephone links were cut. The staff of the airfield were running hither and thither in complete disorder. Several aircraft being serviced in the open presented the Fascist machines with an excellent target. There were several lorries loaded with fuel around the perimeter of the airfield, without any sort of cover. Neither their drivers nor anyone else had considered the danger of leaving them uncamouflaged. Disorganisation spread like pus in an infected wound. The germs which could be harmful to the Republic were multiplying rapidly, hindering the work of those of us who still believed in the eventual triumph of the people and of reason.

"When I wanted to know who was in command I was unable to obtain a positive answer. Neither did anyone know where the leaders were, or who they were. I tried again and again to make contact with Group, but it was useless.

"Several of us manhandled my fighter to the edge of the airfield and concealed it as well as possible. A noise overhead caught my attention: several squadrons of Fiats were flying in from the south-west. The airfield staff began to run and hide.

"I shouted to Manolo, who had just hidden his 'Mosca' by the side of mine, suggesting that we should man the light machine-guns. We had just landed from a sortie, our machines out of fuel and ammunition. The mechanics and armourers were in the shelters when we landed, as the airfield had been bombed only minutes before. Four of us had landed our 'Moscas' amongst the bomb craters. Miraculously we had escaped when we found ourselves beneath enemy fighters without fuel or ammunition.

"Some of our Chatos were circling the airfield, attempting to gain a haven. Without ammunition and low on fuel they were easy prey for the Fiats which came sweeping in, their guns blazing. Manolo and I did our best to protect the Chatos as they landed, banging away with a pair of machine-guns.

"There were five Chatos. One of them, which had a dead engine, was being harried by two Fiats. It came in to land, hit the ground heavily, bounced off again, and went smack into one of the lorries loaded with fuel. There was a tremendous explosion and within two minutes half of Figueras airfield was in flames.

"Manolo and I were situated almost in the centre of the airfield, firing at the Fiats that were attacking the Chatos as they landed, one after the other. Two of the pilots were wounded. When all the Chatos were on the ground we rushed to move them, but a group of German monoplanes arrived to add the finishing touches to the inferno. The Me 109s made a clean sweep. Petrol lorries, aircraft, cars, everything was fuel for the flames, the inevitable product of impotence and fear . . ."

On February 6th it was the turn of Vilajuiga aerodrome, which had received some slight attention the day before, and during that action an Me 109 was lost. When the second attack was launched, two Ratas and three Chatos managed to take off before bombs began to fall on the airfield: by the time the Nationalist attackers were winging their way back to their bases, no less than thirty-five fighters and two bombers had been destroyed on the ground.

On this same date, the pilots of Morato's Group were taken in service buses to visit Barcelona. The journey lasted almost five hours, since they had to make a long detour down the coast, via Tarragona, and cross a large number of temporary bridges. The direct route was impassable, as many of the bridges were still in ruins. According to Larios, Barcelona was filthy and disorganised. Fortunately, these conditions were offset by the current of excitement and relief that prevailed, and shops and market stalls were doing a brisk trade. It was the harbour, in particular, that illustrated how recent was the struggle: bomb-scarred and wreckage-strewn, the masts or upper works of no less than thirty wrecked vessels choked its waters.

The occupation of Catalonia was completed on February 10th, and several of the pilots who had been taken prisoner were set free, with the exception of Mendizábal who, by then, had already been assassinated.

The nine Fiats of 2-G-3 which still remained in Catalonia, were flown to Posadas aerodrome, in Cordoba, on February 15th, where they joined up with the rest of the group. Morato's Group remained in Catalonia to take part in the big victory parade planned to take place in Barcelona on February 21st, and in a naval display at Tarragona a week later. At Barcelona, 3-G-3 flew in formation above the city, traversing the entire length of the Avenida Diagonal with their machines spelling out the letters FET (*Falange Española Tradicionalista*). At Tarragona they roared past the flagship of the Nationalist Fleet, the *Canarias*, their propellers almost cutting the water, as Generalissimo Franco stood on the cruiser's deck in proud salute.

Although the occupation of the island of Minorca had taken place early in February, this operation is worth recording briefly because of the somewhat outstanding part played by the Nationalist Air Force.

On the afternoon of February 8th it was learned in Pollensa that a man named Thomas was leading the uprising which had begun at Ciudadela, on the isle of Minorca, and that he had been wounded.

Fate decreed that the officer in charge of the workshops at Pollensa was Captain Miguel Thomas, brother of the injured man on Minorca. Captain Thomas tried to persuade Captain Carlos Pombo to take him to the island in an He 59, but the leader of Squadron AS-88 would not authorise the flight without consulting his superior officer. Pombo took off on a night reconnaissance sortie off Port de la Selva (Gerona), and when he returned to Pollensa he discovered that another He 59 had taken off for Ciudadela, carrying Commander Noreña and Captain Thomas.

Before leaving Pollensa, Noreña had arranged for three torpedo boats carrying armed soldiers to proceed to the island, and when he reached Ciudadela he took command of the men involved in the uprising, whilst awaiting the arrival of his seaborne army.

Pombo was sent on a second sortie that night, to the area of Mahon, and had been given permission to land at Ciudadela. From there his observer, Lieutenant Romero, went by rubber dinghy to see Noreña, who ordered an immediate return to Mallorca to arrange for a number of resolute officers to be ferried over at once as the morale of the officers in the three battalions at Ciudadela, Ferrerías and San Cristóbal was weakening.

When Pombo arrived back at Pollensa on the morning of the 9th and made contact with the island's authorities, he discovered that Mahon had already surrendered. In fact, at 03.00hrs Luis Gonzalez de Ubieta had decided to embark on the English cruiser *Devonshire* after beginning negotiations with the Nationalist emissary Fernando Sartorius. This marked the end of his recent appointment as the leader of Minorca. About six hundred people followed his lead and another seventy-five went aboard the sailing ship *Carmen Pico*.

Pombo flew over Mahón that morning to find it gay with Nationalist flags, then returned to Ciudadela, where the three torpedo boats had then arrived. In the afternoon a convoy arrived from Tarragona and Noreña handed over command to the Colonel in charge of this expedition.

The Battle of Pozoblanco

When the battle of the Ebro was over, the Central Chief of Staff for the Popular Army prepared an offensive for the Central Armies Group. This was intended to give the Catalonian Armies Group time to reorganise themselves, as they had been very much weakened by the battle and by the repatriation of the International brigades. Even if they mobilised all available troops in Catalonia, it was calculated that they needed to transfer about 30,000 men from the Centre. The arms could enter directly from France.

According to Vicente Rojo, this offensive had been planned by the middle of December. The main action was to be carried out by the Extremadura Army, along the Pozoblanco–Peñarroya line. To support them, two diversionary manoeuvres had been evolved. The first was to be carried out by the Andalusian Army, part of this operation consisting of disembarking a reinforced brigade in Motril; the second was entrusted to the Central Army, whose job was to cut off communications between the Madrid front and Extremadura.

The leader of the Armies Group was opposed to this disembarkation at Motril, which was to be carried out five days before the main action: this operation was finally vetoed, although the troops had already embarked. Also, the need to take supplies to Madrid created transport difficulties, and this delayed the manoeuvre yet again.

The Nationalist leaders were aware of these preparations, and learned that the XVII Corps was in the province of Jaen, with their command post at Mancha Real. Unusual guerrilla activity in Granada and Extremadura indicated that the attack was imminent, but they did not know exactly where this would be launched. At the end of December troop concentrations in the

Pozoblanco sector suggested that this was the chosen area, but the XVII Corps remained an unknown factor, as it had not moved from Jaén and could still attack Granada or Córdoba.

Because of this, two of the reserve divisions, with only nine Russian tanks at their disposal, were placed in Cordoba (to the south and the north of the Guadalquivir) and a third was positioned behind Granada. This exposed the left flank in Extremadura, which was then without reserves. The Generalissimo sent Division 11 (Bartomeu) to this sector, where it was stationed in the Merida-Villanueva de la Serena zone. This division was able to cross the Roman bridge at Medellin twenty-four hours after it had been repaired temporarily, making it possible for them to arrive at the critical moment of the battle. Days later, other reinforcements were using the same bridge: Divisions 74 (Arias), 81 (Ollo) and 41 (González Badía), which had come from Guadalajara, Teruel and Catalonia respectively, the Rodrigo Group from the 71st Division, nine Battalions from the Moroccan Army Corps, nine more from Aragon and ten unattached battalions, together with eleven batteries of artillery.

The attack began on January 5th in the Hinojosa del Duque sector, preceded by a heavy artillery barrage and bombardment from the air. Shortly after this preparatory stage, two divisions of the XII Army Corps (Ibarrola), spearheaded by forty tanks, forced a breech 5 miles (8km) wide between the hills at Trapera and Patuda. By the second day of the offensive they had occupied an area of 96sq miles (250km^2).

The sector under attack was defended by Division 22 (Erquicia) of the Cordoba Army Corps, this Division having to its right and left Divisions 23 (Muñoz Castellanos) and 24 (Rodríguez de la Herran). To face the enemy avalanche Division 122 (Redondo)—reserve Division for the sector—was moved to occupy the second line of defence and the leaders of the Southern Army left the direction of this battle to Redondo. He ordered the other two reserve divisions, No 60 (Jiménez) and 112 (Baturone), to join the action immediately. With these three divisions, plus the remainder of the 22nd Division, a Group was formed and General Muñoz Castellanos, leader of the 23rd Division, was placed in command.

In this sector, on the night of January 6th/7th, the Noria and del Peru sierras, situated on the second defensive line, were lost to the enemy. By bitter fighting Mano de Hierro on the first line of defence, the hill at el Medico on the second, and Sierra Tejonera, to its rear, were held by the Nationalists. This prevented the enemy from expanding the breech made on the previous day, and saved Peñarroya from falling into their hands.

On January 7th Government forces occupied Fuenteovejuna, and by the end of that day they had captured some 193sq miles (500km^2) of territory. Other gains were made by the 47th Division (Recalde) of the XXII Army Corps, and they reached Granja de Torrehermosa on the 8th, representing an advance of 18½ miles (30km). A similar penetration was achieved by column 'F', and these gains marked an unprecedented achievement in Government offensives, gains which were made when their numbers were inferior to those of the opposing forces.

On the Nationalist left flank the Alvarez Rementería Regiment (Antonio), from the 22nd Division, defended the Trapera Sierra until the arrival of the 11th Division on January 6th. This latter Division withstood repeated attacks by the Government forces in the Trapera, Masegara and Torozo sierras, and prevented them from expanding the breech on this flank.

Column 'F', which had discovered that success breeds success, penetrated between the Agrupacion Toral and the XXII Corps on January 7th, and occupied Blázquez and Peraleda de Saucejo. From this point they turned northwards, towards Monterrubio, with the objective of surrounding Divisions 24 and 102 (Castejón), which were holding defensive positions to the east of Cabeza del Buey.

The Nationalist 74th Division arrived in this area on the afternoon of the 6th, and in accordance with specific orders from the Generalissimo, united with Division 11, 40 and 81 to form the García Escámez Agrupación. Their prime task was to attack towards Peraleda and los Blázquez, to relieve the pressure on the 11th Division's flank as quickly as possible.

The XXII Army Corps (Divisions 10, 47 and 70, led by Sampere, Recalde and Arcas), was then occupying more than half of the perimeter of the pocket extending into the Nationalist lines. They did not dare risk advances towards Alanis (the road to Seville), Azuaga (road to Llerena) or Campillo de Llerena (road to Mérida), as long as the enemy held the strong points of sierra Trapera and Mano de Hierro.

On January 11th violent rainstorms helped to paralyse this first phase of the offensive. On the same day the Chief of Staff of the attacking force radioed the following message to the Central Chief of Staff:

"Once again the usual pattern has been repeated. As soon as the subordinate leaders find themselves having to exercise initiative on the field . . . indecision comes, and movement slows down . . . The manoeuvre could have been successful. Reality has proved this to be so; but considerable time has now been lost, and with each passing day the situation becomes more difficult and dangerous."

When this first phase began the only Nationalist aircraft in the South were the Baquera Aero group in Granada, Martínez Mejías' mixed 86-70 Group (which included He 70s, Ju 86s and He 123s) and the Fiat 8-E-3 squadron, then led by Arístides García Lopez, based at Posadas. When the Nationalist Air Force became aware of the huge preparations being made by the enemy, a new provisional squadron was formed, by taking one Fiat from each of the six Spanish squadrons. Led by Simón, this squadron arrived at Posadas on December 30th to reinforce Squadron 8-E-3. Its pilots included Simón, Alcocer, Saiz, Arvizu and Arango, and they were joined later by Acuña, Salvador Serra and Diego Vigueras.

On January 5th the Fiats made two sorties, encountering heavy anti-aircraft fire. On the 6th they were not in operation, but two sorties were made on the 7th and three on the 8th, patrolling the key sectors of Peñarroya, Peraleda de Saucejo and Monterrubio. As the Fiats took off for their second sortie on January 9th, Lieutenant Simón had to abort when his engine failed. Alcocer, Arvizu and Arango continued to the front, where they encountered enemy fighters at Monterrubio. Alcocer shot down one Chato which was confirmed, and Arvizu claimed a probable.

The following day Simón, Alcocer, Vigueras, Saiz, Arango and Acuna were involved in a dogfight at Fuenteovejuna, a combat which was made extremely difficult due to constant intervention by their own anti-aircraft guns. Nevertheless, Simón destroyed one Chato, making his fifth victory (and one which was confirmed by the anti-aircraft crews); Luca de Tena of Squadron 8-E-3 shot down another Chato.

On January 12th the leaders of the 1st and 3rd Squadrons of 2-G-3, Vázquez Sagastizábal and Guerrero, received orders to proceed to the South, and they left Escatrón for Posadas. Upon their arrival, the Fiats of Simón's provisional squadron were integrated into Squadrons 1-E-3 and 3-E-3.

On January 17th, although the weather was still bad, the Extremadura Army resumed their attack. The fundamental objective was to eliminate the defence at sierra Trapera, since it was vital to widen the breech in the Nationalist lines, and to provide reliable lines of communication to reassure the troops which were inside the pocket.

The XVII Army Corps (García Vallejo) attacked energetically from outside, supported initially by Divisions 64 (Calderon) and 73 (Carro). A simultaneous attack was made from inside the pocket by the new Agrupación 'C', formed from Divisions 38 (Fernández Sánchez), 61 (Hortelano) and 71 (Cuerda). Later, the 19th Division ('Juanín') also took part in the attack.

The Nationalist 11th Division did not yield, clinging tenaciously to its positions. To the extent that its strength was reduced by half, which accounted for the proud nickname bestowed by the Andalusians, which began to call them 'Division five and a half'. Their sacrifice was not in vain, for their resistance was to prove decisive to the final outcome of the battle.

On January 19th the three Fiat squadrons were in operation, led by Guerrero, Vázquez Sagastizábal, and Aristides García Lopez. Their mission was to escort He 70s, Savoia S-M.81s and Ju 52s of the 1st Air Brigade, which had been moved to the South, on a bombing sortie over Peraleda de Saucejo. However, they met no enemy fighters on that day, nor the following day. Bad weather prevented air operations on the 21st.

On January 23rd, Mánuel Vázquez Sagastizábal, who had the highest total of victories since the formation of 2-G-3, was killed in combat.

Vázquez, who was known also as 'Patiño', was carrying a cigarette case which Garcia Morato had given him. This was engraved with Morato's initials and as both Vázquez and Morato were similar in appearance, the enemy were convinced that they had killed the latter.

The operational record of 2-G-3 reported these events as follows:

"Escort sortie for the bombers. Before reaching Azuaga, rendezvous point for the aircraft, anti-aircraft fire drew our attention to a group of enemy machines which we attacked. When they scattered we returned to patrol over Azuaga, except for the flight led by Captain Vázquez, which continued to pursue the enemy and managed to bring them to combat between Cabeza Mesada and Hinojosa del Duque. As a result of this Captain Vázquez was shot down. He took to his parachute and landed in the enemy zone where, according to information from Cabeza Mesada, he was seen being carried away on a stretcher. Second Lieutenant Manrique shot down one Chato, and Second Lieutenant Vigueras claimed one probable victory."

On January 24th eight Fiats from Squadron 2-E-3, together with five from Squadron 8-E-3, fought against nine Chatos, of which they destroyed four (Arístides, Muntada, Certeros and Frutos) and claimed two probables (Ibarreche and Luca de Tena). Two Fiats of Squadron 8-E-3, flown by Mendía and Perico Lacalle, were in collision: their pilots escaped by parachute and landed in the enemy zone. Azqueta's engine stalled when he was flying at low level and he made a crash landing, his machine turning turtle. The victories scored by Muntadas and Cesteros brought their individual totals to five each. From that time onwards aerial activity decreased.

The Extremadura Army launched its last attacks on January 23rd. By then, the García Escámez and Muñoz Agrupaciones had already been counter-attacking on both flanks of the pocket for some days. On the 22nd Peraleda de Saucejo was re-captured, Fuenteovejuna on the 25th and on the 27th both Agrupaciones joined forces. By February the 4th the front was re-established more or less on the lines which had existed at the beginning of the Government offensive.

On January 30th, Squadron 1-E-3 was operating under the leadership of Captain Carlos Serra for the first time since his arrival from Catalonia to replace Vázquez.

There were still enemy aircraft operating in the Peñarroya-Fuente Sancha sector. On February 9th Aristides shot down two Chatos and Manrique, Alcocer and Frutos each added one to their scores. Garret and Zorita, both from Squadron 8-E-3, each claimed a probable. With these new victories Manrique and Alcocer each reached a total of five, and they were included in the list of 'aces' in the 19th and 20th positions. The three positions above them were occupied by Simón, Muntadas and Cesteros.

On February 15th the nine Fiats from 2-G-3 flew from Escatrón to Posadas, led by Commander Salas. The independent Squadron 8-E-3 remained at the same aerodrome, but on March 13th they became part of Group 2-G-3, forming its fourth squadron.

The Final Offensive

When the Catalonian campaign was over, the glorious Northern Army was disbanded and all the Nationalist forces were distributed between the Levante Army (Orgaz), the Central Army (Saliquet) and the Southern Army (Queipo de Llano). Dávila was now occupied exclusively at the Ministry of Defence.

The Galician (Aranda), Castille (Varela), Aragón (Moscardó) and Urgel (Muñoz) Army Corps, and the Agrupaciones of Divisions of the Albarracín (Latorre) and Guadalajara (Perales), with a total of twenty divisions, were all integrated in the Levante Army.

The Central Army consisted of the Army Corps from Madrid (Espinosa de los Monteros), Maestrazgo (García Valiño), Navarre (Solchaga), CTV (Gambara) and Toledo (Ponte), and the Agrupaciones of Divisions from Somosierra (Serrador) and the Tagus (Múgica), with a total of twenty-one Infantry Divisions and the 1st Cavalry Division (Monasterio).

The Southern Army still consisted of the Army Corps from Extremadura (Solans), Andalucia (Muñoz Castellanos), Córdoba (Borbón) and Granada (González Espinosa), which were joined by the Moroccan Army Corps (Yagüe), which replaced the García Escámez Agrupacion when these divisions returned to their original Corps. This made a total of sixteen Infantry Divisions and the 2nd Cavalry Division (Gete). To support these divisions there were about 600 tanks and 2,500 field guns. Division 50 (Coco) was still garrisoned in Catalonia, and 151 was in Africa.

So far as the Air Force was concerned, there were plans to organise two more Air Brigades, but this did not come to fruition. The entire Spanish Air Force was distributed between the 1st Air Brigade (Joaquín González Gallarza) and the 2nd (Alfonso de Orleáns), and the Levante Army's Comandancia Principal de Aeronáutica (Apolinar Sáez de Buruaga).

Initially, in the Air Army's General instruction, issued from Saragossa on February 20th, 1939, an order was given for the 1st Air Brigade to operate in Mérida and Azuaga, the 2nd Air Brigade in Veladas (the S-M.79s) and Almoroz (the Ca 310s), the 3rd Air Brigade in Bello and Ojos Negros, the Condor Legion in Ávila and Barcience, and the Legionary Air Force in Matacán, Olmedo, Escalona and Casa Vieja. The Army Co-operation Groups received the following instructions for their deployment:

"Group 4-G-12 will occupy Benquerencia aerodrome, Group 1-G-2 and 5-G-17 Villa del Prado and Groups 4-G-2 and 6-G-15 Teruel." So far as the fighters were concerned, 2-G-3 was to occupy Azuaga aerodrome, 3-G-3 and 5-G-5 Griñón and 6-G-6 Bello.

With this deployment, the 2nd Air Brigade, the Condor Legion, the Legionary Air Force, the Army Co-operation Groups 1-G-2 and 5-G-17, and the fighter Groups 3-G-3 and 5-G-5 were assigned to the Central Army. The Southern Army was supported by the 1st Air Brigade, the 4-G-12 Romeo Group and the 2-G-3 Fiat Group. This left the 3rd Air Brigade (in fact the Levante Air Force) and Groups 4-G-2 and 6-G-15 in Aragón at the disposal of the Levante Army). These transfers were to begin on February 23rd and be completed by March 5th.

Despite these instructions, the 1st Air Brigade retained their 1st Squadron (Eduardo Gonzalez Gallarza) at Peñaflor, although it moved later to Veladas, and No 4 Squadron (Julian Sartorius) was also at Peñaflor. Group 5-G-17 (Baquera), which moved from Granada to the Centre, had some captured Natachas added to its strength.

The Fighter Group 2-G-3 (Salas) and Squadron 8-E-3 (Arístides), remained at Posadas aerodrome, together with the Mixed Group 86-70 (Martínez Mejías).

The 2nd Air Brigade was stationed at del Valle del Tajo and Extremadura aerodromes. No 2 Squadron (Arranz) and 3 (Palacios) were moved from Castejón del Puente to Villanubla, then to Veladas and finally to Mérida; No 6 squadron (Ansaldo) also belonged to this Brigade. Group 4-G-2 (Fernández Pérez) moved to Almorox, and Group 4-G-12 (Pérez Cela) went to Posadas; 6-G-15 (Llop) went from Bell-Puig to Saragossa and later to Almaluez. The Fighter Group 3-G-3 (Barranco) operated from Griñon, near Madrid, where Morato set up the 7th Squadron's Headquarters. Group 5-G-5 was split into two; the He 112 squadron (García Pardo) remained in Almaluez, and the Me 109Bs (Muñoz and Murcia) went to Griñon.

The new No 8 squadron (Frutos) was attached with Groups 8-G-27 (Ibarra), 10-G-25 (Rueda) and 11-G-25 (R. Guerrero) and operated from Saragossa under the Levante Army, in the same way as the groups based at Almaluez (Soria). Group 1-G-2, then equipped with Chatos, went to Villa de Prado.

During the first few days of March the Legionary Air Force placed the *As de Bastos* and *La Cucaracha* Groups in Escalono and Delta (Casa Vieja) respectively. The bombers moved to Matacan and the Army Co-operation aircraft to Olmedo.

The Condor Legion based its fighters at Barcience (Torrijos) and its bombers at Avila, Escalona and Salamanca. These transfers from Saragossa took place on March 11th, and Commander Härle was killed during this movement. On March 5th Von Bonin, Mölder's successor in command of the 3rd Squadron of Me 109s, destroyed the last machine to fall in the Spanish War: a Chato, over Alicante.

In Saragossa, the Condor Legion's three fighter squadrons were equipped with the new Me 109Es, powered by Daimler-Benz DB 601A engines. Both the Me 109E-1 and E-3 were in use, the former having four M.G.17 machine-guns, the latter two M.G.17s in the nose and two M.G.FF 20mm cannons, one in each wing. The highest factory number I located for the Me 109s was 6-136. Higher numbers have been quoted, but these relate to the Me 109F version, which arrived a long time after the war had ended. The Me 109Bs went to the León Air Park, as did the aircraft of the Mixed Group 5-G-5 at a later date.

The Government still had four armies established on a war footing: the Levante (Leopoldo Menendez), the Centre (Segismundo Casado, later Prada), the Extremadura (Escobar), and the Andalusian (Moriones, later Menoyo). The Army Corps I (Barceló, later Gallego), II (Bueno, later Zulueta), III (Oretga, later Fernández Recio) and IV (Mera) formed the Central Army.

In the Catalonian Campaign 21 divisions from the Eastern and Ebro Armies had been lost, a reprise of the earlier Northern Campaign, except that in the latter the losses in men and materials had been in more modest proportions. These 21 Divisions represented some 58 per cent of the 36 Divisions that were engaged at the beginning of the battle.

The Extremadura Army included Army Corps VI (Gallego), VII (Martín Calvo) and VIII (Sáez de San Pedro, later Bertomeu). Army Corps IX (Menoyo, later Gutiérrez de Miguel) and XXII (Bernal Seguar) formed the Andalusian Army, and Corps XIII (Romero, later Fulgencio González

Gómez), XVI (Palacios), XIX (Vidal) and XXI (Güemes) were all part of the Levante Army. This left Army Corps XVII (García Vallejo), XXII (Ibarrola) and the XIV Guerilla Corps (Hungria) in reserve. Thus, it is clear that in terms of infantry divisions the Government still had considerable strength.

In the air it was a different story; here they could no longer provide adequate support. There remained but three squadrons of Natachas, two of Katiuskas, about thirty fighters and a few machines of various types. Miaja was the overall commander for land, sea and air, and the Government's representative; Matallana had become leader of the Armies, with Muedra as Chief of Staff.

At Alicante the assembly of a series of one hundred Ratas was at an advanced stage, and ten had already been handed over. But the loss of Catalonia had meant also the loss of the aircraft factories at Sabadell and Reus, where about two hundred Chatos in various stages of construction were left abandoned.

Negrín assured Casado that there were about six hundred Russian aircraft in France, awaiting transport to Spain, but this could only have been pure imagination. It is true that the arrival of about seventy Ratas was anticipated, as well as about 50 Super-Katiuskas. This version of the Russian SB-2 had radial engines, three-blade propellers and self-sealing fuel tanks. With these latter aircraft the Government hoped to form two new groups of two squadrons. Attempts were also made to strengthen the Government Air Force by purchasing aircraft from other foreign countries. In this way several machines of Seversky and Bellanca manufacture were ordered from the United States, as well as small numbers from other sources, but it was impossible for these to arrive in time, as they could only be transported by sea. Negotiations then taking place between Franco and Daladier's French Government meant that both France and Algeria were closed as transit points for the supply of war materials to the Red Government of Spain.

At the end of the war only 164 aircraft were recovered from Government front line airfields: 36 Natachas, 9 Rasantes, 9 Grumman 'Delfin's', 5 Vultees, 19 Katiuskas, 22 Ratas, 20 Super-Chatos and 44 Chatos. About 50 other aircraft were in reserve, and these and some 100 light aircraft were also taken by the Nationalists. Not all the aircraft remained in Spain, and Spanish pilots returned them via France to European or Algerian aerodromes.

Negrín, President of the Government and Minister of Defence, decided to continue with the war, despite the opposition of a majority of military leaders called to a meeting at Los Llanos aerodrome (Albacete) on February 26th.

On February 27th, France and Britain recognised Franco's Government, which caused Azaña to renounce the Presidency of the Republic. The vacancy was filled provisionally by Martínez Barrio, and under these circumstances, the Central Chief of Staff, Vicente Rojo, who was then in France, decided not to return to the Central Zone.

On March 4th Negrín dismissed General Bernal, the military commander of Cartagena, replacing him by the communist, F. Galan. The following night the troops manning the coastal batteries rebelled and the Fleet left port. The 'Fifth column' took over the Navy's radio transmitter and broadcast an appeal to the Nationalists to provide assistance. A convoy was improvised rapidly and this reached Cartagena when Galán had already mastered the situation, with the help of the Rodríguez Division. The coastal batteries fired at the convoy, sinking the *Castillo de Olite*, exactly one year after the sinking of the *Baleares*. The Fleet, with Buiza in command, remained at sea, and then sailed to Algeria and Tunis, where it was interned at the naval base of Bizerta.

Colonel Segismundo Casado, who was then in Madrid, learned that he had been displaced as leader of the Central Army and had been given instead a department in the Central Government. Concerned that this could be one of several steps to put Communists in power, Casado ordered the immediate mobilisation of several batches of recruits, and formed a National Defence Council, with backing from the unions and political parties except, of course, from those of Communist motivation. General Miaja accepted the presidency of the Council and Julian Besteiro, one of the most outstanding pre-war Socialist leaders, was also a member.

Between March 6th and 11th there was a fierce struggle in Madrid between the Communists and the 'Casadistas' (Casado's followers). This was decided favourably for Casado by the arrival of an expeditionary column from the IV Army Corps, sent by Mera from Guadalajara under orders from Liberino Gonzalez. In the interim period the Communist, Jesús Hernández, political commissary of the Central Group of Armies, had attempted to mobilise the XXII Army Corps, then stationed in Tarancón, but this came to nothing.

By March 15th, when calm had been restored in Madrid, Casado began tentative peace proposals: this led to secret negotiations, which were approved by Franco on the 19th. By this date, however, the Generalissimo had already issued instructions for a final annihilating offensive to all branches of the Nationalist forces. The date for the beginning of this was still not determined, as the results of the negotiations then taking place were still awaited.

The first meeting was held in Burgos, Colonels Garijo and Leopoldo Ortega representing the Government, Colonels Gonzalo and Ungria the Nationalists. A verbal agreement was reached for the hand-over of all Government aircraft on March 25th, and for a cease fire on all fronts on the 27th.

On March 25th the same emissaries returned to Burgos, continuing their negotiations until 18.00hrs when Gonzalo announced that they would be suspended, as the first part of the agreement had not been met. Many of the aircraft that should have been surrendered on that day had been flown to Algeria and, in fact, after the war 59 aircraft were recovered from there.

At 01.00hrs on the 26th Casado sent a cable to Burgos, saying that it had been agreed that all the aircraft would be handed over on the following day. It was then too late, Gonzalo replied to the effect that orders had already been despatched for the offensive to begin. At 16.00hrs Nationalist radios retransmitted the 'concessions' which Franco had agreed with Casado.

The advance on Pozoblanco by the Moroccan and Andalusian Army Corps began on March 26th. On that day 2-G-3 then composed of four squadrons, made three sorties; the first led by Salas and the other two by Guerrero. There was practically no resistance and Salas moved to Grinon, so that he could be one of the first to enter Madrid, where his father was in hiding in an embassy. On March 27th a reconnaissance sortie was carried out, and this was 2-G-3's last operational sortie of the war. The Group's record of operations commented:

"Escort for the 4th and 5th Squadrons which were bombing the railway station at Almadanejos. Once the bombers had withdrawn a reconnaissance of the front was made, and in the Santa Eufemia sector a column of lorries was sighted, advancing along the Almadén road. To the east of the road our forces were advancing in such a way that it was clear they were meeting little resistance."

On March 27th the Navarre, Maestrazgo and CTV Army Corps attacked the Toledo front. Group 3-G-3, joined by Morato and Salas, made one sortie, on the 27th and another on the 28th. On that day Madrid was occupied without a struggle. Prada, last leader of the Central Army, surrendered to the leader of Division 17 (Colonel Losas), in the University Campus.

On March 28th, returning from their last operational sortie, Captain Miguel García Pardo and Lieutenant Rogelio Garcia de Juan were in collision over Almaluez and both were killed. Pardo had survived more than fifty combat sorties: it was ironic that a tragedy of this nature should occur within a few days of the war's end. Worse was to come.

On March 30th Nationalist forces reached Valencia and Casado went aboard the English vessel *Galatea*. On April 1st a Nationalist communiqué was able to announce:

"Yesterday, with the Red Army captive and disarmed, our forces reached their final military objectives. The war has ended."

On April 2nd Morato went to Seville to arrange for the transfer of Vázquez Sagastizábal's remains to his home town. On the following day he returned to Grinon and on April 4th came a major tragedy. A film was being made of the activities of the Condor Legion. In one of the sequences it was planned to show the excitement of an aerial combat, Government versus Nationalist fighters, involving an Me 109, a Rata, a Chato and, of course, Morato in his beloved Fiat 3-51.

The filming had ended and Morato, full of exuberance at a successful conclusion to the war, gave a spontaneous display of aerobatics. It was a delight to watch, skill and an intimate rapport with the Fiat providing smooth and positive manoeuvres that flowed gracefully one into the other. He came down in a steep dive, levelled out and skimmed low across the airfield surface at high speed, then pulled up into a steep climb, rolling as the Fiat nosed upwards into the sky. At the top of its climb the machine stalled but, instead of recovering, it began a spin which was maintained until, seconds later, 3-51 disintegrated into a mass of crumpled wreckage. Unbelievably Morato, hero of the Nationalist Air Force, was dead. Fate was to strike another blow the same day when Commander Ibarra, moving with the 8th Squadron to Azuqueca, was killed in an accident.

On April 5th the senior officers of the Fiat groups accompanied Morato's body on its last journey, to his home town of Malaga where, on April 6th, he was laid to rest, the ceremony attended by practically every resident of the town.

On April 15th several air units moved to Seville to take part in a victory parade on the 17th. On May 19th a final victory parade was held in Madrid. Salas, who had taken command of both Fiat groups following Morato's death, led the formation that triumphantly spelled out the word FRANCO, high above the enthusiastic and cheering crowds that celebrated the return of peace.

On May 31st the Legionary Air Force moved to Tablada, where they handed over all their equipment to the Spaniards. Shortly after they embarked at Cadiz, bound for Genoa, being accompanied by General Kindelan. A few days before their companions in the land forces had left for Naples.

On May 22nd Nationalist Spain bid a grateful farewell to the Condor Legion at León, an event attended by the Chief of Staff. Nine days later its longest serving members embarked at Vigo, accompanied on their return journey by a Spanish commission headed by Generals Aranda and Yagüe.

Epilogue

During the month of July 1939 the Spanish Air Force was reorganised, with the formation of five Air Regions (Central, The Straits, Levante, Pyrenees and Atlantic) and three autonomous Aerial Zones (Canaries, Balearics and Morocco). The Fighter Air Force was divided into nine groups, five of them using Fiats (Nos 21, 22, 23, 28 and 29), one with Super-Chatos—then referred to usually as Super-Curtis (No 24), one with Me 109s (No 25), one with Ratas (No 26) and a mixed group with He 112s and G.50s (No 27).

Fighter Regiment No 21 was formed with Groups 21 and 22, and this was based at Getafe. At Tablada Regiment No 22 was established, this comprising one Fiat group (No 23) and one of Ratas (No 26). The 23rd Regiment consisted of Groups 24 and 25, which had Polikarpov I–15Bs and Me 109s.

Groups 27, 28 and 29 were sent to the three Aerial Zones, where they became identified as the Mixed Regiments Nos 2, 3 and 4, stationed at Melilla (Morocco), Son San Juan (Balearics) and Gando (Canaries) respectively.

Initially, the Fighter School remained at Reus, but was moved later to Morón. The Chatos were used to form the Assault Regiments 32 and 33, and were stationed at Alicante and Villanubla. The old He 51s were assigned to Assault Regiment 31, based at Getafe.

In the middle of this reorganisation the Air Force lost Captain Barranco, another of its veteran fighter leaders, killed in a car accident near Madrid. He was returning from the wedding of Angél Salas, which took place at Oviedo on July 25th. His was not the final loss to the fighter units for several other pilots, including Muntadas, Rey-Stolle and Manrique were killed in accidents within a year of the war's end.

In August 1939 the Air Ministry was formed, with General Yagüe at its head, Barron as Under-Secretary and Moreno Abella as Chief of Staff. Within a few months Yagüe was replaced by Juan Vigón, with Apolinar Sáenz de Buruaga as Under-Secretary and Eduardo González Gallarza as Chief of Staff.

Two years after the end of the war, details of awards for war service, both for the survivors and those killed in action, were published in an Official Bulletin.

Prior to this, few members of the Air Force had received awards for their achievements. Morato had been decorated with the San Fernando Laureate in May 1937, and was posthumously awarded the Military Medal; Bermúdez de Castro, Haya, García Pardo and Vázquez Sagastizábal had also received the Military Medal, and Haya had also been promoted in the year of his death, in recognition of his war service.

On August 7th, 1939, four months after the end of the war, Kindelán put forward the names of the deceased Haya and Vázquez Sagastizábal for the award of the San Fernando Laureate. Yagüe began the necessary formalities, which were made public on December 12th, 1940, and a favourable decision was made in 1942.

Pilots of the bomber and close-support squadrons received no better treatment. The names of José Calderón and José Ugarte were put forward for the San Fernando Laureate at an even later date, and Vara de Rey was given an award after a proposal put forward by Queipo de Llano.

Among the fighter pilots to receive awards were Muñoz, Salas, Salvador and Guerrero, who were given Military Medal and promotion; Cuadra and Senra received promotion; and Arístides García López, Queipo, Carlos Serra, Allende, Simón, Jesús Rubio, Comas, Ibarreche, Bayo, Joaquín Ansaldo, Velasco, O'Connor, Henricourt, Diéguez, Ripollés and Ozores were awarded the Military Medal. Muñoz, Cuadra, Diéguez, Ripolles and Ozores were also commended for their services in Group 1-G-2, before they joined fighter units.

Pilots such as Murcia, leader of a Fiat squadron from December 1937 until the war's end, with a total of 429 operational sorties and five victories, Larios with six, Salvador Serra with four, and others, had to be content with the War Cross. However, two years later the Military Cross with Palms (created in 1942) was given to Murcia, and was also awarded posthumously to all Air Force pilots who had received no higher award. It was not until September 26th, 1944, that the bomber pilot Emilio Jiménez Ugarte received an award for his war service, despite thirty-two months of continuous operations, during which he made 412 sorties totalling 722 flying hours.

It is not surprising that these honours, by the time they were awarded, had lost their true meaning. Indeed, many were so long delayed and ill considered that they caused only disillusionment and bitterness. Promotions for war merits were initially backdated to March 26th, 1937 and March 18th, 1938; thus the Air Force promotional ladder for May 1941 had subsequently to be corrected as at April 1st, 1939. The confusion this caused can be appreciated without difficulty, for many of the service personnel involved had been promoted to a particular rank and had been holding posts related to that rank for some time.

The Military Medals were presented solemnly to the available recipients on Loreto's Day in 1941; nine at Getafe, two at Seville and one at Melilla. Two were never bestowed, those awarded to Munoz and Arístides García López, for these two men disappeared without trace. Henricourt, the Belgian volunteer, received his medal indirectly, for he was no longer in Spain. By then he was flying in the British Royal Air Force, where he added seven more victories to his total before being killed in action. The remaining five, Salas, Allende, Bayo, Ibarreche and O'Connor, also missed the ceremony. Indeed, they were lucky to receive news of the event at all. They, too, were then involved in World War II, on the opposing side to their former colleague, Henricourt. Alongside former allies, the pilots of Germany's *Luftwaffe*, they were then helping to breach the Russian defences of Klin airfield, close to Moscow.

Surely, the English poet, John Milton, had distilled the essence of the situation three centuries earlier, when he penned in a sonnet:

"For what can War but endless War still breed?"

Appendices

1 Fiat C.R.32 Aircraft Used by Spanish Units During the War

(Based on information obtained from the Maestranza Aérea archives at Tablada)

Army No.	*Factory No.*	*Date of Receipt*	*Army No.*	*Factory No.*	*Date of Receipt*
3-51	262	Nov 36	3-76	757	Oct 37
3-52	508	Jan 37	3-77	765	Oct 37
3-53	44	Feb 37	3-78	780	Dec 37
3-54	597	Apl 37	3-79	782	Dec 37
3-55	603	Apl 37	3-80	768	Dec 37
3-56	598	Apl 37	3-81	770	Dec 37
3-57	601	Apl 37	3-82	771	Dec 37
3-58	594	Apl 37	3-83	772	Dec 37
3-59	587	Apl 37	3-84	773	Dec 37
3-60	596	Apl 37	3-85	774	Dec 37
3-61	111	Dec 36	3-86	775	Dec 37
3-62	589	Apl 37	3-87	776	Dec 37
3-63	331	Dec 36	3-88	778	Dec 37
3-64	748	Oct 37	3-89	779	Dec 37
3-65	749	Oct 37	3-90	766	Dec 37
3-66	750	Oct 37	3-91	781	Dec 37
3-67	751	Oct 37	3-92	767	Dec 37
3-68	752	Oct 37	3-93	783	Dec 37
3-69	753	Oct 37	3-94	784	Dec 37
3-70	754	Oct 37	3-95	785	Dec 37
3-71	755	Oct 37	3-96	786	Dec 37
3-72	756	Oct 37	3-97	787	Dec 37
3-73	758	Oct 37	3-98	788	Dec 37
3-74	759	Oct 37	3-99	789	Dec 37
3-75	760	Oct 37	3-100	790	Dec 37

Army No.	*Factory No.*	*Date of Receipt*	*Army No.*	*Factory No.*	*Date of Receipt*
3-101	?	?	3-126	970	Jul 38
3-102	810	?	3-127	971	Jul 38
3-103	811	Jan 38	3-128	974	Jul 38
3-104	812	Jan 38	3-129	975	Jul 38
3-105	813	Jan 38	3-130	976	Jul 38
3-106	814	Jan 38	3-131	977	Jul 38
3-107	815	Jan 38	3-132	978	Jul 38
3-108	816	Jan 38	3-133	979	Jul 38
3-109	817	Jan 38	3-134	980	Jul 38
3-110	818	Jan 38	3-135	982	Jul 38
3-111	819	Jan 38	3-136	983	Jul 38
3-112	820	Jan 38	3-137	984	Jul 38
3-113	821	Jan 38	3-138	985	Jul 38
3-114	822	Jan 38	3-139	987	Jul 38
3-115	823	Jan 38	3-140	990	Jul 38
3-116	929	May 38	3-141	991	Jul 38
3-117	930	May 38	3-142	994	Jul 38
3-118	931	May 38	3-143	1.011	Jul 38
3-119	932	May 38	3-144	1.008	Jul 38
3-120	933	May 38	3-145	1.013	Jul 38
3-121	934	May 38	3-146	1.014	Jul 38
3-122	935	May 38	3-147	1.015	Jul 38
3-123	936	May 38	3-148	1.016	Jul 38
3-124	968	Jul 38	3-149	1.017	Jul 38
3-125	969	Jul 38	3-150	1.018	Jul 38

Note: From July 1938, no new Fiats were received in Spain. 27 aircraft, numbered 3-151 to 3-177, were received from the *Gamba de Ferro* Group, and after the war numbers 3-178 to 3-292 arrived. Hispano-Suiza later built numbers 3-293 to 3-392 in Seville, and re-built two war-damaged aircraft, re-numbered 3-393 and 3-394.

2 Fiat C.R.32 Aircraft Lost by Spanish Units During the War

(Information obtained from Group 2-G-3 and Squadrons 3-E-3 and 4-E-3 operational records and from the Maestranza Aérea archives at Tablada)

Aircraft No.	*Date*	*Pilot*	*Squadron*	*Place*	*Reason*
3-53	23-12-37	R. Jiménez Garrido	3-E-3	Aer. Ávila	Accident
3-56	10- 7-37	Jesús Rubio Paz	1-E-3	Brunete	Combat
3-59	3-38	Luis Noguera	4-E-3	Aragón	Defected
3-62	12- 7-37	N. Bermúdez de Castro	2-E-3	Brunete	Combat
3-63	25- 8-38	J. M.ª Etayo Elizondo	2-E-3	Campanario	Caught fire
3-64	29- 1-38	L. Herrero de Teresa	1-E-3	Teruel	Combat
3-65	14- 7-38	J. L. Bernal de Mérida	5-E-3	Levante	Combat
3-69	3-10-38	J. Salvador Díaz-Benjumea	2-E-3	Ebro	Combat
3-70	12-37	A. Olivera Fernández	2-E-3	?	Accident
3-71	7- 1-39	C. Serra Pablo Romero	2-E-3	Cataluña	Accident
3-75	14- 8-38	José Mesía Lesseps	2-E-3	Ebro	Combat
3-76	21-12-38	J. Romagosa Durán	1-E-3	Caspe	Accident
3-77	2- 1-38	J. M.ª Careaga Urigüen	2-E-3	Teruel	Small-arms fire
3-79	21-12-37	R. Mazarredo Trenor	2-E-3	Tablada	Collision
3-80	21-12-37	R. Giménez Garrido	3-E-3	Tablada	Collision
3-81	12- 1-39	E. Ruiz Hermosilla	1-E-3	Matacán	Accident
3-86	26- 3-38	M. García Díez	3-E-3	Aragón	Small-arms fire
3-87	28-12-37	Antonio López Sert	1-E-3	Teruel	Small-arms fire
3-92	18- 1-38	Pedro Gil Escoaín	4-E-3	Aranda	Accident

Aircraft No.	*Date*	*Pilot*	*Squadron*	*Place*	*Reason*
3-93	7- 2-38	M. Varona Trigueros	4-E-3	Talavera	Collision
3-95	24- 1-38	J. Ibarra Montis	4-E-3	Teruel	Nationalist anti-aircraft fire
3-96	27- 9-38	G. Queipo de Llano Martí	3-E-3	Ebro	Accident
3-97	24- 8-38	F. Arrechea Belzunce	4-E-3	Ebro	Combat
3-99	7- 2-38	Progreso Núñez Martín	4-E-3	Talavera	Collision
3-100	1- 8-38	E. Munaiz de Brea	4-E-3	Ebro	Combat
3-102	24-12-38	R. Mendizábal Amézaga	4-E-3	Cataluña	Combat
3-103	20- 7-38	P. Téllez Rivas	4-E-3	Mérida	Accident
3-104	24- 3-38	J. Jurado González	3-E-3	Aragón	Combat
3-110	11- 4-38	?	3-E-3	?	?
3-114	26- 3-38	A. Figueroa Fernández	3-E-3	Aragón	Small-arms fire
3-115	3-12-38	L. Corsini Beca	4-E-3	Aragón	Accident
3-116	28- 7-38	H. Gautier Larrainzar	4-E-3	Ebro	Small-arms fire
3-118	23- 1-39	M. Vázquez Sagastizábal	1-E-3	Pozoblanco	Combat
3-122	22- 9-38	P. Martínez de Irujo	5-E-3	Ebro	Combat
3-127	14- 8-38	C. Bayo Allessandri	2-E-3	Ebro	Combat
3-135	24- 8-38	J. Chapaprieta Inglada	3-E-3	Ebro	Combat
3-140	2-10-38	A. Oliva Fernández	4-E-3	Ebro	Combat
3-145	31- 8-38	F. Gómez Trenor	8-E-3	Extremadura	Small-arms fire
3-146	24- 1-39	E. Mendía Ruiz	8-E-3	Extremadura	Collision
3-147	24- 1-39	P. Lacalle Orellana	8-E-3	Extremadura	Collision
3-148	10- 3-39	J. Busquets Sindreu	8-E-3	Posadas	?
3-155	19-12-38	R. Bartolomé Chávarri	4-E-3	Cataluña	?
3-170	27- 1-39	L. Márquez Maristany	5-E-3	Pla de Vilanoveta	Accident

Summary

July	1937	2 aircraft	3-56 and 3-62
Dec	1937	5 aircraft	3-53, 3-70, 3-79, 3-80 and 3-87
Jan	1938	4 aircraft	3-64, 3-77, 3-92 and 3-95
Feb	1938	2 aircraft	3-93 and 3-99
March	1938	4 aircraft	3-104, 3-114, 3-59 and 3-86
April	1938	1 aircraft	3-110
July	1938	3 aircraft	3-65, 3-103 and 3-116
Aug	1938	8 aircraft	3-63, 3-75, 3-97, 3-100, 3-122, 3-127, 3-135 and 3-145
Sept	1938	1 aircraft	3-96
Oct	1938	2 aircraft	3-69 and 3-140
Dec	1938	4 aircraft	3-76, 3-102, 3-115 and 3-155
Jan	1939	6 aircraft	3-71, 3-81, 3-118, 3-146, 3-147 and 3-170
March	1939	1 aircraft	3-148
	Total	43 out of	127 (34%)

Note: At the end of the war the Spanish units had 89 Fiats. Amongst the Italian units in the Peninsular and the Balearics, the Fighter School, the Regional Parks and at Hispano-Suiza (where all major repairs were carried out) there were 110 more Fiats, making a total of 199.

If one assumes that the Fiats suffered a similar proportion of losses to those of other Spanish units, this would suggest that approximately 300 machines of this type arrived in Spain. In the review *Avión* the figure has been given as 380, somewhat higher than the number assumed here, and one which would suggest losses of almost 50 per cent.

During the war, Hispano-Suiza of Seville re-built 49 Fiats.

3 Rata Aircraft in Service in the Period February-May 1938

(Based on information supplied by the Group's chief mechanic and by Tarazona Griménez, Spencer and others)

CM-006	4th Squadron
CM-007	4th Squadron
CM-008	At the factory
CM-010	4th Squadron
CM-011	At the factory
CM-012	1st Squadron
CM-013	1st and 2nd Squadron
CM-014	1st Squadron
CM-018	1st Squadron
CM-020	5th Squadron
CM-022	1st and 5th Squadron
CM-023	1st and 4th Squadron
CM-025	Destroyed at Lérida on 23-2-38
CM-027	1st Squadron
CM-028	2nd Squadron
CM-029	2nd Squadron
CM-030	4th Squadron and factory
CM-031	2nd Squadron
CM-034	In reserve
CM-035	2nd Squadron; captured
CM-037	1st and 2nd Squadron

CM-041	2nd and 3rd Squadron
CM-042	1st Squadron
CM-043	1st Squadron
CM-044	4th Squadron
CM-045	1st Squadron
CM-061	2nd, 3rd and 4th Squadron
CM-091	1st and 3rd Squadron
CM-092	5th Squadron
CM-094	2nd Squadron
CM-095	5th Squadron
CM-096	5th Squadron
CM-097	2nd Squadron
CM-098	2nd Squadron
CM-100	5th Squadron
CM-102	5th Squadron
CM-104	2nd and 4th Squadron
CM-105	4th Squadron
CM-107	4th Squadron
CM-108	At the factory
CM-109	1st Squadron and factory
CM-112	4th Squadron
CM-115	1st Squadron
CM-116	5th and 3rd Squadron
CM-117	1st Squadron
CM-118	2nd Squadron
CM-119	3rd and 4th Squadron
CM-120	2nd and 3rd Squadron and at el Prat
CM-121	2nd Squadron
CM-122	2nd Squadron
CM-124	1st, 2nd and 3rd Squadron
CM-125	2nd and 4th Squadron
CM-128	2nd, 5th Squadron and factory
CM-131	2nd Squadron and factory
CM-133	3rd Squadron
CM-134	5th and 3rd Squadron
CM-135	Reserve and 4th Squadron
CM-136	5th, 3rd and 4th Squadron
CM-137	1st and 3rd Squadron
CM-138	1st and 2nd Squadron
CM-139	At Celrá and 5th Squadron
CM-140	5th and 3rd Squadron
CM-141	1st Squadron
CM-143	4th Squadron
CM-146	At the factory
CM-147	1st and 5th Squadron
CM-148	2nd and 3rd Squadron
CM-151	5th Squadron
CM-152	In reserve
CM-154	At factory and 4th Squadron
CM-155	2nd Squadron and reserve
CM-156	1st and 2nd Squadron
CM-157	5th Squadron and at el Prat
CM-158	2nd Squadron and factory
CM-160	5th Squadron
CM-165	5th Squadron and factory
CM-166	?
CM-167	5th Squadron
CM-169	At Valls
CM-170	5th Squadron
CM-171	2nd Squadron
CM-172	5th Squadron
CM-173	2nd Squadron
CM-174	2nd Squadron
CM-175	2nd Squadron
CM-176	2nd Squadron
CM-177	5th Squadron
CM-178	5th Squadron
CM-179	At Valls
CM-182	2nd Squadron

From Nos 001 to 045, 26 remained in service & 19 were destroyed.
From Nos 046 to 090, 1 remained in service & 44 were destroyed.
From Nos 091 to 142, 36 remained in service & 16 were destroyed.
From Nos 143 to 182, 27 remained in service & 13 were destroyed.
Making a *total* of 90 still in service and 92 destroyed.

From this information it seems obvious that aircraft CM-046 to 090 were sent to the North, where they were all lost apart from 061.

There were probably slightly more aircraft in service and less machines destroyed, since I have amended the incomplete lists of aircraft in service. In fact, no machines from the 6th Squadron or from the Fighter School are mentioned.

In the Summer of 1938 a large number of new Ratas with four machine-guns entered the country, similar to the one which had appeared in combat for the first time in May. On August 3rd Tarazona collected No 193. On September 9th No 242 was destroyed; on the 20th of the same month No 257 and on October 3rd Nos 261 and 263 were also destroyed. In 1938, therefore, at least 106 Ratas arrived (Nos 158 to 263).

According to information from the Materials Section, 200 Ratas with two machine-guns and 30 with four machine-guns were acquired from Russia, as well as 70 which never reached Spain. This information agrees partially with that obtained from staff assembling these machines at Celrá.

The dates when the first Ratas probably arrived in Spain were October 1936 for Nos 001 to 031, after December 20th for Nos 032 to 062; Nos 063 to 093 in Spring 1937, and Nos 094 to 142 in the Summer of the same year.

Nos 143 to 157 were assembled in Archena in September 1937. Twelve of these machines went to the new 6th Squadron, which had all Russian pilots.

Nos 158 to 182 must have entered Spain in March 1938, since Nos 158, 160 and 175 were used in operations by the end of that month, and the last ones were ready in May. These all had four machine-guns. Nos 183 to 277 arrived in the Summer of 1938 and others during the Winter period 1938/39.

Of the 100 Ratas built with machinery and staff from the old Hispano-Suiza factory at Guadalajara, which was later established at Alicante, only 10 were in service before the end of the war, and these were numbered from CH-001 onwards. Thirty more were despatched from Jerez de la Frontera after the end of the war. During the war, somewhere in the order of thirty Ratas were rebuilt at Alicante.

At the war's end 22 Ratas were recovered. These were used to form Group No 26, belonging to Fighter Regiment No 22, based at Tablada. These machines were designated 1W and were numbered from 1W-1 to 1W-22; those assembled in Jerez continued these serial numbers up to 1W-52, and some were still flying as late as 1953.

4 Ratas Lost During Several Periods of 1938

(information from the Group's Chief mechanic, from Giménez, Tarazona, Spencer and others)

UP TO FEBRUARY 1938

About 92 planes destroyed (see Appendix 3)

MARCH 1938

March 10th:	CM-141 Caught fire at Caspe	(from 1st Squadron)
	CM-121 Shot down at Alcañiz	(from 2nd Squadron)
March 13th:	CM-102 Caught fire at Caspe	(from 5th Squadron)

March 27th:	CM-135 Caught fire at Lérida	(from 4th Squadron)
	CM-152 Caught fire at Lérida	(from 5th Squadron)
	CM-006 Collided at Alcorisa	(from 4th Squadron)
	CM-044 Collided at Alcorisa	(from 4th Squadron)
March 30th:	CM-155 Disappeared over the front	(from 1st Squadron)

Note Nos CM-006, 043, 045, 109, 128, 135, 137 and 138 were damaged at Lérida.

APRIL 1938

No details available

MAY 1938

During this month the following were damaged:

CM-061	Fuselage damaged (21-5-38 at El Vendrell). Disappeared 3-10-38.
CM-091	Hit by shrapnel at Barcelona.
CM-095	Damaged at Valls; disappeared 23-5-38 (5th Squadron)
CM-100	Damaged at Valls (5th Squadron)
CM-125	Starboard wing damaged 22-5-38. Disappeared 13-9-38
CM-136	Hit by shrapnel at Bell-Puig
CM-151	Landed on top of a 'Chato' (Monjos, 21-5-38)
CM-165	Turned turtle landing at Bell-Puig (23-5-38)—(5th Squadron)
CM-167	Turned turtle landing at Valls (22-5-38)—(5th Squadron)
CM-169	Starboard wing and tail damaged at Valls (22-5-38)
CM-179	Starboard wing and rudder damaged at Valls

JUNE 1938

According to Tarazona only 35 Ratas were then flying. By that time at least 182 had arrived from Spain. The losses must have been in the order of 125, since about 22 planes were undergoing repairs.

SUMMER 1938

According to figures from the Materials Section, in the Summer of 1938 33 per cent of the fighters in the Catalan region were being lost each month, making a total of about 35 machines per month and about 26 pilots. Other sources indicated that the fighters lost in June, July and August were 22, 30 and 22, respectively; 14, 20 and 16 of these in battle, 1, 2 and 0 by anti-aircraft and the rest in accidents.

In accordance with these figures, all the Ratas from the 7 Squadrons (about 90) must have been lost, although many of them saw service months later after they had been repaired; this agrees with the numbers of Ratas imported during the year (at least 120).

According to the same source of information, at the Fighter School there was one fatal accident for every 1,300 hours of flight, or one death for every 37 pupils who left the school. Training as a fighter pilot involved 35 hours in an elementary light aircraft, 22 hours of conversion flight in a more advanced trainer, and 35 hours in a fighter.

SEPTEMBER 3 TO OCTOBER 3, 1938

CM-061 Lost on 3-10-38 (from the 7th Squadron)
CM-125 Lost on 13- 9-38 (from the 7th Squadron)
CM-148 Lost on 23- 9-38 (from the 2nd Squadron)
CM-154 Lost on 13- 9-38 (from the 7th Squadron)
CM-178 Lost on 13- 9-38 (from the 7th Squadron)
CM-190 Lost on 23- 9-38 (from the 3rd Squadron)
CM-192 Lost on 13- 9-38 (from the 1st Squadron)
CM-242 Lost on 9- 9-38 (from the 4th Squadron)
CM-257 Lost on 20- 9-38 (from the 3rd Squadron)
CM-261 Lost on 3-10-38 (from the 3rd Squadron)
CM-263 Lost on 3-10-38 (from the 3rd Squadron)
? Lost on 23- 9-38 (from the 5th Squadron)

Over this period at least 9 other Chatos disappeared, making 21 in all. To this figure has to be added aircraft lost in storms, undergoing repairs, being serviced, etc.

By October 3rd, 1938, at least 277 'Ratas' had entered Spain and of these 177 had been lost and 100 were still in service. Forty machines were lost from October to January, and a similar number in February 1939; the majority were hit by machine-gun fire, or destroyed on the ground. Twenty-two more were recovered at the end of the war.

5 Markings on Government Aircraft

(based on Sanchís' list. Ref: A-127)

FIGHTERS

CA	I-15 Chato
CC	I-15B Super-Chato
CD	Dewoitine 371
CE	Dewoitine 501
CF	Fokker D-XXI
CH	I-16 (Hispano)
CL	Letov S-331
CM	I-16 Rata (Mosca)
CN	Nieuport 52
CS	Seversky P-35
CW	Dewoitine 510

Note: No letters were allocated to the Hawker Fury, Bleriot-SPAD 510, Loire-Nieuport 46 or Bristol Bulldog. Although there were three types of Letov in service, only one was allocated identification letters.

RECONNAISSANCE

RR	S.Z. Rasante	RH	de Havilland D.H.9 (in the schools)
RB	Breguet BR 19 (in the schools)		

Note: No letters were allocated to the Potez 25, used in the North.

ASSAULT

AD Grumman Delfin

LIAISON AND LIGHT BOMBERS

LA	Airspeed Envoy	LL	Aero 101 (Oca)
LB	Bellanca 28-70 (1935)	LN	R5 Natacha
LD	de Havilland D.H.84 Dragon	LR	de Havilland D.H.89 Dragon Rapide
LF	Fokker C-X		
LG	Gourdou-Leseurre 633 B.1 (1932)	LY	de Havilland D.H.90 Dragonfly

Note: No letters were allocated to the Vickers Vildebeest

BOMBERS

BB	Marcel Bloch M.B.210	BP	Potez 54
BF	Fokker F-XVIII	BV	Vultee V-1A
BK	S.B.-2 (Katiuska)		

Note: No letters were allocated to the Fokker F-VII or Potez 63

TRANSPORTS

TA	Avia 51	TL	Latecoère 28
TC	Caudron Goeland	TM	Monospar ST-25
TD	Douglas DC-2	TN	Northrop Delta
TF	Farman F.402	TP	Spartan Executive
TG	Northrop Gamma	TS	Stinson Reliant
TH	de Havilland D.H.37B	TV	Breguet-Wibault Fulgur
TK	Lockheed 9-D		

Note: No letters were allocated to the Potez 56 or 58, de Havilland D.H.83, Consolidated Fleetster, Lockheed Electra, Junkers Ju 52, Percival Gull or Polish RWD-13.

MEDICAL

SF	Farman F.402	SM	Monospar ST-25

SEAPLANES

HD	Dornier-Wal	HS	Savoia S.62
HM	Macchi M.18	HV	Vickers Vildebeest

AMPHIBIANS

XA	Fairchild 91

CAPTURED

FF	Fiat C.R.32	FM	Messerschmitt Me 109
FH	Heinkel He 111	FS	Savoia S-M.81

TRAINING SCHOOL

EA	Caudron C.600	EN	Miles M.3 or M.5
EC	SAAB-Sema 10	EP	de Havilland D.H.82
EE	Hispano-Suiza E-30	EQ	Monocoupe 90-A
EF	Hispano-Suiza E-34	ER	Romano Ro 82
EG	Gil-Pazó GP-1	EU	Morane-Saulnier M.S.60
EJ	Koolhoven FK-51	EW	Focke-Wulf Fw 56
EK	Koolhoven FK-51 *bis*	EX	Bücker Bü 133
EL	Caudron C.272	EY	I-16 Rata (two-seat)
EM	de Havilland D.H.60	EZ	Hanriot H.182

6 Markings on Nationalist Aircraft

(based on Sanchís's list in *Avión*, May 1950, and corrected by the Author)

FIGHTERS

1	Nieuport 52, later Fiat G.50	6	Messerschmitt Me 109
2	Heinkel He 51	7	Romeo Ro 41
3	Fiat C.R.32 (Chirri)	8	I-15 Chato
4	P.W.S.10	9	Arado Ar 68
5	Heinkel He 112		

ASSAULT

10	Breguet Br 19 (Sesqui)	15	Heinkel He 45 (Pavo)
11	Heinkel He 46 (Pava)	16	Breda Ba 65
12	Romeo Ro 37 *bis*	17	Aero 101 (Oca and Praga)
13	Not used	18	Caproni Ca 130 (Capronchino)
14	Heinkel He 70 (Rayo)	19	Henschel Hs 126 (Superpava)

BOMBERS

20	Fokker F-VII and F-XII	25	Heinkel He 51 (Pedro)
21	Savoia S-M.81	26	Junkers Ju 86 (Jumo)
22	Junkers Ju 52	27	Dornier Do 17 (Bacalao)
23	Fiat BR 20	28	Savoia S-M.79
24	Henschel Hs 123 (Angelito)	29	Junkers Ju 87 (Stuka)

LIGHT AIRCRAFT

30	Single-engined	35	Bücker Jungmeister
31	Twin-engined	36	Arado Ar 66
32	Caproni AP-1 (Apio)	37	Fighter school aircraft
33	Bücker Jungmann	38	Gotha Go 145
34	Breda Ba 28		

TRANSPORTS

40	de Havilland Dragon	44	Messerschmitt Me 108 (Taifun)
41	Airspeed Envoy	45	Fokker F-VII and F-XII
42	Two- or three-engined	46	Fieseler Storch (Ciguena)
43	Single-engined	47	Consolidated Fleetster

SEAPLANES

50	Macchi M.41	64	Arado Ar 95
60	Heinkel He 60	70	Dornier-Wal
61	Savoia S.62	71	Heinkel He 59 (Zapatones)
62	Cant Z.501	72	Junkers Ju 52W
63	Fairchild amphibian		

CAPTURED AIRCRAFT

1W	Rata	5W	Grumman Delfin
2W	Super Chato	16W	Rasante
3W	Letov	17W	Natacha
4W	Hawker Fury	20W	Katiuska

7 Fighters Used by Both Sides until the End of 1938

(Author's estimation, based on Appendices 1 to 4, on the highest registered numbers, on information given by Gomez Spencer and Gimenez and various other sources)

NATIONALIST ZONE		*GOVERNMENT ZONE*	
Fiat C.R.32	380—	I-15 Chato	416
Messerschmitt Me 109	96	I-16 Rata	281+
Heinkel He 51 (not counting 75 which were used only in an assault role)	56	Nieuport 52	50
		Dewoitine (three types)	30+
		Bristol Bulldog	11+
Romeo Ro 41 (one- and two-seaters)	13	Letov (three types)	10+
Nieuport 52	10	Koolhoven (not counting those used in an assault role)	10
Arado Ar 69	3	Nieuport (acquired)	4
Heinkel He 112	2	Loire-Nieuport 46	4
		Hawker Fury	3
		Bleriot-SPAD 510	2+
		Boeing P-26	1
		Fokker D-XXI	1
Totals	560—		823+

At the end of March 1939 the following fighters were acquired and entered into service:

NATIONALIST ZONE		*GOVERNMENT ZONE*	
Heinkel He 112	13	I-15B Chato	15
Messerschmitt Me 109E	40	I-16 Rata	6+
Fiat G.50	15	Seversky P-35	(?)
Romeo Ro 41	7	I-153 (similar to the Chato, but with retractable landing gear)	(?)
Fiat C.R. 42 (doubtful)	2		
Totals	77		21+

More than 200 almost completed aeroplanes were left at Sabadell-Reus and many of these flew after the war.

In 1936, 25 'Chatos' arrived in Levante and 30 more in the North. During the first quarter of 1937, three consignments of 31, 11 and 50 arrived, making a total of 92. I have no figures for the second and third parts of the year. During the last quarter, at least 34 'Super Chatos', numbered from CC-001 upwards, were imported and these operated in Teruel.

Of the 'Chatos' built in Catalonia, those numbered up to CA-046 operated in Teruel; CA-129 was flying by June 1938; CA-188 by October 2nd, and CA-235 was handed over at the end of the year. In 1939 the numbers went up to CA-250. This meant that they were handing over completed aircraft at a rate of 45 to 50 per quarter, slightly less than the often quoted figure of one per day, not counting fiestas and Sundays.

8 Nationalist Aircraft Deployment on December 23rd, 1938

(from the archives of the Air Chief of Staff)

197 Fighters	155 Fiat C.R.32	in Escatrón	46
		in Caspe	40
		in Sariñena	38
		in Balearics	15
		in Granada	8
		in Logroño	4
		in Seville	4
	37 Me 109	in La Cenia	32
		in León	5
	2 He 112	in León	2
	3 Ar 69	in La Cenia	3

93 Co-operation aircraft	22 He 51	in Castejón del Puente	13
		in León	5
		in Burgos	3
		in Logroño	1
	7 BR 19	in Tetuán	4
		in Nador	3
	2 He 46	in Castejón del Puente	2
	18 Ro 37	in Candasnos	11
		in Castejón del Puente	7
	10 He 70	in Pallaruelo	4
		in Delta	2
		in Seville	2
		in Tauste	1
		in Buñuel	1
	9 He 45	in Castejón del Puente	6
		in Tauste	3
	11 Ba 65	in Puig Moreno	11
	4 Aero 101	in Granada	3
		in Seville	1
	10 Ca 310	in Candasnos	9
		in Logroño	1

179 Bombers	26 S-M.81	in Huesca (?)	8
		in Balearics	12
		in Seville	6
	23 Ju 52	in Pallaruelo	13
		in Sanjurjo	4
		in Burgos	3
		in La Cenia	2
		in Tauste	1
	11 BR 20	in Puig Moreno	11
	2 Ju 86	in Seville	2
	30 He 111	in Sanjurjo	25
		in León	5
	2 Hs 123	in Seville	2
	19 Do 17	in Buñuel	11
		in Tauste	4
		in Sanjurjo	4
	62 S-M.79	in Valenzuela	25
		in Alfamén	21
		in Balearics	15
		in Puig Moreno	1
	4 Ju 87	in Sanjurjo	4
	22 Seaplanes	in Balearics	18
		in Atalayón	4
	1 Katiuska	in Almorox	1

9 Aircraft Repaired by Hispano-Suiza During the War

Aircraft No. H.S.	*Manufacturers No. (Fiat)*	*Aircraft No. H.S.*	*Manufacturers No. (Fiat)*
A-1	368	A-26	756
A-2	433	A-27	601
A-3	153	A-28	606
A-4	514 *bis*	A-29	230
A-5	84	A-30	729
A-6	610	A-31	95 *bis*
A-7	128	A-32	732
A-8	569	A-33	717
A-9	112	A-34	608
A-10	514	A-35	937
A-11	573	A-36	914
A-12	683	A-37	810
A-13	610	A-38	597
A-14	623	A-39	752
A-15	697	A-40	681
A-16	32	A-41	85
A-17	151	A-42	106
A-18	740	A-43	852
A-19	605	A-44	819
A-20	22 *bis*	A-45	136
A-21	697 *bis*	A-46	594
A-22	843	A-47	573
A-23	605 *bis*	A-48	514
A-24	697	A-49	254
A-25	22		

10 Spanish Air Groups During the War

(Information collected by the author from various sources)

NATIONALIST ZONE

Fighter and Assault

1-G-2	May 1937 (He 51)
2-G-3	May 1937 (Fiat C.R.32)
3-G-3	January 1938 (Fiat C.R.32)
4-G-2	July 1938 (He 51)
5-G-5	January 1939 (mixed He 112 and Me 109B)

Co-operation

1-G-10	October 1936. Disbanded June 1937 (BR 19)
2-G-10	October 1936. Disbanded June 1937 (BR 19)
3-G-10, 4-G-10, 5-G-10 → 1-G-10	October 1936. Re-organised in June 1937 (BR 19). (Later Group 86/70)
→ 2-G-10	October 1936. Re-organised in June 1937 (BR 19)
1-G-11, 2-G-11, 1-G-12 → 3-G-11	January 1937. Changed number designation in June 1937. (He 46)
→ 4-G-12	February 1937. Changed number designation in June 1937 (Ro 37)
→ 5-G-17	June 1937 (Aero 101)
→ 6-G-15	June 1937 (He 45)
7-G-14	October 1937 (He 70)
8-G-18	October 1938 (Ca 310)
9-G-18	October 1938 (Ca 310)

Bomber

Mixed	August 1936. Disbanded in December 1936 (Dragon & Fokker)
1st Junkers	November 1936. Disbanded in May 1937 (Ju 52)
2nd Junkers → 1-G-22	November 1936. Changed number designation in May 1937 (Ju 52)
3rd Junkers → 2-G-22	December 1936. Changed number designation in May 1937 (Ju 52)
→ 3-G-28	August 1937 (S-M.79)
4-G-28	October 1937 (S-M.79)
5-G-28	October 1937 (S-M.79)
6-G-28	June 1938 (S-M.79)
7-G-20	Formed and disbanded in the Summer of 1938
8-G-27	July 1938 (Do 17)
10-G-25	August 1938 (He 111)
11-G-25	February 1939 (He 111)
15-G-21	September 1938 (S-M.81)
16-G-21	September 1938 (S-M.81)
17-G-21	September 1938 (S-M.81)
18-G-21	September 1938 (S-M.81)

Seaplanes

1-G-70	Created in October 1936. Disbanded in April 1938 and re-organised with the same designation in October 1938.
2-G-62—2-G-62/70—2-G-62/73	Created in April 1937. Re-organised and re-designated in April 1938, and again in October 1938.

Note: The Fiat groups began with two squadrons of six aircraft and ended up with three squadrons of nine aircraft. (2-G-3 had four squadrons in March 1939). The assault and co-operation groups consisted of two squadrons, each with six aircraft. (The first Breguet groups had two squadrons, each with three aircraft.) The bomber groups consisted of two squadrons, each with three aircraft.

GOVERNMENT ZONE

Potez Group	Created in August 1936
Marcel Bloch Group	Created in August 1936
Group No 12 (Katiuskas)*	Created in November 1936
Group No 14 (Mixed)	Created in November 1936
Group No 15 (School aircraft)	Created in November 1936
Group No 16	Created at the beginning of 1937
Group No 20 (Natachas)	Created in December 1936
Group No 21 (Ratas)	Created in December 1936
Group No 22 (Mixed)	Created at the beginning of 1937
Group No 23	
Group No 24 (Katiuskas)	Created in the Spring of 1937
Group No 25 (Natachas)	Created in the Spring of 1937
Group No 26 (Chatos)	Created in the Spring of 1937
Group No 27	
Group No 28 (Grumman)	Created in December 1937
Group No 29	
Group No 30 (Natachas)	Created in the Summer of 1937
Group No 71 (Dewoitine, Gourdou, Letov and Aero)	
Group No 72 (Vultee, Potez, DC-2 and D.H.82)	
Group No 73 (Vickers, etc.)	

*Initially mixed.

Note: The fighter groups (Nos 21 and 26) usually consisted of 6 Squadrons of 12 aircraft. In the Ebro, Group 21 ended up with 7 Squadrons, but Group 26 had only 4 Squadrons; in the Central-Southern Zone there were usually one or two Chato Squadrons. Apart from these, there were also the aircraft based at the Fighter and High Speed Flight Schools, and those used by the night operation Squadrons.

The Katiuskas group originally consisted of 3 Squadrons each with 10 machines, but this was later changed to 2 Squadrons each of 15 aircraft. In 1938 there were 4 Squadrons, although the second was soon disbanded, as was the first at the end of the year.

The Natachas groups consisted of 3 Squadrons, although Group 30 had 4 Squadrons after September 1937.

11 Spanish Nationalist Pilots Killed During the War

(Based on the list in *Revista Aeronautica* in 1941, as revised by the author)

In Nieuport 52*s*	
Francisco Cuesta	(September 12, 1936, in Segoria)
Manuel Camino Parladé	(Accident, at Tablada)
In Heinkel He 51*s up to May* 1937	
Alfredo Arija Valenzuela	(December 27, 1936, in Teruel)
Francisco Bofill Dedofeu	(Accident, in Aragón)
Jaime Palmero Palmeta	(April 17, 1937, in Teruel)
In Group 2-*G*-3	
Narciso Bermúdez de Castro	(July 12, 1937, at Brunete)
Antonio López Sert	(December 28, 1937, in Teruel)
Luis Herrero de Teresa	(January 29, 1938, in Teruel)
José Luis Bernal de Mérida	(July 14, 1938, at Sarrión)
José M.ª Etayo Elizondo	(August 25, 1938, in Extremadura)
Pedro Martínez de Irujo	(September 22, 1938, at the Ebro)
José Romagosa Durán	(Accident, at Caspe)
Enrique Ruiz Hermosilla	(Accident, at Matacán)
Manuel Vázquez Sagastizábal	(January 23, 1939, at Pozoblanco)
In Group 3-*G*-3	
Rafael Mazarredo Trenor	(Accident, at Tablada)
Pedro Gil Escoaín	(Accident, at Aranda)
Progreso Núñez Martín	(Accident, at Oropesa)
José Jurado González	(March 24, 1938, at Caspe)
Antonio Figueroa Fernández	(March 26, 1938, at Caspe)
Manuel García Díaz	(March 26, 1938, at Caspe)
Heraclio Gautier Larrainzar	(July 28, 1938, at the Ebro)
Enrique Munaiz de Brea	(August 1, 1938, at the Ebro)
Antonio Olivera Fernández	(October 2, 1938, at the Ebro)
Rafael Mendizábal Amézaga	(December 24, 1938, at Tremp)
In the As de Bastos Group	
Carlos de Haya González	(February 21, 1938, at Teruel)
In Squadron 8-*E*-3	
Francisco Gómez Trenor	(August 31, 1938, in Extremadura)
In Group 5-*G*-5	
Miguel García Pardo	(Accident, at Almaluez)
Rogelio García de Juan	(Accident, at Almaluez)
At training schools	
Manrique Montero Mera	(In Jerez)
Luis Corsini Beca	(In Aragón)
Luis Güervós Martínez	(In Gallur)

12 Spanish Government Fighter Pilots Killed During the War

(Incomplete list based on Tarazona and Tinker's books, on figures supplied by Giménez and Comas, on official bulletins and other sources)

	Date	Place	Reason
Méndez Iriarte, José	6- 8-36	S.ª Madrid	Combat
Andrés Pascual, Antonio	8- 8-36	S.ª Madrid	Combat
González Fernández, Avertano	8- 8-36	S.ª Madrid	Combat
Cabré Plana, José	14- 8-36	Aragón	Combat
Haro López, Antonio de	27- 8-36	Guadix	Combat
Urtubi Ercilla, Félix	9-36	Toledo	Combat
Naranjo	12-36	Manises	Accident
García Herguido, Jesús	6- 1-37	Madrid	Accident
Calderón Sánchez, José	11- 2-37	Jarama	Accident
Bercial Rubero, Luis	20- 2-37	Guadalajara	
Cuartero Pozo, José	12- 3-37		Accident
Blanch, Antonio	13- 3-37	Guadalajara	Accident
Guaza	?	Guadalajara	Accident
Calvo	17- 4-37	Teruel	Accident
Tuya, Luis	16- 4-37	Teruel	Accident
Río Crespo, Felipe del	23- 4-37	Vizcaya	Accident
Baquedano	6-37	Santander	Accident
Pardo Iglesias, Antonio	22- 8-37	Santander	Combat
Ortiz Bueno, Esteban	8-37	Santander	Combat
Magriñá Vidal, Rafael	8-37	Asturias	Combat
Herrera Aguilera, Emilio	2- 9-37	Belchite	Combat
Sardina Pérez, Nicolás			Combat
Gonzalo Obarro, Eloy	19- 9-37	Asturias	Combat
Rodríguez Panadero, Andrés	30- 9-37	Asturias	Combat
Ranz y Díez de Artazcoz, Daniel	30- 9-37	Asturias	Combat
Oreja Moreno, Primitivo	7-10-37	Asturias	Combat
Jornet, Enrique	15-12-37	Teruel	Caught fire
Campoamor Peláez, José M.ª	28-12-37	Teruel	Combat
Frutos González, Luis de	1-38	Teruel	Combat
Pérez García, Antonio	12- 1-38	Teruel	Combat
Chumillas, Francisco	5- 2-38	Teruel	Disappeared
Pinar, Vicente	13- 3-38	Caspe	Accident
Suazo Gare, Conrado	24- 3-38	Caspe-Balaguer	Accident
Villins León, Fernando	24- 3-38	Zaidín	Disappeared
Pérez Pérez, Jesús	24- 3-38	Zaidín	Disappeared
Domingo Hueso, Benigno	24- 3-38	Zaidín	Disappeared
Sánchez, Antonio	24- 3-38	Zaidín	Disappeared
Utrilla	10- 6-38	Levante	Combat

	Date	*Place*	*Reason*
Díaz Pérez, Antonio	10- 6-38	Levante	Combat
Ruiz Gómez, José	25- 6-38	Levante	Combat
Claudín Moncada, Eduardo	5- 7-38	Teruel	Combat
Yuste Gorbatón, Vicente	18- 7-38	Levante	Combat
Belmonte	18- 7-33	Levante	Combat
González Cassola, Eduardo	19- 7-38	Levante	Combat
Fernández Prada, Eduardo	15- 8-38	Ebro	Combat
Gascón Yuste, José	24- 8-38	Ebro	Collision
Nogueira Gordaliza, Antonio	2- 9-38	Ebro	Combat
Araza Sabaté, Manuel	5- 9-38	Ebro	Combat
Correa Antón, José	5- 9-38	Ebro	?
Pascual Gaset, Antonio	5- 9-38	Ebro	Disappeared
San Colom, Jaime	13- 9-38	Ebro	Disappeared
Vega Gómez, Manuel	22- 9-38	Ebro	Disappeared
Margalef Vernet, Luis	23- 9-38	Ebro	Disappeared
Sarriá Calatayud, José	2-10-38	Ebro	Disappeared
Tébar Pérez, Enrique	5-10-38	Ebro	Disappeared
Huerta	7-10-38	Ebro	Disappeared
Beltrán	31-10-38	Ebro	Combat
Paredes	2-11-38	Ebro	Combat
Dosta	6-11-38	Ebro	Combat
Arrés	18-11-38	Cataluña	Combat
Terol	20-11-38	Cataluña	Anti-aircraft fire
Katz, Walter	20-11-38	Cataluña	Anti-aircraft fire
Monjes	24-11-38	Cataluña	Combat
Almodóvar	24-12-38	Cataluña	Combat
Solana, Antonio	8- 6-38	Celrá	Accident
García Esteban, Justo		Fighter School	Accident
Piedra Yébenes, Francisco		Fighter School	Accident
Sampil Fernández, Félix		Reus	Accident
Sampil Fernández, Sebastián		Sabadell	Accident
Alonso Santamaría Roberto	Summer-38	Sabadell	Accident
Castañeda Pardo, Ramón		Fighter School	Accident
Ramos		Los Alcázares	Accident
Corral	28-12-38	Cataluña	Disappeared
Fernández Adalpe, Guillermo	4- 1-39	Cataluña	Disappeared
Carpi Dols, Antonio	11- 1-39	Cataluña	Disappeared
Cairo, Jaime	15- 1-39	Cataluña	Accident
Llovina	16- 1-39	Cataluña	Combat
Fernández	19- 1-39	Cataluña	Disappeared
Cortizo, Sabino	21- 1-39	Cataluña	Combat
Tebar Villar, José	22- 1-39	Cataluña	Combat
Soria Cervera, Antonio	23- 1-39	Cataluña	Combat

13 Spanish Fighter Leaders

(from various sources of information)

NATIONALIST ZONE

Leader of The Fighter Squadron

Joaquin García Morato

Leaders of a Fighter Group (in chronological order)

Joaquín García Morato	(2-G-3 and 3-G-3)
Manrique Montero Mera	(1-G-2)
Angel Salas Larrazábal	(2-G-3)
José Ibarra Montis	(3-G-3)
José Muñoz Jiménez	(5-G-5)
José Barranco del Egido	(3-G-3)

Leaders of Fighter Squadrons (in chronological order)

José Gancedo Sáenz	(Nieuport from Seville)
Angel Chamorro García	(Nieuport from Burgos)
Luis Rambaud Gomá	(Heinkel He 51)
Manrique Montero Mera	(1-E-2 and 4-E-3)
César Martín Campos	(2-E-2 and 3-E-2)
Joaquín García Morato	(1-E-3)
Ángel Salas Larrazábal	(2-E-2 and 2-E-3)
Luis Corsini Beca	(1-E-2)
Julio Salvador Díaz-Benjumea	(1-E-3)
Miguel García Pardo	(2-E-3 and 1-E-5)
Javier Murcia Rubio	(3-E-3 and 1-E-6)
Miguel Guerrero García	(5-E-3)
José Barranco del Egido	(6-E-3)
Heraclio Gautier Larrainzar	(4-E-3)
Gonzalo Queipo de Llano Martí	(4-E-3 and 3-E-3)
José Pazó Montes	(8-E-3)
Arístides García López	(8-E-3)
Mariano Cuadra Medina	(2-E-3)
Rafael Mendizábal Amézaga	(4-E-3)
Manuel Vázquez Sagastizábal	(1-E-3)
Javier Allende Isasi	(4-E-3)
Carlos Serra Pablo Romero	(1-E-3)
Rafael Simón García	(Provisional Fiat School)

GOVERNMENT ZONE

Leaders of The Fighter Squadron (in chronological order)

Ramón Puparelli Francia

Juan Alonso Vega

Isidoro Giménez García

Andrés García de la Calle

Leaders of a Fighter Group (*in chronological order*)

Manuel Cascón Briega	(Group 11 from Getafe)
José Arcega Nájera	(Group 14 mixed)
Ramón Puparelli Francia	(Group 26 Chatos)
Manuel Aguirre López	(Group 21 Ratas)
Juan-J. Armario Álvarez	(Group 26 Chatos)
Eduardo Claudín Moncada	(Group 21 Ratas)
Manuel Zarauza Claver	(Group 21 Ratas)
Juan Comas Borrás	(Group 26 Chatos)
Miguel Zambudio Martínez	(Group 26 Chatos)
Ladislao Duarte Espés (?)	(Group 26 Chatos)
Abelardo Moreno Miró (?)	(Mixed Grumman-Letov Group)
Antonio Urzaiz Guzmán	(Mixed Grumman-Letov Group)
Vicente Castillo Monzo	(Group 26 Chatos)

Leaders of Fighter Squadrons (*in chronological order*)

Avertano González Fernández	(Nieuport 52s)
José Méndez Iriarte	(Nieuport 52s)
Aurelio Villimar Magdaleno	(Mixed Nieuport-Breguet)
Abelardo Moreno Miró	(Mixed Nieuport-Breguet)
Juan Carmona Rey	(Mixed Nieuport-Breguet)
Isidoro Giménez García	(Mixed Nieuport-Breguet)
Manuel Aguirre López	(Mixed Nieuport-Breguet)
Antonio Martín Luna	(Mixed Nieuport-Breguet)
Andrés García de la Calle	(Chatos: at el Jarama)
Roberto Alonso Santamaría	(Chatos: in Aragón)
Javier Jover Rovira	(Chatos: in Andalucía)
Alonso Jiménez Bruguet	(Chatos: replaced by La Calle)
Juan Alonso Vega (?)	(Chatos)
José Riverola Grúas	(Chatos: in the North)
José González Feo	(Bristol Bulldog: in the North)
Andrés Rodríguez Panadero	(Ratas: in the North)
Chindasvinto González García	(Chatos: 2nd Squadron)
Juan Comas Borrás	(Chatos: 3rd Squadron)
Gerardo Gil Sánchez	(Chatos: 2nd Squadron)
Eduardo Claudín Moncada	(Ratas: 1st Squadron)
Manuel Zarauza Claver	(Ratas: 4th Squadron)
Leopoldo Morquillas Rubio	(Chatos: 2nd Squadron)
Ladislao Duarte Espés	(Chatos: 4th Squadron)
José M.ª Bravo Fernández	(Ratas: 3rd Squadron)
Miguel Zambudio Martínez	(Chatos: 3rd Squadron)
Antonio Arias Arias	(Ratas: 4th Squadron)
José Redondo Martín	(Ratas: 1st Squadron)
Francisco Meroño Pellicer	(Ratas: 6th Squadron)
Walter Katz	(Chatos: Night Operations)
Antonio Nieto Sandoval Díaz	(Chatos: 3rd Squadron)
Emilio Ramírez Bravo	(Chatos: 4th Squadron)

Julían Barbero López	(Chatos: 2nd Squadron)
Julio Pereiro Pérez	(Ratas)
Puig Montagut	(Ratas: 7th Squadron)
Vicente Castillo Monzo	(Chatos: 1st Squadron)
Vicente Castillo Monzo	(Chatos: 3rd Squadron)
Francisco Tarazona Torán	(Ratas: 3rd Squadron)
Francisco Viñals Guarro	(Chatos: 2nd Squadron)
Ramón Llorente Castro	(Chatos)
Jaime Torn Roca	(Chatos: 1st Squadron)
Álvaro Muñoz López	(Chatos: 3rd Squadron)
Miguel Castillo Puertas	(Chatos: 4th Squadron)
Nicomedes Calvo Aguilar	(Ratas: 3rd Squadron)
José Falcó San Martín	(Chatos: Night Operations)
Primitivo Pérez García	(Ratas: 7th Squadron)
José M.ª Cano Arnáiz	(Ratas)
Pablo Jiménez Ruiz	(Ratas: 7th Squadron)

14 Nationalist Fighter Pilots Given Important Awards

San Fernando Laureate and Military Medal

Carlos Haya González
Joaquín García Morato
Manuel Vázquez Sagastizábal

Military Medal

Luis Rambaud Gomá
José Gancedo Sáenz
Luis Corsini Beca
José Barranco del Egido
Narciso Bermúdez de Castro
Rafael Mendizábal Amézabal
Antonio Olivera Fernández
José Munoz Jiménez
Ángel Salas Larrazábal
Julio Salvador Díaz-Benjumea
Miguel Guerrero García
Manuel Camino Parladé
Francisco de la Cuesta
Antonio López Sert
Jorge Luis Muntadas Claramunt
Jaime Palmero Palmeta
Arístides García López
Gonzalo Queipo de Llano Martí
Carlos Serra Pablo-Romero
Javier Allende Isasi
Rafael Simón García
Jesús Rubio Paz
Isidro Comas Altadill
Esteban Ibarreche Arriaga
Carlos Bayo Alessandri
Joaquín Ansaldo Vejarano
Joaquín Velasco Fernandez Nespral
Emilio O'Connor Valdivieso
Rodolfo Henricourt
Francisco Diéguez Rodríguez
Jose M. Ripollés Aznares
Ruy Ozores Ochoa
Jesús Fernández Tudela

War Medal with Palms

Javier Murcia Rubio
Rafael Mazarredo Trenor

Luis Herrero de Teresa	Enriques Munaiz de Brea
Progreso Núnez Martín	Pedro Martínez de Irujo
José Jurado González	José M. Etayo Elizondo
Antonio Figueroa Fernández	Francisco Gómez Trenor
Manuel García Díaz	José Romagosa Durán
José Luis Bernal de Mérida	Rogelio García de Juan

Notes: The San Fernando Laureate was awarded to García Morato in Castejón on March 8th, 1938; the Military Medal was placed on his body.

The other San Fernando Laureates were awarded several years after the deaths of those who had qualified for the honour.

The Military Medals were awarded on the Virgin Loreto's Day in 1941. That awarded to Vázquez was placed on his body.

15 Military Record of Joaquín García Morato

Joaquín García Morato had been an outstanding competitor in pre-war aerobatic competitions, and was the author of a book giving primary instruction in aerobatics. He was sent as an instructor to the Flying School at Alcalá de Henares, where he took part in the first Blind Flying Course.

When the war began he was in England, returning from there, across France, to Burgos, from where he flew to Córdoba. He flew Nieuport 52s until receipt of the first Heinkel He 51s. When the Spanish He 51 Squadron was disbanded, he took part in a few bombing raids with Haya and Morau until transferred to Captain Dequal's Fiat Squadron, and finally joined Commander Fagnani's Fiat group.

At the end of December 1936 he formed an autonomous Spanish patrol in Cordoba, together with Salvador and Bermúdez de Castro, and they were joined shortly afterwards by García Pardo. His name was put forward for the award of the San Fernando Laureate after the memorable battle at el Jarama, on February 18th, 1937, and this was bestowed on him one year later.

In April 1937 the patrol was increased to a squadron, joining with Salas' squadron to form group 2-G-3 (May 1937). He continued to lead this group until September of the same year, when he went to Italy. On his return he was named as chief of operations for the 1st Air Brigade, an appointment which he held until the end of June 1938. At that date he assumed command of the second Fiat group (3-G-3) and in November was named as the leader of the Fighter Squadron, a position he retained until his death on April 4th, 1939.

When the war began he had flown for 1,860 hours. During the course of the war he flew another 1,012 hours; carried out 511 operational sorties and was involved in 56 combats during which he gained 40 victories, giving an average of 1 victory for each 1·4 combats and 21 flying hours in fighters. He flew 784 hours in Fiats, 34 in Nieuports, 27 in He 51s, 6 in Me 109s and 5 in He 112s.

During the course of the war he flew more than 30 different types of aircraft.

Morato was an excellent pilot, a good leader and a perfect companion. Small in stature, he had a tremendously likeable character. His prestige was enormous, and with his death the Spanish Air Force lost their indisputable hero.

16 Military Record of Carlos Haya González

Carlos Haya, Morato's brother-in-law, was in many ways his complete opposite. He was tall and serious, and was renowned for his determination and iron will.

When the uprising began, Haya was the leader of the 2nd Breguet Squadron in Group 22 at Tablada. He was then on leave in Málaga as he had just become the father of twins. He joined the forces who were in revolt in Málaga and when these were ordered to return to barracks he boarded a friend's yacht. He went to Jérez, with Diáz Trechuelo, and from there to Tablada in Pablo Atienza's light aircraft. He was the first pilot to fly the DC-2 captured at Tablada when Vara de Rey left, and used this aircraft for transporting troops to the Peninsular, a task which was being carried out at the same time by the Operations Headquarters of the Southern Air Force. On August 2nd, 1936, he bombed Barajas at night, taking off from and returning to Tablada.

On August 11th, 1936, he flew Franco to Burgos and for a short time he was his pilot and adjutant. From October 1936 to March 1937 he was occupied by flying-in essential supplies to Santuario de la Cabeza in the DC-2, a Savoia S-M.81 handed over by the Italians (No 21-20) and Ju 52s sent to Tablada for overhaul.

In March 1937 he was named as leader of the Ju 52 Squadron selected for night operations. This was later divided into two squadrons and became designated as Group 1-G-22. Carrillo, who had also completed the Blind Flying Course, was put in command of the group and Haya remained as leader of the 1st Squadron. In October 1937 Haya asked to be transferred to the Condor Legion, but his request was refused by Franco who considered that Haya was more valuable in the Air Force.

Haya, also good at aerobatics, joined the *As de Bastos* Fiat Group. On February 21st, 1938, after returning from his mother's funeral in Bilbao, he crashed over the Teruel front after colliding with a Chato during combat, and was killed. Haya, together with Ramón Franco and Morato, formed the trio which should have shaped the post-war Spanish Air Army.

When the war began he had flown for 2,425 hours, a figure to which he added 760 hours during the war. He carried out more than 300 operational sorties, 82 of them dropping supplies; I have been unable to ascertain the exact number of war sorties made in fighters, but it must have been in the order of 20 to 25. He had an average of 40 hours flying per month, which was bettered only by Salas.

17 Military Record of Manuel Vázquez Sagastizábal

Manuel Vázquez Sagastizábal was a civil pilot and member of the Seville Aero-Club when the war began. From the outset he belonged to the light aircraft squadron which was led initially by Álvaro Gil Delgado and later by Fernando Medina. He distinguished himself in the campaigns of September and October, to the north of Córdoba, and was promoted from corporal to Second Lieutenant in the latter month. In February 1937 he joined Captain Salas' squadron, and for a few days he flew a Polish PW5 machine until being allocated a Heinkel He 51. With this aircraft he operated from León and Navia; when the squadron was sent to Saragossa, at the end of March, Vázquez moved to Seville and joined Morato's squadron; the first provisional to do so. When 2-G-3 was formed he remained in Salvador's squadron, and in June 1937 his meteoric career as a fighter pilot began, taking him rapidly to third in the list of Nationalist aces, behind Morato and Salvador. When the latter was shot down on October 3rd, 1938, he replaced him as leader of the squadron, until he himself was shot down and killed on January 23rd, 1939, just as the war was ending.

Vázquez had flown for 107 hours when the war broke out, and this figure had reached 1,142 by his death. He flew 657 hours in Fiats and it was in this type of aircraft that he made 324 of his total of more than 400 operational sorties. In the final analysis he had gained an average of 1 victory for each 30 hours flown in Fiats and each 1·8 combats, an average bettered only by Morato.

18 Military Record of José Muñoz Jiménez

José Muñoz Jiménez, 'El Corto' (The Short One) was, as his nickname suggests, far from a giant. He had a poor beginning as a pilot, but his career provides an example of what can be achieved by willpower.

During the pilots' Course at Alcalá he damaged four aircraft in a single day, almost causing the Course to be suspended. In time, however, he became a great pilot, and was particularly outstanding because of his superhuman courage.

When the war began he was sent to join the staff of the Breguet Group in Logrono. He flew in Breguets until the middle of August, usually as Álvarez Pardo's observer, until he went to lead the Dragon-Rapide Squadron in Juan Antonio Ansaldo's Dragon-Fokker Group.

On September 15th he was wounded at the Madrid Sierra and went to hospital. In October he was named as leader of the Spanish Romeo Ro 37 Squadron, which included Murcia and Miguel Guerrero, and remained in this squadron until June 1937, fulfilling an outstanding role at el Jarama.

In the summer of 1937 he flew in the Rayos as second to his cousin Emilio Jiménez Ugarte, and in the autumn he returned to the Romeo Ro 37s as squadron leader, under Negrón's command. In December he became leader of the Heinkel He 51 Group 1-G-2, taking Cuadra as his second. It was in this group that he reached his full potential.

Between December 1937 and September 1938, nine of the group's pilots were killed and seven injured. Their worst day came on March 26th, 1938, when the group were operating in Aragón, and four pilots were injured. One should not conclude from these events that Munõz rashly led his pilots into danger. On the contrary, the affection and respect which all the group's pilots show towards him confirm that Muñoz was an excellent leader.

On August 20th, 1938, he qualified as a Commander. In September he spent a few days at the Fighter School at Gallur, from where he went to La Cenia, to join Mölders' squadron. Durrng November he made 15 operational sorties with this squadron, and at the end of the battle of the Ebro he was named as leader of Group 5-G-5.

At the end of the war he was at Griñón, with the Me 109Bs, and immediately post-war he was made leader of Group 6-G-6 then based at Logroño, later in Melilla. When the *Escuela Superior del Aire* (Advanced Flying School) was formed, he was named as an instructor, a position which he held until July 1941, when he went to Russia.

When Russia was attacked by the forces of Nazi Germany, Spain decided to send a fighter squadron to support the Soviet Air Force. It was agreed that the squadron should be led successively by Salas, Muñoz and Salvador. When his turn came to lead the squadron, Muñoz had made almost 30 operational sorties when, on November 27th, 1941, he was shot down. Forced to escape from a damaged machine by parachute, he baled out at such a low altitude that the canopy of the 'chute was only just beginning to open when he hit the ground and was killed.

When the Uprising began, Muñoz had flown for 971 hours; during the war he flew a further 768 hours and made 402 operational sorties, giving him an average of 23·6 hours and 12·6 sorties per month. He flew 170 hours in He 51s, making 142 sorties; 174 hours and 95 sorties in Ro 37s; 87 hours and 70 sorties in He 70s; 82 hours and 30 sorties in Dragon Rapides; and 79 hours and 34 sorties in fighters. The remaining 30 sorties were made in Br 19s, occupying 72 flying hours.

19 Military Record of Ángel Salas Larrazábal

Ángel Salas Larrazábal, an artillery Lieutenant in 1926, became an observer in 1928 and a pilot in 1929. Because of ability displayed at the Fighter School he was sent to the Martinsyde squadron at Getafe.

At the end of 1930, as the result of an uprising in Cuatro Vientos, led by Ramón Franco and Hidalgo de Cisneros, the Air Force Arm was disbanded and its personnel were returned to their original Arm or Corps, temporarily detached from the Air Force. Shortly afterwards he went to Africa, where he remained until the Uprising, serving first in Tetuan, and later at Cabo Juby and Ifni.

He was promoted to Captain in February 1936, and in July he was with the

Fokker-VII Squadron at Cabo Juby. He learned of the Uprising at Melilla, and decided, together with Escribano, to cross to Spain immediately, each travelling independently. Salas crossed from Getafe to Pamplona the next day, with Tasso and Pardo Pimentel, in Camacho's aircraft. Salas and his companions were imprisoned in Pamplona until released by Nationalist forces.

His first war mission was to liaise between Mola, Franco and Queipo, and on his return he began flying a Dragon which had been bought from a charter company. He mounted a machine-gun on this machine, which he used as a fighter-bomber. In the middle of August he collected the only Fokker-XII to arrive in Vitoria, and ferried this to the Dragon-Fokker Group in Burgos.

He then joined the Nieuport 52 Squadron, achieving his first combat victory at Teruel. He spent a few days in hospital suffering from exhaustion (in one month he had flown for 116 hours during 50 sorties, a figure which was bettered only by Ureña with 180 hours, 24 combat sorties and 101 transport missions).

When he came out of hospital he joined the Dequal Squadron, with which he remained until January 1937. He was then put in command of the PSW Squadron, these aircraft being replaced by Heinkel He 51s only a few days later. He operated in Asturias and Aragón, and it was with this same squadron at Teruel that he was involved in combat with 30 enemy fighters.

At the end of April they were sent to Seville, where the squadron was re-equipped with Fiats. Days later they joined up with the Morato Squadron to form Group 2-G-3. He replaced Morato in the command of this group in September 1937, a position he held until the end of the war. In April 1938 he qualified as a Commander.

Salas had flown for 1,625 hours when the Uprising began. During the war he made 618 sorties, accumulating a total of 1,215 flying hours, and during which he was involved in 49 combats, figures which were not achieved by any other pilot. He flew an average of 20 sorties and 40 hours per month, discounting the two months spent in hospital at the end of 1938. During one wartime sortie he destroyed 3 Katiuskas and a Rata, a figure equalled only by the German Balthasar. He was shot down four times and his aircraft was damaged 117 times in combats fought during the war. He destroyed 48 land vehicles and 16 enemy aircraft, plus one other claimed jointly with another pilot.

At the end of the war he assumed command of the 21st Fighter Regiment and, simultaneously, of the 4th Staff Section. He went to the Advanced Flying School, and from there to Russia heading the 1st expeditionary squadron. In Russia he made 70 operational sorties, during which he destroyed 7 enemy aircraft. These, together with the 17 in Spain, brought his total to 24, a figure equalled only by Morato.

He was later sent as the Air Attaché to Berlin and Paris. In 1956 he converted to turbine powered aircraft and was named Commander of the *Fuerjas Aereas de la Defensa* with the rank of Colonel. When he was promoted to Divisional General he became Commander of the Canaries Air Zone and later Director of Studies at the *Centro Superior de Estudios de la Defensa.* He was promoted to Lieutenant-General in 1966 and was named as Commander of the *Aviación Táctica* and the Straits Air Region (now the 2nd Air Region).

20 Military Record of Julio Salvador Díaz-Benjumea

Julio Salvador Díaz-Benjumea had flown for 550 hours when the war began. He was an artillery Lieutenant in 1930 and became a pupil pilot at Albacete. He showed exceptional ability from early days and was first posted to the Seville Nieuport 52 Squadron, and later to the group at Granada.

In July 1936 he was sent to Gancedo's squadron, at Tablada, and moved with them to Algeciras and Malaga on the morning of the 18th. He then began flying in Nieuport 52s, and quickly moved to Burgos with Senra. When Heinkel He 51s arrived in Seville he, like Morato, joined the Rambaud Squadron, and on August 18th he gained his first two combat victories.

Shortly after he was posted to Dequal's Fiat squadron, which then counted Morato, Salas and García Pardo among its pilots. In December he followed Morato to the south, and they formed the nucleus of the first Spanish Fiat patrol. On February 18th he was with Morato and Bermúdez de Casto at el Jarama and was proposed for the collective Military Medal.

When Group 2-G-3 was formed, Morato made him leader of the 1st Squadron, a position he held until he was shot down over the Ebro, on October 3rd, 1938, and taken prisoner.

During the war he destroyed 24 aircraft and 1 barrage balloon, accumulating 1,066 flying hours in 567 operational sorties. With the Fiats alone he flew 515 sorties totalling 893 hours, which gave him an average of one aircraft destroyed for every 41 flying hours in Fiats. He flew more hours during the war than Morato, Guerrero and Vázquez, despite four months inactivity.

When the war ended he was sent to the 22nd Fighter Regiment (Tablada) and was later named as leader of the Fighter School, which had been moved from Villanubla to Reus and then to Morón, where it remained until it was disbanded in 1953.

He relieved Salas in Command of the expeditionary squadron in Russia, where he remained from March to November 1942. He returned to Morón, remaining there until he was named as Air Attaché in Washington. He was later Director of the *Academia General del Aire*, Chief of Staff for the Straits Air Region, leader of the Defensive Air Forces and second in command of the *Alto Esládo Mayor.*

In November 1969 he was named Air Minister and in 1970 was promoted to Lieutenant-General.

21 Military Record of Miguel Guerrero García

Miguel Guerrero García had much the same beginnings as Julio Salvador. He had, however, accumulated 630 flying hours before the war, rather more than Salvador and, like him, was sent to the Granada Nieuport group. From there he went on a naval pilot's course at Barcelona. This course was in two parts, and having completed the first, Guerrero proceeded on leave to Jaén, where he received orders to assume command of Armilla aerodrome.

It was at this aerodrome that three Nieuports from Getafe landed in error, and were captured. Guerrero, Pérez y Martínez de la Victoria and Bermúdez de Castro virtually commandeered these three machines, and in operations with them shot down four enemy aircraft. He was soon moved to Burgos, where he joined Salvador, Senra and García Pardo. In March 1937 he was transferred to the He 51s, but managed to get Corsini to relieve him in April so that he could join Morato. Never a slim man, he was then so fat that, in his own words, he needed a 'shoehorn' to get him into the cockpit of a Fiat.

When Group 2-G-3 was created he remained in Salvador's squadron until March 1938, when the Group's 3rd Squadron was formed and he was given its command.

The squadron was to be formed with one experienced and two novice pilots culled from the other two squadrons in the group. Guerro was allowed to exercise his choice, but the shrewd García Pardo suggested that he should take Simón, Martínez de Irujo and Ruiz Jiménez, and all three turned out to be good pilots.

During the operations in Extremadura, in August 1938, Guerrero's squadron was stationed at Mérida, where it operated in conjunction with the autonomous Squadron 8-E-3. When Salas went into hospital Guerrero assumed temporary command of the group and, between January 12th and February 15th, of the two squadrons at Posadas aerodrome.

During the war Guerrero accumulated a total of 1,050 flying hours gained in 575 operational sorties: of these totals, 438 sorties totalling 794 flying hours were made in Fiats, 67 sorties and 103 hours in Nieuports. In these aircraft he gained 9 and 4 victories respectively.

At the end of the war he was posted to Group 27, then based at Melilla, and later was sent to replace Salvador as head of the Fighter School. He attended the course on turbine aircraft in 1956, and was named the first leader of the *Ala de Sabres* No 1 (which was later re-designated Ala 11). This was in 1959, 20 years after García Morato's death, and the *Ala de Sabres* was honoured by being allowed to use the insignia of Morato's Squadron. At later dates, Guerrero held the position of Chief of Staff for the Central Air Region, second-in-command of the Levante Air Region and leader of the Canaries Air Zone.

In September 1970 he was promoted to Lieutenant-General and named Commander of the 1st Air Region.

22 Military History of Andrés Garcia La Calle

When the Uprising began, La Calle was a Sergeant pilot in Fighter Group 11, which was then defending Getafe. His record in the Talavera battles was outstanding, and he was promoted to Second Lieutenant on September 3rd, 1936.

At the beginning of February 1937 he was put in command of the first Spanish Chato Squadron. Initially, this consisted of the following pilots: La Calle, Castañeda, Ben Leider, José Calderón, José Allison, Tinker, Dahl, Chang-Selles, Bercial, Ortiz, Gil and Riverola.

On February 7th this squadron moved to the old Hispano Suiza aerodrome in Guadalajara. They began operations at El Jarama, where their activities were outstanding but their losses heavy. José Calderón, Ben Leider and Luis Bercial were killed, and José Allison and Harold Dahl were shot down.

When this battle ended, García La Calle was sent to Russia as an instructor, accompanying the second batch of pilots sent there for training. In his absence Jiménez Bruguet took command of the squadron, which fought at Teruel in April and then went to Biscay.

García La Calle returned to Spain during the battle of Teruel, but for one year he was attached as aide to the Under-Secretary for Air. At the time of the battle of Catalonia he was named as Chief of Staff of the Fighter Squadron, of which he assumed command when Giménez went to El Carmoli. On November 30th, 1938, he was promoted on merit to the rank of Major.

According to Tinker, La Calle gained eleven confirmed victories at El Jarama and was considered by him to be a good leader. This opinion was not shared by Tarazona. La Calle now lives in Mexico.

23 Military History of Isidoro Giménez García

A member of Group 31 stationed at Getafe, he was a Second Lieutenant pilot when the war began. One of his first operational sorties involved reconnaissance of the access roads to Madrid. He continued to operate with his squadron on routine operational patrols until, in the middle of August, he was named leader of the *Alas Rojas* Squadron and sent to Sariñena. On November 18th he was promoted to Captain.

In December he went to Russia with Cascón, Villimar, González Montero, Gumersindo Areán and 200 pilots undergoing training. He returned in July 1937 and took part in the battle of Brunete, when he led a squadron of Natachas which operated successively from Talamanca del Jarama and Santa Cruz de la Zarza aerodromes. He moved with the same squadron to Villar del Arzobispo and later to Barcelona.

In the autumn he was graded as a flying instructor and replaced Félix Sampil as commander of the Fighter School.

He was promoted to Major on June 8th, 1938, and in August he replaced Juan Alonso Vega as commander of the Fighter Squadron, a position he held for most of the battle of the Ebro. During the first few days of the Catalonian campaign he was posted to El Carmolí and remained there until the war was over. He is at present living in Spain.

24 Military History of Manuel Aguirre López

On July 18th, 1936, he was sent to Getafe as a Sergeant pilot. In September he was posted to Andújar, where he was later the leader of the 1st Squadron of Group 21. In November 1936 he was promoted to Lieutenant and shortly afterwards he began flying Chatos.

On April 1st, 1937, he was transferred to Group 16 and he operated with this Group at the Aragón front until he went to Biscay.

He was one of the first Spanish pilots to fly a Rata and at the battle of Belchite he led a patrol in Boris Smirnov's squadron. On September 12th, 1937, he was promoted to Captain and given leadership of a squadron.

Shortly before the battle of Teruel he was made leader of the Rata Group, which then had two Spanish squadrons—(the 1st and 4th, led by Claudín and Zarauza) and four with Russian personnel.

In June 1938 Aguirre gave up leadership of the group, and in October he was named as second-in-command of the Fighter Squadron. In December 1938 he was promoted to Major.

He is now living in Spain.

25 Military History of Juan Comas Borrás

A naval pilot at the beginning of the war, in September 1936 he went for further training at San Javier.

At the end of January 1937 he was posted to Alonso Santamaría's fighter squadron at Lérida, later operating from Castejón and Sarrión. He carried out varied tasks until September 1937 when he was named as leader of the 3rd Chato Squadron based at Figueras, and shortly afterwards was promoted to Lieutenant.

In October his squadron was operating from Reus, and in November from Barracas during the battle of Teruel. In March 1938 he was promoted to Captain.

On September 13th, 1938, he was made commander of Group 26, then based at Valls, later at Sabadell and Monjos. At this latter aerodrome he was wounded during an air raid and transferred to hospital at Villafranca de Panadés, where his left leg was amputated. He was promoted to Commander on November 17th, 1938.

He is now living in Catalonia.

26 Military History of Miguel Zambudio Martínez

When war broke out he went to Reus aerodrome for training where, according to Gayoso, he damaged three Nieuport 52s in a short space of time. In spite of this, he was sent to the Fighter School, and from there to the North on March 23rd, 1937.

When the Northern Campaign ended he was promoted to Lieutenant and in 1938 he was made leader of the 3rd Chato Squadron. In November of the same year he became leader of Group 26, replacing Comas, and was promoted to Captain.

He now lives in France.

27 Military History of Eduardo Claudín Moncada

Claudín was an aeronautical engineering student when the Uprising began.

He was sent to Russia with the first batch of pupil pilots, which embarked on the *Ciudad de Cadiz* at Cartagena at the end of December 1936. This group arrived at Feodosia, in the Crimea, 15 days later. From there they went overland to Kirovabad, to the North of the Caucasus mountains, passing through Rostov and Tiflis.

In May 1937 Claudín returned to Spain, this time the group travelling by boat to Le Havre and across France. He was sent to the Rata Group led successively by Smirnov, Ivanov and Aguirre and, with natural ability as a pilot, he soon made his presence felt: to the extent that by Teruel he was already leading the 1st Squadron.

When the Nationalist offensive began to the south of the Ebro, the Ratas from the 1st Squadron returned to their former aerodrome at Caspe. During these difficult days the squadron operated from Almenar (Lérida), Bell-Puig and Tarragona.

On April 9th, 1938, the Ratas were withdrawn from the front, being moved from Reus to Barcelona, to support the new Minister of Defence (Negrín). In May Claudín was operating at the Castellón front, from Liria, and in the following month he was named as leader of Group 21, to replace Manuel Aguirre. On July 5th, 1938, he was killed in combat at the Teruel front.

28 Military History of Manuel Zarauza Claver

Zarauza, in course of time to become Claudin's successor as leader of Group 21, was another of the pilots who were trained at the beginning of the war to fly Ratas.

He was very small, and Tarazona said that he was almost completely hidden inside the cockpit of an aircraft, which accounted for his nickname of 'The Phantom Pilot'. In the Spring of 1937 he moved to the North with Aguirre's Chato squadron. He was promoted to Lieutenant on November 27th, 1937, and simultaneously named as leader of the 4th Rata Squadron. He was promoted to Captain on March 11th, 1938, and replaced Claudín as leader of Group 21 in July 1938, a position he held until the fall of Catalonia. On December 19th, 1938, he was promoted to Major.

After the war he went to Russia, where he was killed in a flying accident.

29 Military History of José Bravo Fernández

Bravo was an engineering student in Madrid and, like Claudín, learned to fly in Russia. Back in Spain he made a few sorties in a Chato squadron at Brunete, and was then transferred to Belchite, where he operated as a member of the 1st Rata Squadron. An above average pilot, he was soon made a patrol leader.

When the 3rd Squadron of Ratas was re-formed with Spanish personnel, Bravo was made leader of the squadron, with Toquero and Tarazona, veterans from the North, as patrol leaders. He had been promoted to Lieutenant on March 11th, 1938, and was again promoted, to Captain, on May 31st, 1938.

The 3rd Squadron operated from Sagunto throughout the Castellón campaign, from El Vendrell at the time of the attack on the bridgehead at Balaguer, and was based at Camporrobles during the days of the final attack on Valencia. Prior to this they had spent some time in Alicante in defence of the port. During the first few weeks of the Ebro battles they operated from Pla de Cabra, after a brief stay at El Vendrell.

In September Bravo handed over leadership of the 3rd Squadron to Tarazona and shortly afterwards he was named as second-in-command of the group, a post he retained until the end of the Catalonian campaign.

Bravo flew in the Russian Air Force during World War II, and remained in Russia until 1948. He now lives in Spain.

30 Aircraft Destroyed by Nationalist Pilots According to their Unit at the time

(Based on 2-G-3 and 3-G-3 lists, and those published in *Avión* and corrected by the author)

		In Nieuport 52*s*	*In He* 51*s*	*In Fiat Sqdn*	*In Group* 2-*G*-3	*In Group* 3-*G*-3	*In Sqdn* 8-*E*-3	*In Group* 5-*G*-5	*Total*
1	Joaquín García Morato	1	3	19	9	8	—	—	40
2	Julio Salvador Díaz-Benjumea	—	3	3+1	18	—	—	—	24+1
3	Manuel Vázquez Sagastizábal	—	—	—	21⅓	—	—	—	21⅓
4	Arístides García López	—	1	—	12	—	4	—	17
5	Ángel Salas Larrazábal	1	2	4	9⅓	—	—	—	16⅓
6	Miguel Guerrero García	4	—	—	9	—	—	—	13
7	Joaquín Velasco Fernández Nespral	—	—	—	—	11	—	—	11
8	Miguel García Pardo	1	—	1	9	—	—	1	12
9	Carlos Bayo Alessandri	—	—	—	11	—	—	—	11
10	Rodolfo Henricourt	—	—	—	10	—	—	—	10
11	Javier Allende Isasi	—	1	—	6	—	—	—	7
12	Esteban Ibarreche Arriaga	—	—	—	7	—	—	—	7
13	Emilio O'Connor Valdivielso	—	—	—	—	6	—	—	6
14	José Larios Fernández	—	—	—	—	6	—	—	6
15	Javier Murcia Rubio	—	—	—	2	3	—	—	5
16	Jorge Muntadas Claramunt	—	1	—	1	—	3	—	5
17	Rafael Simón García	—	—	—	5	—	—	—	5
18	Abundio Cesteros García	—	—	—	5	—	—	—	5
19	Antonio Manrique Garrido	—	—	—	5	—	—	—	5
20	Luis Alcocer Moreno-Abellá	—	—	—	5	—	—	—	5
21	Jesús Rubio Paz	—	—	—	4	—	—	—	4
22	Ramón Senra Álvarez	1	—	—	3	—	—	—	4

23	Salvador Sera Alorda	—	—	—	4	—	—	—	4
24	Narciso Bermúdez de Castro	1	—	2	1	—	—	—	4
25	Carlos Serra Pablo Romero	—	—	—	3⅓	—	—	—	3⅓
26	Isidro Comas Altadill	—	—	—	3	—	—	—	3
27	Ignacio Alfaro Arregui	—	—	—	—	3	—	—	3
28	José Andrés Lacourt Maciá	—	—	—	—	3	—	—	3
29	José Ruiz-Jiménez Cortés	—	—	—	3	—	—	—	3
30	Joaquín Ansaldo Vejarano	—	1	—	1	—	—	—	2
31	Juan de Frutos Rubio	—	—	—	2	—	—	—	2
32	Rafael Mazarredo Trenor	—	1	—	1	—	—	—	2
33	José M. Muerza Amatrain	—	—	—	—	2	—	—	2
34	Jaime Illera García Lago	—	—	—	2	—	—	—	2
35	Joaquín Pérez y Martínez Victoria	1	—	—	—	—	—	—	1
36	Manrique Montero Mera	—	—	—	—	1	—	—	1
37	Carlos Haya González	—	—	1	—	—	—	—	1
38	José M. Careaga Uriguen	—	—	—	1	—	—	—	1
39	Luis Herrero de Teresa	—	—	—	1	—	—	—	1
40	Álvaro Fernández Matamoros Scott	—	—	—	1	—	—	—	1
41	Juan Prieto Molina	—	—	—	—	1	—	—	1
42	Rafael Mendizábal Amézaga	—	—	—	—	1	—	—	1
43	Jaime Palmero Palmeta	—	1	—	—	—	—	—	1
44	Santiago González Guzmán	—	—	—	—	1	—	—	1
45	Andrés Robles Cebrián	—	—	—	—	1	—	—	1
46	José Romagosa Durán	—	—	—	1	—	—	—	1
47	Luis Recasén y Queipo de Llano	—	—	—	1	—	—	—	1
48	Alfonso Ruibal Sabio	—	—	—	—	1	—	—	1
49	Ramón Luca de Tena	—	—	—	—	—	1	—	1
	Others	—	2	—	2	2	—	—	6
Total		10	16	30+1	179	50	8	1	294+1

31 Aircraft Destroyed by Nationalist Pilots Classified by Types

		Ratas	*Chatos*	*Katiuskas*	*Papagayos*	*Potez*	*Delfin*	*Breguet*	*Nieuport* 52	*Others*	*Total*
1	Joaquín García Morato	5	12	2	9	3	—	3	3	3	40
2	Julio Salvador Díaz Benjumea	3	13	—	4	1	—	2	1	1	24+1
3	Manuel Vázquez Sagastizábal	10	6	$2\frac{1}{3}$	2	1	—	—	—	—	$21\frac{1}{3}$
4	Arístides García López	5	10	—	2	—	—	—	—	—	17
5	Ángel Salas Larrazábal	1	8	$5\frac{1}{3}$	—	1	—	—	—	1	$16\frac{1}{3}$
6	Miguel Guerrero García	2	4	—	3	—	—	1	—	3	13
7	Joaquín Velasco Fdez. Nespral	4	5	—	2	—	—	—	—	—	11
8	Miguel García Pardo	8	2	—	—	—	1	1	—	—	12
9	Carlos Bayo Alessandri	6	5	—	—	—	—	—	—	—	11
10	Rodolfo Henricourt	5	4	—	—	—	1	—	—	—	10
11	Javier Allende Isasi	2	5	—	—	—	—	—	—	—	7
12	Esteban Ibarreche Arriaga	3	4	—	—	—	—	—	—	—	7
13	Emilio O'Connor Valdivielso	3	3	—	—	—	—	—	—	—	6
14	José Larios Fernández	1	4	—	1	—	—	—	—	—	6
15	Javier Murcia Rubio	3	2	—	—	—	—	—	—	—	5
16	Jorge Muntadas Claramunt	1	4	—	—	—	—	—	—	—	5
17	Rafael Simón García	1	3	—	1	—	—	—	—	—	5
18	Abundio Cesteros García	2	3	—	—	—	—	—	—	—	5
19	Antonio Manrique Garido	1	4	—	—	—	—	—	—	—	5
20	Luis Alcover Moreno-Abella	1	4	—	—	—	—	—	—	—	5
21	Jesús Rubio Paz	1	2	—	1	—	—	—	—	—	4
22	Ramón Senra Álvarez	1	2	—	—	—	—	—	1	—	4
23	Salvador Serra Alorda	2	1	1	—	—	—	—	—	—	4
24	Narciso Bermúdez de Castro	1	—	1	1	—	—	—	1	—	4
25	Carlos Serra Pablo Romero	2	1	$\frac{1}{3}$	—	—	—	—	—	—	$3\frac{1}{3}$
26	Isidro Comas Altadill	3	—	—	—	—	—	—	—	—	3
27	Ignacio Alfaro Arregui	3	—	—	—	—	—	—	—	—	3
[illegible]	[illegible]	[illegible]	1	[illegible]	2	[illegible]	—	—	—	—	3

31	Juan de Frutos Rubio	—	2	—	—	—	—	—	—	—	2
32	Rafael Mazarredo Trenor	—	2	—	—	—	—	—	—	—	2
33	José M. Muerza Amatrain	1	1	—	—	—	—	—	—	—	2
34	Jaime Illera García Lago	1	1	—	—	—	—	—	—	—	2
35	Joaquín Pérez y Mnez. Victoria	—	—	—	—	—	—	—	1	—	1
36	Manrique Montero Mera	1	—	—	—	—	—	—	—	—	1
37	Carlos Haya González	—	1	—	—	—	—	—	—	—	1
38	José M. Careaga Uriguen	—	1	—	—	—	—	—	—	—	1
39	Luis Herrero de Teresa	1	—	—	—	—	—	—	—	—	1
40	Álvaro Fdez. Matamoros Scott	1	—	—	—	—	—	—	—	—	1
41	Juan Prieto Molina	1	—	—	—	—	—	—	—	—	1
42	Rafael Mendizábal Amézaga	—	1	—	—	—	—	—	—	—	1
43	Jaime Palmero Palmeta	—	1	—	—	—	—	—	—	—	1
44	Santiago González Guzmán	1	—	—	—	—	—	—	—	—	1
45	Andrés Robles Cebrián	1	—	—	—	—	—	—	—	—	1
46	José Romagosa Durán	1	—	—	—	—	—	—	—	—	1
47	Luis Recasén y Queipo de Llano	—	—	—	1	—	—	—	—	—	1
48	Alfonso Ruibal Sabio	—	—	—	1	—	—	—	—	—	1
49	Ramón Luca de Tena	—	1	—	—	—	—	—	—	—	1
	Others	2	1	2	—	1	—	—	—	—	6
	Total	94	126	14	30	7	2	7	7	7+1	294+1
	Distribution by Units:										
	Group 2-G-3	70	81	7	18	1	2	—	—	—	179
	Group 3-G-3	20	20	1	9	—	—	—	—	—	50
	Group 5-G-5	1	—	—	—	—	—	—	—	—	1
	Squadron 8-E-3	1	7	—	—	—	—	—	—	—	8
	Nieuport 52s	—	—	—	—	—	—	2	3	5	10
	Heinkel He 51s	—	8	1	—	2	—	2	3	—	16
	Fiat Squadron	2	10	5	3	4	—	3	1	2+1	30+1
		94	126	14	30	7	2	7	7	7+1	294+1

32 Infantry Regiments, various Battalions and Special Units existing in July 1936

(Information from the *Military Year Book* 1936)

Infantry Regiments

No 1	Wad-Ras	In Madrid	No 24	Bailén	In Logroño
No 2	León	In Madrid	No 25	San Quintín	In Valladolid
No 3	Castilla	In Badajoz	No 26	Toledo	In Zamora
No 4	Covadonga	In Madrid	No 27	Argel	In Cáceres
No 5	Lepanto	In Granada	No 28	La Victoria	In Salamanca
No 6	Granada	In Seville	No 29	Zamora	In La Coruna
No 7	Pavía	In Algeciras	No 30	Zaragoza	In Lugo
No 8	Vitoria (Later known as the Oviedo Regiment)	In Málaga	No 31	Burgos	In León
			No 32	Milán	In Oviedo
No 9	Otumba	In Valencia	No 33	Cádiz	In Cádiz
No 10	Guadalajara	In Valencia	No 34	Sevilla	In Cartagena
No 11	Tarifa	In Alicante	No 35	Mérida	In Ferrol
No 12	Vizcaya	In Alcoy	No 36	Palma	In Palma de Mallorca
No 13	Badajoz	In Barcelona			
No 14	Alcántara	In Barcelona	No 37	Baleares	In Mahón
No 15	Almansa	In Tarragona	No 38	Tenerife	In Santa Cruz de Tenerife
No 16	Albuera	In Lérida			
No 17	Aragón	In Saragossa			
No 18	Gerona	In Saragossa	No 39	Canarias	In Las Palmas de Gran Canaria
No 19	Galicia	In Jaca			
No 20	Valladolid	In Huesca			
No 21	Valencia	In Santander			
No 22	San Marcial	In Burgos	No 40	Simancas	In Gijon
No 23	América	In Pamplona			

Mountain Battalions

No 1	Chiclana	In Figueras	No 5	Flandes	In Vitoria
No 2	Asia	In Gerona	No 6	Garellano	In Bilbao
No 3	Madrid	In Seo de Urgel	No 7	Arapiles	In Estella
			No 8	Sicilia	In Pamplona
No 4	Ciudad Rodrigo	In Barbastro			

Machine-gun Battalions

No 1	In Castellón	No 3	In Almería
No 2	In Plasencia	No 4	In Manresa

Cyclists' Battalion

In Alcala de Henares

Combat Vehicles Regiment

No 1	In Madrid	No 2	In Saragossa

Presidential Battalion
War Ministry's Group
In Madrid

33 Artillery, Cavalry and Engineering Units in July 1936

(Information from the *Military Year Book* 1936)

Light Artillery Regiments

No 1	In Getafe	1st Division	No 9	In Saragossa	5th Division
No 2	In Vicálcaro	1st Division	No 10	In Calatayud	5th Division
No 3	In Seville	2nd Division	No 11	In Burgos	6th Division
No 4	In Granada	2nd Division	No 12	In Logroño	6th Division
No 5	In Valencia	3rd Division	No 13	In Segovia	7th Division
No 6	In Murcia	3rd Division	No 14	In Valladolid	7th Division
No 7	In Barcelona	4th Division	No 15	In Pontevedra	8th Division
No 8	In Mataró	4th Division	No 16	In La Coruna	8th Division

Heavy Artillery Regiments

No 1	In Córdoba	No 3	In San Sebastián
No 2	In Gerona	No 4	In Medina del Campo

Mountain Artillery Regiments

No 1	In Barcelona	No 2	In Vitoria

Mounted Artillery Regiment
In Campamento

Coastal Artillery Regiments

No 1	In Cadiz	No 3	In Cartagena
No 2	In Ferrol	No 4	In Mahón

Mixed Artillery Groups

No 1	In Palma	No 3	In Las Palmas
No 2	In Tenerife		

Artillery Intelligence Groups

No 1	In Carabanchel	No 3	In Valladolid
No 2	In Barcelona		

Mounted Group
In Oviedo

Anti-aircraft Defence Groups

No 1	In Campamento	No 2	In Saragossa

Cavalry Regiments

No 1	Castillejos	In Saragossa	No 6	Numancia	In Vitoria
No 2	Villarrobledo	In Palencia	No 7	Lusitania	In Valencia
No 3	Calatrava	In Salamanca	No 8	Taxdir	In Seville
No 4	España	In Burgos	No 9	Sabtiago	In Barcelona
No 5	Farnesio	In Valladolid	No 10	Montesa	In Barcelona

Machine-gun and Cannon Group
In Aranjuez

School of Equitation
In Campamento

Remount Centres
In Tetuán de las Victorias (Madrid) and Larache

Breeding Centres
In Jerez and Ecija

Railway Regiments
Nos 1 and 2 In Leganés

Signals Regiment
In El Pardo

Aerostation Regiment
In Guadalajara

Regiment of Mining Engineers
In Madrid

Sappers Regiments

No 1	In Carabanchel	No 5	In Saragossa
No 2	In Seville	No 6	In San Sebastián
No 3	In Valencia	No 7	In Alcalá de Henares
No 4	In Barcelona	No 8	In Gijón

Mixed Groups of Sappers and Signallers

No 1	In Palma	No 3	In Tenerife
No 2	In Mahón	No 4	In Las Palmas

Searchlight Group
In Madrid

Battalion of Bridge-builders
In Saragossa

Central Vehicle Park
In Madrid

34 African Army

(General Gómez Morato)

Eastern Division (General Romerales)
1st Tercio Legion, in Tauima (Lt Col Blanco-Novo)
  1st Bandera (Cdr Alvarez Entrana)
  2nd Bandera (Cdr Carbonell)
  3rd Bandera (Cdr Ricardo Alonso Vega)

Melilla Group of Regulars, No 2. In Nador (Lt Col Barrón)
  1st Tabor (Capt Emperador)
  2nd Tabor (Cdr Rodrigo)
  3rd Tabor (Cdr López Guerrero)

Alhucemas Group of Regulars, No 5. In Segangan (Lt Col Delgano Serrano)
  1st Tabor (Cdr Mizzian)
  2nd Tabor (Cdr Lambea)
  3rd Tabor (Cdr Ríos Capapé)

Eastern Group of African Chasseurs (Col Solans)
  Melilla Chasseurs Battalion No 3 (Lt Col Anel)
  Ceuta Chasseurs Battalion No 7 (Lt Col Aymat)

Cavalry. Six squadrons of Regulars

Eastern Artillery Group
  1st Mobile Group, Melilla
  2nd Mobile Group, Riff
  1st Permanent Group, Melilla
  Machine-gunners Battalion (Cdr Seco)
  Cyclists Detachments, Melilla and Riff
  Melilla Sea Company

Western Division
2nd Tercio Legion, in Dar Riffien (Lt Col Yagüe)
  4th Bandera (Cdr Vierna)
  5th Bandera (Cdr Castejón)
  6th Bandera (Cdr Pimentel)

Tetuan Group of Regulars, No 1. In la Alcazaba (Lt Col Asensio)
1st Tabor (Cdr del Oro)
2nd Tabor (Cdr Serrano)
3rd Tabor (Cdr J. Asensio)

Ceuta Group of Regulars, No 3. In Ceuta (Lt Col Caballero)
1st Tabor (Cdr Rubio Oliver)
2nd Tabor (Cdr Amador de los Ríos)
3rd Tabor (Cdr Civantos)

Larache Group of Regulars, No 4. In Alcazarquivir (Lt Col Romero Bassart)
1st Tabor (Cdr F. García Valiño)
2nd Tabor (Cdr Ansoleaga)
3rd Tabor (Cdr Rodríguez de la Herrán)

Western Group of African Chasseurs
San Fernando Chasseurs Battalion No 1, in Alcazarquivir
Las Navas Chasseurs Battalion No 2, in Larache
Cerinola Chasseurs Battalion No 6, in Tetuan
Serrallo Chasseurs Battalion No 8, in Ceuta

Cavalry. Six squadrons of Regulars

Western Artillery Group (Gautier)
1st Mobile Group, Ceuta-Tetuán
2nd Mobile Group, Larache
Coastal Group, Ceuta

Cyclists Detachments. Ceuta, Tetuán and Larache
Sea Company at Ceuta
Moroccan Sappers Battalion
Moroccan Signals Battalion
Moroccan Vehicle Service

35 Naval Forces on July 18th, 1936

(Information from the Naval Headquarters, 1936)

IN SERVICE
Fleet (Ferrol)
Battleship *Jaime 1* (was at Santander)
Cruiser *Miguel de Cervantes* (Flagship)
Cruiser *Libertad*
Cruiser *Almirante Cervera*
Cruiser *Méndez Núñez* (was in Guinea)

Flotilla of Destroyers (Cartagena)
Destroyer *Churruca* (was in the Straits)
Destroyer *Almirante Valdés*
Destroyer *Sánchez Barcáiztegui*
Destroyer *Lepanto*
Destroyer *Almirante Antequera* (was at Santander)
Destroyer *Almirante Ferrándiz*
Destroyer *Almirante Miranda*
Destroyer *José Luis Díez*
Destroyer *Alcalá Galiano*
Destroyer *Alsedo*
Destroyer *Lazaga*
Destroyer *Velasco* (was at Ferrol)
Flotilla of Submarines (Cartagena and Mahón)
B-1 to B-6
C-1 to C-6

Gunboats
Dato, Canalejas, Laya and *Cánovas del Castillo*

Coastguard vessels
Uad Martin, Uad Kert, Uad Lucus, Uad Muluya, Alcázar, Arcila, Larache, Tetúan and *Xauen*

Torpedo Boats
Nos 2, 3, 7, 9, 14, 16, 17, 19, 20, 21 and 22

Training Vessels
J.S. Elcano and *Galatea*

Various Vessels
Tofiño, C. Casado, Almirante Lobo, Kanguro and *Cíclope* (Also gunboats, tugs and fishery protection vessels)
UNDER CONSTRUCTION (Ferrol Arsenal)
Cruisers *Canarias* and *Baleares*
Minelayers *Júpiter* and *Vulcano*
UNDER CONSTRUCTION (Cartegena Arsenal)
Destroyers *Gravina, Escaño, Císcar, Jorge Juan, Ulloa*
Submarines D-1 to D-4

36 Air Forces in July 1936

MILITARY AIR FORCE

Squadron No 1 (Madrid)

Group No 11 (Nieuport 52s)	In Getafe
Group No 21 (Breguet 19s)	In León
Group No 31 (Breguet 19s)	In Getafe
Three-engined Unit	In Getafe

Squadron No. 2 (Seville)

Group No 12 (Nieuport 52s)	In Granada (Disbanded days before the Uprising)
Group No 22 (Breguet 19s)	In Seville

Squadron No 3 (Barcelona)

Group No 13 (Nieuport 52s)	In el Prat
Group No 23 (Breguet 19s)	In Logroño

Air Forces in Africa

Group No 1 (Breguet 19s)	In Tetuán, Melilla and Larache
Fokker VII Squadron	At Cabo Juby
Seaplane Squadron (Dornier-Wals)	At Melilla

Training Services

Squadron Y-1 (Breguet 19s)	Cuatro Vientos
Squadron Y-2 (Breguet 19s)	Los Alcázares
Seaplane Group No 6 (Dornier-Wals)	Los Alcázares

Material Services

N.W. Regional Park	In León
S. Regional Park	In Seville
S.E. Regional Park	In Los Alcázares

NAVAL AIR FORCE

Reconnaissance Flotilla	(Savoia 62s)
Bomber Squadron	(Dornier-Wals)
Torpedo Squadron	(Vickers Vildebeest)
Combat Squadron	(Martinsydes)
Instruction Squadron	(Hispano E-30s)
Pilot's Training Squadron	(Macchi M 18s, Savoia 62s and Martinsydes)

37 Civil Guard, Carabineers, Security and Riot Corps Forces in July 1936

(Information from the *Military Year Book* 1936 and other sources)

CIVIL GUARD

Zone 1 (*Valencia*)

Tercio No 5	Valencia	Tercio No 20	Guadalajara
Tercio No 7	Saragossa	Tercio No 23	Ciudad Real
Tercio No 15	Murcia		

Zone No 2 (*Córdoba*)

Tercio No 8	Granada	Tercio No 17	Seville
Tercio No 16	Málaga	Tercio No 18	Córdoba

Zone 3 (*Valladolid*)

Tercio No 6	Coruña	Tercio No 12	Burgos
Tercio No 9	Valladolid	Tercio No 13	San Sebastían
Tercio No 10	Oviedo	Tercio No 22	Santander

Zone 4 (*Madrid*)

Tercio No 1	Madrid	Tercio No 11	Badajoz
Tercio No 2	Toledo	Tercio No 14	Madrid
Tercio No 4	Madrid	Tercio No 21	Salamanca

Zone 5 (*Barcelona*)

Tercio No 3	Barcelona	Tercio No 19	Barcelona

Note: Tercio No 24 also existed. This had its headquarters at Santa Cruz, Tenerife, and was to support the Moroccan and Balearics forces. It had a total of 34,320 men in 213 companies.

CARABINEERS

Zone 1 (*Barcelona*)

Command No 1	Barcelona	Command No 3	Huesca
Command No 2	Barcelona		

Zone 2 (*Valencia*)

Command No 4	Valencia	Command No 5	Baleares

Zone 3 (*Alicante*)

Command No 6	Alicante		

Zone 4 (*Almería*)

Command No 7	Almería	Command No 8	Granada

Zone 5 (*Málaga*)

Command No 9	Málaga	Command No 10	Algeciras

Zone 6 (*Seville*)

Command No 11	Cádiz	Command No 12	Seville-Huelva

Zone 7 (*Salamanca*)			
Command No 13	Badajoz	Command No 14	Salamanca-Cáceres
Zone 8 (*Madrid*)			
Command No 15	Madrid-Saragossa-Córdoba	Command No 16	Zamora
Zone 9 (*Coruña*)			
Command No 17	Coruña	Command No 18	Asturias-Santander-Lugo
Zone 10 (*San Sebastían*)			
Command No 19	Guipúzcoa-Vizcaya	Command No 20	Navarra

Note: The Carabineers Corps had a total of 15,790 men in 110 companies.

SECURITY AND RIOT CORPS

There was at least one company of each type in every Spanish province. In the more important provinces there were several companies and in Madrid there were no fewer than 12, one for each district.

Apart from these independent companies there were the Riot Groups, of which there were three in Madrid, three in Barcelona, two in Valencia and one each in Bilbao, Valladolid, Seville, Saragossa, Oviedo, La Coruña, Badajoz, Granada and Burgos.

Note: The Security and Riot Corps had somewhere in the order of 17,500 men distributed between 117 companies.

38 Various Monetary Values in 1936

The value of the dollar had been fixed in 1934 at the present day parity of $35 : 1 ounce of gold, or $1.125 : 1 gram of gold. Since the value of the dollar has not changed since 1936 it is a useful reference.

The relationship between the gold peseta and the dollar, which was 5.18 ptas. to the dollar in 1933 (25 ptas. to the pound sterling), went from just above 8 ptas. during the war, to 9.55 in 1939 and to 10.95 in 1940. In December 1937 export transactions were being carried out at 8.58 ptas. and import transactions at 10.72 ptas.

In 1936 the value of the paper peseta was approximately 55 per cent of the value of the gold peseta.

The value of the pound sterling stayed at the same rate of 4 dollars from 1934 to 1949, the date when it was devalued to 2.8 dollars. Its equivalence with the gold peseta was 32 in 1936 and 38 in 1939. In fact, transactions in the Nationalist Zone were made at 42 ptas. to the pound for exports and 53 ptas. to the pound for imports. The pound was eventually quoted at 100 ptas. The value of the French franc, the lira, the mark and the ruble came down during

World War II, but in 1936 the following values were quoted:

1 French franc	0.50 ptas
1 lira	0.65 ptas
1 mark	3.30 ptas
1 ruble	2.80 ptas

The French franc was devalued at the beginning of October 1936 and was quoted in December 1937 at 0.29 ptas. for exports and 0.36 ptas. for imports. The lira was also devalued on October 5th, 1936.

Initially the Nationalist peseta, as that of the Government, was subjected to 'rubber stamping' to avoid any possibility of an influx of new money in Madrid (which held the Bank of Spain and the Mint) which might cause devaluation. At the beginning of 1937 the 'rubber stamped' peseta was worth twice the Madrid peseta. At a later date new notes went to the Nationalist Zone, but these were printed abroad.

39 The Law of Variation, with the Dates and Numbers of Priests and Clergy Executed

(Calculated on information from Manuel Montero's book)

1st Wave of Terror			*2nd Wave of Terror*		
July 1936			August 1936		
Day 17	1		Day 5	58	
Day 18	2		Day 6	41	
Day 19	10		Day 7	46	
Day 20	31		Day 8	55	
Day 21	25		Day 9	68	
Day 22	37		Day 10	57	
Day 23	60		Day 11	52	
Day 24	85		Day 12	79	
Day 25	102		Day 13	104	
Day 26	69	963	Day 14	94	1,461
Day 27	82	executions	Day 15	96	executions
Day 28	96		Day 16	76	
Day 29	71		Day 17	60	
Day 30	65		Day 18	76	
Day 31	45		Day 19	70	
			Day 20	97	
			Day 21	36	
August 1936			Day 22	63	
Day 1	51		Day 23	73	
Day 2	67		Day 24	53	
Day 3	36		Day 25	57	
Day 4	28		Day 26	50	

SUMMARY OF ALL RECORDED EXECUTIONS

July 17-31, 1936	877		
August 1-31, 1936	2,012		
September 1-30, 1936	1,008		
October 1-31, 1936	536	5,198	
November 1-30, 1936	524		5,425
December 1-31, 1936	236		
1936, Date unknown	5		
1937		172	
1938		43	
1939 (1st Quarter)		12	
Date unknown, but before July 17, 1938		29	
Date unknown		1,343	1,407
Others (In error)		35	
		6,832	6,832

40 Nationalist Divisions

1st Formed in April 1937 (later known as 71 and 11)
1st Formed in October 1937
2nd Formed in April 1937 (later known as 72 and 12)
2nd Was not reformed
3rd Formed in April 1937 (later known as 73 and 13)
3rd Formed in October 1937
4th Formed in April 1937 (later known as 74 and 14)
4th Formed in October 1937
5th Formed in October 1937
11th Previously 1st and 71st (known under this designation from June 1937)
12th Previously 2nd and 72nd (known under this designation from June 1937)
13th Previously 3rd and 73rd (known under this designation from June 1937)
14th Previously 4th and 74th (known under this designation from June 1937)
15th Formed in October 1937
16th Formed in March 1938
17th Formed in March 1938
18th Formed in March 1938
19th Formed in April 1938
20th Formed in May 1938
21st Formed in March 1937
22nd Formed in March 1937
23rd Formed in March 1937 (later known as 31st)
23rd Former Division No 25

24th	Formed in March 1937 (later known as 32nd)
24th	Formed in February 1938
25th	Formed in Summer 1937 (later called 23rd)
26th	Formed in Summer 1937 (later called 33rd)
31st	Former 23rd (known under this designation from Autumn 1937)
32nd	Former 24th (known under this designation from Autumn 1937)
33rd	Former 26th (known under this designation from Autumn 1937)
34th	Formed in November 1938
40th	Formed in May 1938
50th	Formed in May 1938
51st	Formed in April 1937, given this designation in May 1937
52nd	Formed in April 1937, given this designation in May 1937
53rd	Formed in April 1937, given this designation in May 1937 (later 72nd)
53rd	Formed in October 1937
54th	Formed in October 1937
55th	Formed in February 1938
56th	Formed in December 1938
57th	Formed in December 1938
58th	Formed in December 1938
60th	Formed in May 1938
61st	Formed in April 1937 (the 1st, 3rd, 4th and 5th came from here)
61st	Formed in October 1937
62nd	Formed in April 1937 (the 61st, 62nd and 63rd came from here)
62nd	Formed in October 1937
63rd	Formed in October 1937
71st	Former 1st Division, later 11th
71st	Former 75th Division (known by this designation from June 1937)
72nd	Former 2nd Division, later 12th
72nd	Former 53rd Division (known by this designation from June 1937)
73rd	Former 3rd Division, later 13th
73rd	Former 117th Division (known by this designation from October 1937)
74th	Former 4th Division, later 14th
74th	Formed in October 1937
75th	Formed in April 1937 (later known as 71st)
75th	Formed in October 1937
81st	Formed in June 1937
82nd	Formed in June 1937
83rd	Formed in June 1937
84th	Formed in October 1937
85th	Formed in January 1938
102nd	Formed in July 1937
105th	Formed in July 1937
107th	Formed in July 1937
108th	Formed in July 1937
112th	Formed in September 1937
117th	Formed in September 1937 (later known as 73rd)
122nd	Formed in March 1938

150th	Formed in July 1937
151st	Formed in July 1937
152nd	Formed in July 1937

1st Cavalry Formed in November 1937
2nd Cavalry Formed in July 1938

41 Government Divisions

(Details from the Military History Archives)

1st	Formed December 1936 at the Somosierra front
2nd	Formed December 1936 at the Guadarrama front
3rd	Formed December 1936 at the Avila front
4th	Formed December 1936 in Vallecas
5th	Formed December 1936 in el Pardo
6th	Formed December 1936 in Madrid
7th	Formed December 1936 in Madrid
8th	Formed December 1936 in Pozuelo
9th	Formed January 1937 in Aranjuez
10th	Formed January 1937 in Pozuelo
11th	Formed January 1937 in Madrid
12th	Formed February 1937 in Guadalajara
13th	Formed February 1937 in Jarama (initially known as 'A')
14th	Formed March 1937 in Guadalajara
15th	Formed February 1937 in Jarama (initially known as 'B')
16th	Formed February 1937 in Jarama (initially known as 'C')
17th	Formed March 1937 in Guadalajara (initially known as 'C')
18th	Formed March 1937 in Madrid
19th	Formed April 1937 in Extremadura-Córdoba
20th	Formed April 1937 in Jaén-Córdoba
21st	Formed April 1937 in Jaén
22nd	Formed April 1937 in Granada
23rd	Formed April 1937 in Granada
24th	Formed April 1937 in Andalucía
25th	Formed in May 1937 (previously called Jubert)
26th	Formed in May 1937 (previously called Durruti)
27th	Formed in May 1937 (previously called Carl Marx)
28th	Formed in May 1937 (previously called Ascaso)
29th	Formed in May 1937 (previously called Lenin; disbanded in July 1937)
29th	Formed December 1937 in Extremadura
30th	Formed May 1937 (previously called Maciá Companys)
31st	Formed May 1937 in Cataluña
32nd	Formed May 1937 in Cataluña
33rd	Formed May 1937 in Cataluña

34th	Formed April 1937 in Madrid (earlier known as 'A')
35th	Formed April 1937 in Madrid (earlier known as 'B')
36th	Formed May 1937, south of the Tagus
37th	Formed May 1937 in Extremadura
38th	Formed May 1937 in Córdoba
39th	Formed May 1937 in Teruel
40th	Formed May 1937 in Teruel
41st	Formed May 1937 in Teruel (disbanded April 1938)
41st	Formed July 1938 in Extremadura
42nd	Formed May 1937 in Teruel (disbanded February 1938)
42nd	Formed April 1938 in Cataluña
43rd	Formed June 1937 in Cataluña
44th	Formed June 1937 in Cataluña
45th	Formed June 1937 in Madrid
46th	Formed June 1937 in Madrid
47th	Formed June 1937 in Madrid
48th	Formed June 1937 (previously called 1st Basque)
49th	Formed June 1937 (previously called 2nd Basque)
50th	Formed June 1937 (previously called 3rd Basque)
51st	Formed June 1937 (previously called 4th Basque)
52nd	Formed June 1937 (previously called 1st Highland)
53rd	Formed June 1937 (previously called 2nd Highland)
54th	Formed June 1937 (previously called 3rd Highland)
55th	Formed June 1937 (previously called 4th Highland)
56th	Formed June 1937 (previously called Asturian)
57th	Formed June 1937 (previously called Asturian)
58th	Formed June 1937 (previously called Asturian)
59th	Formed June 1937 (previously called Asturian)
60th	Formed June 1937 (previously called Asturian)
61st	Formed June 1937 (previously called Asturian)
62nd	Formed June 1937 (previously called Asturian)
63rd	Formed June 1937 (previously called Asturian)
5th	Basque Formed May 1937 (disbanded in June)
6th	Basque Formed May 1937 (disbanded in June)
63rd	Formed July 1937 in Extremadura
64th	Formed July 1937 in Teruel
65th	Formed July 1937 in Madrid
66th	Formed July 1937 in la Mancha
67th	Formed July 1937 in la Mancha
68th	Formed July 1937 in la Mancha
69th	Formed July 1937 in Madrid
70th	Formed July 1937 in Teruel
71st	Formed January 1938 in Andalucía
72nd	Formed February 1938 in Aragón
73rd	Formed February 1938 in Centro
74th	Formed January 1939 in Cataluña
75th	Guerrillas

76th	Guerrillas
77th	Formed in 1939
48th	Formed April 1938 in Levante
49th	Formed April 1938 in Levante
50th	Formed April 1938 in Levante
51st	Formed April 1938 in Extremadura
52nd	Formed April 1938 in Levante
53rd	Formed April 1938 in Levante
54th	Formed April 1938 in Levante
55th	Formed April 1938 in Cataluña
56th	Formed April 1938 in Cataluña
57th	Not re-formed
58th	Not re-formed
59th	Not re-formed
60th	Formed April 1938 in Cataluña
61st	Formed April 1938 in Levante
62nd	Formed April 1938 in Cataluña
1st	Armoured Vehicle Division Formed in April 1937
2nd	Armoured Vehicle Division Formed in Spring 1938

42 International Battalions

(Based on information in the book by Jacques Delperrie de Bayac)

Battalion	*Designation*	*Formed*	*1st Leader*
1st	German: Edgar André	October 1936	Hans Kahle
2nd	French: Commune de Paris	October 1936	Jules Dumont
3rd	Italian: Garibaldi	October 1936	Randolfo Pacciardi
4th	Slav: Dabrowski	October 1936	Bleslav Ulanovski
5th	11 Nations: Thaelmann	October 1936	Capt. Agard
6th	Franco-Belgian: André Marty	November 1936	Biguiz
7th	Franco-Belgian: Louise Michel	December 1936	?
8th	21 Nations: Tchapaiev	December 1936	Klaus Becker
9th	Nine Nations	December 1936	Stomatov
10th	French: Henri Vuillemin	December 1936	Gaucher
11th	Franco-German: Domingo Germinal	December 1936	Capt Rasquin
12th	Franco-English: Ralph Fox	December 1936	Capt Delassalle
13th	French: Henri Barbusse	December 1936	Capt Putz
14th	British: Saklatvala	February 1937	Tom Wintringham

Battalion	*Designation*	*Formed*	*1st Leader*
15th	Franco-Belgian: 6 Fevrier	February 1937	Gabriel Fort
16th	Balkan: Dimitroff	February 1937	Grebanereff
17th	American: Abraham Lincoln	February 1937	Robert Merriman
18th	German: Hans Beimler	Spring 1937	Heinz Schramm
19th	Austrian: 12 Fevrier	Spring 1937	Emil Reuter
20th	American: George Washington	May 1937	Mirko Markovic
21st	Hungarian: Mathias Rakosi	June 1937	?
22nd	Canadian: Mackensie-Papineau	June 1937	?
23rd	Slav: Palafox	July 1937	Jean Tkaczow
24th	Belgian: Pierre Brachet	October 1937	Roytbord
25th	Slav: Adam Mickiewicz	November 1937	Boleslav Molojec
26th	Czech: Thomas Masaryk	February 1938	?
27th	Yugoslav: Djure Djakovic	February 1938	?
28th	French: Vaillant-Couturier	March 1938	Louis Perrault
29th	Czech-Balkan: Division 45	March 1938	Nicolaides
30th	Italian: Division 35	March 1938	?
31st	Italian-Spanish of the XII Brigade	July 1937	?
32nd	Italian-Spanish of the XII Brigade	July 1937	?
33rd	Italian-Spanish of the XII Brigade	July 1937	?
34th	Italian-Spanish of the XII Brigade	July 1937	?
35th	International of the 86th Brigade	March 1937	Aldo Morandi
36th	International machine-gunners	?	?

Note: These battalions did not all exist simultaneously. At the beginning of March 1938 those numbered 1 to 6, 10, 12, 13, 15 to 27, 29, 30 and 35, and three of those numbered from 31 to 34 were formed. After the Summer of 1937 many of the soldiers were Spanish. There were also 23 International batteries, and some machine-gun, cavalry, medical, transport and signal units in existence.

43 Attacks made by the Rival Air Forces During the First Days of the War

GOVERNMENT AIR FORCE

July 20th	Bombing of Cadiz, Ceuta and Tetuán
July 22nd	Bombing of Toledo and outlying villages
July 23rd	Bombing of Seville and Saragossa
July 26th	Bombing of Saragossa, Córdoba, Cádiz, Seville, Melilla, Ceuta and the Mar Chica airport
July 27th	Bombing of the rebel capitals
July 28th	Bombing of towns in the Peninsular and Africa
August 1st	Bombing of Siétano and Leciñena
August 2nd	Bombing of Siétano and Leciñena
August 3rd	Bombing of Saragossa
August 5th	Bombing of Cordoba
August 7th	Bombing of Algeciras, Cádiz, Ceuta, Larache and Tarife
August 13th	Bombing of Palma by seaplanes
August 22nd	Bombing of Córdoba (58 bombs)
August 24th	Bombing of Oviedo and Huesca
August 25th	Bombing of Oviedo
August 27th	Bombing of Oviedo and Huesca

NATIONALIST AIR FORCE

July 28th	Bombing of Málaga aerodrome
August 13th	Bombing of the *Jaime 1* in Málaga waters
August 14th	Bombing of Badajoz
August 18th	Bombing of the San Sebastian fortifications (forts at Guadalupe and San Marcos, Kursaal, bullring and Mount Igueldo)
August 21st	Bombing of the Simancas barracks
August 27th	Bombing of the aerodromes at Cuatro Vientos and Barajas
August 28th	Bombing of the aerodromes at Cuatro Vientos, Lasarte and the station at Villalba
August 29th	Night attack on Madrid and bombing of Eibar

Index